Lecture Notes in Artificial Intelligence 5044

Edited by R. Goebel, J. Siekmann, and W. Wahlster

Subseries of Lecture Notes in Computer Science

Aditya Ghose   Guido Governatori
Ramakoti Sadananda (Eds.)

Agent Computing and Multi-Agent Systems

10th Pacific Rim International Conference
on Multi-Agents, PRIMA 2007
Bangkok, Thailand, November 21-23, 2007
Revised Papers

 Springer

Series Editors

Randy Goebel, University of Alberta, Edmonton, Canada
Jörg Siekmann, University of Saarland, Saarbrücken, Germany
Wolfgang Wahlster, DFKI and University of Saarland, Saarbrücken, Germany

Volume Editors

Aditya Ghose
School of Computer Science
and Software Engineering
University of Wollongong
Wollongong, NSW, Australia
E-mail: aditya@uow.edu.au

Guido Governatori
National ICT Australia
Queensland Research Laboratory
St Lucia, Queensland, Australia
E-mail: guido.governatori@nicta.com.au

Ramakoti Sadananda
Rangsit University, Bangkok, Thailand
E-mail: r.sadananda@gmail.com

Library of Congress Control Number: Applied for

CR Subject Classification (1998): I.2.11, I.2, C.2.4, D.2, F.3

LNCS Sublibrary: SL 7 – Artificial Intelligence

ISSN   0302-9743
ISBN-10   3-642-01638-3 Springer Berlin Heidelberg New York
ISBN-13   978-3-642-01638-7 Springer Berlin Heidelberg New York

springer.com

© Springer-Verlag Berlin Heidelberg 2009
Printed in Germany

Typesetting: Camera-ready by author, data conversion by Scientific Publishing Services, Chennai, India
Printed on acid-free paper   SPIN: 12606733   06/3180   5 4 3 2 1 0

Aditya Ghose   Guido Governatori
Ramakoti Sadananda (Eds.)

Agent Computing and Multi-Agent Systems

10th Pacific Rim International Conference
on Multi-Agents, PRIMA 2007
Bangkok, Thailand, November 21-23, 2007
Revised Papers

 Springer

Series Editors

Randy Goebel, University of Alberta, Edmonton, Canada
Jörg Siekmann, University of Saarland, Saarbrücken, Germany
Wolfgang Wahlster, DFKI and University of Saarland, Saarbrücken, Germany

Volume Editors

Aditya Ghose
School of Computer Science
and Software Engineering
University of Wollongong
Wollongong, NSW, Australia
E-mail: aditya@uow.edu.au

Guido Governatori
National ICT Australia
Queensland Research Laboratory
St Lucia, Queensland, Australia
E-mail: guido.governatori@nicta.com.au

Ramakoti Sadananda
Rangsit University, Bangkok, Thailand
E-mail: r.sadananda@gmail.com

Library of Congress Control Number: Applied for

CR Subject Classification (1998): I.2.11, I.2, C.2.4, D.2, F.3

LNCS Sublibrary: SL 7 – Artificial Intelligence

ISSN   0302-9743
ISBN-10   3-642-01638-3 Springer Berlin Heidelberg New York
ISBN-13   978-3-642-01638-7 Springer Berlin Heidelberg New York

springer.com

© Springer-Verlag Berlin Heidelberg 2009
Printed in Germany

Typesetting: Camera-ready by author, data conversion by Scientific Publishing Services, Chennai, India
Printed on acid-free paper   SPIN: 12606733   06/3180   5 4 3 2 1 0

Preface

PRIMA has emerged as a major platform for academic and research exchange on agent technologies. The PRIMA workshop series was initiated as a workshop of the Pacific Rim International Conference in Artificial Intelligence (PRICAI) to provide a forum that would bring together research in the areas of agent technology and multi-agent systems, both in the Pacific Rim region and beyond. The inaugural workshop in the series was held in Singapore in 1998, with subsequent meetings in Kyoto (1999), Melbourne (2000), Taipei (2001), Tokyo (2002), Seoul (2003), Auckland (2004), Kuala Lumpur (2005) and Guilin (2006). At the 10th PRIMA in Bangkok in November 2007, the Steering Committee agreed that the series had grown in size and achieved a level of maturity to become a conference series of its own. It was therefore agreed that from Bangkok in 2007 PRIMA would stand for the Pacific Rim International Conference on Multi-Agent Systems.

PRIMA 2007 received 102 valid submissions. Each submission was peer-reviewed by at least three referees selected from the Program Committee. As a result of the selection process, 22 submissions were accepted as full research papers, yielding an acceptance rate of 22.22%. In addition the program included 11 application papers and 16 short papers. A special session on Agent-Oriented Software Engineering (AOSE) was organized by Graham Low from the University of New South Wales (Australia) and Ghassan Beydoun from the University of Wollongong (Australia), where papers were invited from the AOSE community, but put through the same rigourous reviewing process. The papers finally selected for PRIMA 2007 represent a range of themes – expanding the horizons of the agent metaphor, consistent with the way the computing landscape has moved from what was once stand-alone systems to the situation where the real power is realized through distributed, open and dynamic systems. We are faced with new opportunities and great challenges in a computing milieu where intelligent and autonomous agents interacting with one another solve problems of ever-growing complexity and difficulty.

We congratulate and thank the authors of all the papers submitted and the reviewers who carefully reviewed them. We appreciate the academic institutions, especially Rangsit University of Thailand, for hosting and supporting this event. We acknowledge the support rendered by the sponsors, and the members of the committees for doing a splendid job.

November 2007

Aditya Ghose
Guido Governatori
Ramakoti Sadananda

Opening Address

It gives me great pleasure and honor to welcome you all to Rangsit University and to Thailand on the occasion of the 10th Pacific Rim International Workshop on Multi-Agent and Autonomous Agents. As I notice there is a strong distinguished academic community providing a sustained backing to the PRIMA workshop series. I am pleased to have served as Honorary Chairman. In that capacity and as President of Rangsit University, I extend a warm welcome to you all.

Some of you here are also participating in the International Conference on IT for Empowerment (ITE2007). I extend my welcome to you too.

I am a layman as far as the multi-agent systems are concerned. Like every one else I know only one kind of agent: the travel agent. He is the agent of the airlines to me. He enjoys considerable autonomy in the way he charges fees or the way he deals with the airlines. The travel agent is now increasingly embodied in the pages of the worldwide web, thus augmenting effectiveness and efficiency. Well, when you generalize and virtualize this mundane concept of "agency" it emerges as a mighty concept, transcending boundaries of all kinds.

From the program I see your papers addressing a grand spectrum of areas – from human science to biology and from engineering to game theory. You are designing software agents and intelligent agents roaming around the Internet negotiating with one another. The Internet is now the media for the planet. We all operate on the Internet. I do not want to dwell on technical and philosophical aspects of your research. But let me talk to you about a common concern for all of us – no matter where you come from - the threat of climate change. Currently there are world-wide discussions on global warming and the possible serious consequences, means to prevent or mitigate it and/or maybe to face it. The recent Nobel awards recognize that the threat is real and largely manmade. There is an urgent need for collective action. We are in Bangkok and are among the most vulnerable—especially the place we are now assembled in. I ask you – every one of you – as researchers in information technologies, what you can offer.

The situation facing us is complex – especially because while facing the climate crisis, we have to carry the unfinished responsibilities of development. There is still a huge segment of the world population that is undernourished, under-informed and living under unacceptable standards. There is a notion, especially following the Second World War, that typically innovations emerge from the war efforts. We are heading towards a war. But this is war of a different kind. It is not a war of conflict but one of cooperation. The global crisis with all its threats and horrors is pushing us to work together with greater interactions than ever before. You may design agents – the agents who represent us individually and collectively—with skills to negotiate win – win deals for all of us to face the impending manmade catastrophy. This is not utopian. There is boundless potential in intelligent information systems when backed by the strength of the collective minds of all of us.

I see great promise in agent research. I am pleased you have decided to assemble here and I welcome you to our university – especially to our main campus – a few kilometers north of here in the fertile land of Rangsit. Given your fertile mind, interaction with our young students and colleagues will germinate great ideas. I am happy to see that despite being busy in your path-breaking research, you are interested in student research. As an educationist I join you in working for students – in working for the future. I am delighted to see the doctoral mentoring program. This event will go a long way. One of the concerns of our research students, and even the faculty who advise them, is that being in small groups they face frustrating isolation. This is a bane in developing countries, including Thailand where it is hard to get peer-to-peer interaction. A meeting with distinguished researchers like you means a lot to them. It means a lot in terms of building their confidence and in refining their ideas. I am sure there is always benefit in talking to the innocent students whose innocent questions may open new agendas for research. Let me borrow from Shakespeare "it is twice blest: It blessth him that gives and him that takes".

Again with great pleasure and honor I welcome you all to my university, to the city of Angeles and to the land of smiles.

November 2007   Arthit Ourairat

Invited Speakers

Yaser S. Abu-Mostafa, CalTech, USA: Ensemble Learning

One of the core ideas of multi-agents is the accomplishment of a collective task through the contributions of multiple units. The same idea arises in the context of computational learning, where a learning task is accomplished by contributions from an ensemble of learning units. Ensemble learning is a very active area of research, and some of its algorithms such as AdaBoost are in wide use in practical applications. This talk gives the background of ensemble learning and describes its main algorithms. Some of the theoretical questions in ensemble learning parallel those in multi-agents, such as the level of supervision and independence of the individual learners. The key question, however, is why ensemble learning works so well. Several attempts at answering the question theoretically have consequently been shown to be false. Many of these ideas are discussed and it is shown that it is not only a curiosity to answer this question, but an important step in the optimal design of ensemble learning algorithms.

Hideyuki Nakashima, Future University, Hakodate, Japan: Future of Multi-agent Systems Research with Eastern Philosophy

Leon Sterling, University of Melbourne, Australia: Agent-Oriented Modelling for Complex Socio-technical Systems

Agent-oriented software engineering has emerged as an active research area in the past decade. This talk argues that agent concepts are useful from the earliest stages of system conceptualization. The agent paradigm is useful even if systems are implemented without using agent concepts. Examples of agent modes are presented.

Conference Organization

Honorary Chair

Arthit Ourairat

General Chair

R. Sadananda

Program Chairs

Aditya Ghose
Guido Governatori

Doctoral Mentoring Chair

The Duy Bui

Program Committee

Yaser S. Abu-Mostafa	Toru Ishida	Sascha Ossowski
Mike Barley	Kamalakar Karlapalem	Vineet Padmanabhan
Dencho Batanov	Minkoo Kim	Mikhail Prokopenko
Ghassan Beydoun	Yasuhiko Kitamura	Maryam Purvis
Richard Booth	Jean-Luc Koning	Antonino Rotolo
Rafael H. Bordini	Ryszard Kowalczyk	R. Sadananda
Stephane Bressan	Aneesh Krishna	Abdul Sattar
The Duy Bui	Jaeho Lee	Hajime Sawmura
Suresh Chande	Ho-fung Leung	Ali Selamat
Joongmin Choi	Chao-Lin Liu	Liz Sonenberg
John Debenham	Lin Liu	Leon Sterling
Joerg Denzinger	Jyi-Shane Liu	Toshiharu Sugawara
Frank Dignum	Rey-Long Liu	Soo Von-Wun
Virginia Dignum	Alan Liu	Michael Winikoff
Alexis Drogoul	Graham Low	Wayne Wobcke
Atilla Elci	Dickson Lukose	Jung-Jin Yang
Paolo Giorgini	Thomas Meyer	Zili Zhang
Tuong Vinh Ho	S. B. Nair	Dongmo Zhang
Michael C. Horsch	Hideyuki Nakashima	Hans van Ditmarsch
Jane Hsu	Mehmet Orgun	Leon van der Torre

Publicity Chairs

Chattrakul Sombattheera
Aneesh Krishna

Local Organization

Chattrakul Sombattheera
Chom Kimpan
Damrong Indharameesup
Esa Kujansuu
Gyanam Sadananda
Henna Hälinen
HwaJoon Kim
Jaakko Lautarinne
Jeroen Schedler
Julia Jokinen
Malivan Praditeera

Nares Pantaratorn
Panida Yawut
Pitawas Indharameesup
Pongjan Yoopat
Poonphon Suesaowaluk
Prasit Jiyapanichkul
Riku Kestilä
Siriporn Supratid
Suwarin Pattamavorakun
Vannee Suksart
Waewwan Reungthai

External Reviewers

Mohan Baruwal Chhetri
Aliaksandr Birukou
Jeff Blee
Jan Broersen
Volha Bryl
Patrice Caire
Chi-Kong Chan
Timothy Cleaver
Alan Colman
Fabiano Dalpiaz
Hind Fadil
Taro Fukumoto
Masabumi Furuhata
Aurona Gerber
Steve Goschnick
Octavio Gutierrez
Ramon Hermoso Traba
Hoyoung Jeung
Thomas Juan
Kazuki Kobayashi
George Koliadis
Shusuke Kuribara
Ka-man Lam

Jaeho Lee
Louise Leenen
Li Li
Qiang Liu
Lin Liu
Qing Liu
Graham Low
Huiye Ma
Wataru Makiguchi
Melanie Middlemiss
Juliana Mitchell-Wong
Tomokazu Narita
Philippe Pasquier
Laurent Perrussel
Bastin Tony
Roy Savarimuthu
Yohsuke Takahashi
Matteo Vasirani
Bao Quoc Vo
Mengxiao Wu
Zhang Yang
Jung-Jin Yang

Table of Contents

Existence of Risk Strategy Equilibrium in Games Having No Pure Strategy Nash Equilibrium

Ka-man Lam and Ho-Fung Leung

Department of Computer Science and Engineering
The Chinese University of Hong Kong
{kmlam,lhf}@cse.cuhk.edu.hk

Abstract. Two key properties defining an intelligent agent are reactive and pro-active. Before designing an intelligent agent for any multi-agent system, we need to first understand how agents should behave and interact in that particular application, which can be done by modelling the application as a *game*. To analyze these games and to understand how decision-makers interact, we can use a collection of analytical tools known as *Game Theory*. *Risk strategies* is a new kind of game-theoretic strategy. Simulations in previous work have shown that agents using risk strategies are reactive as well as pro-active and thus have better performance than agents using other models or strategies in various applications. However, research on risk strategies has been focusing on formalization, application, and games having pure strategy Nash equilibrium. In this paper, we analyze a game having no pure strategy Nash equilibrium. We find that risk strategy equilibrium may exist even the game does not have pure strategy Nash equilibrium. We then summarize general conditions for the existence of risk strategy equilibrium. Simulation shows that agents using risk strategies also have better performance than agents using other existing strategies in a game having no pure strategy Nash equilibrium.

1 Introduction

Autonomous agents, also known as *intelligent agents*, are agents with reactivity and pro-activeness. Reactivity is the ability that an intelligent agent can react to the changes in the environment instantly, so as to achieve the design objectives. However, if an agent can just react to the environment, the agent will be directed by the environment and deviate from its design objectives very easily. So, an intelligent agent should be able to recognize opportunities and take the initiative to meet its goals. This is Pro-activeness.

In order to design intelligent agents for a multi-agent system that are reactive and pro-active, we need to understand how agents should behave in the system environment. One way to do so is to model agent interaction in that environment as a game. Many human interactions and economic activities can be modeled as games, like auctions, negotiations, bidding, bargaining, and political competition. Game Theory is a tool we can use to model agent interaction as a game, analyze and understand how decision-makers interact in the game.

A. Ghose, G. Governatori, and R. Sadananda (Eds.): PRIMA 2007, LNAI 5044, pp. 1–12, 2009.
© Springer-Verlag Berlin Heidelberg 2009

In game theory, decision-making sometimes takes into account utility only, while sometimes also takes into account probability and uses expected utility maximization. However, experiments [6] show that most of the decision makers violate the Expected Utility Theory [3] when there is risk in the choices. This is because decision makers have attitudes toward risk. However, risk attitude is rarely considered in game analysis. Another key factor affecting a person's decision-making is other people's reputations [19]. At the same time, there are also various models of reputation in the context of multi-agent systems [5,15,17]. These models show that it is also good for agents to make decisions based on other agents' reputations. Again, decision-making based on reputations is also rarely considered in game analysis.

In [9], Lam and Leung propose a new model of decision-making, called *attractiveness maximization*, which uses risk attitude, probability and utility in decision-making. The idea is that instead of calculating the product of probability and utility, some people are attracted by the large amount of gain even the probability of gain is very low, while some people are resisted by the low probability of gain even the amount of gain is very large. Lam and Leung use the risk attitude of a person as a weight on the probability of gain and the amount of gain to calculate the attractiveness of an outcome and the choice in which the outcome has the maximum attractiveness is chosen. They show that the model of attractiveness maximization can be used to explain the Allais paradox [1], which violates the Expected Utility Theory. They also find some properties of the model of attractiveness maximization, which match the human behaviors.

Then, Lam and Leung extend the model of attractiveness maximization and apply the extended model to infinitely repeated games [8,10]. In game decision-makings, reputations of players are considered instead of probability. Then they propose a new kind of strategies and equilibrium called *risk strategies* and *risk strategy equilibrium*. The authors differentiate these new concepts with existing concepts in game theory, like pure strategies, mixed strategies, behavioral strategies, and trigger strategies. Simulation also shows that players using risk strategies outperform players using other game theoretic strategies.

Add to this, Lam and Leung apply risk strategies to design intelligent agents for various multi-agent systems [7,12,13,14], including minority games, resource allocation and the famous Iterated Prisoner's Dilemma. Simulations show that agents using risk strategies are able to react to the opponent as well as to proactively seek for payoff, which match the design objectives of intelligent agents. Simulations also show that agents using risk strategies have better performance than previous models or strategies.

Through analyzing the Iterated Prisoner's Dilemma [14], Lam and Leung also summarize several properties of risk strategy equilibrium in infinitely repeated games. However, those properties hold only for infinitely repeated games in which the constituent strategic game has pure strategy Nash equilibrium. Yet, not every strategic game has pure strategy Nash equilibrium. In this paper, we find out properties of risk strategy equilibrium in infinitely repeated games in which the constituent strategic game has no pure strategy Nash equilibrium.

In the next section, we describe a background of risk strategies, risk strategy equilibrium and their properties. In section 3, analyze a motivating game and summarize the properties of risk strategy equilibrium in infinitely repeated games in which the constituent strategic game has no pure strategy Nash equilibrium. In section 4, we perform simulations and show that risk strategies work better than existing strategies. Lastly, We conclude the paper.

2 Background

2.1 Risk Strategies and Risk Strategy Equilibrium

As suggested by the Expected Utility Theory [3], the risk attitude of a decision-maker affects how the decision-maker values the outcome of a choice. On the other hand, as suggested by the Prospect Theory [6], the risk attitude of a person affects how the person values the probability that an outcome would occur. However, risk attitude is rarely considered in game analysis. Another factor affecting a person's decision-making is other people's reputations [19], which are also rarely considered in game analysis.

In [14], Lam and Leung give formal definitions of risk attitude and reputation and incorporate these two concepts into infinitely repeated games. A **strategic game** is a game in which the players choose their actions once and for all and the players choose their actions simultaneously. When a strategic game is repeated infinitely, the game is called an **infinitely repeated game**.

Definition 1. *An* **infinitely repeated game** *consists of:*

- $N = \{1, 2, \ldots, n\}$ *is the set of players.*
- A_i *is the set of available actions for player i.*
- U_i *is the utility function for player i, where $U_i(a_1, \ldots, a_n)$ returns the payoff of player i for the action profile $(a_1, \ldots, a_n)$.*
- $\succsim_i$ *is the preference relation for player i.*[1]

The kth time that the constituent strategic game is repeated is called *round* k of the infinitely repeated game. In round k, player i chooses action a_i^k and gets a utility of u_i^k, where $u_i^k = U_i(a_1^k, \ldots, a_n^k)$. A sequence of action profiles $(a_1^k, \ldots, a_n^k)_{k=1}^{\infty}$ forms *an outcome O of an infinitely repeated game*, in which player i gets a sequence of payoffs $(u_i^k)_{k=1}^{\infty}$.

In [14], each player is associated with a *risk attitude state* at each round of the game.

---

[1] There are different ways to define preference relations $\succsim_i$ [16]. In this paper, we use limit of means: an outcome O_1, in which player i gets a payoff sequence $(p_i^k)_{k=1}^{\infty}$, is preferred by player i to another outcome O_2, in which player i gets a payoff sequence $(q_i^k)_{k=1}^{\infty}$, denoted as $O_1 \succsim_i O_2$, if and only if $\lim_{T \to \infty} \sum_{k=1}^{T} (p_i^k - q_i^k)/T > 0$.

Definition 2. *In an infinitely repeated game, the* **risk attitude state of a** **player** i **at round** k **of the game,** rs_i^k, *is a 3-tuple* $< r_{i,p}^k, R_i, R_j >$, *where:*

- $r_{i,p}^k$ *is the attitude of player i towards the payoff at round k.*
- R_i *is a tuple* $< r_{i,i,a_1}^k, \ldots, r_{i,i,a_n}^k >$ *where $a_i \in A_i$, which are the attitudes of player i towards his own reputations of choosing each of his available actions at round k.*
- R_j *is a tuple* $< r_{i,j,a_1}^k, \ldots, r_{i,j,a_n}^k >$ *where $a_j \in A_j$, $j \in N$ and $i \neq j$, which are the attitudes of player i towards player j's reputations of choosing each of player j's available actions at round k.*

each of the attitude is a real number in $[0,1]$.

This is to model the kind of human behavior shown in the experiments conducted by Kahneman and Tversky [6]. In these experiments, some people consider payoff as a more important factor in the decision-making process. They are said to be utility-seeking. This can be represented by a player with $r_{i,p}^k = 1$, $r_{i,i,a_i}^k = 0$ for all $a_i \in A_i$ and $r_{i,j,a_j}^k = 0$ for all $a_j \in A_j$. In contrast, some people want to reduce risk as much as possible. They are said to be risk-averse. In a game, there are two ways that a player can reduce risk by considering reputations. First is to consider other players' reputations. Usually, the higher the reputation of a player in choosing a certain action, the more likely the player will choose the same action in future encounter. So by considering other players' reputations, a player can choose a suitable action in response, which reduces the risk undertake. This can be represented by a player with $r_{i,p}^k = 0$, $r_{i,i,a_i}^k = 0$ for all $a_i \in A_i$ and $r_{i,j,a_j}^k = 1$ for some $a_j \in A_j$. Another way is to maintain one's own reputation in choosing a certain action. In this way, a player can attract other players to choose some cooperative actions in future encounters so that potential risk can be lowered. This can be represented by a player with $r_{i,p}^k = 0$, $r_{i,i,a_i}^k = 1$ for some $a_i \in A_i$ and $r_{i,j,a_j}^k = 0$ for all $a_j \in A_j$.

In [14], each available action of each player is associated with a reputation.

Definition 3. *In an infinitely repeated game, the* **reputation of a player** i **in** **choosing an action** $a \in A_i$, **obtained at the end of round** k **of the game,** $rep_{i,a}^k$, *is a real number in $[0,1]$, where $\sum_{a \in A_i} rep_{i,a}^k = 1$.*

This is given by the ratio of the number of times that the player chooses action a out of the previous k rounds of the game.

Elements of a person's risk attitude state are used as a weight of payoff and reputations to calculate the *attractiveness* of an action profile. An action leading to a higher payoff than other actions is more attractive to a utility-seeking player while an action responding to other players' reputable actions or an action that can maintain ones own reputations is more attractive to a risk-averse player. The payoff matrix of a game is then transformed to an **attractiveness matrix** in every round k by Eqt. 1.[2] Then, players choose the most attractive action in response to every other player's most attractive action.

$$Att_i^k(a_1^k, \ldots, a_n^k) = r_{i,p}^k u_i^k + r_{i,i,a_i}^k rep_{i,a_i^k}^k + \sum_{j \in [1,n], j \neq i} r_{i,j,a_j}^k rep_{j,a_j^k}^{k-1} \quad (1)$$

According to [14], a *risk strategy* is a function assigning a risk attitude state to the player in each round of the game. When all players are using their best risk strategies in response to the other players' best response risk strategies, the situation is called a *risk strategy equilibrium*.

Definition 4. *A* **risk strategy** RS_i, *of a player* i *in an infinitely repeated game is a function that assigns a risk attitude state* rs_i^k *to the player in each round* k.

Definition 5. *A* **risk strategy equilibrium** *of an infinitely repeated game is a profile* RS^* *of risk strategies with the property that* $O(RS_{-i}^*, RS_i^*) \succsim_i O(RS_{-i}^*, RS_i)$ *for every risk strategy* RS_i *of player* i, *where* $O(RS_{-i}^*, RS_i^*)$ *is called the* **outcome of the risk strategy equilibrium.**

2.2 Properties of Risk Strategy Equilibrium

In [14], Lam and Leung research some properties of risk strategy equilibrium for infinitely repeated games in which the constituent strategic game has pure strategy Nash equilibrium.

Before we introduce the properties, we recall the definitions of Pareto optimum and domination from [14]. A repetition of the same action profile $(a_1, \ldots, a_n)$ for t rounds is denoted as $(a_1, \ldots, a_n)^t$ and a sequence of action profiles in which the players play $(a_{11}, \ldots, a_{n1})$ for p_1 rounds, ..., $(a_{1t}, \ldots, a_{nt})$ for p_t rounds is denoted as $((a_{11}, \ldots, a_{n1})^{p_1}, \ldots, (a_{1t}, \ldots, a_{nt})^{p_t})$.

Definition 6. *A sequence of action profiles* $((a_{11}, \ldots, a_{n1})^{p_1}, \ldots, (a_{1b} \ldots, a_{nt})^{p_t})$ *is a* **Pareto optimum** *if and only if there exist no non-negative integers* $p_1', \ldots, p_t'$, *where* $\sum_{k=1}^t p_k = \sum_{k=1}^t p_k'$, *such that* $\sum_{k=1}^t p_k' U_i(a_{1k}, \ldots, a_{nk}) \geq \sum_{k=1}^t p_k U_i(a_{1k}, \ldots, a_{nk})$ *for all* $i \in N$.

Definition 7. *A sequence of action profiles* $((a_{11}, \ldots, a_{n1})^{p_1}, \ldots, (a_{1b} \ldots, a_{nt})^{p_t})$ **dominates** *an action profile* $(a_1^*, \ldots, a_n^*)$ *if and only if* $\sum_{k=1}^t p_k U_i(a_{1k}, \ldots, a_{nk}) \geq (\sum_{k=1}^t p_k) U_i(a_1^*, \ldots, a_n^*)$ *for all* $i \in N$.

Property 1. Let $G = < N, (A_i), (U_i) >$ be a strategic game. An indefinite repetition of a sequence of pure strategy Nash equilibria is an outcome of a risk strategy equilibrium in the infinitely repeated game of G if and only if the sequence is a Pareto optimum.

---

[2] As at the beginning of round k, player i does not know what action other players j ($j \in [1, n], j \neq i$) will choose in round k, player i considers other players' reputations $rep_{j,a_j^k}^{k-1}$ obtained at the end of round $k - 1$. $rep_{j,a_j^k}^0$ is the *initial reputations*, which are given to each player at the beginning of the game. In contrast, player i considers his own reputations $rep_{i,a_i^k}^k$ that will be obtained at the end of round k if he chooses action a_i^k in round k.

Player 2

		C	D
Player 1	C	r, r	s, t
	D	t, s	p, p

Player 2

		B	N
Player 1	L	2, -2	-1, 0
	T	1, 1	0, -1

Fig. 1. The Prisoner's Dilemma

Fig. 2. Lying Game

For example, in the Prisoner's Dilemma as shown in Fig. 1 (with $t = 5, r = 3, p = 1, s = 0$), (D, D) is a pure strategy Nash equilibrium. Playing (D, D) in every round of the Iterated Prisoner's Dilemma is also a risk strategy equilibrium.

Property 2. Let $G =< N, (A_i), (U_i) >$ be a strategic game. An indefinite repetition of a sequence of action profiles (but not pure strategy equilibria) is an outcome of a risk strategy equilibrium in the infinitely repeated game of G if and only if the sequence is a Pareto optimum, and dominates all the pure strategy Nash equilibria in G.

In the Iterated Prisoner's Dilemma, playing (C, C) in every round of the game is Pareto optimum. Also, as $U_i(C, C) > U_i(D, D)$ for all $i \in N$, playing (C, C) in every round of the game dominates the pure strategy Nash equilibrium (D, D). This Pareto optimum is an outcome of a risk strategy equilibrium. Also, in a variation of the Iterated Prisoner's Dilemma (with $t = 50, r = 3, p = 1, s = 0$), playing (C, D) and (D, C) alternatively is also a Pareto optimum. As $U_i(C, D) + U_i(D, C) > 2U_i(D, D)$ for all $i \in N$, playing (C, D) and (D, C) alternatively dominates the pure strategy Nash equilibrium (D, D). This Pareto optimum is also an outcome of a risk strategy equilibrium.

3   Risk Strategy Equilibrium in Games Having No Pure Strategy Nash Equilibrium

3.1   Motivating Example: Lying Game

In [11], Lam and Leung propose a trust/honesty model for the semi-competitive environment. In such an environment, agents have incentives to tell the truth as well as to tell lies. However, their discussions are only on a simulative approach. In this paper, we model the semi-competitive environment as a Lying game and give game-theoretic analysis.

In the Lying Game, player 1 can choose to lie or to tell the truth, denote as L and T respectively, while player 2 can choose to believe or not to believe player 1, denote as B and N respectively. The preference relations over the action profiles can be expressed as payoffs, as shown in Fig. 2. If player 1 chooses L, it is better for player 2 to choose N. If player 2 chooses N, it is better for player 1 to choose T. If player 1 chooses T, it is better for player 2 to choose B. If player 2 chooses B, it is better for player 1 to choose L. So, there is no pure strategy Nash equilibrium in this game.

		Player 2	
		B	**N**
Player 1	**L**	0, -2	0, 0
	T	1, $1+rep^0_{1,T}$	1, $-1+rep^0_{1,T}$

		Player 2	
		B	**N**
Player 1	**L**	0, -2	0, 0
	T	1, 2	1, 0

Fig. 3. First round of the Lying Game, transformed using Eqt. 1 and Eqt. 2

Fig. 4. Second round of the Lying Game, transformed using Eqt. 1 and Eqt. 2

Let us denote $rs^k_i =< r^k_{i,p}, < r^k_{i,1,L}, r^k_{i,1,T} >, < r^k_{i,2,B}, r^k_{i,2,N} >>$ as player i's risk attitude state in round k, where $i = 1, 2$. If player 1 wants to be a good man (not to lie) and player 2 chooses his action based on whether player 1 is a good man. Both players care player 1's reputation in choosing T. However, if player 1 lies in the previous round, then player 2 will be cautious to player 1 and care about player 1's reputation in choosing L and his own reputation in choosing N. This is represented by the following risk strategies:

$$rs^k_1 =< 0, < 0, 1 >, < 0, 0 >> \quad \text{for all } k$$

$$rs^k_2 = \begin{cases} < 1, < 0, 1 >, < 0, 0 >> & \text{for } k = 1 \\ < 0, < 1, 0 >, < 0, 1 >> & \text{for } k \geq 2, \text{ and } a^{k-1}_1 = L \\ rs^{k-1}_2 & \text{otherwise} \end{cases} \tag{2}$$

The transformed game of the first round will be the one as shown in Fig. 3. It is more attractive for player 1 to choose T no matter what player 2 chooses. If player 1 chooses T, it is more attractive for player 2 to choose B as $1 + rep^0_{1,T} > -1 + rep^0_{1,T}$. So, player 1 chooses T and player 2 chooses B in round 1.

At the end of round 1, $rep^1_{1,T} = rep^1_{2,B} = 1$ and $rep^1_{1,L} = rep^1_{2,N} = 0$. Both players do not change their risk attitudes according to Eqt. 2. Then, the transformed game of the second round will be the one as shown in Fig. 4. So in round 2, it is also the most attractive for player 1 to choose T no matter what player 2 chooses. If player 1 chooses T, it is also more attractive for player 2 to choose B as $2 > 0$. Again, both players do not change their risk attitudes according to Eqt. 2. Also, $rep^2_{1,T} = rep^2_{2,B} = 1$ and $rep^2_{1,L} = rep^2_{2,N} = 0$ at the end of round 2. Then, the decision-making remains the same in round $k > 2$. As a result, player 1 chooses T and player 2 chooses B in every round of the game. In this case, both players get a payoff of k in k rounds of the game.

Since player 2, using the risk strategy as shown by Eqt. 2, effectively chooses B in every round of the game, then player 1 can increase his one-round payoff by using other risk strategies such that he will choose L instead of T in any round of the game. Say player 1 uses other risk strategies such that he chooses L in round h. Then, player 2 changes his risk attitudes in round $h+1$ according to Eqt. 2. Then it will be more attractive for player 2 to choose N starting from round $h + 1$ no matter what player 1 chooses. Then the best response for player 1 is to choose T starting from round $h + 1$. In this case, player 1 gets a payoff of $1(h - 1) + 2 = h + 1$ in k rounds of the game, where $k > h$. As $\lim_{k \to \infty}(h + 1 - k)/k < 0$, player 1 cannot increase his payoffs for the whole game by using other risk strategies. On the other hand, player 2 is already getting the highest payoff by using Eqt. 2. This is a risk strategy equilibrium.

3.2 Existence of Risk Strategy Equilibrium in Games Having No Pure Strategy Nash Equilibrium

From the Lying Game, we find that a risk strategy equilibrium may exist in an infinitely repeated game even the constituent strategic game has no pure strategy Nash equilibrium.

Property 3. Let $G =< N, (A_i), (U_i) >$ be a strategic game with no pure strategy Nash equilibrium. An indefinite repetition of a sequence of action profiles is an outcome of a risk strategy equilibrium in the infinitely repeated game of G if and only if the sequence is a Pareto optimum, and dominates all other non Pareto optimums in G.

Outline of the proof: Let $G =< N, (A_i), (U_i) >$ be a strategic game. Let a sequence of action profiles be $((a_{11}, \ldots, a_{n1})^{p_1}, \ldots, (a_{1t}, \ldots, a_{nt})^{p_t})$. A risk strategy equilibrium is:

$$
rs_i^k =
\begin{cases}
< r_{i,p}^k = 0, < r_{i,i,a_{it}}^k = 1, r_{i,i,a_i}^k = 0 >, < r_{i,j,a_{jt}}^k = 1, r_{i,j,a_j}^k = 0 >> \\
\quad \text{for } k = p_{t-1} + h(p_1 + \cdots + p_t) + 1 \\
< r_{i,p}^k = 0, < r_{i,i,a_{it}}^k = 0, r_{i,i,a_i}^k = 1 >, < r_{i,j,a_{jt}}^k = 0, r_{i,j,a_j}^k = 1 >> \quad (3) \\
\quad \text{for } a_i^{k-1} = a_{it} \text{ and } a_j^{k-1} \neq a_{jt} \\
rs_i^{k-1} \qquad\qquad\qquad \text{otherwise}
\end{cases}
$$

for all $i, j \in N$, $i \neq j$, $a_i \in A_i$ and $a_i \neq a_{it}$, $a_j \in A_j$ and $a_j \neq a_{jt}$, where h is a non-negative integer and $p_0 = 0$. Then, the players choose $(a_{11}, \ldots, a_{n1})$ for p_1 rounds, $\ldots$, $(a_{1t}, \ldots, a_{nt})$ for p_t rounds repeatedly.

Suppose other players use Eqt. 3 and choose action a_{jt} but player i uses another risk strategy such that he can increase his payoff by action a_i instead of a_{it} in any one round of the game. If so, other players will change their risk attitudes according to Eqt. 3 and will not choose a_{jt} in succeeding rounds of the game. As the sequence of action profiles $((a_{11}, \ldots, a_{n1})^{p_1}, \ldots, (a_{1t}, \ldots, a_{nt})^{p_t})$ is a Pareto optimum, player i cannot increase his payoff by other risk strategies. As a result, Eqt. 3 is a risk strategy equilibrium.

The sequence of action profiles $((a_{11}, \ldots, a_{n1})^{p_1}, \ldots, (a_{1t}, \ldots, a_{nt})^{p_t})$ must be a Pareto optimum. Otherwise, there exists some non-negative integers $p_1', \ldots, p_t'$, where $\sum_{k=1}^t p_k = \sum_{k=1}^t p_k'$, such that $\sum_{k=1}^t p_k' U_i(a_{1k}, \ldots, a_{nk}) \geq \sum_{k=1}^t p_k U_i(a_{1k}, \ldots, a_{nk})$ for all $i \in N$. Then the players can increase their payoffs by using a risk strategy similar to Eqt. 3 by replacing p_1 with $p_1', \ldots, p_t$ with p_t'.

Suppose the sequence of action profiles $((a_{11}, \ldots, a_{n1})^{p_1}, \ldots, (a_{1t}, \ldots, a_{nt})^{p_t})$ does not dominate one of the non Pareto optimum $(a_1', \ldots, a_n')$, we have $\sum_{k=1}^t p_k U_i(a_{1k}, \ldots, a_{nk}) \geq (\sum_{k=1}^t p_k) U_i(a_1', \ldots, a_n')$ for some $i \in N$. Then player i can increase his payoff by using a risk strategy which considers only his own reputation in choosing action a_i and other player j's reputation in choosing action a_j'.

Property 4. Let $G =< N, (A_i), (U_i) >$ be a strategic game with no pure strategy Nash equilibrium. If all the outcomes in G are Pareto optimums, then an indefinite repetition of a sequence of action profiles is an outcome of a risk strategy equilibrium in the infinitely repeated game of G if and only if the sequence is a Pareto optimum.

By Property 3, an indefinite repetition of a sequence of action profiles is an outcome of a risk strategy equilibrium in the infinitely repeated game of G if and only if the sequence is a Pareto optimum and dominates all other non Pareto optimums in G. As there is no non Pareto optimum in G, an indefinite repetition of a sequence of action profiles is an outcome of a risk strategy equilibrium in the infinitely repeated game of G if and only if the sequence is a Pareto optimum.

4   Simulation

In the last section, we find that a game is in equilibrium when both players use risk strategies, even the game has no pure strategy Nash equilibrium. However, the idea of equilibrium is that players are playing the best response given the other players' strategies, which is not ideal in practice. In real situations, players usually do not know in advance what strategies that other players are playing. In this section, we will show that not only a game is in equilibrium when players use risk strategies, players also get high payoffs by using risk strategies without knowing in advance what strategies that other players are playing.

Simulation is done to compare the performance of various strategies. We have 6 strategies for player 1 (and for player 2):

1. *Random*: chooses $L(B)$ or $T(N)$ with probability 0.5.
2. *All_L(All_B)*: chooses only $L(B)$.
3. *All_T(All_N)*: chooses only $T(N)$.
4. *Trigger*: initially chooses $T(B)$, but chooses $L(N)$ whenever the other player chooses $N(L)$ in the previous round, then resume to $T(B)$.
5. *TFT*: initially chooses $T(B)$, and continue to choose $T(B)$ unless the other player chooses $N(L)$ in the previous round.
6. *Risk*: uses Eqt. 4(Eqt. 5).

$$rs_1^k = \begin{cases} < 0, < 0, 1 >, < 0, 0 >> & \text{for } k = 1 \\ < 1, < 0, 0 >, < 0, 0 >> & \text{for } k \geq 1, rep_{2,B}^{k-1} = 1 \\ < 0, < 0, 1 >, < 1, 0 >> & \text{for } k \geq 1, rep_{2,B}^{k-1} \geq rep_{2,N}^{k-1} \\ rs_1^{k-1} & \text{otherwise} \end{cases} \quad (4)$$

$$rs_2^k = \begin{cases} < 0, < 0, 0 >, < 1, 0 >> & \text{for } k = 1 \\ < 1, < 0, 0 >, < 0, 0 >> & \text{for } k \geq 1, rep_{1,L}^{k-1} = 1 \\ < 0, < 1, 0 >, < 0, 1 >> & \text{for } k \geq 1, rep_{1,L}^{k-1} \geq rep_{1,T}^{k-1} \\ rs_1^{k-1} & \text{otherwise} \end{cases} \quad (5)$$

The idea of Eqt. 4 and Eqt. 5 is to be cooperative and care the player's own reputation in choosing T (or B) initially. Then becomes utility-seeking if player

Player 2

Player 1

	Random	All_B	All_N	Trigger	TFT	Risk	Sum of Player 1's payoff
Random	(491, -489)	(1491, -473)	(-510, -490)	(521, -523)	(562, -495)	(1233, -469)	3788
All_L	(527, -1018)	(2000, -2000)	(-1000, 0)	(-997, -2)	(-997, -2)	(-997, -2)	-1464
All_T	(477, -46)	(1000, 1000)	(0, -1000)	(1000, 1000)	(1000, 1000)	(1000, 1000)	4477
Trigger	(489, -492)	(1000, 1000)	(-999, -1)	(1000, 1000)	(1000, 1000)	(1000, 1000)	3490
TFT	(502, -474)	(1000, 1000)	(-999, -1)	(1000, 1000)	(1000, 1000)	(1000, 1000)	3503
Risk	(539, -979)	(1999, -1997)	(0, -1000)	(998, 994)	(998, 994)	(997, 987)	5531
Sum of Player 2's payoff	-3498	-1470	-2492	3469	3497	3516	

Fig. 5. Simulation result

2's (or player 1's) reputation in choosing B (or L) is equal to 1 so as to pro-actively seek for payoff. If player 2 (or player 1) does not always choose B (or L), but player 2's (or player 1's) reputation in choosing B (or L) is greater than that of choosing N (or T), then this risk strategy will care the player's own reputation in choosing T (or N) and player 2's (or player 1's) reputation in choosing B (or L) so as to seek for cooperation (or reduce loss). It can be verified that the game is in risk strategy equilibrium if both players use Eqt. 4 and Eqt. 5.

Each strategy of player 1 will encounter each strategy of player 2 for a game. Each game has 1000 rounds. The result is shown in Fig. 5. Each tuple in the figure denotes the payoffs of player 1 and player 2 in a game respectively. The sum of player 1's payoffs and the sum of player 2's payoffs of each strategy are shown at the end of each row and column respectively.

From the figure, we can see that player 1 gets the highest payoff by using risk strategy, which is about 25% higher than the second largest payoff obtained by using *All_T* strategy. Player 2 also gets the highest payoff by using risk strategy, though it is closely to the second and the third highest payoff. In all games, players using risk strategies are able to get the highest payoff or a payoff very close to the highest payoff.

In particular, if player 2 uses *All_B* strategy, the best response is to use *All_L* strategy, getting a payoff of 2000. We can see that player 1 using risk strategy gets a payoff of 1999, which is very close to the best response. This is because reputations of the opponent are taken into account in decision-making. So if the opponent always chooses L, the player using risk strategy will become payoff-seeking so as to pro-actively seek for payoff. In contrast, other strategies cannot seek for payoff pro-actively. However, if the opponent is using *TFT* or *Trigger* strategies, the opponent will response with an N. As the risk strategy is reactive, the player using risk strategy soon become cooperative again.

If we know in advance what strategy the opponent will use, we can always choose the best strategy to response. For example, if we know that player 2 is using *All_B*, then player 1 should use *All_L*, but it may not be the best response to other strategies. In practice, players do not know what strategies the other players use. However, we can see that players using risk strategies are able to get the highest payoff or a payoff very close to the highest payoff in all cases, without knowing what strategies the opponent is using. This is because we take into account reputations as well as payoff in making decisions. Also, risk strategies are reactive and pro-active, meeting the design objectives of an intelligent agent.

We use *TFT* and *Trigger* strategies for comparison because *TFT* has been a very good strategy for a long time [4] and *Trigger* strategy is a famous strategy for repeated games [2,18]. However, *TFT* and *Trigger* have good performance only if the other player also uses the same strategy. The performance may not be good if the other player uses other strategies. For example, we can see from Fig. 5 that if player 1 gets a payoff of -999 if he uses *TFT* or *Trigger* while player 2 uses *AlL_N*. Another disadvantage of *Trigger* strategy is that players need to make prior agreements before the game start, which is impractical. On the other hand, players using risk strategy get high payoff no matter what strategies the other player uses. Also, piror agreements are not needed.

5   Conclusion

To design intelligent agents that are reactive and pro-active, we can use a collection of analytical tools known as *Game Theory*. *Risk strategies* is a new kind of game-theoretic strategy, which is shown to have better performance than agents using other models or strategies in various applications. Properties of risk strategy equilibrium in games having pure strategy Nash equilibrium are researched in previous work.

In this paper, we analyze the Lying game, which is a game having no pure strategy Nash equilibrium. In this kind of games, we find that risk strategy equilibrium may still exist and we summarize general conditions for the existence. Simulation show that agents using risk strategies also have better performance than agents using other existing strategies in the Lying game. This is not only because reputations as well as payoff are taken into account in decision-making. The more important, risk strategies meet the design objectives of an intelligent agent, being reactive and pro-active.

Acknowledgement

The work described in this paper was supported by a grant from the Research Grants Council of the Hong Kong Special Administrative Region, China (Project No. 413306).

References

1. Allais, M.: Le comportement de l'homme rationnel devant le risque: 367 critique des postulats et axiomes de l'ecole americaine. Econometrica 21, 503–546 (1953)
2. Aumann, R.J., Shapley, L.S.: Long-term competition - a game-theoretic analysis. In: Essays in Game Theory, pp. 1–15. Springer, New York (1994)

3. Bernoulli, D.: Exposition of a new theory on the measurement of risk. Econometrica 22(1), 23–36 (1954)
4. The Prisoner's Dilemma Competition (2005), http://www.prisoners-dilemma.com/
5. Glass, A., Grosz, B.: Socially conscious decision-making. In: Proceedings of the Fourth International Conference on Autonomous Agents, pp. 217–224 (2000)
6. Kahneman, D., Tversky, A.: Prospect theory: An analysis of decision under risk. Econometrica 47(2), 263–291 (1979)
7. Lam, K.M., Leung, H.F.: Behavioral predictors and adaptive strategy for minority games. Physica A (submitted)
8. Lam, K.M., Leung, H.F.: Risk strategies and risk strategy equilibrium in agent interactions modeled as normal repeated 2 by 2 risk games. In: The Eighth Pacific Rim International Workshop on Multi-Agents (2005)
9. Lam, K.M., Leung, H.F.: Expected utility maximization and attractiveness maximization. In: Shi, Z.-Z., Sadananda, R. (eds.) PRIMA 2006. LNCS, vol. 4088, pp. 638–643. Springer, Heidelberg (2006)
10. Lam, K.M., Leung, H.F.: Formalizing risk strategies and risk strategy equilibrium in agent interactions modeled as infinitely repeated games. In: Shi, Z.-Z., Sadananda, R. (eds.) PRIMA 2006. LNCS, vol. 4088, pp. 138–149. Springer, Heidelberg (2006)
11. Lam, K.M., Leung, H.F.: A trust/honesty model with adaptive strategy for multi-agent semi-competitive environments. Autonomous Agents and Multi-Agent Systems 120(3), 293–359 (2006)
12. Lam, K.M., Leung, H.F.: An adaptive strategy for minority games. In: The 6th International Joint Conference on Autonomous Agents and Multiagent Systems (2007)
13. Lam, K.M., Leung, H.F.: An adaptive strategy for resource allocation modeled as minority game. In: The First IEEE International Conference on Self-Adaptive and Self-Organizing Systems, pp. 193–202 (2007)
14. Lam, K.M., Leung, H.F.: Incorporating risk attitude and reputation into infinitely repeated games and an analysis on the iterated prisoner's dilemma. In: The 19th IEEE International Conference on Tools with Artificial Intelligence (2007)
15. Mui, L., Mohtashemi, M., Halberstadt, A.: A computational model of trust and reputation. In: Proceedings of 35th Hawaii International Conference on System Science (2002)
16. Osborne, M.J., Rubinstein, A.: A Course in Game Theory. MIT Press, Cambridge (1994)
17. Rubiera, J.C., Lopez, J.M.M., Muro, J.D.: A fuzzy model of reputation in multi-agent systems. In: Proceedings of the Fifth International Conference on Autonomous Agents, pp. 25–26 (2001)
18. Rubinstein, A.: Equilibrium in supergames. In: Essays in Game Theory, pp. 17–27. Springer, New York (1994)
19. Sartain, A.Q., North, A.J., Strange, J.R., Chapman, H.M.: Psychology – Understanding Human Behavior. McGraw-Hill Book Company, New York (1962)

Multiagent Planning with Trembling-Hand Perfect Equilibrium in Multiagent POMDPs

Yuichi Yabu, Makoto Yokoo, and Atsushi Iwasaki

Graduate School of ISEE, Kyushu University,
744 Motooka, Nishi-ku, Fukuoka, 819-0395, Japan
yabu@agent.is.kyushu-u.ac.jp, {yokoo,iwasaki}@is.kyushu-u.ac.jp

Abstract. Multiagent Partially Observable Markov Decision Processes are a popular model of multiagent systems with uncertainty. Since the computational cost for finding an optimal joint policy is prohibitive, a Joint Equilibrium-based Search for Policies with Nash Equilibrium (JESP-NE) is proposed that finds a locally optimal joint policy in which each policy is a best response to other policies; i.e., the joint policy is a Nash equilibrium.

One limitation of JESP-NE is that the quality of the obtained joint policy depends on the predefined *default policy*. More specifically, when finding a best response, if some observation have zero probabilities, JESP-NE uses this default policy. If the default policy is quite bad, JESP-NE tends to converge to a sub-optimal joint policy.

In this paper, we propose a method that finds a locally optimal joint policy based on a concept called *Trembling-hand Perfect Equilibrium* (TPE). In finding a TPE, we assume that an agent might make a mistake in selecting its action with small probability. Thus, an observation with zero probability in JESP-NE will have non-zero probability. We no longer use the default policy. As a result, JESP-TPE can converge to a better joint policy than the JESP-NE, which we confirm this fact by experimental evaluations.

Keywords: Multiagent systems, Partially Observable Markov Decision Process, Nash equilibrium, Trembling-hand perfect equilibrium.

1   Introduction

Multiagent systems are increasingly being applied to such critical applications as disaster rescues, distributed unmanned air vehicles (UAV), and distributed sensor nets that demand robust, high-performance designs [1,2,3]. In these applications, we need to consider the uncertainty arising from various sources such as partial observability, imperfect sensing, etc. Multiagent Partially Observable Markov Decision Processes (Multiagent POMDPs) are emerging as a popular approach for modeling multiagent teamwork in the presence of uncertainty [4,5,6].

In a single-agent POMDP, a policy of an agent is a mapping of an agent's observation history to actions. The goal is to find an optimal policy that gives the highest expected reward. In a Multiagent POMDP, the goal is to find an optimal

A. Ghose, G. Governatori, and R. Sadananda (Eds.): PRIMA 2007, LNAI 5044, pp. 13–24, 2009.
© Springer-Verlag Berlin Heidelberg 2009

joint policy of agents. Unfortunately, as shown by Bernstein *et al.* [7], the problem of finding an optimal joint policy for a multiagent POMDP is NEXP-Complete if no assumptions are made about the domain conditions. Therefore, a practical policy generation method requires to sacrifice optimality to some extent.

Nair *et al.* [8] propose an algorithm called Joint Equilibrium-based Search for Policy with Nash Equilibrium (JESP-NE) that computes the locally optimal joint policy within a practical runtime. JESP-NE finds a locally optimal joint policy in which each policy is a best response to other policies, i.e., a Nash equilibrium.

One limitation of JESP-NE is that the quality of the obtained joint policy depends on the predefined *default policy*. Assume that there are agent A and B. We first fix agent A's policy and find the best response of agent B. There is a chance that some observation of agent B has zero probability (with the fixed A's policy). In such a case, JESP-NE simply assigns default policy after observation with zero probability. This part of the policy does not affect the expected reward, since the probability that the part of the policy becomes active is zero. However, after finding the best response of agent B, we fix agent B's policy and find the best response of agent A. In this case, part of B's policy (where the default policy is assigned) can be active, since the policy of agent A will change. If the default policy is quite bad, the best response of agent A might be almost identical to the previous policy, so this part of B's policy remains inactive. As a result, JESP-NE converges to a sub-optimal joint policy, which is far from an optimal joint policy.

In this paper, we propose a method that finds a locally optimal joint policy based on a concept called *Trembling-hand Perfect Equilibrium* (TPE) [9]. In finding a TPE, we assume that an agent might make a mistake in selecting its action with small probability. Thus an observation that has zero probability in JESP-NE will have non-zero probability. Therefore, we assign a best response policy rather than the default policy in this part. As a result, the JESP-TPE can converge to a better joint policy than JESP-NE. The experimental results show that JESP-TPE outperforms JESP-NE in settings where the default policy is not good enough.

In the rest of this paper, we first show the multiagent POMDP model used in this paper (Section 2). Next we show an illustrative example, i.e., the multiagent tiger problem (Section 3). Then we describe JESP-NE (Section 4) and JESP-TPE (Section 5). Finally, we show the comparison between the JESP-NE and JESP-TPE through experimental evaluations (Section 6).

2   Model

We follow the Markov Team Decision Problem (MTDP) model [10] as a concrete description of a multiagent POMDP. Given a team of n agents, an MTDP is defined as a tuple: $\langle S, A, P, \Omega, O, R \rangle$. S is a finite set of world states $\{s_1, s_2, \ldots, s_m\}$. $A = \Pi_{1 \leq i \leq n} A_i$, where $A_1, \ldots, A_n$ are the sets of actions for agents 1 to n. A joint action is represented as $\langle a_1, \ldots, a_n \rangle$. $P(s_i, \langle a_1, \ldots, a_n \rangle, s_f)$, the transition function, represents the probability that the current state is s_f, if the previous state is s_i and the previous joint action is $\langle a_1, \ldots, a_n \rangle$.

$\Omega = \Pi_{1 \leq i \leq n} \Omega_i$ is the set of joint observations where Ω_i is the set of observations for agent i. $O(s, \langle a_1, \ldots, a_n \rangle, \omega)$, the observation function, represents the probability of joint observation $\omega \in \Omega$, if the current state is s and the agents' previous joint action is $\langle a_1, \ldots, a_n \rangle$. We assume that an agent's observations are independent of others' observations. Thus the observation function can be expressed as: $O(s, \langle a_1, \ldots, a_n \rangle, \omega) = O_1(s, \langle a_1, \ldots, a_n \rangle, \omega_1) \cdot \ldots \cdot O_n(s, \langle a_1, \ldots, a_n \rangle, \omega_n)$.

Each agent i forms a belief state, $b_i^t \in B_i$, based on its observations seen through time t, where B_i represents the set of possible belief states for the agent. An agent relies on its state estimator function to update its belief state, given the latest observation. Finally, the agents receive a single, immediate joint reward $R(s, \langle a_1, \ldots, a_n \rangle)$ that is shared equally. This joint reward function is central to the notion of teamwork in a MTDP.

Each agent i chooses its actions based on its local policy, π_i, which is a mapping of its observation history to an action. Since we assume agents act as a team, i.e., they are cooperative, we don't need to consider non-deterministic/probabilistic policies. Using a Non-deterministic policy (in other words, using a mixed strategy) makes sense if there exists some adversarial agent. Thus, at time t, agent i will perform action $\pi_i(\boldsymbol{\omega}_i^t)$ where $\boldsymbol{\omega}_i^t = \omega_i^1, \ldots, \omega_i^t$ refers to an observation history of agent i. The important thing to note is that in this model, execution is distributed but planning is centralized. Thus agents don't know each other's observations and actions at runtime but they know each other's policies.

3   Example

We consider a multiagent version of the classic tiger problem introduced in [8]. Two agents are in front of the two rooms and its doors: "left" and "right". Behind one door lies a hungry tiger and behind the other lies untold riches but the agents do not know the position of either. Thus, $S = \{SL, SR\}$, indicating behind which door the tiger is present. The agents can jointly or individually open either door. In addition, the agents can independently listen for the presence of the tiger. Thus, $A_1 = A_2 = \{OpenLeft, OpenRight, Listen\}$. The transition function P, specifies that every time either agent opens one of the doors, the state is reset to SL or SR with equal probability, regardless of the action of the other agent (see Table 1). However, if both agents choose $Listen$, the state is unchanged. The observation function O will return either HL or HR with different probabilities depending on the joint action taken and the resulting world state (see Table 2). For example, if both agents listen and the tiger is behind the left door (state is SL), each agent receives observation HL with probability 0.85 and HR with probability 0.15. Reward function R returns a joint reward (see Table 3). For example, the injury sustained if they opened the door to the tiger is less severe if they open that door jointly than if they open the door alone.

Table 1. Transition function P: * corresponds with either *OpenLeft* or *OpenRight*

Action/Transition	$SL \to SL$ $(SR \to SR)$	$SL \to SR$ $(SR \to SL)$
$\langle *, * \; or \; Listen \rangle$	0.5	0.5
$\langle * \; or \; Listen, * \rangle$	0.5	0.5
$\langle Listen, Listen \rangle$	1.0	0.0

Table 2. Observation function O: * of state corresponds with either *SL* or *SR*, * of action corresponds with *OpenLeft* or *OpenRight*

State	Action	HL	HR	$Reset$
SL	$\langle Listen, Listen \rangle$	0.85	0.15	0.0
SR	$\langle Listen, Listen \rangle$	0.15	0.85	0.0
*	$\langle *, * \; or \; Listen \rangle$	0.0	0.0	1.0
*	$\langle * \; or \; Listen, * \rangle$	0.0	0.0	1.0

Table 3. Reward function R: c corresponds with listen cost, d corresponds with tiger cost, and $d/2$ means the cost when agents jointly open door to tiger

Action/State	SL	SR
$\langle OpenRight, OpenRight \rangle$	$+20$	$-d/2$
$\langle OpenLeft, OpenLeft \rangle$	$-d/2$	$+20$
$\langle OpenRight, OpenLeft \rangle$	$-d$	$-d$
$\langle OpenLeft, OpenRight \rangle$	$-d$	$-d$
$\langle Listen, Listen \rangle$	$-c$	$-c$
$\langle Listen, OpenRight \rangle$	$+10$	$-d$
$\langle OpenRight, Listen \rangle$	$+10$	$-d$
$\langle Listen, OpenLeft \rangle$	$-d$	$+10$
$\langle OpenLeft, Listen \rangle$	$-d$	$+10$

4   JESP with Nash Equilibrium

In this section, we briefly explain Joint Equilibrium-based Search for Policies with Nash Equilibrium (JESP-NE) [8], which introduces the Nash equilibrium concept as a locally optimal approach. The Nash equilibrium is a solution concept of a game where no player has an incentive to unilaterally change strategy. The key idea in JESP-NE is finding the policy to maximize expected reward for other fixed agent's policies. This process is continued until the joint policy becomes a Nash equilibrium.

Algorithm 1 describes the JESP approach for n agents, given an initial belief state b and finite time horizon T. The key idea behind JESP is focusing on the decision problem for one agent at a time and keeping the policies of the other agent fixed; then the free agent faces a complex but normal single-agent POMDP. We repeat this process until we reach an equilibrium.

Within each iteration of JESP, agent i calls the BestResponse function (line 5 in Algorithm 1) to find an individual policy that maximizes the expected joint reward given that the policies of the other agents are fixed. The problem of finding such a best response policy is equivalent to solving a single-agent POMDP. However, a belief state that stores distribution as in the single-agent case, is not a sufficient statistic because agent i must also reason about the other agents' choice of actions, which, in turn, depend on their observation histories. Thus,

---

Algorithm 1. JESP-NE(b, T)

1: initialize $V, \langle \pi_1, \ldots, \pi_n \rangle$
2: **repeat**
3:    *convergence* $\leftarrow$ *true*
4:    **for** $i \leftarrow 1$ to n **do**
5:       $V', \pi'_i \leftarrow$ BESTRESPONSE$(b, \pi_{\neg i}, T)$
6:       **if** $\pi'_i \neq \pi_i$ **then**
7:          *convergence* $\leftarrow$ *false*
8:          $V, \pi_i \leftarrow V', \pi'_i$
9: **until** convergence
10: **return** $V, \langle \pi_1, \ldots, \pi_n \rangle$

Algorithm 2. BESTRESPONSE(b, π_j, T)

1: $val \leftarrow$ GETVALUE$(b, b, \pi_j, 0, T)$
2: initialize π_i
3: $FINDPOLICY(b, b, \langle \rangle, \pi_j, 0, T)$
4: **return** val, π_1

---

at each time t, agent i reasons about the tuple $e^t_i = \langle s^t, \Pi_{j \neq i} \omega_j^t \rangle$, where $\Pi_{j \neq i} \omega_j^t$ represents the observation histories of the other agents. Then multiagent belief state B for agent i given the distribution over initial state $b(s)$ is defined as:

$$B^t_i(e^t_i) = B^t_i(s^t, \Pi_{j \neq i} \omega_j^t) = Pr(s^t, \Pi_{j \neq i} \omega_j^t | \omega_i^t, a_j^{t-1}, b)$$

Having fixed the policy of agent j ($j \neq i$), the best response for agent i can be computed using Algorithm 2. Following the model of the single agent value iteration algorithm, central to dynamic program is the value function over a T-step finite horizon. Value function $V_t(B^t, b)$ represents the expected reward that the team will receive, starting from the most recent belief state b and agent i following an optimal policy from the t-th step. Algorithm 3 constructs the optimal policy by maximizing the value function over possible action choices:

$$V_t(B^t_i, b) = \max_{a_i \in A_i} V^{a_i}_t(B^t_i, b) \tag{1}$$

Function $V^{a_i}_t$ can be computed using the GETVALUEACTION function as follows:

$$V^{a_i}_t(B^t_i, b) = \sum_{e^t} B^t_i(e^t_i) \cdot (R(s^t, \langle a_i, \pi_j(\omega_j, T-t) \rangle)) + \sum_{\omega_i^{t+1} \in \Omega_i} Pr(\omega_i^{t+1} | B^t_i, a_i) \cdot V_{t+1}(B^{t+1}_i)) \tag{2}$$

B^{t+1}_i is the belief state updated after performing action a_i and observing ω_i^{t+1} and is computed using the UPDATE function.

Algorithm 3. GETVALUE(B^t, b, π_j, t, T)

1: **if** $t \geq T$ **then**
2:      **return** 0
3: **if** $V_t(B^t, b)$ is already recorded **then**
4:      **return** $V_t(B^t, b)$
5: $best \leftarrow -\infty$
6: **for all** $a_1 \in A$ **do**
7:      $value \leftarrow$ GETVALUEACTION(B^t, a_i, b, π_j, t, T)
8:      $V_t^{a_i}(B^t, b) \leftarrow value$
9:      **if** $value > best$ **then**
10:         $best \leftarrow value$
11: $V_t(B^t, b) \leftarrow best$
12: **return** $best$

---

5   JESP with Trembling-Hand Perfect Equilibrium

In this section, we introduce Joint Equilibrium-based Search for Policies with Trembling-hand Perfect Equilibrium (JESP-TPE), which finds a locally optimal joint policy that corresponds to a Trembling-hand Perfect Equilibrium (TPE) [9].

5.1   Nash Equilibrium and Trembling-Hand Perfect Equilibrium

JESP-NE obtains a joint policy that corresponds to a Nash equilibrium: i.e., each agent's policy is a best response to other agents' policies. In a Nash equilibrium, no agent has an incentive to unilaterally change strategy, assuming that no other agent changes its policies.

A TPE [1] is proposed as a refinement of the concept of a Nash equilibrium. In a TPE, we assume each agent's policy is a best response to other agents' policies, even if other agents might deviate from the given policies with small probability ϵ.

Definition 1 (Perturbed policy). *A perturbed policy π_i^t for a deterministic policy π_i is a stochastic policy defined as follows: if π_i chooses action a^k in a certain situation, then, for the same situation, π_i^t chooses a^k with probability $1 - \epsilon$, and chooses each action a^j (where $j \neq k$) with probability $\epsilon/(|A_i| - 1)$.*

Definition 2 (Trembling hand perfect equilibrium). *For two agents, a combination of policies $\langle \pi_1, \pi_2 \rangle$ is a TPE if the following conditions hold for all deterministic policies π_1', π_2', and π_1^t, π_2^t, where π_1^t, π_2^t are perturbed policies of π_1, π_2, respectively.*

$$JointReward(\langle \pi_1, \pi_2^t \rangle) \geq JointReward(\langle \pi_1', \pi_2^t \rangle) \qquad (3)$$

$$JointReward(\langle \pi_1^t, \pi_2 \rangle) \geq JointReward(\langle \pi_1^t, \pi_2' \rangle) \qquad (4)$$

---

[1] The definition of a trembling hand perfect equilibrium used in the game theory literature is quite complicated and there exist several alternative definitions [11]. Here, we use a rather simplified definition that matches our model.

Table 4. Policy of agents i and j with finite horizon $T = 2$

$t = 0$		$t = 1$	
observation	action	observation	action
(n/a)	$(Listen, Listen)$	HL	$(OpenRight, OpenRight)$
		HR	$(OpenLeft, OpenLeft)$
		$Reset$	$(OpenLeft, OpenRight)$

As long as ϵ is small enough, if (3) and (4) are satisfied, the following conditions also hold.

$$JointReward(\langle \pi_1, \pi_2 \rangle) \geq JointReward(\langle \pi_1', \pi_2 \rangle)$$
$$JointReward(\langle \pi_1, \pi_2 \rangle) \geq JointReward(\langle \pi_1, \pi_2' \rangle)$$

Thus, a TPE is also a Nash equilibrium, but not vice versa.

First, let us describe a Nash equilibrium in the tiger problem. Table 4 shows a policy for agents i and j in a finite horizon, a listen cost, and a tiger cost ($T = 2$, $c = 2$, $d = 40$). This policy in Table 4 constitutes a Nash equilibrium, because each action of agent i is the best response against j. However, this policy does not satisfy a trembling-hand perfect equilibrium concept. Here, assume that agent j chooses *OpenLeft* by accident at the first step. Then both agents observe *RESET*. Thus agents i and j choose *OpenLeft* and *OpenRight*, respectively and receive rewards of -40: one agent encounters a tiger, while the other finds treasure. Therefore, this policy does not satisfy TPE when an agent may deviate from the given policy with small probability.

Next, we consider a policy that constitutes a TPE. If we change the tuple of the actions for *RESET* as the observation with step $t = 1$ to $(Listen, Listen)$ as the tuple of the actions, all agents receive a -2 reward, which is greater than the other tuple's reward. Therefore, the changed policy constitutes a TPE. Notice that a TPE always constitutes a Nash equilibrium, but not vice versa.

5.2   JESP-TPE

This subsection describes the details of the proposed algorithm.

One limitation of JESP-NE is that the quality of the obtained joint policy depends on the predefined *default policy*, which is used for a branch with zero probability. Let us show an example. Assume there are two agents i and j, the finite horizon $T = 2$, the listen cost is $c = 30$, and the tiger cost is $d = 40$. The initial policy is: first *Listen*, then *OpenLeft* when HR is observed, *OpenRight* when HL is observed, and *OpenLeft* when *Reset* is observed. First, we calculate the best response for agent j as: first *Listen*, then *OpenLeft* when HR is observed, and *OpenRight* when HL is observed. In this case, observation *Reset* has zero probability. In such a case, JESP-NE simply assigns some default policy in this branch. Assume the default policy is always *Listen*. Next we calculate the best response for agent i as: first *Listen*, then *OpenLeft* when HR is observed,

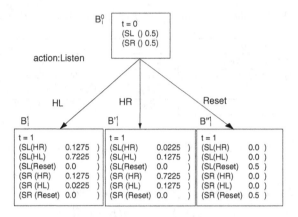

Fig. 1. Trace of tiger scenario

OpenRight when *HL* is observed, and *Listen* when *Reset* is observed. This joint policy is a Nash equilibrium. On the other hand, in JESP-TPE, when calculating the best response of agent j, we assume agent i might take an action that is not specified in the policy with a small probability. Thus, observation *Reset* has non-zero probability. Then, the best response becomes: first *Listen*, then *OpenLeft* when *HR* is observed, *OpenRight* when *HL* is observed, and *OpenLeft* when *Reset* is observed. Next we calculate the best response for agent i as: first *OpenLeft* (or *OpenRight*), then *OpenLeft* when *HR* is observed, *OpenRight* when *HL* is observed, and *OpenLeft* when *Reset* is observed. Here, since agent j chooses *OpenLeft* if *Reset* is observed, the expected utility improves if agent i performs *OpenLeft* (or *OpenRight*) at $t = 1$. Then the best response of agent j becomes: first *OpenLeft*, then *OpenLeft* when *HR* is observed, *OpenRight* when *HL* is observed, and *OpenLeft* when *Reset* is observed. This is a trembling-hand perfect equilibrium, as well as a Nash equilibrium. As shown in this example, by calculating the best response even though some branch that has zero probability, JESP-TPE can converge to a better joint policy than JESP-NE.

Algorithm 4 computes the expected reward for an action, and Algorithm 5 updates the state. Both functions consider the possibility that the other agents may make a mistake and set probabilities which the other agents deviate from the policy to $\epsilon/(|A_j|-1)$ (see lines 5 and 13). Fig. 1 shows different belief states (and possible transitions among them) for agent i in the tiger domain. In this notation, $(SL, (HR))$, which indicates the current world state, is SL, while agent j has observed (HR). JESP-TPE explores the combinations of actions, observations, and histories that the JESP-NE does not consider under the assumption that no agent makes a mistake. Therefore, JESP-TPE can examine policies with belief states that JESP-NE no longer examines (see Fig. 1).

For example, JESP-TPE calculates the probability of 0.5 of episodes $(SL(Reset))$ and $(SR(Reset))$ on belief state B''^1_i, while JESP-NE calculates 0, as shown in Fig. 1, because agent j will probably choose *OpenLeft* or *OpenRight*, although the policy leads j to choose *Listen*. As a result, JESP-TPE

Algorithm 4. $GETVALUEACTION\text{-}TPE(B^t, a_i, b, \pi_j, t, T)$

1: $\delta_j \leftarrow \pi_j(b)$
2: $value \leftarrow 0$
3: **for all** $a_j \in A_j, e^t = \langle s^t, \boldsymbol{\omega}_j \rangle$ s.t. $B^t(e^t) > 0$ **do**
4:    **if** $a_j == \delta_j(\boldsymbol{\omega}_j, T - t)$ **then**
5:       $value \xleftarrow{\pm} B^t(s^t, \boldsymbol{\omega}_j) \cdot R(s^t, \langle a_i, a_j \rangle) \cdot (1 - \epsilon)$
6:    **else**
7:       $value \xleftarrow{\pm} B^t(s^t, \boldsymbol{\omega}_j) \cdot R(s^t, \langle a_i, a_j \rangle) \cdot \frac{1}{|A_j|-1}\epsilon$
8: **for all** $\omega_i \in \Omega_i$ **do**
9:    $B^{t+1} \leftarrow UPDATE(B^t, a, \omega_i, \delta_j)$
10:    $prob \leftarrow 0$
11:    **for all** $a_j \in A_j, s^t, e^{t+1} = \langle s^{t+1}, \boldsymbol{\omega}_j \rangle$ s.t. $B^{t+1}(e^{t+1}) > 0$ **do**
12:       **if** $a_j == \delta_j(\boldsymbol{\omega}_j, T - t)$ **then**
13:          $prob \xleftarrow{\pm} B^t(s^t, \boldsymbol{\omega}_j) \cdot P(s^t, \langle a_1, a_2 \rangle, s^{t+1}) \cdot O_1(s^{t+1}, \langle a_1, a_2 \rangle, \omega_1) \cdot$
         $O_2(s^{t+1}, \langle a_1, a_2 \rangle, \omega_2) \cdot (1 - \epsilon)$
14:       **else**
15:          $prob \xleftarrow{\pm} B^t(s^t, \boldsymbol{\omega}_j) \cdot P(s^t, \langle a_1, a_2 \rangle, s^{t+1}) \cdot O_1(s^{t+1}, \langle a_1, a_2 \rangle, \omega_1) \cdot$
         $O_2(s^{t+1}, \langle a_1, a_2 \rangle, \omega_2) \cdot \frac{1}{|A_j|-1}\epsilon$
16:    $value \xleftarrow{\pm} prob \cdot GETVALUE(B^{t+1}, t + 1)$
17: **return** $value$

Algorithm 5. $UPDATE\text{-}TPE(B^t, a_i, \omega_i, \pi_j)$

1: **for all** e_i^{t+1} **do**
2:    $B^{t+1}(e^{t+1}) \leftarrow 0$
3:    **for all** $a_j \in A_j, s^t \in S$ **do**
4:       **if** $a_j == \delta_j(\boldsymbol{\omega}_j)$ **then**
5:          $B^{t+1}(e^{t+1}) \xleftarrow{\pm} B^t(e^t) \cdot P(s^t, \langle a_i, \ldots, a_j \rangle, s^{t+1}) \cdot O(s^t, \langle a_i, \ldots, a_j \rangle, \omega) \cdot 1 - \epsilon$
6:       **else**
7:          $B^{t+1}(e^{t+1}) \xleftarrow{\pm} B^t(e^t) \cdot P(s^t, \langle a_i, \ldots, a_j \rangle, s^{t+1}) \cdot O(s^t, \langle a_i, \ldots, a_j \rangle, \omega) \cdot \frac{1}{|A_j|-1}\epsilon$
8: normalize B^{t+1}
9: **return** B^{t+1}

---

searches for the policies on all belief states, while JESP-NE only searches for the policies on B_i^1 and B'^1_i.

Notice that Algorithm 4 defines value function $V_t^{a_i}$ that represents the expected reward that the agents will receive when agent i follows action a_i at the t-th step. Also, Algorithm 5 defines agent i's belief state B_i^{t+1} at the t+1-st step when i chooses action a_i and receives observation ω_i^{t+1} at the t-th step.

6 Experimental Results

In this section, we perform an empirical comparison of the JESP-NE and -TPE described in Sections 4 and 5 using the tiger scenario in terms of the expected reward of the obtained policies (see Section 3). We ran the algorithm for an

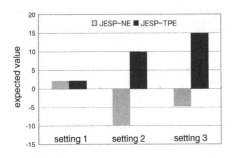

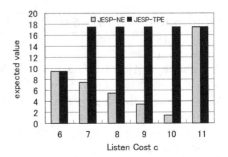

Fig. 2. Expected Reward obtained by the JESP-NE and the JESP-TPE

Fig. 3. Expected reward for listen cost c with tiger cost $d = 14$

initial state chosen randomly, and the initial/default policy is selected as *Listen* for all states. Probability ϵ, with which an agent makes a mistake, is set to a small value, i.e., $1.0E - 13$ so that the expected reward is not affected.

Fig. 2 shows the expected reward of the two JESPs for three different settings where the tiger cost is 20. When we ran the algorithms with a listen cost of 8 and time horizon is 4 (setting 1), both expected rewards are 2.25. Next, we increase the listen cost to 14 (setting 2). JESP-TPE outperforms JESP-NE, i.e., the expected rewards are 10.0 and -9.70. Then we increase the finite horizon to 5, keeping the listen cost of 14 (setting 3). JESP-TPE again outperforms JESP-NE, i.e., the expected rewards are 15.0 and -4.75.

Let us discuss why our proposed algorithm outperforms the JESP-NE in terms of the expected reward under settings 2 and 3. When both algorithms compute the policy at the first iteration, action *Listen* at the first step is the best action. In JESP-NE, state B''^1_i is never reached on Fig. 1 (JESP-TPE changes the policy on B^0_i from *Listen* to either *OpenLeft* or *OpenRight*.

However, in setting 1, the expected reward in JESP-TPE is identical to JESP-NE. Recall that *Listen* is the best action at the first step. Thus, since the policies on B''^1_i are already optimized, the policy does not change even in JESP-TPE. As a result, the expected reward in both algorithms is identical.

Fig. 3 shows the expected reward for a variety of listen costs, i.e., for $1 < c < d$ at $T = 4$ and $d = 14$. We achieve qualitatively similar results when the tiger cost is changed in the range of $[1, 100]$. Thus, we fix it to $d = 14$. For $c \leq 6$ and $c \geq 11$, the expected reward in both algorithms is identical, because they converge at the same equilibrium. For $7 \leq c \leq 10$, JESP-TPE significantly outperforms the JESP-NE, since they converge at different equilibria. In summary, our results suggest that, when the listen cost c is about half of tiger cost d, JESP-TPE is likely to outperform JESP-NE. On the other hand, when c is very small or very large, the expected rewards of both algorithms are about the same.

Furthermore, we examined the trajectories of JESP-NE and -TPE until they converge to an equilibrium. Figs. 4-6 show the expected reward for each iteration. The trajectories in Fig. 4 are exactly identical, since both algorithms converge to the same equilibrium. Fig. 5 shows that JESP-TPE outperforms JESP-NE

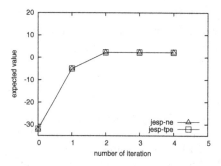

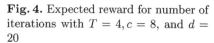

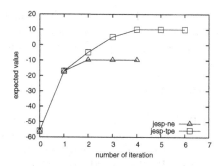

Fig. 4. Expected reward for number of iterations with $T = 4, c = 8$, and $d = 20$

Fig. 5. Expected reward for number of iterations with $T = 4, c = 14$, and $d = 20$

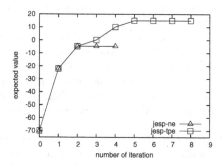

Fig. 6. Expected reward for number of iterations with $T = 5, c = 14$, and $d = 20$

except for the expected reward at the first iteration. JESP-NE converges to an equilibrium at the second iteration, while JESP-TPE does so at the fourth iteration and reaches a better joint policy. Fig. 6 shows a qualitatively similar result to Fig. 5 in setting 3, i.e., the expected reward starts at the same value, and as the iteration continues, JESP-TPE eventually outperforms the JESP-NE.

7   Conclusion

Multiagent POMDPs provide a rich framework to model uncertainties and utilities in complex multiagent domains. Since the problem of finding an optimal joint policy for a multiagent POMDP is NEXP-Complete, we need to sacrifice optimality to some extent. In this paper, we proposed a method that finds a locally optimal joint policy that corresponds to a Trembling-hand Perfect Equilibrium (JESP-TPE), while the existing approach, JESP-NE, finds a joint policy that corresponds to a Nash equilibrium. TPE is stable even if we assume that an agent might make a mistake in selecting its action with small probability, and it is less dependent on the quality of a predefined default policy. The experimental results showed that JESP-TPE outperforms JESP-NE in settings where the default policy is not good enough. In future works, we would like to examine our algorithm in more practical real-world problems.

References

1. Beard, R.W., McLain, T.W.: Multiple uav cooperative search under collision avoidance and limited range communication constraints. In: Proceedings of the 42nd Conference Decision and Control, pp. 25–30. IEEE, Los Alamitos (2003)
2. Nair, R., Tambe, M.: Hybrid BDI-POMDP framework for multiagent teaming. Journal of Artificial Intelligence Research 17, 171–228 (2002)
3. Lesser, V., Ortiz, C., Tambe, M.: Distributed Sensor Networks: A Multiagent Perspective. Kluwer, Dordrecht (2003)
4. Xuan, P., Lesser, V., Zilberstein, S.: Communication decisions in Multiagent cooperation. In: Proceedings of the Fifth International Conference on Autonomous Agents, pp. 616–623 (2001)
5. Goldman, C.V., Zilberstein, S.: Optimizing information exchange in cooperative multi-agent systems. In: Proceedings of the Second International Joint Conference on Agents and Multiagent Systems (AAMAS 2003), pp. 137–144 (2003)
6. Nair, R., Tambe, M., Marsella, S.: Role allocation and reallocation in multiagent teams: Towards a practical analysis. In: Proceedings of the Second International Joint Conference on Agents and Multiagent Systems (AAMAS 2003), pp. 552–559 (2003)
7. Bernstein, D.S., Zilberstein, S., Immerman, N.: The complexity of decentralized control of markov decision processes. In: Proceedings of the 16th Conference on Uncertainty in Artificial Intelligence (UAI 2000), pp. 32–37 (2000)
8. Nair, R., Roth, M., Yokoo, M., Tambe, M.: Communication for improving policy computation in distributed pomdps. In: Proceedings of the Third International Joint Conference on Agents and Multiagent Systems (AAMAS 2004), pp. 1098–1105 (2004)
9. Selten, R.: Reexamination of the perfectness concept for equilibrium points in extensive games. International Journal of Game Theory 4, 25–55 (1975)
10. Pynadath, D.V., Tambe, M.: The communicative multiagent team decision problem: Analyzing teamwork theories and models. Journal of Artificial Intelligence Research 16, 389–423 (2002)
11. Mas-Colell, A., Whinston, M.D., Green, J.R.: Microeconomic Theory. Oxford University Press, Oxford (1995)

MAGEFRAME: A Modular Agent Framework to Support Various Communication Schemas Based on a Self-embedding Algorithm

Quintin J. Balsdon and Elizabeth M. Ehlers

The University of Joahnnesburg: Academy for Information Technology
Tel.: +27 11 559 2847; Fax: +27 11 559 2138

Abstract. The communication techniques used amongst agents in a system is critical to the effectiveness and success of collaboration based actions. Agents which fail to store or communicate information in an effective uniform manner will not be able to accomplish their goals. The aim of the paper is to determine the particular difficulties relating to agent information representation and reconstruction. In addition the paper will discuss whether or not it is profitable for agents to be equipped with the ability to modify their communication style.

Keywords: Agents, Communication, Collaboration, Agent Self-Modification, Embeddable Components, Agent Framework.

1 Introduction

Communication among agents in a system is vital to both the success and maximization of efficiency, or utility, of the agents in the system. Agents that do not communicate *properly*, whether it is in the process of information storage or information communication, will not be able to comprehend a message received and therefore be unable to react to information or respond to a particular message. Agents that do not communicate *effectively* will be prone to inefficiency, which may result in the agents behaving in such a manner that is either measurably insufficient, in the time taken to complete a task, or contradictory to the intention of their inception.

An agent in a multi-agent environment must be able to communicate with two distinct types of agents, the first being an agent which is capable of determining the information that is stored by an agent. This type of agent is generally the original author agent, but is an exclusive assignment. The second type of agent is any agent that is not capable of accessing and determining the type of information stored and is therefore in need of an alternative method of receiving information which is not currently available to it.

It is possible that an agent may have separated components that may be utilized at differing instances of its existence. The concept of embedding agent communication components will be introduced as a possible alternative to an agent having one absolute communicative protocol. The potential benefit from separating distinct styles of communication will be explored. These styles include achieving efficient communication dependant on situational context or to communicate with agents of diverse complexity.

A. Ghose, G. Governatori, and R. Sadananda (Eds.): PRIMA 2007, LNAI 5044, pp. 25–36, 2009.

2 Communication Concerns

The problems that may be encountered during the communication process and the methods of communication will be discussed. Further communication concerns discussed are the composition of messages, the integration of information and the role of the environment.

2.1 Factors Which Play a Significant Role in the Interpretation of a Message

A message is a single formal communication that requires the interpretation of the entity that is involved in its reception. The process of communication is identified by Russell and Norvig as one which involves: intention; generation; synthesis; perception (of the message as a communication unit); analysis; disambiguation and incorporation [1]. Each of the identified stages, should they be hindered, may lead to the modification or corruption of the message that is intended to be sent. The process of successful message transfer is understood to be a period in time after a message has been initiated by a sender and received by the intended recipient, which regards the information transferred in exactly the same manner as the information is regarded by the original sender[1]. Both sender and receiver have significant roles in the successful transmission of a message. The sender involves itself with intention, generation and synthesis, while the receiver is engaged in perception analysis, disambiguation and incorporation [1].

The sender is responsible for three stages in which erroneous communication may occur. In the intentional stage, the *timing* or *purpose* of the message may effect the message adversely. In order to avoid this problem, the receiving agent could perform a *validity check* on the message, which will be aided in sending the actual intentions of the message as well. The generation of the message effects the messages understandability on behalf of the receiving agent. A poorly generated message cannot be clearly disambiguated on the other end. Message synthesis involves the sender and the environment. A message must pass through some medium inside the environment to reach the destined receiver agent.

The receiving agent, upon the delivery of a message, must first separate the message from the medium in which it is transported. After this, the message must have all ambiguity removed, preferably using the context the message was sent in.

Should the receptor agent successfully receive a message that has more than one possible meaning, the best context that can be applied must be used. Rather than have agents calculate what the context of a message should be, some contextual evidence may be provided on behalf of the sender. However, there are some problems with this procedure: the amount of contextual evidence which should be provided, considering the amount of perception the sender has at the specific time of message generation, without overloading the recipient; the determination of the correct evidence to provide the recipient, considering the context as applied to the recipient. These problems were

---

[1] This is not to say that the receiver will *act* in the same way regarding the received information, but rather that the information will *mean the same* to both agents contextually. Each agent may perform different actions, but their premise will be the same information with the same implications.

identified by J. Kant and S. Thiriot, in their paper entitled "Modeling one human decision maker with a multi-agent system: the CODAGE approach", when they stated "due to its bounded rationality, the decision maker cannot represent the whole world" [2].

Information received may have many differing effects on the agent. The receptor agent must determine whether the information is to be discarded, or if the information must be included somehow. The beliefs *must* be consistent with all information that is accepted by the agent, making the communication of a belief vitally important. Any other kind of information sent *must* be consistent with the beliefs, or if the communicated belief is found to be true, all relating beliefs must be negated. The agent will have to determine whether or not it should negate all relating BDI (belief, desire and intention) elements. Message incorporation is an important aspect of the agent communication cycle and will be discussed in further detail.

Communication in complex environments with agents differing in complexity or design is prone to errors along the entire pipeline of communication. Unless these agents are programmed with the ability to modify their behaviour in a manner which avoids these problems, the systems that these agents operate in will continue to require both simple designs and environments. These issues must be addressed individually, but in the most concise manner possible in order to maintain an efficient environment.

2.2 Communication Methodology

Many differing communications styles have been proposed for agents that are required to interact in a system. Since the medium of the environment in question is software-based, the medium that the agents will utilize to communicate in will also be established in the software medium.

In an environment where the activities of agents may be distributed and various communications maybe used, agents may fall into one of two categories: the receiver-initiated and the sender-initiated [3]. In the receiver-initiated method, the agent will confer with other respective agents as to whether they have a message to send. In this type of communication strategy the receiver is introduced as the *actual* initiator in the communication process, although the sending ('intentioning') agent remains the originator. B. Wilkinson and M. Allen identify this method as working well under high system load [3]. The alternative involves the originating agent selecting the agents which ought to receive the message and proceeds in ensuring that those agents receive the message [3].

Agents may employ a strategy where there is no intermediary mechanism. This would typically allow an agent to bypass the environment, due to the fact that the information would travel from agent to agent, regardless of the medium(s) that inhabit the environment. While it may be useful to agents with the same design or easily compatible, the problem would remain that this type of communication is one to one. If an agent would communicate the same message to a group of agents, then the agent would, in the best case scenario, prepare a message and deliver the same message to each member of that group one by one. In the worst case scenario, it may have to prepare a distinctive message for each member and deliver it on a one to one basis. While this technique would work in various systems, the agent may spend more time communicating in complex multi-agent environments than attending to its goals.

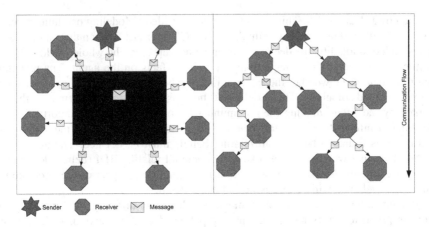

Fig. 1. The difference between a blackboard structure and a chain structure

One proposed communication method is the *blackboard* [4]. A blackboard is typically a sender initiated communication strategy. The main problem with a blackboard is synchronization. An agent may post a message on the blackboard, only for the other agents to respond to that message out of time. A solution to this problem would be to have the agents *subscribe* to the blackboard, so that when a message is posted the blackboard sends a small and identical message to all the subscribing agents. This centralised form of communication is best utilized in environments where there are many agents that are grouped together, to ensure that message consistency is maintained.

Another means of message dissemination would be to use *chains*. A message chain could be formed in the communicating agent groups so that the information is sent out from the sender to the other agents in the group. This would eliminate the use of a blackboard structure and aid the originator agent in such a manner that it would not send the same copy to every receiving agent. A message chain is most optimal in agent groups comprised of a few agents where messages are passed quickly. The problem with the structure is that if one agent fails to send the message then all the agents along its chain will fail, although this method could be enhanced to utilize graph structures rather than tree structures.

There are several methods for sending messages over a medium in a software environment. The two examples given, a blackboard and a chain, as in figure 1 above, illustrate the manners in which a medium may be provided. The latter variety is to create a specific medium inside the environment that is dedicated to message delivery, while the former uses the agents in some mode as the means themselves.

2.3 Message Composition

While delivery has been the focus of most of the discussion up to this point, the composition of a message must be considered. The content of the message itself must be distinguished from the *composition* of the message. The *composition* of the message shall refer to that which makes the message an entirety, in other words, everything that is transmitted from one agent to another. The *content* of a message is used to refer to that which is the focal point, or the purpose behind the intention of the message generation. The content of the message therefore forms a part of the composition of the message.

Since different agents of varying complexity or design must be able to communicate, there must be some base level descriptor of the manner in which the elements that comprise the composition are identified. The structure of the messages must be formalized, so that if agents do not use certain components, the agents will be able to communicate with each other. A tuple[2] will therefore be utilized to represent this structure. Each communicative method must therefore be able to subscribe to the utilization of a tuple. This does not inhibit the freedom of communication that each agent may exhibit in the environment. While all agents will be employing tuples as wrappers, the contents of each compositional element will remain in the originator agent's communicative language. This does not inhibit the 'language' of each agent, but ensures that each 'language' is 'understandable.' The ontology contained within the tuple must be composed of elements that describe the objects in the environment and elements that provide details on the manner in which these objects relate to each other. In this manner any agent may break down these elements to interpret the message.

As stated above, the intention of a message must be communicated in order that the receiver agent may perform a check that would indicate the message's validity. Suppose that an agent, A, wishes a situation to change and sends a message to an agent, B, to stop its current actions and aid agent A. Agent B may receive the message *after* an external force (a force other than agent B) has performed an act in such a manner that the act agent A is requesting of B is no longer necessary. Agent B may examine the intention behind the message and perceive that the intention is no longer valid. Therefore, agent B is not required to consider the message and may continue without regarding the message, which would be the most efficacious use of computer cycles. As previously discussed, an agent may be required to insert multiple intentions into a single message. It must be noted that the intentions of the message must *not contradict* the intentions of the originator agent. However, the message intentions may not *exactly reflect* the agents' intentions as described by the BDI model. The intention of the message may be left blank, in order that an intention is being communicated. There are several purposes for sending a message, as identified by [1, 6]. Table 1 below describes the differing incentives for messages and the effected BDI element.

The message incentive does not denote a complete set of intentions for the recipient. The intention of the message must be communicated in terms of the current state of the environment. While it would be effective for an agent to send the incentive, perhaps to aid in disambiguation or consistency analysis, it would not be as important as the contextual intentions based on the environment.

A further component in the message composition is the element of communication that has an effect on the beliefs, desires or intentions of the agent recipient. The *content*, as opposed to the intentions, is a single entity in the communication. It is not advisable that a message contains various sets of content, since some agents may share some beliefs, desires or intentions and differ on others. The agent must be able to determine whether a message is to be incorporated or discarded based on a combination of the message's intention and the content of the message.

---

[2] "A *tuple* is formed by taking a list of two or more expressions of any types, separating them by commas, and surrounding them by round parenthesis" [5].

Message Incentive	Description	BDI element that is effected
Assertive	Information which pertains to the environment	Beliefs
Directive	Appeal to the receiver to respond in the form of action	Desires
Commitment	An type of acknowledgement which is the response to a directive. Indicates that an agent is dedicated to that action.	Intentions
Permission	An agent which has authority over a group may have to indicate that an action may or may not be performed	Intentions
Declaration	An agent may communicate a formulation that effects the manner in which other agents operate	Beliefs
Expression	A message to communicate feelings	None

Table 1. The different categories of message intentions and their effect on the receiver

A message tuple would look as follows:

$$\langle (i_0...i_m),(j_0...j_n),(c_0...c_p) \rangle$$

Where i is indicative of the incentive constants for the message, j is the list of contextual intentions and c depicts the contents of the message. Each element in the tuple would be represented in the communicating agent's chosen communication schema.

2.4   Information Integration: The Manner in Which New Information Is Assimilated

If the information received contradicts the beliefs of the agent, the agent should consider whether it is going to continue with its current belief system, or negate the belief and accept the information. An agent whose utility is found in computational efficiency would secure a higher utility by rejecting (negating) the information. This is due to the fact that it requires a greater amount of computation effort to not only modify its beliefs, but to modify all existing information stored in the database consistent with the belief. This may be an action resulting in long term utility. If the agent has *direct visible evidence*, which may be communicated in the form of intentions or by what is observed in the environment, that its beliefs are incorrect, it would be better suited to the agent to modify itself than attempt to modify the world based on beliefs that are contrary to the world. Agents *ought* to not have false beliefs due to the fact that beliefs are based on perceptions of the world. However, due to the contextual variance that may be obtained by submitting agents to very dynamic worlds, the fact that agents may be created with inconsistent beliefs remains a possibility.

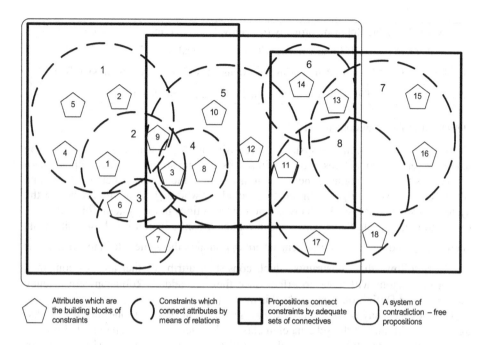

| | Attributes which are the building blocks of constraints | | Constraints which connect attributes by means of relations | | Propositions connect constraints by adequate sets of connectives | | A system of contradiction – free propositions |

Fig. 2. A system of two propositions being introduced to a third

An agent accepting new information must not accept (or assimilate) information that contradicts with its own BDI representations. If the beliefs are to be modified, the agent would have to ensure that the correct course of action is being taken, as discussed above. If the desires or intentions require modification, the new beliefs and desires must not contradict with the agents existing desires and intentions. This means BDI elements of agents must be either *exclusive* or *consistent*. If two elements are exclusive, it means that the two elements have nothing to do with each other; the agent may achieve both elements without affecting the other, regardless of the order of execution. If two elements are to be consistent, the elements have common components, but the achievement of one will aid the achievement of the other.

Consistency may be examined by combining the agent's existing constraints (see figure 2) and the new proposition into a conjunctive formula and checking the formula for contradictions. However, due to the fact that adequate sets of connectives [7] allow for a formula to be represented in several forms, this method, although simple, may become unnecessarily time consuming.

By performing consistency checking using a conjunction, each new proposition will have to be checked for consistency against all existing propositions. This could become computationally intensive when there are many existing propositions. It is proposed that formalism be defined to reduce the amount of checks that will be performed on the set of propositions. Figure 2 depicts a possible situation in the information incorporation process.

> Logic L has the Robinson property (or, equivalently in L the Robinson consistency theorem holds) iff for any theories T, T1 and T2 and types τ, τ_1 and τ_2 with $\tau = \tau_1 \cap \tau_2$, if T1 and T2 are consistent extensions of T respectively in type τ_1 and τ_2, and T is complete in τ, then T1 $\cap$ T2 is consistent in $\tau_1 \cup \tau_2$.

Definition 1: The Robinson property

Consider a contradiction free system of propositions $P_1...P_i$ which are constructed by adequate sets of connectives and contain a subset of constraints $c_1...c_j$. Suppose there is a proposition Q, containing the constraints $q_1...q_k$, which is constructed by the same sets of connectives as $P_1...P_i$. In order to include Q where Q is not already within the system, in such a manner that there are no contradictions in the system, it is only necessary to demonstrate that Q does not introduce a contradiction for those constraints such that q_l and $c_{m...c_n}$ are consistent where q_l contains the same attributes, $a_1...a_p$, as $c_{m...c_n}$. It follows that constraints which consist of attributes that are not contained within the system will have no effect once they are added. Robinsons consistency theorem, as in Definition 1, supports this model [7].

The message may be rejected by the recipient agent based on one instance of disagreement with any of the schema elements. If the agent does not share: a belief consistent with the incentives; a desire that is consistent with the contextual intentions or the contents are inconsistent with the current intentions of the agent, the recipient agent may either reject the information and continue, or assimilate the negation of the content.

2.5   The Role of the Environment

The environment is a crucial aspect of the agents which have dominion over it. Agents must be able to fully function inside their environment in order for them to be efficient.

Agents of differing complexities may be equipped in various ways regarding their communication components. They may have a standard component which must be used, or they may be able to strip itself of some components and equip different components.

The environment must be able to support the variable agent frameworks that may be found inside itself. The environment itself is not *responsible* for managing communication, but rather making sure that communication is possible. Therefore agents must be able to use the components of the other agents to communicate amongst one another. The environment must provide a repository that agents may utilize to encode or decode messages sent by other agents. Agents in the system are then required to *register* their components at the environment communication repository.

While using a communication repository, an agent will have to determine whether it is best to communicate in the receptors communicative language, or to require the receiver of the message to translate the message. If both the agents involved can equip any communication component, then the sender agent may conclude in either manner. However, a situation may possibly arise where either or both agents are unable to strip and equip components. A component repository could be in the form of a complex agent that may perform the translation for the agents, working on a mapping table. A mapping table would simply have the format of the sent message and convert it to the format of the receiver.

3   The Modular AGEnt FRAMEwork (MAGEFRAME)

The agent framework, called MAGEFRAME, enables an agent to embed different communication modules within its structure. The agent model as described by figure 3 is two-fold: each element in the agent process (indicated in a) will be equipped with the same hierarchical structure (indicated by b).

The sensors and actuators are both involved in the agent's proceedings as they are directly related to the environment. With these components the agent is able to formulate and pursue its beliefs, intentions and desires.

The performance element is the core component of the agent structure. The agent will have its overall beliefs, intentions and desires stored in this component. The performance element is responsible for ensuring that the *minimum* utility of the agent is achieved.

The problem generator exists to perceive possible undesirable action patterns and suggest alternative actions [1]. The agent may 'learn', in a primitive manner, by pattern recognition that certain actions always lead to undesirable or least satisfactory results. In this manner the agent may be able to discover a method of achieving its *maximum* utility.

The communication element of the *agent* is designed to deal with the external communications being sent and received through the media within the environment. The component utilizes a structure that allows the embedding of communication components. The embedded communication component within the agent's communication element performs the communication with external agents, while the communication components in all the other agent components manage *internal* communication. This component will either make direct changes to the connections inside the environment or make connections directly with other agents in the environment; this decision is dependant on the environment.

The reactive components ensure that the agent does not allow an unsafe situation to persist. The reactive components will be provided by the environment in a table format that describes the manner in which an agent is to act depending on pre-defined conditions. The agent will not spend computational cycles interpreting inputs that are listed on the table from the environment, for the sake of safety.

The inter-agent communication element describes the manner in which agents are to communicate *internally*. The agent represents information in a standard fashion and sends it directly to the appropriate component. While the performance element concerns itself with utility, the communication element will determine the worthiness of information that is sent inside the agent.

The BDI model contained in each agent module relates to the elements which are most important to that module. In the performance element, there are very few to no beliefs, as it is the beliefs that will inhibit the agent of considering abandoning certain beliefs. The performance element contains all the beliefs that the agent carries. The

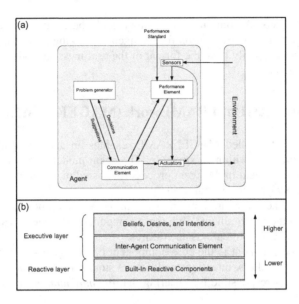

Fig. 3. The MAGEFRAME agent model

communication element carries some of the beliefs of the agent, with which it would determine what may be communicated. In relation to the BDI model, the central component is the performance generator. The performance generator must determine if a BDI element should be discarded or modified. The communication element will then perform the modification.

The MAGEFRAME agent framework differs from its predecessors [1,8] due to the combination of two structures. The agent framework (indicated by figure 3a) supports the lifecycle of the agent. Internally a hierarchical subsumption model (indicated by figure 3b) provides each module in the framework with a standardized process of behaviour that must be followed. The manner of behaviour may be modified by the different embeddable components within the internal structure. However, embedding components is not necessary; the agent is only required to register its communication modules within the environment.

4   Communication Schemas

While an ontology that is flexible enough to be complete in all situations is desirable, this cannot be the final solution. This is due to the fact that all agents may not be equipped with such an ontology, while other agents may not be able to maintain a complete ontology.

In their paper entitled "ANEMONE: an effective minimal ontology negotiation environment", J. van Diggelen, *et al,* state the reason for minimizing an ontology "An ontology that is minimal in size is not bulky and slowly process-able due to superfluous concepts" [9].

Agents utilizing MAGEFRAME are equipped to communicate with other agents that are of the same design and complexity. However, if an agent with a different design or complexity is introduced to the system, all the agents in the system must be able to determine the meaning and context of the messages in the system.

5 A Test Environment

The proposed test environment is a 'lecturer-student world' where students must consult various sources, for example lecturers and textbooks, to achieve the goal of 'passing.' The alternative to 'passing' is 'failing.' This environment is a more complicated environment based on S. Thrun's 'Heaven-hell' world [10]. The environment will use a similar 'success policy' as to the 'Heaven-hell' world, meaning that the agent will always reach its goal, no matter how inefficient the path found may be [10]. The agent may 'fail' several times, however it will be permitted to continue through the environment until it achieves a 'pass' status. The maximum utility for the agent would be to reach the state of 'distinction.'

The agents in the environment, namely the textbook, lecturer and lecture notes, as well as other types of agents communicate in differing styles to one another. Their communication components must be registered in the environment and another 'converter' (tutor) agent will exist as well. The tutor agent translates from one language to another for agents that cannot perform the conversion themselves, although it is not exclusively for this type of agent. More complex agents may determine the usage of the tutor agent is more efficacious than performing the translation themselves.

6 Conclusion

A solution to the communication problem between agents has been proposed. Different issues in the communication process have been discussed, as well as a methodology of communication. Agents must integrate information with great care, as the consistency of their BDI elements is very important. The environment may also play a role in the success or failure of a communication. The agent framework MAGEFRAME has been proposed that not only allows agents of differing complexity to communicate, but may simply be an intermediary communicator for any two agents. Agents may not always use complete language schemas because they tend to be computationally expensive. A test environment for multi-complexity-agent communication and interaction has been identified.

References

1. Russell, S., Norvig, P.: Artificial Intelligence: A Modern Approach. Alan R. Apt, Pearson Education, Inc., London (2003)
2. Kant, J., Thiriot, S.: Modeling one human decision maker with a multi-agent system: the CODAGE approach. In: AAMAS 2006: Proceedings of the Fifth International Joint Conference on Autonomous Agents and Multiagent Systems, Hakodate, Japan, pp. 50–57. ACM Press, New York (2006)

3. Wilkinson, B., Allen, M.: Parallel Programming: Techniques and Applications Using Networked Workstations and Parallel Computers. K. Hargett. Pearson Prentice Hall, Upper Saddle River (2005)

4. Gamatié, A., Gautier, T., Le Guernic, P., Talpin, J.P.: Polychronous design of embedded real-time applications. In: ACM Trans. Softw. Eng. Methodol., vol. 16(2), p. 9. ACM Press, New York (2007), http://0-doi.acm.org.raulib.rau.ac.za:80/10.1145/1217295.1217298

5. Ullman, J.D.: Elements of ML Programming. In: Horton, M. (ed.). Prentice Hall, Upper Saddle River (1998)

6. Singh, M.P.: Agent Communication Languages: Rethinking the Principles. In: Computer, vol. 31(12), pp. 40–47. IEEE Computer Society Press, Los Alamitos (1998), http://dx.doi.org/10.1109/2.735849

7. Mundici, D.: Robinson's Consistency Theorem in Soft Model Theory. In: Transactions of the American Mathematical Society, vol. 263(1), pp. 231–241 (1981) (2007/3/12), http://links.jstor.org/sici?sici=0002-9947%28198101%29263%3A1%3C231%3ARCTISM%3E2.0.CO%3B2-O

8. Huhns, M.N., Rose, J.R., Roy, S.S., Turkett Jr., W.H.: An Agent Architecture for Long-Term Robustness. In: Proceedings of the First International Joint Conference on Autonomous Agents and Multiagent Systems: part 3, vol. 3, pp. 1149–1156. ACM Press, New York (2002)

9. van Diggelen, J., Beun, R., Dignum, F., van Eijk, R.M., Meyer, J.: ANEMONE: an effective minimal ontology negotiation environment. In: AAMAS 2006: Proceedings of the Fifth International Joint Conference on Autonomous Agents and Multiagent Systems, Hakodate, Japan, pp. 899–906. ACM Press, New York (2006)

10. Thrun, S.: Monte Carlo POMDPs. In: Solla, S.A., Leen, T.K., Müller, K.R. (eds.) Advances in Neural Information Processing Systems 12, pp. 1064–1070. MIT Press, Cambridge (2000)

Using Multiagent System to Build Structural Earth Model

Beiting Zhu[1], Zahia Guessoum[2], Michel Perrin[3], Bertrand Braunschweig[1],
Pierre Fery-Forgues[1], and Jean-François Rainaud[1]

[1] Institut Français du Pétrole, 1 & 4, av. de Bois-Préau, 92852 Rueil-Malmaison, France
{Beiting.Zhu,Bertrand.Braunschweig,J-Francois.Rainaud,
Pierre.Fery-Forgues}@ifp.fr
[2] Laboratoire d'Informatique de Paris 6, 104 av. du président Kennedy, 75016 Paris, France
zahia.guessoum@lip6.fr
[3] Ecole des Mines de Paris, 60 boulevard Saint-Michel, 75272 Paris, France
michel.perrin@ensmp.fr

Abstract. Mainly based on seismic data, structural earth models are commonly used for oil & gas reservoir engineering studies. The geometry and the topology of a structural earth model strictly depend on the geological characteristics of its various surfaces. These characteristics constitute the geologists' interpretations of the earth model to be built. In the 3D modeling applications currently used in industry, these interpretations are often registered after the completion of the structural earth model. Therefore further changes in the interpretations can hardly be introduced without reconstructing the structural model from scratch. This situation is dramatic since the only true geometrical information concerning subsurface is that issued from drillings, which daily bring new data. For the above reasons, there is a great interest in providing computer-aided tool for validating and improving geological interpretations to facilitate the geologists' modeling work. This paper presents a distributed problem solving approach, which enables geologists to quickly validate and improve structural earth models by considering new drilling data. This approach is based on a self-organizing multiagent system and on domain-specific expertise.

Keywords: Cognitive agent model, multiagent system, distributed problem-solving, geological interpretation, structural earth modeling.

1 Introduction

Reservoir engineering work for oil & gas exploration and exploitation depends for a good part on the building of reliable earth models. There are many different types of such models. Structural models are built to picture the arrangements of the various geological surfaces. At any phase of a reservoir prospection, the currently available earth models are the major source of information for planning drilling operations. Reliable earth models, which provide subsurface representations close enough to the actual subsurface geology, allow to avoid operational errors that generally induce severe additional drilling operation costs.

A. Ghose, G. Governatori, and R. Sadananda (Eds.): PRIMA 2007, LNAI 5044, pp. 37–48, 2009.
© Springer-Verlag Berlin Heidelberg 2009

Earth model initialization and revision are the results of several experts' cooperation. These experts come from various disciplines, such as: geophysics, structural geology, drilling engineering, etc. They update the earth models by taking into account the drilling data brought daily. Such data, which usually gives rise to modifications of experts' current interpretations, is unpredictable and is imported at any time while the structural model is evolving. Therefore, revising the current model by introducing the new data and the consequent changes becomes an important but hard work. However, in the modeling applications currently used in oil & gas industry, there is no means of registering and supporting the various successive interpretations. Therefore, it is difficult to update the current earth model, which must often be rebuilt from scratch. This task is as more difficult as the earth models' interpretations become numerous. So, it is desirable to study computer-aided solutions, which would provide a help to the modelers for improving the earth model in a semi-automatic way, so as to easily take into account the daily additional information provided by the advancing drillings.

This paper introduces a distributed solution of the above issue, which is realized by a Multi-Agents System based on the eco-problem solving methodology [4]. In eco-problem solving approach, the problem is decomposed into a set of local sub-problems. The problem-solving issue is delegated to a population of independent reactive agents. Their interaction progressively induces a coordination of their behaviors, which finally leads to a stable collective self-organization. The solution of the problem is the direct consequence of this stable organization. Such reactive approach has been applied to resolve complex problems as [2], [3], [8]. Its simplicity allows solving complex problems without predicting an overall strategy.

In this principle, we propose to associate an agent to one geological surface in a structural earth model. Each agent tries to maintain its surface's coherent geological interpretations. For efficiently achieving its tasks, it is built to be cognitive.

This paper is organized as follows. Section 2 introduces the necessary geological background, and details the problem considered in this paper. Section 3 presents our distributed problem-solving approach based on a multiagent model. Section 4 presents a cognitive agent model, which is composed of a behavior model, a communication model, and a knowledge model. Section 5 describes the experimentation operated on two simulated examples defined by domain experts. Finally, some conclusions are presented in Section 6.

2 Structural Earth Modeling Background

In this section we firstly examine how structural earth models are presently built and how their building can be partly automated. We then define at which conditions such models can be improved in view of additional drilling information.

2.1 Structural Earth Model Construction

Earth models related to oil & gas exploration and exploitation basically rest on seismic data. Additional information is provided by the drilling survey data collected along well bore trajectories during reservoir exploration. In order to approximate the modeling result to real nature, earth models should be revised to integrate all the available drilling survey data issued from progressing drillings.

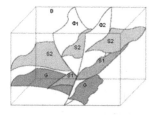   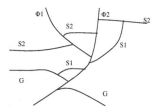

Fig. 1. The left side shows a structural earth model in a 3D block view. The right side shows the same model in a 2D cross-section view. In this model, we have the intersection such as the oldest "on-lap" horizon G interrupts a younger "parallel" horizon S1.

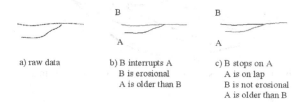

a) raw data

b) B interrupts A
   B is erosional
   A is older than B

c) B stops on A
   A is on lap
   B is not erosional
   A is older than B

Fig. 2. A naïve example showing how geological interpretations affect the topology of two intersecting surfaces [10]

Here we talk about structural earth models, which correspond to mere assemblages of geological surfaces such as horizons and faults. For building purpose, modeler needs to define the all over surface arrangement assemblage, i.e. the topology pattern defining how each of these surfaces intersect the others (cf. Fig. 1).

A structural model's topology pattern depends on the geological characteristics of its various surfaces (such as: erosional or on-lap horizons, constituent faults of a fault network), and on their relative ages. In the sketch b of Fig. 2, B is an "erosional surface" younger than A. B interrupts A. The points located at the right of the intersection between the two surfaces belong to surface B. In the sketch c of Fig. 2, A is an "on lap surface" older than B. B stops on A. The points located at the right of the intersection between the two surfaces belong to surface A.

Joint work operated at IFP[1] and ENSMP[2] [1] has demonstrated an automatic manner to construct a structural earth model by starting from raw geological surfaces (faults or horizons), and from their geological interpretations formalized in a Geological Evolution Schema (GES) [1], [9]. Fig. 3 represents a GES view of the geological scene pictured in Fig. 1. GES is defined as a directed acyclical graph, whose individual nodes correspond to various geological surfaces. The geological characteristics are expressed by attributes putting on the nodes. The arcs linking the nodes correspond to chronological relations, such as S2 is younger than S1, or to topological relations inside a fault network, such as Φ1 stops on Φ2 (cf. Fig. 3).

---

[1] IFP: Institut Français du Pétrole.
[2] ENSMP: École des Mines de Paris.

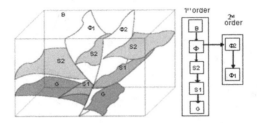

Fig. 3. A geological scene represented in a 3D block, and its associated GES

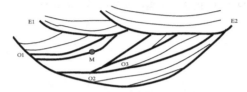

Fig. 4. The next possible neighboring surfaces can be encountered, after marker M, along any drilling trajectory

2.2 The Issue of Validating and Updating Geological Structure Interpretations

The results presented above indicate a new "knowledge-driven" approach for earth modeling work. Our issue is therefore to provide additional tools for facilitating the validation and update of the given geological interpretations, in accordance with new drilling data. This paper provides an agent-based approach, which is to help the geologists to validate the current interpretations expressed in a GES, and then to suggest and to realize possible modifications.

The concerned drilling data refers to an ordered list of markers issued from the geophysicists' interpretation of a drilling log. Each of these markers corresponds to the intersection of a given geological surface (horizon or fault) by a drilling trajectory. The sequence of the markers thus expresses in which order the various geological surfaces are met by the drilling trajectory. Therefore, the marker sequence can be used to check step by step the chronological-topological relations existing between the geological surfaces corresponding two neighboring markers. These relations should strictly be consistent with the geological characteristics of the geological surfaces. Fig. 4 provides a geological scene consisting of a succession of sedimentary sequences, each of which is limited by erosional or on-lap surfaces. By supposing the scene corresponds to an interpreted structure, geologists assume that, along any drilling trajectory, the possible neighbor of marker M can only be located in the surfaces pictured in bolder lines on the figure. In the case that such a neighborhood cannot be validated, the earth model shown on Fig. 4 needs to be revised.

3   A Multiagent Approach

A structural earth model describes an assemblage of geological surfaces. It is considered as consistent *iff* the topology of the all over assemblage is compatible with the

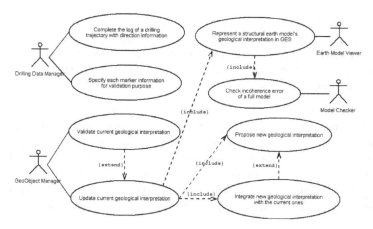

Fig. 5. The use case diagram describing the system requirements

geological age and the geological characteristics of each of the constituent surfaces in this earth model. Experts define these elements in geological structure interpretations. The consistency between the topology and the geological interpretations needs to be checked both locally (among all the interpretations related to one surface) and globally (among all the interpretations related to different surfaces). Therefore, the work defined to validate and to update the geological description of a full structural earth model is actually to validate, to update and to integrate the geological interpretations related to each constituent surface. In this sense, the entities in question are actually the surfaces. Therefore, it is natural to consider the problem in the unit of surface, rather than of the full earth model. Fig. 5 illustrates the system requirements in an UML use case diagram.

The validation and update work needs to be operated in view of real-time drilling information. Since geological surfaces are related by numerous mutual relations, it is difficult to predict how a change concerning the interpretations of a limited part of the earth model will actually propagate throughout the whole model. It is therefore complex to propose an overall revision strategy that takes into account all possible changes in accordance with new drilling information, and permanently keeps the global consistency of the full earth model.

We therefore propose to resolve this problem by using a self-organizing multiagent system. We decompose the global problem related to the full earth model into sub-problems each related to a particular constituent surface. We then associate an autonomous agent with an individual surface, so as to resolve the various sub-problems concerning this surface. By considering a multiagent system as a set of possible organized agents that interact in a common environment [4], we consider that one solution of the global problem will emerge from the agents' self-organization. This distributed approach has two advantages:

1. The problem decomposition that is made allows to deal with smaller and more manageable sub-problems in a relative isolated manner, to limit knowledge acquisition and knowledge modeling scope, and to consequently deal with less complex sub-problems [7].

2. Each autonomous agent associated to an individual surface has the goal of validating and updating the geological interpretations regarding this surface. The agent's autonomic and proactive features allow to automate the decision-making of choosing an appropriate behavior, so as to react to unpredictable situations raised by real-time drilling information.

Our multiagent model is presented in the following way. In Section 3.1, we explain the different types of agents in our system, as well as their goals. In Section 3.2, we introduce the system's organization model, which concerns a micro-macro layered system, and three types of agents' interaction occurring at the micro-level. Besides, according to [13], in order to ensure the emerged solution, it is necessary for a self-organizing multiagent system to find means to control its emergent property. Our control mechanism will be explained through agents' conversation in Section 4.3.

3.1 The Agents

By analyzing the system requirements, we associate one manager with one entity. In the structural modeling domain, the entities in question are geological horizons and geological faults. Therefore, we define an agent *Horizon Manager* for each geological horizon, and an agent *Fault Manager* for each geological fault. Each agent's goal is to validate and to update the geological structural interpretations related to its associated entity. These domain-specific tasks are fulfilled with the help of its knowledge base.

Additionally, three more agents are defined in the system: 1) *Drilling Data Manager*, whose goal is to complete the drilling marker information recorded in a trajectory, and then to distribute them to related *Horizon Managers* or *Fault Managers*; 2) *Earth Model Viewer*, whose goal is to present a GES view corresponding to the full earth model's structural description; 3) *Model Checker*, whose goal is to detect any global inconsistency in the full earth model's structural description that is represented in GES.

3.2 The System Organization

An agent's expertise and information is related to its embedded entity. Thus it sometimes needs to collaborate with others to accomplish its validation and update tasks. In order to describe the agents' interaction, we define our system organization in a micro-macro layered model (cf. Fig. 6).

The micro-level is composed of *Horizon Managers* and *Fault Managers*. For such an agent, each of the local structural interpretations reflects a chronological-topological relation from its associated surface to another agent's. We then consider that two agents linked by such a relation are neighbors. For the maintaining purpose, each agent reacts to the modification in its local neighborhood. But due to the restriction of local information, as well as local problem-solving capacity, agents cooperate by exchanging their information. Agent's interaction is then initiated for different kinds of cooperation, which can be classified into three scenarios:

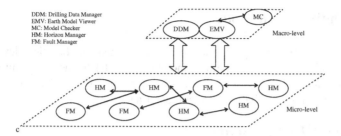

Fig. 6. The multiagent system overview in a micro-macro layered organization model

- **Delegate Check:** A micro-level agent searches to check its current neighborhood, with the partial drilling information distributed from the macro-level. If the agent's local knowledge is not sufficient to fulfill this task, it delegates the check to its current neighbors. This check delegation continues between the neighboring agents at this level, until either a sure result occurs or no more agents are left to delegate.
- **Propose Neighbor:** When a current neighborhood is checked to be invalid, it has to be updated. In that case, a micro-level agent (playing the role of *supplier*) proposes a new neighboring relationship to another micro-level agent (playing the role of *replier*), in regard to the drilling information. Both agents verify if integrating the new relationship into their current neighborhood will give rise to conflicts. In the case that no conflict is detected, the supplier agent waits for a reply (either accept or reject) of the proposal from the replier agent. In case of an acceptance, the neighborhood of the both agents will be updated. In case a conflict is detected, a *Handle Neighboring Conflict* conversation will be initiated immediately.
- **Handle Neighboring Conflict:** When a conflict is detected in a *Propose Neighbor* scenario, either in the supplier side or in the replier side, resolving it involves three micro-level agents: the agent detecting the conflict in its current neighborhood (playing the role of *conflict-holder*); the agent invoking the conflict (playing the role of *conflict-maker*); and the agent capable to solve the conflict (playing the role of *conflict-solver*). The conflict-holder and the conflict-maker roles are respectively played by the proposal's supplier agent and replier agent, or vice versa. The conflict-solver role is played by a current neighbor of the conflict-holder. It is with this agent that the neighboring conflict occurs. In order to handle this conflict, the conflict-holder needs to know the chronological-topological relation between the conflict-solver's surface and the conflict-maker's surface. That is out of its knowledge. So it initiates a *Handle Neighboring Conflict* conversation to send request to the conflict-solver. Once it gets the response, it can handle the conflict by updating its current neighborhood.

The macro-level reflects the view concerning the global earth model. It consists of three agents: *Drilling Data Manager*, *Earth Model Viewer*, and *Model Checker*. The *Drilling Data Manager* is assigned the task of completing and distributing the drilling marker information. So it needs to know all the markers encountered while a drilling progresses inside the full model. The *Earth Model Viewer* presents the global GES view of the earth model, which is in accordance with all the micro-level agents' current neighborhood. Since a GES view assembles various surfaces' interpretations as a directed acyclic graph (DAG). The *Model Checker* is then defined to detect the earth model's global inconsistencies as graph-related problems in a DAG.

4   A Cognitive Agent Model

This section presents the cognitive agent model defined for the micro-level agents. This agent model is developed with a knowledge model for accomplishing the domain-specific tasks, a behavior model for pursuing its goal, and a communication model for controlling its collaboration with other agents.

4.1 Structural Modeling Expertise

In order to accomplish the domain-specific tasks, we have developed two expertise models [12] for *Horizon Manager* and *Fault Manager* respectively. Each one consists of: a structural modeling ontology [14], a set of rule-based inferences [14], and several problem solving methods (PSMs). The ontology is common between the two types of agents. So it is defined out of the agent model, but shared by different agents. The inferences and the PSMs are respectively defined inside *Horizon Manager* and *Fault Manager*, so as to distinguish different reasoning processes for interpreting horizons and faults. An agent's local knowledge is then represented by its expertise model and the existent structural interpretations concerning its embedded surface.

In order to help to well understand how such a cognitive agent reasons, step by step, by using the modeled domain-specific inferences to solve a local problem, we give out two examples. The first example consists of two rules used for deciding a chronological neighborship.

IF   *(surface A is a Fault)* ∧ *(surface B is a Horizon)* ∧ *(surface B is not topographical)*
            ∧ *(surface A and B are in the same geological block)*
THEN   *surface A is older than surface B*
IF   *(surface A is a Horizon)* ∧ *(surface B is a Horizon)* ∧ *(surface A is erosional)*
            ∧ *(surface B is parallel)* ∧ *(surface A and B are in the same geological block)*
THEN   *surface A is younger than surface B*

The second example is illustrated by the PSM shown in Fig. 7. It concerns a *Handle Neighboring Conflict* scenario, in which three agents interact to solve a neighboring conflict: agent A_1 detects conflict in its current neighborhood; A_2 is A_1's current neighbor, with which A_1 is in conflict; agent A_3 proposes to A_1 a new chronological relation, which then causes A_1's conflict. In this situation, A_2 is the agent capable to solve the conflict. We present the *Conflict handling* PSM of A_2, who is supposed to be a *Horizon Manager* in this example. Its objective in this scenario is to provide the conflict-holder A_1 with a conflict-resolving solution.

In this example, by receiving conflict information from the conflict-holder A_1, A_2 tries to solve this conflict by finding a chronological-topological relation with the conflict-maker A_3. The modeled rules implicating such relations for a horizon are used to execute this behavior. A new relation is then proposed to the conflict-maker A_3. By referring to this relation plus the conflict resolution indication rules, A_2 chooses a solution for resolving the received conflict. Accordingly, A_2 keeps or updates its current neighborhood with the conflict-holder A_1, and informs A_1 the decided resolution, so that A_1 knows how to handle its conflict.

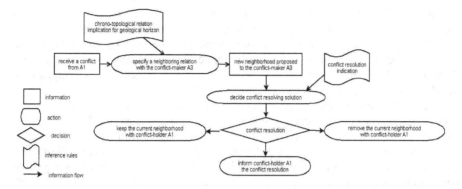

Fig. 7. The problem solving method that represents the reasoning process of solving a neighboring conflict

For the moment, besides *Conflict handling* PSM, we have developed *Delegate Checking*, *Conflict Detecting*, and *Neighborhood Proposing* PSMs for our cognitive agent model. Agents use them to fulfill different local tasks in various interaction scenarios.

4.2 Agent's Behavior Model

Our agent's behavior specifies the eco-agent's meta-behavior, which has been illus-trated by an automaton in [14]. In our system, a cognitive agent's goal consists in ensuring that its local neighborhood, which reflects the geological structure interpreta-tions of its associated surface, is consistent with the marker information recorded along a drilling log. So an agent's satisfaction is dependent on a coherent local neighborhood. To try to be satisfied, agent analyzes and modifies its local neighbor-hood. The modification may raise conflict with its current neighbors. Thus, this agent needs to know the chronological-topological relation between the surface of its cur-rent neighbor, with which the conflict occurs, and the surface of the conflict-maker. It then asks for the help of its neighbor agent. In order to find out this relation, the neighbor agent uses its structure modeling expertise, by considering the geological characteristics of its own surface and that of the conflict-maker. By referring to the found relation, this neighbor agent replies to the conflict-holder agent with a conflict-solving resolution. Meanwhile, it tries to propose this relation to the conflict-maker, and updates its current neighborhood to integrate the new relation. After receiving the resolution, the agent in conflict tries to update its current neighborhood, so as to reach its satisfaction by making this conflict disappear.

4.3 Agent's Prioritized Conversation

Due to the limitation of its local knowledge, an agent needs to communicate with the others which can help it to perform its local tasks. Therefore, several agents are grouped by the message flow circulating in an identified conversation. According to their knowledge, they participate in the conversation with different roles. For exam-ple, in a conversation dedicated to *Propose Neighbor* issue, the agent who proposes a new neighboring relation plays the role of supplier, the agent who accepts or rejects the proposal plays the role of replier. Even though no conflict is raised in the supplier side, the supplier still does not know whether the proposed neighboring relation can be established or not. In that case, it is the replier who is capable to detect the conflicts in its side, to initiate a conflict-solving conversation in need of resolving, and to decide if the proposed relation can be established or not.

Since each agent searches to reach its goal by interacting with others, various conversations simultaneously occur in the system. Therefore an agent needs to know how to select the first conversation in which it should participate with a particular role, so as to decide its behavior in front of different situations. For this reason, we define that each conversation has a priority value, which allows an agent to select an identified conversation with a specified participant role. According to different predefined interaction issues, the priority value of a scenario-typed conversation can be statically distinguished. For example, detecting and solving a neighboring conflict should be executed before validating the current neighborhood with a piece of new drilling marker information. Because it is indispensable to have a stable neighborhood before checking it. Therefore, a *Handle Neighboring Conflict* conversation has priority over a *Delegate Check* conversation.

In front of different scenario-related conversations, the agent selects one having the highest priority to participate. While various conversations are related to a same scenario type, the agent selects the conversation whose related message is the first one in its mail box. By participating in a conversation, agent plays a particular role, which then allows to decide if it is satisfied or if it needs to escape. That then permits to specify the appropriate behaviors it should have in searching for its satisfaction, and in searching for and in performing an escape. An agent quits a conversation when it becomes satisfied in playing its participant role. Meanwhile, it abandons this role. The agent continues to participate in other conversations until there remains no more conversations to join. At that time, the agent plays the role of *validator* in its local environment. And it stays satisfied in case no more drilling marker information comes. While all the agents achieve this state, there is no more interaction occurring in the system, the agents' organization then becomes stable.

Based on the Contract Net protocol [5], we have defined three interaction protocols for modeling the three conversation scenarios: *Delegate Check*, *Propose Neighbor*, and *Handle Neighboring Conflict*. The parameter **timeout** helps to eliminate the conversations that have waited a long time for its participant agents' replies. That permits to avoid having too many interactions at the same time, while the number of *Horizon Manager* and *Fault Manager* grows.

5 Experimentation

The above described approach has been implemented in DIMA platform [6]. In this section, we present the experimentations obtained by testing two simulated examples. Both are composed of a geological scene pictured in cross-section and of the simulated drilling trajectories passing through the earth model. In order to introduce the drilling information into the system, the markers recorded in the drilling logs are written in the XML format.

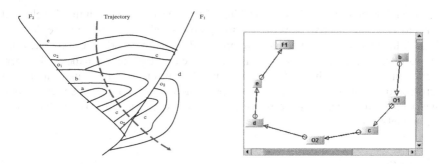

Fig. 8. The left side is the cross-section of a simple geological scene, on which the dotted line represents a 1D sampling trajectory. The right side presents its GES view.

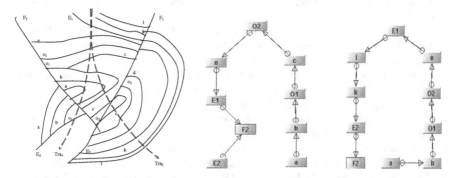

Fig. 9. A geological scene with two simulated drilling trajectories Tra_1, Tra_2. The GES in the middle is resulted from Tra_1. After validating with Tra_2, it evolves to the GES in the right side.

In the first example (cf. Fig. 8), the current GES is empty. By validating with the trajectory, a set of chronological relations are proposed and established. Therefore, a GES corresponding to the model is initialized as shown in the right side.

The second example is tested with a more complex geological scene (cf. Fig. 9), which involves two intersecting faults, parallel, erosional and onlap horizons. In this example, we simulate two trajectories Tra_1 and Tra_2. Tra_2 is more complex, because it meets more surfaces. Moreover, it is more difficult to manage the drilling polarity, such as *from-recent-to-ancient* and *from-ancient-to-recent*, between two successive markers. By considering Tra_1, we have built the model's first GES view. By validating with Tra_2, we have then evolved this initialized GES view (cf. Fig. 9).

6 Conclusion

In this paper, in order to tackle the complexity of predicting global strategy for validating and improving a full earth model's structural description, we proposed to resolve the global problem by favoring the self-organization of cognitive agents, each of which is related to an individual surface in question. Our attention is then focused on acquiring and modeling the adequate knowledge for interpreting each geological surface, and on controlling these agents' interaction. An emergent solution is achieved thanks to agents' collective behaviors. This approach makes the system more flexible, and also facilitates the knowledge acquiring and modeling work. Our approach has been validated with the simulated examples defined by the domain experts. The perspective of this approach can be: 1) detecting the correlation errors in seismic data interpretation; 2) merging the GESs corresponding to the different cross-sections of a same geological model, so as to provide a coherent GES view describing the whole earth model's geology.

References

1. Brandel, S., Schneider, S., Perrin, M., et al.: Automatic Building of Structural Geological Models. Journal of Computing & Information Science & Engineering 5(2), 138–148 (2005)
2. Drogoul, A., Ferber, J., Jacopin, E.: Pengi: Applying Eco-Problem-Solving for Behavior Modelling in an Abstract Eco-System. In: Modeling and Simulation: Proceedings of ESM 1991, Simulation Councils, pp. 337–342 (1991)
3. Dury, A., Le Ber, F., Chevrier, V.: A Reactive Approach for Solving Constraint Satisfaction Problems. In: Rao, A.S., Singh, M.P., Müller, J.P. (eds.) ATAL 1998. LNCS, vol. 1555, pp. 397–411. Springer, Heidelberg (1999)
4. Ferber, J.: Multi-Agent Systems: An Introduction to Distributed Artificial Intelligence. Addison-Wesley, Reading (1999)
5. Foundation for intelligent physical agents: FIPA Contract Net Interaction Protocol Specification. FIPA TC Communication, SC00029H, Geneva, Switzerland (1996–2002)
6. Guessoum, Z., Briot, J.P.: From Active Object to Autonomous Agents. IEEE Concurrency 7(3), 68–78 (1999)
7. Jennings, N., Sycara, K., Wooldridge, M.: A Roadmap of Agent Research and Development. Journal of Autonomous Agents and Multi-Agent Systems 1(1), 7–38 (1998)
8. Ohira, T., Sawatari, R., Tokoro, T.: Distributed Interactions with Compution. In: Agents breaking away, Proc. of Modelling Autonomous Agents in Multi-Agent World (1996)
9. Perrin, M.: Geological Consistency: An Opportunity for Safe Surface Assembly and Quick Model Exploration. 3D Modeling of Natural Objects, A Challenge for the 2000's, 3(pp. 4–5), Nancy France (June 1998)
10. Perrin, M., Zhu, B., Rainaud, J.F., et al.: Knowledge-driven Application for Geological Modelling. Journal of Petroleum Science and Engineering, 89–104 (2005)
11. Ruas, A.: Modèle de généralisation de données géographiques à base de contraintes et d'autonomie. Phd thesis, Université de Marne la Vallée (1999)
12. Schreiber, G., Akkermans, H., Anjewierden, A., et al.: Knowledge Engineering and Management: The CommonKADS Methodology. MIT Press, Cambridge (2000)
13. Serugendo, G., Gleizes, M.-P., Karageorgos, A.: Self-organisation and emergence in MAS: An overview. Informatica 30, 45–54 (2006)
14. Zhu, B., Guessoum, Z., Perrin, M., et al.: Using multiagent systems for validating geological interpretation. In: 2nd IEEE International Conference on Intelligent Computer Communication and Processing, pp. 75–81 (2006)

Agent-Supported Protein Structure Similarity Searching

Dariusz Mrozek, Bożena Małysiak, and Wojciech Augustyn

Silesian University of Technology, Department of Computer Science, Akademicka 16,
44-100 Gliwice, Poland
Dariusz.Mrozek@polsl.pl, Bozena.Malysiak@polsl.pl,
W.August@op.pl

Abstract. Searching for similar proteins through the comparison of their spatial structures requires efficient and fully automated methods and become an area of dynamic researches in recent years. We developed an algorithm and set of tools called EAST (Energy Alignment Search Tool). The EAST serves as a tool for finding strong protein structural similarities in a database of protein structures. The similarity searching is performed through the comparison and alignment of protein energy profiles received in the computational process based on the molecular mechanics theory. This representation of protein structures reduces the huge search space. In order to accelerate presented method we implemented it with the use of Multi Agent System (MAS). This significantly improved the efficiency of the search process. In the paper, we present the complexity of the search process, the main idea of the EAST algorithm and brief discussion on the advantages of its implementation as MAS.

1 Introduction

Proteins are main molecules of life – most of our being has its background in appropriate activity of proteins. Proteins play a very important role in all biological reactions in living cells. Many proteins are enzymes that accelerate (catalyze) biochemical reactions [1]. In consequence, enzymes determine the arrangement and direction of chemical transformations in cells. Proteins can also have other functions, like: energy storage, signal transmission, maintaining of a cell structure, immune response, transport of small bioparticles, regulation of a cell growth and division [2].

An appropriate activity of proteins depends usually on many factors influencing protein spatial structures [4]. Especially, the activity of enzymes in catalytic reactions depends on exposition of some typical parts of their 3D structures called active sites [1], [2]. Conformation and chemical features of active sites allow to recognize and to bind substrates during the catalysis [3], [4]. For these reasons, the study of active sites and spatial arrangement of their atoms is essential while analyzing activity of proteins in particular reactions [5]. The studies can be supported by comparison of one protein structure to other structures (e.g. stored in a database) and can be carried with the use of methods of structural similarity searching. Having a group of proteins indicating strong similarity of selected structural modules one can explore the atomic arrangement of these fragments that take part in respective reactions. Techniques of similarity searching allow seeking the 3D structural patterns in a database of protein structures.

A. Ghose, G. Governatori, and R. Sadananda (Eds.): PRIMA 2007, LNAI 5044, pp. 49–61, 2009.

Unfortunately, this is a very complicated task because of three reasons:

1. proteins are very complex, usually composed of thousands of atoms;
2. the searching process is usually carried through the comparison of a given structure to all structures in a database;
3. number of protein structures in databases, like Protein Data Bank (PDB) [13] rises exponentially every year and is now 44 578 (July 17, 2007).

The first problem is usually solved by decreasing the protein structures complexity in the search process. The most popular methodologies developed so far base on various representations of protein structures in order to reduce the search space. A variety of structure representations were proposed so far, e.g. secondary structure elements (SSE) in VAST [6], locations of the C_α atoms of a protein body and intermolecular distances in DALI [7], aligned fragment pairs (AFPs) in CE [8], or 3D curves in CTSS [9], and many others. These methods are appropriate for homology modeling or function identification. During the analysis of small parts of protein structures that can be active sites in cellular reactions it is required to use more precise methods of comparison and searching. The EAST algorithm [12] that we developed benefit from the dependency between the protein structure and the conformational energy of the structure [10]. In our research, we calculate so called *energy profiles* (EPs) that are distributions of various potential energies along proteins chains (section 2). This reduces the structure complexity. However, a reasonable searching time is still difficult to achieve in the classic client-server architecture.

To solve the problem we decided to reimplement our EAST method to work in the Multi Agent System (MAS). We treat agents as autonomous programs, executed in given place, able to communicate and learn [11]. Since the searching process is carried through the pairwise comparison of given query structure to all structures in a database it is possible to distribute this task to many distinct machines and accelerate entire method. In the paper, we briefly describe the idea of energy profiles (section 2) and our method of similarity searching (section 3), the architecture of the multi-agent system that support the search process (section 4), the environment tests (section 5) and an example of the system usage (section 6).

2   Protein Structure Energy Profiles

In our research on active sites of enzymes, we calculate distributions of conformational energy along amino acid chains of proteins. However, amino acids (peptides) are not directly considered in the calculation process. On the contrary, all performed calculations base on Cartesian coordinates of small groups of atoms that constitute each peptide. Therefore, energy distributions can be seen as forms of representation of protein structures. The distribution of different energies along the protein/enzyme polypeptide chain may be very descriptive for protein function, activity and may reflect some distinctive properties.

Definition 1: We define a single protein energy profile *EP* as a set of energy characteristics of various type of energy, determined for a given protein structure.

$$EP = \left\langle E^{st}, E^{ben}, E^{tor}, E^{vdw}, E^{el}, E^{tot} \right\rangle \tag{1}$$

where: E^{st} denotes a distribution of the bond stretching energy, E^{ben} is a distribution of the angle bending component energy, E^{tor} is a distribution of the torsional angle energy, E^{vdw} is a distribution of the van der Waals energy, E^{el} denotes a distribution of the electrostatic energy. E^{tot} is a distribution of the total energy which is a summary of all component energies in each residue.

Definition 2: The energy distribution E^t, where t is a type of energy, is called *energy characteristics*. Energy characteristics are ordered sets of energy values (so called *energy points*) calculated for groups of atoms of consecutive residues in the polypeptide chain.

Let the R be an ordered set of m residues in the polypeptide chain $R = \left\{ r_1 r_2 r_3 \ldots r_m \right\}$, and X_i^n be a set of atomic coordinates building the ith residue (n is a number of atoms of the ith residue depending on the type of residue), then a simplified protein structure can be expressed by the ordered set of small groups of atoms $X = \left\{ X_1^n X_2^n X_3^n \ldots X_m^n \right\}$.

For the set X we calculate energy characteristics for each type of energy t in the protein energy profile:

$$E^t = \left\{ e_1^t e_2^t e_3^t \ldots e_m^t \right\}, \tag{2}$$

where: e_i^t is an energy point of the ith residue, t is a type of energy.

Energy characteristics (or energy profiles) represent protein structures in a reduced form of ordered sets of energy points, just like other algorithms as sets of positions of C_α atoms. This reduces the search space during the comparison of two protein structures. In our approach, we compute energy characteristics base on the protein atomic coordinates retrieved from the public, macromolecular structure database Protein Data Bank (PDB) [13]. During the calculation we use the TINKER [14] application of molecular mechanics and the Amber [15] force field which is a set of physical-chemical parameters. In this way, we build complete energy profiles as sets of characteristics and store them in our database called Energy Distribution Data Bank (EDB). Afterwards, protein structures can be compared to each other based on their energy profiles, in order to find strong structural similarities, places of discrepancies, or possible mutations.

3 Searching Process with the Use of Energy Profiles

We can use energy profiles to search for structurally similar proteins or search just for some particular parts of their structures. The search process is performed on the energy level with the use of our EAST algorithm and profiles stored in our Energy Distribution Data Bank (EDB). The process is realized through the comparison and alignment of energy characteristics of a query protein and each candidate protein from the EDB. In the comparison we consider only one selected energy type from each EPs. The **alignment** can be thought as the juxtaposition of two energy characteristics that gives the highest number of identical or similar energy points (residues). A *similar* word means that energy points do not have to be identical but they should indicate a similarity with the given range of tolerance. This tolerance is different for different types of energy considered in the search process. As a consequence of a suitable juxtaposition and based on appropriate similarity measures it is possible to evaluate a similarity degree of compared molecules and optionally find regions of dissimilarity. Therefore, the EAST algorithm examines identities, similarities (both are qualified as matches) and disagreements (mismatches) of compared energy points of both energy characteristics. Analogically to the nucleotide or amino acid sequences alignment, some mismatching positions and gaps can appear in the best alignment of energy characteristics. These mismatches and gaps reflect possible evolutionary changes in different organisms.

During the search process with the use of our EAST algorithm a user specifies a query protein (or a part of a molecule) with a known structure. This query-structure is then transformed into the energy profile (EP). Query-molecule EP (QEP) can be compared with other energy profiles stored in the EDB. This is a pairwise comparison – each pair is constituted by the query energy profile QEP and energy profile of the successive molecule from the EDB (candidate energy profile, CEP). In the pairwise comparison, both QEP and CEP are represented by only one chosen energy characteristic (e.g. torsion angle energy, bond stretching energy, electrostatic, or other). During this phase we build a distance matrix D to check the distance between energy characteristics of the query molecule and all candidate molecules.

The distance matrix D allows to compare all energy points of the query molecule energy characteristic $E_A^t = \left(e_{A,1}^t e_{A,2}^t ... e_{A,n}^t \right)$ (part of the QEP) to all energy points of the candidate molecule energy characteristic $E_B^t = \left(e_{B,1}^t e_{B,2}^t ... e_{B,m}^t \right)$ (part of the CEP) and is filled according to the expression (3).

In the energy distance matrix D, the entry d^{AB}_{ij} denotes the distance between energy points of the ith residue of protein A and the jth residue of protein B, and can be expressed as:

$$d_{t,ij}^{AB} = \left| e_{A,i}^t - e_{B,j}^t \right|,$$ (3)

where: t is a type of energy that is considered in the searching.

Based on the distance matrix D we perform the optimization of the alignment path. To optimize the alignment path we use modified, energy-adapted Smith-Waterman method (originally published in [17], with later refinements presented in [18], [19], [20]) that produces the similarity matrix S according to the following rules:

$$\text{for } 0 \leq i \leq n \text{ and } 0 \leq j \leq m:$$

$$S_{i0} = S_{0j} = 0,$$

$$S_{ij}^{(1)} = S_{i-1,j-1} + \vartheta(d_{ij}^{AB}),$$

$$S_{ij}^{(2)} = \max_{1 \leq k \leq n} \{ S_{i-k,j} - \omega_k \},$$

$$S_{ij}^{(3)} = \max_{1 \leq l \leq m} \{ S_{i,j-l} - \omega_l \},$$ (4)

$$S_{ij}^{(4)} = 0,$$

$$S_{ij} = \max_{v=1..4} \{ S_{ij}^{(v)} \},$$

where: ω_k, ω_l are gap penalties for horizontal and vertical gaps of length k and l, respectively, and $\vartheta(d)$ is a function which takes a form of similarity award $\vartheta^+(d_{ij}^{AB})$ for matching energy points ($e_{A,i}^t$ and $e_{B,j}^t$) or a form of mismatch penalty $\vartheta^-(d_{ij}^{AB})$ (usually a constant value) in the case of mismatch (Fig. 1).

The match/mismatch (Fig. 1) is resolved based on distance d_{ij}^{AB} between considered points (stored in the distance matrix D) and additional parameter d_0 called cutoff value. The **cutoff value** is the highest possible difference between energy points $e_{A,i}^t$ and $e_{B,j}^t$ when we treat these two points as similar. The cutoff value determines the range of tolerance for energy discrepancies.

The cutoff value can differ for various types of energy, e.g. for the torsional angle energy the default value was established to d_0=1.4 Kcal/mole based on *a priori* statistics [12]. Default settings for the energy-adapted Smith-Waterman method are: mismatch penalty $\vartheta^-(d_{ij}^{AB})$ =–1/3, affine gap penalty ω_k=1.2+1/3*k [21], where k is a number of gaps and d_{ij} is single cell value of the distance matrix D. The similarity award $\vartheta^+(d_{ij}^{AB})$ for a match depends on distance d_{ij}.

In the scoring function $\vartheta(d)$ in Fig. 1 we have to define two values: a cutoff value d_0, and an identity threshold d_{id}. The **identity threshold** d_{id} is the highest possible difference between energy points when we treat two points as the same. The value of the identity threshold was chosen arbitrary to 0.3-0.5 Kcal/mole during observations of energy characteristics performed for many proteins [12].

The calculation of similarity between two energy points based on their distance is presented in Fig. 1. For each distance we calculate a similarity coefficient (similarity award/penalty for a single match/mismatch). These degrees of similarity are aggregated during the execution of the Smith-Waterman method and contribute to the cumulated *Smith-Waterman Score*. Additional similarity measures are also calculated: *RMSD (Root Mean Square Deviation)* and *Score* [12].

The energy-adapted Smith-Waterman method is one of the most important and time consuming parts of the EAST search algorithm. In the Smith-Waterman method cumulated value of similarity score (*Smith-Waterman Score*) rises when considered energy points match to themselves (are equal or similar with the given range of tolerance d_0), and decreases in regions of dissimilarity (mismatch). Moreover, the energy-adapted Smith-Waterman algorithm with the similarity award/penalty given by a function (not constant values) considers both, number of matching energy points and a quality of the match in the final alignment [16].

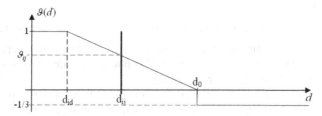

Fig. 1. Similarity award/penalty $\vartheta(d)$ allows to measure the similarity based on the distance between two energy points of compared molecules

4   Architecture of the MAS-EAST Search System

In order to accelerate our EAST algorithm we implemented it in the Multi-Agent System. To this purpose we used JADE (Java Agent DEvelopment Framework) which is an open source platform for peer-to-peer agent based applications. The JADE simplifies the implementation of multi-agent systems through a given middle-ware and through a set of tools that supports the debugging and deployment phases [22]. The most time consuming phase of the EAST algorithm is the optimization (alignment) phase which uses the energy adapted Smith-Waterman method. The method is executed n times for each pair: query molecule vs. candidate molecule, where n is a number of candidate molecules in the EDB. Therefore, the whole alignment task is divided into many subtasks – each one realizes the alignment phase for a smaller group of molecules. In our system we implemented 2 types of agents:

1. **Coordinator Agent, CA** (only one) – responsible for a division of tasks, sequencing and sharing ranges of molecules to compare, and the consolidation of results.
2. **Alignment Agents, AAs** (many) – responsible for the main activity that are: a comparison of a query structure with a portion of structures from the EDB, an appropriate alignment, and similarity measures generation. Each AA does the same alignment task for a different set of candidate molecules from the EDB.

The MAS-EAST searching process consists of the 3 phases:

1. **Initialization** – the parameters of the searching process and query energy characteristic are passed to Alignment Agents (Fig. 2).
2. **Alignment** – each AA performs the alignment for a given range of molecules from the EDB. When an AA finishes its work it returns results to the CA and can get another portion of molecules to work with (Fig. 3).
3. **Consolidation** – the CA consolidates results of alignments obtained from AAs.

The Initialization phase and the Alignment phase are launched sequentially. Nevertheless, the comparison of some portion of structures and consolidation of partial results from the other AAs may occur parallel.

The Initialization phase consists of the following steps (Fig. 2):

1. A user executes the search process (through the GUI) that activates the Coordinator Agent (CA). Searching parameters are passed to the CA.
2. The CA requests appropriate energy characteristic of the Query EP from the EDB.
3. The CA obtains appropriate characteristic as a sequence of energy points.
4. The CA distributes the query energy characteristic and searching parameters to all Alignment Agents (AA).

The Alignment and Consolidation phases consist of the following steps (Fig. 3):

1. The AAs request a portion of data (k candidate molecular structures represented by energy characteristics, CECs) to compare. This portion is called the *package*.
2. The retrieved CECs (package) are sent to AAs.
3. For the query molecule and each candidate molecule from obtained package each AA runs a comparison process including: distance matrices, alignment using energy-adapted Smith-Waterman method, and computation of similarity measures.

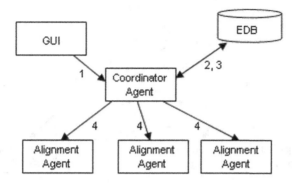

Fig. 2. Communication between agents in the Initialization phase

4. The AAs send results of comparison to the CA. The CA consolidates the partial results asynchronously.
5. The CA sends final results to the user's GUI window and stores them in the EDB (Except of running the searching process, the results can be simply selected from the database when next time any user executes a query with the same searching parameters).

The number of molecules to compare in one package is constant for a searching process, is configurable and is one of the parameters sent in the Initialization phase. Packages are retrieved by AAs continuously until all molecules from the EDB are compared. The CA coordinates the process sending the ranges of molecules to be compared by each AA. The ranges of molecules are disjoint. Therefore, alignment subtasks can be completed independently. If any of the AAs fails its task or disconnects from the system the CA catches the fact and the package of molecules is passed once again to another free AA. There is no need to resolve any conflicts in the situation because results are sent to the CA after the whole package is processed.

We considered other architectures of the system and different interactions between agents in the previous implementations of the MAS-EAST algorithm. In the first implementation, all packages were delivered to AAs by the CA. However, this slowed down the retrieval process, which had to be carried out sequentially. In the second implementation, the CA divided the whole alignment task to the current number of connected AAs. As a result, the number of packages given to each AA was balanced.

This caused many problems, e.g. slower machines completed their tasks much longer than faster machines, a failure of one AA caused a failure of the whole search process, there was no possibility to rescale the alignment task and join additional AAs during the search process. The current implementation (Fig. 2 and Fig. 3) solves all these problems and allows to take over unfinished tasks in the case of failure. In the future, we consider using more Coordinator Agents to secure the system against crashes of the single CA.

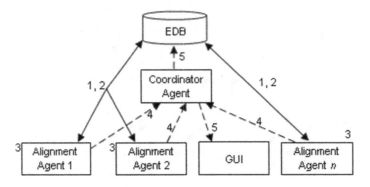

Fig. 3. Communication between agents in the Alignment phase (solid lines) and Consolidation phase (dashed lines)

5 Tests of the MAS-EAST

We tested the agent supported EAST method for many molecules using a set of batch tests. In our experiments we used the EDB database containing 2 240 EPs of proteins from our mirror of the Protein Data Bank (containing more than 44 000 proteins). The subset was chosen arbitrary. Tests were performed with the use of many computers with good performance abilities (from Intel Pentium ® 4 CPU 2.8 GHz, 1GB RAM to Intel ® Core 2 CPU 2.13 GHz, 1 GB RAM). Each agent resided on distinct machine.

Tests confirmed our expectations – the EAST algorithm implemented in the multi agent system is faster than EAST working in standard client-server architecture. The speedup depends on number of Alignment Agents working together to complete the search process. In Fig. 4 we present average execution times (search times) as a function of the number of working Alignment Agents. Results are presented for three molecules that considerably differ with the number of amino acid (residues) in their chains. In Fig. 4 we can observe the execution time decreases with a growing number of working AAs in the system. At first, the decrease is significant, e.g. for 2 working AAs the search process takes half of the time it takes for 1 working AA. For molecule 1QQW the average time we get results is 34 seconds (3AAs), 56 seconds (2AAs), 109 seconds (1 AA). In the client-server implementation of EAST [12] it took 201 seconds but tests were run on slower machine. Afterward, the decrease is not so significant and finally, for 10 working AAs the search process takes about 16 seconds.

The non-linear decrease is probably caused by the communication with the EDB database, data retrieval and delivery. However, this implementation gives us a really good acceleration – for 10 working AAs the average acceleration ratio is 6.33 (7.5 for molecule chains containing 150-450 residues, 3.8 for small molecules up to 100 residues).

In the standard client-server implementation of the EAST algorithm (CS-EAST) we could observe the strong dependency between the average execution time and the length of the query protein chain [16]. Longer protein chains cause the necessity to build bigger distance matrices and elongate the alignment process. In Fig. 5 we show the average execution times as a function of chain lengths for the MAS-EAST implementation, a number of working AAs is constant (for a single series of data).

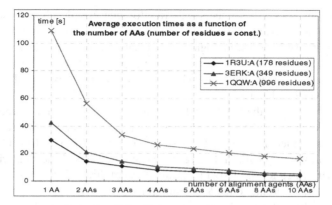

Fig. 4. Average search times as a function of the number of working Alignment Agents for 3 molecules from PDB/EDB: 1R3U (Hypoxanthine-Guanine Phosphoribosyltransferase), 3ERK (Extracellular Regulated Kinase 2), 1QQW (Human Erythrocyte Catalase)

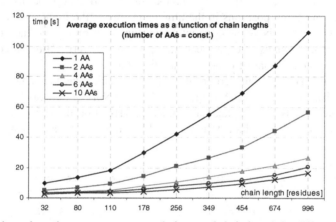

Fig. 5. The dependency between average search times and chain length for different numbers of working Alignment Agents (1, 2, 4, 6, 10 AAs)

In Fig. 5 we can observe the dependency between an execution time and chain length is stronger for the search system with a low number of working AAs. For more AAs working in the system the search time is more independent on chain length. This is an additional advantage of the MAS-EAST implementation.

Our tests shown the type of energy used in the search process does not influence the execution time. The package size during tests was set to 20 molecules. This makes the system more scalable and enables to join additional AAs in the middle of the running process.

6   Example of the System Usage

We tested our method for more than 100 molecules that are in the area of our scientific research. Beneath we present results and analysis of one of the search process performed in our tests. The process was run for query molecule representing the whole protein. However, it can be executed just for the smaller parts of protein structures representing active sites, biological functional domains, 3D motifs or any other structural pattern. The presented example concerns proteins from the RAB family that are members of the bigger group of GTPases – particles that have the ability to bind and hydrolyze GTP molecules.

Therefore, proteins of the RAB family play an important role in intracellular reactions of living organisms. They are elements of the signal pathways where they serve as molecular controllers in the switch cycle between active form of the GTP molecule and inactive form of the GDP. In the Fig. 6 we can see results of the similarity searching process performed for the 1N6H molecule (Crystal Structure Of Human RAB5A). Results are sorted according to the *Score* similarity measure.

Results can be interpreted based on similarity measures: *Score* and *Smith-Waterman Score* (*SW-Score*) – the higher value the higher similarity, *RMSD* – the lower value the better quality of the alignment, and based on output parameters: *Length* – alignment frame, *Matches* – number of aligned energy points, *Match%* – percentage of matching positions in the alignment frame (the higher value the better alignment). Molecules above the horizontal line (Fig. 6) were qualified as similar. The line was inserted manually after the searching process and verification based on similarity measures, annotations of molecules and literature.

The molecule 1HUQ in the group of similar molecules has the same function in mouse organism (*mus musculus*) as query molecule 1N6H in human. The alignment of query molecule 1N6H and candidate molecule 1HUQ on the energy level is presented in Fig. 7. Energy characteristics for both molecules have many matching

```
Best results for job: 2007-07-04 13:13:55
Cut-off: 6.1; id threshold: 0.5; energy type: Charge-charge
S-W type: Fuzzy; mismatch: -0.3334; gap open: 1.2; gap ext.: 0.3334

PDBID Chain Length Matches Match% RMSD     Score     S-W Score
----- ----- ------ ------- ------ ------- -------- ---------
1N6R    A     159     154     96    2.091    73.64    132.84
1N6L    A     162     155     95    2.247    68.98    134.78
1N6O    A     128     126     98    1.914    65.85     98.01
1N6K    A     161     155     96    2.365    65.53    130.45
1N6I    A     154     146     94    2.391    61.06    121.69
1HUQ    A     146     140     95    2.295    61.01    114.89
1N6P    A     136     129     94    2.269    56.85    104.47
1N6N    A     146     137     93    2.488    55.06    110.64
1TU3    A     142     138     97    2.763    49.95     96.85
-----------------------------------------
1GRN    A      28      27     96    3.259     8.29      8.96
1GUA    A      38      32     84    3.960     8.08      4.87
1R8Q    A      26      25     96    3.357     7.45      5.58
...
```

Fig. 6. Results of the similarity searching process with the EAST algorithm (screenshot from the EAST) for molecule 1N6H (Crystal Structure Of Human RAB5A). Parameters – cutoff value: 6.1 Kcal/mole, identity threshold: 0.5 Kcal/mole, energy type: electrostatic.

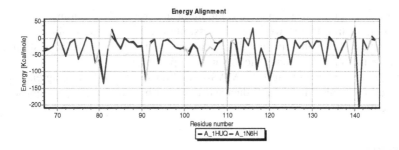

Fig. 7. Alignment of energy characteristics for query molecule 1N6H (Crystal Structure of Human RAB5A) and resultant molecule 1HUQ (Crystal Structure of the Mouse Monomeric GTPase RAB5C). Visible parts: residues 68-145. Grey color (bright line) indicates mismatching parts, no gaps visible.

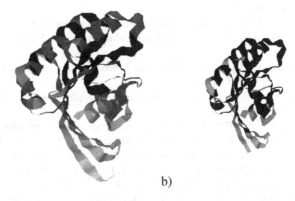

a)   b)

Fig. 8. Comparison of the 3D structures (ribbon representation) of molecules: a) query 1N6H (Crystal Structure of Human RAB5A), b) resultant 1HUQ (Crystal Structure of the Mouse Monomeric GTPase RAB5C). Visualization made with the use of the RasMol [23].

energy points indicating structural similarity. Some parts of these characteristics cover each other what verifies a good quality of the alignment. There are also some parts indicating small conformational differences in the compared structures (e.g. residues 104-110).

The comparison of the 3D structures of query molecule 1N6H and resultant molecule 1HUQ presented in Fig. 8 confirms the similarity of these two molecules.

7 Concluding Remarks

Similarity searching is one of the most frequent tasks performed in bioinformatics database systems. We developed the EAST algorithm of searching for structurally similar proteins (or their parts) with the use of energy profiles. The energy profiles represent protein structures. This reduces the complexity of the search process and is the first acceleration step. The MAS implementation of the EAST algorithm (MAS-EAST) causes additional significant acceleration. Moreover, the MAS implementation guarantees scalability, failure protection, and an automatic balance of the work according to the workstation possibilities. This gives an ability to search great volumes of protein structural data that we expect to have in the nearest future as an effect of mass Nuclear Magnetic Resonance spectrometry.

In the future, we plan to test the MAS-EAST for the EDB containing energy profiles for all molecules in the PDB database and distribute the search problem solution to more computers.

References

1. Fersht, A.: Enzyme Structure and Mechanism, 2nd edn. W.H. Freeman & Co., NY (1985)
2. Dickerson, R.E., Geis, I.: The Structure and Action of Proteins, 2nd edn. Benjamin/Cummings, Redwood City (1981)
3. Lodish, H., Berk, A., Zipursky, S.L., et al.: Molecular Cell Biology, 4th edn. W. H. Freeman and Company, NY (2001)
4. Branden, C., Tooze, J.: Introduction to Protein Structure. Garland (1991)
5. Creighton, T.E.: Proteins: Structures and molecular properties. Freeman, San Fransico (1993)
6. Gibrat, J.F., Madej, T., Bryant, S.H.: Surprising similarities in structure comparison. Curr. Opin. Struct. Biol. 6(3), 377–385 (1996)
7. Holm, L., Sander, C.: Protein structure comparison by alignment of distance matrices. J. Mol. Biol. 233(1), 123–138 (1993)
8. Shindyalov, I.N., Bourne, P.E.: Protein structure alignment by incremental combinatorial extension (CE) of the optimal path. Protein Engineering 11(9), 739–747 (1998)
9. Can, T., Wang, Y.F.: CTSS: A Robust and Efficient Method for Protein Structure Alignment Based on Local Geometrical and Biological Features. In: Proceedings of the 2003 IEEE Bioinformatics Conference (CSB 2003), pp. 169–179 (2003)
10. Burkert, U., Allinger, N.L.: Molecular Mechanics. American Chemical Society, Washington (1980)
11. Wooldridge, M.: Introduction to MultiAgent Systems. Wiley &Sons, Chichester (2002)
12. Mrozek, D., Małysiak, B., Kozielski, S.: EAST: Energy Alignment Search Tool. In: Wang, L., Jiao, L., Shi, G., Li, X., Liu, J. (eds.) FSKD 2006. LNCS, vol. 4223, pp. 696–705. Springer, Heidelberg (2006)
13. Berman, H.M., Westbrook, J., Feng, Z., Gilliland, G., Bhat, T.N., Weissig, H., et al.: The Protein Data Bank. Nucleic Acids Res. 28, 235–242 (2000)
14. Ponder, J.: TINKER – Software Tools for Molecular Design, Dept. of Biochemistry & Molecular Biophysics, Washington University, School of Medicine, St. Louis (June 2001)
15. Cornell, W.D., Cieplak, P., et al.: A Second Generation Force Field for the Simulation of Proteins, Nucleic Acids, and Organic Molecules. J. Am. Chem. Soc. 117, 5179–5197 (1995)
16. Mrozek, D., Małysiak, B., Kozielski, S.: An Optimal Alignment of Proteins Energy Characteristics with Crisp and Fuzzy Similarity Awards. In: Proc. of the IEEE International Conference on Fuzzy Systems (FUZZ-IEEE), pp. 1508–1513 (2007)
17. Smith, T.F., Waterman, M.S.: Identification of common molecular Subsequences. J. Mol. Biol. 147, 195–197 (1981)
18. Gotoh, O.: An Improved Algorithm for Matching Biological Sequences. J. Mol. Biol. 162, 705–708 (1982)

19. Sellers, P.H.: Pattern recognition in genetic sequences by mismatch density. Bull. Math. Biol. 46, 510–514 (1984)
20. Altschul, S.F., Erickson, B.W.: Locally optimal subalignments using nonlinear similarity functions. Bull. Math. Biol. 48, 633–660 (1986)
21. Altschul, S.F., Erickson, B.W.: Optimal sequence alignment using affine gap costs. Bull. Math. Biol. 48(5-6), 603–616 (1986)
22. Bellifemine, F., Caire, G., Poggi, A., Rimassa, G.: JADE, A White Paper (2003), http://jade.tilab.com/papers/2003/WhitePaperJADEEXP.pdf
23. Sayle, R., Milner-White, E.J.: RasMol: Biomolecular graphics for all. Trends in Biochemical Sciences (TIBS) 20(9), 374 (1995)

Merging Roles in Coordination and in Agent Deliberation

Guido Boella[1], Valerio Genovese[1], Roberto Grenna[1],
and Leendert van der Torre[2]

[1] Dipartimento di Informatica, Università di Torino
guido@di.unito.it, valerio.click@gmail.com, grenna@di.unito.it
[2] University of Luxembourg, Luxembourg
leendert@vandertorre.com

Abstract. In this paper we generalize and merge two models of roles used in multiagent systems which address complementary aspects: enacting roles and communication among roles in an organization or institution. We do this by proposing a metamodel of roles and specializing the metamodel to two existing models. We show how the two approaches can be integrated since they deal with complementary aspects: Boella [1] focuses on roles as a way to specify interactions among agents, and, thus, it emphasizes the public character of roles. [2] focuses instead on how roles are played, and thus it emphasizes the private aspects of roles: how the beliefs and goals of the roles become the beliefs and goals of the agents. The former approach focuses on the dynamics of roles in function of the communication process. The latter focuses on agents internal dynamics when they start playing a role or shift the role they are currently playing.

Keywords: Roles, Organizations, O.O. Modeling, MAS, Security.

1 Introduction

In the last years, the usefulness of roles in designing agent organizations has been widely acknowledged. Many different models have been designed. Some of them use roles only in the design phases of a MAS [3], while other ones consider roles as first class entities which exist also during the runtime of the system [4].There are approaches that underline how roles are played by agents [2], other ones on how roles are used in communication among agents in organizations [1]. This heterogeneity of the way roles are dfined and used in MAS risks to be a danger for the interoperability of agents in open systems, since each agent entering a MAS can have a radically different notion of role. Thus, the newly entered agents cannot be governed by means of organizations regulating the MAS. Imposing to all agent designers a single notion of role is a strategy that cannot have success. Rather, it would be helpful to design both multiagent infrastructures that are able to deal with different notions of roles, and to have agents which are able to adapt to open systems which use different notions of roles in organizations. This alternative strategy can be costly if it is not possible to have a general model of role that is compatible, or can be made compatible with other existing concepts.

In this paper we generalize and merge two models of roles used in multiagent systems, in order to promote the interoperability of systems. The research question is: How

A. Ghose, G. Governatori, and R. Sadananda (Eds.): PRIMA 2007, LNAI 5044, pp. 62–73, 2009.

to combine the model of role enactment by [2] with the model of communication among organizational roles of [1]?

We answer these questions by extending to agents a metamodel of roles developed for object oriented systems [5]. The relevant questions, in this case, are: how to introduce beliefs, goals and other mental attitudes in objects, and how to pass from the method invocation paradigm to the message passing paradigm.

Then we specialize the metamodel to model two existing approaches and we show how they can be integrated in the metamodel since they deal with complementary aspects. We choose to model the proposals of [1] and [2] since they are representative of two main traditions. The first tradition is using roles to model the interaction among agents in organizations, and the second one is about role enactment, i.e., to study how agents have to behave when they play a role.

From one side, organizational models are motivated by the fact that agents playing roles may change, for example a secretary may be replaced by another one if she is ill. Therefore, these models define interaction in terms of roles rather than agents. In Boella [1] roles model the public image that agents build during the interaction with other agents; such image represents the behavior agents are publicly committed to. However, this model leaves unspecified, how given a role, its player will behave. This is a general problem of organizational models which neglect that when, for example, a secretary falls ill, there are usually some problems with ongoing issues (the new secretary does not know precisely the thing to be done, arrangements already made etc.). So having a model of enacting and deacting agents surely leads to some new challenges, which could not be discussed, simulated or formally analyzed without this model.

In contrast, the organizational view focuses on the dynamics of roles in function of the communication process: roles evolve according to the speech acts of the interactants, e.g. the commitment made by a speaker or the commands made by other agents playing roles which are empowered to give orders. In this model roles are modeled as sets of beliefs and goals which are the description of the expected behavior of the agent. Roles are not isolated, but belongs to institutions, where constitutive rules specify how roles change according to the moves played in the interactions by the agents enacting them.

Dastani [2] focuses, instead, on how roles are played by an agent, and, thus, on the private aspects of roles. Given a role described in terms of beliefs, goals, and other components, like plans, the model describes how these mental attitudes become the beliefs and goals of the agents. In this approach roles are xed descriptions, so they do not have a dynamics like in the model of [1]. Moreover, when roles are considered inside organizations new problems for role enactment emerge: for example, how to coordinate with the other agents knowing what they are expected to do in their role, and how to use the powers which are put at disposal of the player of the role in the organization. The same role definition should lead to different behaviors when the role is played in different organizations.

In contrast, it species the internal dynamics of the agents when they start playing (or enacting in their terminology) a role or shift the role they are currently playing (called the activated role). So they model *role enacting agents*: agents that know which roles they play, the definitions of those roles, and which autonomously adapt their mental states to play the roles.

Despite the apparent differences, the two approaches are compatible since they both attributes beliefs and goals to roles. So we study by means of the metamodel how they can be combined to have a more comprehensive model of roles.

The paper is structured as follows. In Section 2 we describe the requirements on agents and roles in order to build a metamodel; in Section 3 we formally define the metamodel for roles together with its dynamics; in Section 4 we define the basic notions to model agents that play roles; Section 5 deals with the modeling of enacting agents as in Dastani [2]; Section 6 introduces and models roles to deal with coordination in organizations; in Section 7 we merge Dastani [2] and Boella [1] into the framework introduced in Section 3; Conclusions end the paper.

2   Agents and Roles

Since the aim of this paper is to build a metamodel to promote interoperability, we make minimal assumptions on agents and roles.

The starting point of our proposal is a role metamodel for object orientation. The relation of objects and agents is not clear, and to pass from object to agents we take inspiration from the Jade model [6].

Agents, differently than objects, do not have methods that can be invoked starting from a reference to the object. Rather, they have an identity and they interact via messages. Messages are delivered by the MAS infrastructure, so that agents can be located in different platforms. The messages are modeled via the usual send-receive protocol. We abstract in the metamodel from the details of the communication infrastructure (whether it uses message buffers, etc.). Agents have beliefs and goals. Goals are modeled as methods which can be executed only by the agent itself when it decides to achieve the goal. As said above, we propose a very simple model of agents to avoid controversial issues. When we pass to roles, however, controversial is- sues cannot be avoided. The requirements to cope with both models of roles we want to integrate are: (a) item Roles are instances, associated in some way to their players; (b) roles are described (at least) in terms of beliefs and goals; (c) roles change over time; (e) roles belong to institutions, where the interaction among roles is specified; (f) the interaction among roles specfies how the state of roles changes over time.

In Boella [1] roles are used to model interactions, so agents exchange messages according to some protocol passing via their roles. This means that the agent have to act on the roles, e.g., to specify which is the move the role has to play in certain moment. Moreover, roles interact with each other. Dastanis [2] model specifies how the state of the agent changes in function of the beliefs and goals of the roles it plays. However, it does not consider the possibility that the state of the role change and, thus, it ignores how the agent becomes aware of the changes of beliefs and goals of the role.

To combine the two models we have to specify how the interaction between an agent and its role happens when the agent changes the state of the role or the state of the role is changed by some event. A role could be considered as an object, and its player could invoke a method of the role. However, this scenario is not possible, since the roles are strictly related to the institution they belong to, and we cannot assume that the institution and all the agents playing roles in the institution are located on the same agent platform. So method invocation is not possible unless some sophisticated remote method invocation infrastructure is used. Moreover, the role has to communicate with its player when its beliefs and goals are updated. Given that the agent is not an object, the only way is that a role sends a message to its player. As a consequence, we decide to model the interaction between the agent and the role by means of messages too.

Finally, we have to model the interaction among roles. Since all roles of an institution belong to the same agent platform, they do not necessarily have to communicate via messages. To simplify the interaction, we model communication among roles by means of method invocation.

The fact that roles belong to an institution has another consequence. According to the powerJava [7] model of roles in object oriented programming languages, roles, seen as objects, belong to the same namespace of the institution. This means that each role can access the state of the institution and of the sibling roles. This allows to see roles as a way to specify coordination. In a sense, roles are seen both as objects, from the internal point of view of the institution they belong to, and as agents, from the point of view of their players, with beliefs and goals, but not autonomous. Their behavior is simply to: (1) receive the messages of their players, (2) execute the requests of their player of performing the interaction moves according to the protocol allowed by the institution in that role, (3) send a message to their players when the interaction move performed by the role itself or by some other role results in a change of state of the role.

3   A Logical Model for Roles

In Genovese [5] the model is structured in three main levels: universal, individual and dynamic; here we decide not to talk about the universal level and concentrate ourself on agents dynamics. We dene the formalism of the framework in a way as much general as possible, this gives us an unconstrained model where special constraints are added later.

3.1   Individual Level

This level is composed by a snapshot model that describes in a particular moment the re-lationships between individual players contexts and roles, and a dynamic model which links snapshots and actions modeling how the system changes when an action is exe-cuted. In the formalization of the model we use objects as basic elements upon which the model is based.

Definition 1. A *snapshot model* is a tuple

$$< O, R\_types, I\_contexts, I\_players, I\_roles, Val, I\_contraints$$
$$I_{Roles}, I\_Attributes, I\_Operations, I_{Attr} >$$

- O is a *domain* of objects, for each object o is possible to refer to its attributes and operations through $\pi_{I\_Attr}(o)$ and $\pi_{I\_Op}(o)$, respectively.
- R_types is a set of types of roles.
- I_contexts $\subseteq$ O is a set of institutions (referred as *institutions*).

- I_players $\subseteq$ O is a set of actors (referred as *actors*).
- I_roles $\subset$ O is a set of *roles instances* (referred as *roles_instances*).
- I_Attributes is the set of attributes.
- I_Operations is the set of operations.
- Val is a set of *values*.
- I_constraints is a set of integrity rules that constraint elements in the snapshot.

The snapshot model has also a few functions:

- I_{Roles} is a *role assignment function* that assigns to each role R a relation on I_context x I_players x I_roles.
- I_{Attr} is an *assignment function* which it takes as arguments an object $d \in O$, and an attribute p $\in \pi_{I\_Attr}(d)$, if p has a value $v \in$ Val it returns it, $\emptyset$ otherwise.

Generally, when a role instance x is an individual of the type D, we write $x :: D$. If $a \in \pi_{I\_Attr}(x)$ we write x.a $\in$ I_Attributes as the attribute instance assigned to object x, the same holds for elements in I_Operations. $(i,a,o) \in I_{Roles}(R)$ means: "the object o represents agent a playing the role R in institution i", often writen $R(i,a,o)$, and o is the *role instance*.

3.2   The Dynamic Model

The dynamic model relies on the individual level and denes a structure to properly describe how the framework evolves as a consequence of executing an action on a snapshot. In Section 4 and 5, we describe how this model constraints agentsdynamics.

Definition 2. A *dynamic model* is a tuple

$$< S, TM, Actions, Requirements, D\_constraints, I_{Actions}, I_{Roles_t} \pi_{Req}, I_{Requirements_t} >$$

- S is a set of *snapshots*.
- TM $\subseteq$ S x $\mathbb{N}$: it is a time assignment relationship, such that each snapshot has an associated unique time t.
- Actions is a set of actions.
- Requirements is a set of requirements for playing roles in the dynamic model.
- D_contraints is a set of integrity rules that constraints the dynamic model.
- I_Actions maps each action from Actions to a relation on a set of snapshots P. $I_{Actions}(s,a,t)$ tells us which snapshots are the result of executing action a at time t from a certain snapshop. [1] This function returns a couple in TM that binds the resulting snapshot with time $t + 1$. In general, to express that at time t is carried action a we write a_t.
- About I_{Roles_t}, $R_t(i,a,o)$ is true if there exists, at a time t, the *role instance* $R(i,a,o)$.
- $\pi_{Req}(t,R)$ returns a subset of Requirements present at a given time t for the role of type R, which are the requirements that must be fulfilled in order to play it.

---

[1] Notice that given an action, we can have several snapshots because we model actions with modal logic in which, from a world it is possible to go to more than one other possible world. This property is often formalized through the *accessibility relationship*. Thus, each snapshot can be seen as a possible world in modal logic.

– $I_{Requirements_t}$ is a function that, given (i,a,R,t) returns True if the actor a fills the requirement in $\pi_{Req}(t,R)$ to play the role R in the institution i, False otherwise. We often write $Req_t(i,a,R)$.

Intuitively, the snapshots in S represent the state of a system at a certain time. Looking at $I_{Actions}$ is possible to identify the *course* of actions as an ordered sequence of actions such that $a_1;b_2;c_3$ represents a system that evolves due to the execution of a, b and c at consecutive times. We refer to a particular snapshot using the time t as a reference, so that for instance $\pi_{I\_Attr_t}$ refers to π_{I_Attr} in the snapshot associated with t in TM.

Actions are described using dynamic modal logic [8], in paricular they are modelled through *precondition laws* and *action laws* of the following form:

$$\Box(A \wedge B \wedge C \supset \langle d\rangle\top) \tag{1}$$

$$\Box(A^{'} \wedge B^{'} \wedge C^{'} \supset [d]E) \tag{2}$$

Where the $\Box$ operator expresses that the quantified formulas holds in all the possible words. *Precondition law* (1) specifies the conditions A,B and C that make an atomic action d executable in a state. (2) is an *action law*[2] which states that if preconditions $A^{'},B^{'}$ and $C^{'}$ to action d holds, after the execution of d also E holds.

In addition we introduce *complex actions* which specify complex behaviors by means of *procedure definitions*, built upon other actions. Formally a complex action has the following form: $\langle p_0\rangle\varphi \subset \langle p_1;p_2....;p_m\rangle\varphi$; p_0 is a *procedure name*, ";" is the *sequencing operator* of dynamic logic, and the p_i's, $i \in [1,m]$, are procedure names, atomic actions, or test actions[3].

Now we show some examples of actions that can be introduced in the dynamic model in order to specialize the model.

Role addition and deletion. For role addition and deletion actions we use, respectively $R,i \hookrightarrow_t a$, and $R,i \hookleftarrow_t a$. Then using the notation of dynamic logic introduced above, we write: $\Box(Req_t(i,a,R) \supset \langle R,i \hookrightarrow_t a\rangle\top)$ to express that, if actor a fills the requirements at time t ($Req_t(i,a,R)$ is True), a can execute the role addition action that let him play role of type R.

The above definition gives us the possibility to model that a role assignment introduces a role instance: $\Box(\top \supset [R,i \hookrightarrow_t a]\exists xR_{t+1}(i,a,x))$ or the fact that if a does not already play the role R within institution i, then the role assignment introduces exactly one role instance: $\Box(\neg\exists xR(i,a,x) \supset [R,i \hookrightarrow_t a]\exists!xR_{t+1}(i,a,x))$.

Methods. There are other actions through which is possible to change the model as well, for instance agents may assign new values to their attributes [5].

Here, we will focus on the case in which the attribute's values can be changed by the *objects themselves*. What we will do is to define *methods* of objects with which they can change attributes of their own or those of others. Actually, to simplify the model, we define one single primitive action: $set_t(o_1,o_2,attr,v)$, which means that object o_1

---

[2] Sometimes action laws are called *effect rules* because E can be considered the effect of the execution of d.

[3] Test actions are of the form $\langle\psi?\rangle\varphi \equiv \psi \wedge \varphi$.

sets the value of attr on object o_2 to v at time t. If o_1 and o_2 are autonomous agents, the set$(o_1, o_2, attr, v)$ can be executed only when $o_1 = o_2$.

Now, we will of course have that: $\Box(\top \supset [set_t(o_1, o_2, attr, v)]attr_{t+1}(o_2) = v)$ which means that in any state, after the execution of set, if the action of setting this attribute succeeds, then the relevant object will indeed have this value for that attribute.

Operations. Elements of our framework come with *operations* that can be executed at the individual level in order to change the model dynamically, the semantics of each operations can be given exploiting the actions defined for the dynamic model. Suppose, for instance, to have an object individual $x :: Person$ with x.mail_address attribute, and an operation x.change_mail that changes the value of x.mail_address to its argument. Using the set primitive is possible to define how the model evolves after the execution of x.change_mail operation trough the following axiom:

$[x.change\_mail_t(s)]\varphi \equiv [set_t(x, x, mail\_adress, s)]\varphi$, where x.change_mail$_t(s)$ identifies the action carried by x at time t to execute the instance operation x.change_mail; objects can execute only operations that are assigned to them by I_OS relation. In Section 5 we define exec of certain operations as complex actions because we have to describe a more complex semantics.

4   Enact and Deact Roles

In Dastani [2], the problem of formally defining the dynamics of roles, is tackled identifying the actions that can be done in a *open system* such that agents can enter and leave. Here, four operations to deal with role dynamics are defined: *enact* and *deact*, which mean that an agent starts and finishes to occupy (play) a role in a system, and *activate* and *deactivate*, which means that an agent starts executing actions (operations) belonging to the role and suspends the execution of the actions. Although is possible to have an agent with multiple roles enacted simultaneously, only one role can be *active* at the same time. Before diving into modeling the four basic operations to deal with roles, we need to match our framework with a few concepts defined in [2], following we report a list of elements together with their definition and then how they fit in our meta-model:

- *Multiagent system*: In [2] roles are taken into account at the implementation level of *open MAS*, they belong to the system which can be entered or left by agents dynamically. In our framework is possible to view a system as a context to which are linked all roles that can be played by the agents.
- *Agent role*: A role is a tuple $\langle \sigma, \gamma, \omega \rangle$. Where σ are beliefs, $\gamma \cdot$goals and ω rules representing conditional norms and obligations. This definition specifies a role "in terms of the information that becomes available to agents when they enact the role, the objectives or responsibilities that the enacting agent should achieve or satisfy, and normative rules which can for example be used to handle these objectives" [2]. With this view we define, for *roles* of our framework, a set of complex attributes {beliefs, goals, plans, rules} $\in$ I_Attr togheter with the *operations* that represent actions that an agent can carry out when it *activates* the roles instance choosing it from the set of roles it is playing.
- *Agent type*: We consider an agent type "as a set of agent roles with certain constraints and assume that an agent of a certain type decides itself to enact or deact

a role". To talk about agent types we use *classes* introduced in the framework as a specification of agent instances at the individual level, with this in mind we use the PL relationship to link *agent classes* to *agent roles* (role's classes) so that the set of roles that an agent can enact (play), is constrained by I_PL.

- *Role enacting agent*: "We assume that role enacting agents have their own mental attitudes consisting of beliefs, goals, plans, and rules that may specify their conditional mental attitudes as well as how to modify their mental attitudes. Therefore, role enacting agents have distinct objectives and rules associated to the active role it is enacting, and sets of distinct objectives and rules adopted from enacted but inactive roles". In our framework we define a *role enacting agent* as a instance x having a set of attributes A that represent the internal structures used to deliberate.

$$A = \{\text{beliefs}_a, \text{objectives}_a, \text{plans}_a, \text{rules}_a, \text{enacted\_roles}[], \text{active\_role}\} \in \pi_{I\_Attr}(x)$$

The enacted_roles attribute is a role ordered record where each entry with index i corresponds to a triple $\langle \sigma_i, \gamma_i, \omega_i \rangle$ which represents the set of beliefs, objectives, plans and rules associated to roles instance i enacted by x.

As introduced above, the model in [2] identifies four operations to deal with role dynamics, in order to to grasp the fundamental ideas proposed in the cited paper, we redefine the *enact*, *deact*, *activate* and *deactivate* operations respecting their original meaning. Given an agent x, a role instance $i :: R$ played by x in context c s.t.,

$$\{\text{beliefs}_r, \text{objectives}_r, \text{plans}_r, \text{rules}_r\} \in \pi_{I\_Attr}(i)$$
$$\{\text{beliefs}_a, \text{objectives}_a, \text{plans}_a, \text{rules}_a, \text{enacted\_roles}[], \text{active\_role}\} \in_{SA} \pi_{I\_Attr}(x)$$
$$\{\text{enact}, \text{deact}, \text{activate}, \text{deactivate}\} \in \pi_{I\_Op}(x)$$

Next we report the semantics of each operation exploiting the set primitive:

$$\langle x.\text{enact}_t(i)\rangle \varphi \subset \langle R, s \hookrightarrow x; \text{set}_t(x, x, \text{beliefs}_a, \text{beliefs}_a \cup \text{beliefs}_r);$$
$$\text{set}_t(x, x, \text{enacted\_roles}[i], < \text{objectives}_r, \text{plans}_r, \text{rules}_r >)\rangle \varphi \tag{3}$$

$$\langle x.\text{deact}_t(i)\rangle \varphi \subset \langle R, s \hookleftarrow x; \text{set}_t(x, x, \text{enacted\_roles}[i], \text{null})\rangle \varphi \tag{4}$$

$$\langle x.\text{activate}_t(i)\rangle \varphi \subset \langle \text{set}_t(x, x, \text{active\_role}, \text{enacted\_roles}[i])\rangle \varphi \tag{5}$$

$$\langle x.\text{deactivate}_t(i)\rangle \varphi \subset \langle \text{set}_t(x, x, \text{active\_role}, \text{null})\rangle \varphi \tag{6}$$

5   The Public Dimension of Roles

In Boella-Van der Torre [9] roles are introduced inside institutions to model the interaction among agents. In Boella [1] the model is specifically used to provide a semantics for agent communication languages in terms of public mental attitudes attributed to roles.

The basic ideas of the model are: (1) roles are instances with associated beliefs and goals attributed to them. These mental attitudes are public. (2) The public beliefs and goals attributed to roles are changed by speech acts executed either by the role or by other roles. The former case accounts for the addition of preconditions and of the intention to achieve the rational effect of a speech act, the latter one for the case of commands or other speech acts presupposing a hierarchy of authority among roles. (3) The agents execute speech acts via their roles.

In order to maintain the model simple enough, we model message passing extending the dynamic model with two actions (methods) $\mathsf{send}(\mathsf{x,y,sp})$ and $\mathsf{receive}(\mathsf{y,x,sp})$. Where $\mathsf{send}(\mathsf{x,y,sp})$ should be read as the action carried by x of sending a speech act (sp) to y and $\mathsf{receive}(\mathsf{y,x,sp})$ is the complementary action of y receiving the message from x. It must be underlined that arguments x and y can be agents or roles. A role only listens for the messages sent by the agents playing it:

$$\langle \mathsf{listen(r)} \rangle \varphi \subset \langle \mathsf{P; played\_by(r,x)?; receive(r,x,sp); D} \rangle \varphi$$

These rules define a *pattern* of protocol where P and D have to be read as possible other actions that can be executed before and after the receive. The reception of a message from the agent has the effect of changing the state of other roles. For example, a command given via a role amounts to the creation of a goal on the receiver if the sender has authority (within the system) over it.

$$\Box(authority_{sys}(r, \mathsf{request} \supset [\mathsf{receive}(r, x, \mathsf{request}(r, r', \mathsf{act})))]\mathbf{G}_t^r(\mathsf{act}))^4$$

To produce a speech act, the agent has to send a message to the role specifying the illocutive force, the receiver and the content of the speech act:

$$\langle \mathsf{communicate(a)} \rangle \varphi \subset \langle \mathsf{P; send(x,r,sp); D} \rangle \varphi$$

6   The Combined Model

The two models presented above model complementary aspects of roles: the public character of roles in communication and how agents privately adapt their mental attitudes to the roles they play.

In this section we try to merge the two approaches using the metamodel we presented. On the one hand, Boella's model [1] is extended from the public side to the private side, by using Dastani [2] as a model of role enacting. In this way, the expectations described by the roles resulting from the interaction among agents can become a behavior of agents and they do not remain only a description. On the other hand, Dastanis model [2] is made more dynamic. In the original model the role is given as a fixed structure. The goals of agent can evolve according to the goal generation rules contained in it, but the beliefs and goals described by the role cannot change. This is unrealistic, since during the activity of the agent enacting its role, it is possible that further information are put at disposal of the role and that new responsibilities are assigned, etc.

In order to merge the two models within the same framework, we need to add (complex) actions which are able to grasp the dynamics introduced in [1] and [2]. Interactions among agents is done through message passing and, in particular, through actions send and receive introduced in section 6. Next we are going to introduce all the speech-acts and complex actions which are needed to grasp the combined model and then we introduce a running example to clarify their use defining a *course* of actions in the dynamic

---

[4] $\mathsf{request}(r, r', \mathsf{act})$ means: role r asks to r''s player to do act. $authority_{sys}(r, \mathsf{request})$ expresses that role r has the authority to make a request within system sys.

model defined in section 3.2. An agent who wants to play a role within an *open system* has to ask to the system for a role instance; this process is handled by two speech act: ask_to_play(R) and accept_to_play(r,A), where the first one is sent from the agent to the system in order to ask to play a role of type R, whereas the second is sent from the system to the agent, together with the identifier of the role instance r and a set A of other role instances present in the system, in order to inform the agent with which roles is possible to interact. Next we report the two *effect rules* associated:

$$\Box(\top \supset [\text{receive}(s,x,\text{ask\_to\_play}(R));\text{send}(s,x,\text{accept\_to\_play}(r,A)] \\ \text{played\_by}_{\text{sys}}(r,x,s) \tag{7}$$

$$\Box(\top \supset [\text{send}(x,s,\text{ask\_to\_play}(R));\text{receive}(x,s,\text{accept\_to\_play}(r,A)] \\ \text{played\_by}_{\text{ag}}(r,x,s)) \tag{8}$$

Where s is the system, x the agent, and r a role instance of type R. In this section we use x,y,z... to denote agents, s for the system and r,r',r''...for role instances. Notice that played_by$_{\text{sys}}(r,x,s)$ and played_by$_{\text{ag}}(r,x,s)$ refer to two different infrastructures; in Rule 7 is the system that, after having acknowledged the agent request, knows that x is going to play r, whereas in Rule 8 is the agent that becomes aware of the play relation between x and r. To link the two predicates with the logical model introduced in Section 3 we have that: played_by$_{\text{sys}}(r,x,s) \wedge$ played_by$_{\text{ag}}(r,x,s) \rightarrow R(s,x,r)$. When we are dealing with a single system we can omit s writing played_by$_{\text{sys}}(r,x)$ and played_by$_{\text{ag}}(r,x)$. To enact a role, an agent, provided the identifier of the role instance it wants to enact, has to send a message to the role and to wait till the role replies with the information about the state of the role: its beliefs, goal, plans, etc. When the state is received, the agent can enact the role in the same way described by Rule 3 in Section 5. In order to model such interaction we introduce two complex actions tell_enact, accept_enact and two speech acts accept_enact and inform_enact. Following the specification of the complex actions:

$$\langle \text{tell\_enact}(x,r)\rangle\varphi \subset \langle \text{played\_by}_{\text{ag}}(r,x)?;(\text{send}(a1,r1,\text{enact}(x,r)))\rangle\varphi \tag{9}$$

$$\langle \text{accept\_enactment}(r,x)\rangle\varphi \subset \langle \text{receive}(r,x,\text{enact}(x,r));\text{played\_by}_{\text{sys}}(r,x)?; \\ \text{send}(r,x,\text{inform\_enact}(<\text{beliefs}_r,\text{objectives}_r,\text{plans}_r,\text{rules}_r>)))\rangle\varphi \tag{10}$$

When the agent receives the specification of the role he wishes to enact, it can internalize them as in Rule 3:

$$\Box(\top \supset [\text{receive}(x,r,\text{inform\_enact}(<\text{beliefs}_r,\text{objectives}_r,\text{plans}_r,\text{rules}_r>))] \\ \mathbf{B}^x(\text{beliefs}_r) \wedge x.\text{enacted\_roles}[r] =<\text{objectives}_r,\text{plans}_r,\text{rules}_r>)^5 \tag{11}$$

In this combined view is possible that role's specifications change dynamically, in that case it is up to the role to send a message to its player each time its state is updated:

$$\langle \text{udpate\_state}(r,x)\rangle\varphi \subset \langle \text{played\_by}_{\text{sys}}(r,x)?;(\neg\mathbf{G}_t^r(q) \wedge \mathbf{G}_{t+1}^r(q))?; \\ \text{send}(r,x,\text{inform\_goal}(q)))\rangle\varphi \tag{12}$$

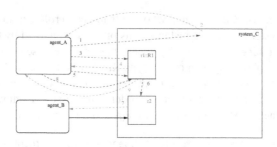

Fig. 1. Roles in MAS

Last but not least, we need to model the deactment of a role respecting the formalization as in Rule 4, therefore we introduce two speech acts deact, ok_deact and a complex action confirm_deact defined as follows:

$$\langle \text{confirm\_deact}(r,x) \rangle \varphi \subset \langle \text{receive}(r,x,\text{deact}); \text{played\_by}_{sys}(r,x)?;$$
$$\text{send}(r,x,\text{ok\_deact}) \rangle \varphi \qquad (13)$$

After sending ok_deact, the system will not consider anymore agent x as player of r:

$$\Box(\top \supset [\text{confirm\_deact}(r,x)]\neg\text{played\_by}_{sys}(r,x) \qquad (14)$$

If it is possible for the agent to deact the role, it will receive an ok_deact from its role:

$$\Box(\top \supset [\text{receive}(x,r,\text{ok\_deact})]x.\text{enacted\_roles}[r] = \text{null} \wedge \neg\text{played\_by}_{ag}(r,x)) \quad (15)$$

Fig. 1 depicts two agents which interact through roles in an open system. At time t the system has already agent_B that enacts role r2 as represented by the black arrow which goes from agent_B to r2. Following the course of actions that describe how the system evolves:

1. At time t+1 agent_A asks to institution system_C to play a role of type R1:
   $\text{send}_{t+1}(\text{agent\_A}, \text{system\_C}, \text{ask\_to\_play}(R1))$
2. At time t+2 system_C replies to agent_A assigning to him the role instance r1:
   $\text{send}_{t+2}(\text{system\_C}, \text{agent\_A}, \text{accept\_to\_play}(r1, \{r2\}))$
3. At time t+3 agent_A wants to enact (internalize) role r1: $\text{tell\_enact}_{t+3}(\text{agent\_A}, r1)$
4. At time t+4 role r1 receives the speech act from agent_A asking for enactment and accepts it, replying to agent_A with its specifications:
   $\text{accept\_enactment}_{t+4}(r1, \text{agent\_A})$
5. Once that agent_A has enacted the role as in Rule 3 it decides, at time t+5, to activate it and then to ask to the agent playing r2 to do an action act. In other words: $\text{send}_{t+5}(\text{agent\_A}, r1, \text{request}(r1, r2, \text{act}))$. When r1 receives a send from agent_A asking for an act of r2, first it checks if the sender has the authority in the system to ask such an act, if so r2 acquires the goal to do act:
   $\Box(\text{authority}_{sys}(r', \text{act}) \supset [\text{receive}(r, \text{agent\_A}, \text{request}(r, r', \text{act}))]\mathbf{G}^{r'}(\text{act}))$. Is important to underline that because role internals are public to other roles in the same system, it is always possible for r1 to check or modify r2's goals. So, at time t+6 we have: $\text{receive}_{t+6}(r1, \text{agent\_A}, \text{request}(r1, r2, \text{act}))$

6. Now that r2 has updated its internal state (i.e. its goals) it must inform its player agent_B: update_state$_{t+7}$(r2, agent_B) Where update_state is modeled as in Rule 12
7. At time t+8 agent_A decides to deact the role r1: send$_{t+8}$(agent_A, r1, deact)
8. Finally, at time t+9, r1 confirm the deact: confirm_deact$_{t+9}$(r1, agent_A)

7 Conclusions and Further Works

In this article we merged two representative roles models in MAS by introducing a metamodel taken from Genovese [5] and adapting it to agents. In particular, we added representations of typical agents mental attitudes and a framework to deal with message passing. The model has been specialized in order to describe both public and private dimensions of roles (Boella, Dastani [[1,2]). Finally, we merged the two dimensions defining a group of actions together with their semantics and we modeled a running example to show a possible course of events.

Further works point in two main directions: adapting the proposed metamodel to other roles approaches like Omicini [10], and introducing a formal proof theory of roles' actions dynamics and related aspects starting from Baldoni et al [8].

References

1. Boella, G., Damiano, R., Hulstijn, J., van der Torre, L.: Acl semantics between social commitments and mental attitudes. In: Procs. of Workshop on Agent Communication (2006)
2. Dastani, M., van Riemsdijk, B., Hulstijn, J., Dignum, F., Meyer, J.J.: Enacting and deacting roles in agent programming. In: Odell, J.J., Giorgini, P., Müller, J.P. (eds.) AOSE 2004. LNCS, vol. 3382, pp. 189–204. Springer, Heidelberg (2005)
3. Zambonelli, F., Jennings, N., Wooldridge, M.: Developing multiagent systems: The Gaia methodology. IEEE Trans. of Software Engineering and Methodology 12(3), 317–370 (2003)
4. Colman, A., Han, J.: Roles, players and adaptable organizations. Applied Ontology (2007)
5. Genovese, V.: Towards a general framework for modelling roles. In: Normative Multi-agent Systems. Number 07122 in Dagstuhl Seminar Proceedings (2007)
6. Bellifemine, F., Poggi, A., Rimassa, G.: Developing multi-agent systems with a FIPA-compliant agent framework. Software – Practice And Experience 31(2), 103–128 (2001)
7. Baldoni, M., Boella, G., van der Torre, L.: Interaction between Objects in powerJava. Journal of Object Technology 6, 7–12 (2007)
8. Baldoni, M., Baroglio, C., Martelli, A., Patti, V.: Reasoning about interaction protocols for customizing web service selection and composition. Journal of Logic and Algebraic Programming, special issue on Web Services and Formal Methods 70(1), 53–73 (2007)
9. Boella, G., van der Torre, L.: The ontological properties of social roles in multi-agent systems: Denitional dependence, powers and roles playing roles. Artificial Intelligence and Law Journal (AILaw) (2007)
10. Omicini, A., Ricci, A., Viroli, M.: An algebraic approach for modelling organisation, roles and contexts in MAS. Applicable Algebra in Engineering. Communication and Computing 16, 151–178 (2005)

Planning Actions with Social Consequences

Hsueh-Min Chang[1] and Von-Wun Soo[1, 2]

[1] Department of Computer Science, National Tsing Hua University
101, Section 2, Guangfu Road, Hsinchu 300, Taiwan
[2] Department of Computer Science and Information Engineering,
National University of Kaohsiung
700, Kaohsiung University Road, Kaohsiung 811, Taiwan
{pchang,soo}@cs.nthu.edu.tw

Abstract. In an environment with multiple autonomous agents, the perform-ance of an action may have effects on the beliefs and goals of the witnessing agents in addition to the direct effects. The awareness of such mental effects is critical for the success of a plan in multi-agent environments. This paper pro-vides a formulation of social plans, and show that social planning can be done by including models of other agents' minds in the planning domain. A social planning agent is constructed based on automatic generation of PDDL (Plan-ning Domain Description Language) domains from knowledge about other agents.

1 Introduction

Automated planning is an important research topic for designing agents that achieve their goals by modifying the environment through a sequence of actions. In multi-agent environments, the planning problem is complicated by the fact that multiple agents may modify the shared environment concurrently so that their plans may dis-rupt or reinforce each other. Interference among plans is the foundation of much multi-agent planning research, including plan coordination [6] and counterplanning [15], in which an agent strives to achieve its goal despite or possibly due to the inter-ference from others.

However, it is often overlooked in planning that an action can have *social influ-ences* on other agents. In other words, an action can cause changes not only in the physical environment but also in the mental states of other agents, either deliberately or accidentally. Like plan interferences, social influences also impact agent planning, albeit on a different level. The difference can be seen in the following cases, where agent A plans to assassinate agent B with a knife:

Agent C also has a plan that needs the knife.

Guard agent D sees A with a knife and decides to block A's entry to B's house.

Both situations can cause the plan of A to fail, but the reasons are different. In case (i), the plans of agents A and C conflict (i.e. interfere negatively) with each other. In case (ii), however, D has no plan that conflicts with A's plan at first, but generates a new conflicting goal upon perceiving a knife on A. Thus, D's blocking the entry is a *social consequence* of A's walking to the door. If A hopes to succeed, he should have constructed a plan that explicitly avoids being witnessed when carrying the knife. Since each action can arouse certain reactions from other agents, it is easy to see that

A. Ghose, G. Governatori, and R. Sadananda (Eds.): PRIMA 2007, LNAI 5044, pp. 74–85, 2009.

agents who ignore the mental effects of actions will be blind to many further social consequences, and often fail to produce a feasible plan.

A closely related concept to social consequences is *social actions*, which Castelfranchi defines as those actions that "deal with another entity as an agent, i.e. an active, autonomous, goal-oriented entity." [3] He further divides social actions into *weak* and *strong* ones. Weak social actions are based on beliefs, but not goals, about others' minds or actions. For instance, in case (i), if A believes that C intends to take the knife, A's taking another weapon is a weak social action, for it is based on A's own belief about C's goal but is not to change it. A strong social action, however, is directed by social goals, i.e. goals to change or maintain the mental states of others. For instance, in case (ii), if A chooses to take an alternative entrance or to drug the guard out of his consciousness, A is performing a strong social action directed by the social goal that D has no goal to block A's entrance. The model of social actions therefore distinguishes between the problem of plan coordination, which requires solely weak social actions, and the problem of *social planning* introduced in this paper. Social planning extends conventional planning by including social consequences as a part of its action effects, and thus requires strong social actions.

In this work, we put the concepts into practice by presenting an implementation of social planning. Since social planning extends the state space to the internal states of agents, the planning agent must treat the internal mechanisms of other agents as part of the world causality. For example, an agent's perceiving a particular object causes its belief state to change, and the new belief state activates the motivational mechanism [11] to generate a new goal state, which can be translated into a new physical state of the world through actions. Essentially, the agent builds a model of other agents and simulates their mental processes in order to reason about what actions he can perform in order to bring about certain mental states of others. However, since mental states are not directly accessible, social planning will cause the well-known *ramification problem* ([2] and [8], for example), which states that actions can have indirect effects which is context-dependent and can be potentially unbounded.

The implementation of the social planning agent takes a representation-oriented approach that leverages the expressive power of the Planning Domain Description Language (PDDL) [7][12] to describe agent perception, mental states, belief revision and desire generation in a limited but useful way. In particular, PDDL provides a *derived predicates* construct that can represent the deduction from physical states to mental states. The social planning agent translates its model of other agents to PDDL files, and uses one of the state-of-the-art general-purpose planners to do the actual planning. Details of domain translation are presented in Sect. 3. One of the potential applications of social planning is on the interactive drama domain, as is demonstrated in section 4, in which social planning agents are used to simulate a simplified version of Othello, a famous play by William Shakespeare.

2 Analysis of Social Planning

Social planning can be viewed as basically classical single-agent planning enhanced with consideration on the social consequences of actions. The product of social planning is often (but not always) a *social plan*, which contains (a) actions by other agents and (b) actions by self that motivate these other agents to act. Although a social plan is a multi-agent plan, social planning is done from a single-agent perspective, utilizing actions by others only as a means to achieve its own goal. This sets social planning apart from many forms of multi-agent planning that assumes the agents are designed to be a part of a cooperative system whose objective is to maximize the team utility, such as in [9].

In effect, social planning enhances classical planning in two ways. On one hand, *active social planning* aims to invoke others' goals that positively contributes to the plan, making it possible to construct plans for goals that an agent cannot achieve by itself. On the other hand, *passive social planning* aims to prevent a goal that is detrimental to the plan from being generated, and thus helps detect plans that work in single-agent settings but no longer works when other agents are present. Note that purely passive social planning can result in nonsocial plans because its ultimate aim is to trigger no beliefs and goals at all. This fact leads to subtleties about the identification of social actions, as will be shown in Sect. 2.2. In the remainder of the section, we will use a simple motivational, goal-oriented agent to illustrate the nature of social planning.

2.1 Formulation of Social Plans

We begin by describing an agent with naïve rule-based belief revision and motivation functions. Although decidedly simple, the agent is motivated, i.e. can generate goals autonomously, and thus satisfies the basic requirement of social planning.

Definition 1 (Description of an agent)
Let P be the set of all atomic propositions. Let R be the set of first-order sentences. An agent ag_1 is a 4-tuple $(B_{ag1}, G_{ag1}, BRR_{ag1}, MR_{ag1})$, where B_{ag1} P is ag_1's beliefs, G_{ag1} P is ag_1's goals, BRR_{ag1} R is a set of belief revision rules, and MR_{ag1} R is a set of motivation rules. The rules have the form $x \to p$, where x is a first-order proposition and p P is the derived atom. A belief revision rule derives a belief from beliefs, while a motivation rule derives a goal from beliefs.

The agent will gain perceptual input from the environment, update the belief set using BRR_{ag1}, and then update the goal set using MR_{ag1}. If any new goal is added, the agent searches for a plan for the goal. A social planning agent (denoted ag_1 in this section) can thus have an internal model of another agent (denoted ag_2) using the explicit representation.

Definition 2 (Model of another agent)
Agent ag_1's model about another agent ag_2 is a 4-tuple $M_{ag2} = (B_{ag2}, G_{ag2}, BRR_{ag2}, MR_{ag2})$, where $B_{ag2} = \{p \mid believes(ag_2, p)$ $B_{ag1}\}$ is ag_1's model about ag_2's beliefs, $G_{ag2} = \{p \mid hasGoal(ag_2, p)$ $B_{ag1}\}$ is ag_1's model about ag_2's goals. BRR_{ag2} and MR_{ag2} are the modeled belief revision functions and motivation functions, respectively.[1]

The social planning agent ag_1 can then infer how a percept changes the internal state of ag_2. However, ag_1 also needs a perception model to estimate whether the effects of its action are actually perceived by ag_2. Note that it is the environment, not the agents, who dictate the range of perception. We assume that for any event e P, the environment provides the truth value of the predicate $perceives(ag, e)$. With the above models, now we can derive the mental changes as a result of an action. To calculate the mental effect, ag_1 simulates an instance of ag_2 by adopting ag_2's beliefs, goals and mental state transition rules. Then ag_1 gives the simulated ag_2 some hypothetical

---

[1] We adopt the naming convention that predicates are in lower case while functions are capitalized.

percepts which would result from the action, and observes the mental state change. It first applies the belief revision rules to derive the belief effects.

Definition 3 (Belief effects of an action on one agent)
Let $P\text{-}Eff(action)$ be the set of physical effects of $action$. The set of belief addition by an action $action$ on an agent ag_2 is $B\text{-}Add(action, M_{ag2}) = \{p \mid pP, p\ B_{ag2}, \{q \mid qP\text{-}Eff(action), perceives(ag_2, q)\} \cup B_{ag2} \cup BRR_{ag2} \vdash p\}$. The set of belief deletion is $B\text{-}Del(action, M_{ag2}) = \{p \mid p\ B_{ag2}, \{q \mid qP\text{-}Eff(action), perceives(ag_2, q)\} \cup B_{ag2} \cup BRR_{ag2} \nvdash p\}$.

The belief effects thus include an add list and a delete list. The add list contains atoms that can be derived but was not originally believed, while the delete list contains ones that was originally believed but cannot be derived after an action is conducted. After the beliefs of ag_2 are updated, motivation rules are applied to derive new goal effects.

Definition 4 (Goal effects of an action on one agent)
Let B_{ag2}' be the belief set updated with $B\text{-}Add(action, M_{ag2})$ and $B\text{-}Del(action, M_{ag2})$. The set of goal additions by the action $action$ on an agent ag_2 is $G\text{-}Add(action, M_{ag2}) = \{p \mid p\ P, p\ G_{ag2}, B_{ag2}' \cup MR_{ag2} \vdash p\}$. The set of goal deletions is $G\text{-}Del(action, M_{ag2}) = \{p \mid p\ G_{ag2}, B_{ag2}' \cup MR_{ag2} \nvdash p\}$.

Now we turn to actions that consume rather than produce mental effects. For an agent who plans its own actions, the actions only need to satisfy the physical precondition. However, if the plan involves actions of other agents (which we will call *foreign actions*), the planning agent must motivate these agents to perform them. Riedl and Young [14] are among the first to propose this additional intentional requirement in planning, although their planner is not based on the perspective of an individual agent. In short, the intentional precondition of an action is that either the performer is self or the performer desires any of the physical effects of the action by other agents.

Definition 5 (Intentional precondition)
The intentional precondition of an action performed by agent ag is the disjunction of members of the set $M\text{-}Precond(action, ag) = \{goal(ag, p) \mid p\ P\text{-}Eff(action)\} \cup \{self(ag)\}$.

The total precondition is the thus conjunction of the physical precondition and the intentional precondition. Finally, we derive our definition of social plans as containing one or more foreign actions, whose intentional preconditions are supported by some other actions. For convenience, we adopt the convention in plan-space planning (e.g. POP) that there is a *finish* action whose precondition is the goal of the plan. Thus, if the goal of the plan is a social goal, *finish* is considered a foreign action, and the plan a social plan.

Definition 6 (Social plan)
Let $Actions(plan)$ be the set of all actions in $plan$. $social(plan)$. $(a1, a2\ Actions\text{-}(plan)), \{\ (p, ag), (goal(ag, p)\ M\text{-}Precond(a1, M_{ag})\ p\ G\text{-}Add(a2, M_{ag})))$.

2.2 Relationship between Social Actions and Social Plans

When analyzing a social plan, one may be tempted to regard it as the combination of three types of actions: social, non-social and foreign actions. While an action whose effects include some intentional precondition of another action is clearly social, one that does not is not necessarily nonsocial. Here we provide two reasons why the such an action could still be social:

1. *The action belongs to a subplan that causally supports a social action.* Thus, the action still can be regarded as driven by a social goal, albeit indirectly. This rises the question of the *degree* of sociality.

2. *The action is chosen because alternatives are known to cause negative social consequences.* The action could be regarded as driven by a social goal to keep another agent from generating a goal, and thus social. However, if the action is considered *before* the bad alternatives which are therefore never considered, can it still be said to be directed by a social goal?

In essence, Castelfranchi's social action is a concept based on the agent's subjective judgment about whether it is "dealing with another entity as an agent." Whether an action is social depends on the agent's way of thinking, such as its choice of planning algorithm. Thus, it is simpler to regard social planning as incorporating social consequences than as producing social actions. On the other hand, a social plan is a structural concept. A plan is social because its structure involves other agents; how it is generated is irrelevant.

2.3 Social Planning as a Case of the Ramification Problem

Social planning relies on mental effects, which are always indirect because agents have no direct access to others' minds [8]. They are also highly context-dependent; who the witnesses are and what they have in mind decide the mental effects of an action, as shown in Definition 3 and 4. These facts classify social planning as an instance of the long recognized ramification problem, which concerns the indirect consequences of an action. A variety of methods have been proposed to (partially) solve the ramification problem in planning, including deductive planning [2] and external theorem provers [8], among others. However, completely specifying the action ramifications can be difficult. In social planning, an action can cause mental effects, which motivate another agent to perform some action, which in turn can be perceived by yet another agent, and so on, resulting in a chain of reaction. An agent with knowledge about the mental states of a society can in principle predict the future of the society by modeling the agents' actions step by step while checking whether their interaction changes their goals and thus the course of their actions. *The total effect of an action is thus the difference between how the society would evolve with and without that action.* Luck and d'Inverno [10] called agents capable of modeling the society *sociological agents*. Unfortunately, the butterfly effects[2] of an action could be broad in scope and infinite in time, making it difficult to find a sound and complete social planner. In the next section, we will introduce a method that compiles a limited representation of the social planning problem and then solve it with a sound and complete planner.

---

[2] It is commonly said that a flap of wings of a butterfly could produce a tornado far away.

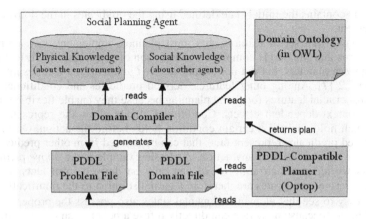

Fig. 1. The architecture of the social planning agent

3 Social Planning through Domain Compilation

This section presents an implementation of social planning agents based on planning domain compilation. An assumption of automated planning is that the causality of the world is encoded in a domain-description language, which allows the specification of planning operators as triggers of state change. Therefore, planning can control the social consequences in multi-agent environments *if the planning domain includes agency as part of world causality*. Based on this observation, we have developed a social planning agent without resorting to a special-purpose planner[3]. Instead, the agent leverages the expressive power of PDDL to represent a social planning problem as a standard planning problem, and uses a general-purpose planner to solve it. Fig. 1 shows the architecture of the agent who plans socially with domain compilation techniques. Before planning, the agent compiles its beliefs and the ontology schema into PDDL files. A compatible planner then takes the files as input, plans, and returns the result to the agent. Domain compilation is based on the formulations of mental effects and preconditions in Sect. 2. It generates a partial representation of the social planning problem with an inherent bias towards active social planning. The remainder of this section will briefly introduce PDDL and describe the details of domain compilation into PDDL.

3.1 Introduction to PDDL

McDermott et al. [12] created the first version Planning Domain Description Language (PDDL) in an attempt to provide a standard language for specifying planning problems in the International Planning Competition. PDDL has since been revised several times for the need of the competition. As a result, most mainstream planners now adopt PDDL documents as input format.

Two PDDL documents are needed for a planning problem. The *domain* file defines the predicates, actions and their preconditions and effects for a planning domain. The

---

[3] This is not to say that social planning cannot benefit from a special-purpose planner.

problem file contains the initial state defined using the predicates in the domain, and a goal statement.

PDDL has a rich set of features, and most planners implement only a subset of PDDL. Barros and Musse [1] compiled a comparison of supported PDDL features for several modern planners, but did not include *derived predicates*, a features introduced in version 2.2 [7]. Among other features, derived predicates and conditional effects are the most crucial features for social planning because they enable flexible representation of context-dependent effects. Conditional effects allow the representation of effects which holds only if a certain condition holds before the action. On the other hand, derived predicates represent facts that can be derived from other predicates, but can never be direct effects of any action. A classic example is the *above* predicate in the blocks world, in which *above(a, b)* can only be derived from facts like *on(a, c)on(c, b)*. Derived predicates are therefore a partial solution to the ramification problem. It is easy to see that elements of mental states also possess the properties of derived predicates because no action can directly infuse a belief in an agent; actions can only produce percepts, from which beliefs are derived. Optop [13] and Marvin [5] are two of the planners that provide the best support for derived predicates.

3.2 Automated Domain Compilation

Fig. 2 lists the mapping between a motivated agent and the corresponding PDDL constructs that describe the agent. A domain compiler (DC) compiles the domain ontology and each part of the agent into PDDL. The generation of regular predicates and actions from the domain ontology is rather straightforward and thus is omitted. Specific processes required by social planning are discussed in the following.

Representing beliefs and goals. Since PDDL is unable to represent nested literals like *belief(Emilia, holds(Desdemona, Handkerchief))*, DC must generate additional predicates like *b_holds(Emilia, Desdemona, Handkerchief)* for each predicate as a workaround. Similarly, DC generates *p_holds* for percepts and *g_holds* for goals.

Perception. Any change to the mental state starts from perception. Thus, agents whose plan relies on foreign actions must have some control on the perception of other agents. We make the assumptions that agents have a perception range, and that they perceive all events happening within that range. Accordingly, an action produces percepts if and only if either of the following conditions holds: (a) the action is performed within the perception range of some other agent, (b) the action causes an object to enter the perception range of some agent. The performance of an action produces two types of events: an *action event* represents the performance of an action, while *state events* represent the changed state after the performance of the action.

PDDL implementation of perception. Percepts are represented in PDDL as conditional effects of an action because an action successfully invokes percepts only when the geographic relationship between agents is valid.[4] The following expression in terms of PDDL represents the conditional state event of performing *drop(actor, thing, place)*:

---

[4] Although one might be tempted to describe percepts as derived predicates dependent on geographic relations, doing so will cause existing percepts to *disappear* when the supporting geographic conditions no longer hold!

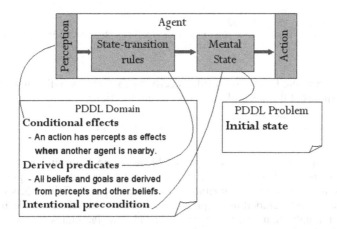

Fig. 1. The mapping between agents and the PDDL constructs

```
(forall (?other)
   (when (and (in ?other ?place) (in ?actor ?place))
         (and (p_in ?other ?thing ?place)
              (not (p_holds ?other ?thing ?actor)))))
)
```

The action *goto* is more complex because it involves location change, and its corresponding code is too long to be listed here. Basically, performing a *goto* will cause the actor to perceive all (observable) predicates describing everything in the new place, and cause everyone in the new place to perceive all predicates describing the actor. Therefore, domain compilation has to list all predicates as the condition effects of goto.

Belief revision and goal generation. Belief revision is the process of updating beliefs according to the percepts. There are two types of predicates for beliefs: *action event belief* and *state belief*, in correspondence with the two types of percepts. In addition to directly reflecting percepts, state beliefs can also be derived from existing ones using belief revision rules. For example, the social knowledge may describe agents as having a belief revision rule like the following one:

$loves(ag_1, ag_2)$. $t, precious(t)$ $gives(ag_1, ag_2, t)$ $man(ag_1)$ $woman(ag_2)$

Note that $gives(ag_1, ag_2, t)$ is an action event belief, while others are state beliefs.

However, a social planning agent adopts the rule not to revise its own beliefs, but to reason about how to activate it for other agents in order to change their minds. Therefore, the subjective rule needs to be transformed into a relative one, in which each literal becomes a belief of some particular agent. The resulting axiom is as follows:

. $subject, belief(subject, loves(ag_1, ag_2)$.$t, belief(subject, precious(t))$ $belief(subject, gives(ag_1, ag_2, t))$ $belief(subject, man(ag_1))$ $belief(subject, woman(ag_2))$

DC uses the same procedure to compile motivation rules for describing goal generation.

PDDL implementation of belief revision and goal generation. Beliefs and desires are described as PDDL derived predicates of the form (:derived P F), meaning that predicate P holds iff formula F holds. Here is an example of the above belief of *love*, specifying both sources of belief:

```
(:derived (b_loves ?s ?a1 ?a2)
   (or (p_loves ?s ?a1 ?a2)
       (exists (?t) (and (b_precious ?s ?t) (b_gives ?s ?a1 ?a2 ?t)
                         (b_man ?s ?a1) (b_woman ?s ?a2)))))
)
```

Below is a compiled motivation rule specifying that agents will generate goals to get precious things at the same place as his current location.

```
(:derived (g_holds ?s ?t)
   (and (b_precious ?s ?t) (exists (?p) (and (in ?s ?p) (in ?t ?p)))
)
```

Action selection. An agent will attempt to achieve the goals through actions. To represent the relationship between goals and actions, DC extends action preconditions according to the formulation of *intentional precondition* in Definition 5, which states that an action *can* be included in the plan only if some of its effects are desired by the performer. Although the use of intentional preconditions facilitates active social planning, it also leads to limitations in passive social planning. The reason is as follows. A satisfied precondition merely implies that the action is feasible, not that the action is necessary. This goes contrary to the fact that when an agent desires some effect of an action, the agent *will* perform it, unless there is an alternative action that provides the same effect. Thus, other agents' actions whose intentional preconditions are accidentally satisfied during planning will be performed. A normal planner will simply choose not to include these actions in the plan if they are irrelevant or detrimental to the goal, but that they will still be performed is not changed.

PDDL implementation of action selection. The PDDL is exactly modeled after Definition 5. For the *drop* action that has the physical effects $in(thing, place)$ □ □$holds(actor, thing)$, the intentional precondition is

```
(or (self ?actor)
    (g_in ?actor ?thing ?place) (g_not_holds ?actor ?thing ?actor))
```

Macro actions. Another problem is that the other agent may need more than one action to achieve the goal. To model this, social planning agent may have to plan for other agents and check interferences among all plans. Since plan coordination is outside the scope of this paper, we use macro actions to bypass the problem. Macro actions represent a sequence of actions to achieve a goal, like plan libraries. They have the same format as regular actions, except that they can only be performed by other agents. An example in our domain is *steal-for*, which represents walking to the victim, stealing something, walking to the master, and give it to the master.

PDDL implementation of macro preconditions. The PDDL for macro actions is not different from that for regular actions in terms of perceptual effects. The only difference is that macro actions do not have the *self* disjunct in their intentional preconditions.

Problem generation. Whenever a social planning agent chooses a goal to plan for, DC creates a PDDL problem file containing the goal and the agent's social and physical beliefs as the initial state. The translation process for beliefs to PDDL simply involves dumping all beliefs as PDDL literals. A physical belief has the form (holds Iago Handkerchief), while (g_holds Cassio Cassio Handkerchief) represents a social belief that Cassio desires to hold the handkerchief. With the domain and problem files, the planner can connect the actions to produce a plan.

4 Implementation Results

The implementation is based on our ontology-based agent environment, which uses OWL models to describe the knowledge schema and action specification. Details about the system can be found in [4]. The domain compiler translates OWL models to PDDL files. Both the agents and the domain compiler are implemented in Java and use sockets to connect to McDermott's Optop planner, which runs on Lisp.

4.1 The Othello Scenario

We draw our inspiration from Shakespeare's Othello, a prime example of shrewd social planning. A vastly simplified version of it is used as the scenario for demonstration. Here is our mundane version:

A soldier Iago have long resented General Othello and plotted to make him suffer by having him kill his own wife, Desdemona. To carry out his plan, Iago first asked his wife Emilia in the garden to steal a handkerchief Othello gave Desdemona. Emilia stole it from Desdemona and gave it to Iago. Iago then deliberately planted the handkerchief in the lieutenant Cassio's room, expecting that Cassio would pick it up, and Cassio did it. Othello, under the advice of Iago, then paid a visit to Cassio. Seeing the handkerchief on Cassio, he was enraged by jealousy. He killed Cassio immediately and ended up going to Desdemona's room to kill her as well.

All the characters are modeled as autonomous motivated agents, but Iago is the only social planning agent among them. The scenario contains 9 objects, 6 actions, 1 macro action, and 16 basic predicates, each of which has 3 extended versions: belief, goal and precept. The actions are `goto`, `pickup`, `drop`, `kill`, `request_in`, and `request_holds`, the latter two being communicative actions representing a request to adopt a goal to be in somewhere or to hold something. The macro action is `steal_for`. One belief predicate, `b_loves`, is derived from a motivation rule of folk psychology basically stating that when an agent C finds a gift given to person A to be on person B of an opposite sex, C believes that A loves B. Two goal predicates, `g_holds` and `g_dead`, are derived from two motivation rules, greed and jealousy. The greed rule states that an agent will desire to take away precious things in his residing location, and the jealousy rule states that an agent will desire to kill his wife and her lover, if the lover is not the agent himself.

4.2 Results and Performance

In the simulations, both active and passive social planning plays a part in Iago's plan. In a simulation run in which Iago's goal was *hasGoal(Othello, dead(Desdemona))*, Iago did produce a plan, but this plan included an action to carry the handkerchief to Othello's home, resulting in the deaths of both Desdemona and Iago himself, the latter being an undesirable side effect. To correct this, the goal is conjoined with *hasGoal(Othello, dead(Iago))* to enforce the passive social planning to remove the side effect. On a 3.0 GHz Pentium 4 computer running CLISP, Optop takes 10.2 seconds to find a correct plan. The domain compiler needs to be ported to work with Marvin [5], whose support on conditional effects is limited. We have not finished the porting, but our initial experience is that Marvin takes excessive time in preprocessing the domain. The output of Optop is presented in the following with adjusted indentation. However, it comes up with a plan that is slightly different from the original scenario in that Iago requests Cassio to visit Othello, not vice versa.

```
(#<Planning-problem-solution / length 7 / score 7 [NIL]
      (#/(REQUEST_HOLDS_0 IAGO_0 EMILIA_0 IAGO_0 HANDKERCHIEF_0)
    #/(STEAL_FOR_0 EMILIA_0 HANDKERCHIEF_0 IAGO_0)
    #/(GOTO_0 IAGO_0 GARDEN_0 HOME_0)
    #/(DROP_0 IAGO_0 HANDKERCHIEF_0 HOME_0)
    #/(REQUEST_IN_0 IAGO_0 CASSIO_0 CASSIO_0 PALACE_0)
    #/(PICKUP_0 CASSIO_0 HANDKERCHIEF_0 HOME_0)
  #/(VISIT_0 CASSIO_0 HOME_0 PALACE_0))>) ;
```

5 Conclusion

When multiple motivated agents inhabit the same environment where they can see each other, effects of an action will enter the witnesses' minds and change their beliefs and goals and could thus initiate a series of reactions. Since actions may have social ramifications, an agent can no longer be oblivious of others while making plans. Instead, they should use actions to motivate others to conduct parts of the plan, and avoid actions with negative social consequences. The formulation of social plans takes into consideration of the dependence relation between actions of self and actions of others in a plan. Although a sound and complete social planner is very difficult to produce, we show that a reduced social planning problem can be represented using a standard domain description language. The implementation of social planning agents demonstrates that social planning through planning domain compilation can be done with a general purpose planner. Since social planning makes no assumption about whether agents are cooperative or competitive, improved understanding of the problem, its logical characterization and its computational properties could shed lights on how human-like agents interact socially in general.

Acknowledgment

This work is supported by the National Science Council of Taiwan under grant number NSC 96-2628-E-007-044-MY3.

References

1. Barros, L.M., Musse, S.R.: Planning algorithms for interactive storytelling. Comput. Entertain. 5 (2007)
2. Bibel, W.: Let's Plan it Deductively! Artif. Intell. 103, 183–208 (1998)
3. Castelfranchi, C.: Modeling Social Actions for AI agents. Artif. Intel. 103, 157–182 (1998)
4. Chang, P.H.-M., Chien, Y.-H., Kao, E.C.-C., Soo, V.-W.: A Knowledge-Based Scenario Framework to Support Intelligent Planning Characters. In: Panayiotopoulos, T., Gratch, J., Aylett, R.S., Ballin, D., Olivier, P., Rist, T. (eds.) IVA 2005. LNCS, vol. 3661, pp. 134–145. Springer, Heidelberg (2005)
5. Coles, A.I., Smith, A.J.: Marvin: Macro-actions from reduced versions of the instance. In: IPC4 Booklet, Fourteenth International Conference on Automated Planning and Scheduling (2004)
6. Cox, J., Durfee, E.H.: An Efficient Algorithm for Multiagent Plan Coordination. In: Proceedings of the 4th International Joint Conference on Autonomous Agents and Multi-Agent Systems (AAMAS 2005), pp. 828–835. ACM Press, NY (2005)

7. Edelkamp, S., Hoffmann, J.: PDDL2.2: The Language for the Classical Part of the 4th International Planning Competition. Technical Report 195. Albert-Ludwigs-Universität, Institut für Informatik, Freiburg, Germany (2004)

8. Field, D., Ramsay, A.: How to Change a Person's Mind: Understanding the Difference between the Effects and Consequences of Speech Acts. In: Proceedings of 5th Workshop on Inference in Computational Semantics (IcoS-5), Buxton, England, pp. 27–36 (2006)

9. Grosz, B., Hunsberger, L., Kraus, S.: Planning and Acting Together. AI Magazine 20, 23–34 (1999)

10. Luck, M., d'Inverno, M.: Plan Analysis for Autonomous Sociological Agents. In: Castelfranchi, C., Lespérance, Y. (eds.) ATAL 2000. LNCS, vol. 1986, pp. 182–197. Springer, Heidelberg (2001)

11. Luck, M., d'Inverno, M.: Motivated behaviour for goal adoption. In: Zhang, C., Lukose, D. (eds.) DAI 1998. LNCS, vol. 1544, pp. 58–73. Springer, Heidelberg (1998)

12. McDermott, D., Ghallab, M., Howe, A., Knoblock, C., Ram, A., Veloso, M., Weld, D., Wilkins, D.: PDDL - The Planning Domain Definition Language. Technical Report CVC TR-98-003/DCS TR-1165. Yale Center for Computational Vision and Control (1998), http://www.cs.yale.edu/~dvm

13. McDermott, D.: The Optop Planner. In: IPC4 Booklet, Fourteenth International Conference on Automated Planning and Scheduling (2004)

14. Riedl, M.O., Young, R.M.: An Intent-Driven Planner for Multi-Agent Story Generation. In: Proceedings of the Third International Joint Conference on Autonomous Agents and Multi-Agent Systems (AAMAS 2004), pp. 186–193. IEEE Computer Society, Washington (2004)

15. Rowe, N., Andrade, S.: Counterplanning for Multi-agent Plans using Stochastic Means-Ends Analysis. In: Proceedings of the IASTED Artificial Intelligence and Applications Conference, pp. 405–441 (2002)

Layered Cooperation of Macro Agents and Micro Agents in Cooperative Active Contour Model

Noriko Matsumoto, Norihiko Yoshida, and Shuji Narazaki

Division of Mathematics, Electronics and Informatics
Saitama University, Saitama 338-8570, Japan
noriko@ss.ics.saitama-u.ac.jp

Abstract. We have proposed *Multi-Snake*, which realizes boundary detection in image recognition with the layered cooperation of micro agents and macro agents. Cooperation in a set of micro agents constructs the behavior of a macro agent, and cooperation of the micro agents are integrated to cooperation of the macro agents. This mechanism makes the application more dynamic and flexible. Our previous proposals dealt with cooperation between some macro agents of the same kind. This paper focuses on the cooperation of macro agents of different kinds: sensor-based macro agents and model-based macro agents. We show that our proposal makes estimation improved and more robust. We verify the effectiveness of our proposal through some experiments using artificial images and real images.

1 Introduction

Image recognition and feature extraction are still difficult to solve although there have been many proposals applying various techniques including agents techniques. Accurate boundary detection in an image is one of the most important problems in image recognition, however it is also still difficult.

One of the most popular boundary detectors is Active Contour Model "Snake", proposed by Kass et al. [1]. The principle of Snake is an energy-minimizing spline for estimating the closest contour of a target object in an image gradually from an initial contour. This principle can be considered as a boundary detector realized by cooperation in an aggregate of many micro agents, that is, the contour is a single macro agent which consists of a set of micro agents. There have been some proposals concerned with cooperation of macro agents. In this paper, we discuss layered cooperation which integrates the cooperation of the micro agents, who construct a macro agent, to the cooperation of the macro agents. In this way, we can produce the macro cooperation from the micro cooperation. The layered cooperation make this application more dynamic and flexible.

We have proposed Multi-Snake, the improvement of Snake in this manner. This proposal so far has been concerned with cooperation of macro agents of the same kind, and we verified its effectiveness [2,3,4]. Our another paper [5] presented some preliminary idea on cooperation of macro agents of different kinds, namely, sensor-based macro agents and model-based macro agents. In

A. Ghose, G. Governatori, and R. Sadananda (Eds.): PRIMA 2007, LNAI 5044, pp. 86–97, 2009.
© Springer-Verlag Berlin Heidelberg 2009

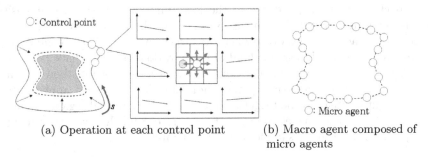

(a) Operation at each control point   (b) Macro agent composed of
micro agents

Fig. 1. Principle of Snake

this paper, we investigate some fundamental aspects on cooperation of macro agents of different kinds based on cooperation of micro agents.

2   Active Contour Model, Snake

Snake is a deformable contour $v(s) = [x(s), y(s)], s \in [0, 1]$ that moves to minimize an energy function E_{snake}. The energy E_{snake} consists of an internal force $E_{int}(v(s))$ and an external force $E_{ext}(v(s))$. $E_{int}(v(s))$ indicates elasticity and smoothness of the contour, and $E_{ext}(v(s))$ is derived from the image along the contour $v(s)$ so as to be attracted to a certain edge. Snake is formulated as minimizing a spline of the energy function as follows:

$$E_{snake} = \int \{E_{int}(v(s)) + E_{ext}(v(s))\}ds \qquad (1)$$

$$E_{int}(v(s)) = (\alpha|v_s(s)|^2 + \beta|v_{ss}(s)|^2) \; / \; 2 \qquad (2)$$

$$E_{ext}(v(s)) = -\gamma|\nabla I(v(s))|^2 \qquad (3)$$

where $v_s(s)$ and $v_{ss}(s)$ denote the first and second derivative of the contour with respect to s, ∇I is image intensity gradient, and each α, β, and γ are weight coefficients. It means the value of this energy function gets smaller, if the shape of the closed contour is more circular, if the circumference length is shorter, or if the intensity gradient is larger. However, this tendency depends on the parameter settings.

In general, Snake transforms the contour to minimize E_{snake} from an initial closed contour provided by a user, and searches the target boundary. Snake calculates the changes of the function value at each point, namely each control point, on the closed contour, and moves the control point to a direction whose energy gradient is the steepest as shown in Figure. 1(a). Therefore, it can be considered that each control point is a micro agent and, the contour is a single macro agent as an aggregate of the micro agents (Figure. 1(b)).

Snake searches the target boundary sequentially from the initial contour, so that it tends to be influenced extremely by the initial contour. Snake also has a drawback of strong dependence to the local information, which is intensity gradient along the closed contour, as expressed in the formula (3). Hence, the detection accuracy becomes worse when the target image consists of complicated features. In order to address this kind of issue, various methods have been proposed using some macro agents distributed in space, such as a method dividing an image into several uniform regions beforehand [6], a method applying two Snakes simultaneously to the target region and the background region [7], and a method making some Snakes compete or cooperate [8,9]. However, they require strict positioning of many sample points for the initial contour(s).

3 Multi-Snake

The original Snake has some drawbacks of its strong dependence on the parameters, the target features and the target image as mentioned above. In order to address these drawbacks, we have proposed *Multi-Snake*, an improvement of Snake by applying the agent technique, with the layered cooperation mechanism [2,3,4]. This method uses several macro agents in parallel, each of which runs its own Snake, to detect the boundary of a single target object. Each macro agent does a different estimation being based on different solution space, using different parameters, or being applied to closely-related different images. This cooperation of macro agents are realized by the cooperation of micro agents, that is, *Multi-Snake* has two layers as shown in Figure 2 (a) and (b). Some micro agents, which are located at the same control point on the contour, exchange their intermediate contour estimation with each other periodically, and adjust their own contour estimations. This approach realizes robust estimation against noises and textures, and improves estimation qualities.

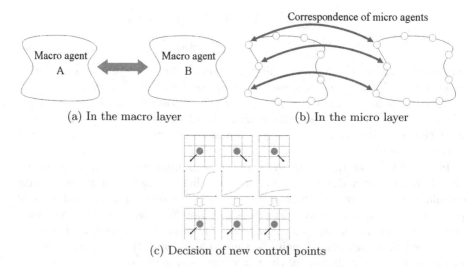

(a) In the macro layer   (b) In the micro layer

(c) Decision of new control points

Fig. 2. Cooperation mechanism of Multi-Snake

When the gradient (the first derivative) of the energy function calculated in a certain macro agent gets small, this means the agent gets near to a local minimum or the global minimum. However, if the gradient in another agent still keeps large at the same control point, it is supposed that the agent is not at the global minimum but at a local minimum. Accordingly, in the micro agent layer, each corresponding micro agent exchanges with each other the direction which gives the largest energy gradient among its eight-neighbors, and follows the direction which gives the largest gradient among the values from all the micro agents. This scheme is shown in Figure 2(c). This exchange takes place at every moment when the micro agents move control points. This cooperation of the micro agents layer realizes the cooperation of the macro agents layer.

4   Model-Based Snake

As mentioned above, *Multi-Snake* has two layers as shown in Figure 2 (a) and (b), and we have verified its effectiveness, but using macro agents of the same kind so far. To improve the estimation quality even more, we discuss cooperation of macro agents of different kinds [5], namely sensor-based macro agents and model-based macro agents. First, we introduce model-based Snake.

Snake is prone to complex shapes, concave boundaries, and pointed boundaries. In particular, the concave boundaries cannot be detected by adjusting its parameters only, and this problem is still left as a big problem. This is caused by the energy potential as shown in Figure 3 (a), in which arrows express the forces to attract Snake to the target. A user must place an initial contour on the region very close to the target concave region so as to make Snake converge to the concave. Once Snake escapes from the energy potential to attract to the concave, it is inevitable to transform into a straight line as shown in Figure 3 (b). This is the core of the problem. In order to solve this kind of problem, we have an observation that the initial contour placed by a user implies (or can be given easily) some information of the target shape.

There have been some methods using a model as information of the target shape; for example, a proposal determines E_{int} which is suitable for the target shape by presenting the prototype beforehand [10,11], or another proposal determines a range of acceptable shape divergence by estimating the average shape of target and the unevenness of shape [12,13,14,15,16]. In particular, Matsuzawa [16] adopts the symbolized information, such as "corner", "curve", "segment", and "arc", which is obtained from the shape of initial contour. Based on this symbolized information, this method assigns these shape information to each control point of Snake respectively, and makes control of Snake reflect the shape knowledge of target region. This approach has an advantage of its ability which can include the model with the process of boundary detection without giving up Snake's advantages of the ability of general-purposeness and handiness. Based on this approach, we have considered modeling the fragment shapes

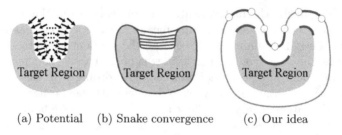

(a) Potential   (b) Snake convergence   (c) Our idea

Fig. 3. Around a concave boundary region

of the initial contour to bring in the model to the control of Snake. Matsuzawa's symbolization cannot describe the fine features, although control Snake by the target model acquired from the shape information in an initial contour. Hence, we use the curvature at each region more concretely.

Our model-based Snake, which we call *Curvature Snake*, selects the feature points from the initial contour, and models the curvature among the feature points. We bring in this curvature to Snake as a model.

Curvature Snake uses the energy function as follows:

$$E_{CS} = \int \{E_{int}(v(s)) + E_{ext}(v(s)) + E_{model}(v(s))\} ds \qquad (4)$$

$$E_{model} = \delta |E^0_{curv} - E_{curv}| \qquad (5)$$

where E^0_{curv} is the initial curvature calculated on a feature point on the initial contour. These initial feature points are placed on the contour at an equal interval (Δs) as shown in Figure 4 (a). E_{curv} is the current curvature calculated on a feature point on the current contour at each moment. When the current curvature approximates to the model (the initial curvature), E_{model} gets smaller, therefore Curvature Snake can hold the information from the initial contour.

When we notice the details of transformation of Snake, namely the movement of the control points, there is a case that the control points move along the contour. Therefore, this method needs a mechanism corresponding between a model and the current feature point. At each moment, the current feature point is selected from the control point which is on the base-line. *Curvature Snake* calculates E_{CS} (Form.(4)) only when it is on the feature points. When on the other control points, it calculates the original energy function only. There would be various kinds of base-lines, such as the normals in the initial contour, or the line drawn from a gravity center of the initial contour; here we use the latter, because the feature points gather to concave region according to the convergence as shown in Figure 4 (b).

Now, we describe the calculation of curvature from the feature points. The initial feature points is determined as the points dividing the initial contour at an equal interval Δs (Figure 4(a)). From these feature points, the calculation uses the first and second derivative as follows:

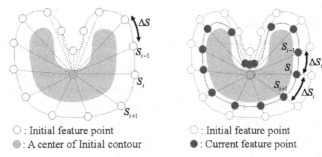

○ : Initial feature point   ○ : Initial feature point
● : A center of Initial contour   ● : Current feature point

(a) Initial feature points and base-lines (b) Current feature points

Fig. 4. Principle of *Curvature Snake*

$$\frac{dx_i}{ds} \approx \frac{x_{i+1} - x_{i-1}}{2\Delta s} \qquad\qquad \frac{d^2x_i}{ds2} \approx \frac{x_{i+1} - 2x_i + x_{i-1}}{\Delta s2}$$

$$\frac{dy_i}{ds} \approx \frac{y_{i+2} - y_{i-1}}{2\Delta s} \qquad\qquad \frac{d^2y_i}{ds2} \approx \frac{y_{i+1} - 2y_i + y_{i-1}}{\Delta s2}$$

where $\dfrac{dx_i}{ds}$ and $\dfrac{d^2x_i}{ds^2}$ is called x_s, x_{ss}, the curvature k_i of feature point S_i is defined as follows:

$$k_i = \frac{y_{ss}x_s - x_{ss}y_s}{(x_s^2 + y_s^2)^{\frac{3}{2}}}$$

On the contrary, the current feature point in the detection process at time t cannot use the same equation as mentioned above, because its interval between the feature points is different respectively (Fig. 4(b)). However, the current curvature need not be completely exact, so that it is approximated during the detection process as follows:

$$\frac{dx_i}{ds} \approx \frac{x_{i+1} - x_{i-1}}{\Delta s_{i-1} + \Delta s_i} \qquad\qquad \frac{d^2x_i}{ds2} \approx \frac{x_{i+1} - 2x_i + x_{i-1}}{\Delta s_{i-1} \cdot \Delta s_i}$$

$$\frac{dy_i}{ds} \approx \frac{y_{i+2} - y_{i-1}}{\Delta s_{i-1} + \Delta s_i} \qquad\qquad \frac{d^2y_i}{ds2} \approx \frac{y_{i+1} - 2y_i + y_{i-1}}{\Delta s_{i-1} \cdot \Delta s_i}$$

where Δs_i is the arc between the feature point S_i and S_{i+1} as shown in Fig. 4(b).

5   Curvature Multi-Snake

Now we propose the layered cooperation of sensor-based agents and model-based agents, namely, the original Snake agents and *Curvature Snake* agents. We call this cooperation "*Curvature Multi-Snake (CMS)*". *Multi-Snake* has two layers as shown in Figure 2 (a) and (b), and *CMS* also has two layers.

In *CMS*, the original Snake cooperates with *Curvature Snake* at the feature points, because there are cases that the only *Curvature Snake* cannot keep the smoothness of the contour depending heavily on the shape of initial contour at each feature point.

At a feature point which crosses the base-line, each micro agents exchanges with each other the direction which gives the largest energy gradient among its eight-neighbors, and follows the direction which gives the largest gradient among the values from all the micro agents in the same manner of *Multi-Snake*. The differences between *Multi-Snake* and *CMS* is only the occasion of when the cooperation is happen. *CMS* makes agent cooperate only at the feature points.

The overall detection procedure of *CMS* is as follows:

Set an initial contour (by user)
Find the center of initial contour
Divide the initial contour at an equal interval (Δs)
Repeat for each control point on the contour
    If the control point is on the base-line
        Make Original Snake cooperate with *Curvature Snake*
    Else
        Find a new control point using the original energy
Until converged.

Preserving the model at each feature point by *Curvature Snake*, *CMS* is able to overcome the difficulty of boundary detection without giving up Snake's advantage of the smooth result contour by this cooperation performed only on the feature points.

6   Experiments

In order to verify the effectiveness of our proposal, we performed several experiments about *Curvature Snake* and *CMS*. In these experiments, we used artificial images (100×100 pixels) and real images (640×480 pixels) which have 256 levels of intensity for each color at each pixel.

First, we show results of experiments using some artificial images. Figure 5 (a) presents the initial contour in a solid black curve, (b) is the results of the original Snake with (α, β, γ) shown under the pictures, and (c) is the results of the single *Curvature Snake* with $(\alpha, \beta, \gamma, \delta)$. In this experiment, *Curvature Snake* does not cooperate with the original Snake on the feature points, but uses the energy function E_{CM} only. On other control points, it performs the same as the original Snake. The purpose of this is to verify the effectiveness of the model force E_{model} added to the energy function. In this picture, the result of boundary detection are shown in a solid black curve, the red pixels on each contour are the feature points. The number of feature points is thirty. As shown in (c), *Curvature Snake* failed to exhibit enough accuracies even with preserving shape. This is caused by the lack of desired effects of the model, namely the lack of appropriate correspondence between initial feature points and the current feature points. This result means that the single *Curvature Snake* has the target shape which cannot coordinate with the feature points as desired by a user. It depends on the target shape or the movement of control points.

Then, we show how *CMS* influences the result accuracy when it makes original Snake of parameters (α, β, γ) cooperate with *Curvature Snake* of parameters

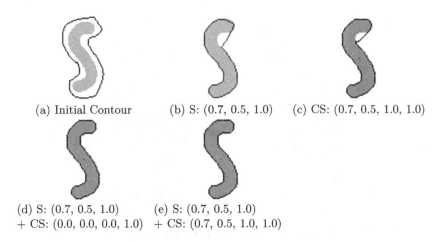

(a) Initial Contour   (b) S: (0.7, 0.5, 1.0)   (c) CS: (0.7, 0.5, 1.0, 1.0)

(d) S: (0.7, 0.5, 1.0)   (e) S: (0.7, 0.5, 1.0)
+ CS: (0.0, 0.0, 0.0, 1.0)   + CS: (0.7, 0.5, 1.0, 1.0)

Fig. 5. The results of Curvature Snake and CMS

$(0.0, 0.0, 0.0, \delta)$. In this case, *Curvature Snake* is not affected by E_{int} and E_{ext}, so that the micro agents of original Snake cooperate with a model-based micro agent which depends on E_{model} only at each feature point. (d) is the result of this case, and the parameters are shown under the pictures. This result shows the improvement of the accuracy of detection boundary. Additionally, we performed the experiments in which original Snake is cooperated with *Curvature Snake* with parameters $(\alpha, \beta, \gamma, \delta)$ instead of $(0.0, 0.0, 0.0, \delta)$. (e) exhibits enough accuracies as well as the experiments as in (d). In these experiments of *CMS*, we checked which agents were chosen, and confirmed tendency to choose the original Snake agent as its convergence progressed.

In the experiments of the single *Curvature Snake* (Figure 5 (c)), the process of boundary detection is performed with parameters $(\alpha, \beta, \gamma, \delta)$, so that Snake is certainly influenced by the model force. On the contrary, the process in *CMS* ((d),(e)) chooses better suited agents according to both the contour shape and the image force at each moment. This means that *CMS* adjusts the influence of the model-based agents dynamically, consequently reduces the undesired trans-formation of the contour in concave regions, and at the same time can detect more smooth boundaries than the single *Curvature Snake*.

However, *CMS* cannot exhibit enough accuracy with all parameter sets. There are some cases which failed to detect the concave region, for example we show that results in Figure 6 (a) and (b). *CMS* can improve its accuracies by increasing macro agents of original Snake whose parameter sets are different respectively. We performed the experiments of *CMS* employing three agents, namely two sensor-based agents and one model-based agent. Figure 6 (c) show the result, and through this experiment, we confirmed that *CMS* using three agents improved the stability of concave detection and also the dependence on a parameter set by reducing a tendency of boundary detection that parameters have. We also performed another experiment employing three agents, that is one sensor-based agent and two model-based agents, and (d) shows its result. This experiment also improved the accuracy of boundary detection.

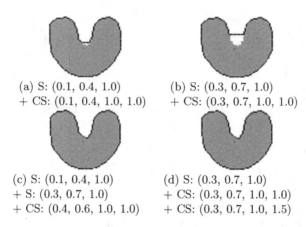

(a) S: (0.1, 0.4, 1.0)
  + CS: (0.1, 0.4, 1.0, 1.0)

(b) S: (0.3, 0.7, 1.0)
  + CS: (0.3, 0.7, 1.0, 1.0)

(c) S: (0.1, 0.4, 1.0)
  + S: (0.3, 0.7, 1.0)
  + CS: (0.4, 0.6, 1.0, 1.0)

(d) S: (0.3, 0.7, 1.0)
  + CS: (0.3, 0.7, 1.0, 1.0)
  + CS: (0.3, 0.7, 1.0, 1.5)

Fig. 6. The results of CMS with 3 agents

Table 1. Performance

Point num	Loop	Time	Time/Loop
Original Snake	103	0.157	0.00152
CMS 10	98	0.422	0.00431
CMS 20	78	0.359	0.00460
CMS 30	62	0.328	0.00529

We adopted thirty feature points in the above-mentioned experiments. Here we show the effect of changing the number of feature points for the detection result. Figure 7 is the result of CMS using the different number of feature point, and Table 1 shows the performance of this experiment. In this regard, we use two agents, one is an original Snake agent with parameter (0.6, 0.4, 1.0) and another is a *Curvature Snake* agent with parameter (0.6, 0.4, 1.0, 1.0). As in Figure 7, the number of feature points affects its result of boundary detection. In Table 1, "Loop" denotes the number of loops and "Time/Loop" denotes the execution time of one loop. The Time/Loop of *CMS* is about three times longer than that of original Snake. It is because of both of curvature calculation on each feature point and calculation of E_{model} and k_i.

Next, Figure 8 is the result of *CMS* using real images. (a) presents the intensity of the image by color gradation, and (b) is the initial contour in black. In this case, the number of control points is 1784 and the number of feature points is 180. (c) is the result of original Snake of parameter (0.6, 0.4, 0.5), and (d) is the result of *CMS* that original Snake of parameter (0.6, 0.4, 0.5) cooperating with *Curvature Snake* with (0.6, 0.4, 0.5, 1.5). Even with *CMS*, it failed to exhibit enough accuracies with these parameter sets. This is caused by the undesired correspondence between the initial and current feature points. The target boundary has some concave regions, and this kind of targets needs some additional technique to correspond between them. Another reason is that the energy potential in the concave region is small. The intensity gradient is small

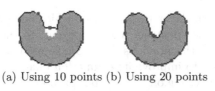

(a) Using 10 points (b) Using 20 points

Fig. 7. Effects of the Number of Representative Points

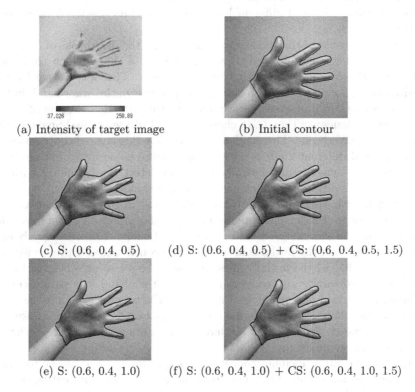

(a) Intensity of target image   (b) Initial contour

(c) S: (0.6, 0.4, 0.5)   (d) S: (0.6, 0.4, 0.5) + CS: (0.6, 0.4, 0.5, 1.5)

(e) S: (0.6, 0.4, 1.0)   (f) S: (0.6, 0.4, 1.0) + CS: (0.6, 0.4, 1.0, 1.5)

Fig. 8. CMS: $(\alpha, \beta, \gamma) + (\alpha, \beta, \gamma, \delta)$ applied to real image

between the target region and the background, and as a result, the force to attract to concave becomes smaller. Because the energy potential is formed by the intensity gradient and the parameters. When γ is set larger, (e) is the result of original Snake with (0.6, 0.4, 1.0), and (f) is the result of *CMS* that it cooperates with *Curvature Snake* with (0.6, 0.4, 1.0, 1.5). Through this experiment, *CMS* realized the improvement of stability in the concave region, and we confirmed the improvement of the accuracy.

7 Conclusions

Snake's principle can be considered as a boundary detector realized by cooperation in an aggregate of many micro agents, and according to this point, we have proposed *Multi-Snake*, the layered cooperation which integrates the cooperation of the micro agents, who construct a macro agent, to the cooperation of the macro agents. However, the previous *Multi-Snake* used some macro agents of the same kind. In order to improve its estimation quality, and to solve Snake's vulnerability with concave regions, this paper proposed *Curvature Snake*, which adopts a curvature-based shape model based on information out of the initial contour, and also proposed *Curvature Multi-Snake*, layered cooperation of micro agents and macro agents of different kinds. We verified its effectiveness through some experiments.

In the experiments of the single *Curvature Snake*, the drawbacks of Snake to the concave region was improved. However, there is a shape which could not exhibit enough accuracy even with *Curvature Snake*. This was caused by the undesired correspondence between the feature points. On the other hand, in the experiments of *CMS* improved the accuracy. In the detection process of *CMS*, we confirmed a tendency that *CMS* chose the agent of the original Snake in the last stages of convergence. This tendency shows that this layered cooperation of macro agents of different kinds is not only improving its accuracy but also this method is more dynamic and flexible. *CMS* can detect the boundary without giving up Snake's advantage which can obtain the smooth boundary.

In general, such kind of the complex shapes used in the experiment of real image is difficult for Snake, and imposes a great deal of labors on a user to set the initial contour and parameters suited for the target shape. *Curvature Snake* and *CMS* also need to set the initial contour with the contrivance for preserving the target shape. That is, the initial contour needs to be set to preserve the target shape such as concavity and convexity. On the other hand, the parameters is set through a certain amount of trial and error. *Curvature Snake* has the force to preserve the shape, so the internal energy E_{int} lessen its grip on Snake. As a result, *Curvature Snake* and *CMS* have an advantage that makes easier to determine parameters for users.

If the initial contour includes concave regions, there is a case of one-to-many correspondence, namely an initial feature point and some current feature points. We dealt with this issue by selecting the feature point whose interval is shortest between the initial feature point and the current feature point. If *Curvature Snake* and *CMS* failed to detect the boundary because of this kind of correspondence, it will be preventable issue by cooperating with *Curvature Snake* of different number of feature points.

References

1. Kass, M., Witkin, A., Terzopoulos, D.: Snakes: Active contour model. Int.J. Computer Vision 1(4), 321–331 (1988)
2. Matsumoto, N., Yoshida, N., Narazaki, S.: Active Contour Model with Decentralized Cooperative Processing. IIEEJ 34(6), 747–752 (2005)
3. Matsumoto, N., Yoshida, N., Narazaki, S.: Cooperative Active Contour Model and Its Application to Remote Sensing. In: Proc. ACM 21st Annual Symp. on Applied Computing, pp. 44–45 (2006)

4. Matsumoto, N., Yoshida, N., Narazaki, S.: Improvement of Active Contour Model with Decentralized Cooperative Processing and Its Application to Remote Sensing. International Journal of Knowledge-Based and Intelligent Engineering Systems 11(3), 169–179 (2007)
5. Matsumoto, N., Yoshida, N., Narazaki, S.: Curvature Multi-Snake: Cooperative Snakes with Curvature-Based Simple Modeling. In: Proceedings of International Workshop on Advanced Image Technology 2007, pp. 632–637 (2007)
6. Etoh, M., Shirai, Y., Asada, M.: Active Contour Extraction Based on Region Descriptions Obtained from Clustering. IEICE Transactions(D-II) J75-D-II(7), 1111–1119 (1992)
7. Zhu, S., Yuille, A.: Region competition: Unifying snakes, region growing, and bayes/MDL for multiband image segmentation. IEEE Trans., PAMI 18(9), 884–900 (1996)
8. Wada, T., Nomura, Y., Matsuyama, T.: Cooperative Distributed Image Segmentation. IPSJ Journal 36(4), 879–891 (1995) (in Japanese)
9. Matsuzawa, Y., Abe, T.: Region Extraction Using Competition of Multiple Active Contour Models. IEICE Transactions(D-II) J83-D-II(4), 1100–1109 (2000) (in Japanese)
10. Staib, L., Duncan, J.: Boundary finding with parametrically deformable models. IEEE Trans. PAMI 14(11), 1061–1075 (1992)
11. Umeyama, S.: Contour extraction using a complex autoregressive model. Systems and Computers in Japan 28(1), 66–73 (1997)
12. Cootes, T., Taylor, C., Cooper, D., Graham, J.: Active Shape models – Their Training and Application. Computer Vision and Image Understanding 61(1), 38–59 (1995)
13. Lai, K., Chin, R.: Deformable contours: Modeling and extraction. IEEE Trans. PAMI 17(11), 1084–1090 (1995)
14. Wang, Y., Staib, L.: Boundary finding with prior shape and smoothness models. IEEE Trans. PAMI 22(7), 738–743 (2000)
15. Olstad, B., Torp, A.: Encoding of a priori information in active contour models. IEEE Trans. PAMI 18(9), 863–872 (1996)
16. Matsuzawa, Y., Abe, T., Kumazawa, I.: Active Contour Model Using Shape Information Obtained from Initial Contour. IEICE Transactions(D-II) J85-D-II(9), 1436–1445 (2002)

Contextual Agent Deliberation in Defeasible Logic

Mehdi Dastani[1], Guido Governatori[2], Antonino Rotolo[3],
Insu Song[2], and Leendert van der Torre[4]

[1] Department of Information and Computing Sciences, University of Utrecht
[2] School of Information Technology and Electrical Engineering, The University of Queensland
[3] CIRSFID, University of Bologna
[4] Université du Luxembourg, Computer Science and Communication

Abstract. This article extends Defeasible Logic to deal with the contextual deliberation process of cognitive agents. First, we introduce meta-rules to reason with rules. Meta-rules are rules that have as a consequent rules for motivational components, such as obligations, intentions and desires. In other words, they include nested rules. Second, we introduce explicit preferences among rules. They deal with complex structures where nested rules can be involved.

1 Introduction

Logic is used in agent oriented software engineering not only for specification and verification, but also for programming deliberation and meta-deliberation tasks. For this reason, Defeasible Logic (DL) [1,2] has been extended with, amongst others, rule types, preferences [7], and actions [5,7]. In rule based cognitive agents, for example in defeasible logic, detailed interactions among cognitive attitudes like beliefs, desires, intentions and obligations are represented by rules, like the obligation to travel to Paris next week leading to a desire to travel by train (r_1), or by preferences, such that if the desire to travel by train cannot be met, than there is a desire to travel by plane (p_1). Patterns of such interactions are represented by rule priorities (obligations override desires or intentions – for social agents) [3,9] rule conversions (obligations behave as desires – for norm internalizing agents) [7], and so on.

As interaction among mental attitudes becomes more complicated, the new challenge in agent deliberation languages is the coordination of such interactions. For example, at one moment an obligation to travel may lead to the desire to travel by train (r_1), whereas at another moment it may lead to a desire to travel by plane (r_2). Such coordination may be expressed by making the context explicit in rules r_1 and r_2, and defining when rule r_1 has higher priority than rule r_2, or it can be defined as a combination of rule r_1 and preference p_1 [5].

In this paper we raise the question how, as a further sophistication to coordinate the interaction among mental attitudes, to define the proof theory of nested rules (see [11] for a general theory of nested rules, [6] for theory of nested rules with time) and preferences among rules. Surprisingly, this complex language gives us just the right expressive power to describe a wide class of interaction phenomena: the rule leading to desire to travel by train may be preferred to the rule leading to a desire to travel by plane (r_1 is preferred to r_2), maybe as a second alternative, or the train rule may even

A. Ghose, G. Governatori, and R. Sadananda (Eds.): PRIMA 2007, LNAI 5044, pp. 98–109, 2009.

be replaced by the plane rule (r_1 into r_2), maybe due to experienced train delays. The new language can be used to describe a new class of patterns of the coordination of interaction, for example when social agents turn into selfish agents, maybe when the agent does not have sufficient resources. Due to space limitations, we focus only on the formal aspects of the new logic.

Finally, the definitions of the deliberation logics developed here are much more complex than the definitions of temporal logics traditionally used in agent based software engineering for specification and verification, since they contain rules, preferences, non-monotonic proof system, and so on. However, whereas these temporal logics have a relatively high computational complexity, deliberation logics have to be efficient – with at most linear complexity (in the number of rules). Moreover, interaction patterns in such temporal logics have focussed on a relatively small class of agent types such as, for example, realisms and commitment strategies in BDI-CTL [4,10], whereas a much broader class has been studied in the more expressive deliberation logics.

This paper is organized as follows. We first give some general intuitions of how the logical system works and define the formal language we use to contextualise the deliberation of cognitive agents. A running example will help us illustrate the system. The second step consists in describing the logical machinery for reasoning about contextualised agents. This requires to provide proof procedures to derive goals (desires, intentions, and obligations) as well as to derive rules for proving goals. A further example concludes the paper.

2   Contextualising Cognitive Agents

The basic deliberative process uses rules to derive goals (desires, intentions, obligations) based on existing beliefs, desires, intentions and obligations (beliefs concern the knowledge an agent has about the world: they are not in themselves motivations for action). Contextualising the deliberation requires to provide the agent with a mechanism for reasoning about rules for goals, which are conditioned to some additional factors. In the simplest case, this can be done by adding such factors as new antecedents of the rules to be contextualised. But transformations may be problematic when complex reasoning patterns are considered. The framework of this paper is based on the following assumptions:

Modalities: The system develops a constructive account of the modalities corresponding to mental states and obligations: rules are meant to devise the logical conditions for introducing them. Modalities may have a different logical behaviour. (Consider the special role played by belief rules, which here are not contextualised and permit to derive only unmodalised literals, whereas the other rule types allow for deriving modalised conclusions.) [7,9,5].

Conversions: Possible conversions of a modality into another can be accepted, as when the applicability of rule leading to derive, for example, OBLp (p is obligatory) may permit, under appropriate conditions, to obtain INTp (p is intended) [7,9].

Preferences: Preferences can be expressed in two ways: using standard DL superiority relation over rules and the operator $\otimes$. Operator $\otimes$ [8] applies to literals [5] as well as to rules, and captures the idea of violation. A $\otimes$-sequence such as $\alpha \otimes \beta \otimes \gamma$

means that α is preferred, but if α is violated, then β is preferred; if β is violated, then the third choice is γ.

Meta-rules: Meta-rules permit to reason about rules for deriving goals. This is the main device for contextualising the provability of goals and requires to introduce nested rules.

We extend the language of Defeasible Logic with the modal operators BEL, INT, DES and OBL, and the non-classical connective $\otimes$. We divide the rules into meta-rules, and atomic rules. Atomic rules are in addition divided into rules for beliefs, desires, intentions, and obligations. For $X \in \{C, \text{BEL}, \text{INT}, \text{DES}, \text{OBL}\}$, where $\{\text{BEL}, \text{INT}, \text{DES}, \text{OBL}\}$ is the set of modalities and C stands for contextual or meta-rules, we have that $\phi_1, \ldots, \phi_n \rightarrow_X \psi$ is a *strict rule* such that whenever the premises $\phi_1, \ldots, \phi_n$ are indisputable so is the conclusion ψ. $\phi_1, \ldots, \phi_n \Rightarrow_X \psi$ is a *defeasible rule* that can be defeated by contrary evidence. $\phi_1, \ldots, \phi_n \rightsquigarrow_X \psi$ is a *defeater* that is used to defeat some defeasible rules by producing evidence to the contrary.

Definition 1 (Language). *Let* PROP *be a set of propositional atoms and* Lab *be a set of labels.*

- *The set of modal operators is* $\text{MOD} = \{\text{BEL}, \text{OBL}, \text{INT}, \text{DES}\}$;
- *The set of literals is* $\text{L} = \text{PROP} \cup \{\neg p \mid p \in \text{PROP}\}$. *If q is a literal, $\sim q$ denotes the complementary literal (if q is a positive literal p then $\sim q$ is $\neg p$; and if q is $\neg p$, then $\sim q$ is p);*
- *The set of modal literals is*

$$\text{MLit} = \{Xl, \neg Xl \mid l \in L, X \in \{\text{DES}, \text{INT}, \text{OBL}\}\};$$

- *The set of $\otimes$-expressions is*

$$PREF = \{l_1 \otimes \cdots \otimes l_n : n \geq 1, \{l_1, \ldots, l_n\} \subseteq L\}.$$

We also write $\bigotimes_{i=1}^n l_i$ for $l_1 \otimes \cdots \otimes l_n \in$ Pref.
- *The set of labeled atomic rules is* $\text{Rule}_{atom} = \text{Rule}_{atom,s} \cup \text{Rule}_{atom,d} \cup \text{Rule}_{atom,dft}$, *where for $X \in \text{MOD}$*

$$\text{Rule}_{atom,s} = \{r : \phi_1, \ldots, \phi_n \rightarrow_X \psi \mid r \in \text{Lab}, A(r) \subseteq L \cup \text{MLit}, \psi \in L\}$$
$$\text{Rule}_{atom,d} = \{r : \phi_1, \ldots, \phi_n \Rightarrow_X \psi \mid r \in \text{Lab}, A(r) \subseteq L \cup \text{MLit}, \psi \in \text{Pref}\}$$
$$\text{Rule}_{atom,dft} = \{r : \phi \rightsquigarrow_X \psi \mid r \in \text{Lab}, A(r) \subseteq L \cup \text{MLit}, \psi \in \text{Pref}\}$$

- *the set of labeled rules is*

$$\text{Rule} = \text{Rule}_{atom} \cup \{\neg(r : \phi_1, \ldots, \phi_n \rhd_Y \psi) \mid (r : \phi_1, \ldots, \phi_n \rhd_Y \psi) \in \text{Rule}_{atom},$$
$$\rhd \in \{\rightarrow, \Rightarrow, \rightsquigarrow\}, Y \in \{\text{DES}, \text{INT}, \text{OBL}\}\}$$

By convention, if r is a rule, $\sim r$ denotes the complementary rule (if $r : \phi_1, \ldots, \phi_n \rhd_X \psi$ then $\sim r$ is $\neg(r : \phi_1, \ldots, \phi_n \rhd_X \psi)$; and if $r : \neg(r : \phi_1, \ldots, \phi_n \rhd_X \psi)$ then $\sim r$ is $r : \phi_1, \ldots, \phi_n \rhd_X \psi$).
- *the set of $\otimes$-rules is*

$$Q = \{a_1 \otimes \cdots \otimes a_n \mid n \geq 1, \{a_1, \ldots, a_n\} \subseteq \text{Rule}\}$$

– *The set of labeled meta-rules is* $\text{Rule}^C = \text{Rule}^C_s \cup \text{Rule}^C_d \cup \text{Rule}^C_{dft}$, *where, for* $X \in \{\text{DES}, \text{INT}, \text{OBL}\}$

$$\text{Rule}^C_s = \{r : \phi \to_C \psi \mid r \in \text{Lab}, \phi \subseteq \text{L} \cup \text{MLit}, \psi \in \text{Rule}^X\}$$
$$\text{Rule}^C_d = \{r : \phi \Rightarrow_C \psi \mid r \in \text{Lab}, \phi \subseteq \text{L} \cup \text{MLit}, \psi \in Q\}$$
$$\text{Rule}^C_{dft} = \{r : \phi \rightsquigarrow_C \psi \mid r \in \text{Lab}, \phi \subseteq \text{L} \cup \text{MLit}, \psi \in Q\}$$

– *We use some abbreviations, such as superscript for mental attitude or meta-rule, subscript for type of rule, and* $\text{Rule}[\phi]$ *for rules whose consequent is* ϕ, *for example:*

$$\text{Rule}^{\text{BEL}} = \{r : \phi_1, \dots, \phi_n \triangleright_{\text{BEL}} \psi \mid (r : \phi_1, \dots, \phi_n \triangleright_{\text{BEL}} \psi) \in \text{Rule}, \triangleright \in \{\to, \Rightarrow, \rightsquigarrow\}\}$$
$$\text{Rule}_s[\psi] = \{\phi_1, \dots, \phi_n \to_X \psi \mid \{\phi_1, \dots, \phi_n\} \subseteq \text{L} \cup \text{MLit}, \psi \in \text{L}, X \in \text{MOD}\}$$

Other abbreviations are the following. We use $r_1, \dots, r_n$ *to label (or name) rules,* $A(r)$ *to denote the set* $\{\phi_1, \dots, \phi_n\}$ *of antecedents of the rule* r, *and* $C(r)$ *to denote the consequent* ψ *of the rule* r. *For some* i, $1 \leq i \leq n$, *such that* $c_i = q$, $R[c_i = q]$ *and* $r^X_d[c_i = q]$ *denote, respectively, the set of rules and a defeasible rule of type* X *with the head* $\otimes^n_{i=1} c_i$ *such that* $c_i = q$.

A defeasible agent theory consists of a set of *facts* or indisputable statements, a set of rules for beliefs, a set of meta-rules, a *superiority relation* $>$ among rules saying when one rule may override the conclusion of another rule, and a conversion function c saying when a rule of one type can be used also as another type. Belief rules are the reasoning core of the agent. Rules for goals (desires, intentions, and obligations) are viewed in any theory as meta-rules with an empty antecedent and a consequent consisting of a $\otimes$-sequence of rules for goals.

Definition 2 (Contextual Defeasible Agent Theory). *A contextual defeasible agent theory is a structure* $D = (F, R^{\text{BEL}}, R^C, >, c)$ *where*

– $F \subseteq \text{L} \cup \text{MLit}$ *is a finite set of facts,*
– $R^{\text{BEL}} \subseteq \text{Rule}^{\text{BEL}}$,
– $R^C \subseteq \text{Rule}^C$,
– $> \subseteq (\text{Rule} \times \text{Rule}) \cup (R^C \times R^C)$, *the superiority relation, is an acyclic binary relation over the set of rules;*
– $c \subseteq \text{MOD} \times \text{MOD}$ *is a set of conversions.*

For readability reasons, we sometimes omit arrows for meta-rules $r^{\Rightarrow c}$ with the empty body. That is, a defeasible meta-rule $\Rightarrow_C (p \to_{\text{INT}} q)$ is just represented as $p \to_{\text{INT}} q$.

This extension of DL makes it possible to express ordered preferences over different options for contextualising rules for goals. In fact, we may have meta-rules such as the following:

$$r : a \Rightarrow_C (r' : b \Rightarrow_{\text{OBL}} c) \otimes \neg (r'' : d \Rightarrow_{\text{INT}} f \otimes g)$$

Intuitively, meta-rule r states that, under the condition a, we should infer rule r' stating that c is obligatory if b is the case; however, if this rule is violated (i.e., if, given b we obtain $\neg c$) then the second choice is to derive the negation of rule r'', which would imply to intend f, as a first choice, or g as a second choice, if d is the case.

The following running example illustrates the contextual defeasible agent theory.

Example 1. (RUNNING EXAMPLE). Frodo, our Tolkienian agent, intends to be entrusted by Elrond to be the bearer of the ring of power, a ring forged by the dark lord Sauron. Frodo has the task to bring the ring to Mordor, the realm of Sauron, and to destroy it by throwing it into the fires of Mount Doom. Given this task, if Frodo does not destroy the ring, he is obliged to leave the Middle Earth, while, if his primary intention is not to destroy it, but he does accomplish the task anyway, he will intend to go back to the Shire. If Frodo is a brave hobbit, rule r_0 should hold, which states the intention to kill Sauron; however, if r_0 is violated, then rule r_3 should not hold. On the other hand, if Frodo is selfish, that he has the intention to be entrusted implies that he has also the intention to kill Elrond. However, if he has this last intention, he is not obliged destroy the ring if he is obliged to be the ring bearer. As facts of the theory, we know that Frodo intends to be entrusted by Elrond, that he is selfish and brave at the same time, and that he does not kill Sauron.

$F = \{$INT*Entrusted*, *Selfish*, *Brave*, $\neg$*KillSauron*$\}$

$R = \{r_1 :$ OBL*Mordor* $\Rightarrow_{\text{OBL}}$ *DestroyRing* $\otimes$ *LeaveMiddleEarth*

$\quad\quad r_2 :$ INT*RingBearer* $\Rightarrow_{\text{OBL}}$ *Mordor*

$\quad\quad r_3 :$ INT*RingBearer* $\Rightarrow_{\text{INT}}$ $\neg$*DestroyRing* $\otimes$ *BackToShire*

$\quad\quad r_4 :$ *Entrusted* $\Rightarrow_{\text{OBL}}$ *RingBearer*

$\quad\quad r_5 :$ *Brave* $\Rightarrow_C$ $(r_0 : \emptyset \Rightarrow_{\text{INT}}$ *KillSauron*$)$ $\otimes$

$\quad\quad\quad\quad\quad\quad\quad\quad \neg(r_3 :$ INT*RingBearer* $\Rightarrow_{\text{INT}}$ $\neg$*DestroyRing* $\otimes$ *BackToShire*$)$

$\quad\quad r_6 :$ *Selfish* $\Rightarrow_C$ $(r_7 :$ INT*Entrusted* $\rightarrow_{\text{INT}}$ *KillElrond*$)$

$\quad\quad r_8 :$ *Selfish*, INT*KillElrond* $\Rightarrow_C$ $(r_9 :$ INT*RingBearer* $\Rightarrow_{\text{OBL}}$ $\neg$*DestroyRing*$)\}$

$>= \{r_3 > r_1, r_5 > r_8\}$

$c = \{c(\text{OBL}, \text{INT})\}$

3   Reasoning about Contextual Deliberation

Let $X \in \{C, \text{BEL}, \text{DES}, \text{INT}, \text{OBL}\}$. Proofs are sequences of literals, modal literals, and rules together with so-called proof tags $+\Delta$, $-\Delta$, $+\partial$ and $-\partial$. Given a defeasible agent theory D, $+\Delta_X q$ means that a conclusion q is provable in D using only facts and strict rules for X, $-\Delta_X q$ means that it has been proved in D that q is not definitely provable in D, $+\partial_X q$ means that q is defeasibly provable in D, and $-\partial_X q$ means that it has been proved in D that q is not defeasibly provable in D.

Before presenting proof procedures to derive specific tagged literals and rules in a contextual agent theory, we need to introduce some auxiliary notions.

Definitions 3 and 4 are propaedeutic for Definition 5 (which defines the set of meta-rules supporting the derivation of a chosen rule) and Definition 6 (which defines the maximal-provable sets of rules that are provable in a theory).

Definition 3 (Sub Rule). *Let $r \in$ Rule be an atomic rule and $\triangleright \in \{\rightarrow, \Rightarrow, \leadsto\}$. The set Sub$(r)$ of sub-rules is defined as follows:*

- $Sub(r) = \{A(r) \rhd_X \otimes_{i=1}^{j} a_i | C(r) = \otimes_{i=1}^{n} a_i, j \leq n\}$, if r is atomic
- $Sub(r) = \{\neg(A(r) \rhd_X \otimes_{i=1}^{j} a_i) | C(r) = \otimes_{i=1}^{n} a_i, j \leq n\}$, otherwise

E.g., given $r : (a \rightarrow_{INT} b \otimes c)$, $Sub(r) = \{a \rightarrow_{INT} b, a \rightarrow_{INT} b \otimes c\}$.

Definition 4 (Modal Free Rule). *Given an atomic rule r, the modal free rule $L(r)$ of r is obtained by removing all modal operators in $A(r)$.*

For example, given $r : INTa \rightarrow_{INT} b$, $L(r)$ is $r : a \rightarrow_{INT} b$.

Definition 5 (Rule-Supporting Rules). *Let D be a contextual agent theory. The set $R^C \langle r^{\rhd x} \rangle$ of supporting rules in R^C for a non-nested rule $r^{\rhd x} \in$ Rule is:*

- *if $r^{\rhd x} \in$ Rule$_{atom}$ and $\forall a \in A(r) : a = Xb \in$ MLit,*

$$R^C \langle r^{\rhd x} \rangle = \bigcup_{s^{\rhd x} \in Sub(r^{\rhd x})} \left(R^C[c_i = s^{\rhd x}] \cup \bigcup_{Y:c(Y,X)} R^C[c_i = L(s^{\rhd Y})] \right)$$

- *otherwise*

$$R^C \langle r^{\rhd x} \rangle = \bigcup_{\forall s^{\rhd x} \in Sub(r^{\rhd x})} R^C[c_i = s^{\rhd x}]$$

For example, a meta-rule $\Rightarrow_C (a \Rightarrow_{INT} b \otimes c) \otimes (a \Rightarrow_{INT} d)$ supports the following rules: $(a \Rightarrow_{INT} b)$, $(a \Rightarrow_{INT} b \otimes c)$, and $(a \Rightarrow_{INT} d)$.

Definition 6 (Maximal Provable-Rule-Sets). *Let D be a contextual agent theory. The maximal provable-rule-sets of non-nested rules that are possibly provable in D is, for $X \in \{DES, INT, OBL\}$,*

$$RP^X = \left\{ Sub(c_i) | C(r) = \bigotimes_{i=1}^{n} c_i, r \in R^C \right\} \cup$$

$$\left\{ Sub(L(c_i^{\rhd Y})) | \forall Y \text{ such that } sc(Y,X), C(r) = \otimes_{i=1}^{n} c_i^{\rhd x}, r \in R^C, \text{ and} \right.$$

$$\left. \forall a \in A(r) : a = Xb \in \text{MLit} \right\}$$

$$RP^{BEL} = \{Sub(r) | r \in R^{BEL}\}.$$

Since we want to derive rules for goals, this requires defining when two rules are incompatible. In this regard, notice that defeasible rules and defeaters for goals may have $\otimes$-expressions as their consequents, which is something we do not have for strict rules. Accordingly, the notion of incompatibility has to take also into account when two $\otimes$-expressions occur in the the heads of two rules.

Definition 7. *Two non-nested rules r and r' are incompatible iff r' is an incompatible atomic rule of r or r' is an incompatible negative rule of r.*

1. *r' is an incompatible atomic rule of r iff r and r' are atomic rules and*
   - *$A(r) = A(r')$, $C(r) = \otimes_{i=1}^{n} a_i$ and*
   - *$C(r') = \otimes_{i=1}^{m} b_i$, such that $\exists j, 1 \leq j \leq n, m, a_j = \sim b_j$ and, $\forall j' \leq j, a_{j'} = b_{j'}$.*

2. r' *is an incompatible negative rule of r iff either r or r' is not an atomic rule and*
   - $A(r) = A(r')$, $C(r) = \bigotimes_{i=1}^{n} a_i$ *and*
   - $C(r') = \bigotimes_{i=1}^{m} b_i$, *such that $N = min\{n,m\}, \forall j \leq N, a_j = b_j$.*

Definition 8. *Let D be a contextual agent theory and r a non-nested rule. The set of all possible incompatible rules for $r^{\triangleright X}$ is:*

$$IC(r^{\triangleright X}) = \{r' | r' \in RP^X, \ r' \text{ is incompatible with } r^{\triangleright X}\}$$

Definitions 9 and 10 define, respectively, when a literal or a rule is provable (and non-provable: rejected), and when a rule is applicable (and non-applicable: discarded). Both notions are used in the proof procedures presented in the remainder.

Definition 9 (Provable). *Let $\# \in \{\Delta, \partial\}$, $P = (P(1), \ldots, P(n))$ be a proof in a contextual agent theory D, and $X \in \{DES, INT, OBL\}$. A literal $q \in L$ or a rule $r \in Rule$ are $\#$-provable in P if there is an initial sequence $P(1), \ldots, P(m)$ of P such that either*

1. *q is a literal and $P(m) = +\#_{BEL} q$ or*
2. *q is a modal literal $X p$ and $P(m) = +\#_X p$ or*
3. *q is a modal literal $\neg X p$ and $P(m) = -\#_X p$ or*
4. *$r^{\triangleright X}$ is a rule in RP^X and $P(m) = +\#_c r^{\triangleright X}$;*

A literal $q \in L$ or a rule $r \in Rule$ are $\#$-rejected in P if there is an initial sequence $P(1), \ldots, P(m)$ of P such that either

1. *q is a literal and $P(m) = -\#_{BEL} q$ or*
2. *q is a modal literal $X p$ and $P(m) = -\#_X p$ or*
3. *q is a modal literal $\neg X p$ and $P(m) = +\#_X p$ or*
4. *$r^{\triangleright X}$ is a rule in RP^X and $P(m) = -\#_c r^{\triangleright X}$.*

Definition 10. *Let D be a contextual agent theory. Applicable rules and discarded rules are defined as follows:*

1. *A rule $r \in R^{BEL} \cup R^C$ is applicable iff $\forall a \in A(r)$:*
   - *if $a \in L$ then $+\partial_{BEL} a \in P(1..n)$, and*
   - *if $a = Xb \in MLit$ then $+\partial_X a \in P(1..n)$.*
2. *A rule $r \in R[c_i = q]$ is applicable in the condition for $\pm \partial_X$ iff*
   - *$r \in R^X_{atom}$ and $\forall a \in A(r)$: if $a \in L$ then $+\partial_{BEL} a \in P(1..n)$, and if $a = Zb \in MLit$ then $+\partial_Z a \in P(1..n)$; or*
   - *$r \in R^Y_{atom}$ and $c(Y,X) \in c$ and $\forall a \in A(r)$: $+\partial_X a \in P(1..n)$.*
3. *A rule r is discarded in the condition for $\pm \partial_X$ iff either:*
   - *if $r \in R^{BEL} \cup R^C \cup R^X$ then either*
     $\exists a \in A(r) : -\partial_{BEL} a \in P(1..n)$ or
     $\exists Xb \in A(R), Xb \in MLit$ and $-\partial_X b \in P(1..n)$; or
   - *if $r \in R^Y$, then $\exists a \in A(r) : -\partial_X a \in P(1..n)$.*

Notice that the notion of applicability needs to take conversions into account.

Remark 1. Conversions affect applicability of rules. In many cases we want that this possibility can be admitted:

$$+\Delta_{\text{INT}} GoToRome, GoToRome \rightarrow_{\text{BEL}} GoToItaly \mathrel{\vert\!\sim} +\Delta_{\text{INT}} GoToItaly$$
$$+\partial_{\text{INT}} GoToRome, GoToRome \Rightarrow_{\text{OBL}} VisitVatican \mathrel{\vert\!\sim} +\partial_{\text{INT}} VisitVatican$$

The first rule states that the agent believes that going to Rome strictly implies going to Italy; if we can derive that the agent has the intention to visit Rome, we have reasons to say that a rational agent may have the intention to visit Italy. The second rule says that visiting Rome defeasibly implies the obligation to visit Vatican City. With norm-complying agents, agent's intention to visit Rome rationally implies to having the intention to go to Vatican City.

Example 2. Suppose we allow a deontic rule to be converted into a rule for intention, i.e. $c(\text{OBL}, \text{INT})$. Consider rule $r : a, b \Rightarrow_{\text{OBL}} p$: if $\partial_{\text{INT}} a$ and $\partial_{\text{INT}} b$, then r is applicable in the proof condition for $+\partial_{\text{INT}}$.

Before providing proof procedures to derive rules, let us introduce specific proof tags for this purpose. Remember that $\rhd$ denotes either $\rightarrow$, $\Rightarrow$ or $\rightsquigarrow$ to simplify our presentation. $\pm\Delta_C r^{\rhd x}$ means that rule $r \in R^X$ is (is not) definitely provable using meta-rules; $\pm\partial_C r^{\rhd x}$ means that rule $r \in R^X$ is (is not) defeasibly provable using meta-rules. In general, $\pm\Delta_C^{\rhd x}$ and $\pm\partial_C^{\rhd x}$ mean, respectively, definitive (non-)provability of rules for X, and defeasible (non-)provability of rules for X.

Let us see proof procedures to derive rules. In this perspective, however, we have to be careful, as we can distinguish between strict and defeasible derivations of non-nested strict and defeasible rules. Given a contextual agent theory D, a non-nested rule r is strictly provable in D when it is strictly derived using a meta-rule such as $a \rightarrow_C r$. A rule r is defeasibly provable in D when it is defeasibly derived using a meta-rule such as $a \rightarrow_C r$ and $a \Rightarrow_C r$. When a strict atomic rule $a \rightarrow_{\text{INT}} b$ is defeasibly derived, it acts as a defeasible rule $a \Rightarrow_{\text{INT}} b$.

Proof procedures for the strict derivation of atomic rules in a contextual defeasible agent theory D are as follows:

$+\Delta_C^{\rhd x}$: If $P(i+1) = +\Delta_C r^{\rhd x}$ then
(1) $X = \text{BEL}$ and $r^{\rhd x} \in R^{\text{BEL}}$ or
(2) $\exists s \in R_s^C \langle r^{\rhd x} \rangle \ \forall a \in A(s) \ a$ is Δ-provable.

$-\Delta_C^{\rhd x}$: If $P(i+1) = -\Delta_C r^{\rhd x}$ then
(1) $X \neq \text{BEL}$ or $r^{\rhd x} \notin R^{\text{BEL}}$ and
(2) $\forall s \in R_s^C \langle r^{\rhd x} \rangle \ \exists a \in A(r) : a$ is Δ-rejected.

Strict derivations of rules are based on the following intuition. If the rule r we want to derive is for belief, r must be in the set of belief rules of the theory. Otherwise (for the other rule types), r must be proved using a strict meta-rule whose antecedents are strictly provable. Defeasible derivations of rules are based on the following procedures.

$+\partial_C^{\rhd x}$: If $P(n+1) = +\partial_C r^{\rhd x}$, then

(1) $+\Delta_C r^{\rhd x} \in P(1..n)$, or

(2) (1) $\forall r'' \in IC(r^{\rhd x})$, $\forall r' \in R_s^C \langle r'' \rangle$, r' is discarded and

    (2) $\exists t \in R^C \langle c_i = r^{\rhd x} \rangle$ such that

        (1) $\forall i' < i$, $c_{i'}$ is applicable,

        (2) $\forall i' < i$, $C(c_{i'}) = \bigotimes_{k=1}^n b_k$, such that $\forall k : +\partial_{\mathrm{BEL}} \sim b_k \in P(1..n)$,

        (3) t is applicable, and

    (3) $\forall r'' \in IC(r^{\rhd x})$, $\forall s \in R^C \langle d_i = r'' \rangle$

        (1) if $\forall i' < i$, $d_{i'}$ is applicable, $C(d_{i'}) = \bigotimes_{k=1}^n a_k$ s.t. $\forall k : +\partial_{\mathrm{BEL}} \sim a_k \in P(1..n)$, then

            (1) s is discarded, or

            (2) $\exists z \in R^C \langle p_i = r''' \rangle$: $r''' \in IC(C(s))$ s.t. $\forall i' < i$, $p_{i'}$ is applicable, and

                $C(p_{i'}) = \bigotimes_{k=1}^n d_k$ s.t. $\forall k : +\partial_{\mathrm{BEL}} \sim d_k \in P(1..n)$ and z is applicable and $z > s$.

$-\partial_C^{\rhd x}$: If $P(n+1) = -\partial_C r^{\rhd x}$, then

(1) $-\Delta_C r^{\rhd x} \in P(1..n)$, and

(2) (1) $\exists r' \in R_s^C \langle r'' \rangle$ such that $r'' \in IC(r^{\rhd x})$, r' is applicable or

    (2) $\forall t \in R^C \langle c_i = r^{\rhd x} \rangle$

        (1) $\exists i' < i$ such that $c_{i'}$ is discarded, or

        (2) $\exists i' < i$ such $C(c_{i'}) = \bigotimes_{k=1}^n b_k$ and $\exists k : -\partial_{\mathrm{BEL}} \sim b_k \in P(1..n)$,

        (3) t is discarded, or

    (3) $\exists s \in R^C \langle d_i = r'' \rangle$ such that $\forall r'' \in IC(r^{\rhd x})$, such that

        (1) $\forall i' < i$, $d_{i'}$ is applicable, $C(d_{i'}) = \bigotimes_{k=1}^n a_k$ s.t. $\forall k : +\partial_{\mathrm{BEL}} \sim a_k \in P(1..n)$, and

            (1) s is applicable, and

            (2) $\forall z \in R^C \langle p_i = r''' \rangle$ such that $r''' \in IC(C(s))$ $\exists i' < i$, $p_{i'}$ is discarded or

                $C(p_{i'}) = \bigotimes_{k=1}^n d_k$ s.t. $\exists k : -\partial_{\mathrm{BEL}} \sim d_k \in P(1..n)$ or z is discarded or $z \not> s$.

Remark 2. The defeasible proof of a rule runs in three phases. We have to find an argument in favour of the rule we want to prove. Second, all counter-arguments are examined (rules for the opposite conclusion). Third, all the counter-arguments have to be rebutted (the counter-argument is weaker than the pro-argument) or undercut (some of the premises of the counter-argument are not provable). Let us exemplify positive proof conditions $(+\partial_C^{\rhd x})$ step by step. Suppose we want to derive $r : \mathrm{INT}a \rightarrow_{\mathrm{INT}} b$, namely, that $X = \mathrm{INT}$ and $\rhd = \rightarrow$. We have the following options. Condition (1): r is definitely provable; or, Condition (2): We use a strict or defeasible meta-rule to derive r. This must exclude, as a precondition, that any rule, which is incompatible with r, is definitely supported: (condition 2.1). That is, rules such as

$$r' : \neg(\mathrm{INT}a \rightarrow_{\mathrm{INT}} b) \qquad r'' : \mathrm{INT}a \rightarrow_{\mathrm{INT}} \neg b \qquad r''' : a \rightarrow_{\mathrm{OBL}} \neg b$$

should not be supported, if we have that r (the rule we want to prove) is applicable, $+\partial_{\mathrm{INT}}a$ and $c(\mathrm{OBL}, \mathrm{INT})$, namely, if we may convert a rule for obligation into one for intention. In fact, if we have this conversion, r'' behaves like a rule for intention. With this done, condition (2.2) states that there should exist a meta-rule such as

$$t : d \Rightarrow_C (w : p \Rightarrow_{\mathrm{OBL}} q) \otimes (r : \mathrm{INT}a \rightarrow_{\mathrm{INT}} b)$$

such that t is applicable, $+\partial_{\mathrm{BEL}}d$, and the first choice, rule w, is violated, namely that $+\partial_{\mathrm{BEL}}p$ and $+\partial_{\mathrm{BEL}}\neg q$. But this fact must exclude that any meta-rule s supporting an incompatible conclusion against r is applicable (see condition 2.3.1.1). Alternatively, if

s is applicable, we have to verify that there exists a meta-rule z supporting r such that z is applicable and is stronger that s (see condition 2.3.1.2). Notice that when we say that that a meta-rule supports a rule, we take into account that meta-rules may have $\otimes$-rules in their consequents. For example, if s is as follows

$$s : d \Rightarrow_C (w : b \rightarrow_{\text{DES}} c) \otimes r' : \neg(\text{INT}a \rightarrow_{\text{INT}} b),$$

but we prove $-\partial_{\text{BEL}} \neg c$, this means that w cannot be violated and so s cannot be used to attack the derivation of r: in this case, using s, we could only prove rule w.

Given the above proof conditions for deriving rules, the following are the procedures for proving literals. Notice that each time a rule r is used and applied, we are required to check that r is provable.

$+\Delta_X$: If $P(i+1) = +\Delta_X q$ then
(1) $Xq \in F$, or $q \in F$ if $X = \text{BEL}$, or
(2) $\exists r \in \text{Rule}_s^X[q] : +\Delta_C r$ and $\forall a \in A(r)$ a is Δ-provable or
(3) $\exists r \in \text{Rule}_s^Y[q] : +\Delta_C r$, $\forall a \in A(r)$ a is Δ-provable and $c(Y,X)$.

$-\Delta_X$: If $P(i+1) = -\Delta_X q$ then
(1) $Xq \notin F$, or $q \notin F$ if $X = \text{BEL}$, and
(2) $\forall r \in \text{Rule}_s^X[q] : -\Delta_C r$ or $\exists a \in A(r) : a$ is Δ-rejected and
(3) $\forall r \in \text{Rule}_s^Y[q] : -\Delta_C r$, or if $c(Y,X)$ then $\exists a \in A(r)$ a is Δ-rejected.

$+\partial_X$: If $P(n+1) = +\partial_X q$ then
(1) $+\Delta_X q \in P(1..n)$ or
(2) (1) $-\Delta_X \sim q \in P(1..n)$ and
    (2) $\exists r \in \text{Rule}_{sd}[c_i = q]$ such that $+\partial_C r$, r is applicable, and
        $\forall i' < i, +\partial_{\text{BEL}} \sim c_{i'} \in P(1..n)$; and
    (3) $\forall s \in \text{Rule}[c_j = \sim q]$, either $-\partial_C s$, or s is discarded, or
        $\exists j' < j$ such that $-\partial_{\text{BEL}} \sim c_{j'} \in P(1..n)$, or
        (1) $\exists t \in \text{Rule}[c_k = q]$ such that $+\partial_C t$, t is applicable and
            $\forall k' < k, +\partial_{\text{BEL}} \sim c_{k'} \in P(1..n)$ and $t > s$.

$-\partial_X$: If $P(n+1) = -\partial_X q$ then
(1) $-\Delta_X q \in P(1..n)$ and either
(2) (1) $+\Delta_X \sim q \in P(1..n)$ or
    (2) $\forall r \in \text{Rule}_{sd}[c_i = q]$, either $-\partial_C r$, or r is discarded or
        $\exists i' < i$ such that $-\partial_{\text{BEL}} \sim c_{i'} \in P(1..n)$; or
    (3) $\exists s \in \text{Rule}[c_j = \sim q]$ such that $+\partial_C s$, s is applicable and
        $\forall j' < j, +\partial_{\text{BEL}} \sim c_{j'} \in P(1..n)$, and
        (1) $\forall t \in \text{Rule}[c_k = q]$ either $-\partial_C t$, or t is discarded, or
            $\exists k' < k$ such that $-\partial_{\text{BEL}} \sim c_{k'} \in P(1..n)$ or $t \not> s$.

Example 3. (RUNNING EXAMPLE, CONTINUED). The fact that Frodo has the intention to be entrusted by Elrond makes it possible to derive $+\Delta_{\text{INT}} Entrusted$. Since we have the conversion $c(\text{OBL}, \text{INT})$, this would make both r_2 and r_3 applicable. However, r_5 and r_6, too, are applicable. Rule r_6 permits to derive r_7, which is applicable, as Frodo has the intention to be entrusted. This allows in turn for the derivation of the intention to kill Elrond, which makes r_8 applicable. Here we have a conflict between r_5 and r_8, but the former is stronger. On the other hand, r_5 states, as a first choice, that Frodo has the intention to kill Sauron. But this intention is violated, as $\neg KillSauron$ is a fact, which makes it possible to derive $+\Delta_{BEL}\neg KillSauron$ and so $+\partial_{BEL}\neg KillSauron$. Thus we have to derive the second choice, namely, the negation of r_3. In this way, even if r_3 is stronger than r_1, the applicability of meta-rule r_5 makes r_3 inapplicable.

4   Context-Detection: A Further Example

Context can play as a disambiguating function in agent communication. For example, when an agent A receives a command "On" from another agent B, the meaning of the message usually depends on the common context between the two agents. Without context information, the command "On" is too ambiguous because "On" could mean many things, for example, turn on a water tap, turn on a light, turn on a projector, or run a weekly meeting presentation.

To show how contexts can be detected and decisions can be made using contextual information within our reasoning model, we consider a simple theory representing an office assistant that can help office workers to control their modernized office environment for non-interrupted work flow:

$$F = \{MRoom, Monday, Morning, onProjector\}$$

$$R^{BEL} = \{r_1 : MRoom, Monday, Morning \Rightarrow_{BEL} CWMeeting$$
$$r_2 : MRoom, Monday, Morning \Rightarrow_{BEL} \neg CDMeeting$$
$$r_3 : MRoom, Morning \Rightarrow_{BEL} CDMeeting$$
$$r_4 : onProjector \rightarrow_{BEL} \neg trunOnProjector\}$$

$$R^C = \{r_5 : CWMeeting \Rightarrow_C (MessageOn \Rightarrow_{INT} turnOnProjector \otimes$$
$$openWMPresentation \otimes openDMPresentation)$$

$$r_6 : CDMeeting \Rightarrow_C (MessageOn \Rightarrow_{INT} turnOnProjector \otimes$$
$$openDMPresentation \otimes openWMPresentation)\}$$

Herein, rules r_1 and r_2 say that if the assistant agent is in a meeting room (*MRoom*) and it is Monday morning, then usually the context is that of a weekly meeting (*CWMeeting*) and not of a daily meeting (*CDMeeting*). However, rule r_3 says that if the assistant agent is in a meeting room in the morning, then the context is usually that of a daily meeting. That is, r_1, r_2, and r_3 are used to detect the context. Once the context is determined, the assistant agent can properly process the command "On". For instance, r_5 says that if it is a weekly meeting, enable the following rule:

$$MessageOn \Rightarrow_{INT} trunOnProjector \otimes openWMPresentation \otimes openDMPresentation$$

meaning that, if the agent receives a command "On", then the agent usually should form the intention to turn on the data projector, but if it cannot be turned on (because it is already turned on), then it should try to open a weekly meeting presentation file.

However, for some reason, if the weekly meeting presentation cannot be run (maybe it is just a daily meeting), then it should try to open a daily meeting presentation file.

On the other hand, r_6 says that if it is a daily meeting, enable the following rule:

$$Message\_On \Rightarrow_{INT} trunOnProjector \otimes openDMPresentation \otimes openWMPresentation$$

This rule sasys that, in this context, opening a daily meeting presentation file (*openDMPresentation*) has higher priority than opening a weekly meeting presentation file (*WMPresentation*). With the given theory, the office agent will conclude $+\partial_{INT}$ *openWMPresentation* if it receives *Message_On* because it is a weekly meeting and a projector is already turned on. This example clearly illustrates how contextual information is naturally represented within our reasoning model. That is, contextual information can be used to enable certain rules and to change priority between deliberations.

5   Summary

We extended Defeasible Logic to deal with the contextual deliberation process of cognitive agents. First, we introduce meta-rules to reason with rules. Meta-rules are rules that have, as a consequent, rules to derive goals (obligations, intentions and desires): in other words, meta-rules include nested rules. Second, we introduce explicit preferences among rules. They deal with complex structures where nested rules can be involved to capture scenarios where rules are violated. Further research are the development of a methodology to use the language, and a formal analysis of the logic.

References

1. Antoniou, G., Billington, D., Governatori, G., Mahe, M.J.: Representation results for defeasible logic. ACM Transactions on Computational Logic 2(2), 255–287 (2001)
2. Antoniou, G., Billington, D., Governatori, G., Maher, M.J.: Embedding Defeasible Logic in Logic Programming. Theory and Practice of Logic Programming 6(6), 703–735 (2006)
3. Broersen, J., Dastani, M., Hulstijn, J., van der Torre, L.: Goal generation in the BOID architecture. Cog. Sc. Quart. 2(3-4), 428–447 (2002)
4. Cohen, P.R., Levesque, H.J.: Intention is choice with commitment. Artif. Intell. 42(2-3), 213–261 (1990)
5. Dastani, M., Governatori, G., Rotolo, A., van der Torre, L.: Programming cognitive agents in defeasible logic. In: Sutcliffe, G., Voronkov, A. (eds.) LPAR 2005. LNCS (LNAI), vol. 3835, pp. 621–636. Springer, Heidelberg (2005)
6. Governatori, G., Padmanabhan, V., Rotolo, A.: Rule-based agents in temporalised defeasible logic. In: Yang, Q., Webb, G. (eds.) PRICAI 2006. LNCS (LNAI), vol. 4099, pp. 31–40. Springer, Heidelberg (2006)
7. Governatori, G., Rotolo, A.: Defeasible logic: Agency, intention and obligation. In: Lomuscio, A., Nute, D. (eds.) DEON 2004. LNCS, vol. 3065, pp. 114–128. Springer, Heidelberg (2004)
8. Governatori, G., Rotolo, A.: Logic of violations: A Gentzen system for reasoning with contrary-to-duty obligations. Australasian Journal of Logic 4, 193–215 (2006)
9. Governatori, G., Rotolo, A., Padmanabhan, V.: The cost of social agents. In: Proc. AAMAS 2006, pp. 513–520 (2006)
10. Rao, A.S., Georgeff, M.P.: Decision procedures for bdi logics. J. Log. Comput. 8(3), 293–342 (1998)
11. Song, I., Governatori, G.: Nested rules in defeasible logic. In: Adi, A., Stoutenburg, S., Tabet, S. (eds.) RuleML 2005. LNCS, vol. 3791, pp. 204–208. Springer, Heidelberg (2005)

Real-Time Moving Target Search

Cagatay Undeger[1] and Faruk Polat[2]

[1] Savunma Teknolojileri Muhendislik ve Tic.A.S., 06510 Ankara, Turkey
[2] Middle East Technical University, 06531 Ankara, Turkey
cundeger@stm.com.tr, polat@ceng.metu.edu.tr

Abstract. In this paper, we propose a real-time moving target search algorithm for dynamic and partially observable environments, modeled as grid world. The proposed algorithm, Real-time Moving Target Evaluation Search (MTES), is able to detect the closed directions around the agent, and determine the best direction that avoids the nearby obstacles, leading to a moving target which is assumed to be escaping almost optimally. We compared our proposal with Moving Target Search (MTS) and observed a significant improvement in the solution paths. Furthermore, we also tested our algorithm against A* in order to report quality of our solutions.

Keywords: Path Planning, Real-Time Search, Moving Target Search.

1 Introduction

Pursuing a moving target is one of the most challenging problems in areas such as robotics, computer games, etc. Off-line and incremental path planning algorithms are not able to handle moving targets in real-time, and most of the on-line search algorithms are specifically designed for partially observable environments with static targets. The most well known algorithm for moving targets is Moving Target Search (MTS) [2], which maintains a heuristic table that contains estimated costs of paths between every pair of coordinates.

In this paper, we propose a new moving target search algorithm, Real-Time Moving Target Evaluation Search (MTES), which is build on Real-Time Target Evaluation Search [9] developed for partially observable environments with static targets. MTES is able to estimate the distance to the target considering the intervening obstacles and discard some non-promising alternative moving directions in real-time in order to guide the agent to a moving target. The method sends virtual (non-physical) rays away from the agent in four directions, and determines the obstacles that the rays hit. For each such obstacle, we extract its border and determine the best direction that avoids the obstacle if the target is blocked by the obstacle. Hence, we have a number of directions each avoiding an obstacle hit by a ray. Then by using these directions and a resolution mechanism, a single moving direction is determined. To show the performance of our algorithm, we compared MTES with MTS-c, MTS-d and A*. For the experiments, we randomly generated grids of different types, and developed a successful prey algorithm (Prey-A*) in order to challenge the algorithms used in the experiments. The results showed that MTES produces near optimal solutions, and outperforms MTS-c and MTS-d significantly.

A. Ghose, G. Governatori, and R. Sadananda (Eds.): PRIMA 2007, LNAI 5044, pp. 110–121, 2009.

The related work is given in Section 2. In section 3, MTES is described in details. In Section 4, the performance analysis of MTES is presented. Finally Section 5 is the conclusion.

2   Related Work

Off-line path planning algorithms [6] are hard to use for large dynamic environments and for moving targets because of their time requirements. One way to make these algorithms more efficient is to change them from off-line to incremental [7,4] in order to avoid re-planning from scratch. Although these algorithms work fine with partially observable environments, they are sometimes not efficient enough and usually not capable of handling moving targets. There are also a number of on-line approaches [5,3,8,9,2]. As a matter of fact, only few of these on-line algorithms can be adapted against a moving target.

Moving Target Search (MTS) [2] is a well known real-time algorithm for pursuing a moving target, which is built on Learning Real-Time A*. The algorithm maintains a table of heuristic values, presenting the function $h(x,y)$ for all pairs of locations x and y in the environment, where x is the location of the agent and y is the location of the target. The original MTS is a poor algorithm in practice because when the target moves, the learning process has to start all over again. Therefore, two MTS extensions namely *Commitment to Goal* (MTS-c) and *Deliberation* (MTS-d) [2] are proposed to improve the solution quality. In order to use the learned table values more effectively, MTS-c ignores some of the target's moves, and MTS-d performs an off-line search while in a heuristic depression.

When we look at the prey algorithms, we usually cannot see very successful studies. Mostly the focus is on the predators, and the prey algorithms commonly use hybrid techniques mixing the reactive strategies [1,2]. Since these strategies are not challenging enough for our algorithms, we developed an off-line strategy, which is slow but more powerful with respect to its escape capability.

3   Moving Target Search

3.1   Problem Description

In our study, the environment is a grid world, where any grid cell can either be free or obstacle. There is a single agent (predator) that aims to reach a static or moving target (prey). Both are randomly located far from each other in non-obstacle grid cells. The predator is expected to reach the prey from a short path avoiding obstacles in real-time. We assume that the predator knows the prey's location all the time, but has limited perception, and is only able to sense the obstacles around him within a square region centered at the agent location. The size of the square is $(2v+1)$x$(2v+1)$, where v is the **vision range**. We used the term *infinite vision* to emphasize that the agent has unlimited sensing capability and knows the entire grid world before the search starts. The unknown parts of the grid world is assumed to be free of obstacle by the agent, until it is explored. Therefore, when we say an obstacle, we refer to the known part of that obstacle. The agent can only perform four actions in each step; moving to a free neighbor cell in north, south, east or west direction. The prey has unlimited perception and knows all the grid world and the location of the predator all the time. The search continues until the predator reaches the prey.

3.2 MTES Algorithm

MTES makes use of a heuristic, Real-Time Target Evaluation (RTTE-h), which analyzes obstacles and proposes a moving direction that avoids these obstacles and leads to the target through shorter paths. To do this, RTTE-h geometrically analyzes the obstacles nearby, tries to estimate the lengths of paths around the obstacles to reach the target, and proposes a moving direction. RTTE-h works in continuous space to identify the moving direction, which is then mapped to one of the actual moving directions (north, south, east and west). MTES repeats steps in Algorithm 1 until reaching the target or detecting that target is inaccessible.

In the first step, MTES calls RTTE-h heuristic function, which returns a moving direction and the utilities of neighbor cells according to that proposed direction. Next, MTES selects one of the neighbor cells on open directions with the minimum *visit count*, which stores the number of visits to the cell. If there exists more than one cell having the minimum *visit count*, the one with the maximum utility is selected. If utilities are also the same, then one of them is selected randomly. After the move is performed, the *visit count* of the previous cell is incremented and the cell is inserted into the *history*. The set of previously visited cells forms the *history* of the agent. History cells are treated as obstacles. Therefore, if the agent discovers a new obstacle during the exploration and realizes that the target became inaccessible due to history cells, the agent clears the history to be able to backtrack.

Algorithm 1. An Iteration of MTES Algorithm

 1: Call RTTE-h to compute the proposed direction and the utilities of neighbor cells.
 2: **if** a direction is proposed by RTTE-h **then**
 3:      Select the neighbor cell with the highest utility from the set of non-obstacle neighbors with the smallest visit count.
 4:      Move to the selected direction.
 5:      Increment the visit count of previous cell by one.
 6:      Insert the previous cell into the history.
 7: **else**
 8:      **if** History is not empty **then**
 9:          Clear all the History.
10:          Jump to 1
11:      **else**
12:          Destination is unreachable, stop the search with failure.
13:      **end if**
14: **end if**

In moving target search problem, the target may sometimes pass through the cells the agent previously walked through. In such a case, there is a risk that the history blocks the agent to reach the target since history cells are assumed to be obstacles and may close some gateways required to return back. If this situation occurs at some point, the agent will surely be able to detect this at the end, and clear the history, opening all the closed gateways. Therefore, the algorithm is capable of searching moving targets without any

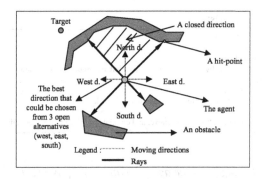

Fig. 1. Sending rays to split moving directions

additions. As a matter of fact, the only drawback of the history is not the possibility that it can block the way to the target entirely, but it can sometimes prevent the agent to reach the target through shorter paths by just closing some of the shortcuts. To reduce the performance problems of this side effect, the following procedure is applied. Assuming that (x_1, y_1) and (x_2, y_2) are the previous and newly observed locations of the target, respectively, and R is the set of cells the target could have visited in going from (x_1, y_1) to (x_2, y_2), the algorithm clears the history along with visit counts when any cell in set R appears in history or has non-zero visit count. In the algorithm, R can be determined in several ways depending on the required accuracy. The smallest set has to contain at least the newly observed location of the target, (x_2, y_2). One can choose to ignore some of the set members and only use (x_2, y_2) to keep the algorithm simple.

The RTTE-h heuristic method in Algorithm 2 propagates four diagonal rays away from the agent location (line 2 in Algorithm 2) to split north, south, east and west moving directions as shown in Fig 1. The rays move outwards from the agent until they hit an obstacle or maximum ray distance is achieved. Four rays split the area around the agent into four regions. A region is said to be closed if the target is inaccessible from any cell in that region. If all the regions are closed, the target is unreachable from the current location. To detect closed regions, the boundary of the obstacle is extracted (line 4) and analyzed (line 5). Next, the obstacle border is re-traced from both left and right sides to determine geometric features of the obstacle (line 6). These features are evaluated and a moving direction to avoid the obstacle is identified (line 7). After all the obstacles are evaluated, results are merged to propose a final moving direction (line 9).

The obstacle border extraction and closed direction detection phases of the algorithm use the same methods presented in [8,9]. The geometric features of an obstacle are determined in two phases: left analysis and right analysis (line 6 in Algorithm 2). In left/right analysis, the known border of the obstacle is traced edge by edge towards the left/right sides starting from the hit point, making a complete tour around the obstacle border. During this process, several geometric features of the obstacle are extracted, which are described in Definitions 1 to 8 and illustrated in Fig. 2.

Definition 1 (Outer left most direction). *Relative to the ray direction, the largest cumulative angle is found during the left tour on the border vertices. In each step of the trace, we move from one edge vertex to another on the border. The angle between the*

Algorithm 2. RTTE-h Heuristic

1: Mark all the moving directions as open.
2: Propagate four diagonal rays.
3: **for** each ray hitting an obstacle **do**
4:     Extract the border of the obstacle by tracing the edges from left side until making a complete tour around the obstacle.
5:     Detect closed directions.
6:     Extract geometric features of the obstacle.
7:     Evaluate the results and determine a direction to avoid the obstacle.
8: **end for**
9: Merge individual results, propose a direction to move, and compute utilities of neighbor cells.

---

two lines (TWLNS) starting from the agent location and passing through these two following vertices is added to the cumulative angle computed so far. Note that the added amount can be positive or negative depending on whether we move in counter-clockwise (ccw) or clockwise (cw) order, respectively. This trace (including the trace for the other geometric features) continues until the sum of the largest cumulative angle and the absolute value of smallest cumulative angle is greater than or equal to 360. The largest cumulative angle before the last step of trace is used as the outer left most direction.

Definition 2 (Inner left most direction). *The direction with the largest cumulative angle encountered during the left tour until reaching the first edge vertex where the angle increment is negative and the target lies between TWLNS. If such a situation is not encountered, the direction is assumed to be $0 + \varepsilon$, where ε is a very small number (e.g., 0.01).*

Definition 3 (Inside of left). *True if the target is inside the polygon whose vertices starts at agent's location, jumps to outer left most point, follows the border of the obstacle to the right and ends at the hit point of the ray.*

Definition 4 (Inside of inner left). *True if the target is inside the polygon that starts at agent's location, jumps to the inner left most point, follows the border of the obstacle to the right and ends at the hit point of the ray.*

Definition 5 (Behind of left). *True if the target is in the region obtained by sweeping the angle from the ray direction to the outer left most direction in ccw order and the target is not inside of left.*

Definition 6 (Outer-left-zero angle blocking). *True if target is in the region obtained by sweeping the angle from the ray direction to the outer left most direction in ccw order.*

Definition 7 (Inner-left-zero angle blocking). *True if target is in the region obtained by sweeping the angle from the ray direction to the inner left most direction in ccw order.*

In right analysis, the border of the obstacle is traced towards the right side and the same geometric properties listed above but now symmetric ones are identified. In the right analysis, additionally the following feature is extracted:

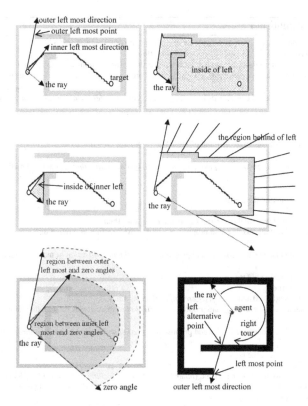

Fig. 2. Geometric features of obstacles

Definition 8 (Left alternative point). *The last vertex in the outer left most direction encountered during the right tour until the outer right most direction is determined (see Fig. 2).*

In obstacle evaluation step (line 7 in Algorithm 2), if an obstacle blocks line of sight from agent to target, we determine a moving direction that avoids the obstacle meanwhile reaching the target through a shorter path. Method is given in Algorithm 3, which requires path length estimations given in Definitions 9 to 11.

Definition 9 (d_{left}). *The approximated length of the path which starts from the agent location, jumps to the outer left most point, and then follows the path determined by Algorithm 4 (see Fig. 3).*

Definition 10 ($d_{left.alter}$). *The approximated length of the path which starts from the agent location, jumps to the outer right most point, and then to the outer left most point, and finally follows the path determined by Algorithm 4 (see Fig. 3).*

Definition 11 ($d_{left.inner}$). *The approximated length of the path passing through the agent location, the inner left most point, and the target (see Fig. 3).*

Algorithm 3. Evaluation Phase

1: **if** (*behind of left* and not *inside of right*) or (*behind of right* and not *inside of left*) **then**
2:      **if** *outer left most angle* + *outer right most angle* ≥ 360 **then**
3:          **if** distance from agent to *outer left most point* is smaller than distance from agent to *left alternative point* **then**
4:              Assign estimated distance as $min(d_{left}, d_{right.alter})$ and propose *outer left most direction* as moving direction
5:          **else**
6:              Assign estimated distance as $min(d_{left.alter}, d_{right})$ and propose *outer right most direction* as moving direction
7:          **end if**
8:      **else**
9:          **if** $d_{left} < d_{right}$ **then**
10:             Assign estimated distance as d_{left} and propose *outer left most direction* as moving direction
11:         **else**
12:             Assign estimated distance as d_{right} and propose *outer right most direction* as moving direction
13:         **end if**
14:     **end if**
15:     Mark obstacle as blocking the target
16: **else if** *behind of left* **then**
17:     **if** Target direction angle $\neq 0$ and *outer-right-zero angle blocking* **then**
18:         Assign estimated distance as d_{left} and propose *outer left most direction* as moving direction
19:     **else**
20:         Assign estimated distance as $d_{right.inner}$ and propose *inner right most direction* as moving direction
21:     **end if**
22:     Mark obstacle as blocking the target
23: **else if** *behind of right* **then**
24:     **if** Target direction angle $\neq 0$ and *outer-left-zero angle blocking* **then**
25:         Assign estimated distance as d_{right} and propose *outer right most direction* as moving direction
26:     **else**
27:         Assign estimated distance as $d_{left.inner}$ and propose *inner left most direction* as moving direction
28:     **end if**
29:     Mark obstacle as blocking the target
30: **else**
31:     **if** (*inside of left* and not *inside of right*) and (*inner-left-zero angle blocking* and not *inside of inner left*) **then**
32:         Assign estimated distance as $d_{left.inner}$ and propose *inner left most direction* as moving direction
33:         Mark obstacle as blocking the target
34:     **else if** (*inside of right* and not *inside of left*) and (*inner-right-zero angle blocking* and not *inside of inner right*) **then**
35:         Assign estimated distance as $d_{right.inner}$ and propose *inner right most direction* as moving direction
36:         Mark obstacle as blocking the target
37:     **end if**
38: **end if**

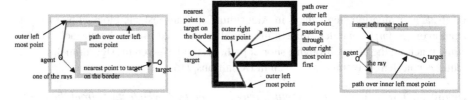

Fig. 3. Examples of d_{left} (left), $d_{left.alter}$ (middle) and $d_{left.inner}$ (right)

Algorithm 4 is internally used in computations of d_{left} and $d_{left.alter}$, and the subfunction *isoutwardsfacing* is called for detecting if a border segment, whose both ends touch the line passing through the *outer left most point* and the target point, is outwards facing (see Fig. 4). The estimated target distances over right side of the obstacle are

---

Algorithm 4. Path length estimation

Require: t : target point
Require: s : outer left most point
Require: n : the nearest point to the target
Require: $+$: next border point (left of)
Require: $-$: previous border point (right of)
Require: $insert(p)$: inserts a point to the estimated path
Require: $clasify(p_1, p_2, p_3)$: if the edge formed by the points p_1, p_2, p_3 does a left turn then returns true, else returns false
Require: $isoutwardsfacing(side, p_1, p_2)$: see Algorithm 5
1: **let** $prev = s$
2: **let** $prevleft = true$
3: $insert(s)$
4: **for** each border point v between $s+$ and n **do**
5:    **if** $v = n$ **then**
6:      **if** $isoutwardsfacing(prevleft, prev, t)$ **then**
7:        $insert$(all border points between $prev+$ and v)
8:      **end if**
9:      $insert(t)$
10:      **return** length of estimated path
11:    **end if**
12:    **let** $vleft = $ not $clasify(s, t, v)$
13:    **if** $prevleft \neq vleft$ **then**
14:      **let** $z = $ intersection point of lines (s, t) and $(v-, v)$
15:      **if** not $isoutwardsfacing(prevleft, prev, z)$ and z is between $prev$ and t **then**
16:        $insert(t)$
17:        **return** length of estimated path
18:      **end if**
19:      **if** $isoutwardsfacing(prevleft, prev, z)$ **then**
20:        $insert$(all border points between $prev+$ and v)
21:      **else**
22:        $insert(v)$
23:      **end if**
24:      **let** $prev = v$
25:      **let** $prevleft = vleft$
26:    **end if**
27: **end for**

Algorithm 5. The function $isoutwardsfacing(side, p_1, p_2)$

Require: t : target point
Require: s : outer left most point
Require: $len(n_1, n_2)$: returns distance between points n_1 and n_2
Require: $positive(m)$: if $len(m, t) \leq len(s, t)$ or $len(m, t) \leq len(s, m)$ then returns true, else returns false
Require: $slen(m)$: if $positive(m)$ then returns $+len(s, m)$ else returns $-len(s, m)$
1: **if** $(side$ and $slen(p_1) < slen(p_2))$ or $($not $side$ and $slen(p_1) > slen(p_2))$ **then**
2:    **return** true
3: **else**
4:    **return** false
5: **end if**

---

similar to those over left side of the obstacle, and computed symmetrically (the terms *left* and *right* are interchanged).

In the merging phase (line 9 in Algorithm 2), the evaluation results for all obstacles are used to determine a single moving direction [9]. This proposed direction will be passed to MTES algorithm (Algorithm 1) for final decision.

The complexity of MTES is $O(w.h)$ per step, where w is the width and h is the height of the grid world. Since increasing the grid size decreases the efficiency, a **search depth** (d) can be introduced in order to limit the worst case complexity. A search depth is a rectangular area of size $(2d + 1)$x$(2d + 1)$ centered at agent location, which makes the

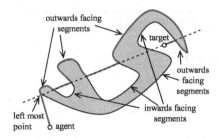

Fig. 4. Exemplified path length estimation, and outwards/inwards facing segments

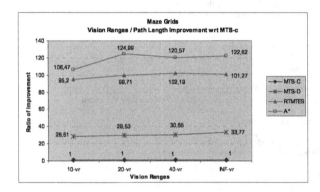

Fig. 5. Average of path length results of maze grids for increasing vision ranges

algorithm treat the cells beyond the rectangle as non-obstacle. With this limitation, the complexity becomes $O(d^2)$.

4   Performance Analysis

In this section, we present our experimental results on MTS-c, MTS-d, MTES and A*. As being an o-line algorithm, we executed A* in each step from scratch. For the test runs, we used 9 randomly generated sample grids of size 150x150. Six of them were the *maze* grids, and three of them were the *U-type* grids [8,9]. For each grid, we produced 15 different randomly generated predator-prey location pairs, and made all the algorithms use the same pairs for fairness. Our tests are performed with 10, 20, 40 and infinite vision ranges and search depths. To test the algorithms, we developed a deliberative off-line prey algorithm (Prey-A*), which is powerful but not very efficient. To prevent the side effects caused by the efficiency difference, the predator and the prey are executed alternately in performance tests. We also assumed that the prey is slower than the predator, and skips 1 move after each 7 moves.

With respect to vision ranges and search depths, the averages of path lengths on maze grids are given in Figures 5 and 6, and the averages of path lengths on U-type grids are given in Figures 7 and 8, respectively. In the charts, the horizontal axis is either the vision range or the search depth, and the vertical axis contains the path length

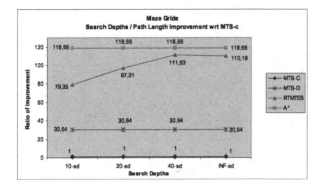

Fig. 6. Average of path length results of maze grids for increasing search depths

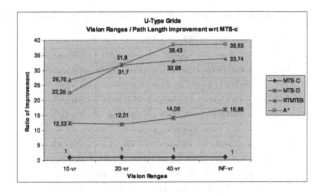

Fig. 7. Average of path length results of U-type grids for increasing vision ranges

of MTS-c divided by that of the compared algorithm. The results showed that MTES performs significantly better than MTS-c and MTS-d even with small search depths, and usually offers near optimal solutions that are almost as good as the ones produced by A*. Especially in U-type grids, MTES mostly outperforms A*. When we examined this interesting result in details, we observed that they behave very differently in sparse parts of the grid. MTES prefers performing diagonally shaped manoeuvres for approaching targets located in diagonal directions, whereas A* prefers performing L-shaped manoeuvres in such cases. Since the agents are only permitted to move in horizontal and vertical directions, these two manoeuvre patterns have equal path distances to a static target, but for a moving target, the strategy difference significantly affects the behavior of the prey in U-type grids and sometimes makes A* worse than MTES.

We also examined the step execution times of the algorithms running on an AMD Athlon 2500+ computer. In Table 1, the worst case and the average number of moves executed per second are shown. The rows are for the compared algorithms and the columns are for the search depths. We see that MTS-c and MTS-d have low and almost

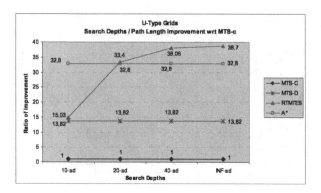

Fig. 8. Average of path length results of U-type grids for increasing search depths

Table 1. Worst case and average number of moves/second for increasing search depths

Maze grids

Depth	10-sd	20-sd	40-sd	INF-sd
MTS-c	1063/2676	1063/2676	1063/2676	1063/2676
MTS-d	937/2412	937/2412	937/2412	937/2412
MTES	531/1101	212/692	82/413	23/283
A*	20/189	20/189	20/168	20/189

U-type grids

Depth	10-sd	20-sd	40-sd	INF-sd
MTS-c	1063/2855	1063/2855	1063/2855	1063/2855
MTS-d	1062/2498	1062/2498	1062/2498	1062/2498
MTES	793/1257	400/747	133/348	57/233
A*	8/104	8/104	8/104	8/104

constant step execution times whereas the efficiency of MTES is tied to the search depth and obstacle ratio, and hence the appropriate depth should be chosen according to the required efficiency. A* is the worst as expected.

5   Conclusion

In this paper, we have examined the problem of pursuing a moving target in grid worlds, introduced a moving target search algorithm, MTES, and presented the comparison results of MTS-c, MTS-d, MTES and A* against a moving target controlled by Prey-A*. With respect to path lengths, the experiments showed that MTES performs significantly ahead of MTS-c and MTS-d, and competes with A*. In terms of step execution times, we observed that MTS-c and MTS- d are the most efficient algorithms, and almost spend constant time in each move. But their solution path lengths are usually unacceptably long. MTES follows MTS, and its efficiency is inversely proportional to the increase in obstacle density. Finally, A* is always the worst.

References

1. Goldenberg, M., Kovarsky, A., Wu, X., Schaeffer, J.: Multiple agents moving target search. In: Int'l. Joint Conf. on Artificial Intelligence, IJCAI, pp. 1536–1538 (2003)
2. Ishida, T., Korf, R.: Moving target search: A real-time search for changing goals. IEEE Trans. Pattern Analysis and Machine Intelligence 17(6), 97–109 (1995)
3. Koenig, S., Likhachev, M.: Real-time adaptive a*. In: 5th Int'l. Joint Conf. on Autonomous Agents and Multiagent Systems, pp. 281–288 (2006)
4. Koenig, S., Likhachev, M., Sun, X.: Speeding up moving-target search*. In: 6th Int'l. Joint Conf. on Autonomous Agents and Multiagent Systems (2007)
5. Korf, R.: Real-time heuristic search. Artificial Intelligence 42(2-3), 189–211 (1990)
6. Russell, S., Norving, P.: Artificial Intelligence: a modern approach. Prentice Hall, Inc., Englewood Cliffs (1995)
7. Stentz, A.: The focussed D* algorithm for real-time replanning. In: Proceedings of the Int'l. Joint Conference on Artificial Intelligence (1995)
8. Undeger, C., Polat, F.: Real-time edge follow: A real-time path search approach. IEEE Transaction on Systems, Man and Cybernetics, Part C 37(5), 860–872 (2007)
9. Undeger, C., Polat, F.: Rttes: Real-time search in dynamic environments. Applied Intelligence 27, 113–129 (2007)

Formalizing Excusableness of Failures in Multi-Agent Systems

Eugen Staab and Thomas Engel

Faculty of Sciences, Technology and Communication, University of Luxembourg,
6, rue Richard Coudenhove Kalergi, L-1359 Luxembourg
Tel.: 00352-466644-5319
{eugen.staab,thomas.engel}@uni.lu

Abstract. To estimate how much an agent can be trusted, its *trustworthiness* needs to be assessed. Usually, poor performance of an agent leads to a decrease of trust in that agent. This is not always reasonable. If the environment *interferes* with the performance, the agent is possibly not to blame for the failure. We examine which failures can be called *excusable* and hence must not be seen as bad performances. Knowledge about these failures makes assessments of trustworthiness more accurate. In order to approach a formal definition of *excusableness*, we introduce a generic formalism for describing environments of Multi-Agent Systems. This formalism provides a basis for the definition of *environmental interference*. We identify the remaining criteria for *excusableness* and give a formal definition for it. Our analysis reveals that *environmental interference* and a strong commitment of the performing agent do not suffice to make a failure *excusable*.

Keywords: Multi-agent systems, trust, dynamic environments, service-oriented computing, mobile ad hoc networks.

"Both types of mistake - trusting too well and not well enough - can be costly." [1]

1 Introduction

In Multi-Agent Systems (MAS) the assessment of agents in terms of trustworthiness is an important topic in research [2, 3, 4, 5, 6]. Many trust-models use experiences made with interaction partners as basis for assessments. But – as Ramchurn et al. point out [2] – only few models account for the context in which the behavior of other agents was assessed.

In [7] Falcone and Castelfranchi present a comprehensive study of trust in Multi-Agent Systems. They mention that "when x trusts the internal powers of y, it also trusts his abilities to create positive opportunities for success, to perceive and react to the external problems". A profound investigation on the causality in the other direction though could not be found in literature, i.e. which experiences should be used to diminish or augment the trust in y.

A. Ghose, G. Governatori, and R. Sadananda (Eds.): PRIMA 2007, LNAI 5044, pp. 122–133, 2009.

An example shows why this is important. Assume the trustworthiness of agent a and agent b is assessed at time t_1 and time t_2 respectively. Even if the performances of agents a and b are the same, if the environment has changed between time t_1 and t_2, agent a may succeed while b fails. The agent who was assessed during the disadvantageous setting is most likely trusted less than the other one. This is an incorrect perception of reality and a sophisticated trust-model should not have this characteristic.

We therefore introduce the property of *excusableness*. If an agent performs well but the environment interferes (such that the agent does not accomplish the task), the failure should not generally be classified as bad performance of the agent; in some cases the failure is *excusable*. *Excusable* failures are those which are wrongly used for diminishing the trust in the failing agent. So if the evaluation of experiences is seen as classification problem then *excusable* failures would belong to the set of false negatives[1]. In our work this set is identified by developing a theoretical understanding of *excusableness* and by providing a definition for it. This definition and all requisite definitions are given from an objective or external viewpoint. In this way, the paper contributes to the conceptual analysis of trust and its assessment. To make the results suitable for the use in formal trust-models, all definitions are presented both informally and formally – by the use of predicate logic.

By the definition of *excusableness*, knowledge about *excusable* failures can make assessments of trustworthiness more accurate. That is important both for the assessing agent and for the agent being assessed. The paper does not address how this knowledge can be obtained, i.e. how *excusableness* can be measured in practice. Further we do not investigate moral or legal aspects of the property.

For many definitions in this paper we provide examples for the purpose of illustration and to demonstrate the appropriateness of the formalisms. The setting for the examples are Mobile Ad Hoc Networks (MANETs) [8]. A MANET consists of mobile nodes communicating over wireless technologies. The network does not rely on a pre-existing infrastructure as it cannot be predicted how the nodes will move over time.

In the next section we introduce a generic formalism for describing environments of Multi-Agent Systems. Using this formalism, *environmental interference* and *riskiness* of performances are introduced in Sect. 3. In Sect. 4 the criteria for *excusableness* are derived and a formal definition is given. We have a look at the work that has been done on related topics in Sect. 5. Conclusions are drawn and an outlook on future work is given in Sect. 6 and 7 respectively.

2   Formalizing the Environment

An environment is described through a set of *environmental variables* and the relations between them. The set of variables is constructed by taking the power set of all *atomic variables* where *atomic variables* are those which are not composed

---

[1] False positives cannot be defined symmetrically and therefore shall be investigated separately.

from other variables. Agents are variables, too. Each environmental variable has a certain *intensity* depending on time. *Intensity* is a degree of strength (over time) with which the variable influences its environment. The relations between the environmental variables are expressed as their *exposure* among each other. A variable may be exposed to another one heavily or not at all. The influence one variable has on another one could then be calculated on the basis of intensity of the influencing variable and the exposure of the influenced variable towards the influencing variable. However this will not be an issue of this paper.

An environment Ψ can formally be described as a triple $\langle \Omega, I_\Omega, E_\Omega \rangle$, where:

- The set Ω contains all environmental variables ω. The set Ω is constructed as power set of all *atomic variables*. Each environmental variable is then a set consisting of atomic variables and/or other composed variables. The set of agents (each agent is a variable), denoted by $\mathcal{A}$, is contained in Ω, so $\mathcal{A} \subseteq \Omega$.
- The set I_Ω contains for each variable $\omega \in \Omega$ a function which represents ω's intensity over time. Every such function $\iota_\omega : \mathbb{R} \rightarrow [0, \infty)$ maps points in time t to the intensity of the environmental variable. The intensity of a variable can range from its minimum 0 (no intensity at all) to ∞. We call a function ι_ω the *intensity-function of variable* ω.
- The set E_Ω contains for each variable $\omega_i \in \Omega$ a function which represents the exposure of ω_i to all other variables. For a point in time t and an environmental variable ω_j such a function $\varepsilon_{\omega_i} \in E_\Omega$ returns the exposure of ω_i to ω_j at time t. The function is of the form $\varepsilon_\omega : (\Omega * \mathbb{R}) \rightarrow [0, 1]$. A variable can be totally exposed to another one (1) or not at all (0). We call a function ε_{ω_i} the *exposure-function of variable* ω_i.

Example 1 (Environment). Let the nodes of a MANET be the set of agents $\mathcal{A}$. As agents are environmental variables each one has an intensity-function which represents the radiation power of an agent's network card. When an agent a doesn't send at time t, its intensity-function is zero, i.e. $\iota_a(t) = 0$. The exposure between two agents a and b depends on their distance. If their distance changes over time the exposure-functions $\varepsilon_a(b, t)$ and $\varepsilon_b(a, t)$ change (in the same way). So the movement of variables can completely be described by the exposure-functions. Other variables are for instance walls; their intensity-function is constant and depends on the material and the thickness of the wall.

3   Interference and Riskiness

In this section we introduce the concepts of *interference* and *riskiness*. Both are important for the definition of *excusableness* given in Sect. 4.

3.1   Interference with Actions

Interference addresses the impact the environment has on the actions of an agent. More precisely it describes the case in which the environment is the *critical* cause for a failure in an agent's performance. *Critical* means that if this cause had not been given, the agent would have succeeded. If there are n environmental variables $\omega_1, ..., \omega_n$ only together causing a failure, then the variable $\omega = \bigcup_{i=1}^{n} \omega_i$ interferes with the action.

To express *interference* formally we first need to define two predicates, namely *perform* and *success*.

Definition 1 (Performance). *Let A be the set of agents within the set of variables of Ψ and $a \in A$. The predicate $perform(a, \alpha, t, t', \Psi)$ marks the attempt of agent a to perform an action α in an environment Ψ within time-frame $[t, t']$, i.e. the performance starts at time t and ends at time t'.*

The predicate *perform* does not say *how much* it was attempted to perform α; so this effort is left unparameterized for the sake of simplicity. It suffices to assume that if this predicate is used more than once in a formula then the effort is the same for each agent for which the predicate is used.

Example 2 (Performance). In a MANET an agent attempts to send a packet if it sends the packet with the radiation power of its network card.

Definition 2 (Success). *Let A be the set of agents within the set of variables of Ψ and $a \in A$. The predicate $success(a, \alpha, t, \Psi)$ marks the successful accomplishment of an action α through agent a in an environment Ψ at time t. It always holds: $success(a, \alpha, t', \Psi) \Rightarrow \exists t < t'.perform(a, \alpha, t, t', \Psi)$.*

Example 3 (Success). An agent in a MANET succeeds to send a packet if it is received without errors.

We are now ready to formalize the predicate $interfere(\omega, a, \alpha, t, t', \Psi)$. Recall that $\iota_\omega(t)$ returns the intensity of variable ω at time t. We use the notation $I_\Omega[\iota_\omega(t) := y]$ to denote the substitution of the value of ι_ω to be y at time t.

Definition 3 (Interference of Variables with Actions). *An environmental variable ω interferes with the attempt of an agent a to perform an action α within time-frame $[t, t']$ in an environment Ψ, iff the agent does not succeed but would have succeeded if ω had had a lower intensity.*

We write $interfere(\omega, a, \alpha, t, t', \Psi)$ and have

$$interfere(\omega, a, \alpha, t, t', \Psi) \equiv perform(a, \alpha, t, t', \Psi) \wedge \neg success(a, \alpha, t', \Psi)$$
$$\wedge \exists y < \iota_\omega(t), \Psi' = \langle \Omega, I_\Omega[\iota_\omega(t) := y], E_\Omega \rangle.$$
$$(perform(a, \alpha, t, t', \Psi') \Rightarrow success(a, \alpha, t', \Psi')).$$

The first line of the formula only guarantees that the action is not successfully performed – if it was, there would be no interference. The other two lines enforce the existence of a threshold for the intensity of the interfering variable; if ω had an intensity below this threshold the action would have been successfully accomplished. That excludes the possibility that the agent is not motivated or incapable. Note that the exposure towards the interfering variable needs not to be considered, as the intensity of it can be set to zero, causing the overall influence of the variable to become zero, too (regardless of how much other variables are exposed to it). Analogously a definition could be given using only exposure.

Example 4 (Interference). Imagine an agent in a MANET tries to send a packet to another agent. They are separated by a wall which interferes with the transmission. If the wall was not there or maybe only thinner (i.e. the intensity-function lower), the transmission would have been successful. Another example is the collision of transmissions between two agents using the IEEE 802.11 radio technology and another agent using the Bluetooth radio technology. As they both operate on the 2.4 GHz ISM band an interference is quite possible [9]. If one of the sending agents had not sent (thus the intensity-function would have had value 0) the other transmission would not have been interfered.

The definition for *interference* given above, referred to one specific environmental variable. This can be generalized to apply for an entire environment by quantification over the environmental variables. We use the symbol $*$ as wildcard character:

Definition 4 (Interference with Actions). *An environment* $\Psi = \langle \Omega, *, * \rangle$ *interferes with the attempt of an agent a to perform an action α within time-frame $[t, t']$ in that environment Ψ, iff there is at least one variable ω which interferes with the performance.*
We write $interfere(a, \alpha, t, t', \Psi)$ *and have*

$$interfere(a, \alpha, t, t', \Psi) \equiv \exists \omega \in \Omega.interfere(\omega, a, \alpha, t, t', \Psi).$$

3.2   Interference with Tasks

In the previous section a definition for *interference* of an environment with an atomic action α was given. Now we can proceed to the problem of interference with the accomplishment of a task, e.g. one agent asks another agent to fulfill a task for it. Such a task can consist for instance in delivering products or solving problems. Generally speaking a task can be accomplished by the sequential execution of one or more atomic actions. The interesting thing here is that every agent may have its own way to carry out the task. The environment possibly interferes with only some ways to solve the task but not with others. Note that for a rational agent following the BDI-architecture [10, 11] such a task would be a *desire* and could be accomplished by the execution of nested *plans*.

A task τ can be fulfilled through the successful execution of a sequence σ_τ of atomic actions. We represent such a sequence σ_τ as a set of triples (t, t', α), $0 \leqslant t \leqslant t'$, associating time-frames with atomic actions, e.g.

$$\sigma_\tau = \{(t_0, t'_0, \alpha_0), (t_1, t'_1, \alpha_1), ..., (t_n, t'_n, \alpha_n)\}.$$

The points of time given in that sequence are not absolute but relative to the point at which the execution of the sequence starts. So if one assumes the above sequence to be chronologically ordered, then $t_0 = 0$.

The successful execution of the atomic actions within their associated time-frames leads to the fulfillment of task τ. As we already stated, there can be more than one way to solve a task. The set of all these sequences for one specific τ is written as S_τ. Each agent a has its own set of sequences S_τ^a for each task τ.

The definition for *interference* of the environment with a certain sequence σ_τ through an agent a is straightforward (based on definition 4). The only thing to take care of is that the relative dates in the sequence need to be added to the starting point of the execution.

Definition 5 (Interference with Sequences). *An environment Ψ interferes with the attempt of an agent a to perform a sequence σ_τ in that environment Ψ starting at t_0 iff it interferes with at least one atomic action of the sequence.
We write $interfere(a, \sigma_\tau, t_0, \Psi)$ and have*

$$interfere(a, \sigma_\tau, t_0, \Psi) \equiv \exists (t, t', \alpha) \in \sigma_\tau . interfere(a, \alpha, t_0 + t, t_0 + t', \Psi).$$

Accordingly the predicates *perform* and *success* of Def. 1 and 2 respectively can be adapted to sequences of actions. We then have $perform(a, \sigma_\tau, t, t', \Psi)$ instead of $perform(a, \alpha, t, t', \Psi)$ and $success(a, \sigma_\tau, t, \Psi)$ instead of $success(a, \alpha, t, \Psi)$.

Finally it is possible to state in which cases the environment interferes with the attempt of an agent to fulfill a task τ. In order to perform a task τ within a given time-frame, an agent selects a certain sequence σ_τ. This choice is based on observations on the environment, i.e. observations on the intensity- and exposure-functions of the respective environment Ψ. The choice is represented by the function $select_a(\tau, t_0, t_1, O_\Psi)$ with domain $(\mathcal{T} * \mathbb{R} * \mathbb{R} * \mathcal{O}_\Psi)$ and the set of according sequences S_τ^a as codomain; here $\mathcal{T}$ denotes the set of all tasks and $\mathcal{O}_\Psi$ the set of all possible sets of observations O_Ψ on Ψ. Each agent $a \in \mathcal{A}$ has its own function $select_a$ because every agent may have a different strategy to select a sequence and a different set of sequences S_τ^a.

Definition 6 (Selection). *The function $select_a(\tau, t_0, t_1, O_\Psi)$ returns the selection for a sequence of tasks $\sigma_\tau \in S_\tau^a$ an agents makes in order to accomplish a task τ in the time-frame $[t_0, t_1]$.*

Let $O_\Psi^{a,t}$ denote the set of observations on Ψ to which a had access to until time t. Then the environment *interferes* with the attempt of agent a to fulfill a task τ in an environment Ψ within time-frame $[t_0, t_1]$, iff the following holds:
$\left(select_a(\tau, t_0, t_1, O_\Psi^{a,t_0}) = \sigma_\tau\right) \Rightarrow interfere(a, \sigma_\tau, t_0, \Psi)$.

3.3   Riskiness

Before a sophisticated agent selects a sequence of actions σ_τ in order to fulfill a task τ, it makes a risk assessment for the possible choices. The interest of the agent may be to minimize the risk of a failure (if he wants to appear trustworthy) or to minimize its costs or both. Its risk assessment is based on a set of observations on the environment:

Definition 7 (Riskiness). *The function $risk(a, \sigma_\tau, t_0, O_\Psi^{a,t_0}, \Psi)$ returns the probability which an agent a, given observations O_Ψ^{a,t_0} on Ψ, assigns to the event that the sequence of actions σ_τ will interfere with the environment Ψ when executed by agent a at time t_0.*

Example 5 (Riskiness). Let τ denote the task to securely transfer a packet in a MANET. The probability that this will be accomplished successfully by using a simple substitution cipher for encryption is very low; it saves computation-costs for the sending agent but the risk that it will be compromised is very high. Let's write σ_τ for this approach. Public key cryptography is computationally more expensive but much more secure [12]. The risk is much lower. We write ς_τ for the second approach. For a sufficiently sophisticated agent a we get for a general environment: $risk(a, \varsigma_\tau, t_0, O_\Psi^{a,t_0}, \Psi) \ll risk(a, \sigma_\tau, t_0, O_\Psi^{a,t_0}, \Psi)$.

4   Excusableness

Excusableness identifies cases in which bad performances of agents are wrongly used to decrease the trust in these agents; therefore only *failures* can be *excusable*. It can be argued that assessments that account for *excusableness* are more credulous because certain bad experiences are ignored. In fact, the opposite is true: by ignoring only *excusable* failures, the difference between agents that are really trustworthy and those which are not is amplified. This has consequences on the social structures of a MAS and, since Castelfranchi et al. [13] identified trust as "relational capital", agents start to care more about their image as trustee.

In the following we analyze the factors that can cause an agent to fail and identify the criteria that make a failure *excusable*. Consequently the definition of *excusableness* is given.

4.1   Criteria

An agent can fail in performing a task as a consequence of one or more of the following four factors:

- The *ability* of the agent,
- the possibly *interfering* environment in which the agent performs,
- the *willingness* and
- the *commitment* of the agent.

Ability If an agent fails to perform a task due to general inability, the trust in that agent should be diminished. If its abilities do not change, the agent will never succeed in the future; other agents should be preferred to it (the agent should be trusted less).

When the environment interferes with the performance of one agent, that does not imply that the same environment would interfere with another agent's actions. One agent might be more robust than another agent and thus should be trusted more; therefore robustness belongs as well to the abilities of an agent. That demands for a definition of *excusableness* in respect to a reference set of agents. Only if no other agent of the reference set succeeded under the same conditions, a failure might be *excusable*. This reference set can consist for instance of all agents in a MAS or only the adjacent agents in a network.

Interference. As listed above, three causes for a failure come from the inside of an agent, namely the ability, the willingness and the commitment of an agent. If these are the only causes for a failure, the reason for failing must be one of reluctance, inability (in respect to the environment) or an insufficient level of commitment. These causes though demand for a decrease of trust in that agent as they can clearly be attributed to the agent itself. The environmental interference is the only external causation and thus must be a precondition for *excusableness*. As defined in Def. 3, *interference* implies that the agent is not generally unable to perform the task: the agent would succeed under different circumstances. The ability of the agent itself is thereby already guaranteed if *interference* is demanded.

In a *dynamic setting*, the trustworthiness of an agent should be independent of the environment in which the agent is assessed. Otherwise, if the environment of the agent changes, the trust in that agent developed earlier ceases to be consistent with the agent's recent trustworthiness. In a *static setting* however, the environment of an agent stays always the same. In that case, the agent's environment should be attributed to the agent itself and wouldn't make failures *excusable*. Therefore our definition addresses only *dynamic settings*.

Willingness. A capable agent that is unwilling to perform a task cannot be trusted as it will certainly fail due to reluctance. This directly implies that a failure as a result of unwillingness is not *excusable*. *Willingness* is already implicit in the predicate of *interference* (see Sec. 3.1). With *willingness* we address the willingness of an agent to perform the task. It does not address how much the performing agent is ready to invest – the next issue:

Commitment. An agent can select a way, out of a set of alternative approaches, to accomplish a task τ. Assume the selected approach σ_τ is less costly for the agent, but, to its knowledge, riskier than another approach ς_τ; further assume the agent fails because the approach was risky. Then, of course, the failure is not *excusable*. As Falcone and Castelfranchi [7] put it: "When x trusts y, x is just assuming that other motivations will prevail over his [y's] economic interests or other selfish goals". Therefore, given a measure for riskiness as defined in Def. 7, the definition for *excusableness* has to require that the performing agent knew no approach that was thought to be less risky and would have succeeded.

4.2 Definition

At this point we are equipped with all the necessary formalisms to give a formal definition of the *excusableness*-property as derived in the previous section. Note that the selection of a sequence of actions made by the failing agent is based on the observations he had access to until time t_0. To stay comparable, the agents from the reference set need to be equipped with the same set of observations as the failing agent. Recall that ε_ω is the function that describes the exposure of the variable ω towards other variables. Also remember that $O_\Psi^{a,t}$ is the set of observations on Ψ to which a had access to until time t.

Definition 8 (Excusableness). *The failure of an agent a in performing a task τ in time-frame $[t_0, t_1]$ and environment $\Psi = \langle \Omega, I_\Omega, E_\Omega \rangle$ is excusable in respect to a group of agents B iff both*

1. *no other agent in B would succeed in performing τ under the same conditions and*
2. *for the sequence of actions σ_τ selected by agent a it both holds:*
   (a) σ_τ is interfering with the environment and
   (b) there is no alternative sequence of actions ς_τ with which agent a would have succeeded and which is assessed by a to be less risky than σ_τ.

We write $excusable(a, B, \tau, t_0, t_1, \Psi)$ with $\Psi = \langle \Omega, I_\Omega, E_\Omega \rangle$ and have

$$
\begin{aligned}
excusable(a, B, &\tau, t_0, t_1, \Psi) \equiv \\
&\forall b \in B, \Psi' = \langle \Omega, I_\Omega, E_\Omega[\varepsilon_b := \varepsilon_a] \rangle . &(1.)\\
&\quad select_b(\tau, t_0, t_1, O_\Psi^{a, t_0}) = \sigma_\tau^b \Rightarrow \big(perform(b, \sigma_\tau^b, t_0, t_1, \Psi') \\
&\qquad\qquad\qquad\qquad\qquad\qquad \Rightarrow \neg success(b, \sigma_\tau^b, t_1, \Psi') \big) \\
\wedge\, select_a(\tau, &t_0, t_1, O_\Psi^{a, t_0}) = \sigma_\tau^a \Rightarrow \big(interfere(a, \sigma_\tau^a, t_0, \Psi) &(2.(a))\\
\wedge\, \forall \varsigma_\tau \in S_\tau^a . (&risk(a, \varsigma_\tau, t_0, O_\Psi^{a, t_0}, \Psi) < risk(a, \sigma_\tau^a, t_0, O_\Psi^{a, t_0}, \Psi) &(2.(b))\\
&\Rightarrow (perform(a, \varsigma_\tau, t_0, t_1, \Psi) \Rightarrow \neg success(a, \varsigma_\tau, t_1, \Psi)))\big).
\end{aligned}
$$

Example 6 (Excusableness). Let the four agents a, b, c and d be nodes in a MANET (as shown in Fig. 1). All of them are equipped with the same network cards and send with the same transmitting power. For the purpose of the example they are arranged in a line-topology a-b-c-d, i.e. agent a can only communicate with b, b also with c, d only with c. Now imagine a requests b to deliver a packet to c before time t. Agent b sends the packet repeatedly until time t but c doesn't receive it as d is sending at the same time: the messages sent by b and d collide and c cannot receive any of them (this is also known as the *Hidden Terminal Problem* [14]). So b fails in delivering the packet to c. The question is whether this failure should be used by a to diminish its trust in b. That shouldn't be the case as it could not have been passed off better under these circumstances; this failure should be *excusable*. Let's check whether each condition required by Def. 8 is true:

1. No one else would have succeeded: Every packet sent with the same transmitting power would have collided with the packet coming from d (and no other agent could send with a higher transmitting power).
2. (a) The environment did interfere: If the intensity with which the agent d sent would have been 0, then b would have succeeded.
   (b) There was only one possibility for b to send the packet to c: No less risky alternatives were available to b which would have succeeded.

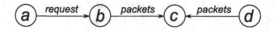

Fig. 1. The *Hidden Terminal Problem* in a MANET

Hence, according to the definition of *excusableness* it is indeed an *excusable* failure. In addition, all three conditions are necessary because if any of them was dropped the trust should be diminished and thus the failure should not be classified as *excusable*:

1. If another agent had succeeded, then a should trust more in that agent than in b concerning the fulfillment of that task.
2. (a) If the environment did not interfere, a failure would imply either b's inability or its unwillingness: the trust in b should be diminished.
   (b) If b had sent with a higher transmitting power and would have succeeded in that case, a could expect b to have done so. Agent b's motivation not to do so would be to save energy – but that is no excuse: agent a should diminish its trust in b.

5   Related Work

The question about *excusability* is strongly related to the research field of *causality* (see e.g. Pearl [15]). In the definition of interference (Def. 3) for example, we use *counterfactuals*: if the environment had been different, the agent would have succeeded – to express this we use two different instances of an environment Ψ of which one is not happening. As the definition of *excusableness* demands, one precondition is the relativity towards the abilities and commitments of other agents. This draws *excusableness* out of the field of pure *causality*.

Ramchurn et al. [2] give an overview on the research done in the field of trust in MAS. They point out that many trust models do not take into account in which context assessments of trustworthiness are made. They refer to Molm et al. [16] which state that information captured under certain conditions can become worthless under different conditions. This shows the importance of defining *excusableness* in dependence of a time-frame $[t_0, t_1]$ (at another time the failure might not be *excusable*).

In Şensoy and Yolum [5], experiences about past interactions are always associated with the environment within which they are made. This enables agents to evaluate their experiences context-sensitively. Similarly Hussain et al. [17] let their trusting peers assimilate recommendations of others based on the context and the time of the according interaction. Both approaches do not account for *excusable* failures but present frameworks that could be extended accordingly.

Falcone and Castelfranchi [7] present a comprehensive study on trust in Multi-Agent Systems. They discuss the importance of trust for MAS and analyze the elements forming a mental state of trust. They make a distinction of *external* and *internal* factors for trust. With *internal* factors they mean *ability, willingness* and *commitment*. With *external* they mean the environmental influence. They mention the reciprocal influence between external and internal factors. In a similar direction Boella and van der Torre [18] investigate the motivations of agents when they violate norms. They state that a sophisticated system of trust dynamics would not "decrease the trust if the other agent did its best to fulfill the promise, but failed due to circumstances beyond its control". The last two papers [7] and [18] agree with our understanding of trust; the authors examine the impact of environmental factors for trusting agents and more general for the phenomenon trust. They do not address the problem of how experiences should be used in the process of developing trust. Furthermore they do not account for the relative aspect of an agent's *ability*.

6   Conclusion

In this paper we introduced the notion of *excusableness* and developed a formal definition for it. A failure shall be called *excusable* iff it should not be used to diminish the trust in the failing agent. When breaking this proposition down into a set of factors we found out that three conditions must be given such that a failure can be called *excusable*:

1. No other agent from a reference set of agents would have been able to succeed under the same conditions.
2. The environment has interfered with the performance of the failing agent.
3. No other way to accomplish the task was assessed by the failing agent to be less risky and would have succeeded.

It is concluded that environmental interference and a strong commitment of the performing agent do not yet imply *excusableness*. The relation of the failing agent towards other agents is as well essential in order to make a failure *excusable*. Further we pointed out that in dynamic settings *excusableness* has a different meaning than in static settings. In the latter case, the environment of an agent can be interpreted as part of the agent itself. Then environmental interference becomes part of the agent's inability and doesn't make a failure *excusable*.

An important question is how knowledge about *excusable* failures can be obtained in practice. As the definition of *excusableness* reveals, it is a quite complex property. Thus, in practice it will be hard to gather all the needed information to clearly state whether a failure is *excusable* or not. This fact promotes either an approach using statistical data analysis and/or a trade-off is made which however still improves the accuracy of trust-assessments.

7   Future Work

Currently we are working on a statistical mechanism that subtracts environmental interference in a reputation system iff it occurred for all assessed agents in the same reference groups. The approach ignores the riskiness-precondition as trade-off; this is acceptable when the reasonable assumption is made that agents do not agree on their risk-strategies over time. The assessing agents collaborate in order to collect as much information as possible. It is planned to verify the improvement within the Agent Reputation and Trust (ART) Testbed Architecture [19].

References

1. Friedman, B., Kahn Jr., P.H., Howe, D.C.: Trust online. Commun. of the ACM, 34–40 (2000)
2. Ramchurn, S.D., Huynh, T.D., Jennings, N.R.: Trust in multi-agent systems. Knowledge Engineering Review, 1–25 (2004)
3. Huynh, T.D., Jennings, N.R., Shadbolt, N.R.: An integrated trust and reputation model for open Multi-Agent systems. Autonomous Agents and Multi-Agent Systems, 119–154 (2006)
4. Castelfranchi, C., Falcone, R.: Principles of trust for MAS: Cognitive anatomy, social importance, and quantification. In: Proceedings of ICMAS 1998, pp. 72–79 (1998)
5. Şensoy, M., Yolum, P.: A context-aware approach for service selection using ontologies. In: Proceedings of AAMAS 2006, pp. 931–938 (2006)
6. Teacy, W.T.L., Patel, J., Jennings, N.R., Luck, M.: TRAVOS: Trust and reputation in the context of inaccurate information sources. Autonomous Agents and Multi-Agent Systems, 183–198 (2006)
7. Falcone, R., Castelfranchi, C.: Social trust: a cognitive approach. Trust and deception in virtual societies, 55–90 (2001)
8. Haas, Z.J., Deng, J., Liang, B., Papadimitratos, P., Sajama, S.: Wireless ad hoc networks. In: Perkins, C.E. (ed.) Ad Hoc Networking, pp. 221–225. Addison-Wesley, Reading (2001)
9. Vilovic, I., Zovko-Cihlar, B.: Performance analysis of wireless network using bluetooth and IEEE 802.11 devices. In: Proceedings of Elmar 2004, pp. 235–240 (2004)
10. Bratman, M.: Intentions, Plans, and Practical Reason. Harvard University Press (1987)
11. Georgeff, M., Ingrand, F.: Decision-making in an embedded reasoning system. In: Proceedings of IJCAI 1989, pp. 972–978 (1989)
12. Schneier, B.: Applied cryptography, 2nd edn. Protocols, algorithms, and source code. C. John Wiley & Sons, Inc., Chichester (1995)
13. Castelfranchi, C., Falcone, R., Marzo, F.: Being trusted in a social network: Trust as relational capital. In: Stølen, K., Winsborough, W.H., Martinelli, F., Massacci, F. (eds.) iTrust 2006. LNCS, vol. 3986, pp. 19–32. Springer, Heidelberg (2006)
14. Yoo, J., Kim, C.: On the hidden terminal problem in multi-rate ad hoc wireless networks. In: Kim, C. (ed.) ICOIN 2005. LNCS, vol. 3391, pp. 479–488. Springer, Heidelberg (2005)
15. Pearl, J.: Causality: models, reasoning, and inference. Cambridge University Press, Cambridge (2000)
16. Molm, L.D., Takahashi, N., Peterson, G.: Risk and trust in social exchange: An experimental test of a classical proposition. American Journal of Sociology (2000)
17. Hussain, O.K., Chang, E., Hussain, F.K., Dillon, T.S., Soh, B.: Context and time based riskiness assessment for decision making. In: Proceedings of AICT/ICIW 2006, p. 104. IEEE Computer Society, Los Alamitos (2006)
18. Boella, G., van der Torre, L.: Normative multiagent systems and trust dynamics. In: Trusting Agents for Trusting Electronic Societies at AAMAS 2004, pp. 1–17 (2004)
19. Fullam, K., Klos, T., Muller, G., Sabater, J., Topol, Z., Barber, K.S., Rosenschein, J., Vercouter, L.: The agent reputation and trust (ART) testbed architecture. In: Workshop on Trust in Agent Societies at AAMAS 2005, pp. 50–62 (2005)

Design and Implementation of Security Mechanisms for a Hierarchical Community-Based Multi-Agent System

Kenichi Takahashi[1], Yoshiki Mitsuyuki[2], Tsunenori Mine[2], Kouichi Sakurai[1,2], and Makoto Amamiya[2]

[1] Institute of Systems & Information Technologies/KYUSHU,
2-1-22 Momochihama, Sawara-ku, Fukuoka 814-0001, Japan
{takahashi,sakurai}@isit.or.jp
[2] Faculty of Information Science and Electrical Engineering, Kyushu University,
744 Motooka, Nishi-ku, Fukuoka 819-0395, Japan
{mitsu,mine,amamiya}@al.is.kyushu-u.ac.jp

Abstract. Recently, several community-based systems have been developed; however, almost all such systems have been developed as Web-server-based systems. Thus, server administrator can easily eavesdrop on user communications, since they have to send/receive information through the server. Therefore, we propose multi-agent-based peer-to-peer (P2P) system wherein each peer manages his/her information and exchanges it with other peers directly. This, thus, resolves the problems posed by Web-server-based systems; however, we have to consider attacks from malicious third parties. This study designs and implements security protocols/mechanisms for a hierarchical community-based multi-agent system. Furthermore, if we consider a practical use case, we should be able to demonstrate that the proposed system can be implemented by combining it with existing security techniques for more reliable and rapid deployment. Finally, we evaluate the performance of the proposed security system and present an example application.

1 Introduction

The evolution of the Internet has made it difficult to discover target information, further, the nature of the Internet, which allows everyone to easily contribute, has made it difficult to ensure the reliability of information. This imposes the inference of reliability of information on users. Therefore, community-based systems have been developed. In a community-based system, users with common interests and/or objectives organize a community. They can communicate efficiently on the topics within a community. Furthermore, these communities also facilitate the secure exchange of privacy-related information by restricting communications to within a community.

Almost community-based systems are developed as Web-server-based systems. These systems enforce security by employing public key infrastructure (PKI), https, access controls mechanisms, etc. However, since users have to send/receive

A. Ghose, G. Governatori, and R. Sadananda (Eds.): PRIMA 2007, LNAI 5044, pp. 134–145, 2009.

information through a server, server administrator can eavesdrop on their communications. Moreover, a vulnerability in the server may threaten the privacy of all users.

Therefore, we propose a multi-agent based peer-to-peer (P2P) system wherein each peer manages his/her information and exchanges it with other peers directly. P2P systems can be divided into pure P2P systems such as Gnutella and hybrid P2P systems such as Napster. Hybrid P2P systems employ one or more special peers who provide a special service such as resource discovery and/or indexing of peers, while pure P2P systems do not employ special peers. With regard to a community-based system, a hybrid P2P system is more suitable since special peers organize communities.

In the proposed system, the formation of a community depends on a special peer, but each peer in the community can exchange their information directly. This, thus, remedies the problems posed by Web-server-based systems; however, we have to consider attacks from malicious third parties, such as eavesdropping, message alteration, spoofing. In this study, we design and implement security protocols/mechanisms for a hierarchical community-based multi-agent system. Furthermore, if we consider a practical use case, we should be able to demonstrate that the proposed system can be implemented by combining it with existing security techniques for more reliable and rapid deployment.

2   Related Work

In [11], an agent-community-based P2P information retrieval system is proposed; in this system, agent communities manage and look up information efficiently. In [15], a group-based reputation system is proposed, wherein peers evaluate the credibility of a given peer based on his/her local trust information or references from within the group. However, these do not consider security.

In [4,13], the security functions for a few multi-agent-based applications have been discussed. In [7], SAgent is proposed for protecting the computations of mobile agent applications in a potentially hostile environment. Also, several researches [10,16] have discussed mobile agent security. These, however, do not take a community structure into consideration.

Most security researches in P2P systems have focused on anonymity or trust relationships; however, very few have focused on security countermeasures against attacks such as eavesdropping message alteration, and spoofing [17]. In [1,3] , these security concerns with regard to community-based system have been focused on. [3] allows a peer to change the security policy flexibly based on applications; however, it does not indicate what type of security techniques are required in particular application. [1] focuses on the security on information sharing; however, in this system, a peer has to create a digital signature for each message. Moreover, these studies do not evaluate the performances of the proposed systems.

JXTA [14] provides certain functions for the development of secure P2P systems; it requires developers to determine and combine security functions for an application. The Globus Project provides the Globus Security Infrastructure (GSI) [6], which is a security framework for grid computing applications. Groove [5] provides spontaneous shared spaces in which a small group of collaborators can securely exchange information. However, these frameworks do not take a hierarchical community structure into considerations.

3 A Hierarchical Community-Based Multi-Agent System

We represent a user as an agent managing his/her information and supporting activities. These agents who have common interests and objectives organize a community. In the proposed model, a community is also defined as one agent; thus, communities can also organize a community. Therefore, our model allows a hierarchical community structure (Fig. 1) [18]. This nature matches that of real societies. For example, each company consists of certain departments with each department comprising certain sections and each section comprises certain staff. As in real societies, a community has a representative, named portal agent. A portal agent is responsible for organizing a community and subsequently providing services for new agent participation, deregistration, and channels to actualize communication from outside the community to within and vice versa. However, the portal agent does not restrict the communications of agents within the community. Thus, agents can communicate with each other freely and directly. This nature protects agents within a community from risks of information leakage caused by a portal agent.

3.1 Levels of Information Security

An agent manages not only non-privacy-related information but also privacy-related information to support his/her activities. Thus, each agent is responsible for releasing the appropriate information to only the appropriate partner in an appropriate manner. This implies that each agent should protect his/her information by appliying the appropriate cryptographic techniques according

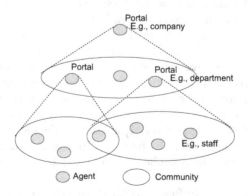

Fig. 1. Hierarchical community structure

to levels of information security. With regard to a system with a hierarchical community structure, we can define four levels of information security:

Closed information, which cannot be released to any agent.

Partner-limited information, which can be released to only those agents who satisfy a specific condition.

Community-limited information, which can be released to only those agents in the same community.

Open information, which can be released to all agents.

We do not discuss which levels of information security should be applied to a particular information entity, since this depends on the application being considered. Information should be protected in an appropriate manner based on the level of information security.

3.2   Attacks and Corresponding Countermeasures

We have to consider the prevention of attacks from malicious third parties, such as eavesdropping, message alterations and spoofing. Since closed information cannot be released to any agent, we do not need to consider preventive counter-measures for safeguarding this type of information against these attacks. However, in the case of the other levels of information security, we have to consider to prevent these attacks.

With regard to eavesdropping, no preventive countermeasure are required for open information as it can be released to all agents. However, community-limited and partner-limited information require preventive countermeasures. Community-limited information can be released to only agents in the same community; thus, agents in the same community should be able to access the information but other agents should not. On the other hand, partner-limited information can be released to only those agents who satisfy a particular condition; thus, only an agent who satisfies a specific condition should be able to access the information. Therefore, we introduce the group and P2P keys for encryption/decryption of community-limited and partner-limited information, respectively.

In order to protect against message alteration and spoofing, all types of information require preventive countermeasures. We can use a digital signature for this purpose; however, the creation and verification of a digital signatures require high computational power. In this case, we believe that it would suffice to detect the spoofing when an attack may occur. For example, when we gather price information of a product for the price comparison, influence from information spoofed by a malicious third party is small; but, when we buy the product, the information harms our wallet. Therefore, we propose a mechanism wherein a sender attaches a hash value generated from the content of a message with secret information (e.g. random number) to the message. When the receiver wants to verify whether the message was spoofing or not, he/she requests the secret information (signed by a digital signature) from the sender. On receiving this secret information, if the hash value of the message matches that generated from the secret information, the message can be considered non-spoofed.

Digital signatures indicate that a particular information entity has been created by someone who possesses a key for its creation; however, it does not indicate who the key belong to. Usually, a certificate authority (CA) keeps a record of which belongs to who by offline communication, ID/password authentication, etc. In the proposed system, a portal agent assumes this role. Therefore, a portal agent specifies requirements for new agent participations. When an agent wishes to join a community, he/she has to provide information that satisfies the specified requirements. Then, the portal agent issues a digital certificate for the agent's key. The agent can thus prove that the key is recognized by the portal agent by displaying his/her digital certificate.

3.3   Necessary Protocols

We need to design and implement the following protocols for the prevention of attacks from malicious third parties:

Participation in a community. It is necessary to prepare for activities of new agents wishing to join a community. Each community has specific requirements for participation, for example, ID/password, invitation from a friend (e.g., mixi [12]), etc. Therefore, a portal agent needs to check whether new agent satisfies the requirements, issue a digital certificate for the new agent's public key, and provides the group key. Note that the information for satisfying these requirements may also be sensitive.

Group key communication. It provides a secure channel for communication among agents from the same community. The sender embeds secret information into a message as the evidence of his/her message. Thus, he/she can prove that the message belongs to him/her. Further, it is also necessary to encrypt and decrypt community-limited information using a group key.

Mutual authentication and P2P communication. It provides for the mutual authentication and secure communication between two agents. Mutual authentication is achieved by verifying the digital certificate of each agent. Further, two agents need to share a common key (P2P key) for the encryption and decryption of partner-limited information. After sharing a P2P key, they can exchange partner-limited information securely. Moreover, they can detect whether the group key communication have been spoofed by exchanging secret information.

Leaving a community. When an agent leaves a community, his/her digital certificate should be invalidated. Then, his/her digital signature should be recorded in the certificate revocation list (CRL).

Group key updation. When community members change, updated group key is necessary for forward and backward security.

CRL Reference. Some digital signature may be come invalid before their expiry period. Therefore, an agent may want to refer to the CRL periodically.

Although we have designed all of the above protocols, this paper presents only participation in a community, group key communication, and mutual authentication and P2P communication.

3.4   Security Techniques

We use the following techniques for the design and implementation of the proposed security.

Public key cryptosystem. This algorithm utilizes a public-secret key pair. A message encrypted using the public key can only be decrypted using the secret key and vice versa. In this study, the public and secret keys of agent X are depicted as PK_x and SK_x, respectively. The encryption and decryption of a message M using a key K are represented as $E_K(M)$ and $D_K(M)$, respectively.

Common key cryptosystem. This algorithm utilizes the same key (common key) for message encryption and decryption. Thus, the sender and receiver of a message have to share a common key in advance. Moreover, the algorithm is much faster than the public key cryptosystem. In this study, a common key between agents X and Y is represented as CK_{xy}.

Digital signature. A digital signature is created using a secret key (of public key cryptosystem). Since only an agent who knows the secret key can create the digital signature for a message, other agents can confirm that the message is created by the agent who has the secret key. This study represents the digital signature of message M using a secret key SK_x as $Sign_{SK_x}(M)$.

Message authentication code (MAC). MAC is used for the detection of message alteration by using a hash function. The MAC for message M is represented as $MAC(M)$.

Digital certificate. A digital certificate binds a public key with an identity. It is issued by the CA (a portal agent in our system). In this study, the digital certificate created by a portal agent P (who possesses the secret key SK_p) for a public key PK_x is represented as $Cert_{SK_p}(PK_x)$.

Group key. The group key is shared among the agents belonging to the same community and enables them to encrypt and decrypt a message. In this study, the group key of community C is represented as GK_c.

Hash chain. A hash chain is a sequence of hash values computed by adapting the hash function n times. In this study, the hash chain with seed S is represented as $H^1(S), H^2(S), ..., H^n(S)$. Even if $H^i(S), where\ i \le n$, is known to other agents, they cannot compute any $H^j(S), where\ j < i$.

4   Design of Security Protocols

We designed the protocols for participation in a community, group key communication, and mutual authentication and P2P communication.

4.1   Participation in a Community

With regard to participation in a community, it is necessary to check whether new agent satisfies the requirements for community participation or not, issue a digital certificate for the new agent's public key, and provides the group key. Therefore, we designed the protocol shown in Fig. 2.

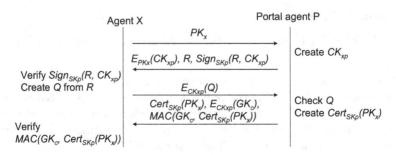

Fig. 2. Protocol for participation in a community

1. When an agent X wishes to participate in a community C, X sends PK_x to the portal agent P of C.
2. P creates a common key CK_{xp} and responds by sending $E_{PK_x}(CK_{xp})$, requirements for participation R, and $Sign_{SK_p}(R, CK_{xp})$.
3. X decrypts $E_{PK_x}(CK_{xp})$ using SK_x and verifies the integrity of CK_{xp} and R using $Sign_{SK_p}(R, CK_{xp})$. Next, X creates a qualification Q for R and sends $E_{CK_{xp}}(Q)$ to P.
4. P decrypts $E_{CK_{xp}}(Q)$ and checks whether Q satisfies R. If it is satisfied, P creates $Cert_{SK_p}(PK_x)$ and responds by sending $Cert_{SK_p}(PK_x)$, $E_{CK_{xp}}(GK_c)$, and $MAC(GK_c, Cert_{SK_p}(PK_x))$.
5. X decrypts $E_{CK_{xp}}(GK_c)$ and verifies the possibility of message alteration using $MAC(GK_c, Cert_{SK_p}(PK_x))$. Also, X creates a hash chain $H^1(S_x)$, $H^2(S_x)$, ..., $H^n(S_x)$.

Thus, only those agents who satisfy requirements for community participation can obtain the digital certificate and group key. However, in this protocol, X has to know PK_p before the protocol start. If the qualification is one provided from the administrator of C such as ID/password, X can receive PK_p together with ID/password from the administrator. Otherwise, X receives $PK_?$ from an agent (who is usually P, but may be a malicious third party) and has to believe $PK_?$ is PK_p. If $PK_?$ is not PK_p, X may participate in his/her unintended community. However, there is definitely no way to solve this problem, because there is no information to distingush P and a malicious third party.

4.2 Group Key Communication

With regard to group key communication, message encryption using a group key and preventive countermeasures against spoofing are necessary. The proposed system provides two countermeasures against spoofing: One simply involves using a digital signature; however, it requires much amount of computations in order to create a digital signature for each message. The second involves the usage of a hash chain, a sender attaches $MAC(M, H^{n-m}(S))$ to the m-th message M. Subsequently, the receiver stores the $MAC(M, H^{n-m}(S))$ and M pair. When the receiver needs to verify whether the message has been spoofed, he/she can do it by obtaining $H^{n-m}(S)$ from the sender (using P2P communication).

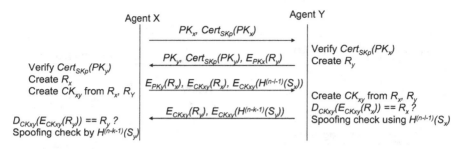

Fig. 3. Protocol for mutual authentication and P2P communication

4.3   Mutual Authentication and P2P Communication

A protocol for mutual authentication between agents X and Y is shown in Fig. 3.

1. Agent X sends PK_x and $Cert_{SK_p}(PK_x)$, which is the digital certificate provided by a portal agent P to agent Y.
2. Y verifies $Cert_{SK_p}(PK_x)$ using PK_p. Here, only when Y trusts P, the result of verification evaluates to true. Next, Y generates a random number R_y and responds by sending PK_y, $Cert_{SK_p}(PK_y)$, and $E_{PK_x}(R_y)$.
3. X verifies $Cert_{SK_p}(PK_y)$ and generates a random number R_x. Next, the agent X decrypts $E_{PK_x}(R_y)$ using SK_x. Then, X can create a P2P key (common key) CK_{xy} using R_x and R_y. Finally, X sends $E_{PK_y}(R_x)$, $E_{CK_{xy}}(R_x)$, and $E_{CK_{xy}}(H^{n-l-1}(S_x))$ to Y, where l is the number of messages already sent by X as group key communication. Here, $E_{CK_{xy}}(H^{n-l-1}(S_x))$ is optional. It is required only when Y wishes to verify the messages in group key communication have been spoofed.
4. Y decrypts $E_{PK_y}(R_x)$ using SK_y and creates a P2P key CK_{xy} using R_x and R_y. Subsequently, CK_{xy} is surely shared if and only if the decryption of $E_{CK_{xy}}(R_x)$ yields R_x. Finally, Y responds by sending $E_{CK_{xy}}(R_y)$ and $E_{CK_{xy}}(H^{n-k-1}(S_y))$, where k is the number of messages already sent by Y as group key communication. $E_{CK_{xy}}(H^{n-k-1}(S_y))$ is also optional. Moreover, Y can verify whether the messages in group key communication have been spoofed using $MAC(M, H^{n-i-1}(S_x))$ generated using $H^{n-i-1}(S_x)$, where $i > l$.
5. X decrypts $E_{CK_{xy}}(R_y)$. Subsequently, CK_{xy} is surely shared if and only if the decryption of $E_{CK_{xy}}(R_y)$ yields R_y. X can also verify whether the messages in group key communication have been spoofed.

Thus, X and Y share the P2P key CK_{xy} and can exchange partner-limited information securely between them in P2P fashion.

4.4   Considerations of a Hierarchical Community Structure

There are two types of a community structure; upper communities handle important information and lower communities handle important information. For

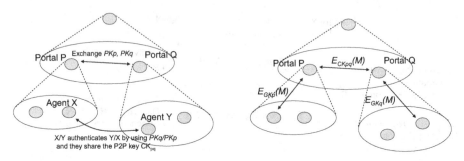

Fig. 4. Mutual authentication and P2P key sharing between agents beloing to different communities (left), and group key communication between agents belonging to different communities (right)

example, the hierarchical community structure representing a company organization handles important information in executive meetings than one in the meeting in each section. However, the community comprising friends (e.g., mixi) handles important information in the lower communities. Thus, security requirements differ with the type of community structure.

A portal agent manages this type of security requirement as a policy. When an upper community handles important information, the portal agent prohibits to forward group key communication messages from the upper community to the lower communities. On the other hand, when lower communities handle important information, the portal agent prohibits to forward group key communication messagess from the lower community to the upper community. Note that if an agent expricitly specifies that message forwarding to an upper/lower community should be allowed, the policy will be neglected.

We have to also consider group key and P2P communications between agents belonging to different communities. These communications are kept secure by formulating an agreement between the communities. In the process of agreement, portal agents P and Q of each community exchange each public key PK_p and PK_q, and change their policy to allow message forwarding from the opposite community. Consequently, agents belonging to different communities are able to authenticate each other and share a P2P key. They can, thus, do P2P communications securely (left panel in Fig. 4). Moreover, when lower communities handle important information, group key communication messages between agents belonging to different communities should be protected. Therefore, the portal agents have to share a P2P key. Then, the messages exchanged between the communities are protected by encryption using the P2P key (right panel in Fig. 4). Thus, messages exchanged between agents belonging to different communities are protected.

5   Performance Testing

We implemented the proposed security mechanisms using Java and evaluated their performances.

Table 1. Results of performance tests (average of 1000 times)

Participation	Group key communication	P2P key sharing with mutual authentication	P2P communication
27.93 ms	1.77 ms	35.21 ms	1.52 ms

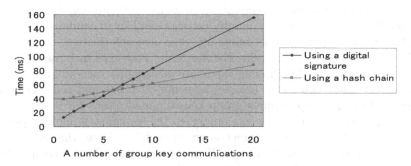

Fig. 5. Performances of two anti-spoofing countermeasures (average of 100 times)

In our implementation, we used 1024-bit RSA as the public key cryptosystem, 128-bit AES as the common key cryptosystem, and SHA-256 as the hash function, which are included in Java Cryptography Extention (JCE) [8]. Further, we used the AES key as group key.

Our performance tests were conducted on a 100 Base-T local network comprising two PCs running Solaris 10 x86 and Java version 1.5.0_12 with a Pentium4 4GHz CPU and 2GB memory. We set up no requirements for participation, and 128 byte messages were used in group key and P2P communications. The average results of the performance tests are shown in table 1.

These results show that 35 agents can participate in the same community, an agent can perform mutual authentication and share P2P key with 28 agents, and an agent can send/receive over 500 messages per second in group key and P2P communication. This implies that in the proposed system, all agents belonging to a community comprising 100 agents can send over 5 multicast messages to the community per second.

We also compared the performances of two anti-spoofing countermeasures. The result of this comparison are shown in Fig. 5.

When authentication is required after 6 group communications, using a hash chain proves to be more efficient. This is because it reduces the number of digital signature verifications.

6   An Application Example

Nowadays, various business matching services are being actively used and gaining popularity [2,9]. Since these services are developed as Web-server-based systems, all information is stored on the Web site. Thus, companies may not be willing to use sensitive information for business matching. Therefore, a P2P-based system is more suitable for business matching services. Therefore, we implemented the proposed security mechanisms using Java and developed a business matching system for small-and-medium-sized companies.

In the developed business matching system, the requirements for participation in a community are ID and a password pair check. A company can obtain the ID and password by closing a contract with the administrator of the community. The top community comprises two sub-communities, software and semiconductor community; semiconductor community consists of 12 small communities.

An agent participates in the community, exchanges information, and advances business matching semi-automatically. There are two steps in business matching: The first step involves finding candidate business partners from within the community; The second step involves agreeing on terms and contracting the business. The first step requires group key communications for restricting information access to within the community. In the second step, more important information related to the contract is exchanged, therefore, this information should be protected from others by P2P communication. Thus, a company can advance business matching while protecting information.

7   Conclusion

In this study, we have designed and implemented security mechanism for a hierarchical community-based multi-agent system. The proposed system realizes the following: (1) protection of information based on four levels of information security, (2) each community can define unique requirements for participation, and (3) two anti-spoofing methods. Furthermore, we have considered a practical use case, and our security mechanisms can be implemented using Java classes. The results of the performance tests shows that our system allows all agents belonging to a community comprising 100 agents send over 5 multicast messages to the community per second. We believe that this capacity is sufficient for several applications.

Acknowledgments

This research was supported by the Strategic Information and Communications R&D Promotion Programme under grant 052310008.

References

1. Berket, K., Essiari, A., Muratas, A.: PKI-Based Security for Peer-to-Peer Information Sharing. In: Proc. of 4th International Conference on Peer-to-Peer Computing, pp. 45–52 (2004)
2. Business Mall, http://www.b-mall.ne.jp/
3. Detsch, A., Gaspary, L., Barcellos, M., Cavalheiro, G.: Towards a Flexible Security Framework for Peer-to-Peer based Grid Computing. In: Proc. of the 2nd workshop on Middleware for grid computing, pp. 52–56 (2004)

4. FIPA MAS Security white paper, http://www.fipa.org/index.html
5. Groove, http://www.groove.net/
6. GT Security (GSI), http://www.globus.org/toolkit/security/
7. Gunupudi, V., Tate, S.R.: SAgent: A Security Framework for JADE. In: Proc. of 5th International Joint Conference on Autonomous Agents and Multiagent Systems, pp. 1116–1118 (2006)
8. Java Cryptography Extension (JCE), http://java.sun.com/products/jc
9. Jetro TTPP, https://www3.jetro.go.jp/ttppoas/indexj.html
10. McDonald, T., Yasinsac, A.: Application Security Models for Mobile Agent Systems. In: Proc. of International Workshop on Security and Trust Management, pp. 38–53 (2005)
11. Mine, T., Matsuno, D., Kogo, A., Amamiya, M.: Design and implementation of agent community based peer-to-peer information retrieval method. In: Klusch, M., Ossowski, S., Kashyap, V., Unland, R. (eds.) CIA 2004. LNCS (LNAI), vol. 3191, pp. 31–46. Springer, Heidelberg (2004)
12. mixi, http://mixi.jp/
13. Poslad, S., Calisti, M., Charlton, P.: Specifying standard security mechanisms in multi-agent systems. In: Falcone, R., Barber, S., Korba, L., Singh, M.P. (eds.) AAMAS 2002. LNCS, vol. 2631, pp. 227–237. Springer, Heidelberg (2003)
14. Project JXTA, http://www.jxta.org/
15. Tian, H., Zou, S., Wang, W., Cheng, S.: A group based reputation system for P2P networks. In: Yang, L.T., Jin, H., Ma, J., Ungerer, T. (eds.) ATC 2006. LNCS, vol. 4158, pp. 342–351. Springer, Heidelberg (2006)
16. Tsai, J., Ma, L.: Security Modeling of Mobile Agent Systems. J. of Ubiquitous Computing and Intelligence 1, 73–85 (2007)
17. Wallach, D.: A survey of peer-to-peer security issues. In: Okada, M., Pierce, B.C., Scedrov, A., Tokuda, H., Yonezawa, A. (eds.) ISSS 2002. LNCS, vol. 2609, pp. 253–258. Springer, Heidelberg (2003)
18. Zhong, G., Amamiya, S., Takahashi, K., Mine, T., Amamiya, M.: The Design and Implementation of KODAMA System. IEICE Transactions INF. & SYST. E85-D(4), 637–646 (2002)

A Need for Biologically Inspired Architectural Description: The Agent Ontogenesis Case

Terence L. van Zyl and Elizabeth M. Ehlers

Academy of Information Technology, University of Johannesburg,
University Rd., Auckland Park, South Africa
tvzyl@meraka.org.za, emehlers@uj.ac.za

Abstract. Biologically inspired complex adaptive systems (BICAS) have and will continue to move from research laboratories into industry. As the abstractions presented by biologically inspired systems move into industry, systems architects will be required to include the abstractions in their architectural descriptions (ADs) in order to communicate the design to system implementers. The paper argues that in order to correctly present the architectures of BICAS an additional set of biologically inspired views will be required. The paper then describes a set of additional biologically inspired architectural views for use when describing the architecture of BICAS. Finally the paper constructs a set of viewpoints for the biologically inspired views and demonstrates their use in agent ontogenesis. The paper also demonstrates the usage of a number of techniques for describing the architecture of BICAS.

Keywords: Architectural Description, Agent Ontogenesis, Biologically Inspired Complex Adaptive Systems, Architectural Views.

1 Introduction

Multi-agent systems, artificial neural networks, autonomic computing, swarm intelligence, genetic algorithms, genetic programs, artificial ontogeny, and computational embryology have one thing in common. Each of them presents a biologically inspired computing paradigm. These abstractions of biological systems have provided much inspiration in the development of complex adaptive systems. In general biologically inspired complex adaptive systems (BICAS) describe at multiple levels of abstraction the small scale interaction of agents and how that interaction gives rise to a large scale system [1], [2]. In the case of artificial neural networks, the small scale agents are neurons that interact to give rise to a large scale pattern recognition.

As BICAS move from research laboratories into industry the need for formal methodologies to describe their design arises [3]. The architects of industrial software systems will be required to translate abstract concepts of biology into concrete architectural descriptions (ADs) that can be used by system implementers. Many modelling and design techniques have been proposed [4], [5], [6], [7], [8], [9], [10]. The purpose of the paper is to present additional views for documenting the architecture of BICAS.

A. Ghose, G. Governatori, and R. Sadananda (Eds.): PRIMA 2007, LNAI 5044, pp. 146–157, 2009.
© Springer-Verlag Berlin Heidelberg 2009

The novel contribution of the paper consists of two parts. First an argument is presented in which the short comings of current ADs are highlighted with respect to biologically inspired systems. A set of additional views are presented to facilitate the documenting of biologically inspired complex adaptive agents, a type of biologically inspired complex adaptive system. Secondly an approach to the architectural description of systems that have dynamic architectures that change with time, follow a partially-deterministic path, and are self-adaptive is described.

The paper is organised as follows. Section 2 provides background to the topics discussed in the paper. In section 3 a case for biologically inspired ADs is presented. In section 4 an architectural description viewpoint for agent ontogenesis is presented. Finally section 5 looks at related and future work.

2   Background

In the background section, the main concepts, terminology, and ideas presented in the paper are defined. The section first explores some concepts relating to the field of biology, then looks at ADs, and finally agent ontogenesis.

2.1   Biology: Genetics, Phylogeny, Ontogeny, and Morphology

In biology the field of genetics is primarily concerned with the study of the genetic constitution of an individual, group, or class of living organisms [11], [12]. The term genetic used here refers to those traits of individuals that are affected or determined by their genes [12]. In short a gene is a hereditary unit that determines a particular characteristic or trait in an organism [12], [13]. Characteristics and traits are either morphological (structure) or behavioural.

The genes of an individual provide the complete make-up of an organism and are called the individual's genotype [13]. Inspecting the genotype tells what species an organism is and what traits and characteristics are present in the organism. An organism's traits include for example in a fish's genotype fins and in a dog's genotype lungs [11], [14].

The environment is a secondary force that has an influence on the resultant traits and characteristics of an organism. The environment's influence is throughout the entire life of an organism and gives rise to the concept of an individual's phenotype. An individual's phenotype is the result of its genotype and environmental factors that together bring about adaptation and change during the development and continued existence of the individual [11], [14]. The genetics driving the genotype and phenotype of an individual is not a random process, but rather is brought about by the historical ancestry of the individual as studied in phylogeny.

Phylogeny is the study of, phylogenesis, the evolutionary development of a species or group of organisms through a succession of forms [13]. The succession of forms is brought about by the processes of evolution. The result of phylogenesis is a change in the genetic make-up (genotype) of a species. By changing the genotype phylogenesis allows a species to adapt to changes in its environment.

Ontogeny describes the study of the biological process, ontogenesis, that starts with the activation of a single cell and results in a complex mature adult individual

[15]. In other words ontogeny investigates the "developmental model" of an individual organism from the earliest embryonic stage to maturity [13]. The ontogenesis of an organism can be divided into discreet stages, each of which is characterised by the onset of a particular developmental phenomenon [15]. Ontogenesis is guided by a number of biological processes and structures that express themselves over time. Some of the processes guiding ontogenesis include genetics (discussed above), morphogenesis, and epigenesis (both discussed further below).

Epigenesis, relating to epigenetics, is concerned with the expression of genes through interaction with the environment. Epigenesis states that an organism's genotype is not the sole deciding factor in the organism's eventual behaviour or morphology. Epigenetics is concerned with all genetics where the environment plays a role in deciding which genes are expressed and how expression takes place. Examples of epigenetic processes are the central nervous system, immune system, and endocrine system [16]. Many of the learning processes of an individual are shaped by epigenesis.

Finally morphology studies those processes concerned with the structure, shape, and form of an individual. Morphogenetics is concerned with how the morphology of an individual comes about.

The section has explored some of the biological processes involved in shaping and guiding the evolution and development of biological individuals. In the following section the software engineering practice of architectural description is reviewed.

2.2 Architectural Descriptions (ADs)

Software architecture is "the fundamental organisation of a system embodied in its components, their relationships to each other, and to the environment, and the principles guiding the systems design and evolution" [17]. The collection of products that are used to document an architecture are referred to as the architectural description [17]. Fundamental to all software development life cycles is the ability of stakeholders to communicate amongst each other. A system's architectural description provides one such communication tool [17].

An architectural description is composed by combining a collection of products. One of the products used in an architectural description is called a view. A view is a representation of a whole system from the perspective of a related set of concerns [17]. In order to use a view a viewpoint is established [18]. A viewpoint is a pattern or template from which to develop individual views by establishing the purposes and audience for a view and the techniques for its creation and analysis [17].

In summary architecture provides a mechanism, through views and viewpoints, which allows for the production of ADs for software systems. The architectural description guides the software system's design and evolution [19]. In the following section the concepts outlined in agent ontogenesis are defined.

2.3 Agent Ontogenesis

Compositional self-adaptation is dynamic structural self-adaptation of component based software [20]. For the purpose of discussion a software component is briefly described as a "unit of independent deployment and third–party composition" [21]. The actions that constitute compositional self-adaptation include component addition, component removal, connector addition, connector removal, and component composition. Dynamic here refers to actions that occur at runtime. Component based agent design provides a framework for the design and development of agents from basic building blocks, or components [22], [23].

The authors are researching agent ontogenesis. In agent ontogenesis biologically inspired complex adaptive agents are developed starting from a single component and through compositional self-adaptation and self-organisation arrive at a complex mature developed individual. The actions that constitute compositional self-adaptation and self-organisation are akin to discreet developmental events underlying the developmental model of the agent. It is important to note that the agent is exposed to its environment during its entire developmental process. Being exposed to the environment means that activities such as learning and exploration are present at all stages of the developmental process. Agent ontogenesis describes a method to arrive at a biologically inspired complex adaptive agent. In the next section a case for biologically inspired ADs is presented.

3 The Case for Biologically Inspired Architectural Description

The argument presented in the paper shows that current ADs provide inadequate abstractions for the description of BICAS and that additional views are required. The argument first looks at the shortcomings of current ADs. Secondly the field of genetics is described. Thereafter agent ontogenesis is presented as a case that needs additional biologically inspired views. Finally the additional biologically inspired views are presented as viewpoints.

3.1 Shortcomings of Current ADs with Respect to Biologically Inspired Systems

The abstractions presented by the various biologically inspired systems provide novel insight into the eventual architecture. The need for biologically inspired views becomes apparent when discussing notion such as supervised learning, genetic programs, or agent ontogenesis. In the case of agent ontogenesis the need for a view that describes the developmental events that result in the adult individual and the continued events that constitute its adaptation until death is apparent.

It is natural to describe a neural network in terms of its topology and the architecture of the individual neurons. However if the architecture is communicated to system implementers then the implementation of a neural network from only the above set of views is insufficient. A neural network is not only the result of its static architecture but is also as a result of the training set used in its learning. Both the static structure and the learning mechanism need to be fully described in the architectural description of the neural network. Current ADs are incapable of capturing the additional details required in both of these examples. For a brief expose of current views the reader is referred to [24].

Some might argue that the views presented in popular methodologies such as Krutchen 4+1, reference model for open distributed processes (RM-ODP), and rational unified process (RUP) provide sufficient abstractions to include BICAS [19], [25], [26]. In designing complex systems, architects use abstractions as a mechanism to filter unwanted details. The abstractions allow architects to view systems at various levels of complexity and using various idioms. Abstractions are later translated into concrete and well understood patterns as is the case with pipes and filters or service oriented architectures [27]. The use of abstractions become ever more important when designing the architecture of BICAS. BICAS use abstractions such as animats, agents, neurons, and genetic algorithms [2].

Abstractions are essential to the understanding of the goals of the architecture. An example of the abstraction to concrete concept translation is seen in multi-agent systems (MAS). Many MAS implementations, implement agents as objects despite fervent denial by the practitioners that objects and agents are one and the same [28], [29]. In order to take advantage of an agent based system, the abstraction of agent is required. In the section biologically inspired architectural views are explored.

3.2 The Biologically Inspired Views

The views presented in the section should not be taken in isolation but should be used in addition to the already established views of other software design methodologies such as kruchten 4+1, RUP, or RM-ODP [19], [25], [26]. The set of views proposed here should be used in situations where the need for abstractions are essential or where the views presented are insufficient to describe the required architecture.

3.2.1 The Phylogenetic View

The phylogenetic view is the architectural view relating to, or characteristic of phylogenesis. The phylogenesis of an agent refers to the development of a genotype of the agent through a succession of forms. Typical biologically inspired systems that are described using the phylogenetic view include genetic algorithms and genetic programs. *In summary the phylogenetic view is not concerned with the architectural dynamics of an individual but rather with the architectural dynamics as one individual evolves into another individual from generation to generation.*

3.2.2 The Ontogenetic View

The ontogenetic view describes the ontogenesis of the agent. The view describes a sequential time series of developmental events. Each developmental event triggers a dynamic reconfiguration of the agent's components. The actions that constitute reconfiguration include component addition and subtraction, connection addition and subtraction, and various composition actions. Artificial embryology is an example of a BICAS that requires an ontogenetic view to describe the developmental process. RM-ODP, Kruchten 4+1, and RUP do not include a view where time series developmental events can be modelled [19], [25], [26]. *In summary the ontogenetic view is used to describe how the architecture of an individual changes with respect to time.*

3.2.3 The Epigenetic View

The epigenetic view describes the epigenesis of a system. The epigenesis of a system involves all those aspects of a system where the type, organisation, behaviour and structure of the components and connectors that constitute the architecture of a system are influenced by environmental feedback. The types of BICAS that would require the epigenetic view include neural networks, and swarm intelligence. In the epigenetic view those features of a system, relating to self-organisation and self-adaptation are modelled. Both self-organisation and self-adaptation rely on environmental feedback to shape the system's architecture. *In summary the epigenetic view describes how the architecture of an individual changes with respect to changes in the environment.*

3.2.4 The Morphogenetic View
The morphogenetic view is an architectural view used for describing the structure of the components and connectors that make-up an agent. The morphogenetic view describes the static structure of an agent's components and connectors and also how the structure can change over time. All the components that make up an agent refer to the genotype of the agent. Each component can be designed using more common views. *In summary the morphogenetic view describes the structure of the individual agent and how that structure can change.*

3.2.5 The Environmental View
The environment is a first order abstraction in many BICAS [30], [31], [32]. It includes all the entities outside of the agent that the agent is able to receive feedback from. The feedback includes not only software and hardware infrastructure and middleware but also other agents. In the case of reinforcement learning the rewards will be described in the environmental view. Multi agent systems use the environment for communication amongst other functionality [31].

The section has explored a number of additional views not available in common ADs. In the following section the use of some of these views are complemented with viewpoints and examples.

4 Agent Ontogeny, a Viewpoint Example

To model a system using a specific view requires the establishment of an associated viewpoint [17]. The associated viewpoint provides the mechanism for constructing and using a view. The section describes some of the biologically inspired views outlined in the paper. In order to model a viewpoint a diagram, some text, or a set of diagrams and or text are required to describe the view.

Agent ontogenesis described in section 2.3 is an example of a biologically inspired complex adaptive agent. The architectural description of agent ontogenesis requires the introduction of views not previously required in the description of traditional systems. The need for these additional views stems from the biological abstractions used in designing these agents.

Agent ontogeny presents a biologically inspired system that exhibits a dynamic architecture. The architecture presented by agent ontogeny is not only dynamic but is also temporally dependent. In addition to being dynamic and temporally dependent the architecture is also partially-deterministic. The partially-deterministic nature comes as a result of the interaction between the agent and its environment during development. The section uses the example of agent ontogenesis. The viewpoints for the morphogenetic view, ontogenetic view, and epigenetic view are partially declared and an example is given for each view.

4.1 The Ontogenetic Viewpoint

The ontogenetic view is primarily concerned with how the architecture changes over time. Therefore the ontogenetic view requires a time series description of when the architecture will change. In order to describe the ontogenetic view the use of Adaptive-Linear Temporal Logic (A-LTL) is employed as described by [33]. The A-LTL is used to describe the time series adaptation of a telemanufacturing negotiating agent's ontogenesis. A telemanufacturing negotiating agent is an agent that negotiates on behalf of a human for rapid prototyping resources [34]. The example in formula 1 shows an agent starting with a reasoning component and then adding a bidding component. Finally an agent communication language (ACL) component is added as shown in formula 2. The set of adaptation requests are denoted by the time sequence ($T0_{REQ}$, $T1_{REQ}$, ... , Tn_{REQ}). Where $T0_{REQ}$ denotes the first time interval request up to Tn_{REQ} at which stage the agent is fully developed.

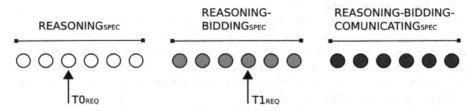

Fig. 1. Ontogenetic view of a telemanufacturing negotiating agent's initial development events

$$ADAPT1 = (REASONING_{SPEC} \wedge \lozenge T0_{REQ}) \rightharpoonup REASONING\text{-}BIDDING_{SPEC} \qquad (1)$$

Where $\wedge$ indicates an "and" operation, $\lozenge$ indicates "eventually", and $\rightharpoonup$ indicates an "adaptation". $REASONING_{SPEC}$ is an architectural specification with a single reasoning component and $REASONING\text{-}BIDDING_{SPEC}$ is an architectural specification with reasoning and bidding components. Formula 1 states that the system initially satisfies $REASONING_{SPEC}$. After receiving an adaptation request $T0_{REQ}$ the system adapts to satisfy $REASONING\text{-}BIDDING_{SPEC}$.

$$ADAPT2 = (ADAPT1 \wedge \lozenge T1_{REQ}) \rightharpoonup REASONING\text{-}BIDDING\text{-}ACL_{SPEC} \qquad (2)$$

At a later stage the system receives a $T1_{REQ}$ adaptation request. $T1_{REQ}$ causes the system in state ADAPT1 from formula 1 to satisfy $REASONING\text{-}BIDDING\text{-}ACL_{SPEC}$. Where $REASONING\text{-}BIDDING\text{-}ACL_{SPEC}$ indicates an architectural specification that includes reasoning, bidding and ACL components. The graphical representation of the above set of formula can be seen in figure 1.

4.2 The Epigenetic Viewpoint

The epigenetic view is primarily concerned with how environmental feedback changes the architecture both parametrically and structurally. The epigenetic viewpoint uses UML state diagrams to describe the adaptation state transitions due to environmental changes. The state diagram representing the agent epigenetic view can be

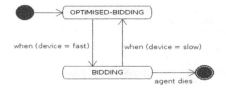

Fig. 2. Epigentic view of telemanufacturing negotiating agent responding to the environment

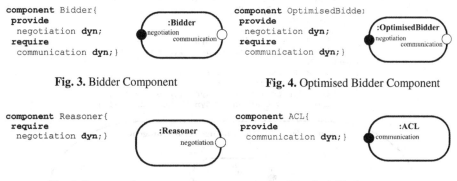

Fig. 3. Bidder Component

Fig. 4. Optimised Bidder Component

Fig. 5. Reasoner Component

Fig. 6. ACL Component

seen in figure 2. "OPTIMISED-BIDDING$_{STATE}$" and "BIDDING$_{STATE}$" are the states. The environmental events that trigger the transitions between the states are "when (device = slow)" and "when (device = fast)".

4.3 The Morphogenetic Viewpoint

The morphogenetic viewpoint describes the morphogenesis of a system, that is the morphology and how it can change. The morphogenetic viewpoint is described using a Darwin like notation and visualisation [35]. The Darwin notation is informally extended to include an *unbind* declaration and modes for the purposes of demonstration as described by [36]. The *event* declaration is also informally included. The *event* declaration acts in the same way as *when* however it guards for event states.

The choice of Darwin over Dynamic Wright as an architectural description language (ADL) is due to its simplicity [37]. Note that the names of the events triggering reconfigurations correspond to events described in both the epigenetic view and the ontogenetic view. Figure 3 declares a bidding component and figure 4 declares an optimised bidding component, both provide negotiation and requiring communication. In figure 5 a reasoner component is declared that requires negotiation. In figure 6 an ACL component is declared that provides communication. Finally in figure 7 the components are combined to form a Telemanufacturing-Negotiating-Agent-Ontogenesis component.

```
component Telemanufacturing-Negotiating-Agent-Ontogenesis {
            provide NegotiationSkills;
            require telemanufacturingEnvironment;

            instR1:Reasoning;
            instB1:dyn Bidder;
            instB2:dyn OptomisedBidder;
            inst A1:dyn ACL;

            event REASONING-BIDDING:
                bind R1.negotiation -- dyn B1.negotiation;
            event REASONING-BIDDING-ACL:
                bind B1.communication -- dyn A1.communication;
            event OPTIMISED-BIDDING:
                unbind B1.communication;
                unbind R1.negotiation;
                bind R1.negotiation -- dyn B2.negotiation;
                bind B2.negotiation -- dyn A1.communication;
            event BIDDING:
                unbind B2.communication;
                unbind R1.negotiation;
                bind R1.negotiation -- dyn B1.negotiation;
                bind B1.negotiation -- dyn A1.communication; }
```

Fig. 7. Telemanufacturing Negotiating Agent Ontogenesis

In figure 7, the dotted lines indicate potential binding, the keywords presented in bold have the following meanings:

- **component** *<name>* := component type
- **provide** *<serviceName>* := port for a service provided by a component
- **require** *<serviceName>* := port for a service required by a component
- **inst** *<instanceName>:<componentType>* := instances of component
- **dyn**: dynamic declaration and binding
- **bind** *<com1>.<port>--<com2>.<port>* := binding between components
- **unbind** *<com1>.<port>* := performs the opposite action of bind
- **event** *<eventName>* := waits for specified event then performs operation

For a detailed description of Darwin the reader is referred to [35]. In the following section a comparison to agent oriented software engineering is made.

5 Comparison with Agent Oriented Software Engineering

Agent oriented software engineering (AOSE) proposes a methodology for analysing, designing, and building complex software systems. AOSE is an active research area, with many methodologies, that propose engineering software systems using autonomous agents as a point of departure [39], [40], [41].

The field of AOSE has until now focused more on actual architectural solutions, analyses and designs and less on architectural description as put forward in the paper. Further due to this solution driven approach, many AOSE methodologies are biased towards a certain agent design philosophy such as the emphasis on beliefs, desires, and intentions (BDI) highlighted in the paper by Wooldridge [42].

Also apparent in some agent oriented design methodologies is the presentation of abstractions relating mainly to the agent as an entity, agent interactions, and the agent environment [43],[44]. Although the agent, agent interactions, and agent environment are essential for the architectural description of multi-agent systems, the extension to other BICAS are not apparent when notions such as evolution (phylogenesis), ontogenesis, and learning (epigenesis) need to be presented. The architectural views described in the paper are sufficient to describe most views of multi-agent system presented by current AOSE approaches along with any additional view requirements highlighted by the arguments around BICAS presented above.

The section has described some of the differences between current AOSE approaches and the ADs put forward by the paper. The authors realise that an approach that augments current AOSE with agent oriented architectural description techniques, such as the use of an ADL, is an open research area that should be explored.

6 Conclusion and Discussion

The paper highlights the need for additional formalism and mechanisms for describing the architecture of systems that use BICAS. As these BICAS move from the laboratory into industry the need for mechanisms for describing their architecture will increase. The paper argues that biologically inspired views present the best opportunity for describing BICAS. The benefit of using biologically inspired views is due to the abstractions used by architects being maintained during the architectural process.

The paper defines a number of additional views including a phylogenetic view, an ontogenetic view, an epigenetic view, a morphogenetic view, and the environmental view. The paper concludes by using an example of agent ontogenesis for a telemanufacturing negotiating agent and defining a number of viewpoints to describe the architecture of the agent.

In the future ADs need to be extended in order to make them sufficiently rich so as to facilitate their use as first class entities in a software systems construction. Model driven architecture (MDA) tries to achieve this richness by providing formalisms and tools surrounding ADs so as to facilitate code generation from models of a system [45]. Future research hopes to use sufficiently rich ADs of a system as the basis for the complete implementation of agent ontogenesis in the way that DNA and genetics provides a complete encoding for living organisms.

References

1. Gell-Mann, M.: What is Complexity? Complexity, 1 (1995)
2. Cliff, D.: Biologically-Inspired Computing Approaches to Cognitive Systems: A Partial Tour of the Literature. HPL-2003-11 (2003)
3. Luck, M., McBurney, P., Shehory, O., et al.: Agent technology: Computing as interaction (A roadmap for agent based computing) (2005)
4. Andronache, V., Scheutz, M.: Integrating Theory and Practice: The Agent Architecture Framework APOC and its Development Environment ADE, pp. 1014–1021 (2004)
5. Cervenka, R., Greenwood, D., Trencansky, I.: The AML Approach to Modeling Autonomic Systems. ICAS 0, 29 (2006)
6. Faulkner, S., Kolp, M.: Towards an Agent Architectural Description Language for Information Systems
7. Li, J., Mao, X., Shu, Y.: An OO-Based Design Model of Software Agent, pp. 434–440 (2005)
8. Pagliarecci, F., Spalazzi, L., Capuzzi, G.: Formal Definition of an Agent-Object Programming Language. CTS 0, 298–305 (2006)
9. Shan, L., Zhu, H.: Modelling and Specifying Scenarios and Agent Behaviour, p. 32 (2003)
10. Tahara, Y., Ohsuga, A., Honiden, S.: Pigeon: A Specification Language for Mobile Agent Applications. AAMAS 03, 1356–1357 (2004)
11. Hunter, L., Lathrop, R.H.: Guest Editors' Introduction-Computer Science and Biology: An Unlikely Pair. IEEE Intelligent Systems 17, 8–10 (2002)
12. King, R.C., Stansfield, W.D., Mulligan, P.K.: A dictionary of genetics. Oxford University Press, US (2006)
13. Oxford english disctionary. Oxford University Press, Oxford (2007)
14. Hartl, D., Jones, E.: Genetics: Analysis of Genes and Genomes, 6th edn. Jones & Bartlett (2005)
15. Balon, E. K.: Epigenesis of an Epigeneticist: The Development of some Alternative Concepts on the Early Ontogeny and Evolution of Fishes. Guelph Ichthyology Reviews 1 (1990)
16. Sipper, M., Sanchez, E., Mange, D., et al.: A Phylogenetic, Ontogenetic, and Epigenetic View of Bio-Inspiredhardware Systems. IEEE Transactions on Evolutionary Computation 1, 83–97 (1997)
17. IEEE Recommended Practice for Architectural Description of Software-Intensive Systems. IEEE Std 1471-2000 (2000)
18. Hilliard, R.: Viewpoint Modeling. In: Proceedings of 1st ICSE Workshop on Describing Software Architecture with UML (2001)
19. Kruchten, P.: The 4+1 View Model of Architecture. IEEE Softw. 12, 42–50 (1995)
20. McKinley, P.K., Sadjadi, S.M., Kasten, E.P., et al.: Composing Adaptive Software. Computer 37, 56–64 (2004)
21. Grone, B., Knopfel, A., Tabeling, P.: Component Vs. Component: Why we Need More than One Definition, pp. 550–552 (2005)
22. Rakotonirainy, A., Bond, A.: A Simple Architecture Description Model, p. 278 (1998)
23. Wang, M., Wang, H.: Intelligent Agent Supported Flexible Workflow Monitoring System, pp. 787–791 (2002)
24. Land, R.: A Brief Survey of Software Architecture. Malardalen Real-Time Research Center, Malardalen University, Vasteras, Sweden, Tech. Rep. (2002)
25. Putman, J.R.: Architecting with rm-odp. Prentice Hall PTR (2000)

26. Kruchten, P.: The rational unified process: An introduction. Addison-Wesley Professional (2003)
27. Shaw, M., DeLine, R., Klein, D.V., et al.: Abstractions for Software Architecture and Tools to Support them. IEEE Trans. Softw. Eng. 21, 314–335 (1995)
28. Jennings, N.R.: An Agent-Based Approach for Building Complex Software Systems. Commun. ACM 44, 35–41 (2001)
29. Wooldridge, M.: Intelligent Agents: The Key Concepts, pp. 3–43 (2002)
30. Beer, R.D.: The Dynamics of Active Categorical Perception in an Evolved Model Agent. Adapt. Behav. 11, 209 (2003)
31. Weyns, D., Omicini, A., Odell, J.: Environment as a First Class Abstraction in Multiagent Systems. Auton. Agents Multi-Agent Syst. 14, 5–30 (2007)
32. Okuyama, F.Y., Bordini, R.H., da Costa, R., Carlos, A.: ELMS: An Environment Description Language for Multi-Agent Simulation. In: Environments for Multi-Agent Systems, pp. 91–108 (2005)
33. Zhang, J., Cheng, B.H.C.: Using Temporal Logic to Specify Adaptive Program Semantics. The Journal of Systems & Software 79, 1361–1369 (2006)
34. van Zyl, T.L., Marais, E., Ehlers, E.M.: An implementation of resource negotiating agents in telemanufacturing. In: Sixth International Symposium on Tools and Methods of Competitive Engineering (2006)
35. Magee, J., Kramer, J.: Dynamic Structure in Software Architectures, pp. 3–14 (1996)
36. Kramer, J., Magee, J.: Self-Managed Systems: An Architectural Challenge, pp. 259–268 (2007)
37. Allen, R., Douence, R., Garlan, D.: Specifying and Analyzing Dynamic Software Architectures. Fundamental Approaches to Software Engineering, 21 (1998)
38. Bradbury, J.S., Cordy, J.R., Dingel, J., et al.: A Survey of Self-Management in Dynamic Software Architecture Specifications, pp. 28–33 (2004)
39. Jennings, N.R., Wooldridge, M.: Agent-Oriented Software Engineering. Handbook of Agent Technology. Springer, Heidelberg (2000)
40. Wooldridge, M.J., Jennings, N.R., Kinny, D.: The Gaia methodology for agent-oriented analysis and design. Autonomous Agents and Multi-Agent Systems, 285–312 (2000)
41. Wood, M.F., DeLoach, S.A.: An overview of the multiagent systems engineering methodology. In: Ciancarini, P., Wooldridge, M.J. (eds.) AOSE 2000. LNCS, vol. 1957, pp. 207–221. Springer, Heidelberg (2001)
42. Wooldridge, M., Ciancarini, P.: Agent-Oriented Software Engineering: The State of the Art. In: Ciancarini, P., Wooldridge, M.J. (eds.) AOSE 2000. LNCS, vol. 1957, pp. 1–28. Springer, Heidelberg (2001)
43. Odell, J.J., Van Dyke Parunak, H., Bauer, B.: Representing Agent Interaction Protocols in UML. In: Ciancarini, P., Wooldridge, M.J. (eds.) AOSE 2000. LNCS, vol. 1957, pp. 121–140. Springer, Heidelberg (2001)
44. Weyns, D., Holvoet, T.: A reference architecture for situated multiagent systems. In: Environments for Multiagent Systems III, 3th International Workshop, E4MAS, Hakodate, Japan (2006)
45. Frankel, D.: Model driven architecture. Wiley, New York (2003)

Multi-Agent Based Web Search with Heterogeneous Semantics*

Rui Huang[1,2] and Zhongzhi Shi[1]

[1] Key Laboratory of Intelligent Information Processing
Institute of Computing Technology, Chinese Academy of Sciences
P.O. Box 2704-28, 100190 Beijing, China
Tel.: +86-10-62600508
[2] Graduate School of the Chinese Academy of Sciences, 100049 Beijing, China
{huangr,shizz}@ics.ict.ac.cn

Abstract. Relevance ranking is key to Web search in determining how results are retrieved and ordered. As keyword-based search does not guarantee relevance in meanings, semantic search has attracted enormous and growing interest to improve the accuracy of relevance ranking. Recently heterogeneous semantic information such as thesauruses, semantic markups and social annotations have been adopted in search respectively for this purpose. However, although to integrate more semantics would logically generate better search results in respect of semantic relevance, such integrated semantic search mechanism is still in absence and to be researched. This paper proposes a multi-agent based semantic search approach to integrate both keywords and heterogeneous semantics. Such integration is achieved through semantic query expansion, meta search of expanded queries in varieties of existing search engines, and aggregation of all search results at the semantic level. With respect to the great volumes of distributed and dynamic Web information, this multi-agent based approach not only guarantees efficiency and reliability of search, but also enables automatic and effective cooperations for semantic integration. Experiments show that the proposed approach can effectively integrate both keywords and heterogeneous semantics for Web search.

Keywords: Semantic Search, Multi-Agent System, Relevance Ranking, Semantic Web, Social Annotation.

1 Introduction

Relevance ranking is key to search mechanisms, according to which potentially related documents are retrieved and ordered. As keyword-based search does not guarantee relevance in meanings, search with semantic information, also known as semantic search, has recently attracted enormous and growing research focuses to improve the accuracy of relevance ranking [1,2,3,4].

* This work is supported by National Basic Research Programme (No.2007CB311004, No.2003CB317004), 863 National High-Tech Program (No.2006AA01Z128, No. 2007AA01Z132), National Natural Science Foundation of China (No.90604017, No. 60435010, No. 60775035) and Innovation Fund of the Institute of Computing Technology (No.20060250).

A. Ghose, G. Governatori, and R. Sadananda (Eds.): PRIMA 2007, LNAI 5044, pp. 158–170, 2009.
© Springer-Verlag Berlin Heidelberg 2009

Heterogeneous semantics have been adopted for search. Latent semantics are induced from statistics of terms in documents, and then used for semantic similarity computing [5]. Thesauruses provide explanations of words and phrases as well as the synonyms and antonyms for search [6,7]. The Semantic Web [8] comprises well-defined semantic markups written in standard languages as RDF[1] and OWL[2]. Thus it supports semantic inference in search [9,10]. Recent Web 2.0 [11] embraces more social semantics to boost search. For example, the Del.icio.us[3] social bookmark services enable search with tags assigned by users as social annotations [12] to their shared web bookmarks.

It is expected that to integrate more semantics would logically generate better search results in respect of semantic relevance. As all kinds of semantic information represent some meanings, to understand more of them would generate more proper and intensive semantics for search. It is also demanding to include both semantic and keyword information in search. Keywords and semantics are closely interrelated with each other, and they together represent more exact meanings. Moreover, semantic information is more scarce on the Web compared with keyword information, and the majority of users are inclined to contribute their documents or express their information needs in terms of keywords.

However, to the best of our knowledge, no current search mechanism achieves such expected integration of both keywords and heterogeneous semantics. These heterogeneous semantic models differ in their semantic representation standards, relevance ranking criteria, and even suitable search mechanisms. To build a uniform semantic representation and search mechanism is almost impossible, due to the diversified and dynamic semantic information on current open Web.

Therefore, a practical approach is to develop an efficient and effective framework to integrate varieties of existing keyword and semantic search engines, and construct a uniform measurement for semantic correlativities and similarities among all keywords and heterogeneous semantics.

This paper proposes such a multi-agent based statistical semantic search approach to integrate both keywords and heterogeneous semantics on the Web. A multi-agent architecture is developed for distributed and dynamic integration and cooperation of varieties of existing search engines. Semantic probabilities are defined to calculate semantic relationships among both keywords and heterogeneous semantics. Experiments show that the proposed approach can effectively integrate both keywords and heterogeneous semantics for Web search.

Rest of the paper is organized as follows. Section 2 describes the motivation example. Section 3 discusses the related work. Section 4 details the approach with framework overview, fundamental definitions of semantic probabilities, and main algorithms of indexing, knowledge learning, query expansion and results aggregation. Section 5 presents the preliminary experimental results. Conclusions and future works are included in Section 6.

---

[1] http://www.w3.org/TR/rdf-primer/

[2] http://www.w3.org/TR/2004/REC-owl-features-20040210/

[3] http://del.icio.us

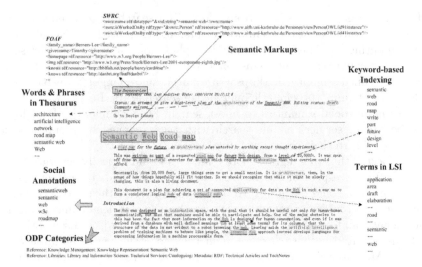

Fig. 1. Heterogeneous Semantics

Table 1. Semantic Search Examples

Using	Query	Related Semantics	Example Results *(not ordered)*
None	semantic web	None	*"Semantic Web - Wikipedia"*, *"W3C Semantic Web"*, *"Semantic Web Road Map"*.
Thesaurus	semantic web	S:(adj)semantic... "semantic analysis" S:(n)network,web...	*"Semantic Web Road Map"*, *"Latent Semantic Analysis"*, *"Semantic Networks"*.
Category (e.g.ODP)	semantic web	categories "Reference: ... Semantic Web", "...RDF..."	*"Semantic Web Road Map"*, *"Semantic Web: Why RDF is more than XML"*.
Ontology (e.g.[3])	(semantic web) ⊓∃isWorkedOn By(Person)	swrc:name, swrc: isWorkedOnBy, foaf: :Person, foaf:name	*<foaf:name> Tim Berners-Lee </foaf:name>, <foaf:name> Eric Miller</foaf:name>.*
Tag (e.g.[4])	semantic web	related tags such as "semantic","web", "semanticweb","w3c"	*"W3C Semantic Web"*, *"FOAF project"*, *"Semantic Web Road Map"*.

2   Motivation Example

To illustrate the problem of heterogeneous semantics on the Web, we start with an example webpage "Semantic Web Road Map"[4]. Figure 1 illustrates heterogeneous semantics and Table 1 gives semantic search examples for the webpage.

In Figure 1, keyword-based indexing (e.g. Google[5]) includes keywords as *"semantic"* and *"web"*. LSI(Latent Semantic Indexing) [5] indexes similar terms as *"web"* and *"map"*. Look up the WordNet[6] thesaurus, we get words and phrases

---

[4] http://www.w3.org/DesignIssues/Semantic.html

[5] http://www.google.com

[6] http://wordnet.princeton.edu/

as *"network"* and *"semantic web"*. ODP (Open Directory Project [7]) categorizes the webpage to *"Reference:...Semantic Web..."* and *"...RDF..."*. Semantic markups provide more detailed semantics such as *"<swrc:name..."* specifically describes *"semantic web"* using the SWRC[8] ontology. Del.icio.us users tag the webpage with *"semanticweb"*, *"w3c"*, etc.

All these heterogeneous semantics represent some meanings of the webpage, which can be used in semantic search. In Table 1, ODP uses categories, [3] uses ontologies and semantic markups, and [4] uses social annotations to boost search.

However, we might expect the machine to automatically trace all kinds of related semantics (*e.g. "semantics" in Table 1*) from simple keyword queries (*e.g. semantic web*), and integrate all these keywords and heterogeneous semantics search and inference results (*e.g. "Example Results" in Table 1*).

Therefore, a powerful mechanism to integrate both keywords and heterogeneous semantics is needed, in order to make the most of Web information for semantic search. This is the goal of our multi-agent based statistical approach.

3 Related Work

The scientific literature offers various solutions to semantic search, which can be roughly classified into four subcategories according to different semantics used. (1) Latent semantic based methods [5]. (2) Thesaurus based methods, such as for query expansion [6] and similarity computing [7]. (3) Ontology and semantic markup based methods, supporting logical inference of semantic relations [9,10]. Recent efforts focus more on combination of semantic inference and keyword-based search [2,3,13]. (4) Social annotation based methods [4,12,14,15].

Our approach intends to integrate heterogeneous semantics in all these four subcategories. In this sense, it's different with all current works, though based on them. Two kinds of most related works are [2,3] and [4,12,15]. [2] proposes to tightly integrate semantic inference and text retrieval, which is followed by works as [3] besides ours. However in [2], such integration is achieved only in retrieved results and through feedback mechanisms, while our work automatically expands the query with both related keywords and semantics before search. Our model also differs with [3] which uses centralized mechanisms and fuzzy description logic (DL) to integrate inference and retrieval. We adopt multi-agents and statistical computing to integrate both existing search mechanisms and heterogeneous semantics. [12] enlightens our statistical semantic relationship measurement, yet their work mainly focuses on social relationships of users. Hence we include textual information for analysis rather than pure resource links. Though [15] also explores semantic relationships, it targets at enterprise search and mainly uses annotations as feedbacks, while our approach is designed for the open Web and uses heterogeneous semantics for query expansion and relevance ranking.

To integrate varieties of existing search engines, we extend traditional works on multi-agent based meta search mechanisms [16,17,18]. [16] and [18] include

---

[7] http://dmoz.org/
[8] http://ontoware.org/projects/swrc/

user model database or user dictionary in order to more exactly understand user intentions (semantics), yet they do not semantically integrate all search results. [17] sheds some light on integration of disparate tourist information and service resources, though the integration is mainly based on ontologies. Our work is among the first to not only expand semantics of queries, but also integrate both keyword and heterogeneous semantic search results. Moreover, we aim at integrating search engines of heterogeneous semantic information, rather than only integrating results of keyword-based search engines.

Work on query expansion, detailed in [19], is also related to our work. Characteristics of our spread activation [20] based semantic query expansion is that, we use both keywords and heterogeneous semantics for query expansion.

Another relevant research domain is semantic integration, surveyed in [21]. Most current semantic integration is based on certain formalized and structured representations such as data schemas or ontologies [22]. Some pioneer works such as [23] explore emergent semantics for semantic interoperability. To the best of our knowledge, this paper is the first attempt to integrate semantics of different semantic models varied from ontologies to social annotations, though we merely calculate potential semantic correlativities for searching instead of obtaining exact semantic mappings or matchings.

4   Multi-Agent Based Statistical Semantic Search

4.1   Overview

Figure 2 illustrates the semantic search system framework based on multi-agent environment MAGE [24]. The main idea is to first calculate semantic probabilities (defined in section 4.2) among all keywords and semantics, second expand the original query with such calculated semantic relationships, then distribute the expanded queries to multiple search engines for search, and finally integrate all search results according to their semantic relevance rankings.

In Figure 2, the original *document corpus* contains some documents of both keywords and heterogeneous semantics, and the *semantic knowledge base* contains some prior semantic knowledge. The *keyword-semantic indexing agent* builds the keyword-semantic indexes (see section 4.3). The *semantic knowledge learning agent* calculates statistical semantic knowledge and enriches the *semantic knowledge base* (see section 4.4). When a new query is issued or relevance feedbacks are given, the *semantic query expansion agent* generates a list of expanded queries using keyword-semantic indexes and the semantic knowledge (see section 4.5). This query list is then distributed to varieties of *search agents* in the system for search and inference. Then the *semantic result aggregation agent* integrates all keywords and semantics search and inference results, according to their semantic relevance rankings calculated with user-specified modulative aggregation parameters (see section 4.6). If newly found documents accumulate over a threshold number, update the corpus and repeat steps of keyword-semantic indexing and semantic knowledge learning.

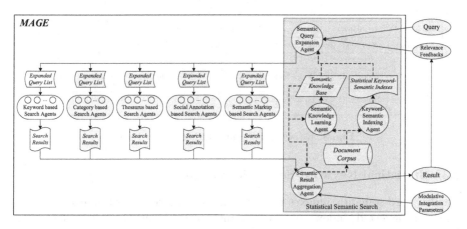

Fig. 2. Multi-Agent Based Statistical Semantic Search Framework

4.2   Fundamental Definitions

We mainly consider semantic occurrence, cooccurrence and conditional probabilities. Traditional definitions of probabilities are recasted with respect to the semantic annotation space of both keywords and heterogeneous semantics.

By semantic annotation space, we mean the whole set of semantic annotations $SA = (sa_1, \cdots, sa_p)$. A semantic annotation $sa = [T, S]$ is a pair which defines that the semantic unit (the minimum unit that represents certain complete and clear semantics) list S annotates meanings of the term list T. $\forall s_j \in S$ semantically occurs in sa, represented as $s_j \vdash_{sa}^{S}$. $\forall t_i \in T$ semantically occurs in sa, represented as $t_i \vdash_{sa}^{T}$. If $s_j \vdash_{sa}^{S} \wedge t_i \vdash_{sa}^{T}$, then t_i and s_j semantically cooccur in sa, represented as $< t_i, s_j > \vdash_{sa}$.

Definition 1 (Semantic Occurrence Probability). *$\forall t \in T$, $P(t) \in [0,1]$ denotes the semantic occurrence probability that term t semantically occurs in SA. $\forall s \in S$, $P(s) \in [0,1]$ denotes the semantic occurrence probability that semantic unit s semantically occurs in SA.*

Definition 2 (Semantic Cooccurrence Probability). *$\forall < t, s >$ where $t \in T \wedge s \in S \wedge SA = [T, S]$, $P(< t, s >) \in [0,1]$ denotes the probability that term t semantically cooccurs with semantic unit s in SA.*

Definition 3 (Semantic Conditional Probability). *$P(t/s) = \frac{P(<t,s>)}{P(s)} \in [0,1]$ denotes the semantic conditional probability of term t given semantic unit s, $P(s/t) = \frac{P(<t,s>)}{P(t)} \in [0,1]$ denotes the semantic conditional probability of semantic unit s given term t.*

Remark 1. *Probabilities as $P(T)$, $P(S)$, $P(T/s)$ $P(t/S)$, $P(T/S)$ can also be defined and inferred from the above definitions and equations, omitted here.*

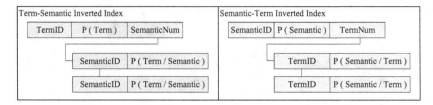

Fig. 3. Keyword-Semantic Indexes Structure

4.3   Statistical Keyword-Semantic Indexing

The keyword-semantic indexes consist of a pair of interrelated indexes: a term-semantic inverted index and a semantic-term inverted index, shown in Figure 3.

Term-semantic inverted index is ordered by "TermID" unique to each term, while semantic-term inverted index is ordered by "SemanticID" unique to each semantic unit. $P(Term)$ is the semantic occurrence probabilities of "Term". "SemanticNum" stores the length of "SemanticID" links, indicating the total number of related "SemanticID"s. $P(Term/Semantic)$ is the semantic conditional probability of term $Term$ given semantic unit $Semantic$. Similar structure holds for semantic-term inverted index. The two interrelated inverted indexes compose the keyword-semantic indexes of statistical semantic correlativity network.

4.4   Semantic Knowledge Learning

Besides thesaurus and ontologies, the semantic knowledge base also contains learned knowledge about semantic similarity matrixes. These matrixes are learned through Algorithm 1 from the cooccurrence statistics of the document corpus. The idea is similar with LSI [5]. Singular value decomposition (SVD) is applied to cooccurrence probability matrixes for dimension reduction. Then, similarity matrixes are re-constructed from the decomposed matrixes with reduced dimension, representing latent semantic similarities among all terms and semantics. Four such learned matrixes form the semantic similarity knowledge.

Algorithm 1. Semantic similarity matrixes learning

1: Construct original cooccurrence probability matrix M: $M[i][j] = P(< T[i], S[j] >)$
2: Singular value decomposition: $M = U\Sigma V^T$, where U and V are orthogonal matrixes, and $\Sigma = diag(\sigma_1, \cdots, \sigma_r)$ is a diagonal matrix
3: Dimension reduction: $\Sigma' = diag(\sigma_1, \cdots, \sigma_{r'}, 0_{r'+1}, \cdots, 0_r)$
4: Reconstruct the term-semantic similarity matrix: $M_{TS} = U\Sigma' V^T$, $M_{ST} = M_{TS}^T$
5: Compute the term-term similarity matrix: $M_{TT} = M_{TS} M_{ST}$
6: Compute the semantic-semantic similarity matrix: $M_{SS} = M_{ST} M_{TS}$
7: All four matrixes form the final semantic similarity matrix: $M = \begin{bmatrix} M_{TT} & M_{TS} \\ M_{ST} & M_{SS} \end{bmatrix}$

4.5   Statistical Semantic Query Expansion

Algorithm 2 for statistical semantic query expansion extends traditional query expansion [19] to use both terms and semantic units. Three steps of semantic computing, semantic inference and query expansion are involved.

Algorithm 2. Statistical semantic query expansion

Inputs: (a) parsed query Q of ($Type$: whether term or semantic unit, ID: term or semantic unit ID, W: weight of the term or semantic unit in query); (b) keyword-semantic indexes I_{TS}, I_{ST}; (c) prior semantic knowledge base KB.
Outputs: expanded query Q' of ($Type$, ID, CP: semantic conditional probability).
Constants: (a) $\theta \in [0, 1]$: threshold for acceptable semantic conditional probability;
  (b) $\kappa \in [0, 1]$: activation decay factor for semantic conditional probability
Mid-results: (a) term list T of (ID, CP); (b) semantic unit list S of (ID, CP).
Step 1. $(T, S) \leftarrow$ Semantic computing(Q, I_{TS}, I_{ST});
Step 2. $(S) \leftarrow$ Semantic inference(KB, S);
Step 3. $(Q') \leftarrow$ Query expansion(T, S).

Semantic computing Algorithm 3 finds all related terms and semantic units in the keyword-semantic indexes. From the original query vector, all related keywords and semantic units are traced through iterative calling of subfunction "*addList*". That is, if the decayed (decay each link with κ) semantic conditional probability of a keyword or semantic unit given the query vector exceeds the threshold θ, then the keyword or semantic unit is considered semantically related to the original query and added to the expanded query list.

Algorithm 3. $(T, S) \leftarrow$ Semantic computing(Q, I_{TS}, I_{ST})

1: **for all** term $+t \in Q$ **do**
2:   addList($t.ID$, $t.W$, 1, θ, κ, T, S, I_{TS}, I_{ST})
3: **end for**{terms that should be included in the search results}
4: **for all** term $-t \in Q$ **do**
5:   addList($t.ID$, $t.W$, -1, θ, κ, T, S, I_{TS}, I_{ST})
6: **end for**{terms that should be excluded in the search results}
7: **for all** semantic unit $+s \in Q$ **do**
8:   addList($s.ID$, $s.W$, 1, θ, κ, S, T, I_{ST}, I_{TS})
9: **end for**{semantic units that should be included in the search results}
10: **for all** semantic unit $-s \in Q$ **do**
11:   addList($s.ID$, $s.W$, -1, θ, κ, S, T, I_{ST}, I_{TS})
12: **end for**{semantic units that should be excluded in the search results}
   SUBFUNCION: addList(int id, float $condprob$, int $include$, float $threshold$, float $decayfactor$, List L_1, List L_2, Index I_1, Index I_2)
1: $L_1.add(id, include * condprob)${When $List.add(id, x)$, if (id, y) already exists, then $y \leftarrow y + x$.}
2: **for** $i = 0$ to $I_1[id].LinkNum$ **do**
3:   **if** ($decayfactor * I_1[id].Link[i].CP$) $\geq threshold$ **then**
4:     addList($I_1[id].Link[i].ID$, ($decayfactor * I_1[id].Link[i].CP$), $include$, $threshold$, ($\kappa * decayfactor$), L_2, L_1, I_2, I_1)
5:   **end if**
6: **end for**

Semantic inference is processed in Algorithm 4 to query and infer related semantic units using thesauruses and ontologies in the semantic knowledge base. Existing approaches can be applied such as query based on semantic markup languages [25], semantic similarity measure for objects in ontologies [26].

Algorithm 4. $(S) \leftarrow$ Semantic inference(KB, S)

1: **for all** semantic unit $s_i \in S$ **do**
2:     **for all** queried/inferred related semantic unit ns_j in KB **do**
3:         **if** $s_i.CP * M_{SS}[ns_j][s_i] \geq threshold$ **then**
4:             S.add$(ns_j.ID, s_i.CP * M_{SS}[ns_j][s_i]))$
5:         **end if**$\{M_{SS}$ is the semantic-semantic Semantic Similarity Matrix in $KB\}$
6:     **end for**
7: **end for**

Finally, Algorithm 5 constructs the semantically expanded query with all possibly related terms and semantic units, along with their degree of semantic relativity (normalized to $[0, 1]$) with the original query.

Algorithm 5. $(Q') \leftarrow$ Query expansion(T, S)

1: $maxCP \leftarrow \max(\max(\|t_i.CP\| \,|t_i \in T), \max(\|s_j.CP\| \,|s_j \in S))$
2: **for all** term $t \in T$ **do**
3:     $Q'.add("Term", t.ID, (t.CP/maxCP))$
4: **end for**
5: **for all** semantic unit $s \in S$ **do**
6:     $Q'.add("Semantic", s.ID, (s.CP/maxCP))$
7: **end for**

4.6   Search Results Aggregation

Search result aggregation is based on both statistical semantic similarity and inference semantic similarity.

Let $\|T\| = m$ be the total number of keywords and $\|S\| = n$ be the total number of semantic units in the semantic annotations space. The expanded query Q' is a $1 * (m + n)$ matrix $q = [q_T \; q_S]$. Each result document $d \in D$ is a $(m + n) * 1$ matrix $d = [\begin{smallmatrix} d_T \\ d_S \end{smallmatrix}]$. Then statistical semantic similarity of document d with query q is calculated as $SS(q, d) = qMd = [q_T \; q_S][\begin{smallmatrix} M_{TT} & M_{TS} \\ M_{ST} & M_{SS} \end{smallmatrix}][\begin{smallmatrix} d_T \\ d_S \end{smallmatrix}]$.

Through semantic inference knowledge as well as calculated semantic conditional probabilities, more semantic results can be found through probabilistic inference. Inferred semantic similarity $IS(q, d)$ of document d with query q can be calculated following methods in [27,26].

Therefore semantic similarity of document d with query q is calculated as $Sim(q, d) = \alpha * SS(q, d) + (1 - \alpha) * IS(q, d)$, where α is a user-specified modulative integration parameter.

5   Experiments

5.1   Datasets

The approach is experimented with heterogeneous semantic datasets on the Web. The WordNet thesaurus of 147,249 unique strings [9] are used not only for

---

[9] http://wordnet.princeton.edu/obtain

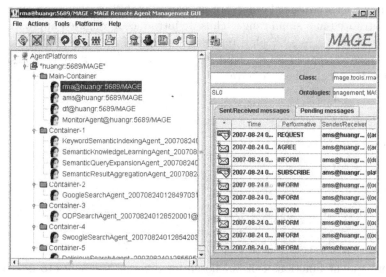

Fig. 4. Semantic search system on MAGE

stemming but also as prior semantic knowledge. ODP data of 730,416 categories and 4,792,967 links obtained May, 2007 [10] are included. As for semantic web data, we collect 347 example ontologies on the Web, and use the 10,429,951 RDF triples extracted from Swoogle cache June, 2005 [11]. We also crawled a sample of Del.icio.us data during May, 2007, consisting of 459,143 social annotations covering 28,704 different links, 184,136 different users and 54,460 different tags.

5.2   Preliminary Results

Figure 4 is a snapshot of the system running on MAGE. Container-1 holds the statistical semantic search subsystem, while container 2-5 include four different kinds of search engines for both keyword and heterogeneous semantic search. Currently, Google, ODP search, Swoogle and Del.icio.us search are employed.

Current experiments included 13,849,511 keywords and 97390 semantic units. Statistics about frequencies of these keywords and semantic units in semantic annotations are:

KEYWORDS:
count= 1.3849511E7
min= 9.999000099990002E-5
max= 1.0
average= 0.001790676941583935
meansquare= 0.006570170094960456

deviation= 3.9960611167178325E-5

SEMANTICS:
count= 97390
min= 9.999000099990002E-5
max= 1.0
average= 0.2546462675839461
meansquare= 0.47206660327193767

deviation= 0.15800215633024237

---

[10] http://rdf.dmoz.org/rdf/
[11] http://ebiquity.umbc.edu/resource/html/id/126/10M-RDF-triples

Such frequencies can not be directly used in probability calculation, as they are too centralized in a small range. Thus we introduce a weighted approach for calculation. $W(t \vdash^T_{sa=[T,S]}) \in [0,1]$ represents weight of $t \vdash^T_{sa}$, $W(s \vdash^S_{sa=[T,S]}) \in [0,1]$ represents weight of $s \vdash^S_{sa}$, and $W(< t,s >\vdash_{sa=[T,S]}) \in [0,1]$ represents weight of $< t,s >\vdash_{sa}$. Then we have:

$$P(t) = \frac{\sum_{k=1}^{\|SA\|} W(t\vdash^T_{sa_k})}{\|SA\|}, \qquad P(s) = \frac{\sum_{k=1}^{\|SA\|} W(s\vdash^S_{sa_k})}{\|SA\|}$$

$$P(< t,s >) = \frac{\sum_{k=1}^{\|SA\|} W(<t,s>\vdash_{sa_k})}{\|SA\|}$$

$$P(t/s) = \frac{\frac{\sum_{k=1}^{\|SA\|} W(<t,s>\vdash_{sa_k})}{\|SA\|}}{\frac{\sum_{k=1}^{\|SA\|} W(s\vdash^S_{sa_k})}{\|SA\|}} = \frac{\sum_{k=1}^{\|SA\|} W(<t,s>\vdash_{sa_k})}{\sum_{k=1}^{\|SA\|} W(s\vdash^S_{sa_k})}$$

$$P(s/t) = \frac{\frac{\sum_{k=1}^{\|SA\|} W(<t,s>\vdash_{sa_k})}{\|SA\|}}{\frac{\sum_{k=1}^{\|SA\|} W(t\vdash^T_{sa_k})}{\|SA\|}} = \frac{\sum_{k=1}^{\|SA\|} W(<t,s>\vdash_{sa_k})}{\sum_{k=1}^{\|SA\|} W(t\vdash^T_{sa_k})}$$

Different weight functions can be chosen for different strategies to interpret the degree of semantic similarity in social annotations. According to the statistics of keywords and semantics in our experiments, we choose weight function $Weight(freq) = \lg(freq^{\frac{1}{e}} * 9 + 1)$ where $freq \in [0,1]$ is the frequency of the term or semantic unit in the semantic annotation.

For the example query "semantic web" in section 2, our system finds an ordered list of related keywords and semantics, including keywords as "web", "semantic", "rdf", "ontology", "xml" etc, and semantics as "semantic", "rdf", "reference", "category:topic", "web2.0", "srwc:isworkedonby" etc. Therefore the search can be processed on all keywords and semantic information.

6   Conclusion

This paper develops a multi-agent based approach for heterogeneous semantic search on the Web. We construct a multi-agent based system to integrate varieties of existing keyword and semantic search engines, and propose a semantic-probability based statistical measure to integrate semantic relationships among both keywords and heterogeneous semantics. Through semantic query expansion, expanded meta search of multiple search engines, and semantic aggregation of all results, our approach uses both keywords and heterogeneous semantics in search. With respect to the great volumes of distributed and dynamic Web information, the proposed approach not only guarantees efficiency and reliability of search, but also enables automatic and effective cooperations for semantic integration. Preliminary experimental results show that varieties of search mechanisms, as well as both keywords and semantics can be effectively integrated for Web search.

In the future, we will focus on evaluation and optimization of semantic similarity computing and semantic relevance rank aggregation algorithms.

References

1. Guha, R., Mccool, R., Miller, E.: Semantic search. In: Proceedings of WWW 2003, pp. 700–709 (2003)
2. Mayfield, J., Finin, T.: Information retrieval on the semantic web: Integrating inference and retrieval. In: SIGIR 2003 Semantic Web Workshop (2003)
3. Zhang, L., Yu, Y., Zhou, J., Lin, C., Yang, Y.: An enhanced model for searching in semantic portals. In: Proceedings of WWW 2005, pp. 453–462 (2005)
4. Bao, S., Wu, X., Fei, B., Xue, G., Su, Z., Yu, Y.: Optimizing web search using social annotations. In: Proceedings of WWW 2007, pp. 501–510 (2007)
5. Furnas, G.W., Deerwester, S., Dumais, S.T., et al.: Information retrieval using a singular value decomposition model of latent semantic structure. In: Proceedings of SIGIR 1988, pp. 465–480 (1988)
6. Voorhees, E.M.: Query expansion using lexical semantic relations. In: Proceedings of SIGIR 1994, pp. 61–69 (1994)
7. Tollari, S., Glotin, H., Maitre, J.L.: Enhancement of textual images classification using segmented visual contents for image search engine. Multimedia Tools and Applications 25(3), 405–417 (2005)
8. Berners-Lee, T., Hendler, J., Lassila, O.: The semantic web. Scientific American 284(5), 34–43 (2001)
9. Cohen, S., Mamou, J., Kanza, Y., Sagiv, Y.: Xsearch: A semantic search engine for XML. In: Proceedings of VLDB 2003, pp. 45–56 (2003)
10. Ding, L., Finin, T., Joshi, A., Peng, Y., Pan, R., Reddivari, P.: Search on the semantic web. IEEE Computer 10(38), 62–69 (2005)
11. O'Reilly, T.: What is web 2.0: Design patterns and business models for the next generation of software. O'Reilly, Sebastopol (2005), http://www.oreilly.com/
12. Wu, X., Zhang, L., Yu, Y.: Exploring social annotations for the semantic web. In: Proceedings of WWW 2006, pp. 417–426 (2006)
13. Rocha, C., Schwabe, D., de Aragao, M.P.: A hybrid approach for searching in the semantic web. In: Proceedings of WWW 2004, pp. 374–383 (2004)
14. Hotho, A., Jäschke, R., Schmitz, C., Stumme, G.: Information retrieval in folksonomies: Search and ranking. In: Sure, Y., Domingue, J. (eds.) ESWC 2006. LNCS, vol. 4011, pp. 411–426. Springer, Heidelberg (2006)
15. Dmitriev, D.A., Eiron, N., Fontoura, M., Shekita, E.: Using annotations in enterprise search. In: Proceedings of WWW 2006, pp. 811–817 (2006)
16. Müller, M.E.: An intelligent multi-agent architecture for information retrieval from the internet (1999)
17. Chiu, D.K.W., Leung, H.-f.: Towards ubiquitous tourist service coordination and integration: a multi-agent and semantic web approach. In: Kishino, F., Kitamura, Y., Kato, H., Nagata, N. (eds.) ICEC 2005. LNCS, vol. 3711, pp. 574–581. Springer, Heidelberg (2005)
18. Koorangi, M., Zamanifar, K.: A distributed agent based web search using a genetic algorithm. International Journal of Computer Science and Network Security 7(1), 65–76 (2007)
19. Khan, M.S., Khor, S.: Enhanced web document retrieval using automatic query expansion. Journal of the American Society for Information Science and Technology 55(1), 29–40 (2004)
20. Crestani, F.: Application of spreading activation techniques in information retrieval. Artificial Intelligence Review 11(6), 453–482 (1997)

21. Noy, N.F.: Semantic integration: a survey of ontology-based approaches. ACM SIGMOD Record 33(4), 65–70 (2004)
22. Gruninger, M., Kopena, J.B.: Semantic integration through invariants. AI Magazine 26(1), 11–20 (2005)
23. Aberer, K., CudréMauroux, P., Hauswirth, M.: The chatty web: emergent semantics through gossiping. In: Proceedings of WWW 2003, pp. 197–206 (2003)
24. Shi, Z., Zhang, H., Cheng, Y., Jiang, Y., Sheng, Q., Zhao, Z.: Mage: An agent-oriented programming environment. In: Proceedings of IEEE International Conference on Cognitive Informatics (ICCI 2004), pp. 250–257 (2004)
25. Chu-Carroll, J., Prager, J., Czuba, K., Ferrucci, D., Duboue, P.: Semantic search via xml fragments: A high-precision approach to ir. In: Proceedings of SIGIR 2006, pp. 445–452 (2006)
26. Maguitman, A.G., Menczer, F., Roinestad, H., Vespignani, A.: Algorithmic detection of semantic similarity. In: Proceedings of WWW 2005, pp. 107–116 (2005)
27. Stojanovic, N., Struder, R., Stojanovic, L.: An approach for the ranking of query results in the semantic web. In: Fensel, D., Sycara, K.P., Mylopoulos, J. (eds.) ISWC 2003. LNCS, vol. 2870, pp. 500–516. Springer, Heidelberg (2003)

Reasoning about Norms, Obligations, Time and Agents

Jan Broersen[1] and Leendert van der Torre[2]

[1] University of Utrecht, The Netherlands
[2] Computer Science and Communication, University of Luxembourg, Luxembourg

Abstract. Reasoning about norms and time is of central concern to the regulation or control of the behavior of a multiagent system. In this paper we introduce a representation of normative systems that distinguishes between norms and the detached obligations of agents over time, leading to a simple and therefore practical way to reason about norms, obligations, time and agents. We consider the reasoning tasks to determine whether a norm is redundant in a normative system and whether two normative systems are equivalent. In the former case the redundant norm might be removed. In the latter case one norm might be replaced by the other. It is well known that properties concerning iterated or deontic detachment no longer hold when reasoning with multiple agents or with obligations over time. Yet, earlier approaches to reasoning about norms rarely consider the intricacies of time. We show how norms can be used to define the persistence of obligations of agents over time. We illustrate our approach by discussing three ways to relate norms and obligations of agents over time. Also we show how these three ways can be characterized.

1 Introduction and Running Examples

Reasoning about norms and time is of central concern to the regulation or control of the behavior of a multiagent system [7, 8]. Norms in multiagent systems come in varying forms, are used for various reasons, and are meant for varying domains. There are norms in law books meant to govern the behavior of communities. Each member of the community is subject to the same norms, and often it is explicitly stated that the norms should not discriminate between members of the society. Contracts constitute another kind of norms. A contract explicitly links agents, for instance a buyer and a seller, to distinct norms. Yet another category is formed by norms describing organizations. Such norms are usually linked to roles used to structure organizations.

However, due to the philosophical problem known as Jorgenson's dilemma [20], which roughly says that a proper logic of norms is impossible because norms do not have truth values, most formal systems reasoning about norms and time [2, 27, 18, 24, 19, 20, 16, 9] are restricted to obligations, prohibitions and permissions only, and do not consider the norms explicitly. These logics might be used, for example, to reason about obligations and permissions following from a legal code without representing the legal code itself. Systems without explicit norms are difficult to use in multiagent systems, but systems that explicitly represent norms of the system usually do not provide a way to reason about them. For example, there is no way to decide whether a norm is redundant in a normative system, or whether two normative systems are equivalent. Ways to reason about the norms [20, 21, 15] do not consider the intricacies of time.

A. Ghose, G. Governatori, and R. Sadananda (Eds.): PRIMA 2007, LNAI 5044, pp. 171–182, 2009.

We use an example of David Makinson [20] as a running example in this paper. He illustrates the intricacies of temporal reasoning with norms, obligations and agents by discussing the iteration of detachment, in the sense that from the two conditional norms "if p, then obligatory q" and "if q, then obligatory r" together with the fact p, we can derive not only that q is obligatory, but also that r is obligatory.

First, Makinson argues that iteration of detachment often appears to be appropriate. He gives the following example, based on instructions to authors preparing manuscripts.

Example 1 (Manuscript [20]). Let the set of norms be "if $25x15$, then obligatory *text*12" and "if *text*12, then obligatory *refs*10", where $25x15$ is "The text area is 25 by 15 cm", *text*12 is "The font size for the main text is 12 points", and *refs*10 is "The font size for the list of references is 10 points". If the facts contain $25x15$, then we want to detach not only that it is obligatory that *text*12, but also that it is obligatory that *refs*10.

Second, he argues that iteration of detachment sometimes appears to be inappropriate by discussing the following example, which he attributes to Sven Ove Hansson.

Example 2 (Receipt [20]). Let instances of the norms be "if owe_{jp}, then obligatory pay_{jp}" and "if pay_{xy}, then obligatory $receipt_{pj}$" where owe_{jp} is "John owes Peter \$1000", pay_{jp} is "John pays Peter \$1000", and $receipt_{pj}$ is "Peter gives John a receipt for \$1000". Intuitively Makinson would say that in the circumstance that John owes Peter \$1000, considered alone, Peter has no obligation to write any receipt. That obligation arises only when John fulfils his obligation.

Makinson observes that there appear to be two principal sources of difficulty here. One concerns the passage of time, and the other concerns bearers of the obligations. Sven Ove Hansson's example above involves both of these factors. "We recall that our representation of norms abstracts entirely from the question of time. Evidently, this is a major limitation of scope, and leads to discrepancies with real-life examples, where there is almost always an implicit time element. This may be transitive, as when we say "when b holds then a should eventually hold", or "... should simultaneously hold". But it may be intransitive, as when we say "when b holds then a should hold within a short time" or "... should be treated as a matter of first priority to bring about". Clearly, iteration of detachment can be legitimate only when the implicit time element is either nil or transitive. Our representation also abstracts from the question of bearer, that is, who (if anyone) is assigned responsibility for carrying out what is required. This too can lead to discrepancies. Iteration of detachment becomes questionable as soon as some promulgations have different bearers from others, or some are impersonal (i.e. without bearer) while others are not. Only when the locus of responsibility is held constant can such an operation take place." [20]

In this paper we show how to reason about norms in these circumstances. In Section 2 we consider obligations that have to be obeyed immediately. In Section 3 obligations are preserved until they are obeyed. To predict the behavior of a normative multiagent system, in Section 4 we investigate the interaction with belief sets of agents. Finally, in Section 5 we suggest how our approach can be extended to reason about abilities, games, norm revision, and other complex phenomena relevant for temporal reasoning about norms and obligations in multi-agent systems.

2 Instantaneous Obligations

Our approach to reason about norms, obligations, time and agents involves three steps. Inspired by an approach advocated by Sergot and Craven [26], we assume a branching temporal structure that represents how propositions change over time, and we use an algorithm that, given the input of the branching temporal structure and a set of norms, yields a labeling of the temporal structure with obligations. Moreover, we reason about the norms to determine norm redundancy or equivalence of normative systems.

For the temporal structures we use trees, i.e., possibly infinite branching time temporal structures. The reason is that branching time structures are used most often, where the branches represent uncertainty or alternative actions of the agents, and seem to be the most convenient and flexible to model a wide variety of examples.

Definition 1 (Temporal structure). *Let L be a propositional language built on a set of atoms P. A temporal structure is a tuple $T = \langle N, E, \models \rangle$ where N is a set of nodes, $E \subseteq N \times N$ is a set of edges obeying the properties of a tree, and $\models \subseteq N \times L$ is a satisfaction relation for nodes and propositional formulas of L closed under propositional logic.*

The following example illustrates a possible temporal structure for the manuscript example.

Example 3 (Manuscript, continued from Example 1). The temporal structure in Figure 1 must be read as follows. A circle visualizes a node of the temporal structure, and the words within the circle visualize the propositions which are true at that node. An arrow from one node to another one visualizes that the latter node can be reached from the former. In the temporal structure, the root of the tree is visualized on the left hand side, and four distinct nodes can be reached from it. In all these nodes we have that $25x15$, which visualizes that the text area is 25 by 15 cm. Then we have or have not *text12*, the font size for the main text is 12 points or not, and we have or have not *refs10*, the font size for the list of references is 10 points or not. For all these four nodes we can reach an additional node visualized on the right hand side of the figure, in which we no longer have $25x15$.

For the normative system we consider only regulative norms like obligations and prohibitions, since they are the most basic and often used kind of norms. Though normative systems may have a complicated structure including, for example, permissive, constitutive and procedural norms [5, 6], they always contain at least such regulative norms. Extensions with, for example, explicit sanctions, as well as other kinds of norms, are left for further research. Following conventions in input/output logic [21, 22], we write a conditional norm "if i, then o is obligatory" as a pair of propositional formulas (i, o).

Definition 2 (Normative system). *A norm "if i, then obligatory o" is represented by a pair of formulas of L, and written as (i, o). It is also read as the norm "if i, then forbidden $\neg o$." A normative system S is a set of norms $\{(i_1, o_1), \ldots, (i_n, o_n)\}$.*

Example 4 (Manuscript, continued from Example 3). The normative system contains two norms and is represented by $\{(25x15, text12), (text12, refs10)\}$.

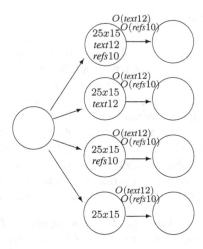

Fig. 1. Labeling of the temporal structure using the manuscript normative system $\{(25x15, text12), (text12, refs10)\}$ with instantaneous obligations. The obligation $O(refs10)$ is detached in all $25x15$ nodes, also where $text12$ is false. None of the obligations persists in time.

Norms are used to detach obligations. The detached obligations are a propositional labeling[1] of the temporal structure.

Definition 3 (Obligation labeling). *An obligation labeling is a function* $O : N \rightarrow 2^L$.

The following example illustrates how the norms of the manuscript example 1 are used to label our branching time structure. As is always done in the deontic logic literature, we distinguish between so-called factual and deontic detachment [18]. The former is based on a match between the condition of the norm and the facts, and the latter kind is based on a match between the condition and the obligations. As discussed in the introduction, for the manuscript example we want both kinds of detachment.

Example 5 (Manuscript, continued from Example 4). The obligation $O(text12)$ is detached in all nodes where $25x15$. This is called factual detachment, since the condition of the norm is factually true in the node. The obligation $O(refs10)$ is detached in all $25x15$ nodes, also where $text12$ is false, because $text12$ is in $O(n)$. This kind of detachment is therefore called deontic detachment. None of the obligations persist in time.

The way we label the temporal structure determines the meaning of the norms. Our semantics can thus be considered a kind of operational semantics. We assume that the obligatory formulas at a node are a deductively closed set, representing the ideal alternative for the node. This logical closure is not visualized in Figure 1. Consequently, since in this paper we focus on temporal reasoning with norms, we do not consider contrary-to-duty norms stating what should hold in sub-ideal nodes [12, 13] or dilemmas stating various optimal alternatives for a node [28]. For a discussion on the various problems with such norms and approaches such as priorities to deal with these problems, see [14].

---

[1] Instead we could have introduced an obligation modality with a standard semantics. However this propositional approach avoids some unnecessary complications.

Definition 4 (Instantaneous norm semantics). *The instantaneous norm semantics of a normative system S is the unique obligation labeling $O : N \to 2^L$ such that for each node n, $O(n)$ is the minimal set such that:*

1. *for all norms (i, o) and all nodes n, if $n \models i$ or $i \in O(n)$, then $o \in O(n)$.*
2. *if $O(n) \models \varphi$ then $\varphi \in O(n)$, where $\models$ is logical consequence for propositional logic.*

We now define how to reason about norms, obligations and time. A norm is redundant when it does not affect the labeling of the temporal structure.

Definition 5 (Norm redundancy). *In normative system S, a norm $(i, o) \in S$ is redundant if and only if for all temporal structures, the obligation labeling of S is the same as the obligation labeling of $S \setminus \{(i, o)\}$.*

The definition of norm redundancy is used to define equivalence of normative systems.

Definition 6 (Equivalence normative systems). *Two normative systems S_1 and S_2 are equivalent if and only if each norm of S_1 is redundant when added to S_2, and vice versa.*

Reasoning about normative systems is illustrated in the manuscript example.

Example 6 (Manuscript, continued from Example 5). The norm $(25x15, refs10)$ is redundant in normative system $\{(25x15, text12), (text12, refs10), (25x15, refs10)\}$ due to deontic detachment. Consequently, $\{(25x15, text12), (text12, refs10), (25x15, refs10)\}$ and $\{(25x15, text12), (text12, refs10)\}$ are equivalent normative systems. In general, if a norm can be derived using transitivity from the other rules, then it is redundant.

Another property for reasoning about norms is reasoning by cases, saying that if the normative system contains (i_1, o) and (i_2, o), then the norm $(i_1 \vee i_2, o)$ is redundant. The following result characterizes *all* properties which hold for normative systems. For space reasons, we do not detail the proofs of this and following theorems.

Theorem 1 (Redundant norms). *In a normative system S, a norm $(i, o) \in S$ is redundant under the instantaneous semantics when we can derive it from $S \setminus \{(i, o)\}$ using replacement of logical equivalents in input and output, together with the following rules:*

$$\frac{(i_1, o)}{(i_1 \wedge i_2, o)} SI \quad \frac{(i, o_1 \wedge o_2)}{(i, o_1)} WO \quad \frac{(i, o_1)(i, o_2)}{(i, o_1 \wedge o_2)} AND \quad \frac{(i_1, o)(i_2, o)}{(i_1 \vee i_2, o)} OR \quad \frac{(i, o_1), (i \wedge o_1, o_2)}{(i, o_2)} CT$$

Proof. Let $I(n) = \{\phi \mid n \models \phi\}$ be the set of propositions true at node n, and let $S(I(n)) = \{o \mid i \in I(n), (i, o) \in S\}$. Then $O(n) = \cup\{V \mid S(I(n)) \subseteq V \supseteq S(V), V \text{ complete}\}$. The result follows from the characterization of out_4 in input/output logic [21].

Example 7 (Manuscript, continued from Example 5). Assume that $text12$ is obligatory too for 20x15. $\{(20x15, text12), (25x15, text12), (text12, refs10), (25x15, refs10)\}$ is equivalent to $\{(20x15 \vee 25x15, text12), (text12, refs10)\}$, because we can derive $(20x15 \vee 25x15, text12)$ from $(20x15, text12)$ and $(25x15, text12)$ using OR, and vice versa we can derive $(20x15, text12)$ and $(25x15, text12)$ from $(20x15 \vee 25x15, text12)$ using SI.

3   Persistence: Preserving Obligations Until They Are Fulfilled

We now turn our attention to Makinson's second example involving time and agents. The normative system has the same logical structure as the normative system of the manuscript example, but the intended temporal structure contains sequential nodes.

Example 8 (Receipt, continued from Example 2). Consider the temporal structure in Figure 2. From the root node visualized on the left side of the figure we can access only one node, in which "John owes Peter $1000", owe_{jp}. From this node, we can reach three other nodes, one in which "John pays Peter $1000", pay_{jp}, another one in which "Peter gives John a receipt for $1000", $receipt_{pj}$, and a third one in which neither happens. The norms are "if owe_{xy}, then obligatory pay_{xy}" (owe_{xy}, pay_{xy}), and "if pay_{xy}, then obligatory $receipt_{yx}$" ($pay_{xy}, receipt_{yx}$). Here x and y are variables ranging over the set of agents, in the sense that each norm is treated as a set of proposition based norms, for each instance of the agent variables.

As discussed in the introduction, we do not want to have iterated or deontic detachment, in the sense that Peter is not obliged to give John a receipt until he has given him the money. Moreover, in contrast to the instantaneous semantics, if John pays Peter, then Peter has to give John the receipt directly or *at some point in the future*. We postpone the definition of deadlines in the present framework [10] for further research.

Example 9 (Receipt, continued from Example 8). Consider the desired labeling of the temporal structure in Figure 2. In the circumstance that John owes Peter $1000 but he has not paid him yet, Peter does not have the obligation to write a receipt. That obligation arises only when John fulfils his obligation by paying Peter. Consequently, we have factual detachment without iterated or deontic detachment. Moreover, for each norm, we have that if the condition is true in a node, then the obligation holds for the node itself. Moreover, if the obligation is not fulfilled, then it also holds for all successor nodes.

Again, in addition to factual detachment and persistence, we assume that the obligatory formulas at a node are a deductively closed set. This logical closure is not visualized in Figure 2, and it implies that we do not consider contrary-to-duty norms stating what should hold in sub-ideal nodes or dilemmas stating various optimal alternatives for a node.

Definition 7 (Persistent norm semantics). *The persistent norm semantics of a normative system S is the unique obligation labeling $O : N \to 2^L$ such that for each node n, $O(n)$ is the minimal set such that:*

1. *for all norms (i, o), all nodes n_1 and all paths $(n_1, n_2, \ldots, n_m)$ with $m \geq 1$, if $n_1 \models i$ and $n_k \not\models o$ for $1 \leq k \leq m - 1$, then $o \in O(n_m)$*
2. *if $O(n) \models \varphi$ then $\varphi \in O(n)$*

Redundance and equivalence for persistent obligations is analogous to reasoning about instantaneous obligations in Definition 5 and 6. We have the following result.

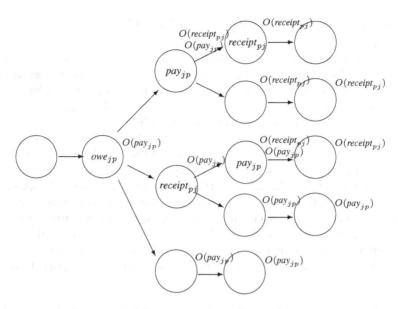

Fig. 2. Labeling of the temporal structure using the receipt normative system $S = \{(owe_{xy}, pay_{xy}), (pay_{xy}, receipt_{yx})\}$ with persistent obligations. The obligation $O(receipt_{pj})$ is not detached in all owe_{jp} nodes, only when pay_{jp} is true. All the obligations persists in time, until they are fulfilled.

Theorem 2 (Redundant norms). *In a normative system S, a norm $(i, o) \in S$ is redundant under the persistence semantics when we can derive it from $S \setminus \{(i, o)\}$ using replacement of logical equivalents in input and output, together with the following rules:*

$$\frac{(i_1, o)}{(i_1 \wedge i_2, o)} SI \qquad \frac{(i, o_1 \wedge o_2)}{(i, o_1)} WO \qquad \frac{(i_1, o)(i_2, o)}{(i_1 \vee i_2, o)} OR$$

The theorem shows that the redundancy for persistent obligations is weaker in two respects from redundancy for instantaneous obligations. First, we no longer have redundancy of transitivity because we no longer have deontic detachment. Second, we no longer have the conjunction rule AND, as illustrated by Example 10.

Example 10 (Receipt, continued from Example 9). Consider the normative systems $S_1 = \{(owe_{xy}, pay_{xy} \wedge receipt_{yx})\}$, $S_2 = \{(owe_{xy}, pay_{xy}), (owe_{xy}, receipt_{yx})\}$ and $S_3 = \{(owe_{xy}, pay_{xy}), (owe_{xy}, pay_{xy} \rightarrow receipt_{yx})\}$. If $n \models owe_{jp} \wedge pay_{jp} \wedge \neg receipt_{pj}$, then we have $O(n)$ is the consequence set of $pay_{jp} \wedge receipt_{pj}$. Hence, at node n we cannot discriminate among the three normative systems. However, we have for any successor node of n that using S_1 we have $pay_{jp} \wedge receipt_{pj} \in O(m)$, because the obligation for $pay_{jp} \wedge receipt_{pj}$ persists, using S_2 we have only $receipt_{pj} \in O(m)$, because we have that only the obligation for $receipt_{pj}$ persists, and using S_3, we have only $pay_{jp} \rightarrow receipt_{pj} \in O(m)$, because only the obligation for $pay_{jp} \rightarrow receipt_{pj}$ persists. The example also illustrates that the three normative systems S_1, S_2 and S_3 are *not* equivalent.

4   Beliefs and Subjective Obligations of Agents

In normative multi-agent systems we usually consider a subjective obligation $O_a p$, which can be read as "Agent a is obliged to see to it that p'. Obviously we can replace the objective modality Op in the previous two sections by such subjective obligations, such that, for example, the norm (owe_{xy}, pay_{xy}) detaches the obligation $O_j(pay_{jp})$ in owe_{jp} nodes. This does not affect the definitions or results.

Moreover, in multi-agent systems we usually make a distinction between subjective knowledge or belief, represented by $K_a p$ or $B_a p$ and objective knowledge or belief, as represented by operators for common knowledge or common belief. The subjective versions of knowledge and belief are relevant for predicting the behavior of a normative multi-agent system, since agents will react only to obligations they know or believe they have [25]. In this section we therefore consider a subjective obligation $O_a p$ read as "agent a believes to be obliged to see it that p". We replace the objective truth function $\models$ by a subjective belief function B. We assume that all the agents know the norms of the normative system, and therefore we do not relativize the normative system to the set of agents.

Definition 8. *Let A be a set of agents. An epistemic temporal structure is a tree $\langle N, E, B \rangle$ where N is a set of nodes, $E \subseteq N \times N$ is a set of edges obeying the properties of a tree, and $B : A \times N \to 2^L$ is a partial function such that $B(a, n)$ contains at least the tautologies and is deductively closed in L.*

The following example illustrates the temporal structure and a normative system for a situation with subjective beliefs.

Example 11 (Promise, continued from Example 2). Consider the temporal structure in Figure 3, which zooms in on the first step of the receipt example. Instead of considering only the situation in which "John owes Peter $1000", owe_{jp}, we consider also the situation in which "John promised Peter $1000", $promise_{jp}$. We assume that John is obliged to pay Peter $1000 in either of these two cases. Moreover, we consider three distinct belief sets of John: either he believes that he owes John $1000, or he promised John $1000, or he believes he either owes or promised $1000 to Peter, without remembering which of these two cases hold. The normative system is $\{(owe_{xy}, pay_{xy}), (promise_{xy}, pay_{xy})\}$.

Definition 9. *An agent-node labeling is a function $O : A \times N \to 2^L$.*

The labeling procedure for subjective obligations is obtained by replacing references to the facts by references to the belief states of agents.

Definition 10 (Persistent subjective norm semantics). *The persistent subjective norm semantics of a normative system S is the unique obligation labeling $O : A \times N \to 2^L$ such that for each node n, $O(a, n)$ is the minimal set such that:*

1. *for all norms (i, o), all nodes n_1 and all paths $(n_1, n_2, \ldots, n_m)$ with $m \geq 1$, if $i \in B(a, n_1)$ and $o \notin B(a, n_k)$ for $1 \leq k \leq m - 1$, then $o \in O(a, n_m)$*
2. *if $O(a, n) \models \varphi$ then $\varphi \in O(a, n)$*

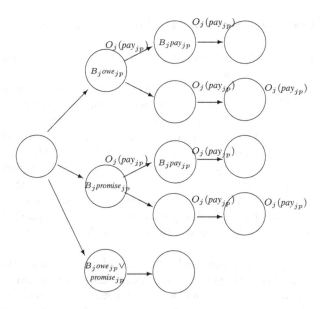

Fig. 3. Labeling of the temporal structure using the 'promise' normative system $S = \{(owe_{xy}, pay_{xy}), (promise_{xy}, pay_{xy})\}$ with persistent subjective obligations. The obligation $O_j(pay_{jp})$ is detached in $B_j owe_{jp}$ nodes and in $B_j promise_{jp}$ nodes, but not in $B_j(owe_{jp} \vee promise_{jp})$ nodes. All the obligations persist in time, until they are fulfilled.

Example 12 (Promise, continued from Example 11). The labeling obtained by the algorithm is visualized in Figure 3. The obligation $O_j(pay_{jp})$ is detached in $B_j owe_{jp}$ nodes and in $B_j promise_{jp}$ nodes, but not in $B_j(owe_{jp} \vee promise_{jp})$ nodes. All the obligations persist in time, until they are fulfilled.

The following theorem shows that redundancy for subjective obligations is weaker than redundancy for persistent obligations, because reasoning by cases no longer holds.

Theorem 3 (Redundant norms). *In a normative system S, a norm $(i, o) \in S$ is redundant under the subjective semantics when we can derive it from $S \setminus \{(i, o)\}$ using replacement of logical equivalents in input and output, together with the following rules:*

$$\frac{(i_1, o)}{(i_1 \wedge i_2, o)} SI \qquad \frac{(i, o_1 \wedge o_2)}{(i, o_1)} WO$$

Summarizing, if the norms refer to the belief states of agents rather than the objective facts, we lose reasoning by cases. If reasoning by cases is desired for subjective obligations too, then we have to close normative systems explicitly under the OR rule. In other words, we have to add the norm $(owe_{xy} \vee promise_{xy}, pay_{xy})$ explicitly to the normative system $\{(owe_{xy}, pay_{xy}), (promise_{xy}, pay_{xy})\}$.

5   Further Research: Extensions for Multi-Agent Systems

For the instantaneous semantics we can reuse results obtained within the input/output logic framework and extend the normative system with permissive norms [23], constitutive norms like counts-as conditionals [17] and procedural norms [6]. Moreover, we can introduce hierarchies of normative systems with multiple authorities [1]. To deal with contrary-to-duty reasoning and dilemmas we can use constraints [22].

Moreover, we can extend the language of normative systems to refer to obligations which do not refer to the same moment in time, but which hold in the future, by replacing the propositional language L by, for example, LTL or CTL.[2] For example, using a modal operator F to refer to any future node, we may model the receipt example by the normative system $\{(owe_{jp}, Fpay_{jp}), (pay_{jp}, Freceipt_{pj})\}$.[3] Moreover, we can refer to explicit time using for example nominals in our language referring to specific nodes. We can also extend our norms with an explicit deadline "if i, then obligatory o before d," $(i, o < d)$ [10].

Another issue are dyadic obligations, which we can introduce to model the situation where obligations might be fulfilled before they are detached. In particular, a property of the persistent obligations is that when Peter gives the receipt to John before John has given him the money, maybe because they are in a long standing relationship and Peter trusts John, or maybe because Peter wrongly believed that Peter already transferred the money, then after Peter gives him the money, the obligation to write a receipt is still detached, and persists indefinitely! This is illustrated by the obligation $O(receipt_{pj})$ in the third node on the righthand side of Figure 2. We can define an alternative labeling without this property using a labeling with dyadic obligations $O(o|c)$, read as "o is obligatory in context c."

Of particular interest for normative multiagent systems is the extension of our approach with the abilities or powers of the agents. If we label each edge by a (possibly complex) action of the agents, then we can define power of agents using ATL. In this way, we may be able to solve problem of ATL that the power of an agent is a very strong notion, which in reality it holds only under conditions.

Finally, we can extend normative systems with a new kind of norms (i, α), where α refers to an action. In that representation, conditional actions can be represented by $O(a; b)$. We label edges instead of nodes. If we label both nodes and edges, then we have both ought-to-be and ought-to-do, and therefore we have to deal with constraints between them, like the green-green-green constraint of Sergot and Craven [26].

---

[2] There are many alternatives to the temporal structures we use in our paper, such as infinite trees only, non-branching or linear structures only, or finite state machines instead of trees. The adaptation of our approach to these other temporal structures is left for further research.

[3] Our labeling algorithm solves a problem encountered in approaches to reasoning about obligations over time without an explicit normative system [11, 9]. With an explicit normative system, moreover, Example 10 illustrates that our algorithm implies that obligations persist only when they are detached from an explicit norm. Without an explicit normative system, we can only decide among the three normative systems when pay_{jp} and $receipt_{pj}$ contain temporal references which can be used to distinguish among them [11, 9].

6 Summary

Reasoning about norms and time is of central concern to the regulation of multiagent system behavior [7, 8]. In particular, for the study of social norms emerging in societies enforcing desirable group behavior, the design of legal norms to meet institutional goals in electronic institutions, the design of organizational norms to structure organizations and regulate agents playing a role in the organization, and the study of norms in contracting in electronic commerce. In this paper we show that the distinction between norms and obligations leads to a simple and therefore practical way to reason about norms, obligations of agents and time, and we illustrate our approach by discussing three ways to relate norms and obligations over time. Also we show how these three can be characterized, generalizing the non-temporal input/output logic framework. Our approach to reasoning about norms, obligations, time and agents takes three steps.

1. We assume a branching temporal structure representing how propositions change over time, where the branches represent either uncertainty or alternative actions of the agents. Such a temporal structure can be generated using a formal language, like, for example, in model checkers such as Mocha [3] or action logics such as the causal calculator [4].

2. We use an algorithm that, given the input of the branching temporal structure and a set of norms, produces as output a labeling of the temporal structure with obligations. The algorithm determines the meaning of the norms, and it may therefore be considered an operational semantics of the norms. We give formal definitions for the possible labelings, enabling us to say when norms are equivalent or redundant.

3. A norm is redundant in a normative system, if removing the norm from the normative system does not change the labeling produced by the algorithm. Two normative systems are equivalent, when adding a norm of one normative system to the other one makes this added norm redundant.

In particular, we consider three ways to generate obligations and study their logics. First we consider an instantaneous norm semantics, where the generated obligations have to be obeyed immediately. In this case, iterated detachment holds, as well as reasoning by cases. The second semantics states that obligations are preserved until they are obeyed. In this case, iterated detachment no longer holds, but reasoning by cases does. Finally, we investigate the interaction with belief sets of particular agents at time points, and we show that reasoning by cases no longer holds.

We suggest how our approach can be extended to reason about abilities, games, norm revision, and other complex phenomena relevant for temporal reasoning about norms and obligations in multi-agent systems. Moreover, to study the relation between the logic of norms in this paper and existing temporal deontic logics (also known as logics of normative propositions), we can define temporal deontic logics for our temporal structures, and relate the redundancy of norms to logical properties of these temporal structures.

References

1. Alchourrón, C.E., Makinson, D.: Hierarchies of regulations and their logic. In: Hilpinen, R. (ed.) New Studies in Deontic Logic, pp. 125–148. Reidel (1981)
2. Alchourrón, C.E., Bulygin, E.: Normative Systems. Springer, Wien (1971)

3. Alur, R., Henzinger, T.A., Mang, F.Y.C., Qadeer, S., Rajamani, S.K., Tasiran, S.: Mocha: Modularity in model checking. In: Y. Vardi, M. (ed.) CAV 1998. LNCS, vol. 1427, pp. 521–525. Springer, Heidelberg (1998)
4. Artikis, A., Sergot, M., Pitt, J.: Specifying electronic societies with the causal calculator. In: Giunchiglia, F., Odell, J.J., Weiss, G. (eds.) AOSE 2002. LNCS, vol. 2585, pp. 1–15. Springer, Heidelberg (2003)
5. Boella, G., van der Torre, L.: An architecture of a normative system. In: Procs. of AAMAS 2006, pp. 229–231. ACM Press, New York (2006)
6. Boella, G., van der Torre, L.: Substantive and procedural norms in normative multiagent systems. Journal of Applied Logic (2008)
7. Boella, G., van der Torre, L., Verhagen, H. (eds.): Computational and Mathematical Organization Theory. Selected papers from NORMAS 2005 (2006)
8. Boella, G., van der Torre, L., Verhagen, H. (eds.): Normative Mulit-agent systems, Procs. of NORMAS 2007, Dagstuhl Seminar proceedings 07122 (2007)
9. Broersen, J., Brunel, J.: What I fail to do today, I have to do tomorrow: a logical study of the propagation of obligations. In: Proceedings CLIMA VIII. LNCS. Springer, Heidelberg (2007)
10. Broersen, J., Dignum, F., Dignum, V., Meyer, J.-J.: Designing a deontic logic of deadlines. In: Lomuscio, A., Nute, D. (eds.) DEON 2004. LNCS, vol. 3065, pp. 43–56. Springer, Heidelberg (2004)
11. Brunel, J., Bodeveix, J.-P., Filali, M.: A state/Event temporal deontic logic. In: Goble, L., Meyer, J.-J.C. (eds.) DEON 2006. LNCS, vol. 4048, pp. 53–68. Springer, Heidelberg (2006)
12. Chisholm, R.: Contrary-to-duty imperatives and deontic logic. Analyse 24, 33–36 (1963)
13. Forrester, J.: Gentle murder, or the adverbial samaritan. The Journal of Philosophy 81, 193–197 (1984)
14. Hansen, J., Pigozzi, G., van der Torre, L.: Ten philosophical problems in deontic logic. In: Proceedings of Normative Multi-agent Systems, NORMAS 2007 (2007)
15. Hansen, J.: Sets, sentences, and some logics about imperatives. Fundam. Inform. 48(2-3), 205–226 (2001)
16. Horty, J.: Agency and Deontic Logic. Oxford University Press, Oxford (2001)
17. Jones, A., Sergot, M.: A formal characterisation of institutionalised power. Logic Journal of IGPL (1996)
18. Loewer, Belzer: Dyadic deontic detachment. Synthese 54, 295–318 (1983)
19. Makinson, D.: Five faces of minimality. Studia Logica 52, 339–379 (1993)
20. Makinson, D.: On a fundamental problem of deontic logic. In: McNamara, P., Prakken, H. (eds.) Norms, Logics and Information Systems. New Studies on Deontic Logic and Computer Science, pp. 29–54. IOS Press, Amsterdam (1999)
21. Makinson, D., van der Torre, L.: Input-output logics. Journal of Philosophical Logic 29(4), 383–408 (2000)
22. Makinson, D., van der Torre, L.: Constraints for input-output logics. Journal of Philosophical Logic 30(2), 155–185 (2001)
23. Makinson, D., van der Torre, L.: Permissions from an input-output perspective. Journal of Philosophical Logic 32(4), 391–416 (2003)
24. Meyer, J.J.C.: A different approach to deontic logic: Deontic logic viewed as a variant of dynamic logic. Notre Dame Journal of Formal Logic 29(1), 109–136 (1988)
25. Pacuit, E., Parikh, R., Cogan, E.: The logic of knowledge based obligation. Knowledge, Rationality and Action 149(2), 311–341 (2006)
26. Sergot, M.J., Craven, R.: The deontic component of action language nC+. In: Goble, L., Meyer, J.-J.C. (eds.) DEON 2006. LNCS, vol. 4048, pp. 222–237. Springer, Heidelberg (2006)
27. van Eck, J.: A system of temporally relative modal and deontic predicate logic and its philosophical applications. logique et analyse 25, 339–381 (1982)
28. van Fraassen, B.: Values and the heart's command. The Journal of Philosophy (1973)

An Agent Modeling Method Based on
Scenario Rehearsal for Multiagent Simulation

Shohei Yamane and Toru Ishida

Department of Social Informatics, Kyoto University
Yoshida-Honmachi, Sakyo-ku, Kyoto, 606-8501, Japan
yamane@ai.soc.i.kyoto-u.ac.jp,
ishida@i.kyoto-u.ac.jp

Abstract. Multiagent Systems are potential computational systems for various practical applications, tools, and so on. Multiagent simulation is one of the remarkable application to evaluate several kinds of phenomena. In order to design an agent for multiagent simulation, it is important to reflect user's opinion. However, if a user is not computer professional or does not have technical knowledge of agent logics and programming language, it is hard for him/her to implement his/her own opinion. Participatory design is a promising approach to incorporate user's opinion in the agent design and modification process. In this paper, we propose rehearsal oriented testing for implementation of participatory design. By the rehearsal oriented testing, it becomes possible to carry out anytime modification of agent's scenario, which describe its behavior during simulation. For rehearsal oriented testing, we set operators for modifying scenarios, which is described using finite state machine model. We also design interaction protocol between a user and an agent to smoothly get information through the user-agent dialog for modifying operators. Under this protocol, an agent informs a user about what kind of information is required.

1 Introduction

Multiagent Systems are potential computational systems for various practical applications, tools, and so on. Multiagent simulation is one of the remarkable application to evaluate several kinds of phenomena. In order to design an agent for multiagent simulation, it is important to reflect user's opinion. For agents which provide services for humans, the quality of services will be improved by taking account of users' preference. For agents which simulate users, the agents' behavior can be similar to them.

Participatory design is a promising approach to incorporate user's opinion in design process. There are some researches which try to apply participatory design to multiagent systems. Participatory simulations are examples of such researches[1][2].

In a participatory simulation, users participate in the simulation as avatars in the simulation. Log data of the simulation and interviews with participants using a videotaped simulation are used to construct agent models[3].

A. Ghose, G. Governatori, and R. Sadananda (Eds.): PRIMA 2007, LNAI 5044, pp. 183–194, 2009.

Applying users' opinion is important not only in the designing process but also in the maintenance process. It is ineffective to repeat the process of agent design whenever the modification or extension of agent models are required. If users can modify/extend agents' behavior by themselves, it is easy to effectively implement their own opinion on agents. However, if a user is not computer professional or does not have technical knowledge of agent logics and programming language, it is hard for him/her to implement his/her own opinion. This research proposes rehearsal oriented testing so that users who are not computer professionals can modify/extend agents' behavior. In this research, we propose rehearsal oriented testing to help users, who are not computer professionals or do not have technical knowledge of agent logics and programming language, to modify and extend agents' behavior. In this paper, we use metaphor of rehearsal for drama in order to construct rehearsal oriented testing methodology. A user modifies/extends agents' behavior as a director directs actors.

In this paper, we addresses the following two issues to realize rehearsal oriented testing.

Setting of modification operators. We should reveal targets of modification and then we set modification operators required to modify them.

Design of an interaction protocol. In order to modify/extend an agent's behavior through dialog between a user and an agent, we design an interaction protocol based on defined modification operators.

This paper is organized as follows. Section 2 explains what users do in rehearsal oriented testing. Section 3 explains a interaction protocol between a user and an agent for rehearsal oriented testing. Section 4 explains possible applications of rehearsal oriented testing. Section 5 concludes this paper with our future work.

2   Rehearsal Oriented Testing

Our main motivation for introducing rehearsal oriented testing is modification of agents' behavior which designed based on participatory simulation approach. Participatory simulations incorporate avatars which are characters operated by humans as in computer games in multiagent simulations. Agents which simulate humans are designed on the basis of log data of avatars and interviews to the humans. In this case, users of rehearsal oriented testing are human subjects of participatory simulations. The user monitors the agent's behavior which simulates him/her and modifies the agent's behavior if it is different from the user's expectation.

In rehearsal oriented testing, each user plays a role as a director and an agent play role as an actor. Monitoring agents, a user modifies their behavior like a director supervises actors. Even if a user is not a computer professional, he/she can modify agents' behavior by rehearsal oriented testing.

Figure 1 shows an overview of an interface for rehearsal oriented testing. To perform rehearsal oriented testing, a simulation environment should be

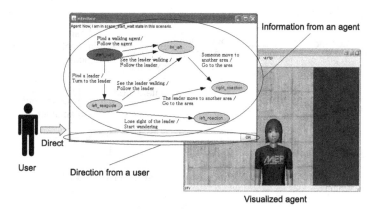

Fig. 1. Interface for rehearsal oriented testing

visualized in order for a user to monitor agents' behavior. In Figure 1, we used
FreeWalk/Q^1[4] to visualize the simulation.

A user can check whether there are problems in an agent's behavior through
monitoring of the visualized simulation. When a user finds a problem, he/she
interrupts the agent's behavior then starts interaction in order to modify the ongoing behavior. That is to say, a user tries to conduct modification. In Figure 1,
an agent opens a window which displays the agent's remark by text and information available for the user. In this example, the agent is asking its user to
specify what it should do to fix the problem next and showing its plan described
in state transition diagram. We explain more detail about interaction between
a user and an agent in the rest of this section. The user gives direction to the
agent based on given information through the window by typing a text. For
example, assume a case that a user tells his/her agent to turn around because
it is getting stuck at the corner. In this case, the user and the agent interact
via window displaying state transition diagram. When the user finishes scenario
modification, the agent closes the window and restart from the modified state.
To put it concretely, the agent can resolve deadlock.

2.1   Scenario Description

In this research, we use a method which separates an agent's external behavior
(interaction with other agents and environment) as a scenario from its internal
mechanism[5].

A part of an agent which is to be a target of modification in rehearsal oriented
testing becomes clear by separating scenarios from the agent's internal model.
Only scenarios are targets of modification in rehearsal oriented testing. Agents'
internal models are implemented by computer professionals in order to realize
actions requested from scenarios on the simulation environment. On the other
hand, since scenarios describe only agents' external (and visible) behavior, users

---

[1] http://www.ai.soc.i.kyoto-u.ac.jp/freewalk/

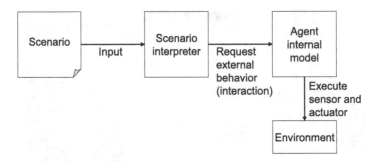

Fig. 2. Separate a scenario from an internal model

who are not computer professional can easily understand them. Users modify scenarios in order to work agents desirably for them.

Figure 2 shows architecture which separates a scenario from an agent's internal model. As shown in Figure 2, a scenario which describes an agent's external behavior is input to a scenario interpreter and the scenario interpreter requests behavior of the agent. The agent internal model executes sensors and actuators according to the request. We use scenario description language Q to describe agent scenarios. Using Q, novice at using computer can describe agent scenarios based on extended finite state machine model. Detailed specification of Q is represented in [6].

2.2 Processes of Scenario Rehearsal

We focused on two features of rehearsal in theater to realize rehearsal oriented testing. One is direction during performance. In rehearsal, actors perform in the same way as public performance and a director monitors them. If the director finds a problem in the actor's performance, he/she directs the actor to fix the problem. Then he/she restarts performance to check whether the modification succeeds and to find another problem. Second feature is sharing of context. A director and actors share information such as a situation in a stage, other actors' position and scripts. Based on these features, we construct rehearsal oriented testing methodology. Rehearsal oriented testing consists of two main processes. One is finding problems in a multiagent simulation, and the other is modifying the problems.

Running a multiagent simulation and find a problem. The multiagent simulation runs and each agent behave in accordance with its scenario. This multiagent simulation should be visualized. A user monitors the visualized multiagent simulation and checks whether there are problems in the agents' behavior. If the user finds a problem, he/she interrupts the multiagent simulation.

Modifying a problem found. If a user finds a problem, he/she interrupts the simulation in order to modify the problem. The user tells the agent the way in which the user wants it to behave. The agent modifies its scenario based on the user's direction and context in the simulation. When the user finishes modification, he/she restarts the simulation.

The first process will be mostly realized by visualization and faculties of a multiagent system. Therefore, in the rest of this paper, we focus on second process: how to modify problems in agent scenarios.

2.3   Setting of Modification Operators for Finite State Machine

In this paper, we use finite state machine model to describe agent scenarios. Finite state machine is easy to describe and understand by representing state transition diagram. This will help people who are not computer professionals to understand operation of scenarios.

When a user designs interactions of agents, he/she first describes scenarios described on the basis of finite state machines. Then the user modifies them by rehearsal oriented testing. Therefore, modification operators of rehearsal oriented testing must include operators enough to modify a finite state machine.

Typically, state transition model is defined as $\langle Q, C, A, q_0 \rangle$ where Q is a set of states, C is a set of events can be observed by an agent, A is a set of actions can be executed by the agent, Δ is a set of state transition functions and $q_0 \in Q$ is an initial state. We express a condition of scenario execution $s_t \in S$ at time t as $s_t = \langle Q, C, A, \Delta, q_0, \delta_t, q_t \rangle$. where δ_t is a state transition which is running at time t and q_t is a state which a scenario is in at time t.

Using this definition, scenario modification operators modify s_t. In other words, each element of s_t is considered as a target of modification. However, not all of the elements can be targets of the modification. C is a set of events which an agent can observe and A is a set of actions which an agent can execute in its environment. These are implemented as faculties of a multiagent system. Rehearsal oriented testing aims to refine agents' behavior under given multiagent systems. For this reason, C and A can not be targets of the modification. As to q_0, since it is an initial state of the scenario, it seems unlikely that the user changes the initial state when the multiagent system is running. For this reason, q_0 can not be a target of the modification. In addition, a user must not change δ_t and q_t because they are the conditions of scenario execution. Excepting for these elements, the modification in rehearsal oriented testing targets Q and Δ. For Q and Δ of a scenario, possible modification operations are adding, modifying and deleting them. As to Q, since modifying a state means modifying state transitions which transit from and to the state, we consider only about adding and deleting it.

From above reasons, there are following five modification operators.

Adding a state. A user specifies a state to be added.

Deleting a state. A user specifies a state to be deleted.

Adding a state transition. A user specifies all element of a state transition (a current state, an event, an action and a next state).

Modifying a state transition. A user specifies a state transition to be modified and how to modify each element of it.

Deleting a state transition. A user specifies a state transition to be deleted.

In rehearsal oriented testing, a user gives an agent the information required for modification through dialog with the agent.

3 Interaction Protocol

In rehearsal oriented testing, a user modifies agent scenarios through dialog with agents using condition of scenarios and simulation environment at a certain moment in the simulation. However, it is very difficult to figure out a user's intention from completely free interaction. Therefore we have to give constraints on their interaction. In addition, a user can understand what he/she should do to modify its scenario by following the interaction protocol. In this section, we explain about the protocol. This interaction protocols should be natural and simple as rehearsal in order to reduce cost of rehearsal oriented testing.

We use context in a simulation to make dialog simple and natural interaction between a user and agents. In concrete terms, if a user starts modification in time t, $q_t \in Q, \delta_t \in \Delta$ of agent scenarios can be used as the context. Previously, we explained that targets of modification by rehearsal oriented testing are states and transition functions of agent scenarios. A user has to specify a state to be deleted in deleting state, current state and next state in adding state transition, current state and next state of transition function to be modified in modifying state transition and transition function to be deleted in deleting state transition respectively. Dialog between a user and an agent can be more simple using q_t, δ_t in these modification cases.

Let q_c be a state which a user is modifying and let δ_c be a state transition which a user is modifying in rehearsal oriented testing. At the time t when a user starts the modification, q_t is assigned to q_c and δ_t is assigned to δ_c. For deleting state, q_c is used for deleted state. For adding state transition, q_c is used for current state. For modifying and deleting state, δ_c is used for state transition to be modified or deleted.

We design interaction protocol taking into account the context explained above. At the moment when a user starts modification, scenario execution condition can be classified into two. One is an agent is executing an action in a transition function. The other is an agent is waiting some events in a certain state. We explain interactions which start from each condition.

Figure 3 shows the interaction protocol when a modification starts. As explained above, at the moment when the modification starts, an agent is executing action in a certain state transition or waiting events in a certain state. The interaction is first divided into two according to which condition an agent is in.

If the agent is executing an action, a user can modify a state transition which includes the action. In this case, the state transition is δ_c. When the user finishes modifying the state transition or the user does not want to modify the state transition, the user can move to modification of a state. When the user move to modification of the state, the current state of the state transition δ_c is assigned to q_c.

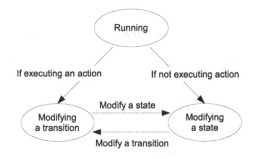

Fig. 3. Interaction protocol when the modification starts

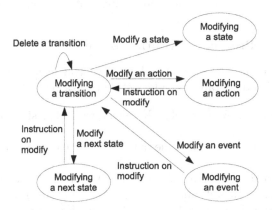

Fig. 4. Interaction protocol for modifying and deleting a state transition

If the agent is waiting events in a certain state, the user starts interaction to modify the state. The state is assigned to q_c. The user can add a state, delete a state and add a state transition in this case. When the user wants to modify or delete a state transition, he/she specify the state transition and move to interaction to modifying the state transition assigning the state transition to δ_c.

3.1 Interaction Protocol in Executing State Transition

Figure 4 shows an interaction when an agent is executing state transition. A user can modify and delete a state transition in this protocol.

Modification of a state transition. A user first selects an event, an action or a next state of the state transition to be modified. Then the user gives instruction on how to modify it. The user repeats this interaction if he/she wants to modify more.

Deletion of a state transition. A user can delete δ_c by telling the agent to delete the state transition.

When a user wants to modify state such as adding a state transition, he/she can tell the agent to modify a state. In this case, a current state of the state transition δ_c is assigned to q_c.

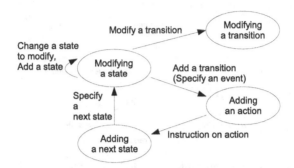

Fig. 5. Interaction protocol for adding and deleting states and adding state transitions

3.2   Interaction Protocol in Waiting Events

Figure 5 shows the interaction protocol while waiting events in a certain state. A user can add/delete a state and add a state transition.

Addition of a state. A user tells the agent to add a state then the agent creates a new state.

Deletion of a state. A user specifies a state to be deleted and the agent deletes it.

Addition of a state transition. First, q_c is selected as a current state. Then an agent asks a user information required for a state transition. In the interaction protocol shown in Figure 5, the user first specifies an event to be observed. And then the user specifies an action and at last the user specifies a next state.

If a user wants to modify or delete a state transition which has q_c as a current state, the user specifies the state transition and moves to interaction to modify the state transition which is shown in Figure 4.

4   Example

We show an example of rehearsal oriented testing using an evacuation simulation. The simulation is performed as follows. There are dozens of agents in a room. The agents start escaping from the room when they hear sound of a siren. This simulation finishes when all the agents go out from the room. A user monitors this simulation and checks if all the agents can go out.

Let us suppose a situation that one agent does not move while the other agents are heading to an exit. First, a user analyzes what is happening through visualized simulation. Visualized simulation is shown in Figure 6. The user finds that the agent is facing a wall. Then the user speaks to the agent to know what the agent is doing. The agent shows its scenario in response and says "Now I am in **searching** state in this scenario." Figure 7 show the scenario. In this case, the scenario is in **searching** state. The agent is looking for another agent or an

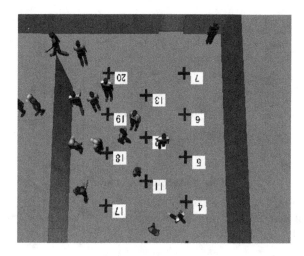

Fig. 6. Evacuation simulation

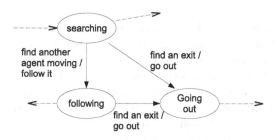

Fig. 7. Initial scenario

exit in this state. From this scenario and visualized agent which is facing the wall, the usercan see the agent does not move since it can find nothing.

Next, the user modifies this problem based on the analysis above. The agent should turn around if it can not find anything in **searching** state. Therefore the user and the agent talk in order to modify scenario as follows. When the dialog starts, a state of the interaction protocol is **Modifying a state** state in Figure 5. The user request to add an action when the agent can not find anything saying "Please add an action when you can do nothing in a few seconds." Then the agent says "What should I do when I can do nothing in a few seconds?" and the interaction protocol transits to **Adding an action** state. The user says "Please turn around." and the agent replies "Please specify a next state." according to the interaction protocol. The user says "**searching** state." in order for the agent to back to search turning around. Modified scenario in this way is shown in Figure 8. The new state transition in **searching** state was added.

This example shows how to find and modify a problem of a scenario by rehearsal oriented testing. Visualized simulation and information about a scenario from an agent are available for a user. The user identify a problem from these information and decide how to modify it. In addition, dialog based on the

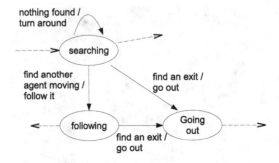

Fig. 8. Modified scenario

interaction protocol helps a user to know what an agent needs to modify the scenario properly.

5   Application

In this paper we proposed rehearsal oriented testing in order to modify agent scenarios for multiagent simulation. However, we believe there are many other applications using rehearsal oriented testing.

Rehearsal oriented testing can be applied to control of robots. In order to do this, we have to activate a robot using an agent system and install interfaces required to talk with humans such as a speaker and a microphone. Furthermore, implementing faculties explained in this paper, we can perform rehearsal oriented testing to the robot. For example, by saying "When I say 'Please fetch a newspaper' to you, go outside..." to the robot, a user can extend the robot's behavior. In addition, if there is no newspaper outside, the robot can do nothing because it does not know what it should do. Then the user can modify the robot's behavior by saying "If there is no newspaper..." to the robot.

Rehearsal oriented testing includes a process in which a user talks to an agent to know state of an agent scenario. Taking advantage of this, when an interesting event occurs in a simulation, rehearsal oriented testing can be used as a tool to inspect what is happening in the simulation. In order to realize this, rehearsal oriented testing should be able to target more than one agent at the same time. In addition, rehearsal oriented testing should show the user not only a scenario execution condition of the agent, but also history of interaction with other agents and environment.

6   Conclusion and Future Work

In this paper, we proposed rehearsal oriented testing in order for novice at using computer to modify agent scenarios. In particular, we focused on interaction protocol between a user and an agent under which a user can modify his/her agent scenario through the interaction.

We accomplished the following two goals to realize rehearsal oriented testing.

Setting of modification operators. We set the modification operators for rehearsal oriented testing. If scenarios are described on the basis of finite state machines, they are addition of a state, deletion of a state, addition of a state transition, modification of a state transition and deletion of a state transition.

Design of an interaction protocol. Under this protocol, an agent tells a user what kind of directions the user can give in order for the user to know modification procedure. In addition, this protocol realizes more natural dialog using context in a simulation.

Rehearsal oriented testing is one process of development of a multiagent system. Development tools and methodologies for multiagent systems have been studied for years[7][8]. In contrast to these researches, our research aims to help users who are not computer professionals to make agents behave properly. Users, such as participants of participatory simulations and users of service agents, have only to consider interaction scenarios of agents and the agents which behave according to the scenarios are implemented by computer professionals.

In rehearsal oriented testing, a human finds and modifies agent scenarios based on visualized behavior of agents. This is effective if the user wants to modify behavior of one agent or simple interaction such as one-on-one interaction. However, it is difficult to find out a problem from many scenarios which interact with each other. For this purpose, techniques which help us to analyze interaction between the agents such as those implemented in [9] are required.

Our future works also include learning of directions from a user in rehearsal oriented testing. Rehearsal oriented testing is a method to modify and extend agent models which are designed from some sort of techniques such as participatory simulations. However, different from theaters in which limited situations can exist, there can exist enormous situations in a multiagent simulation. It is not realistic to simulate immense situations in the simulation and perform rehearsal oriented testing for each situation. Therefore, we have to make agents which not only follow a user's directions but also learn them. The agents deduce the user's intention based on the learning and updates its scenario autonomously. If this mechanism is realized, we can make agents which adapt its scenario to a situation which is not considered in designing the agents and a change of their environment.

Acknowledgment

This research was partially supported by a Grant-in-Aid for Scientific Research (A) (18200009, 2006-2008) from Japan Society for the Promotion of Science (JSPS) and a Grant-in-Aid for JSPS Fellows.

References

1. Drogoul, A., Vanbergue, D., Meurisse, T.: Multi-agent Based Simulation: Where Are the Agents? In: Sichman, J.S., Bousquet, F., Davidsson, P. (eds.) MABS 2002. LNCS, vol. 2581, pp. 1–15. Springer, Heidelberg (2003)
2. Guyot, P., Drogoul, A., Lemaitre, C.: Using emergence in participatory simulations to design multi-agent systems. In: Proceedings of The Fourth International Joint Conference on Autonomous Agents and Multi-Agent Systems (AAMAS) (2005)
3. Murakami, Y., Sugimoto, Y., Ishida, T.: Modeling human behavior for virtual training systems. In: The Twentieth National Conference on Artificial Intelligence (AAAI 2005) (2005)
4. Nakanishi, H., Ishida, T.: FreeWalk/Q: Social interaction platform in virtual space. In: ACM Symposium on Virtual Reality Software and Technology (VRST 2004), pp. 97–104 (2004)
5. Ishida, T.: Q: A scenario description language for interactive agents. IEEE Computer 35(11), 42–47 (2002)
6. Ishida, T., Yamane, S.: Introduction to scenario description language Q. In: International Conference on Informatics Research for Development of Knowledge Society Infrastructure (ICKS 2007). IEEE Computer Society, Los Alamitos (2007)
7. Wooldridge, M., Jennings, N.R., Kinny, D.: The Gaia methodology for agent-oriented analysis and design. Autonomous Agents and Multi-Agent Systems 3(3), 285–312 (2000)
8. Nwana, H.S., Ndumu, D.T., Lee, L.C., Collis, J.C.: ZEUS: a toolkit and approach for building distributed multi-agent systems. In: Etzioni, O., Müller, J.P., Bradshaw, J.M. (eds.) Proceedings of the Third International Conference on Autonomous Agents (Agents 1999), pp. 360–361 (1999)
9. Ndumu, D.T., Nwana, H.S., Lee, L.C., Collis, J.C.: Visualising and debugging distributed multi-agent systems. In: Proceedings of the Third International Conference on Autonomous Agents (Agents 1999), pp. 326–333 (1999)

Fast Partial Reallocation in Combinatorial Auctions for Iterative Resource Allocation

Naoki Fukuta[1] and Takayuki Ito[2]

[1] Shizuoka University, Hamamatsu Shizuoka 4328011, Japan
fukuta@cs.inf.shizuoka.ac.jp
http://whitebear.cs.inf.shizuoka.ac.jp/
[2] Nagoya Institute of Technology, Gokiso-cho Nagoya 4668555, Japan

Abstract. In this paper, we propose enhanced approximation algorithms of combinatorial auction that are suitable for the purpose of periodical reallocation of items. Our algorithms are designed to effectively reuse the last solutions to speeding up initial approximation performance. We show experimental results that show our proposed algorithms outperform existing algorithms in some aspects when the existing bids are not deleted. Also, we propose an enhanced algorithm that effectively avoids undesirable reuse of last solutions in the algorithm. This is especially effective when some existing bids are deleted from the last cycle. Furthermore, our algorithms satisfy two desirable properties: WPM for final results and Weak-WPM for intermediate results.

1 Introduction

Combinatorial auctions, one of the most popular market mechanisms, have a huge effect on electronic markets and political strategies. For example, Sandholm et al. [1] proposed a market using their innovative combinatorial auction algorithms. It is well-known that the FCC tried to employ combinatorial auction mechanisms for assigning spectrums to companies [2].

Resource allocation for agents on ubiquitous computing environment is a good example to understand the needs of short time approximation of combinatorial auctions. On ubiquitous computing environment, there are typically limited amount of resources(sensors, devices, etc.) that do not cover all needs for all agents. Due to some reasons (physical limitations, privacy reasons, etc.), most of the resources cannot be shared with other agents. Furthermore, agents will use two or more resources at a time to realize desirable services for users. Of course each agent provides services to its own user, agent may be self-interested. Therefore, combinatorial auction mechanism is suitable for such situation since it is well-known mechanism for effective resource allocation to self-interested agents. Here, consider there are 256 resources, 100 agents, and each agent has 100 to 200 bids, there will be 10,000 to 20,000 bids for 256 goods in an auction. On ubiquitous computing scenario, physical location of users are always changing, resources should be reallocated in a certain period to catch up those changes. For better usability, the time period of resource reallocation will be 0.1 to several

A. Ghose, G. Governatori, and R. Sadananda (Eds.): PRIMA 2007, LNAI 5044, pp. 195–206, 2009.

seconds depending on services provided there. Therefore, it is strongly demanded to get winners of an auction within such extremely short time period.

In general, the optimal winner determination problem of combinatorial auction is NP-hard[3]. Thus, much work focuses on tackling the computational costs for winner determination [4][3][1]. These works basically try to achieve the optimal solution in winner determination. Although these works can be used for attaining approximated solutions and they perform well in certain conditions, there remain possibilities for further improvements focused on approximation.

Some works [5] [6] [7] try to achieve *approximate* solutions in winner determination. A recent well-known theoretical work is Lehmann et al. [5]. In [5], they proposed a greedy approximation algorithm that relaxes economic efficiency and proves the truthfulness in a certain condition. The paper [5] rather focuses on the more elegant theoretical aspects, i.e., giving truthfulness for an auction mechanism with approximated allocations of items. However, it is well known that the performance of [5] is really nice that can successfully handle a very large number of bids and goods in an auction. Also, it is well known that the approximation algorithms presented in [6] and [7] generally perform very well even if the number of bids is relatively large. Recently, we proposed a set of extended approximation algorithms that are based on Lehmann's approach. In [8], we showed that our algorithm perform well when the number of bids is very large and there is hard time constraint. Also we reported detailed comparisons of our algorithms and existing algorithms(e.g., [9]).

However, since those existing algorithms are 'offline' algorithms, we need to re-calculate the winners when some bids are added to or deleted from the auction even when the modification of bids is little. It will be helpful when the most recent results can be reused to the approximation process of the current auction. However, those algorithms did not consider about reusing past approximated results for performance improvement.

In this paper, we propose enhanced approximation algorithms of combinatorial auction that are suitable for the purpose of periodical reallocation of items we mentioned above.

This paper is organized as follows. In section 2, we present some necessary backgrounds about our research, including definition of the problem and existing algorithms. Section 3 describes our proposed algorithms that are designed to effectively reuse the last results to speeding up initial approximation performance after the modification of bids in the auction. In Section 4, We show experimental results that shows our proposed algorithms outperform existing algorithms in some aspects when the existing bids are not deleted. Also, we report the effectiveness of an enhanced algorithm that effectively avoid undesirable reuse of last solutions in the algorithm. In Section 5, we show our algorithms satisfy two desirable properties: WPM for final results and Weak-WPM for intermediate results. In Section 6, we show related works to clarify our contributions in this paper. Finally, section 7 concludes the paper.

2 Preliminaries

2.1 Combinatorial Auction

Combinatorial auction is an auction mechanism that allows bidders to locate bids for a bundle of items rather than single item. The winner determination problem is defined as follows[3] : The set of bidders is denoted by $N = 1, \ldots, n$, and the set of items by $M = \{m_1, \ldots, m_k\}$. $|M| = k$. Bundle S is a set of items : $S \subseteq M$. We denote by $v_i(S)$, bidder i's combinatorial bid for bundle S. An allocation of the items is described by variables $x_i(S) \in \{0, 1\}$, where $x_i(S) = 1$ if and only if bidder i wins the bundle S. An allocation, $x_i(S)$, is feasible if it allocates no item more than once,

$$\sum_{i \in N} \sum_{S \ni j} x_i(S) \le 1$$

for all $j \in M$. The winner determination problem is the problem to maximize total revenue

$$\max_X \sum_{i \in N, S \subseteq M} v_i(S) x_i(S)$$

for feasible allocations $X \ni x_i(S)$.

Throughout this paper, we only consider the auctions that are single-sided, with a single seller and multiple buyers to keep the simplicity of discussions. It can be extended to the reverse situation with a single buyer and multiple sellers, and the two-sided cases[10].

2.2 Lehmann's Greedy Winner Determination

Lehmann's greedy algorithm [5] is a very simple but powerful linear algorithm for winner determination on combinatorial auctions. Here, a bidder declaring $< a, s >$, with $s \subseteq M$ and $a \in \mathcal{R}_+$ will be said to put out a bid $b = < a, s >$. Two bids $b = < a, s >$ and $b' = < a', s' >$ conflict iff $s \cap s' \neq \emptyset$. The greedy algorithm can be described as follows: (1)The bids are sorted by some criterion. The paper[5] proposed sorting the list L by descending average amount per good. More generally, they proposed sorting L by a criterion of the form $a/|s|^c$ for some number c, $c \ge 0$, possibly depends on the number of goods, k. (2) A greedy algorithm generates an allocation. L is the sorted list in the first phase. Walk down the list L, accepting bids if the goods demanded are still unallocated and not conflicted.

In the paper[5], they argued that $c = 1/2$ is the best parameter for approximation when the norm of worst case performance is considered. Also they have shown that the mechanism is truthful when single-minded bidders are assumed and their proposed pricing scheme is used.

2.3   Hill-Climbing Search

In [8], we have shown that hill-climbing approach performs well when an auction has a massively large number of bids. In this section, we summarize our proposed algorithms.

Lehmann's greedy winner determination could succeed specifying the lower bound of the optimality in its allocation[5]. The straightforward extension of the greedy algorithm is to construct a local search algorithm that continuously updates the allocation so that the optimality is increased. Intuitively, one allocation corresponds to one state of a local search.

The inputs are *Alloc* and *L*. *L* is the bid list of an auction. *Alloc* is the initial greedy allocation of items for the bid list.

1: **function** LocalSearch(*Alloc, L*)

2:    *RemainBids*:= *L* - *Alloc*;

3:    **for each** $b \in RemainBids$ as sorted order

4:      **if** b conflicts *Alloc* **then**

5:        *Conflicted*:=*Alloc* - *consistentBids*({b}, *Alloc*);

6:        *NewAlloc*:= *Alloc* - *Conflicted* + {b};

7:        *ConsBids*:=

8:          consistentBids(*NewAlloc, RemainBids*);

9:        *NewAlloc*:=*NewAlloc*+*ConsBids*;

10:       **if** *price(Alloc)* < *price(NewAlloc)* **then**

11:         **return** LocalSearch(*NewAlloc,L*);

12:    **end for each**

13:    **return** *Alloc*

The function *consistentBids* finds consistent bids for the set *NewAllocation* by walking down the list *RemainBids*. Here, a new inserted bid will wipe out some bids that are conflicted with the inserted bid. So there will be free items to allocate after the insertion. The function *consistentBids* tries to insert the other bids for selling the higher value goods as many as possible.

2.4   Local Search for Multiple Values of the Sorting Criterion c

The optimality of allocations got by Lehmann's algorithm (and the followed hill-climbing) deeply depends on which value was set to the bid sorting criterion c. Lehmann et al. reported $c = 1/2$ is the approximately best value. But the optimal values for each auction are varied from 0 to 1 even if the number of items is constant. Here, we use an enhancement for our local search algorithm with parallel search for the sorting criterion c. In the algorithm, the value of c for Lehmann's algorithm is selected from a pre-defined list. It is reasonable to select c from neighbors of $1/2$, namely, $C = \{0.0, 0.1, \ldots, 1.0\}$. The results are aggregated and the best one (that has highest revenue) is selected as the final result.

2.5   Other Approximation Approaches

Zurel and Nisan[6] proposed a very competitive approximate winner determination algorithm for combinatorial auctions. The main idea is a combination of approximated positive linear program algorithm for determining initial allocation and stepwise random updates of allocations.

Hoos[7] proposed that a generic random walk SAT solver may perform well for approximation of combinatorial auctions. In [7], Casanova algorithm has been proposed for the purpose of approximating winner determination. It is based on scoring each search state using the revenue-per-good of the corresponding allocation.

3   Enhanced Approximation Algorithms

3.1   Fast Partial Reallocation by Using Last Result

In the setting of periodical resource re-allocation scenario, winner determination occurs when some bids are revised. Theoretically, we need to recalculate winners even if only one bid is changed in the auction. However, in some cases, it is useful to re-use winners of previous auction when the change is small so that it has small effects to the next winner determination process. Following simple algorithm reuses the approximation result in last cycle when recalculation is needed due to change of bids in the auction. Here, we assume winners of the last cycle (*LastWinners*) and bidset of the last cycle (*LastBids*) are known.

```
1: Function PartialReallocationA(LastBids,LastWinners,CurrentBids)
2:    AddedBids := CurrentBids - (LastBids ∩ CurrentBids);
3:    DeletedBids := LastBids - (LastBids ∩ CurrentBids);
4:    Winners := LastWinners;
5:    foreach d ∈ DeletedBids
6:      if d ∈ Winners then
7:        Winners := Winners − d;
8:    foreach a ∈ AddedBids
9:      foreach w ∈ Winners
10:       if b(w) = b(a) and v(w) < v(a) then
11:         Winners := Winners − w + a;
12:   Winners := LocalSearch(Winners,CurrentBids);
13:   return Winners
```

At the first step, the algorithm deletes winners that no longer valid due to deletion of bids. And then, some winner bids are replaced by newly added bids. Note that we only replace when the bundle of bids are just equal to avoid ordering problem of newly added bids. Modification of a bid through cycles will be treated as a combined operation of deletion of previous bid and addition of the renewed bid.

3.2   Eliminating Bad Reallocations within Short Overhead

Generally speaking, performance of reusing partial result of similar problem depends on the problem. Therefore, in some cases, reuse of last result may cause performance decreases. To avoid such a situation, we slightly modified our algorithm to switch initial allocation by evaluating its performance.

Here, the modified algorithm simply compares the reused result with greedy allocation. Then, the better one is used for the seed of Hill-climbing improvement. Note that both our reallocation algorithm and greedy allocation algorithm complete their executions in very short time. Therefore, the computational overhead is expected to be negligible.

```
1:  Function PartialReallocationX(LastBids,LastWinners,CurrentBids)
2:      AddedBids := CurrentBids - (LastBids ∩ CurrentBids);
3:      DeletedBids := LastBids - (LastBids ∩ CurrentBids);
4:      Winners := LastWinners;
5:      foreach d ∈ DeletedBids
6:        if d ∈ Winners then
7:            Winners := Winners − d;
8:      foreach a ∈ AddedBids
9:        foreach w ∈ Winners
10:           if b(w) = b(a) and v(w) < v(a) then
11:               Winners := Winners − w + a;
12:     GreedyWinners := GreedySearch(CurrentBids);
13:     if price(Winners) =< price(GreedyWinners) then
14:         Winners := GreedyWinners;
15:     Winners := LocalSearch(Winners,CurrentBids);
16:     return Winners
```

4   Experimental Results

We implemented our algorithms in a C program for the following experiments. We also implemented the Casanova algorithm in a C program. However, for the following experiments, we used Zurel's C++ based implementation that are shown in [6]. The experiments were done with above implementations to examine the performance differences among algorithms. The program was employed on our Mac with Mac OS X 10.4, CoreDuo 2.0GHz CPU, and 2GBytes of memory.

We conducted several experiments. In each experiment, we compared the following search algorithms. "greedy(C=0.5)" uses Lehmann's greedy allocation algorithm with parameter ($c = 0.5$). "greedy-3" uses the best results of Lehmann's greedy allocation algorithm with parameter ($0 \leq c \leq 1$ in 0.5 steps). "HC(c=0.5)" uses a local search in which the initial allocation is Lehmann's allocation with $c = 0.5$ and conduct the hill-climbing search shown in the previous section. "HC-3" uses the best results of the hill-climbing search with parameter

$(0 \leq c \leq 1$ in 0.5 steps). Also, we denote Casanova algorithm as "casanova" and Zurel's algorithm as "Zurel".

In the following experiments, we used 0.2 for epsilon value of Zurel's algorithm in our experiments. This value appears in [6]. Also we used 0.5 for np and 0.15 for wp on Casanova that appear in [7]. Note that we set $maxTrial$ to 1 but $maxSteps$ to ten times of the number of bids in the auction.

We conducted detailed comparisons among our past presented algorithms and other existing algorithms mentioned above. The detail of the comparisons has shown in [9] and [11]. In [9] and [11], we prepared datasets having 20,000 bids in an auction. The datasets were produced by CATS[12] with default parameters in 5 different distributions. It contains 100 trials for each distribution. Each trial is an auction problem with 256 items and 20,000 bids[1].

However, since CATS common datasets provide only static bids for an auction, we prepared an extended usage for those datasets to include dynamic changes of bids in an auction.

Procedure: In each auction, the bid set is divided into 10 blocks by the order of bid generation (i.e. bid id). The bid set is modified totally 10 times and the modification will be done in each 1 second. In each period of 1 second, a block is marked as hidden so that bids within these marked blocks are treated as 'deleted bids'. For example, at first period, the first block is marked as hidden so left bids (second to 10th blocks) are used for winner determination. After 1 second, the mark is moved to second block (i.e. first, and third to 10th blocks are used) and the winner determination process is restarted due to this change. Here, we can see it as the bids in first block are newly added to the auction and the bids in second block are deleted from the auction. This process is repeated until the mark has been moved to the 10th block. And finally, all marks are cleared and the winner determination process is restarted with full bids in the auction. Ordinary algorithms should be completely restarted in each cycle. However, when we use our proposed reallocation algorithms, some intermediate results can be reused in the next cycle in the same auction.

Since the bid set in last period is completely equal to the bids of the auction, the result last periods can be compared to our previous experimental results.

Table 1 shows the experimental result on the dataset with 20,000 bids in an auction focused on the execution time of short time approximation. Due to difficulty of attaining optimal values, we normalized all values as Zurel's results equal 1. The name of each distribution is referred from [12]. We prepared cut-off results of Casanova and HC. For example, "casanova-10ms" denotes the result of Casanova within 10 milliseconds. Also we prepared a variant of our algorithm that has a suffix of '-seq' or '-para'. The suffix '-seq' denotes the algorithm is completely executed in sequential that is equal to be executed on a single CPU computer. For example, greedy-3-seq denotes that the execution time is just the sum of execution times of three threads. The suffix '-para' denotes the algorithm

---

[1] Due to difficulty of preparing dataset, we only prepared 5 distributions. Producing dataset with other distributions is difficult in feasible time. More detailed experimental results are shown in [9].

Table 1. Time Performance on 20,000bids-256items

	L2		L3		L4		L6		L7	
greedy(c=0.5)	1.0002	(23.0)	0.9639	(19.0)	0.9417	(23.0)	0.9389	(23.4)	0.7403	(22.1)
greedy-3-seq	1.0003	(69.1)	0.9639	(59.2)	0.9999	(72.9)	0.9965	(67.8)	0.7541	(66.8)
greedy-3-para	1.0003	(26.4)	0.9639	(20.9)	0.9999	(28.4)	0.9965	(26.0)	0.7541	(25.5)
HC(c=0.5)-100ms	1.0004	(100)	0.9741	(100)	0.9576	(100)	0.9533	(100)	0.8260	(100)
HC-3-seq-100ms	1.0004	(100)	0.9692	(100)	1.0000	(100)	0.9966	(100)	0.8287	(100)
AHC-3-seq-100ms	-		0.9690	(100)	1.0006	(100)	0.9974	(100)	1.0225	(100)
XHC-3-seq-100ms	-		0.9813	(100)	1.0005	(100)	0.9987	(100)	1.0217	(100)
HC-3-para-100ms	1.0004	(100)	0.9743	(100)	1.0001	(100)	0.9969	(100)	0.9423	(100)
AHC-3-para-100ms	-		0.9741	(100)	1.0006	(100)	0.9977	(100)	1.0249	(100)
XHC-3-para-100ms	-		0.9820	(100)	1.0006	(100)	0.9988	(100)	1.0249	(100)
HC(c=0.5)-1000ms	1.0004	(1000)	0.9856	(1000)	0.9771	(1000)	0.9646	(1000)	1.0157	(1000)
HC-3-seq-1000ms	1.0004	(1000)	0.9804	(1000)	1.0003	(1000)	0.9976	(1000)	1.0086	(1000)
AHC-3-seq-1000ms	-		0.9795	(1000)	1.0007	(1000)	0.9982	(1000)	1.0266	(1000)
XHC-3-seq-1000ms	-		0.9830	(1000)	1.0006	(1000)	0.9991	(1000)	1.0266	(1000)
HC-3-para-1000ms	1.0004	(1000)	0.9856	(1000)	1.0006	(1000)	0.9987	(1000)	1.0240	(1000)
AHC-3-para-1000ms	-		0.9847	(1000)	1.0008	(1000)	0.9990	(1000)	1.0272	(1000)
XHC-3-para-1000ms	-		0.9853	(1000)	1.0008	(1000)	0.9996	(1000)	1.0272	(1000)
Zurel-1st	0.5710	(11040)	0.9690	(537)	0.9983	(2075)	0.9928	(1715)	0.6015	(1795)
Zurel	1.0000	(13837)	1.0000	(890)	1.0000	(4581)	1.0000	(4324)	1.0000	(3720)
casanova-10ms	0.2583	(10)	0.0069	(10)	0.0105	(10)	0.0202	(10)	0.2577	(10)
casanova-100ms	0.2583	(100)	0.0069	(100)	0.0105	(100)	0.0202	(100)	0.2577	(100)
casanova-1000ms	0.5357	(1000)	0.1208	(1000)	0.0861	(1000)	0.1486	(1000)	0.7614	(1000)

(each value in () is time in milliseconds)

is completely executed in parallel manner, the three independent threads are completely executed in parallel. Here, we used ideal value for '-para' since our computer has only two core in the CPU. The actual execution performance will be between '-seq' and '-para'.

Additionally, we added results with the name 'AHC-' or 'XHC-' in the same table. They are the average approximated results of the last periods of auctions with our proposed algorithms `PartialReallocationA` and `PartialReallocationX`, respectively[2].

In most distributions, Zurel-1st takes more than 1 second but the obtained optimality is lower than greedy-3-seq. However, our proposed 'HC-3' performs better or slightly lower although their computation times are shorter than Zurel-1st and Zurel, excluding L3. Surprisingly, in most cases, the results of 'XHC-3-seq-100ms' are better than 'HC-3-seq-1000ms' while their spend computation time are only 1/10. This fact shows that our 'XHC-3' could reuse approximated results of previous cycles effectively.

Figure 1 shows the average performance curves of 'HC-3-para', 'AHC-3-para', and 'XHC-3-para'. In Figure 1, average performances of algorithms in each distribution are separately plotted. Since it can be viewed that each 1-sec period has its own auction problem, the optimal total revenue cannot be a fixed value in the whole period. For this reason, the plotted performances are normalized as the result of HC-3-para-1000msec be 1 in each 1-sec period. For example, when the value in the time 2100msec was 0.95, it means that the total revenue of approximated result was 95 percent of the maximum approximated value

---

[2] We omitted the results of L2 for 'AHC' and 'XHC' since the obtained results of HC(c=0.5)-100ms are good enough and it is easily predicted to get the same performance by our 'AHC' and 'XHC'.

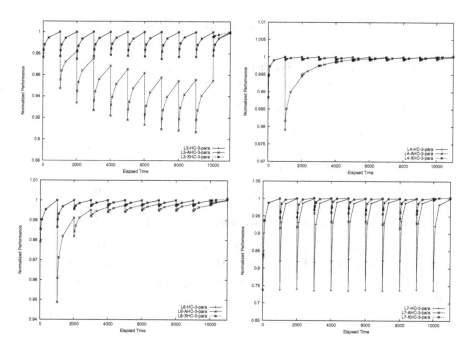

Fig. 1. Perfromance Changes on 10-fold periodical bid replacement

attained within the period starting from 2000msec to 3000msec by 'HC-3-para'. Therefore we can see how each algorithm can improve the approximated results in each cycle.

On L7, both 'AHC-3' and 'XHC-3' perform very well compared to 'HC-3'. However, on L3, L4, and L6, the performance of 'AHC-3' is far worse than 'HC-3' excluding the final period. This is because the deletion and addition of bids in the same time will cause a mis-choice of initial allocations in each cycle when there is no 'bad reallocation avoiding mechanism' within the algorithm. In contrast, 'XHC-3' only reuses the results of last cycle when it is better than the vanilla greedy result. Actually, the results of 'XHC-3' are constantly better than 'AHC-3' and there is no performance decrease compared to 'HC-3' in any time of the period.

5 Discussion

In real world, a loser who might be a winner in the optimal allocation could know the winner's bidding price in an approximate allocation after the auction finishes. This loser might place a higher price than the winner's even if they placed bids on the same bundle. This could result in "unfair" allocations for bidders. Therefore, we proposed two desirable properties, Winner-Price-Monotonicity and Weak-Price-Monotonicity to avoid 'unfair' allocations[11].

Definition 1. (Winner-Price-Monotonicity: WPM) *For two bundles* B *and* B', *if* $B \subseteq B'$ *and* $v_i(B) > v_j(B')$, *then* j *must not win bundle* B'.

Definition 2. (Weak-Winner-Price-Monotonicity: Weak-WPM) *For one bundle* B, *if* $v_i(B) > v_j(B)$, *then* j *must not win bundle* B.

We gave proofs about following propositions in [11].

Proposition 1. *Our proposed determination algorithms, except for the simulated annealing-based algorithm, produce allocation* W_{fin} *that satisfies WPM when the algorithm reaches an end.*

Proposition 2. *In terms of any allocations that are achieved during computation (as an anytime algorithm), our proposed winner determination algorithms, except for the simulated annealing-based algorithm, satisfy Weak-WPM.*

We designed our newly proposed algorithms ('AHC-3' and 'XHC-3') to keep these desirable properties. Here, we show that above propositions can also be applied to the proposed reallocation algorithms. For this purpose, we give Lemma 1 and its proof below.

Lemma 1. *Our proposed initial winner set reallocation algorithm satisfies Weak-WPM.*

Proof for Lemma 1. Consider about function `PartialReallocationA`, when $LastBids = LastWinners = \emptyset$, it is equal to simple Lehmann's greedy allocation. Therefore, initial allocation for initial cycle ($LastBids = LastWinners = \emptyset$) satisfies WPM.

In function `PartialReallocationA`, $DeletedBids$ will be deleted from $Winners$ when they are included in last winners ($LastWinners$). Here, recall the definitions of WPM and Weak-WPM, there is no effect about deleting bids from winners. A special example about it is that when $Winners = \emptyset$, it satisfies WPM and Weak-WPM since they only consider about *invalid winners*. Therefore, the deletion mechanism will not take effect about WPM and Weak-WPM.

Also, in function `PartialReallocationA`, last winners ($Winners$) are replaced by most higher one when bids for just same bundle are newly added. Here, it is guaranteed that all winner bids in $Winners$ are placing highest prices for the bundles. Therefore, there is no bid $b'(x) \in Winners$ such that $v'(x) < v(X) \in CurrentBids$.

Note that some bids will be added to $Winners$ such that they do not conflict to the current bids in $Winners$. Here, since we used Lehmann's greedy algorithm for this purpose, and the fact that the procedure for filling bids for non-allocated bundles will not break Weak-WPM[11], this will not break Weak-WPM.

From above, any initial winner set generated by our reallocation algorithm satisfies Weak-WPM.

Also any initial winner set generated in function `PartialReallocationX` satisfies Weak-WPM. Since it is same winner set in function `PartialReallocationA` or attained by simple Lehmann's greedy allocation, and both satisfies at least Weak-WPM. □

Recall the proof in [11] and the proof about above lemma 1, it is clear that proposition 2 is satisfied for our proposed reallocation algorithms. Also, it is easy to extend the proof in [11] to the proof of proposition 1 for our proposed reallocation algorithms[3].

6 Related Work

There have been a lot of works on the optimal algorithm for winner determination in combinatorial auctions[13]. Recently, Dobzinski et,al. proposed improved approximation algorithms for auctions with submodular bidders[14]. Lavi et,al, reported an LP based algorithm that can be extended to support the classic VCG[15]. Those researches are mainly focused on theoretical aspects. In the contrast to those papers, we rather focus on experimental and implementation aspects. Those papers did not present experimental analysis about the settings with large number of bids we presented in this paper. Also, Guo[16] proposed local-search based algorithms for large number of bids in combinatorial auction problems. However, their approach needs to adjust some parameters to make the algorithms perform satisfactory that is not necessary in our algorithms.

CPLEX is a well-known, very fast linear programming system. In [6], Zurel et, al. evaluated the performance of their presented algorithm with many data sets, compared with CPLEX, and other existing implementations. While the version of CPLEX used in [6] is not up-to-date, the shown performance of Zurel's algorithm is approximately 10 to 100 times faster than CPLEX. Therefore, the performance of Zurel's and ours shown in this paper will be competitive enough to CPLEX and similar systems.

Above approaches are based on offline algorithms and there are no considerations about addition and deletion of bids in their approximation processes. Although our algorithms are not strict online algorithms, it is possible to reuse the last results when bids are modified and recalculation is necessary.

7 Conclusions

In this paper, we proposed enhanced approximation algorithms of combinatorial auction that are suitable for the purpose of periodical reallocation of items. Our proposed algorithms effectively reuse the last solutions to speeding up initial approximation performance. The experimental results showed that our proposed algorithms outperform existing algorithms in some aspects when the existing bids are not deleted. However, we found that in some cases reuse of last solutions may cause worse performance compared to ordinary approximation from scratch. We proposed an enhanced algorithm that effectively avoids undesirable reuse of last solutions in the algorithm. We showed this is especially effective when some existing bids are deleted from the last cycle. Furthermore, We showed that our proposed algorithms satisfy two desirable properties: WPM for final results and Weak-WPM for intermediate results.

---

[3] Due to space limitation, detailed proofs are omitted.

References

1. Sandholm, T., Suri, S., Gilpin, A., Levine, D.: Cabob: A fast optimal algorithm for winner determination in combinatorial auctions. Management Science 51(3), 374–390 (2005)
2. McMillan, J.: Selling spectrum rights. The Journal of Economic Perspectives (1994)
3. Cramton, P., Shoham, Y., Steinberg, R.: Combinatorial Auctions. MIT Press, Cambridge (2006)
4. Fujishima, Y., Leyton-Brown, K., Shoham, Y.: Taming the computational complexity of combinatorial auctions: Optimal and approximate approarches. In: Proc. of the 16th International Joint Conference on Artificial Intelligence (IJCAI 1999), pp. 548–553 (1999)
5. Lehmann, D., O'Callaghan, L.I., Shoham, Y.: Truth revelation in rapid, approximately efficient combinatorial auctions. Journal of the ACM 49, 577–602 (2002)
6. Zurel, E., Nisan, N.: An efficient approximate allocation algorithm for combinatorial auctions. In: Proc. of the Third ACM Conference on Electronic Commerce (EC 2001), pp. 125–136 (2001)
7. Hoos, H.H., Boutilier, C.: Solving combinatorial auctions using stochastic local search. In: Proc. of the AAAI 2000, pp. 22–29 (2000)
8. Fukuta, N., Ito, T.: Towards better approximation of winner determination for combinatorial auctions with large number of bids. In: Proc. of The 2006 WIC/IEEE/ACM International Conference on Intelligent Agent Technology(IAT 2006), pp. 618–621 (2006)
9. Fukuta, N., Ito, T.: Short-time approximation on combinatorial auctions – a comparison on approximated winner determination algorithms. In: Proc. of The 3rd International Workshop on Data Engineering Issues in E-Commerce and Services (DEECS 2007), pp. 42–55 (June 2007)
10. Parkes, D.C., Cavallo, R., Elprin, N., Juda, A., Lahaie, S., Lubin, B., Michael, L., Shneidman, J., Sultan, H.: Ice: An iterative combinatorial exchange. In: The Proc. 6th ACM Conf. on Electronic Commerce (EC 2005) (2005)
11. Fukuta, N., Ito, T.: Periodical resource allocation using approximated combinatorial auctions. In: Proc. of The 2007 WIC/IEEE/ACM International Conference on Intelligent Agent Technology (IAT 2007) (2007)
12. Leyton-Brown, K., Pearson, M., Shoham, Y.: Towards a universal test suite for combinatorial auction algorithms. In: Proc. of EC 2000, pp. 66–76 (2000)
13. de Vries, S., Vohra, R.V.: Combinatorial auctions: A survey. International Transactions in Operational Research 15(3), 284–309 (2003)
14. Dobzinski, S., Schapira, M.: An improved approximation algorithm for combinatorial auctions with submodular bidders. In: SODA 2006: Proceedings of the seventeenth annual ACM-SIAM symposium on Discrete algorithm, pp. 1064–1073. ACM Press, New York (2006)
15. Lavi, R., Swamy, C.: Truthful and near-optimal mechanism design via linear programming. In: 46th Annual IEEE Symposium on Foundations of Computer Science (FOCS 2005), pp. 595–604 (2005)
16. Guo, Y., Lim, A., Rodrigues, B., Zhu, Y.: A non-exact approach and experiment studies on the combinatorial auction problem. In: Proc. of HICSS 2005, p. 82.1 (2005)

Deliberation Process in a BDI Model with Bayesian Networks

Moser Silva Fagundes[1], Rosa Maria Vicari[1], and Helder Coelho[2]

[1] Instituto de Informática Universidade Federal do Rio Grande do Sul (UFRGS)
Po. B 15.064 91.501-970 Porto Alegre RS Brasil
Tel./Fax: +55 51 33166161
{msfagundes,rosa}@inf.ufrgs.br
[2] Faculdade de Ciências Universidade de Lisboa
Campo Grande 1749-016 Lisboa Portugal
hcoelho@di.fc.ul.pt

Abstract. This paper presents a way to perform the deliberation process in a BDI model with Bayesian networks. The assemblage of mental states and Bayesian networks is done by viewing beliefs as networks, and desires and intentions as particular chance variable states that agents pursue. We are particulary concerned with the deliberation about which states of affairs the agents will intend. Perception, planning and execution of plans lie outside the scope of this paper. Our proposal introduces the notion of threshold function to change the agent behavior, and we also discuss the intention selection and the compatibility verification among proactive mental states.

Keywords: BDI Architecture, Bayesian Networks, Deliberation.

1 Introduction

Several decisions we have to take in our everyday life demand a large amount of information, which frequently is imprecise and incomplete. Like human beings, resource-bounded cognitive agents that inhabit complex and dynamic environments face the uncertainty phenomenon.

The AI (Artificial Intelligence) community has made relevant efforts to develop computational models for cognitive agents capable of dealing with uncertainty, since several real world agent applications require that capability. Among these efforts, we include the specification of uncertain beliefs [1], the implementation of intention reconsideration as a partially observable Markov decision process [2], the specification of general probabilistic models of cognition [3,4] and the promotion of interoperability of uncertain knowledge between Bayesian agents [5].

This work is particulary concerned with the deliberation process, responsible for generating the intentions to be pursued by the agent. Efforts have been done in order to enable the deliberation under uncertain conditions. To the best of our knowledge, most researches addressing that issue employ decision theory principles to select intentions (frequently abstracted by the notion of action plans) [6,7].

A. Ghose, G. Governatori, and R. Sadananda (Eds.): PRIMA 2007, LNAI 5044, pp. 207–218, 2009.

Our main contribution is the specification of a deliberation process that takes into account probabilistic information through the usage of Bayesian networks to abstract the mental states. Inside our deliberation, the uncertainty is considered to decide if an agent believes that a state can be achieved and if desires and intentions are compatible. The deliberation also uses the causality feature of Bayesian networks to seek the establishment of conditions where desires are feasible.

In addition, we discuss the different behaviors (*cautious* and *bold*) that can be obtained by adjusting the parameters used inside the deliberation. The terms *cautious* and *bold* agents were previously used by Kinny and Georgeff [8] in their experiments about intention reconsideration and commitment strategies, taking into account the rate of change of the environment. In the context of this work, we use the notions of boldness and cautiousness to qualify the agent's behavior.

The remaining of this paper is organized as follows: section two presents the background for our research; section three presents the assemblage of mental states and Bayesian networks; section four describes the deliberation process; section five presents the related work; and in the section six it is presented our conclusion and future work.

2   Background

We employ Bayesian networks [9,10], also called belief networks, to represent beliefs in our model. They are graphical models that represent causality between variables, allowing the performance of reasoning under conditions of uncertainty in a consistent, efficient, and mathematically sound way. Formally, they consist of directed acyclic graphs and a set of conditional probability distributions. Each node corresponds to a chance variable which has a finite set of mutually exclusive states. The directed arcs specify the causal relation between the variables, and each variable has a conditional probability distribution.

In Figure 1, we illustrate the *Movies or Soccer* Bayesian network, which we use throughout the paper to exemplify how mental states are interpreted by the deliberation process. This very didactic example models the beliefs about the agent going to the movies or playing soccer (beliefs about the agent itself carrying out these activities), and beliefs about the weather and the soccer players (external environment elements). The agent believes that a rainy weather is not a good condition to play soccer, but it is a good call to go to the movies. It also believes that sunny days are good to play soccer, but they were not made to stay in a room watching movies. Finally, our agent believes that soccer games additionally require a group of players. The network and the conditional probability tables illustrated in Figure 1 were specified in order to express these beliefs.

Regarding beliefs, it is worth to stress the different interpretations of probabilities in different stages of the Bayesian inference. In Figure 2, we illustrate three stages in the Bayesian inference. The first stage corresponds to the conditional probability table defined by the system designer. The P(Movies|Weather) means the degree of belief (probability) about Movies if a particular state of Weather

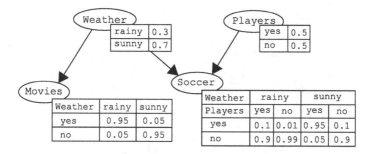

Fig. 1. *Movies or Soccer* Bayesian network

P(Movies|Weather) =

	Weather=rainy	Weather=sunny
Movies=yes	0.95	0.05
Movies=no	0.05	0.95

P(Movies,Weather) = P(Movies|Weather)P(Weather)

	Weather=rainy	Weather=sunny
= Movies=yes	0.285	0.035
Movies=no	0.015	0.665

$$P(\text{Movies}) = \sum_{\text{Weather}} P(\text{Movies,Weather})$$

= Movies=yes	0.32
Movies=no	0.68

Fig. 2. Conditional probability table, computed joint distribution and marginalized table for the variable Movies

occurs with certainty (hard evidence perception). The second stage corresponds to the computed joint distribution for Movies and Weather. The computation was performed taking into account the current probabilities of the states of the variable Weather (P(Weather=rainy)=0.3 and P(Weather=sunny)=0.7). Finally, in the third stage, we obtain the current probability of each state of Movies by marginalizing out Weather of P(Movies,Weather). By this it means that the agent believes with some degree of certainty that a particular state will occur. Throughout the paper, we show how these probabilistic information are used by the deliberation process.

Differently from the Bayesian networks, which is a formalized model for representing knowledge, there is not a unique BDI model for agency. In this paper, we specify the deliberation process through algorithms. In order to better contextualize our contribution, we use as starting point the agent control loop specified by Wooldridge [11]. Figure 3 shows the complete control loop, which consists of perception, belief revision function, option selection, filter function, planning, and finally, action plan execution.

```
Algorithm: Agent Control Loop Version 3
01
02  B:=B₀;
03  I:=I₀;
04  while true do
05      get next percept ρ;
06      brf(B,ρ);
07      D:=options(B,I);
08      I:=filter(B,D,I);
09      Π:=plan(B,I);
10      execute(Π);
11  end-while
```

Fig. 3. BDI Agent control loop [11]

We are particulary concerned with the deliberation, decomposed by the authors in `options` and `filter` functions (lines 7–8). The option (desire) selection consists of understanding which desires are available, while the filtering consists of choosing among incompatible desires. For more information about the BDI agent control loop, including more sophisticated versions, see [11].

3 Representing Mental States

Our agents represent the Intentional content of the desires through particular states of variables. Consequently, desires become a subset of beliefs. Differently from beliefs, we use a data structure to make explicit the Intentional content of the desires. By assuming that, we leave outside of the research scope the question "Where do desires come from?". In other words, the application designer or domain expert specifies which variable states might be desired. In the *Movies or Soccer* example, the desires are represented by end nodes, however it is not mandatory.

The first requirement for a desire become an intention is the belief support. In other words, the agent will not desire a state unless it believes it is possible to achieve that state. It is done by checking the computed marginal probability (see Figure 2). Consider the example depicted in Figure 4, where the agent will desire the state `Movies=yes` because it believes the current world conditions (`Weather=rainy`) support this desire. According to its beliefs, to play soccer is not an option, unless the weather gets sunny. One could argue that our agent will only desire something that is true in the present moment, however this interpretation is not correct. Actually, a high probability associated with a unobserved state does not mean that the state has occurred. It just means that the conditions imposed by the parent variables hold and the state might occur with some degree of certainty. However, in some circumstances, these desired states might never happen unless the agent acts in order to achieve them.

A *proactive* behavior is exhibited by the agent when it pursues states of world where desires become feasible. More specifically, this behavior consists of achieving particular states of parent variables (conditions) based on the values of the conditional probability table of the desired state. They can be viewed as desires connected to a desire through causality.

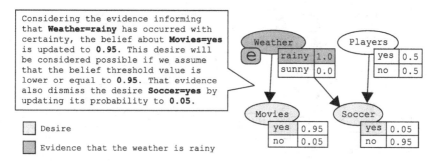

Considering the evidence informing that **Weather=rainy** has occurred with certainty, the belief about **Movies=yes** is updated to **0.95**. This desire will be considered possible if we assume that the belief threshold value is lower or equal to **0.95**. That evidence also dismiss the desire **Soccer=yes** by updating its probability to **0.05**.

☐ Desire

■ Evidence that the weather is rainy

Fig. 4. Supporting desires through beliefs

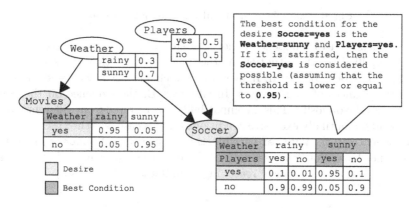

The best condition for the desire **Soccer=yes** is the **Weather=sunny** and **Players=yes**. If it is satisfied, then the **Soccer=yes** is considered possible (assuming that the threshold is lower or equal to **0.95**).

☐ Desire

■ Best Condition

Fig. 5. Conditions for a desire

In Figure 5, we illustrate an example where Soccer=yes is a desire. It has two conditions, which will be evaluated by the agent (it will decide if it believes or not in the conditions). After evaluating these conditions, the agent realizes that Weather=sunny and Players=yes is the best condition. Assuming that conditions might be seen as desires, it is possible to model conditions of conditions through causal relations, giving rise to a multilevel reasoning.

It is important to point out that the desire probability caused by the establishment of the conditions has to be higher than the belief *threshold value* (minimum probability value required to an agent believe that the state will be observed). For example, it would be a waste of time to bring about the conditions Weather=rain and Player=no because they establish a state of world where the desire Soccer=yes become almost impossible. That threshold issue is discussed in detail in the deliberation process section.

Intentions correspond to states of affairs that agents have committed to bring about. This commitment makes the BDI agents to check intentions for incompatibility (mutually exclusive). In our approach, incompatibility is detected when an evidence indicating the achievement of an intention affects negatively other intention by decreasing its chances.

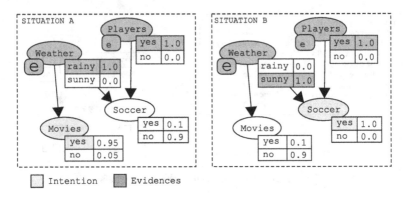

Intention   Evidences

Fig. 6. Example of incompatibility among intentions

Figure 6 shows two independent network situations, where an incompatibility is exemplified. In the situation A, the agent believes that the state `rainy` of `Weather` has been observed. It increases the chances of `Movies=yes` and decreases the chances of `Soccer=yes`. In situation B, the evidence on the state `sunny` causes the opposite. This incompatibility has resulted from different states that depend on mutually exclusive conditions (in this case, `Weather`). Even without an evidence on the `Weather` variable, the achievement of `Soccer=yes` would decrease the chances of `Movies=yes` (first by diagnostic reasoning, from `Soccer` to `Weather`, and then by causal reasoning from `Weather` to `Movies`).

4   Deliberation Process

In the deliberation process BDI agents examine which desires are possible, choose between competing desires, and commit to achieving them. The selection of possible desires done by the `options` function, illustrated in Figure 7, has two parameters: beliefs and intentions. It begins by obtaining the desires (goals), which are defined in the design-time. After that, the `SD` (selected desires) variable is initialized. In the line 5, each unintended desire is checked for its compatibility with the current intentions (`compatible` function call). The next step consists of selecting which desires the agent believes that can be achieved given the current state of world (`believe` function call, line 6). Desires considered compatible are added to the `SD` vector (line 7).

If a desire `d` is refused by the `believe` function, then it is checked by the `parent-options` function (line 10) in order to establish a state of world where that desire `d` become feasible. For example, assume that the desire `Soccer=yes` is refused by the `believe` function. By checking its conditional probability table (see Figure 1), the agent realizes that the degree of belief about `Soccer=yes` goes to 0.95 if the conditions `Weather=sunny` and `Players=yes` are established. The `parent-options` function is capable of establishing conditions of conditions by using the causal relations and conditional probability tables of Bayesian networks. We omit here the algorithm of the `parent-options` function for reasons of space.

```
01  options: (Bel B, Int I) → Des
02      Des D:= get desires;
03      Des SD:=null;
04      for each d ∈ D do
05          if d ∉ I and compatible(B,d,I) then
06              if believe(B,d) then
07                  add d to SD;
08              end-if
09              else
10                  if parent-options(B,I,d) then
11                      add d to SD;
12                  end-if
13              end-else
14          end-if
15      end-for
16      options:=SD;
17  end-options
```

Fig. 7. Function that selects the options (desires)

```
18  believe: (Bel B, Des d) →boolean
19      boolean result:=true;
20      if probability(d,B) < belief threshold then
21          result:=false;
22      end-if
23      believe:=result;
24  end-believe
25
26  compatible:(Bel B, Des D, Int I) →boolean
27      boolean result:=true;
28      simulate achievement of D;
29      for each i ∈ I do
30          if not believe(B,i) then
31              result:=false;
32          end-if
33      end-for
34      undo simulation;
35      compatible:=result;
36  end-compatible
```

Fig. 8. Function to select desires that the agent believes that can be achieved, and function to check desires incompatible with the current intentions

In Figure 8, we show the **believe** and the **compatible** functions. The **believe** function verifies if the computed marginal probability of the desired state is lower than the *belief threshold value*. If it is lower, then the agent does not believe that state can be achieved.

The **compatible** function has three parameters: the beliefs, the desires to be verified and the intentions. The verification for incompatibility begins by simulating a fake hard evidence indicating the occurrence of the desire. It is done by associating the fake evidence with the node state representing that desire, followed by the performance of a probabilistic inference over the Bayesian networks. The intentions affected by the simulated achievement of the desire are verified with the **believe** function. If it returns false (the agent does not believe that the intention can be achieved given the current state of world), the desire is considered incompatible. After simulating the achievement of the desire, the

```
37  filter:(Bel B, Des D, Int I) → Int
38     boolean compatible:=true;
39     sort D ascending by belief probability;
40     for each dn ∈ D do
41        simulate achievement of dn and its desired conditions;
42        for each dm ∈ D do
43           if index(dm) > index(dn) then
44              if not believe(B,dm) then
45                 compatible:=false;
46              end-if
47           end-if
48        end-for
49        undo simulation;
50        if compatible then
51           add dn and its desired conditions to I;
52        end-if
53     end-for
54     filter:=I;
55  filter-end
```

Fig. 9. Filter function that selects intentions from competing desires

changes on the network are undone and the beliefs about the current world situation are reestablished.

In Figure 9, we show the `filter` function. It outputs the agent intentions after choosing between competing desires based on beliefs and current intentions. It begins by sorting the desires from lower to higher computer marginal probability (line 39). Here, we employ the same strategy used to detect incompatibility in the `compatible` function. We simulate the achievement of a desire and verify the remaining ones for incompatibility. Among incompatible desires, we select the one with higher probability according to the sort initially performed.

4.1 Tuning the Agent Behavior

We use the terms cautious and bold to describe the agent behavior in the following three situations inside of the deliberation process: to decide if the agent believes in particular states, to decide if desires are incompatible with intentions and to decide if desires are incompatible among themselves.

The first decision that the agent faces in the deliberation process consists of deciding if it believes that a potential desire can be achieved given the current state of the world. This decision, specified in the `believe` function (Figure 8, line 20), is done by comparing the current value of the computed marginal probability of the potential desire with a *threshold value*. The threshold indicates the minimum value to believe that the potential desired can be achieved. By increasing the threshold value, we obtain a more cautious behavior since the agent will desire only under high degrees of certainty. By decreasing the threshold value, a bolder behavior is obtained.

The last two situations (illustrated in Figure 9 and in Figure 8, respectively) concern with the incompatibility detection. In both cases, the mental states are considered incompatible if the achievement of one affects negatively the achievement of the other by decreasing its chance of success (computed marginal probability). The chance of success is estimated by calling the `believe` function.

But the following question arises: "How significant is this decrease?". It depends on the agent's behavior. A cautious agent will tolerate lower degrees of incompatibility. On the other hand a bold agent will tolerate higher degrees of incompatibility.

Outside the deliberation process, the `believe` function can be used to implement a open-minded agent, since this commitment strategy consists of keeping intentions while the agent believes that it is possible to achieve them. It is worth to point out that the single-minded and the open-minded commitment strategies can be used in the intention selection also. We used the open-minded strategy since the agent has to believe in the state to desire it and consequently to intend it. If we employ a function to verify if the agent believes that the state is impossible, we obtain a single-minded behavior.

5   Related Work

We deal with the integration of two well established areas, namely BDI agency and Bayesian networks. Since the eighties, several significant research concerning these areas have been developed. Among them, we selected the following related ones.

A natural question that arises is: "Why not Influence diagrams [12]?". To address this question we present the following reasons:

- Our approach allows the adjustment of behavior (cautious and bold) in the generation of desires and verification of compatibility among mental states.
- The Influence diagrams represent actions within diagrams, however they are limited in the sense that they require the specification of a predefined sequence of actions. It reminds an embedded means-end reasoning, however without advanced planning features. Our approach enables the usage of different planning techniques since we consider means-end reasoning and deliberation as distinct processes.
- Bayesian networks are quite simpler than Influence diagrams since the last one include the decision and utility concepts and their edges have different semantics (functional, conditional and informational). From the perspective of our deliberation process, it is required to specify the networks and the potential desires.

Concerning uncertainty representation for agency, the related work [5] proposes an architecture for interoperability among Bayesian agents. It specifies an ontology that models the Bayesian network domain, and an agent internal architecture capable of dealing with that ontology. Processes such as Bayesian inference, knowledge manipulation (update and query) and perception handler are proposed. However, this work does not deal with goal-oriented reasoning.

In order to allow the implementation of cognitive agents that can deal with uncertain information, the research developed by [1] investigates the usage of

Dempster-Shafer theory to incorporate uncertainty in BDI-type agent programming languages. The authors discuss how uncertain beliefs can be represented and reasoned with, and how they can be updated with uncertain information. Despite the fact that this work provides a formal basis to represent uncertain mental states, it does not focus on the deliberation process under uncertainty.

The work developed by Rao and Georgeff [6] provides an unifying framework for BDI agents by bringing together theory, systems and applications. The authors transform decision trees, and appropriate deliberation functions, to an equivalent model that represents beliefs, desires and intentions as separate accessibility relations over sets of possible worlds. The resulting model contains two types of information, represented by the probabilities across worlds (belief-accessibility relation) and the payoffs assigned to paths (desire-accessibility relation). The deliberation function, such as maximizing expected utility, selects one or more best sequences of actions, which correspond to the agent's intentions. The approach adopted by [6] differentiates from ours in the sense that they employ the expected utility maximization to select actions. We employ uncertain beliefs (variable states and conditional probabilities) to select intentions and check for incompatibities among mental states.

BayesJason [13] is an extension of the Jason [14] tool that addresses the integration of Bayesian networks and BDI agents. Jason is a java-based AgentSpeak(L) [15] interpreter. The BayesJason implements a probabilistic module for Jason, allowing BDI agents to act on uncertain environments. To allow the programming of Bayesian networks within the Jason, the AgentSpeak(L) grammar was modified and extended. Although integrating Bayesian networks and BDI model, the BayesJason uses the Bayesian networks in the context of the intention selection (plans in the AgentSpeak(L) systems). It does not use that knowledge representation to verify the compatibility among mental states, neither to bring about states of world where desires can be achieved.

6   Conclusion and Future Work

We have presented a BDI deliberation process over Bayesian networks, interpreting the mental states through that probabilistic knowledge representation. We focused on the deliberation, leaving outside the research scope issues such as performance measurements, methodology of development, uncertainty on perceptions, and planning.

Our proposal of compatibility verification eliminates the necessity of an explicit specification of which mental states are incompatible. By using causal relations and conditional probabilities, the agent infers the degree of incompatibility. Actually, the incompatibilities are implicitly specified in the network, for example in the desires with mutually exclusive conditions.

It was highlighted which decisions inside the deliberation can be adjusted to obtain different behaviors under uncertainty, enabling the employment of other Artificial Intelligence techniques, including affective computing [16], by future work to compute the threshold values.

Despite the fact that the deliberation does not take into account the meaning of the chance variables, that process is strongly dependent of the conditional probabilities and causal relations. It enables the reuse of that process, but it leaves the application dependent on the designer knowledge and know-how, what happens in other agent development frameworks.

We choose to represent intentions separated from plans. By this we mean that our intentions correspond to states of affairs (Intentional contents) instead of sequences of actions that lead the agent to those states. This choice fits exactly in the Wooldridge's loop, which distinguished the notions of deliberation and means-end reasoning. However, we believe that the serial execution of deliberation and means-end reasoning limits the model in the sense that the agent will have to wait the plan function call to realize that some states can not be achieved. For example, our agent would have to wait for the plan function call to realize that it can not change the weather. Previous work, including PRS-like systems [17], propose plan libraries in order to guarantee the agent reactivity. The same plan libraries could be employed just to check action plans instead of reacting.

Future work on the deliberation process improvement is threefold. The first research direction consists of experimenting different AI techniques to implement the threshold function. Currently, we are working on the modification of the Tileworld [18] testbed to experiment our model in that uncertain domain. The second one is concerned with modifications on the control loop, covering commitment strategies, intention reconsideration and scheduling between deliberation and means-end reasoning. The third research direction consists of integrating the Bayesian network ontology [5] in our agent architecture. This integration will make possible to perform an ontological reasoning over the knowledge representation (Bayesian networks) and over the domain knowledge (concepts associated with chance variables, corresponding to the knowledge about the application domain).

References

1. Kwisthout, J., Dastani, M.: Modelling uncertainty in agent programming. In: Baldoni, M., Endriss, U., Omicini, A., Torroni, P. (eds.) DALT 2005. LNCS, vol. 3904, pp. 17–32. Springer, Heidelberg (2006)
2. Schut, M.C., Wooldridge, M., Parsons, S.: Reasoning about intentions in uncertain domains. In: Benferhat, S., Besnard, P. (eds.) ECSQARU 2001. LNCS, vol. 2143, pp. 84–95. Springer, Heidelberg (2001)
3. Tenenbaum, J.B., Griffiths, T.L., Kemp, C.: Theory-based bayesian models of inductive learning and reasoning. Trends in Cognitive Sciences 10(7), 309–318 (2006)
4. Baker, C., Tenenbaum, J.B., Saxe, R.: Bayesian models of human action understanding. In: Neural Information Processing Systems, pp. 99–106 (2005)
5. Santos, E.R., Fagundes, M.S., Vicari, R.M.: An ontology-based approch to interoperability for Bayesian agents. In: Proceedings of the International Conference on Autonomous Agents and Multiagent Systems, Honolulu, Hawaii, pp. 1304–1306. ACM Press, New York (2007)

6. Rao, A.S., Georgeff, M.P.: BDI-agents: from theory to practice. In: Proceedings of the 1st International Conference on Multiagent Systems, San Francisco, pp. 312–319 (1995)
7. Ambroszkiewicz, S., Komar, J.: A model of BDI-agent in game-theoretic framework. In: Model Age Workshop, pp. 8–19 (1997)
8. Kinny, D., Georgeff, M.: Commitment and effectiveness of situated agents. In: International Joint Conference on Artificial Intelligence, pp. 82–88 (1991)
9. Pearl, J.: Belief networks revisited. Artificial Intelligence 59(1-2), 49–56 (1993)
10. Jensen, F.V.: Bayesian Networks and Decision Graphs. Springer, Heidelberg (2001)
11. Wooldridge, M.: Reasoning about Rational Agents. Intelligent Robots and Autonomous Agents. MIT Press, Cambridge (2000)
12. Cowell, R.G., Dawid, A.P., Lauritzen, S.L., Spiegelhalter, D.J.: Probabilistic Networks and Expert Systems. Springer, Heidelberg (1999)
13. Calcin, O.G.P.: BayesJason: Bayesian networks and Jason interpreter. In: Iberoamerican Workshop on Multi-Agent Systems (2006)
14. Bordini, R.H., Fisher, M., Visser, W., Wooldridge, M.J.: Verifiable multi-agent programs. In: Dastani, M., Dix, J., El Fallah-Seghrouchni, A. (eds.) PROMAS 2003. LNCS, vol. 3067, pp. 72–89. Springer, Heidelberg (2004)
15. Rao, A.S.: Agentspeak(l): Bdi agents speak out in a logical computable language. In: Perram, J., Van de Velde, W. (eds.) MAAMAW 1996. LNCS, vol. 1038, pp. 42–55. Springer, Heidelberg (1996)
16. Picard, R.A.: Affective Computing. MIT Press, Cambridge (1997)
17. Georgeff, M.P., Ingrand, F.F.: Decision-making in an embedded reasoning system. In: Proceedings of the 11th International Joint Conference on Artificial Intelligence, Detroit, MI, pp. 972–978 (August 1989)
18. Pollack, M.E., Ringuette, M.: Introducing the tileworld: Experimentally evaluating agent architectures. In: Proceedings of the 8th National Conference on Artificial Intelligence, pp. 183–189 (1990)

An Asymmetric Protocol for Argumentation Games in Defeasible Logic

Jenny Eriksson Lundström[1], Guido Governatori[2],
Subhasis Thakur[2], and Vineet Padmanabhan[3]

[1] Dept. of Information Science, Computer Science Division, Uppsala University, Sweden
[2] School of ITEE, The University of Queensland, Brisbane, Australia
[3] Dept. of Computer & Information Sciences, University of Hyderabad, India
jenny.eriksson@dis.uu.se, {guido,subhasis}@itee.uq.edu.au,
vineetcs@uohyd.ernet.in

Abstract. Agent interactions where the agents hold conflicting goals could be modelled as adversarial argumentation games. In many real-life situations (e.g., criminal litigation, consumer legislation), due to ethical, moral or other principles governing interaction, the burden of proof, i.e., which party is to lose if the evidence is balanced [22], is *a priori* fixed to one of the parties. Analogously, when resolving disputes in a heterogeneous agent-system the unequal importance of different agents for carrying out the overall system goal need to be accounted for. In this paper we present an asymmetric protocol for an adversarial argumentation game in Defeasible Logic, suggesting Defeasible Logic as a general representation formalism for argumentation games modelling agent interactions.

1 Introduction

Adversarial situations arise when agents in pursuit of their goals interact with other agents pursuing goals of a conflicting nature. In a setting where issues need to be resolved, the agent interaction could be modelled as an adversarial argumentation game. Argumentation games are defeasible, meaning that an argument put forward by one of the agents in support of a conclusion could be defeated by contrary evidence and arguments put forward by the other agent. Thus, the agents are to resolve the dispute by putting forward the arguments that will enable the best outcome for their cases. Using a symmetrical protocol an argumentation game between homogeneous (equally strong) parties could be modelled. However, as in many real-life settings, also in agent systems disputes arise where the claims of the agents involved in the interaction (e.g., regarding distribution of a scarce resource) are of unequal importance to the overall goal of the agent system, and thus need to be handled accordingly. In addition, as in many real-life situations the evidence presented by the parties of a dispute may be inconclusive and the accompanying arguments incoherent. Thus, a majority of the disputes has to be resolved by higher-level principles guiding the interaction. One important principle is referred to as the burden of proof, *cf. e.g.* [22].

To accommodate for a correct outcome of argumentation games in heterogeneous agent systems, we present an asymmetric protocol for adversarial argumentation games.

A. Ghose, G. Governatori, and R. Sadananda (Eds.): PRIMA 2007, LNAI 5044, pp. 219–231, 2009.
© Springer-Verlag Berlin Heidelberg 2009

The paper is organized as follows: In Section 2 we present argumentation games and their setup. In Section 3 we highlight the most relevant features of defeasible logic. We discuss the formalization of argumentation games using defeasible logic as presented in [25] in Section 4. Section 5 presents the asymmetrical protocol for argumentation games. We use a criminal litigation setting to illustrate and discuss some of the benefits of the model. Section 6 presents some related work. In Section 7 we conclude.

2   Argumentation Games

Consider an adversarial argumentation (dialogue) game as an interaction between two parties, the *Proponent* and the *Opponent*. The two parties debate over a topic. Each equipped with a set of arguments the parties take turn in putting forward a subset of these arguments, i.e., *move*, with the sole purpose of justifying their claim. The game is governed by a protocol for admissible moves and the winning conditions. For the proponent a basic protocol for an argumentation game is that the arguments of the move attack the previous move of the adversary, and that the main claim follows from the arguments assessed as currently valid. For the opponent goes that an admissible move has to attack the previous move of the adversary, and that the main claim is not derivable. Even though more complex winning criteria could be devised, by a basic protocol, a player wins the argumentation game when the other party is out of admissible moves.

3   Defeasible Logic

Defeasible Logic (DL) [18,1,2] is a simple, flexible, rule based non-monotonic formalism able to capture different and sometimes incompatible facets of non-monotonic reasoning [3], and efficient and powerful implementations have been proposed [17,12].

Knowledge in DL can be represented in two ways: facts and rules. *Facts* are represented either in form of states of affairs (literal and modal literal) and actions that have been performed. Facts are represented by predicates. For example, "Tweety is a penguin" is represented by $Penguin(Tweety)$. A *rule* describes the relationship between a set of literals (premises) and a literal (conclusion), and we can specify how strong the relationship is. As usual rules allow us to derive new conclusions given a set of premises. We distinguish between *strict rules*, *defeasible rules* and *defeaters* represented, respectively, by expressions of the form $A_1, \ldots, A_n \rightarrow B$, $A_1, \ldots, A_n \Rightarrow B$ and $A_1, \ldots, A_n \rightsquigarrow B$, where $A_1, \ldots, A_n$ is a possibly empty set of prerequisites (causes) and B is the conclusion (effect) of the rule. We only consider rules that are essentially propositional. Rules containing free variables are interpreted as the set of their ground instances.

Strict rules are rules in the classical sense: whenever the premises are indisputable then so is the conclusion. Thus they can be used for definitional clauses. An example of a strict rule is "Penguins are birds", formally: $Penguin(X) \rightarrow Bird(X)$.

Defeasible rules are rules that can be defeated by contrary evidence. An example of such a rule is "Birds usually fly": $Bird(X) \Rightarrow Fly(X)$. The idea is that if we know that X is a bird, we may conclude that X can fly *unless other evidence suggest she may not*.

Defeaters are a special kind of rules. They are used to prevent conclusions, not to support them. For example: $Heavy(X) \leadsto \neg Fly(X)$. This rule states that if something is heavy then it might not fly. This rule can prevent the derivation of a "fly" conclusion. On the other hand it cannot be used to support a "not fly" conclusion.

DL is a "skeptical" non-monotonic logic, meaning that it does not support contradictory conclusions. Instead DL seeks to resolve conflicts. In cases where there is some support for concluding A but also support for concluding $\neg A$, DL does not conclude either of them (thus the name "skeptical"). If the support for A has priority over the support for $\neg A$ then A is concluded. No conclusion can be drawn from conflicting rules in DL unless these rules are prioritized. The *superiority relation* among rules is used to define priorities among rules, that is, where one rule may override the conclusion of another rule. For example, given the defeasible rules

$$r : Bird(X) \Rightarrow Fly(X) \qquad r' : Penguin(X) \Rightarrow \neg Fly(X)$$

which contradict one another, no conclusive decision can be made about whether a Tweety can fly or not. But if we introduce a superiority relation $\succ$ with $r' \succ r$, then we can indeed conclude that Tweety cannot fly since it is a penguin.

We now give a short informal presentation of how conclusions are drawn in DL. Let D be a theory in DL (i.e., a collection of facts, rules and a superiority relation). A *conclusion* of D is a tagged literal and can have one of the following four forms:

$+\Delta q$ meaning that q is definitely provable in D (*i.e.*, using only facts and strict rules).
$-\Delta q$ meaning that we have proved that q is not definitely provable in D.
$+\partial q$ meaning that q is defeasibly provable in D.
$-\partial q$ meaning that we have proved that q is not defeasibly provable in D.

Strict derivations are obtained by forward chaining of strict rules, while a defeasible conclusion p can be derived if there is a rule whose conclusion is p, whose prerequisites (antecedent) have either already been proven or given in the case at hand (i.e., facts), and any stronger rule whose conclusion is $\neg p$ has prerequisites that fail to be derived.

Formally a DL theory (as formalized by [5]) is a structure $D = (F, R, \succ)$ where F is a finite set of factual premises, R a finite set of rules, and $\succ$ a superiority relation on R. Given a set R of rules, we denote the set of all strict rules in R by R_s, the set of strict and defeasible rules in R by R_{sd}, the set of defeasible rules in R by R_d, and the set of defeaters in R by R_{dft}. $R[q]$ denotes the set of rules in R with consequent q. In the following $\sim p$ denotes the complement of p, that is, $\sim p$ is $\neg q$ if $p = q$, and $\sim p$ is q if p is $\neg q$. For a rule r we will use $A(r)$ to indicate the body or antecedent of the rule and $C(r)$ for the head or consequent of the rule. A rule r consists of its antecedent $A(r)$ (written on the left; $A(r)$ may be omitted if it is the empty set) which is a finite set of literals, an arrow, and its consequent $C(r)$ which is a literal.

Provability is based on the concept of a derivation (or proof) in D. A derivation is a finite sequence $P = (P(1), \ldots, P(n))$ of tagged literals. Each tagged literal satisfies some proof conditions. A proof condition corresponds to the inference rules corresponding to one of the four kinds of conclusions we have mentioned above. $P(1..i)$ denotes the initial part of the sequence P of length i. Here we state the conditions for strictly and defeasibly derivable conclusions (see [1] for the full presentation of the logic):

If $P(i+1) = +\Delta q$ then
    (1) $q \in F$, or
    (2) $r \in R_s[q]$, $\forall a \in A(r) : +\Delta a \in P(1..i)$.

If $P(i+1) = +\partial q$ then
    (1) $+\Delta q \in P(1..i)$, or
    (2) (2.1) $\exists r \in R_{sd}[q] \forall a \in A(r) : +\partial a \in P(1..i)$ and
         (2.2) $-\Delta \sim q \in P(1..i)$ and
         (2.3) $\forall s \in R[\sim q]$ either
                (2.3.1) $\exists a \in A(s) : -\partial a \in P(1..i)$ or
                (2.3.2) $\exists t \in R_{sd}[q] \; \forall a \in A(t) : +\partial a \in P(1..i)$ and $t \succ s$.

4   Dialogue Games in Defeasible Logic – A Symmetric Protocol

In [25] we presented a model for an argumentation game in DL using a basic symmetric protocol for adversarial dispute. We parse a dialogue into defeasible rules utilizing time of the dialogue as the time of the rule. In order to resolve the dispute, the agents take turn in putting forward arguments from a private knowledge base, i.e., a finite set of (defeasible) arguments in support of their claim. At each time step, an agent is allowed to put forward any of its arguments (rules) that has precedence over any contradictory defeasible rule of the previous steps.

In this symmetric protocol we assume that if at time t_2 we have a *valid* rule $w \in R_{sd}^{t_2}$ which contradicts a defeasible rule $s \in R_d^{t_1}$ of time t_1 and $t_2 > t_1$ then the strength of w is greater than s. The expression $a@t$ denotes that the expression a being put forward or upgraded at time t.

$$(w \succ s)@t \text{ iff } (w,s) \in \succ \text{ or } w \in R^{t'}[P], s \in R^t[\neg P] \text{ where } t' < t$$

A common public knowledge base holds the common knowledge, which is a theory in defeasible logic. The sets of agreed common knowledge construct the theories $T_1, T_2, \ldots, T_n$ respectively as the undefeated defeasible rules from the previously adjacent step are strengthened into strict rules and the defeated defeasible rules are removed. Thus, if P is the conclusion of a defeasible rule of the adjacent previous step t_{i-1}, regardless of its origin, the agreed common knowledge is created by strengthening the status of rules from defeasible to strict in the adjacent next step t_{i+1} if:

$$\exists r \in R_d^{t'}[P] \; t' < t \; \forall t'' : t' < t'' < t \; R_{sd}^{t''}[\neg P] = \emptyset \text{ and } \forall a \in A(r) : +\Delta a@t$$

The proof procedures of the defeasible logic are applied to the critical literal at each time step, thus determining the burden of proof and the outcome of the argumentation game. The first theory $T_1 = (\{\}, R_d^1, \succ)$ is created from the arguments (ARG_1) presented by the first player, and the second theory $T_2 = (\{\}, R_d^2, \succ)$ is created through modifications of T_1 by the arguments (ARG_2) presented by player 2. The transition rules from the first theory to the second theory were devised as follows:

1. If $r \in R_d^1$ and $\forall s \in ARG_2, \neg C(s) \neq C(r) \wedge \neg C(s) \notin A(r)$, then $r \in R_d^2$.
2. All rules of ARG_2 are added to T_2 as defeasible rule. Here we assume that ARG_2 is valid and that a valid argument, by the above defined precedence relations, is stronger than any contradictory argument of the previous step.

At time n, $n > 2$ theory T_n is created through modification of T_{n-1} by arguments (ARG_n) of the player who has to play at that step. The rules for transition from T_{n-1} to T_n are

1. If $r \in R_s^{n-1}$ then $r \in R_s^n$.
2. If $r \in R_d^{n-2}$ and $\forall s \in ARG_{n-1}, \neg C(s) \neq C(r) \wedge \neg C(s) \notin A(r)$, then $r \in R_s^n$; otherwise $r \notin R^n$. Here we should note that the player will not oppose its previous argument. Thus, all unchallenged rules of time $n - 2$ are upgraded as strict rules at time n.
3. If $r \in R_d^{n-1}$ and $\forall s \in ARG_{n-1}, \neg C(s) \neq C(r) \wedge \neg C(s) \notin A(r)$, then $r \in R_d^n$. Unchallenged defeasible rules of time $n - 1$ are added to T_n as defeasible rules.
4. All rules of ARG_{n-1} are added to T_n as defeasible rules. Here we assume that ARG_{n-1} is valid and that a valid argument, by the above defined precedence relations, is stronger than any contradictory argument of previous step.

The winning criteria for a basic game are devised as an agent to be winning if the claim q is definitely proven $+\Delta q$ at any time step. If an agent at any step of the game proves $+\partial A$ the burden of production as well as persuasion of $-\partial A$, or $-\Delta A$ or $+\Delta \neg A$ or $+\partial \neg A$ are placed on the other party.

Using a symmetric protocol, a dispute between equally strong parties could be modelled as an argumentation game and resolved accordingly. However, in many situations ethical, moral or other reasons (cf., e.g., criminal litigation[1]) advocate for special concerns to be taken on behalf of one of the parties. To accommodate such settings, asymmetric protocols are required.

5 Dialogue Games in Defeasible Logic – An Asymmetric Protocol

Here we present an asymmetric model for adversarial argumentation games between two parties: the *Prosecutor* and the *Defendant*. As in the symmetric protocol, we parse the dialogue into defeasible rules utilizing time of the dialogue as the time of the rule. Each agent has at its disposition a private knowledge base consisting of a finite set of defeasible arguments in support of their claim (the critical literal). Initiated by the prosecutor, the parties take turns in presenting their arguments. At each time step the proof procedures are applied to the critical literal. The outcome of an argumentation game is determined by the final stage of the game, whilst the intermediate stages are illustrating the situation for the current situation. For common sense reasons, as an argument put forward cannot be revoked from impacting the argumentation, we do not allow for backtracking.

The winning criteria for a basic game are devised as an agent to be winning if the claim q is definitely proven $+\Delta q$ at any time step. However, analogously to the burden

---

[1] "Homo praesumitur bonus donec probetur malus" lat: Innocent until proven guilty. The adoption of this presumption of innocence in many national statutes results in that the defendant of a criminal litigation only is required to at most produce an exception to the accusation.

of persuasion, which imposes a requirement of providing a justified (i.e., strongly de-feating) argument for the issue on which the burden rests (based on rebutting defeat) [22], we require of the prosecutor a strong defeat of any argument (including the criti-cal literal) presented by the defendant. Thus, if the prosecutor at any step of the game proves $+\partial A$, the prosecutor still holds the burden to produce proof of $+\Delta A$ in order to win. For the defendant only a burden of production of an exception $+\partial\neg A$, (being subsumed by $-\partial A$, $-\Delta A$ or $+\Delta\neg A$) is imposed. If the defendant at any step of the game proves the exception $+\partial\neg A$, the burden of persuasion placed on the prosecutor necessitates the proof of $+\Delta A$ (including $-\partial\neg A$) in order for the prosecutor to win.

In the symmetric protocol, regardless of its origin, time brings strengthening of un-defeated rules from defeasible to strict. Here we require that the strengthening of rules originating from the prosecutor only occurs when the rule could be derived from argu-ments already put forward by the defendant. In other cases, undefeated rules from the previously adjacent step presented by the prosecutor remain as defeasible rules in the common knowledge base. Defeated rules are removed at each step. As we do not al-low the prosecutor to repeat arguments and the arguments put forward have to strongly defeat any arguments put forward by the defendant, the game will terminate.

In the symmetric protocol at each step any agent in turn to move can present an argument if its strength is stronger than contradictory defeasible rules of the previous steps. In our asymmetrical distribution of the burden of proof, the defendant is allowed to present an argument that merely weakly defeats the argument of the prosecutor of the previous steps. As consequence the defendant could remain with the same argument for fulfilling his burden of production of an assumption $+\partial\neg A$ as response to $+\partial A$.

The strength of an argument is determined by either previously known superiority relationships or validity of that rule. Adhering to the above presented syntax, we write $y_i \in R_x^{t_j}|x \in \{d,s,sd\}$. Here y is a rule identifier with the subscripts $i \in \{p,d\}$ where p means that the origin of the rule is the prosecutor and d means that the origin of the rule is the defendant. In the following, unless needed, the indexing is left out for readability reasons.

If $\forall r \in R_s^{t_i}[q]$ and $\forall s \in R_d^{t_i}[\neg q]$, then $(r \succ s)@t_i$

We consider that the rule strength of a strict rule is greater than the rule strength of a defeasible rule.

$(w_d \succ s_p)@t$ iff $(w_d, s_p) \in \succ$ or $s_p \in R^{t'}[P]$ and $w_d \in R^{t''}[\neg P]$, where $t' < t'' < t$

For defeasible rules presented by *the defendant* we simply assume that if at time t_2 we have a *valid* rule $w_d \in R^{t_2}$ which contradicts a defeasible rule $s_p \in R^{t_1}$ of time t_1 and $t_2 > t_1$ then the strength of w_d is greater than s_p. This fits well with the burden of persuasion being placed on the prosecutor. We utilize defeasible logic to determine strength of a new rule presented by the players.

$(s_p \succ w_d)@t$ iff $(s_p, w_d) \in \succ$ or $w_d \in R^{t'}[\neg P]$ and $s_p \in R^{t''}[P]$ and $\forall a \in A(s) :$
$+\Delta a@t$, where $t' < t'' < t$
else
$(w_d \succ s_p)@t$ iff $(w_d, s_p) \in \succ$ or $w_d \in R^{t'}[\neg P]$ and $s_p \in R^{t''}[P]$ and $\exists a \in A(s) :$
$-\Delta a@t$, where $t' < t'' < t$

As the prosecutor holds the burden of persuasion, we assume that unless the rule priority is set, that only if at time t_2 we have a *valid* rule $s_p \in R^{t_2}$ which contradicts a defeasible rule $w_d \in R^{t_1}$ of time t_1 and $t_2 > t_1$ and the rule presented by the prosecutor *strongly defeats* the rule of the defendant then the strength of the argument s_p of the prosecutor is *greater* than the argument of the defendant w_d. In all other situations the opposite goes, thus rendering the strength of the argument s_p of the prosecutor *weaker* than the argument of the defendant w_d.

In this asymmetric protocol the criteria for strengthening the rule strength of a defeasible rule to a strict rule are devised as follows:

$$\exists r \in R_d^{t'}[P] \; t' < t \; \forall t'' : t' < t'' < t \; R_{sd}^{t''}[\neg P] = \emptyset \text{ and } \forall a \in A(r) : +\Delta a @ t$$

If P is the conclusion of a defeasible rule $r \in R_d^{t'}$ of the adjacent previous step t' and the rule was presented by the *defendant* then we can upgrade the rule status from defeasible to strict in the next time step t if no counterarguments are presented by the prosecutor at time t''. For $t^{Even} < t^{Odd} < t$

$$\exists r \in R_d^{t^{Odd}}[P], R_{sd}^{t^{Even''}}[\neg P] = \emptyset \text{ and } \forall a \in A(r) : +\Delta a @ t \text{ and}$$
$$1) \; \exists r \in R_{ds}^{t^{Even}}[P] \text{ and } \forall a \in A(r) : +\Delta a @ t, \text{ or}$$
$$2) \; +\partial[P] @ t \, from R_{ds}^{t^{Even}}$$

However, if P is the conclusion of a defeasible rule $r \in R_d^{t^{Odd}}$ of the adjacent previous step t^{Odd} and the rule was presented by the *prosecutor* then we can upgrade the rule status from defeasible to strict in next step only in the case of no counterarguments being presented by the defendant at the adjacently following time t^{Even} *and* the defeasible (or strict) rule r has been put forward by the defendant *or* the conclusion P follows defeasibly from the defeasible or strict rules $R_{ds}^{t^{Even}}$ presented by the defendant at the adjacently following time t^{Even}.

An argumentation game is initiated at time 1 by the prosecutor putting forward arguments (ARG_1) from its private knowledge into the common knowledge base to prove its claim (critical literal) A. As the parties take turns in presenting their arguments, at time 2 the defendant agent responds to the accusations. We allow arguments in the form of valid defeasible rules being as strong or stronger than at least some rules of theory T_1. The common sets of argument construct the theories $T_1, T_2, T_3, \ldots, T_n$ respectively where the subscripts indicate the time at which the common sets of argument are constructed. As all arguments in the private knowledge base of the agents are defeasible, in the first two theories the common set of arguments consists only of defeasible rules from both time 1 and time 2, according to the following transition rules:

Let the first theory $T_1 = (\{\}, R_d^1, \succ)$ be created from arguments (ARG_1), the operative plea of prosecutor, and the second theory $T_2 = (\{\}, R_d^2, \succ)$ be created through modifications of T_1 by arguments (ARG_2) from the defendant. Now the transition rules from the first theory T_1 to the second theory T_2 are as follows:

1. If $r \in R_d^1$ and $\forall s \in ARG_2, \neg C(s) \neq C(r) \wedge \neg C(s) \notin A(r)$, then $r \in R_d^2$.
2. All rules of (ARG_2) are added to T_2 as defeasible rules. Under the assumption of (ARG_2) be valid and that, by the above defined precedence relations, any valid argument from the defendant is stronger than its contradictory argument (from the

prosecutor) of the adjacent previous step. As all unchallenged rules of the prosecutor are added to T_2 as defeasible rules T_2 now consists of all unchallenged rules of the prosecutor and all arguments (ARG_2) of the defendant.

At time $n = 2m + 1$ $(m > 0)$, theory T_n is created through modification of T_{n-1} by arguments (ARG_n) of the prosecutor. Accounting for the heterogeneity of the parties we capture the asymmetrical burden of proof by the following rules for transition from theories T_{n-1} to T_n:

1. If $r \in R_d^1$ and $\forall s \in ARG_{n-1}, \neg C(s) \neq C(r) \wedge \neg C(s) \notin A(r)$, and 1) $r \in R_d^{n-1}$ or 2) $R_d^{n-1} \vdash C(r)$, then $r \in R_s^n$.
2. If $r \in R_d^{n-2}$ and $\forall s \in ARG_{n-1}, \neg C(s) \neq C(r) \wedge \neg C(s) \notin A(r)$, then $r \in R_d^n$. Here we should note that, in contrast to the symmetric protocol, even though the defendant has not actively challenged these arguments and the prosecutor will not oppose its previous argument by the rules of the game, we find it to be a too strong presumption to strengthen the rule status of these rules to strict rules. Thus, unless the argument is acknowledged by the defendant (see transition rule 1.), all unchallenged rules of time $n - 2$ of the prosecutor remain as defeasible rules at time n.
3. If $r \in R_d^{n-1}$ and $\forall s \in ARG_n, \neg C(s) \neq C(r) \wedge \neg C(s) \notin A(r)$, then $r \in R_d^n$. All unchallenged defeasible rules of time $n - 1$ (originating from the defendant) are added as defeasible rules at time n.
4. If $r \in R_d^{n-1}$ and $\forall s \in ARG_n, \neg C(s) = C(r) \wedge \neg C(s) \notin A(r)$, and $r \succeq s$ then $r \in R_d^3$. For removal is required that all rules of the defendant have to be strongly defeated by the prosecutor. Thus, also the defeasible rules of time $n - 1$ (originating from the defendant) of equal or stronger strength are added as defeasible rules at time n.
5. If $r \in ARG_n$ and $\forall s \in R_d^{n-1}, \neg C(s) \neq C(r) \wedge \neg C(s) \notin A(r)$, then $r \in R_d^n$. All unchallenged rules of (ARG_n) are added to T_n as defeasible rules.
6. If $r \in ARG_n$ and $\forall s \in R_d^{n-1}, \neg C(s) = C(r) \wedge \neg C(s) \notin A(r)$ and $r \succeq s$, then $r \in R_d^n$. All rules of (ARG_n) that are of higher priority, i.e., strongly defeat the arguments of the defendant are added to T_n as defeasible rules. Here due to the burden of production of the prosecutor, all arguments added are required to either be unchallenged or to strongly defeat all previous arguments of the defendant. This way, by putting forward new arguments, the prosecutor could strengthen its claim.

As a result T_n consists of the unchallenged defeasible rules of T_{n-2} of the prosecutor, the unchallenged defeasible rules and the rules of by T_{n-1} of the defendant that are challenged by (ARG_n) but found equally strong or stronger, and the unchallenged defeasible rules of the prosecutor from (ARG_n).

At time $n = 2m$ $(m > 1)$, theory T_n is created through modification of T_{n-1} by arguments (ARG_n) of the defendant. The transitions from T_{n-1} to T_n are devised as follows:

1. If $r \in R_d^{n-1}$ and $\forall s \in ARG_n, \neg C(s) \neq C(r) \wedge \neg C(s) \notin A(r)$, then $r \in R_s^n$. The defendant will not oppose its previous argument by the rules of the game. Thus, all the unchallenged defeasible rules R_d^{n-1} are upgraded as strict rules, i.e., facts, at time n.
2. If $r \in R_d^{n-1}$ and $\forall s \in ARG_n, \neg C(s) \neq C(r) \wedge \neg C(s) \notin A(r)$, then $r \in R_d^n$. All unchallenged defeasible rules R_d^{n-1} are added as defeasible rules at time n. As already stated, the defendant cannot challenge her own rules presented in R_d^{n-1}.

3. All rules of (ARG_n) are added to T_n as defeasible rules. In contrast to arguments, e.g., (ARG_{n-1}) originating from the prosecutor, as (ARG_n) originates from the defendant we merely require that all rules of (ARG_n) are valid and at least as strong (or stronger) than any of its contradictory arguments presented by the prosecutor.

An Example – Presumption of Innocence. The asymmetric model of argumentation game defeasible logic is illustrated by elaboration on the example of [25]. Consider a particular argumentation game between the prosecutor Alice and the defendant Bob. Alice is trying to convict Bob by proving A and Bob is claiming $\neg A$. At each step they maintain a current set of rules (CR_t, where t is the time). Here a rule consists of its name $R'i$ (where $R'i$ indicates that the rule belongs to the current set CR_t as opposed to the rules present in the private knowledge bases of the parties denoted by R_i), its antecedent $A(r)$, which is a finite set of literals, an arrow, its consequent $C(r)$, which is a literal and $@t_x|x \in \{1,2,3,\ldots,n\}$ denotes the time of the rule, which is updated at each step. Alice initiates the game at time t_1 by presenting her first move as

$$R1 : \emptyset \Rightarrow B \qquad R2 : B \Rightarrow A$$

This will generate two defeasible rules as $R'1(\emptyset \Rightarrow B)@t_1$, $R'2(B \Rightarrow A)@t_1$. Thus at time t_1 $CR_{t_1}=[R'1, R'2]$ and we can prove $+\partial A@t_1$. Now at next time point, Bob gets its chance to disprove A. At time t_2, Bob presents the following argument,

$$R3 : \emptyset \Rightarrow D \qquad R4 : D \Rightarrow \neg A$$

This will generate two new defeasible rules as $R'3(\emptyset \Rightarrow D)@t_2$ $R'4(D \Rightarrow \neg A)@t_2$. Now, Bob only attacks $R'2$ presented by Alice at previous step by $R'4$ and $R'2$ is removed from CR_{t_2}. Note that as $t_2 > t_1$, the strength of $R'4$ is greater than $R'2$ according to the strength determination rule for the defendant. At time t_2, $R'1$ remains unchallenged but as this rule is not utilized even as a premise in the reasoning of Bob it does not commit Bob to this rule, (leaving Bob the possibility to dismiss this rule by contesting it at a later time or Alice to present evidence to strengthen this rule by the strength determination rule). Thus, the rule remain in CR_{t_2} as $R'1(\emptyset \Rightarrow B)@t_2$. This is in contrast to the symmetric protocol where $R'1$ as unchallenged is changed to a strict rule $R'1(\emptyset \rightarrow B)@t_2$ (a fact) regardless of its origin. Note that we change the time stamp of the rule from t_1 to t_2 to indicate that it is member of CR_{t_2} at time t_2. Thus, $CR_{t_2} =[R'1, R'3, R'4]$. The proof at time t_2 is $+\partial \neg A$ (which implies that we also have $-\Delta A$ as the latter rule $R'4$ is stronger than $R'2$ in accordance to the first strength determination rule.

Next at time t_3, in order to defeat the arguments presented by Bob, Alice presents the following arguments:

$$R5 : B \Rightarrow \neg D \qquad R6 : \emptyset \Rightarrow E \qquad R7 : E \Rightarrow A$$

So the translated defeasible rules are $R'5(B \Rightarrow \neg D)@t_3$, $R'6(\emptyset \Rightarrow E)@t_3$, $R'7(E \Rightarrow A)@t_3$. Now the CR_{t_3} is $[R'1, R'3, R'4, R'6]$ as the rule $R'4$ is stronger than $R'7$ and the rule $R'3$ is stronger than $R'5$ according to the transition rule as neither the argument $R'7$ nor $R'5$ can strongly defeat $R'4$ or $R'3$ respectively and thus they are removed. So the proof at this time point remain $+\partial \neg A$. If Alice cannot present any additional arguments strongly defeating $R'4$ in the next step the rule $R'4$ is strengthened into a strict rule resulting in the proof of $+\Delta \neg A$. Thus, in contrast to the symmetric protocol example where Alice wins the game as she were able to upgrade the defeasible rules supporting the proof of $+\partial A$ by use of the rule priority assumption in 5, she would need the rule to be strongly defeated as e.g by addition of a rule $R'i : E \Rightarrow \neg D$ to prevent the rule $R'4$ from being strengthened into a strict rule at time t_4. As this is not the case, Bob wins the game at time t_4 and is acquitted from the criminal charge of A.

Another Example – Beyond Reasonable Doubt. Consider a second argumentation game between the prosecutor Alice and the defendant Bob. Alice is still trying to convict Bob by proving A and Bob is claiming $\neg A$. Again Alice initiates the game at time t_1 by presenting her first move as

$$R1 : \emptyset \Rightarrow B \qquad R2 : F \Rightarrow A$$

This will generate two defeasible rules as $R'1(\emptyset \Rightarrow B)@t_1$, $R'2(F \Rightarrow A)@t_1$. Thus at time t_1 $CR_{t_1} = [R'1, R'2]$ and we have proof $+\partial A@t_1$. Now at next time point, Bob gets its chance to disprove A. At time $t_2(t_2 > t_1)$, Bob presents the following argument,

$$R3 : E \Rightarrow D \qquad R4 : B, D \Rightarrow \neg A$$

This will generate two new defeasible rules as $R'3(E \Rightarrow D)@t_2$, $R'4(B, D \Rightarrow \neg A)@t_2$. Now, Bob only attacks $R'2$ presented by Alice at previous step by $R'4$ and $R'2$ is removed from CR. As $t_2 > t_1$, the strength of $R'4$ is greater than $R'2$ according to the strength determination rule for the defendant. Thus, $CR_{t_2} = [R'1, R'3, R'4]$. The proof at time t_2 is $-\partial A$, which includes that we also have $-\Delta A$ as the latter rule $R'4$ is stronger than $R'2$.

Next at time t_3, Alice presents the following arguments,

$$R5 : \neg E \Rightarrow \neg D \qquad R6 : \emptyset \Rightarrow \neg E \qquad R7 : B \Rightarrow A$$

The translated defeasible rules are $R'5(\neg E \Rightarrow \neg D)@t_3$, $R'6(\emptyset \Rightarrow \neg E)@t_3$, $R'7(B \Rightarrow A)@t_3$. Now $CR_{t_3} = [R'1, R'4, R'5, R'6, R'7]$ as $R'3$ is strongly defeated by $R'5$ and $R'6$ and thus, it is removed. At time t_3, $R'1$ remains unchallenged and as it is utilized as a premise in the reasoning of Bob and thus commits Bob to this rule (which is justified as Bob could not be allowed to rely on not actively presented inconsistencies), presented by the prosecutor Alice it is strengthened into a strict rule (i.e., a fact) as $R'1(\emptyset \rightarrow B)@t_3$. So the proof at this time point is $+\partial A$ as the rule is stronger according to the transition rules. If Bob does not present valid arguments in the next step Alice wins the game as from Bob's argumentation her claim is corroborated.

6   Related Work

In this paper we augment the model of dialogue games in defeasible logic of [25]. The work is based on ALIS [22], and we are inspired by [14] as we have separated the knowledge of the players into (1) private knowledge and (2) public knowledge. The common public knowledge forms the common set of arguments, which is a theory in defeasible logic. As such our model in contrast to [22] provides a closer approximation of argumentation games for the agent setting, as the agent could choose at what time and which parts of its arguments (i.e., private knowledge) be disclosed to its opponent.

Substantial work have been done on argumentation games in the AI and Law-field. [4] presents an early specification and implementation of an argumentation game based on the Toulmin argument-schema without a specified underlying logic. [8] presented The Pleadings Game as a normative formalization and fully implemented computational model, using conditional entailment. The goal of the model was to identify issues in the argumentation rather than as in our case elaborating on the status of the main claim. The dialectic proof procedures presented by [7] focus on minimizing the culprit of argumentation. The proof procedures are expressed as metalogic programs. Our use of defeasible logic establishes a difference as to the syntactic limitations as the approach in [7] is built on assumptions that are atomic, whereas in our framework the arguments are expressible as rules of propositional defeasible logic, not being directly applicable in the abstract argumentation framework underlying [6]. DiaLaw [16] is a two player game, in which both players make argument moves. The model combines exchange of statements and exchange of arguments, dealing with rhetorical as well as psychological issues of argumentation. However, the main focus for the two players is to convince each other rather than defeating an adversarial as in our case. The abstract argumentation systems of [26,27] study arguments as the object of defeat. The results however are more related to stable semantics than sceptical as in the defeasible logic utilized in our framework and the study is devised as meta games for changing the rules of argumentation games.

Modelling argumentation games in defeasible logic has been addressed by [14,13,15]. [15], in contrast to our work, focuses on persuasion dialogues in a cooperative setting. It includes in the process cognitive states of agents such as knowledge and beliefs, and presents some protocols for some types of dialogues (*e.g.* information seeking, explanation, persuasion). The main reasoning mechanism is based on basic defeasible logic (cf. Section 3), while ignoring recent development in extensions of defeasible logic with modal and epistemic operators for representing the cognitive states of agents [10,11]. [14] provides an extension of defeasible logic to include the step of the dialogue in a way very similar to what we have presented in the paper. A main difference is that the resulting mechanism just defines a metaprogram for an alternative computational algorithm for ambiguity propagating defeasible logic while the logic presented here is ambiguity blocking. In [13], the authors focus on rule sceptic characterizations of arguments and propose the use of sequences of defeasible (meta) theories, while using meta-reasoning (meta-rules or high level rules) to assess the strength of rules for the theories at lower levels.

7   Conclusion

In this paper Defeasible Logic is used to capture an asymmetric protocol for argumentation games. We have shown that our model provides for a closer approximation of argumentation games for heterogeneous agent settings. The agent characteristics or the agents' relative importance in fulfilling the overall goal of the system could be captured, while all the same the agent is allowed to argue its case in the best way it knows, *e.g.* choosing at what time any subset of its arguments (*i.e.* private knowledge) be disclosed to its adversary.

References

1. Antoniou, G., Billington, D., Governatori, G., Maher, M.J.: Representation results for defeasible logic. ACM Transactions on Computational Logic 2(2), 255–287 (2001)
2. Antoniou, G., Billington, D., Governatori, G., Maher, M.J.: Embedding Defeasible Logic in Logic Programming. Theory and Practice of Logic Programming 6(6), 703–735 (2006)
3. Antoniou, G., Billington, D., Governatori, G., Maher, M.J., Rock, A.: A family of defeasible reasoning logics and its implementation. In: Proc. ECAI 2000, pp. 459–463 (2000)
4. Bench-Capon, T.J.M.: Specification and Implementation of Toulmin Dialogue Game. In: Proc. JURIX 1998, Nijmegen, GNI, pp. 5–20 (1984)
5. Billington, D.: Defeasible logic is stable. J. Log. and Comput. 3, 370–400 (1993)
6. Dung, P.M.: On the acceptability of arguments and its fundamental role in nonmonotonic reasoning, logic programming, and n–person games. Artif. Intel. 77, 321–357 (1995)
7. Dung, P.M., Kowalski, R.A., Toni, F.: Dialectic proof procedures for assumption-based, admissible argumentation. Artif. Intel. 170, 114–159 (2006)
8. Gordon, T.: The Pleadings Game: An artificial Intelligence Model of Procedural Justice. Artif. Intel. and Law 2(4) (1993)
9. Governatori, G., Maher, M.J., Billington, D., Antoniou, G.: Argumentation semantics for defeasible logics. J. Log. and Comput. 14(5), 675–702 (2004)
10. Governatori, G., Rotolo, A.: Defeasible logic: Agency, intention and obligation. In: Lomuscio, A., Nute, D. (eds.) DEON 2004. LNCS (LNAI), vol. 3065, pp. 114–128. Springer, Heidelberg (2004)
11. Governatori, G., Rotolo, A., Padmanabhan, V.: The cost of social agents. In: Proc. AAMAS 2006, pp. 513–520. ACM Press, New York (2006)
12. Grosof, B.N.: Representing e-commerce rules via situated courteous logic programs in RuleML. Electronic Commerce Research and Applications 3(1), 2–20 (2004)
13. Eriksson Lundström, J., Hamfelt, A., Fischer Nilsson, J.: A Rule-Sceptic Characterization of Acceptable Legal Arguments. In: Proc. ICAIL 2007, pp. 283–284. ACM Press, New York (2007)
14. Hamfelt, A., Eriksson Lundström, J., Fischer Nilsson, J.: A metalogic formalization of legal argumentation as game trees with defeasible reasoning. In: Proc. ICAIL 2005, pp. 250–251. ACM Press, New York (2005)
15. Letia, I.A., Varic, R.: Defeasible protocols in persuasion dialogues. In: Proc. WE-IAT 2006. IEEE, Los Alamitos (2006)
16. Lodder, A.R.: DiaLaw: On Legal Justification and Dialogical Models of Argumentation. Artif. Intel. and Law 8(2-3), 265–276 (2000)
17. Maher, M.J., Rock, A., Antoniou, G., Billington, D., Miller, T.: Efficient defeasible reasoning systems. International Journal of Artificial Intelligence Tools 10(4), 483–501 (2001)
18. Nute, D.: Defeasible logic. In: Handbook of Logic in Artificial Intelligence and Logic Programming, vol. 3, pp. 353–395. Oxford University Press, Oxford (1994)
19. Prakken, H.: Modelling defeasibility in law:logic or procedure? Fundamenta informaticae, 253–271 (2001)
20. Prakken, H., Sartor, G.: Rules about rules: Assessing conflicting arguments in legal reasoning. Artif. Intel. and Law, 331–368 (1996)

21. Prakken, H., Sartor, G.: Presumptions and burdens of proof. In: Proc. Jurix 2006, pp. 21–30. IOS Press, Amsterdam (2006)
22. Prakken, H., Sartor, G.: Formalising arguments about the burden of persuation. In: Proc. ICAIL 2007, pp. 97–106. ACM Press, New York (2007)
23. Prakken, H.: Relating protocols for dynamic dispute with logics for defeasible argumentation. Synthese 127, 187–219 (2001)
24. Roth, B., Riveret, R., Rotolo, A., Governatori, G.: Strategic Argumentation: A Game Theoretical Investigation. In: Proc. ICAIL 2007, pp. 81–90. ACM Press, New York (2007)
25. Thakur, S., Governatori, G., Padmanabhan Nair, V., Eriksson Lundström, J.: Dialogue games in defeasible logic. In: Orgun, M.A., Thornton, J. (eds.) AI 2007. LNCS (LNAI), vol. 4830, pp. 497–506. Springer, Heidelberg (2007)
26. Vreeswijk, G.: Abstract Argumentation Systems. Artif. Intel. 90, 225–279 (1997)
27. Vreeswijk, G.: Representation of formal dispute with a standing order. Artif. Intel. and Law 8(2/3), 205–231 (2000)

On the Design of Interface Agents for a DRT Transportation System

Claudio Cubillos, Sandra Gaete, and Guillermo Cabrera

Pontificia Universidad Católica de Valparaíso
Escuela de Ingeniería Informática
Av. Brasil 2241, Valparaíso, Chile
claudio.cubillos@ucv.cl, sandra.gaete@gmail.com, guillermo.cabrera@ucv.cl

Abstract. This work tackles the design and development of interface agents present in a flexible transportation system devoted to the planning, scheduling and control of passenger trips. In particular, the agent-oriented software engineering methodology (AOSE) PASSI was used. The interface agents devoted to interaction with customers and drivers are explained in detail and their prototypes are shown. The present work gives continuity to previous research in the field of transportation services and agent systems design.

1 Introduction

The need to cover more diffuse travel patterns, varying periods of low demand, city-peripheral journeys, as well as commuting trips often make conventional public transport systems unable to guarantee the level of service required to address the user needs. The use of Demand-Responsive Transport services (DRTS), where routes, departure times, vehicles and even operators, can be matched to the identified demand allows a more user-oriented and cost effective approach to service provision.

On the other hand, software agents are defined as autonomous entities capable of flexible behavior denoted by reactiveness, pro-activeness and social ability [1]. Multiagent systems (MAS) consist of diverse agents that communicate and coordinate generating synergy to pursue a common goal. This higher level of abstraction has allowed agents to tackle the increasing complexity of nowadays open software systems. Under such an scenario, the agent paradigm has leveraged as an important modeling abstraction, in areas such as web and grid service, peer to peer and ambient intelligence architectures just to mention some cases.

The present work describes the design of a multiagent system using a particular AOSE methodology called PASSI [2] for the passenger transportation under a flexible approach. It gives continuity to our past research [3] [4] on heuristics for solving scheduling of passenger trips. In particular the paper focuses in describing the design of the interface agents for the main actors; Customer and Driver, providing a practical case of GUI agents' modeling with PASSI.

A. Ghose, G. Governatori, and R. Sadananda (Eds.): PRIMA 2007, LNAI 5044, pp. 232–242, 2009.

2 Related Work

In general terms, Agent research on in the Intelligent Transportation Systems (ITS) domain has deserved an increasing interest. One of the ITS fields is in the Advanced Transportation Information System (ATIS), where Kase and Hattori [6] proposed the InfoMirror application that provides agent-based information assistance to drivers through car navigation systems or on-board PCs. A distributing route guidance system was presented by Adorni [7], which allowed dynamic route searching using the coordination capabilities of MAS.

Another ITS field is Bus-holding control, which tackles the coordination of multiple lines of fixed-route buses and the different stops, seeking the global optimality. In 2001, Jiamin et al. [8] proposed a distributed bus-holding control approach in which a MAS negotiation between a Bus Agent and a Stop Agent was conducted based on marginal cost calculations.

Deserves to be mentioned that in the above solutions no agent development methodology is used for specifying the system, mainly due to a lack of maturity of those methodologies at that time. Therefore, the aim of this work is to provide an experience in the design of multiagent systems using the PASSI methodology and to present the design of interface agents specific for the demand-responsive passenger transportation domain.

3 Flexible Public Transport Services

Demand Responsive Transport (DRT) services can be seen as an element of a larger intermodal service chain, providing local mobility and complementary to other conventional forms of transportation (e.g. regular buses and trams, regional trains). In this context, DRT provides a range of Intermediate Transport solutions, filling the gap between traditional public bus services and individual taxis.

The DRT service can be offered through a range of vehicles including regular service bus, mini-bus, maxi-vans, buses and vans adapted for special needs and regular cars. The use of each vehicle type depends on the transport service to offer, the covered area and the target users. The aim aim is to meet the needs of different users for additional transport supply. The use of flexible transport services, where routes, departure times, vehicles and even operators, can be matched to the identified demand allows a more user-oriented and cost effective approach to service provision. The adaptation of the transport services to match actual demand enables cost savings to the operators, society and passengers.

With respect to process implementation and management, the flexibility of the system is expressed along two main directions: on one hand, users of DRT systems must be provided with user-friendly instruments for accessing the services (such as information, reservation, query update) in several different flexible ways (the so called "anywhere and anytime" access). On the other hand, the organization providing flexible services must be itself flexible, with the capability of managing dynamic relationships in a pool of transport resources (vehicles), which may sometimes have to change to better adapt the transport supply to the dynamic demand.

4   The Agent-Based Transportation System

The system prototype was designed following the Process for Agent Societies Specification and Implementation (PASSI) which is made up of five models containing twelve steps in the process of building multi-agent. Please refer to [2] for a more detailed description on the whole PASSI methodology. Models were developed with the PTK (Passi Toolkit [14]) add-on for Rational Rose and was implemented over the Jade Agent Platform[9], which provides a full environment for agents to work. For a more detailed description on the agent architecture and the planning & scheduling mechanism please refer to [5] and [3]. In the following the general architecture will be explained for then detailing the interface agents in the next sections.

As outlined in the PASSI section, the methodology starts capturing the system's requirements through use cases, for then grouping them together to conform the agents. The diagram in Figure 1 shows part of the use cases and agents involved in the system. Due to space restrictions some of the supporting agents are expressed as actors.

By starting from the transport operator side, we find the Vehicle, which is an interface agent (with a GUI) in charge of providing the monitoring of the route-schedule planned for the vehicle. In addition, it can inform the Driver about any changes to the initial schedule and can be used by him to inform any eventuality (e.g client no show, delay, detour, etc) that may happen regarding the trip and the customers. In particular its interface has been designed to work on-board the vehicle through a touch screen. This agent will be further detailed on a next section.

The Schedule agent is the one in charge of managing the trip plan (work-schedule) of the vehicle. In addition, the agent is also responsible of making trip proposals upon Planner request and in case of winning will have to update its actual plan to include the new trip. Upon changes (due to vehicle or client events) informed either by the Vehicle or the Planner agent, the Schedule agent will update the plan and reschedule the remaining requests.

The Client is the second interface agent with a GUI, providing the connection between the end-user (Customer) and the transportation system. Through it, the Customer can request a trip by giving a description of the desired transportation service by means of a *Trip Request Profile*. In addition, using a *Client Profile* it is possible to create and manage personalized services profiles with diverse characteristics and preferences common to the different trips requested by the user.

After a service has been contracted, the Customer can also communicate events to the system (e.g. a delay, a change on the agreed service, or simply cancel). In a similar way, the system can communicate with the Customer, informing him about any eventuality that may happen (e.g. a traffic jam or vehicle break down) which may imply a delay or change in the service to be provided. This agent will be also detailed on a next section.

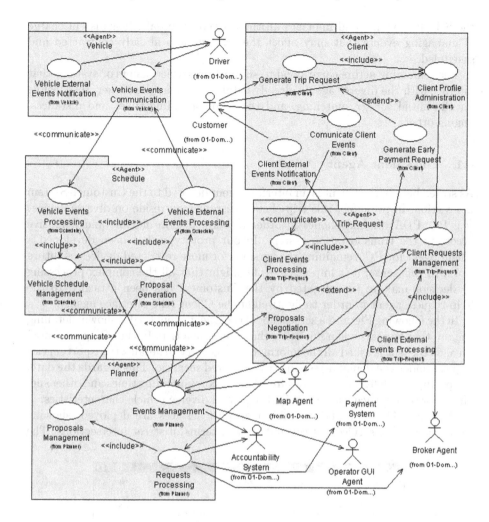

Fig. 1. Portion of the Agents' Identification Diagram

Other relevant agent is the Trip-Request, which acts as a proxy representing the Customer in the process of contracting a transportation service. In fact, the trip-request agent is involved in all the interaction of the Customer (through the interface agent) with the transportation system. Its activities regard the management of the client transportation requests, including any negotiation or selection of proposals coming from the Planner, together with processing any events generated by the Customer or by the system. As residing on a device with more processing power (such as a PC), this agent may have diverse degrees of autonomy for taking decisions on the trip proposal to choose and how to react when faced to eventualities.

Finally, the Planner agent processes all the customers' requests coming through their Trip-request agents. It initiates a contract-net (CNP) [15] with the Schedule agents and manages all the arrived proposals. It is also in charge of managing events that may affect the trip services already contracted and scheduled.

The remaining actors correspond to supporting-service agents or systems that interact with the diverse agents already detailed, such as the broker, responsible for the initial service matching, and the map, providing times and distances, among others.

4.1   The Client Agent

As stated before, the Client is an interface agent devoted to the Customer-System interaction. In principle, this trip-client assistant may reside on diverse devices (e.g PC, PDA, mobile phone) in order to allow a more flexible and pervasive access to the transportation system. In our prototype, has been developed a Client agent for PC, remaining the versions for more restricted devices as future work. In this sense, it is important to highlight that all the complex processing or decision-making (if delegated by the Customer) has been attached to the Trip-request agent in order to lightweight the Client (the interface agent).

In the following Figure 2 a screenshot of the Client agent GUI is shown, detailing the tab that appears when initiating the request of a trip. In the "Request Data" area, on the left, is asked all the information necessary to detail a transport service request under the demand-responsive considered scenario. This regards the date, the pickup and delivery points (addresses), the corresponding times and other specific information such as the required seats and diverse vehicle characteristics.

On the right hand, the available transport services are deployed, showing for each selected service the covered area in terms of street intersections. The

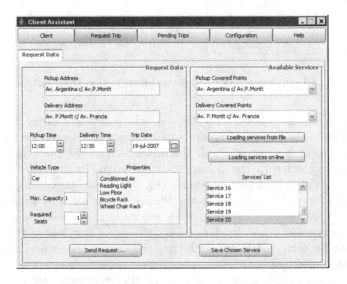

Fig. 2. Client agent GUI showing the "Request Data" tab in the "Request Trip" menu

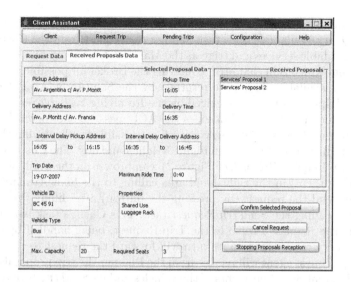

Fig. 3. Client agent GUI showing the "Received Proposals Data" tab in the "Request Trip" menu

services' list can be imported from the system (on line) or from a local file. At the bottom, the Customer can send the trip request and save the services' list.

The following Figure 3 corresponds to a screenshot of the Client agent GUI detailing the "Received Proposals Data" tab which appears as an answer after sending the request for a trip. In this form are displayed all the transportation alternatives found to be capable of performing the service. The list of alternatives is on the right-hand box and by selecting on each of them the left area (Selected Proposal Data) displays the details of such proposal. The data involved concerns the address and requested time for pickup and delivery. In addition, a time window is specified for the pickup and for the delivery in order to make more flexible the service and tackle possible differences with the original schedule.

Other relevant data provided regards the vehicle ID and type, the required seats, together with diverse specific properties, such as the capacity, bicycle rack, shared/individual use, among others. It is important to mention that all the concepts involved in the specification of the services make part of a Domain Ontology specific for this transportation domain (for further details on the ontology please refer to [5]).

The PASSI methodology used for the modeling considers a *Task Specification* step. In this activity the scope is to focus on each agents behavior, decomposing it into tasks which usually capture some functionality that conforms a logical unit of work. Therefore for each agent an activity diagram is developed, containing what that agent is capable of along the diverse roles it performs. In general terms, an agent will be requiring one task for handling each incoming and outgoing message.

In the following Figure 4 a portion of the Task Specification Model for the Client Agent is depicted. The diagram shows six tasks that constitute the main Client agent capabilities devoted to the process of requesting a transportation service. The *SendQueryAvailableService* task handles the request from the Customer to search for available services and triggers the *ManageClientQuery* task of the Trip-Request agent which is in charge of requesting the Broker for possible transportations services available. These are returned by the *SendActualAvailableService* task of the Trip-request and is received by the *ReceivingAvailableService* task of the Client which processes and decodes the ACL message and forwards the services' list to the *ShowAvailableService* task responsible for displaying the list in the proper form as already shown in Figure 3 right-hand box. The Customer, when making a trip Request Profile (see Figure 2), can browse on the available services (after loading them) in the right-hand area calling to the *ShowAvailableService* task or can send the request (by pressing the button) after filling the left-hand information, calling the *SendTripRequest* task. This Client's task is responsible for sending the *Request Profile* to the Trip-Request, being handled by its *ManageClientQuery* task, which on its turn will forward the request to the Planner.

The Trip-request agent will receive from the Planner the trip proposals coming from the different Schedule agents of the vehicles and its *SendTripProposals* task will send them to the Client. On its turn, the Client will receive and handle the proposals through its *ShowTripProposals* task, also responsible for displaying them on the appropriate form area as already shown on Figure 3.

In this way, the Customer will be able to select the best alternative according to his preferences and will click the "Confirm Selected Proposal" button on the GUI (see Figure 3 first button lower-right corner). This action will call the *SendChosenProposal* task of the Client responsible of forwarding the selected proposal to the Trip-request agent, which on its turn will forward it to the Planner, who is in charge of communicating the proposals' acceptance/rejection to the diverse Schedule agents that made bids.

4.2   The Vehicle Agent

As mentioned earlier, the Vehicle agent constitutes an interface agent for the Driver - Transportation System interaction. From the Agents' identification Diagram of Figure 1, it is possible to see that the Vehicle is responsible for allowing the communication of incoming events to the Customer and of vehicle events to the transportation system.

The following Figure 5 shows a screenshot of the Vehicle agent GUI, detailing the actual vehicle itinerary with expected times. On a first view, we can realize that the layout is minimalistic with simple shapes as buttons. This is because the Vehicle agent is intended to be on-board the transportation vehicle (car, van, maxi-taxi, etc.). Hence, the interfaces developed to be used in touch screens.

On the left side appears the timetable, providing the expected times (e.g. 10:00, 10:30, 11:00 and so on) of the places to visit (either pickup or delivery points). These can be scrolled up or down with the square buttons in the lower part.

On the right hand the interface is divided in three. A header on the top, showing the present date and time plus a square led that blinks when a change

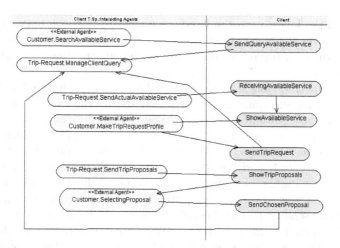

Fig. 4. Part of the Task Specification Model for the Client Agent, showing the flow of tasks involved in the trip request processing

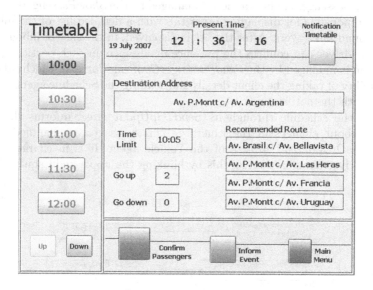

Fig. 5. Vehicle agent GUI showing the main screen with the itinerary

to the itinerary is carried out by the system and needs to be communicated to the driver. On the middle-right are shown the details of the entry selected on the left hand (the 10:00 in this particular case). It provides the destination address to reach, the time limit for departure in that place (10:05) for not arriving late to the next destination (at 10:30 in this case) and the number of passengers that go up and down in this stop. Additionally, it is provided the best route in order to arrive from the actual position of the vehicle to the required destination.

Finally on the footer part, the interface deploys three touch buttons; the first allows to confirm passengers presence at the stop, the second to inform a delay or anticipation with respect to the schedule and the third one to turn back to the main menu.

The Task Specification Model for the Vehicle agent is depicted in Figure 6. This activity diagram contains five tasks that specify the labour carried out by the agent. The task *ObtainEventData* manages the notification of events received from the Driver when touching the *Inform Event* button of the Vehicle GUI (on Figure 5). The task handles the GUI processing of the notification at low-level, the notification details and forwards them to the *SendEventNotification* task. This task is responsible for translating the event notification and related data into an ACL message in alignment with the transportation domain ontology and finishes by sending to the Schedule agent the ACL message with the given event notification. The *Inform Event* button display another screen that allows to notify a delay due to a detour, a traffic jam, or a vehicle breakdown.

On each stop the driver must confirm to the transportation system the presence or absence of the clients (*Confirm Passengers* button on Figure 5). For this, the driver's passenger confirm action is managed by the *ShowPassengersList* task which is responsible for displaying other tab with a detailed list of the inbound and outbound passengers. After the list is displayed, in the case of inbound customers the driver can confirm the presence or absence on each particular case. This action is managed by the *SendPassengerConfirmation* task which takes the responsibility of taking the client details and sending the Schedule agent an ACL Message with the notification.

Finally, the schedule through its *SendTripUpdate* task informs the Vehicle agent about changes in the itinerary. This messages are handled by the *ShowDetailsOfUpdatedTrip* task of the Vehicle agent. It is in charge of notifying the driver about a change, this by blinking the upper-right square led on

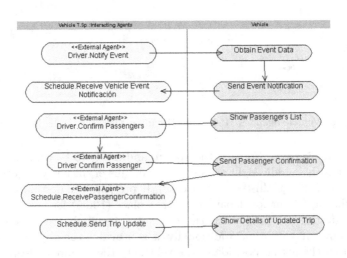

Fig. 6. Task Specification model for the Vehicle Agent

the screen (on Figure 5) together with updating the timetable in order to reflect the changes.

5   Conclusions

The presented work tackled the design description of interface agents using PASSI withing the context of a complete system for passenger transportation under a demand-responsive approach. The methodology used allowed an appropriate level of specification along its diverse phases. The focus was centered on the specification of the interface agents for the main actors involved with the system: Customers and Drivers; The Client and Vehicle Interface Agent prototypes were detailed providing an in-depth example of agent design & implementation using the AOSE PASSI.

Additionally, the design enables showing how are articulated the Requirements model, providing a functional description of the system in terms of use-cases, the identification of agents' roles through sequence diagrams and the identification of agents'tasks.

Future work considers to perform usability tests on the interface agents in order to improve the quality of them, together with considering the development of client agents for mobile devices (e.g. palm or cellular phone). Other issue regards the system openness with the implementation of a high-level communication mechanism in order to provide a dynamic participation in such a system.

Acknowledgement

This work is part of Project No. 209.746/2007 entitled "Coordinación en una sociedad multiagente dedicada a la programación y control bajo ambiente dinámico", funded by the Pontifical Catholic University of Valparaíso (www.pucv.cl).

References

1. Weiss, G.: Multiagent Systems: A Modern Approach to Distributed Artificial Intelligence. MIT Press, Massachusetts, USA (1999)
2. Burrafato, P., Cossentino, M.: Designing a multiagent solution for a bookstore with the passi methodology. In: Fourth International Bi-Conference Workshop on AgentOriented Information Systems (AOIS 2002) (2002)
3. Cubillos, C., Crawford, B., Rodríguez, N.: Distributed planning for the on-line dial-a-ride problem. In: Preparata, F.P., Fang, Q. (eds.) FAW 2007. LNCS, vol. 4613, pp. 124–135. Springer, Heidelberg (2007)
4. Cubillos, C., Rodriguez, N., Crawford, B.: A study on genetic algorithms for the DARP problem. In: Mira, J., Álvarez, J.R. (eds.) IWINAC 2007. LNCS, vol. 4527, pp. 498–507. Springer, Heidelberg (2007)
5. Cubillos, C., Gaete, S.: Design of an agent-based system for passenger transportation using PASSI. In: Mira, J., Álvarez, J.R. (eds.) IWINAC 2007. LNCS, vol. 4528, pp. 531–540. Springer, Heidelberg (2007)

6. Kase, N., Hattori, M.: InfoMirror - Agent-based Information Assistance to Drivers. In: IEEE\IEEJ\JSAI Intelligent Transportation Systems Conference Proceedings, pp. 734–739 (1999)
7. Adorni, G.: Route Guidance as a Just-In-Time Multiagent Task. Journal of Applied Artificial Intelligence 10(2), 95–120 (1996)
8. Zhao, J., Dessouky, M., Bukkapatnam, S.: Distributed Holding Control of Bus Transit Operations. In: IEEE Intelligent Transportation Systems Conference Proceedings, Oakland - USA, pp. 976–981 (August 2001)
9. Bellifemine, F., et al.: JADE - A FIPA Compliant Agent Framework. C SELT Internal Technical Report (1999)
10. Bürckert, H., Fischer, K., et al.: TeleTruck: A Holonic Fleet Management System. In: 14th European Meeting on Cybernetics and Systems Research, pp. 695–700 (1998)
11. Fischer, K., Müller, J.P., Pischel, M.: Cooperative Transportation Scheduling: An application Domain for DAI. Journal of Applied Artificial Intelligence 10 (1996)
12. Kohout, R., Erol, K., Robert, C.: In-Time Agent-Based Vehicle Routing with a Stochastic Improvement Heuristic. In: Proc. Of the AAAI/IAAI Int. Conf., Orlando, Florida, pp. 864–869 (1999)
13. Perugini, D., Lambert, D., et al.: A distributed agent approach to global transportation scheduling. In: IEEE/ WIC Int. Conf. on Intelligent Agent Technology, pp. 18–24 (2003)
14. PASSI Toolkit (PTK), http://sourceforge.net/projects/ptk
15. Smith, R.G., Davis, R.: Distributed Problem Solving: The Contract Net Approach. In: Proceedings of the 2nd National Conference of the Canadian Society for Computational Studies of Intelligence (1978)

Supporting Requirements Analysis in Tropos: A Planning-Based Approach

Volha Bryl, Paolo Giorgini, and John Mylopoulos

University of Trento, DIT,
via Sommarive 14, Povo (TN) 38050, Italy
bryl@dit.unitn.it, paolo.giorgini@unitn.it, jm@cs.toronto.edu

Abstract. Software systems are becoming more and more part of human life influencing organizational and social activities. This introduces the need of considering the design of a software system as an integral part of the organizational and social structure development. Alternative requirements and design models have to be evaluated and selected from a social perspective finding a right trade-off between the technical and social dimension. In this paper, we present a Tropos-based approach for requirements analysis, which adopts planning techniques for exploring the space of requirements alternatives and a number of social criteria for their evaluation. We describe the tool-supported analysis process with the help of a case study (the e-voting system), which is a part of a project funded by the Autonomous Province of Trento.

1 Introduction

Unlike their traditional computer-based cousins, socio-technical systems include in their architecture and operation organizational and human actors along with software ones. Moreover, human, organizational and software actors in such systems rely heavily on rich inter-dependencies to other actors in order to fulfill their respective objectives. Not surprisingly, an important element in the design of socio-technical systems is the identification of a set of dependencies among actors which, if respected by all parties, will fulfill all objectives.

Let's make the problem more concrete. KAOS [5] is a state-of-the-art requirements elicitation technique that starts with stakeholder goals and through a systematic, tool-supported process derives functional requirements for the system-to-be and a set of assignments of leaf-level goals (constraints, in KAOS terminology) to external actors so that if the system-to-be can deliver the functionality it has been assigned and external actors deliver on their respective obligations, stakeholder goals are fulfilled. However, there are (combinatorially) many alternative assignments to external actors and the system-to-be. How does the designer choose among these? How can we select an optimal, or "good enough" assignment? What is an optimal assignment? The KAOS framework remains silent on such questions. Alternatively, consider the $i*$ and Tropos frameworks for modeling and analysis of early requirements of agent-oriented systems [1,11]. In $i*$/Tropos, goals are explicitly associated with external stakeholders and they can be delegated to other actors or the system-to-be. Or, they can be decomposed into subgoals that are delegated to other actors. In this setting, selecting a set of assignments

A. Ghose, G. Governatori, and R. Sadananda (Eds.): PRIMA 2007, LNAI 5044, pp. 243–254, 2009.
© Springer-Verlag Berlin Heidelberg 2009

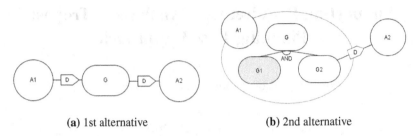

(a) 1st alternative   (b) 2nd alternative

Fig. 1. Sample problem: two alternative models

is more complex because delegations can be transitive and iterative. "Transitive" means that actor A may delegate goal G to actor B who in turn delegates it to actor C. "Iterative" means that an actor A who has been delegated goal G, may choose to decompose it (in terms of an AND/OR decomposition) and delegate its subgoals to other actors.

To illustrate the problem, consider the design task in Figure 1 where actor A_1 has to achieve goal G, which can be refined into two subgoals G_1 and G_2. The actor can decide to achieve the goal by itself or delegate it to actor A_2. In both cases, there are a number of alternative ways that can be adopted. For instance, A_1 can decide to delegate to A_2 the whole G (Figure 1a), or a part of it (Figure 1b). The diagrams follow Tropos modelling notation with circles representing actors, big dashed circles representing actors' perspective, and ovals representing goals (interconnected by AND/OR-decomposition links). Social dependencies among actors for goals are represented by D-labelled directed links. Even for such a simple example, the total number of alternative requirements models is big, and a systemized approach and tool support for constructing and evaluating such networks of delegations would be beneficial.

We are interested in supporting the design of socio-technical systems, specifically the design of a set of inter-actor dependencies intended to fulfill a set of initial goals. The support comes in the form of a tool that is founded on an off-the-shelf AI planner to generate and evaluate alternative assignments of actor dependencies to identify an optimal design.

Specifically, our tool solves the following problem: given a set of actors, goals, capabilities, and social dependencies, the tool generates alternative actor dependency networks on the basis of the following steps, which may be interleaved or used inside one another:

- Check problem-at-hand: (a) Analyze actor capabilities: check whether existing actors possess enough capabilities to collectively satisfy their goals; (b) Analyze actor inter-dependencies: check whether existing dependencies between actors allows them to fulfill all given goals.
- Explore alternative dependency networks: (a) With the help of planning algorithms construct assignments of goals to actors that leads to the satisfaction of the actors' goals; (b) Evaluate alternatives by assessing and comparing them with respect to a number of criteria, provided by the designer.

The idea of casting the problem of designing a set of delegations for a socio-technical system into a planning one has already been presented in [4,3]. In addition, [3] proposes a preliminary approach to the evaluation of alternatives. However, what was missing in these works, is the systematic process of requirements analysis to support the design of socio-technical systems. In this paper, we present such a tool-supported process, which combines formalization and analysis of an organizational setting, the use of planning techniques [3], and a concrete set of optimality criteria to evaluate the produced requirements models. The approach is illustrated with the help of a case study involving an e-voting system, developed for the Autonomous Province of Trento. We also report on preliminary experimental results aimed to evaluate the scalability of the prototype tool.

The rest of the paper is structured as follows. Sections 2 and 3 present the baseline for this research [3,4], namely, in Section 2 the details on applying planning techniques to requirements models construction are given, and in Section 3 criteria and procedures for evaluating those models are discussed. Section 4 presents the general process schema of the proposed requirements analysis approach. This is followed by the explanations on how the inputs to the process are organized and analyzed in Section 5. Section 6 introduces the e-voting case study and illustrates the whole approach on its basis, which is followed by summarizing remarks and discussion on the future work directions in Section 7.

2   Using Planning to Construct Requirements Models

The task of constructing delegation networks can be framed as a *planning problem*: selecting a suitable design corresponds to selecting a plan that satisfies actors' and organizational goals [3]. In general, AI (Artificial Intelligence) planning [10] is about automatically determining the course of actions (i.e. a plan) needed to achieve a certain goal where an action is a transition rule from one state of the world to another. A specification language is required to represent the planning domain, i.e. the initial and the desired states and the actions.

The following predicates are used to formally represent the initial and the desired states of the world (i.e. the organizational setting). The predicates take variables of three types: `actors`, `goals` and `goal types`.

To typify goals, `type(goal, g_type)` predicate is used. Actor capabilities are described with can `satisfy(actor, goal)` and `can_satisfy_gt(actor,g_type)` predicates meaning that an actor has enough capabilities to satisfy either a specific goal, or a goal of a specific type. Dependencies among actors are reflected by `can_depend_on(actor, actor)` and `can_depend_on_gt(actor, actor, g_type)` predicates, which mean that one actor can delegate to another actor the fulfilment of any goal or, in the latter case, any goal of a specific type. Predefined ways of goal refinement are represented by `and/or_decomposition(goal, goal, ..)` predicates. Initial actor desires are represented with `wants(actor, goal)` predicate. When a goal is fulfilled `satisfied(goal)` predicate becomes true for it. In Figure 2a the example presented in Figure 1 (hereafter referred to as *sample problem*) is formalized using the above described predicates.

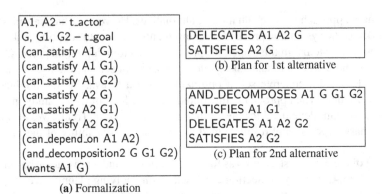

(a) Formalization

A1, A2 – t_actor
G, G1, G2 – t_goal
(can_satisfy A1 G)
(can_satisfy A1 G1)
(can_satisfy A1 G2)
(can_satisfy A2 G)
(can_satisfy A2 G1)
(can_satisfy A2 G2)
(can_depend_on A1 A2)
(and_decomposition2 G G1 G2)
(wants A1 G)

DELEGATES A1 A2 G
SATISFIES A2 G

(b) Plan for 1st alternative

AND_DECOMPOSES A1 G G1 G2
SATISFIES A1 G1
DELEGATES A1 A2 G2
SATISFIES A2 G2

(c) Plan for 2nd alternative

Fig. 2. Sample problem: formalization and plans

A plan, which is constructed to fulfill actors and organizational goals, comprises the following actions: (a) *Goal satisfaction*, (b) *Goal delegation*, and (c) *Goal decomposition*. Actions are described in terms of preconditions and effects, both being conjunctions of the above mentioned predicates and/or their negations. If a precondition of an action is true in the current state, then the action is performed; as a consequence of an action, a new state is reached where the effect of the action is true.

When the problem domain and the problem itself are formally represented, a planner is used to produce a solution. Having analyzed a number of available o-the-shelf planners (see [4] for the details), we have chosen LPG-td [7], a fully automated system for solving planning problems, which supports PDDL 2.2 specification [6], for implementing our planning domain. In Figure 2b-c two plans for the sample problem generated by LPG-td are shown.

A set of experiments, which we do not report here due to the space limits, were conducted with LPG-td to assess the scalability of the approach. The key point of the experiments was to identify the complexity limits (in terms of number of goals, actors and actor dependencies, depth of goal decomposition trees, etc.) which the planner could handle. The obtained results justify the use of planning in the requirements engineering domain as, according to our experience, requirements models of real life case studies stay within the complexity limits which our planning approach is able to manage. In [3] we have presented P-Tool, an implemented prototype to support the designer in the process of exploring and evaluating alternatives. The tool has the interface for the input of actors, goals and their properties. LPG-td is built in the tool, and is used to generate alternative requirements structures, which are then represented graphically using Tropos notation.

3   Evaluating Requirements Models

After a requirements model has been constructed, it can be evaluated from the two perspectives, global (i.e. the perspective of the designer), and local (i.e. the perspective of an individual actor). The perspective of the designer will normally include a number of non-functional requirements, which he wants to be met. E.g., these might be security concerns, efficiency, maintainability, user friendliness, etc. Evaluation is either quantitative, or qualitative, depending on whether one can "measure" the requirement in terms of numbers, or there exists just a relative scale to compare two models. An example of quantitative criteria would be a "fair", or homogeneous distribution of workload among the actors, with a variance as a measure of it. An example of qualitative criteria could be user friendliness, meaning that the expertise of the designer allows him to say that organizing the process in this way is "more user friendly" than in this other.

An example of a local evaluation criterium we consider in this paper, is related to workload distribution. We assume that each actor, either human or software, wants to minimize the number and complexity of goals it/he/she needs to satisfy. Complexity of a goal for an actor measures the effort required to achieve the goal. Complexity has to be defined explicitly for leaf goals, i.e. for those goals that could be assigned to actors that have capabilities to satisfy them. There is no need to define or calculate complexity for a goal that is to be further decomposed and delegated. Complexity is "local" in a sense that the same goal can have different complexity values for different actors. For each actor there is a maximum complexity it can handle, i.e. the sum of complexity values for all the goals this actor is assigned should be less than some predefined threshold, namely, maximum complexity. If this condition is violated the actor might be willing to deviate from the imposed assignment.

After the complexity and maximum complexity values are defined, the evaluation procedure, which preliminary version was presented in [3], is as follows.

1. A plan P is generated by the planner.
2. Plan complexity values for each actor are calculated, by summing up the complexity values for all the goals this actor is assigned.
3. Actors whose plan complexity values are greater than the corresponding maximum complexity values are identified.
4. One of these actors is selected, namely, actor a_{max} which has the maximum difference δ between plan complexity and maximum complexity values.
5. A subset of actions $P_{dev} \subset P_{a_{max}}$ is formed with the total cost greater or equal to δ, where $P_{a_{max}}$ denotes those actions of P in which a_{max} is involved.
6. The definition of the planning problem is changed in order to avoid the presence of actions contained in P_{dev} during the next planning iteration.
7. The procedure re-starts with the generation of a next plan.

4   Requirements Analysis: A General Schema

Our proposal is to structure the requirements analysis process to support a designer in constructing and evaluating requirements models. The general schema of the process is presented in Figure 3. A preliminary description of an organizational setting, which is provided by a designer in terms of actors, goals and social relations, is analyzed and iteratively improved so as to output a model that guarantees the fulfillment of stakeholder goals and is good-enough with respect to a number of criteria. In the following we give details on the process steps and their interrelations. Most of the process steps can be

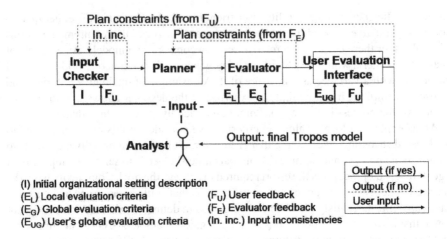

Fig. 3. Requirements analysis process: a general schema

automated, however, the presence of a human designer is inevitable the design process for socio-technical systems can be supported by tools but cannot be automated.

As a first step, it is checked whether there exist at least one assignment of goals to actors that leads to the satisfaction of top-level goals. **Input checker** analyzes the organizational setting, detects inconsistencies, and proposes possible improvements, which then are either approved, or rejected, or modified by the designer. In particular, it is checked whether available actors possess enough capabilities to collectively satisfy their goals, and whether the relationships between actors permit this to happen. To analyze actor capabilities means to check that for each goal it is possible to find an actor capable of achieving each of its AND-subgoals or at least one of its OR-subgoals. To analyze actor interdependencies means to check whether a goal can be delegated from an actor who wants to achieve it to an actor who is capable of achieving it. Given a network of delegations between the actors, it is checked whether there exists a path between two actors. In Section 5, we give details on analyzing and dealing with missing capabilities, while the second kind of analysis is not covered in the paper.

After the input is checked, the first possible alternative is generated by the **Planner** component, which exploits AI planning algorithms to search for a solution as described in Section 2.

An alternative generated by the planner is then assessed by the **Evaluator** with respect to a number of criteria. These criteria are defined by the designer and refer to the optimality of the solution either from a global perspective (e.g. assessing the overall security or efficiency), or from the local perspectives of stakeholders (e.g. assessing the workload distribution). Evaluation criteria and procedures were discussed in Section 3. If evaluation reveals that an alternative is not acceptable, then the **Evaluator** provides feedback to the **Planner** in order to formulate constraints for the generation of the next alternative. If no further alternative can be generated, the current description of an organizational setting is changed according to the constraints identified by the Evaluator, and then is analyzed by the Input checker, and so on, iteratively.

Note that the output of the evaluation process needs to be approved by a human designer. **User evaluation interface** presents the selected alternative to the designer together with the summarized evaluation results. Another task of this component is to provide the designer with the interface for giving his feedback on why the selected alternative does not satisfy him. On the basis of this feedback the constraints for the generation of the next alternative are formulated and forwarded to the **Planner**. The result of the application of the approach is a new requirements model, which is, ideally, optimal or, in practice, good-enough with respect to all the local and global criteria, and is approved by the designer. After obtaining one satisfiable alternative it is possible to repeat the process to generate others, reusing already obtained constraints.

5   Input Analysis

The input to the proposed requirements analysis process is provided by the designer, and can be logically divided into the following two categories. Firstly, it is an organizational setting description, i.e. actors, their goals and capabilities, dependencies among actors, possible ways of goal refinements (decompositions of a goal into AND/OR-subgoals). The second category contains evaluation criteria, either qualitative or quantitative, e.g. preferences or cost bounds, as discussed in Section 3.

As it was stated in Section 4, the description of an organizational setting can be analyzed with respect to capabilities of available actor and actor connectivity. In this section the process of analyzing actor capabilities is explained, while actor connectivity analysis is outside the scope of this paper.

Firstly, a "capability tree" for each high-level organizational goal is constructed. A "capability tree" is based on a goal model [1], which organizes goals in a tree structure reflecting AND- and OR-decompositions. In addition, a list of actors capable of achieving a goal is associated with each leaf node of a tree. Nodes with no associated actors are marked as unsatisfiable with the goal which causes the problem included in the label (*unsat : goal*). Otherwise, a node is marked as satisfiable (*sat*). After that, labels are propagated bottom-up to the root goal according to the following rules. If all OR-subgoals or at least one AND-subgoal of a goal is marked *unsat*, then the goal is also marked *unsat*, and sat otherwise. When an *unsat* label is propagated, the goals that cause unsatisfiability problem are accumulated together; at the end the label might look as *unsat : $(G_1$ or $G_2)$ and G_3*, meaning that to satisfy the root goal we need to find the ways to satisfy G_3 and either G_1 or G_2.

After a capability tree has been built and *sat/unsat* labels propagated, it becomes clear whether the root goal can be satisfied, and if not, what are the missing capabilities. There are two ways to deal with missing capabilities:

- Add a new capability to an existing actor. Such a decision could be based on the actual capabilities of this actor. Namely, if this actor is already capable of achieving one or several goals of the same type, it is likely that it could manage the new goal as well.
- If there is no way to add the missing capability to one of the existing actors, a new actor might be introduced.

6 E-Voting Case Study

The focus of the case study is on modelling requirements for an electronic based voting system that is to be introduced in the Autonomous Province of Trento by the next provincial elections (to be held in 2008). The Province is funding the ProVotE project [9], which has the goal of providing a smooth transition from the paper based voting system to new technologies. The project includes partners from the public administration, research centers and academia, and local industries.

6.1 Description

Voting in Italy consists of the following stages [8]: (a) Identification and registration of a voter at a polling station; (b) Casting a vote; (c) Counting votes and tabulating the results; (d) Transmission of the results to the offices responsible for data aggregation; (e) Sum and proclamation of the elected representatives.

Introducing the new technologies in all these stages not only changes the way in which votes are collected and processed, but also roles and responsibilities of the actors involved. One of the ProVotE activities was the extensive UML modelling of existing paper based voting procedures [8] in order to provide a baseline for the definition of new procedures. Obviously, there are many ways in which the paper based system might be transformed into an e-voting system, and thus, many alternative configurations should be analyzed and compared. However, UML modelling approach, being process-oriented, does not provide support for such an analysis. To complement UML modelling in tackling the above problems, Tropos modelling approach has been used, which provides a clear visual representation of the organizational setting (actors, goals, actor dependencies) combining the perspectives of different stakeholders[1].

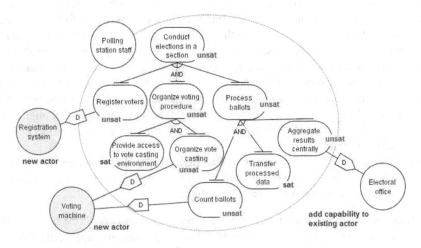

Fig. 4. Case study: conduct elections in a section

---

[1] See [2] for the discussion on why and how UML and Tropos modelling approaches are applied together in ProVotE.

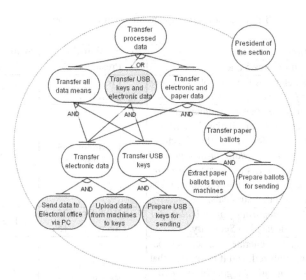

Fig. 5. Case study: transfer processed data

Example 1. In Figure 4 the diagram representing the viewpoint of the *polling station staff* on the voting process is shown[2]. As presented in the diagram, the root level goal, *conduct election in a section*, is decomposed into the three AND-subgoals, two of which are then further decomposed. Some of the subgoals (*provide access to vote casting environment*, and *transfer processed data*) can be satisfied by the *polling station staff*. For the achievement of other goals the *polling station staff* depends on the other actors, either organizations, or humans, or software systems, e.g. the goal *register voters* is delegated to the *registration system* actor.

Example 2. The second example concerns the goal *transfer processed data,* and the *president of the section,* the leading member of the *polling station staff,* who is responsible for satisfying this goal, see Figure 5. Elections are conducted with the help of several *voting machines* installed in standard voter cabins in each polling station. A voter expresses his/her choice with the help of a touch-screen, and then a ballot is printed, approved by the voter and stored inside a machine. At the end of an election day, data from voting machines are collected on the special purpose USB keys, one per machine, and printed paper ballots are extracted from the machines (more details are given in [8]). Thus, there are three pieces of data that could be transferred from the *polling station* to the *Electoral office*, namely, USB keys, electronic data these keys contain, and paper ballots.

6.2   Illustrating the Process

Capability analysis. Figure 4 depicts a capability tree for *conduct elections in a section* goal, in which two leaf goals are assigned sat labels, namely, *provide access to*

---

[2] For the moment sat/unsat labels should be ignored, the necessary explanations will be given in Section 6.2.

Table 1. Case study: plans and their evalaution

#	Description	Actor : Workload	Who deviates
1	Depicted in Figures 5 and 6a	President: **20**	President
2	President delegates the goal of *preparing USB keys for sending* to Secretary.	President : 15 Secretary : 5	Designer
3	Designer decides that to maintain the required security level all the data means should be transferred to the Electoral office. *Transfer all data means* goal is adopted, Secretary is in charge of *preparing USB keys for sending*, President takes care of all the other subgoals.	President : **35** Secretary : 5	President
4	The goal of *preparing paper ballots for sending* is delegated to Secretary.	President : **25** Secretary : 15	President
5	No plan can be generated, so actors capabilities are analyzed, and it is inferred that Scrutineer can satisfy a goal of *extracting paper ballots from voting machines*. This goal is delegated to Scrutineer, see Figure 6b.	President : 15 Secretary : 15 Secretary : 10	–

vote casting environment and *transfer processed data*, meaning that *polling station staff* possesses enough capabilities to satisfy both of them. After *sat/unsat* labels are propagated, it becomes clear that the goal *conduct elections in a section* cannot be satisfied due to the fact that the *polling station staff* is not able (or need extra support) to *register voters*, *count ballots*, and *aggregate the results centrally*[3]. To address the missing capability problems, the following steps are performed. Firstly, the capability to *aggregate the results centrally* is added to the existing actor, *Electoral office*; in the initial input setting this data could be omitted just by mistake, and such kind of input analysis helps to correct the errors. Secondly, two new actors are introduced to deal with *register voters* and *count ballots* goals, *registration system* and *voting machine*, respectively. These new actors are the parts of the new e-based voting system, specifying the requirements to which is what we aim at.

Planning and evaluation. In Table 1 the iterations of the planning and evaluation procedure applied to the case study are presented. When evaluating the workload, it is assumed that the goals *send data to Electoral office via PC* and *prepare USB keys for sending* are considered to be not very complex goals with the complexity value equal to 5 units for each of the two goals. The other three leaf goals are considered to be more complex with the complexity value equal to 10 units. For the sake of simplicity the complexity values for the same goal are the same for all actors. Maximum complexity values are the same for all the actors and are equal to 15 units.

---

[3] Extensions of *unsat* labels (which accumulate the goals that cause unsatisfiability problem as it was described in Section 5) are omitted for the sake of presentation simplicity.

```
OR_DECOMPOSES PRES
   TR TRALL TREP TREK
AND_DECOMPOSES PRES
   TREK TRE TRK
AND_DECOMPOSES PRES
   TRE UPLOADONK SENDE
SATISFIES PRES UPLOADONK
SATISFIES PRES SENDE
AND_DECOMPOSES PRES
   TRK UPLOADONK PREPAREK
SATISFIES PRES PREPAREK
```

(a) Initial Plan

```
OR DECOMPOSES PRES
   TR TRALL TREP TREK
AND DECOMPOSES PRES
   TRALL TRE TRK TRP
AND DECOMPOSES PRES
   TRP EXTRACTP PREPAREP
DELEGATES PRES SCRU EXTRACTP
SATISFIES SCRU EXTRACTP
DELEGATES PRES SECR PREPAREP
SATISFIES SECR PREPAREP
AND DECOMPOSES PRES
   TRE UPLOADONK SENDE
SATISFIES PRES UPLOADONK
SATISFIES PRES SEND
AND DECOMPOSES PRES
   TRK UPLOADONK PREPAREK
DELEGATES PRES SECR PREPAREK
SATISFIES SECR PREPAREK
```

(b) Final Plan

Fig. 6. Transfer data: the initial and the final plans

7 Conclusions and Future Work

In this paper we have proposed a structured Tropos based requirements analysis process which focuses on exploring and evaluating alternative requirements models. Planning techniques are adopted for constructing alternative dependency networks, which are then evaluated with respect to a number of criteria. Evaluation criteria represent either a designers point of view, or assess the models from the local perspectives of organizational actors. The approach is illustrated with the help of the case study taken from the ongoing project, which is about introducing e-based voting system in Autonomous Province of Trento.

The priority among the possible future work directions is on further implementation and testing the tool which supports all steps of the design process. Other important research directions include the further development of evaluation metrics, with a focus on local evaluation metrics; elaborating on the input analysis to address all the situations in which no solution is available; exploiting advances in AI planning by incorporating some of the evaluation metrics into the planning process; further experiments regarding the scalability and usability of the proposed approach.

Acknowledgements

This work has been partially funded by EU Commission, through the SENSORIA and SERENITY projects, by MEnSA-PRIN project, and also by the Provincial Authority of Trentino, through the MOSTRO project.

References

1. Bresciani, P., Giorgini, P., Giunchiglia, F., Mylopoulos, J., Perini, A.: Tropos: An agent-oriented software development methodology. JAAMAS 8(3), 203–236 (2004)
2. Bryl, V., Ferrario, R., Mattioli, A., Villafiorita, A.: Evaluating Procedural Alternatives in an e-Voting Domain: Lesson Learned. Technical Report DIT-07-005, University of Trento (2007)
3. Bryl, V., Giorgini, P., Mylopoulos, J.: Designing cooperative IS: Exploring and evaluating alternatives. In: Meersman, R., Tari, Z. (eds.) OTM 2006. LNCS, vol. 4275, pp. 533–550. Springer, Heidelberg (2006)
4. Bryl, V., Massacci, F., Mylopoulos, J., Zannone, N.: Designing security requirements models through planning. In: Dubois, E., Pohl, K. (eds.) CAiSE 2006. LNCS, vol. 4001, pp. 33–47. Springer, Heidelberg (2006)
5. Dardenne, A., van Lamsweerde, A., Fickas, S.: Goal-directed requirements acquisition. Science of Computer Programming 20, 3–50 (1993)
6. Edelkamp, S., Hoffmann, J.: Pddl2.2: The language for the classical part of the 4th international planning competition. Technical Report 195, University of Freiburg (2004)
7. LPG Homepage. LPG-td Planner, http://zeus.ing.unibs.it/lpg/
8. Tiella, R., Villafiorita, A., Tomasi, S.: Specification of the Control Logic of an eVoting System in UML: the ProVotE experience. In: CSDUML 2006 (2006)
9. Villafiorita, A., Fasanelli, G.: Transitioning to eVoting: the ProVotE project and Trentino's experience. In: EGOV 2006 (2006)
10. Weld, D.S.: Recent Advances in AI Planning. AI Magazine 20(2), 93–123 (1999)
11. Yu, E.S.-K.: Modelling strategic relationships for process reengineering. PhD thesis, University of Toronto (1996)

Towards Method Engineering for Multi-Agent Systems: A Validation of a Generic MAS Metamodel

Graham Low[1], Ghassan Beydoun[3], Brian Henderson-Sellers[2],
and Cesar Gonzalez-Perez[1,2]

[1] School of Information Systems, Technology and Management,
University of New South Wales, Sydney, Australia
[2] Faculty of Information Technology, University of Technology of Sydney, Sydney, Australia
[3] Faculty of Informatics, University of Wollongong, Wollongong, Australia

Abstract. It is a widely accepted premise that no single methodology can be suitable for all Multi-Agent System (MAS) software projects. This premise is playing a significant role in the appearance of new methodologies at an increasing pace. To effectively harness the software engineering knowledge of methodologies, method engineering is an appealing approach. It focuses on project-specific methodology construction from existing method fragments and it requires a generic product-focussed metamodel to serve as a representational infrastructure to unify existing methodologies into a single specification. As part of its ongoing validation towards method engineering for MAS development, we present our generic metamodel and illustrate in this paper its wide applicability with respect to 10 methodologies extant agent-oriented. This validation provides further evidence to support the use of our metamodel towards the construction of situated MAS methodologies.

1 Introduction

Multi Agent Systems (MAS) are a new class of distributed parallel software systems that have proved effective in the following core tasks: automating management of information within businesses (e.g. computer network management applications [1]), building computational models of human societies to study emergent behaviour [2–4] and building cooperative distributed problem solving [5,6].

The building blocks of a MAS are intelligent, autonomous and situated software entities: agents. The agent, the concept of agency and the MAS abstractions offer a promise of making software systems easier to embed within our daily lives as suggested in [7]. However, it is widely acknowledged that for agents to be accepted into the mainstream of software development, suitable development methodologies are required. As a testimony to this, agent-oriented methodologies are being published at an increasing rate. We have identified more than a dozen, examples being Gaia [8], Adelfe [9], Prometheus [10] and PASSI [11].

Formal arguments refuting that a single methodology is sufficient, regardless as to how well thought out it might be, have recently appeared [7]. We support such arguments, in our work, rather than the suggestions that combining existing methodologies

A. Ghose, G. Governatori, and R. Sadananda (Eds.): PRIMA 2007, LNAI 5044, pp. 255–267, 2009.

into one comprehensive methodology is the answer e.g. [12]. We believe the latter will prove to be impossible, because the sets of assumptions underlying each methodology are likely to be inconsistent and irreconcilable. In [13], we proposed an alternative to empower MAS software developers to create methodologies from existing (method) fragments (self-contained components); this activity is known in software engineering as method engineering [14]. Method engineering approaches have been successful in object-oriented development due to widely accepted modelling languages and the constructs of OO software systems and development processes e.g. [15]. With the objective of applying method engineering for developing a MAS, in [13] we synthesised and introduced a process-independent metamodel for an agent-oriented modelling language to describe software components of any MAS. This metamodel is the first to focus on conceptual and ontological underpinnings rather than being constrained for use in a single methodological approach. It is widely applicable, without any constraining prerequisites; it will be able to be used to describe work products required in most methodologies. At the system level, we did not make any assumptions about agents beyond their essential properties: *autonomy*, *situatedness* and *interactivity*. Any other non-definitional agent characteristic, visible at the system level, suggests a methodology-specific feature. For instance, *adaptivity* is non-definitional. Adelfe's [16] adaptive system design requires learning agents. Thus, some concepts in Adelfe's metamodel are too specific to be included in our metamodel. At the agent level, we intend our metamodel to be comprehensive enough to describe any type of agent (reactive, planning). In other words, to describe a given methodology, not all aspects of our metamodel will be needed. Our metamodelling approach is iterative and comprises two iterative phases: synthesis and validation. To validate our metamodel in [13], we verified that it can be successfully used to obtain metamodels underlying Islander [17] and TAO [18]. We sketched how our metamodel can generate both of them. That preliminary validation reinforced our case for method engineering and constituted early evidence that our method engineering proposal for MAS development is plausible and it is one step closer to being realised. In this paper, we undertake further validation of our metamodel by ensuring that the metamodel supports the key AOSE concepts considered by [19] when evaluating 10 extant and well-known methodologies: Gaia [8], Tropos [20], Adelfe's [16], Prometheus [10], PASSI [11], MAS-CommonKADS [21], MASE [22], RAP [23] MESSAGE [24] and Ingenias [25].

The rest of this paper is organised as follows: In Section 2, we present our metamodel and how it was synthesized. In Section 3, we present our validation while in Section 4 we conclude, pinpointing where the metamodel can be improved as a result of the evaluation and describe future work.

2   MAS Metamodel for Method Engineering

The full details of the synthesis of our metamodel is presented in [13]. In this section, we briefly overview that synthesis process and then present our actual metamodel before we undertake its validation in Section 3.

Table 1. Design-time concepts and their definitions

Term	Definition
Action Specification	Specification of an action, including any preconditions and postconditions.
Agent Definition	Specification of the initial state of an agent just after it is created.
Convention	Rule that specifies an arrangement of events expected to occur in a given environment.
Environment Statement	A statement about the environment.
Facet Action Specification	Specification of a facet action in terms of the facet definition it will change and the new value it will write to the facet.
Facet Definition	Specification of the structure of a given facet, including its name, data type and access mode.
Functional Requirement	Requirement that provides added value to the users of the system.
Message Action Specification	Specification of a message action in terms of the message schema and parameters to use.
Message Schema	Specification of the structure and semantics of a given kind of messages that can occur within the system.
Non-Functional Requirement	Requirement about any limits, constraints or impositions on the system to be built.
Ontology	Structural model of the application domain of a given system.
Ontology Aggregation	Whole/part relationship between two ontology concepts.
Ontology Concept	Concept included in a given ontology.
Ontology Relationship	Relationship between ontology concepts.
Ontology Specialisation	Supertype/subtype relationship between two or more ontology concepts.
Performance Measure	Mechanism to measure how successful the system is at any point in time.
Plan Specification	An organised collection of action specifications.
Requirement	Feature that a system must implement.
Role	Specification of a behavioural pattern expected from some agents in a given system.
System	Final product of a software development project.
Task	Specification of a piece of behaviour that the system can perform.

2.1 Overview of Our Metamodel Synthesis

We ensured that our metamodel is a consensual picture of what a MAS looks like. The resultant metamodel covered as many features of a MAS as possible. In its synthesis, the behavioural characteristics of agents in a wide range of MASs were considered. The metamodel describes the behaviour of any agent. We anticipated that any methodology can be successfully generated using our metamodel. We aimed to maximise coverage (inclusion of as many MAS concepts as possible) and generality (wide acceptance and familiarity to methodologists). To construct our generic metamodel, we decided on the set of concepts that will be used, describing entities in any MAS and the relationships amongst them. This set of concepts and their definitions was rooted in the existing literature related to MAS and MAS methodologies. Because of the sheer size of this literature, we could not be sure that the initial set of examined references was comprehensive. We continuously considered additional references during the metamodelling process. This necessitated that our metamodelling process be iterative. This process consisted of the following steps undertaken iteratively: **Step 1**: Decide on the set of general concepts relevant to any MAS and its model. See Tables 1–2 for a list of concepts from this step. **Step 2**: Decide on definitions worth considering. **Step 3**: Reconcile differences between definitions where possible, giving hybrid definitions. **Step 4**: Designate the chosen concepts into two sets: run-time concepts and design-time concepts. Each set has two scopes: system-related or agent internals related scope. **Step 5**: Identify the relations within both the design-time and run-time sets produced in Step 4, to produce the actual metamodel. These steps did not depend on any single software development methodology.

Table 2. Run-time concepts and their definitions

Term	Definition
Action	Fundamental unit of agent behaviour.
Agent	A highly autonomous, situated, directed and rational entity.
Belief	An environment statement held by an agent and deemed as true in a certain timeframe.
Desire	An environment statement held by an agent, which represents a state deemed as good in a certain timeframe.
Environment	The world in which an agent is situated.
Environment History	The sequence of events that have occurred between the environment start-up and the present instant.
Environment Statement	A statement about the environment.
Event	Occurrence of something that changes the environment history.
Facet	Scalar property of the environment that is expected by the agents contained in it.
Facet Action	Action that results in the change of a given facet.
Facet Event	Event that happens when the value of a facet changes.
Goal	Ultimate desire.
Intention	A committed desire.
Message	Unit of communication between agents, which conforms to a specific message schema.
Message Action	Action that results in a message being sent.
Message Event	Event that happens when a message is sent.
Obligation	Behaviour expected from an agent at some future time.
Plan	An organised collection of actions.

3   Our Generic Metamodel

Our metamodel is complete as far as describing the internal structure of single agents is concerned (according to our three definitional properties of agents). However, not all concepts in the metamodel have to be used by a given methodology. Some issues are left to the methodology or the developers, e.g. how plans are generated and dumped, how beliefs are maintained and shared, verification and validation of the system. In connecting all concepts into one coherent metamodel, we omitted all relations which are too specific, relating to some special kind of agent. We also ensured that the set of terms was self-contained, that is, concepts may only depend on each other in this set. The metamodel is summarized below (for full details see [13]).

It has two layers: design-time and runtime layers and can have one of two scopes: system related or agent related. The metamodel is presented in four diagrams to clearly group classes into the four different areas of concern: design-time system related classes, runtime system-related (environment) classes, design time agent-internals classes and run-time agent-internals classes.

Fig. 1 shows the classes (and associated relationships) of the metamodel that are directly related to the description of a MAS, i.e. design-time system-related classes. These classes are concerned with features that can only be perceived by looking at the whole system at design time: Role, Message schema, Task, Agent Definition, Ontology plus environment access points.

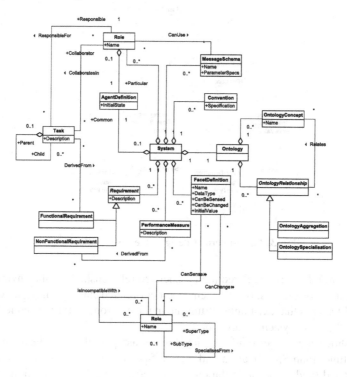

Fig. 1. System related design-time classes after [13]

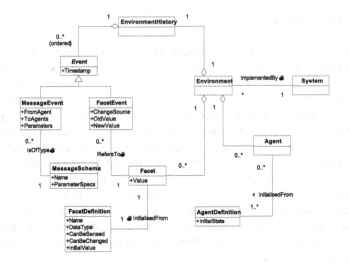

Fig. 2. Run-time, environment-related classes after [13]

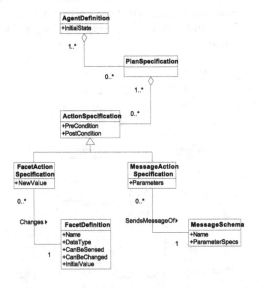

Fig. 3. Agent-internals design-time classes after [13]

Fig. 2 shows the classes related (and associated relationships) to the environment in which agents "live", that is, run-time environment-related classes. These are concerned with MAS features that exist only at runtime in the environment: Environment History, Event together with system access points.

Fig. 3 shows the classes (and associated relationships) related to the agent internals at design time: Plan Specification and Action Specification. Finally, Fig. 4 shows the classes related (and associated relationships) to agent internals at run-time: Plan, Action, Desire (and Belief) and Intention.

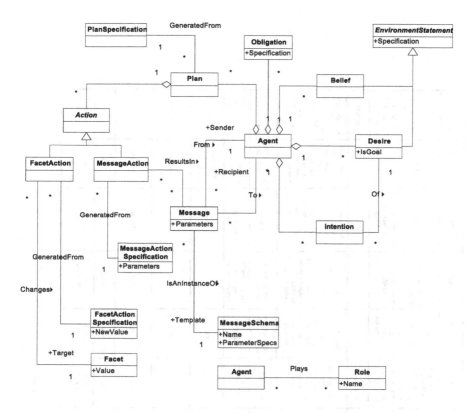

Fig. 4. Agent-internals design-time classes after [13]

4   Metamodel Validation

We are concerned with external consistency and completeness of the metamodel [as discussed earlier, internal consistency is ensured during its creation]. External validation is designed to ensure external consistency with existing methodologies and ensure that the metamodel can generate all prominent methodologies. Generally, internal consistency is a strong indicator of external consistency as demonstrated and highlighted in Beydoun et al. [26]. In our validation, we directly undertook an external consistency check against the explicit and implicit metamodels of methodologies available in the literature. We validated our metamodel using TAO and Islander as reported in [13]. In this section, we determine if our metamodel supports the key AOSE concepts considered by [19] when evaluating 10 extant and well-known methodologies (shown in Table 3).

Tran and Low [19, 27] developed an evaluation framework by identifying and integrating the evaluation criteria from various feature analysis frameworks, including those for assessing conventional system development methodologies [28-30], Object Agency Inc. [31] and those for evaluating AOSE methodologies [32-35]. The former category provides a well-established list of generic system engineering features to be considered, while the latter presents various agent-oriented and MAS-specific aspects

	GAIA	TROPOS	MAS-COMMONAKADS	PROMETHEUS	PASSI	ADELFE	MASE	RAP	MESSAGE	INGENIAS
Development lifecycle	Iterative within each phase but sequential between phases	Iterative and incremental	Cyclic risk-driven process	Iterative across all phases	Iterative across and within all phases (except for coding and ... analysis,...	Rational Unified Process (RUP)	Iterative across all phases	RUP	RUP	Unified software development process
Coverage of the lifecycle	Analysis and Design	Analysis and Design	Analysis and Design	Analysis and Design	Analysis, Design and Implementation	Analysis, Design and Implementation	Analysis and Design	Analysis and Design	Analysis and Design	Analysis, Design and Implementation
Development perspective	Top-down	Top-down	Hybrid	Bottom-up	Bottom-up	Top-down	Top-down	Hybrid	Hybrid	Hybrid
Application domain	Independent (business process management, GIS, traffic simulation)	Independent (e-business systems, knowledge management, health IS)	Independent (Flight reservation, automatic control)	Independent (holonic manufacturing, online bookstore)	Independent (distributed robotics applications, online bookstore)	Dependent - adaptive systems (adaptive intranet system, timetabling system)	Independent (distributed planning, database integration system, computer virus immune system, automatic control)	Dependent - distributed organizational IS (supply chain management, enterprise resource planning)	Independent (network management, operational systems, knowledge management systems)	Independent (collaborative information filtering, personal computer management, robot battles)
Size of MAS	<= 100 agent classes	Not specified	Not specified, but possibly any size	Any size	Not specified	Not specified, but possibly any size	<= 10 agent classes	Any size	Not specified, but possibly any size	Not specified, but possibly any size
Agent nature	Heterogeneous	BDI-like agents	Heterogeneous	BDI-like agents	Heterogeneous	Adaptive	Not specified but possibly heterogeneous	Reactive agents	Heterogeneous	Agents with goals and states
Support for verification and validation	No	Yes	Mentioned but no explicit steps/guidelines provided	Yes	Yes	Yes	Yes	No	Mentioned as future enhancement	Yes
Ease of understanding of the process	High	High	High	High	High	High	High	High	High	High
Usability of the methodology	Medium	Medium	Medium	High	High	High	High	Medium	Medium	High
Refinability	Yes	Yes	Yes	Yes	Yes	Yes	Yes	Yes	Yes	Yes
Approach towards MAS development	a. OO b. RO (OrO)	a. i* modelling framework b. NRO	a. KE b. NRO	a. OO b. NRO	a. OO b. RO	a. OO b. NRO	a. OO b. RO (GO)	a. OO b. RO	a. OO b. RO (GO and BO)	a. OO b. RO

Fig. 5. Comparison of Concepts

Table 3. Support of Concepts by Generic Metamodel

Concepts	Support by FAML metamodel
System goal	Not supported
System task/behaviour	Task class
Use case scenario	Not supported
Role	Role class
Domain conceptualization	Ontology classes
Agent goal/task	Task class
Agent-role assignment	Role Specification between Role and Agent Definition classes
Agent belief/knowledge	Belief, Intention and Desire classes
Agent capability/service	
Agent plan/reasoning rule/problem solving method	Plan class
Agent percept/event	Event class
Agent architecture	Agent Definition class
Agent acquaintance	Role Relationship classes
Interaction protocol	Not supported
Content of exchanged messages	Message class
Inter-agent contract/commitment	Message class
System architecture	Not supported
Organizational structure/inter-agent social relationship	Organization: not supported Inter-agent social relationship: handled via roles
Environment resource/facility	Environmental level classes
Environment characterization	Environmental level classes
Agent aggregation relationship	Extension of Agent Definition class
Agent inheritance relationship	Extension of Agent Definition class
Agent instantiation	Agent class
Agent instances deployment	Agent Definition class
Ontology	Ontology classes
Mobile agents	Not supported

for assessment. They also added several evaluation criteria that are not included in existing frameworks, e.g. "support for mobile agents" and "support for ontology". They conducted a survey to substantiate the relevance of the proposed criteria and to make the necessary refinements to the criteria specification.

The framework consists of:

– *Process Related Criteria*: evaluating an AOSE methodology's development process.
– *Technique Related Criteria*: assessing the methodology's techniques to perform development steps and/or to produce models and notational components.
– *Model Related Criteria*: examining the capabilities and characteristics of the methodology's models and notational components including the concepts represented by the models, the quality of notational components and the agent characteristics supported by the models.
– *Supportive Feature Criteria*: evaluating a variety of high-level methodological capabilities.

This structure highlights the framework's attention to all three major components of a system development methodology, i.e. process, models and techniques.

Tran and Low [19] used the feature analysis technique to evaluate 10 well known AOSE methodologies. The concepts related criteria are particularly relevant to our validation of the generic metamodel. Two additional criteria included in supportive-feature criteria are considered: ontology and support for mobile agents.

The "Concepts" criterion in Table 3 evaluates the modelling capability of an AOSE methodology by examining which concepts the methodology's models are capable of capturing/representing both at design time and run time. A list of "standard" AOSE concepts was used as an assessment checklist. If a methodology supports the modelling of a particular concept, the name of the model or notational component (i.e. diagram) that represents that concept is indicated. If a concept appears in many different models or diagrams within the methodology, the model or diagram that represents the concept as the principal modelling element is specified. Table 4 examines the support of the generic.

5   Discussion, Summary and Future Work

In [13] we provided a process-independent metamodel for an agent-oriented modelling language to describe software components of any MAS and showed how our metamodel can be refined to express metamodels underlying known MAS descriptors: MAS-ML (representing TAO) and Islander. As a result of that preliminary evaluation we noted an extension of our metamodel entailing new (dynamic) relationships amongst roles and between roles, as well as dynamic constructs such as Environment History to monitor message flows as described in [36]. This paper extends that evaluation to provide further evidence for the expressive power of our language constructed as a formalised synthesis of the implicit modelling approaches found in a number of existing agent-oriented methodologies.

Based on the analysis in this paper, the initial version of the generic FAML metamodel was found to support most of the features in Gaia [8], Tropos [20], Adelfe's [16], Prometheus [10], PASSI [11], MAS-CommonKASDS [21], MASE [22], RAP [23] MESSAGE [24] and Ingenias [25]. However, it was found to be deficient with respect to goal analysis, organizational structure, support for mobile agents, interaction protocol and system architecture (Table 4). We suggest adding support for goal analysis and organizational structure. However, for interaction protocol and system architecture, we view these as too methodology specific. They can be elaborated or constructed from our metamodel concepts. Support for mobile agents is the basis for future work. Beyond these extensions, we will undertake further validation against the underlying metamodels of a number of prominent methodologies, including Ingenias [25] and Tropos [20]. We also plan to further identify and exemplify its individual elements in the analysis of an actual P2P retrieval MAS application.

Beyond the metamodel validation, the next step of our work is to create a complementary generic process metamodel and to situate the presented agent-oriented modelling language within a full method engineering framework. The modelling language will be stored in a repository as a collection of method fragments, which will be subsequently linked to other method fragments describing potential activities, tasks, techniques (i.e. process aspects), teams and roles (i.e. people aspects). Thus, a complete methodological framework will be provided, which will be able to support the generation of complete, custom-made agent-oriented methodologies using the tenets of method engineering.

Acknowledgement

This work is supported by a GoldStar Award from University of New South Wales and the Australian Research Council.

References

1. Horlait, E.: Mobile Agents for Telecommunication Applications (Innovative Technology Series: Information Systems and Networks). Kogan Page, Portland (2004)
2. Guessoum, Z., Rejeb, L., Durand, R.: Using adaptive Multi-Agent Systems to Simulate Economic Models. In: AAMAS 2004. ACM, New York (2004)
3. Ferber, J., Drogoul, A.: Using Reactive Multi-Agent Systems in Simulation and Problem Solving. In: Avouris, L.G.N.M. (ed.) Distributed AI: Theory and Praxis. Kluwer, Brussels (1992)
4. Tidhar, G., et al.: Using Intelligent Agents in Military Simulation or Using Agents Intelligently. In: 11th Conference on Innovative Applications of Artificial Intelligence Papers (IAAI 1999), Orlando,Florida. MIT Press, Cambridge (1999)
5. Hunsberger, L., Grosz, B.J.: A combinatorial auction for collaborative planning. In: 4th International Conference on Multi-Agent Systems (ICMAS 2000) (2000)
6. Hogg, T., Williams, C.: Solving the Really Hard Problems with Cooperative Search. In: 11th National Conference on Artificial Intelligence, Washington, DC, USA. MIT Press, Cambridge (1993)
7. Edmonds, B., Bryson, J.: The Insufficiency of Formal Design Methods - the necessity of an experimental approach. In: AAMAS 2004. ACM, New York (2004)
8. Wooldridge, M., Jennings, N.R., Kinny, D.: The Gaia Methodology for Agent-Oriented Analysis and Design. In: Autonomous Agents and Multi-Agent Systems, The Netherlands. Kluwer Academic Publishers, Dordrecht (2000)
9. Bernon, C., Gleizes, M.-P., Peyruqueou, S., Picard, G.: ADELFE: A methodology for adaptive multi-agent systems engineering. In: Petta, P., Tolksdorf, R., Zambonelli, F. (eds.) ESAW 2002. LNCS, vol. 2577, pp. 156–169. Springer, Heidelberg (2003)
10. Padgham, L., Winikoff, M.: Developing Intelligent Agent Systems. A Practical Guide, vol. 1, p. 225. J. Wiley & Sons, Chichester (2004)
11. Cossentino, M., Potts, C.: A CASE tool supported methodology for the design of multi-agent systems. In: International Conference on Software Engineering Research and Practice (SERP 2002), Las Vegas, NV, USA (2002)
12. Bernon, C., Cossentino, M., Gleizes, M.-P., Turci, P., Zambonelli, F.: A study of some multi-agent meta-models. In: Odell, J.J., Giorgini, P., Müller, J.P. (eds.) AOSE 2004. LNCS, vol. 3382, pp. 62–77. Springer, Heidelberg (2005)

13. Beydoun, G., et al.: Developing and Evaluating a Generic Metamodel for MAS Work Products. In: Garcia, A., et al. (eds.) Software Engineering for Multi-Agent Systems IV: Research Issues and Practical Applications, pp. 126–142. Springer, Berlin (2006)

14. Brinkkemper, S.: Method Engineering: Engineering of Information Systems Development Methods and Tools. Information and Software Technology 38(4), 275–280 (1996)

15. Henderson-Sellers, B., Simons, A., Younessi, H.: The OPEN Toolbox of Techniques, Harlow (Essex), UK. The OPEN Series. Addison-Wesley Longman, Amsterdam (1998)

16. Bernon, C., Gleizes, M.-P., Peyruqueou, S., Picard, G.: ADELFE: A methodology for adaptive multi-agent systems engineering. In: Petta, P., Tolksdorf, R., Zambonelli, F. (eds.) ESAW 2002. LNCS, vol. 2577, pp. 156–169. Springer, Heidelberg (2003)

17. Esteva, M., Cruz, D.d.l., Sierra, C.: ISLANDER: an electronic institutions editor. In: International Conference on Autonomous Agents & Multiagent Systems (AAMAS 2002), Italy. ACM, New York (2002)

18. da Silva, V.T., Choren, R., de Lucena, C.J.P.: Using the MAS-ML to model a multi-agent system. In: Lucena, C., Garcia, A., Romanovsky, A., Castro, J., Alencar, P.S.C. (eds.) SELMAS 2003. LNCS, vol. 2940, pp. 129–148. Springer, Heidelberg (2004)

19. Tran, Q.N.N., Low, G.C.: Comparison of Ten Agent-Oriented Methodologies. In: Giorgini, B.H.-S.P. (ed.) Agent-Oriented Methodologies, pp. 341–367. Idea Group, Hershey (2005)

20. Giunchiglia, F., Mylopoulos, J., Perini, A.: The tropos software development methodology: Processes, models and diagrams. In: Giunchiglia, F., Odell, J.J., Weiss, G. (eds.) AOSE 2002. LNCS, vol. 2585, pp. 162–173. Springer, Heidelberg (2003)

21. Iglesias, C.A., Garijo, M.: The Agent-Oriented Methodology MAS- CommonKADS. In: Henderson-Sellers, B., Giorgini, P. (eds.) Agent-Oriented Methodologies, pp. 46–78. IDEA Group Publishing (2005)

22. DeLoach, S.A., Kumar, M.: Multi-Agent Systems Engineering: An Overview and Case Study. In: Henderson- Sellers, B., Giorgini, P. (eds.) Agent-Oriented Methodologies, pp. 236–276. IDEA Group Publishing (2005)

23. Firby, R.J.: Adaptive Execution in Dynamic Domains. Yale University, Yale (1989)

24. Garijo, F.J., Gomez-Sanz, J.J., Massonet, P.: The MESSAGE Methodology for Agent-Oriented Analysis and Design. In: Henderson-Sellers, B., Giorgini, P. (eds.) Agent-Oriented Methodologies, pp. 203–235. IDEA Group Publishing (2005)

25. Pavon, J., Gomez-Sanz, J., Fuentest, R.: The INGENIAS Methodology and Tools. In: Henderson-Sellers, B., Giorgini, P. (eds.) Agent-Oriented Methodologies, pp. 236–276. IDEA Group Publishing (2005)

26. Eydoun, G., et al.: Cooperative Modeling Evaluated. International Journal of Cooperative Information Systems 14(1), 45–71 (2005)

27. Tran, Q.-N.N., Low, G., Williams, M.-A.: A preliminary comparative feature analysis of multi-agent systems development methodologies. In: Bresciani, P., Giorgini, P., Henderson-Sellers, B., Low, G., Winikoff, M. (eds.) AOIS 2004. LNCS, vol. 3508, pp. 157–168. Springer, Heidelberg (2005)

28. Wood, B., et al.: A Guide to the Assessment of Software Development Methods, Software Engineering Institute, Carnegie Mellon University (1988)

29. Jayaratna, N.: Understanding and Evaluating Methodologies: NIMSAD, a Systematic Framework. McGraw-Hill, New York (1994)

30. Olle, T.W., Sol, H.G., Tully, C.J.: Information Systems Design Methodologies - A Feature Analysis. Elsevier Science Publishers, Amsterdam (1983)
31. Inc., T.O.A. A Comparison of Object-Oriented Development methodologies (1995), http://www.toa.com/smnn?mcr.html
32. Shehory, O., Sturm, A.: Evaluation of modeling techniques for agent-based systems. In: Proceedings of the 5th International Conference on Autonomous Agents (2001)
33. O'Malley, S.A., DeLoach, S.A.: Determining when to use an agent-oriented software engineering paradigm. In: Wooldridge, M.J., Weiß, G., Ciancarini, P. (eds.) AOSE 2001. LNCS, vol. 2222. Springer, Heidelberg (2002)
34. Cernuzzi, L., Rossi, G.: On the Evaluation of Agent-Oriented Modeling Methods. In: Proceedings of the OOPSLA Workshop on Agent-Oriented Methodologies (2002)
35. Sabas, A., Badri, M., Delisle, S.: A Multidimentional Framework for the Evaluation of Multiagent System Methodologies. In: Proceedings of the 6th World Multiconference on Systemics, Cybernetics and Informatics (SCI 2002) (2002)
36. Beydoun, G., Debenham, J., Hoffmann, A.: Using Messaging Structure to Evolve Agents Roles. In: Barley, M., Kasabov, N. (eds.) Intelligent Agents and Multi-Agent Systems VII, pp. 18–30. Springer, Australia (2005)

Entrainment in Human-Agent Text Communication

Ikuko Kanashiro[1], Kazuki Kobayashi[1], and Yasuhiko Kitamura[2]

[1] Graduate School of Science and Technology, Kwansei Gakuin University
2-1 Gakuen, Sanda, Hyogo, 669-1337 Japan
[2] School of Science and Technology, Kwansei Gakuin University,
2-1 Gakuen, Sanda, Hyogo, 669-1337 Japan
{i_kanashiro,kby,ykitamura}@ksc.kwansei.ac.jp

Abstract. Non-verbal information such as utterance speed and switching pause create an impression of the speaker. If intelligent agents could handle such non-verbal information properly, the quality of interactions between agents and human users would improve. Entrainment is a phenomenon in which brainwave synchronization is established by means of periodic stimulus. It is reported that non-verbal information expressed by an individual entrains that expressed by another in voice communication. We have interest in how an agent can affect people though entraining the non-verbal information in text communication. Text is much easier for agents to handle than voice. Through experiments, we show that the utterance speed of an agent can entrain the duration of switching pauses used by human subjects.

Keywords: Human-agent text communication, switching pause, utterance speed, entrainment.

1 Introduction

People communicate by not only verbal information but also the non-verbal information such as the volume, pitch, and speed of the utterances and switching pause which is the silence between turns [7,8]. The non-verbal information, as well as the verbal information, creates an impression of the speaker [13]. For example, many bank clerks speak slowly and clearly. This way of speaking creates an impression of credibility which is an important attribute for bank clerks. On the other hand, TV shopping casters speak rhythmically and rapidly to introduce commercial products. The viewers receive a lot of commercial information in a short time and are tempted to buy the products. This is an effective way for TV casters to sell products.

Nagaoka et al. [1] show that the duration of the switching pauses used by a speaker in voice communication can determine his/her impression. If the duration is short, he/she appears to be unkind, and if it is long, he/she appears to be unreliable. Thus, the non-verbal information is important in creating an impression of the speaker and to make the listener take the action desired by the speaker. An intelligent agent that could handle non-verbal information properly would improve the quality of interactions between the agent and human users [10,11].

This concept also permits non-verbal information to be used to entrain the partner. In voice communication, Watanabe et al. [4] report that breathing frequency

A. Ghose, G. Governatori, and R. Sadananda (Eds.): PRIMA 2007, LNAI 5044, pp. 268–277, 2009.

establishes entrainment between two persons when they talk to each other smoothly. Nagaoka[2, 3] showed that switching pauses are entrained in voice communication. Entrainments between an artifact and people have also been observed. Komatsu et al. [5] report that utterance speed is entrained in voice communication between a person and a computer given the situation that the person and the computer interchangeably read sentences written in a script. If we can utilize entrainment properly, we can develop an artificial agent that can create desirable impressions by its non-verbal information [9].

Conventional works deal with entrainment in voice communication, but this paper deals with text communication. Text is much easier to be handled by agents than voice. Conventional text communication systems such as chat systems or messengers fail to well represent non-verbal information. Our solution is a chat system that changes that rate at which it displays individual characters in a message to alter the utterance speed.

This paper shows how an agent can entrain non-verbal information such as utterance speed and switching pauses in text communication with humans. We believe that the result will lead to the development of agents that can create affective impressions by utilizing non-verbal information.

Section 2 introduces a chat system that can control utterance speed. Section 3 shows how an agent can entrain the utterance speed and the switching pause of human users and we discuss the result in Section 4. We conclude this paper in Section 5 with our future work.

2 Chat System That Reflects Utterance Speed

Users receive no impression of utterance speed in conventional chat systems because the systems display the whole message at once when received. We developed a chat system that can control the utterance speed.

The utterance time per character (or just "utterance time") T [msec/char] is defined as

$$T = \frac{1}{V} = \frac{(T_2 - T_1)}{C} \tag{1}$$

where T_1 is the time when the sender starts typing his/her message, T_2 is the time when he/she finishes typing it, and C is the number of characters in the message. The utterance speed V [char/msec] is defined as the inverse of T.

Fig. 1 shows the components of the chat system that reflects the utterance speed of the message creator. Users A and B send messages to each other through client programs A and B, respectively. When user A inputs a message using client program A, the client sends it with the user's name and the utterance time to client program B through the server program. When client program B receives the message, it types the characters in the message one by one according to utterance time T. User B sends back his/her messages to user A and the message is processed likewise. This system allows each user to feel the utterance speed of his/her counterpart. The server program which mediates the client programs stores the history of chat data between users in a log file.

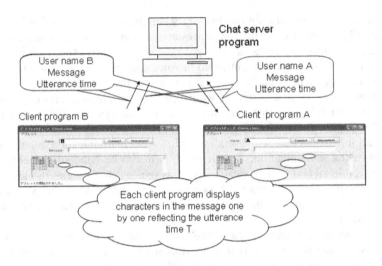

Fig. 1. Components of chat system that reflects utterance speed

3 Experiment

We here examine how an agent can entrain the non-verbal information in text communication with subjects. The non-verbal information in voice communication has
various modalities such as volume, pitch, and speed, but text communication is limited
to just speed and switching pause. We examine how these two factors can establish
entrainment.

3.1 Experiment System

We replaced a client program of the chat system shown in Fig. 1 by an agent as
shown in Fig. 2. The agent automatically sends messages to a subject. It doesn't
interpret the content of replies from the subject but merely uses them as cues for
creating its next message. When the agent receives a cue, it reads the message (m_i),
utterance time (ut_i), and switching pause (sp_i) stored in the setting file. It then applies
the switching pause and sends the message with the utterance time specified to the
subject.

The agent has no physical appearance like an avatar and all communication is
through a chat interface as shown in Fig. 3.

The subject receives a series of questions from the agent. We prepared only easy
questions such as asking for the subject's name, age, preferences, and so on, in order to
make him/her reply quickly. We didn't use tough questions that would need time to
reply because they may hinder smooth communication between the agent and the
subject. As shown in Table 1, we prepared 52 questions and stored them with corresponding utterance time and switching pause in a setting file.

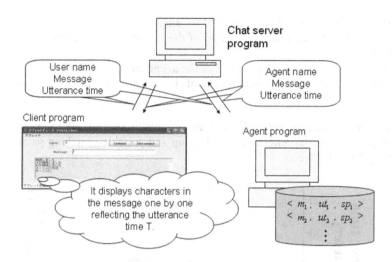

Fig. 2. Experimental system

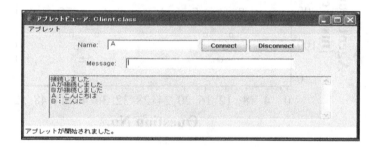

Fig. 3. User interface

Table 1. Example of questions from the agent

Question	Utterance Speed	Switching Pause
(1) Hello. May I ask you some questions? What is your name?	500.00	0.00
(2) What is your nickname?	462.50	0.00
(3) How old are you?	425.00	0.00
(4) …	…	…

3.2 Procedure

In this experiment, we examined how an agent can entrain non-verbal information expressed by subjects. Non-verbal information in text communication is limited to utterance speed and switching pause, so we examined how these factors establish entrainment. We assessed entrainment by measuring the following correlations.

(1) Correlation between utterance speed of the agent and that of the subjects
(2) Correlation between utterance speed of the agent and switching pause of the subjects
(3) Correlation between switching pause of the agent and that of the subjects
(4) Correlation between switching pause of the agent and utterance speed of the subjects

40 university students participated in this experiment as subjects. We separated them into two groups; variable utterance speed group and variable switching pause group; each group had 20 subjects.

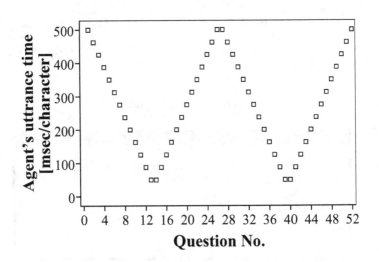

Fig. 4. Variable utterance time: agent

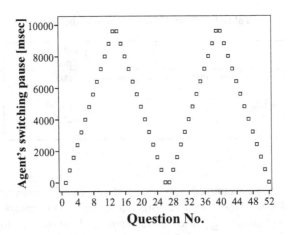

Fig. 5. Variable switching pause: agent

Each subject in the variable utterance speed group chatted with the agent whose utterance time varied from 50[msec/character] to 500[msec/character] in 13 steps of 37.5[msec/character] and with two peaks as shown in Fig. 4. The switching pause was fixed at 0[msec].

Each subject of the variable switching pause group chatted with the agent whose switching pause varied from 0[msec] to 9600[msec] with 13 levels separated by 800[msec] with two peaks as shown in Fig. 5. The utterance time was fixed at 0[msec/character] in this group so each message was displayed in its entirety.

3.3 Results

We plot variations between the utterance speed of the agent and that of subjects in Fig. 6(a). The vertical axis represents the utterance time of the agent and the horizontal axis represents that of the subjects.

Multiple-regression was used to determine the variations between the utterance speed of the agent and that of a subject [12]. We used the utterance speed of subjects as outcome variable, that of the agent and subjects as predictor variable. Subject was treated as categorical factor using dummy variable with 19 degrees of freedom. The p value from t test for the regression slope of the utterance speed of the agent was used to determine the probability of the analysis. The magnitude of correlation coefficient between the utterance speed of the agent and that of subjects was calculated as square root of (sum of squares for the utterance speed of the agent) / (sum of squares for the utterance speed of the agent + residual sum of squares). The sign of the correlation coefficient was given by that of the regression coefficient for the utterance speed of the agent. The correlation with correlation coefficient of 0.049 (p=0.111) was found, but this correlation is not significant.

Fig. 6(b) shows variations between the utterance time of the agent and the switching pause of the subjects. The correlation coefficient is 0.661 (p<0.01), so the correlation is significant and relatively strong.

Fig. 6(d) shows variations between the switching pause of the agent and that of the subjects. The correlation coefficient is -0.05 (p=0.109), so the correlation is not significant. Fig. 6(c) shows variations between the switching pause of the agent and the utterance time of the subjects. The correlation coefficient is 0.071 (p<0.05), so this correlation is significant but weak.

Table 2 summarizes the experiment's results. The utterance speed of the agent entrains the switching pause of the subjects but the other combinations do not yield any significant entrainment.

Table 2. Summary of experiment's results

		Subjects	
		utterance speed	switching pause
Agent	utterance speed	no significant correlation	relatively strong correlation
	switching pause	weak correlation	no significant correlation

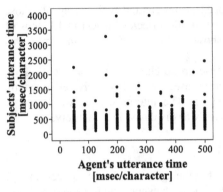

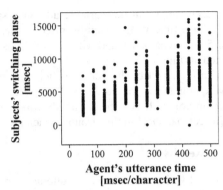

(a) Correlation between the utterance time of the agent and that of the subjects.

(b) Correlation between the utterance time of the agent and the switching pause of the subjects.

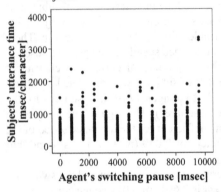

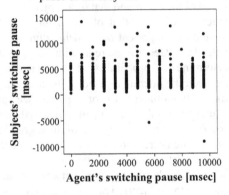

(c) Correlation between the switching pause of the agent and the utterance time of the subjects.

(d) Correlation between the switching pause of the agent and that of the subjects.

Fig. 6. Correlations of the utterance time and the switching pause between the agent and the subjects

4 Discussion

4.1 Typing Ability of Subjects

The above results show there is a relatively strong correlation between the utterance time of the agent and the switching pause of the subjects, but there is no significant correlation between the utterance time of the agent and that of the subjects. We discuss here the failure of the utterance time to establish entrainment.

Table 3 shows the correlations between utterance time of the agent and that of each subject. It indicates that 5 of the 20 subjects showed significant correlations ($p < 0.05$), though the correlation was weak. Fig. 7 shows the correlation between the utterance time of the agent and that of the subject (No.5) who showed the strongest correlation.

Table 3. Correlation between the utterance time of the agent and that of each subject

No.	Correlation coefficient	p	No.	Correlation coefficient	p
1	0.009	0.955	11	0.061	0.698
2	0.215	0.161	12	0.326	0.018*
3	0.084	0.607	13	-0.088	0.538
4	0.306	0.043*	14	0.382	0.010*
5	0.481	0.002**	15	0.206	0.150
6	0.198	0.197	16	0.203	0.209
7	0.300	0.041*	17	0.062	0.684
8	0.009	0.951	18	-0.012	0.942
9	-0.055	0.724	19	0.211	0.155
10	0.102	0.517	20	0.143	0.320

$* p < 0.05.$ $** p < 0.01.$

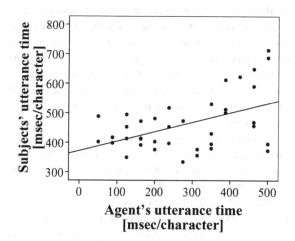

Fig. 7. Correlation between the utterance time of the agent and that of subject No.5 whose correlation is strongest in the group

The reason why most subjects were not entrained by the agent may be due to their limited typing ability. Although the subjects may have been entrained with regard to utterance speed, they may not have been able to express it because of their limited typing ability. In future work, we would like to perform this experiment again using some approach to offset the subjects' typing skills.

4.2 Switching Pause of the Agent

The experiment showed that the switching pause of the agent failed to establish entrainment. The reason may reflect how the subjects interpreted the switching pause of the agent. After this experiment, some subjects said they thought the chat system or the network was out of order. The subjects thought that the change in switching pause was merely due to a system problem but not due to the agent.

4.3 Affective Influence on Subjects

Changes in the agent's utterance speed influenced the subjects. In the experiment, the utterance speed of the agent entrained the switching pause of the subjects. The increased utterance speed of the agent goaded the subjects to replying more quickly. In future work, we need to examine the affective influence of the agent's utterance speed on the subjects in detail, for example by using a questionnaire survey or by measuring biometrics such as sweating or cardiac rate.

5 Summary

Communication between people involves not only verbal information but also non-verbal information, and the non-verbal information also creates an impression of the speaker. We find that entrainment can be established by non-verbal information.

Conventional studies on entrainment consider voice communication between two people or between a person and an agent, but we deal with entrainment in text communication. In this paper, we examined how the two factors of non-verbal information, utterance speed and switching pause, can entrain the responses of human subjects. For this experiment, we developed a chat system which uses typing speed to be used as an indicator of utterance speed.

We conducted an experiment to show that the utterance speed of an agent entrains the switching pause of subjects. We could not observe any other significant entrainment among the other combinations of utterance speed and switching pause. We can conclude that the utterance speed is effective in establishing entrainment, and that switching pause is entrained by the utterance speed.

In future work, we will examine the affective influence of utterance speed on people. We expect this work is lead to that development of interface agents that affectively interact with human users through the use of non-verbal information in text communication.

References

1. Nagaoka, C., Draguna, M., Komori, M., Nakamura, T.: The Influence of Switching Pauses on Interpersonal Perception in Dialogues. In: Proc. of Human Interface 2002, pp. 171–174 (2002) (in Japanese)
2. Nagaoka, C., Draguna, M., Komori, M., Kawase, S., Nakamura, T.: The Mutual Influence of the Speakers' Switching Pauses in Dialogues. In: Proc. of Human Interface 2001, pp. 221–224 (2001) (in Japanese)
3. Nagaoka, C., Komori, M., Nakamura, T.: The interspeaker influence of the switching pauses in dialogue. Japanese Journal of Ergonomics 38(6), 316–323 (2002)
4. Watanabe, T., Okubo, M.: Physiological Analysis of Entrainment in Face-to-Face Communication. In: Proceedings of the Seventh International Conference on Human-Computer Interaction, pp. 411–414 (1997)

5. Komatsu, T., Morikawa, K.: Entrainment in the Rate of Utterance in Speech Dialogs Between Users and an Auto Response System. Journal of Universal Computer Science 13(2), 186–198 (2007)
6. Fogg, B.J.: Persuasive Technology: Using Computers to Change What We Think and Do. Morgan Kaufmann, San Francisco (2003)
7. Vargas, M.F., Words, L.T.: An Introduction to Nonverbal Communication. Iowa State University Press (1987)
8. Patterson, M.L.: Nonverbal Behavior: A Functional Perspective. Springer, Heidelberg (1983)
9. Picard, R.: Affective Computing. MIT Press, Cambridge (1997)
10. Cassell, J., Sullivan, J., Prevost, S., Churchill, E.: Embodied Conversational Agents. MIT Press, Cambridge (2000)
11. Prendinger, H., Ishizuka, M. (eds.): Life-Like Characters. Springer, Heidelberg (2004)
12. Bland, J.M., Altman, D.G.: Calculating correlation coefficients with repeated observations: Part 1 – correlation within subjects. Brit. Med. J. 310, 446 (1995)
13. Reeves, B., Nass, C.: The Media Equation. CSLI Publications (1998)

A Driver Modeling Methodology
Using Hypothetical Reasoning
for Multiagent Traffic Simulation

Yusuke Tanaka, Yuu Nakajima, Hiromitsu Hattori, and Toru Ishida

Department of Social Informatics, Kyoto University
Yoshida Honmachi, Sakyo-ku, Kyoto, 606-8501 Japan
{ytanaka,nkjm}@ai.soc.i.kyoto-u.ac.jp, {hatto,ishida}@i.kyoto-u.ac.jp

Abstract. We propose how to acquire driver's individual operation models using the three-dimensional driving simulator in order to implement distinct personalities on each agent. In this paper, operation models are defined as sets of prioritized operation rules, each of which consists of the world as observed by a driver and his/her next operation according to the observation. Each driver might have different set of rules and their priorities. We apply a method to acquire individual operation models using hypothetical reasoning. Because of the method, we are able to obtain operation models which can explain driver's operation during driving simulation. We show some operation models acquired from aged/young human drivers, and then clarify the proposed method can catch each driver's characteristics.

1   Introduction

Multiagent-based traffic simulation has been considered as one of the promising approach to analyze traffic flow [1,2]. In the multiagent traffic simulation, each human driver is modeled as an agent, which has common properties for driving. In the real world, there is a variety of drivers, such as aged drivers, novice drivers, and so on. In order to incorporate such variety of driver's properties into the traffic simulation, it is required to develop techniques to construct human driver's operation model [3,4,5].

We propose how to acquire driver's individual operation models using the three-dimensional driving simulator in order to implement distinct personalities on each agent. In this paper, we define an operation model as sets of prioritized operation rules, each of which consists of the world as observed by a driver and his/her next operation according to the observation. Each driver might have different set of rules and their priorities. In this paper, we address the following two research issues:

1) **Forming individual operation models from driving simulation log**
   In order to acquire diverse driver models, we extract individual operation models from driving simulation log data.

A. Ghose, G. Governatori, and R. Sadananda (Eds.): PRIMA 2007, LNAI 5044, pp. 278–287, 2009.

2) Efficient acquisition of individual operation models

In order to form individual operation models, time-consuming tasks are required, such as recruitment of examinees, analysis of simulation log data. Therefore, we try to enable formation of operation models from little log data and operation rules, which are extracted through the interview with the small number of examinees.

For achieving these two issues, we apply a method using hypothetical reasoning for modeling driver's operation [6]. To put it concretely, driver's operation models are acquired according to the following process; 1) acquisition of examinees' behavior, 2) formal description of the observations in predicate logic, 3) extraction of operation rules through the interviews, and 4) construction of operation models from collected behavior and operation rules based on hypothetical reasoning.

From the viewpoint of traffic engineering, it is sometimes unclear what operation rules are used by an individual driver when he/she is driving a vehicle. In contrast, we can acquire operation models with only operation rules by using a method based on hypothetical reasoning.

The remainder of the paper is organized as follows. First, we describe the modeling process using hypothetical reasoning with log data resulting from driving simulation. Second, we define technical terms used in this paper, and then formalize our target problem by using the defined terms for hypothetical reasoning. Then, we apply a learning method using hypothetical reasoning to driving simulations for acquisition of operation models. Finally, concluding remarks are given in the final section and we also discuss possible future directions.

2   Modeling Process Using Driving Simulation Log

We explain an agent modeling process using hypothetical reasoning in our research. In the process, first, we conduct driving simulation on the three-dimensional driving simulator. Then, we acquire an examinee's operation model, a set of operation rules, by explaining the examinee's behavior observed in one or more driving simulations. However, the obtained operation rules may exhibit some incompatibility. Therefore, we hypothesize whether each operation rule is employed by the target examinee, and choose the assumptions that pass hypothetical reasoning, which offers the consistent selection of hypotheses. The result of hypothetical reasoning is a set of compatible operation rules employed by the target examinee. Some log data are not explained using operation rules, and then such data is removed. Details of an agent modeling process is as follows (also shown in Figure 1):

1) **Accumulation of driving log:** Conduct driving simulations where each examinee drives a virtual car on the driving simulator.
2) **Log data cleaning:** Eliminate operation log data which cannot be explained by operation rules.
3) **Formal description of the observations:** Collect an observation from log data in driving simulations and describe the observations in predicate

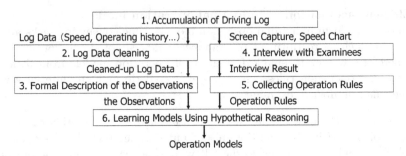

Fig. 1. Modeling Process

logic. In this paper, "observation" means the world (environment) which is observed by an examinee.

4) **Interview with examinees:** Interview with examinees using screen capture during driving simulation and kinds of charts.

5) **Collecting operation rules:** Collect operation rules constituting domain knowledge from the result of interview. In this paper, each operation rule represents what examinees observed and how they operated during simulations.

6) **Learning models using hypothetical reasoning:** Acquire candidate operation models using hypothetical reasoning with the domain knowledge and the observations. As we mentioned above, operation models are defined as sets of prioritized operation rules.

In this paper, we focus on how to acquire operation models using hypothetical reasoning from log data resulting from driving simulations.

3 Formalization of the Problem in Driving Simulation

In this section, in order to apply hypothetical reasoning to the acquisition of operation models, we formally define operation rules, observations, and operation models.

3.1 Operation Rules

We describe an operation rule as a condition-action rule. The condition part of a rule describes an examinee's operation and the action part describes situation observed by an examinee. If and only if all conditions are satisfied, the action part of the rule could be executed. Example 1 shows a description of operation rules.

Example 1: Description of operation rules
$rule_1$: if $Curve(x),InSight(x,\text{self})$ then $LoosenAccel(\text{self})$
$rule_2$: if $Uphill(x),InSight(x,\text{self})$ then $StrengthenAccel(\text{self})$
$rule_3$: if $MoreThanDesiredSpeed(\text{self})$ then $LoosenAccel(\text{self})$

$rule_1$: if an examinee(self) sees($InSight$) a curve $x(Curve)$, he/she releases the accelerator($LoosenAccel$). $rule_2$: if an examinee sees an uphill road $x(Uphill)$, he/she depresses the accelerator($StrengthenAccel$). $rule_3$: if the speed of examinee's vehicle is over his/her desired speed($MoreThanDesiredSpeed$), he/she releases the accelerator.

3.2   Observation

The observation, which is included in log data, is described in predicate logic according to the time line. We use road shape, driving speed, and acceleration pedal operation as observations. An example of the description of observation is as follows:

Example 2: Description of observation
$Curve(Curve_2) \wedge InSight(Curve_2, \text{self}) \wedge Uphill(Uphill_3) \wedge$
$On(Uphill_3, \text{self}) \wedge Accelerate(\text{self}) \wedge MoreThanDesiredSpeed(\text{self}) \wedge$
$StrengthenAccel(\text{self}) \Rightarrow Do(LoosenAccel(\text{self}))$

This observation means that an examinee releases the accelerator when the examinee sees $Curve_2$, his/her vehicle is running on $Uphill_3(On)$, he/she is increasing speed($Accelerate$), the speed of vehicle is over his/her desired speed, and he/she depresses the accelerator. In this example, Do is a predicate meaning that he/she initiates an operation.

3.3   Operation Model

An operation model consists of sets of prioritized operation rules which are actually used by an examinee. If the condition part of an operation rule is satisfied, the rule is available to use. If there are many usable rules, the one which has the highest priority is chosen. Example 3 shows a description of an operation model.

Example 3: Description of operation model
$(rule_1, rule_2, rule_3, rule_2 \preceq rule_1)$

The meaning of this example is as follows. An examinee uses $rule_1$, $rule_2$, and $rule_3$. The priority of $rule_1$ is higher than that of $rule_2$, and thus when both of the condition part of $rule_1$ and $rule_2$ are satisfied at the same time, he/she uses $rule1$.

4   Detail of Driver Modeling

In this section, we are showing how to apply hypothetical reasoning to the acquisition of examinee's operation models in driving simulation.

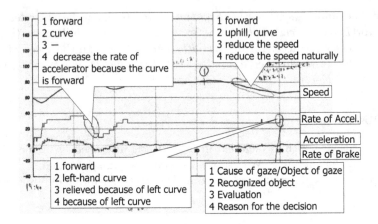

Fig. 2. Log data with the result of the Interviews

4.1   Driving Simulation

In our research, we try to acquire log data from aged examinees and young examinees, and then investigate their decision making process to determine their operation. During driving simulation, each examinee drives 11km road including diverse road alignments. In order to focus on the relationship between each examinee's operations and road conditions, we choose solo driving scenario. Through the investigation, we analyze the relationship between each examinee's operations and road conditions.

Figure 2[1] shows an example of log data with answers at post simulation interview. The horizontal axis denotes the elapsed time, and the vertical axis denotes speed (km/h), acceleration (m/ss), the rate of acceleration/brake(%).

4.2   Collecting and Cleaning-Up Log Data

In this research, we use the following data to construct operation models.

1) **Time(s):** The elapsed time from the beginning of driving simulation.
2) **Mileage(km):** The mileage from the start point.
3) **Speed(km/h):** The speed of examinee's vehicle
4) **Rate of Accel./Brake(%):** The rate of acceleration/braking, *i.e.*, accelerator/brake pedal position. When an examinee does not step on the pedal, the rate is 0%, and he/she fully steps on the pedal, the rate is 100%.

During driving simulation, there is a possibility of examinee's unintentional/ meaningless operation. For example, an examinee sometimes increases the speed without any explicit reasons. Currently, we only have a method to acquire models from examinee's intentional operation. This is because an operation rule consists

---

[1] The log data is offered by Iida Lab., Osaka University.

of intentional operation and surrounding environment, so that it is impossible to explain an unintentional operation by using operation rules. Therefore, we eliminate unintentional operation log before the step for acquiring operation models. Currently, we take the following two policies for the elimination.

1) **Elimination of unintentional operations**
   In general, it is practically difficult to execute intentional operations in short time. Thus, we eliminate such operations from log data. We empirically eliminate operations which are subsequently executed within 2 seconds (shown in Figure 3).

2) **Elimination of operations unrelated to surrounding environment**
   An examinee sometimes continuously executes operations until he/she can recognize the change of surrounding environment. For example, when an examinee wants to reduce the speed, he/she steps on the brake several times. This is because it takes time to get to the desired speed. In such case, there are many moves in log data due to the continuous operations. Therefore, we use only the first operation and eliminate subsequent operations. Empirically, we eliminate operations subsequently executed within 3.5 seconds (also shown in Figure 3).

4.3   Description of Observation

We describe observations, extracted from log data, based on predicate logic. In this paper, we pick up observations which could affect examinees' operations, and define the following predicates.

$Straight(x)$, $Curve(x)$, $Uphill(x)$, $Downhill(x)$: x is straight/curve/ uphill/downhill

$On(x, y)$: y is running on x

$Finish(x, y)$: y is running at the end of curve x

$InSight(x, y)$: y can see x

$Sharp(x)$, $Slow(x)$: x($e.g.$ curve, slope) is sharp or slow

$MoreThanDesiredSpeed(x)$, $LessThanDesiredSpeed(x)$: the speed of vehicle x is over the desired speed

$MoreThanCurveSpeed(x, y)$: the speed of vehicle y is too high to safely drive in curve x

$Accelerate(x)$, $Decelerate(x)$: the vehicle x is accelerating/decelerating

$KeepAccel(x)$: x keeps the rate of acceleration

$StrengthenAccel(x)$: x is increasing the rate of acceleration

$LoosenAccel(x)$: x is decreasing the rate of acceleration

$ReleaseAccel(x)$: x is releasing the accelerator

$Brake(x)$: x is stepping on the brake

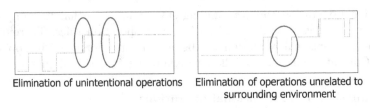

Elimination of unintentional operations   Elimination of operations unrelated to
                                            surrounding environment

Fig. 3. Types of Elimination

4.4   Interview

We interview an examinee with a chart which shows speed/acceleration/rate of accelerator and brake. Additionally, we use screen capture of an examinee's screen in order to help him/her to remember his/her behavior during simulation. In the interview, we ask about the following four points:

1) **Cause of gaze/Object of gaze:** The reason why an examinee gazes something or the thing what an examinee gazes.
2) **Recognized object:** The thing what an examinee recognizes
3) **Evaluation:** The feeling that an examinee has
4) **Reason for the decision:** The reason of examinee's decision making

In this paper, we have an interview on some points where the speed/acceleration is drastically changed (5km/h, 5m/ss) or his/her rate of acceleration is drastically changed (10%). Examples of answers to above four points are shown in Figure 2.

4.5   Extraction of Operation Rules

We analyze the result of interview and log data, then we generate an operation rule which can denote an examinee's generic operation. We extract the condition part of a rule by analyzing the result of interview (cause of gaze, recognized object). We extract the action part of a rule by analyzing examinee's operations for the condition. In this paper, we extract operation rules from aged and young examinees. As a result, the following operation rules are extracted.

$rule_1$: if an examinee sees a curve ahead, he/she releases the accelerator
$rule_2$: if an examinee sees a curve ahead and the speed of vehicle is too high to drive the curve, he/she releases the accelerator
$rule_3$: if an examinee sees a sharp curve ahead and the speed of vehicle is too high to drive the curve, he/she releases the accelerator
$rule_4$: if an examinee is driving at the end of a curve, he/she depresses the accelerator
$rule_5$: if an examinee sees an uphill ahead, he/she depresses the accelerator
$rule_6$: if an examinee sees a downhill ahead, he/she releases the accelerator
$rule_7$: if an examinee is driving on an uphill, he/she depresses the accelerator
$rule_8$: if an examinee is driving on a downhill, he/she releases the accelerator

$rule_9$: if the speed is over the desired speed, an examinee releases the accelerator

$rule_{10}$: if an examinee is driving on a straight road and the speed is under the desired speed, he/she depresses the accelerator

$rule_{11}$: if an examinee depresses the accelerator and then the vehicle is accelerating, he/she keeps the rate of the accelerator

$rule_{12}$: if an examinee releases the accelerator and then the vehicle is decelerating, he/she keeps the rate of the accelerator.

4.6   Operation Models

In this section, we show operation models acquired by our proposed method.

Example 1: Operation model acquired from the aged examinee A04

$(\{rule_7, rule_8, rule_{11}, rule_{12}\}, rule_7 = rule_8 \preceq rule_{11}, rule_7 = rule_8 \preceq rule_{12})$

This model means that the aged examinee A04 used four operation rules ($rule_7$, $rule_8$, $rule_{11}$, $rule_{12}$). Figure 4(a) shows the order of priorities of these rules. In this figure, the direction of an arrow describes the order of priority between rules. An rule with an arrow-head has the higher priority. For example, the priority of $rule_{11}$ is higher than that of $rule_7$ and $rule_8$. $rule_7 = rule_8$ means that $rule_7 \preceq rule_8$ and $rule_8 \preceq rule_7$ are approved. In the figure, an arrow in both direction shows that the priorities of both rules are same.

Example 2: Operation model acquired from the aged examinee A20

$(\{rule_5, rule_7, rule_9, rule_{11}, rule_{12}\}, rule_5 = rule_7 = rule_9 \preceq rule_{11},$
$rule_5=rule_7=rule_9\preceq rule_{12})$

This model means that the aged examinee A20 used five operation rules ($rule_5$, $rule_7$, $rule_9$, $rule_{11}$, $rule_{12}$). Figure 4(b) shows the order of priorities of rules. Because the order of priorities of three rules ($rule_5$, $rule_7$, $rule_9$) are same, this model represents that the examinee depressed or released the pedal when he/she saw an uphill and the speed of his/her vehicle was over the desired speed. Therefore, it would appear that he/she could not always sense an uphill and the driving speed was over his/her desired speed.

Example 3: Operation model acquired from the young examinee Y01

$(\{rule_7, rule_{11}\})$

This simple model (Figure 4(c)) means that the young examinee Y01 drove based on only two operation rules ($rule_7$, $rule_{11}$). Because the condition part of these rules could not be satisfied at the same time, the order of priorities of these rules are not fixed.

Example 4: Operation model acquired from the young examinee Y08

$(\{rule_7, rule_8, rule_9, rule_{11}, rule_{12}\}, rule_7\preceq rule_8=rule_9, rule_7\preceq rule_{12})$

This model (Figure 4(d)) means that the young examinee Y08 used five operation rules ($rule_7$, $rule_8$, $rule_9$, $rule_{11}$, $rule_{12}$). Figure 4 shows the order of priorities of these rules. Because the priority of $rule_9$ is higher than that of $rule_7$, it

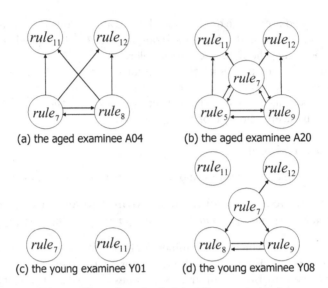

Fig. 4. The order of priorities of operation rules

would appear that the examinee wanted to keep his/her desired speed instead of keeping up the speed on an uphill.

In this research, operation models of a young examinee usually consists of less numbers of operation rules. On the other hand, the models of an aged examinee consists of more numbers of rules. That is to say, an young examinee tends to drive a vehicle based on simple driving model and an aged one tends to drive a vehicle based on relatively complex model.

5   Conclusion

For conducting multiagent-based traffic simulation, one of the central issue is how to model an agent including diverse characteristics of a human driver. For achieving this issue, we proposed a method to acquire operation models using hypothetical reasoning, and then showed acquired operation models from aged/young human drivers. The main contributions of this paper are the following two points:

1) **A method to acquire operation models from log data in driving simulation**

We have proposed a method to acquire operation models of an individual examinee using log data in driving simulation. In the proposed method, first the interview is conducted to catch the reasons of behaviors during driving simulation, and operation rules are described using predefined predicates. Then, we use hypothetical reasoning to acquire characteristic operation models. The acquired model is sets of prioritized operation rules.

2) Reduction of modeling cost

Actually, having the interview and log data analysis are time-consuming task. However, in our method, firstly operation rules are acquired from some examinees. Then, all acquired rules are usable for explaining any examinee's log data. We do not need to interview all examinees and analyze all log data, so thus we could cut out troublesome modeling cost.

In the proposed method, it is possible to acquire promising operation models if an examinee takes simple "intentional" operations. That is to say, when we use straightforward log data, the proposed modeling process using hypothetical reasoning could work well. If there is noise data, *i.e.* "unintentional" operations, it becomes difficult to accurately acquire operation model. Our possible future work includes: improving noise-canceling method in order to acquire more sophisticated operation model; incorporating more information (condition) into operation rules; implementation of the models, operating on traffic simulation, based on the acquired operation models; analyzing the validity of the models for practical traffic simulation by making evaluation experiments.

Acknowledgment

The authors would like to thank K. Iida for making this work possible. This research was partially supported by a Grant-in-Aid for Scientific Research (A) (18200009, 2006-2008) from Japan Society for the Promotion of Science (JSPS).

References

1. Paruchuri, P., Pullalarevu, A.R., Karlapalem, K.: Multi agent simulation of unorganized traffic. In: Proceedings of The First International Joint Conference on Autonomous Agents and Multiagent Systems (AAMAS 2002), pp. 176–183 (2002)
2. Balmer, M., Cetin, N., Nagel, K., Raney, B.: Towards truly agent-based traffic and mobility simulations. In: The Third International Joint Conference on Autonomous Agents and Multiagent Systems (AAMAS 2004), pp. 60–67 (2004)
3. Espie, S.: Vehicle-driven simulator versus traffic-driven simulator: the inrets approach. In: Driving Simulation Conference (DSC 1999), pp. 367–376 (1999)
4. Bonabeau, E.: Agent-based modeling: Methods and techniques for simulating human systems. Proceedings of the National Academy of Sciences of the United States of America 99(10), 7280–7287 (2002)
5. Fernlund, H., Gonzalez, A.J., Gerber, W.J., DeMara, R.F., Georgiopoulos, M.: Learning tactical human behavior through observation of human actor. IEEE Transactions on Systems, Man and Cybernetics (2005)
6. Murakami, Y., Sugimoto, Y., Ishida, T.: Modeling human behavior for virtual training systems. In: The 20th National Conference on Artificial Intelligence (AAAI 2005), pp. 127–132 (2005)

Analysis of Pedestrian Navigation
Using Cellular Phones

Yuu Nakajima[1], Takatoshi Oishi[1], Toru Ishida[1], and Daisuke Morikawa[2]

[1] Department of Social Informatics, Kyoto University
Yoshida-Honmachi, Sakyo-ku, Kyoto, 606-8501, Japan
{nkjm,oishi,ishida}@ai.soc.i.kyoto-u.ac.jp
[2] KDDI R&D Laboratories Inc.
2-1-15 Ohara, Fujimino, Saitama, 356-8502, Japan
morikawa@kddilabs.jp

Abstract. Navigation services for pedestrians are spreading in recent years. Our approach to provide personal navigation is to build a multi-agent system that assigns one guiding agent to each human. This paper attempts to demonstrate a design implication of the guiding agent. In the navigation experiment where a pedestrian using a map on a GPS-capable cellular phone was guided by a distant navigator, we observed the communication between them by conversation analysis. The result suggests that information required by a pedestrian were the current location, the current direction and a proper route toward a destination. The communications between a pedestrian and a navigator were based on a navigation map or a movement history. When a pedestrian did not understand the map adequately, navigation sometimes failed due to the lack of communication basis.

1 Introduction

Traveling in an unfamiliar city is a daily task for ordinary people. For instance, they look for meeting spots or shops in unfamiliar cities. These days, more and more pedestrians use cellular phones as information sources for route guidance. Pedestrians use cellular phones in two ways as information sources. One is displaying a map showing the current location, and the other is consulting with a distant navigator via voice conversations.

Due to the popularity of and improvement in sensor devices and network devices, environments that support ubiquitous computing are spreading. In such environments, it is possible to provide personal navigation that suits the properties, the location and the context of each user [1]. We built evacuation navigation system based on multi-agent server, which assigns one guiding agent to each human. In this system, an agent can provide a personalized navigation map considering the current location and the surrounding environment [2][3].

Some people may not be able to reach their destination even if they use such navigation systems. People who are not good at reading maps should ask others for help. This paper assumes that pedestrians take part in evacuation drill with

A. Ghose, G. Governatori, and R. Sadananda (Eds.): PRIMA 2007, LNAI 5044, pp. 288–297, 2009.

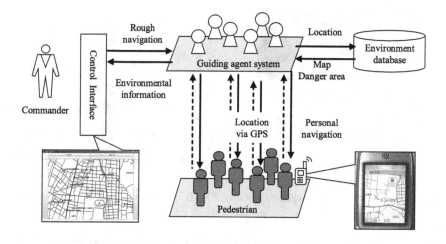

Fig. 1. Large-scale evacuation guide system with guiding agents

the evacuation navigation system. To demonstrate requirements of the guiding agent, we address the following two issues.

Analysis of information required by pedestrian. To examine a design implication of the guiding agent, it is necessary to investigate the information requirements of pedestrians when they use a navigation map.

Analysis of communication between pedestrian and navigator. A pedestrian cannot be always guided into a proper route by a distant navigator. Investigation of failure cases is needed in order to examine the limitation of remote navigation. We analyze the communication between the pedestrian and the navigator using conversation analysis[1].

2   Large-Scale Evacuation Guide System

We produced a large-scale evacuation guide system based on large scale agent platform and GPS-capable cellular phones. Fig. 1 depicts system architecture of pedestrian navigation system [3]. In a navigation system which uses ubiquitous information infrastructure on a city, the system can acquire information of each individual user in real time. However, quantity of the information becomes enormous. There occurs a problem that a human who control system cannot handle all the information. Our approach is that a human gives rough navigation to agents and the agents give precise navigation to each person. We aim at realizing a mega scale navigation system using GPS-capable cellular phones.

The control interface was implemented based on transcendent communication architecture. Transcendent communication is proposed as the method for navigation in public spaces [5]. In transcendent communication, the distribution of

---

[1] Conversation analysis is a methodology for studying social interaction. It was principally developed by Harvey Sacks and Emanuel Schegloff [4].

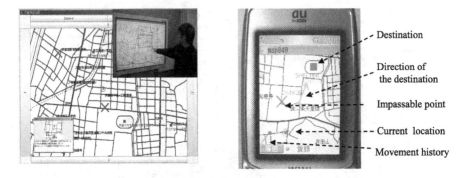

Fig. 2. User interface of navigation system   **Fig. 3.** Navigation map on cellular phone

evacuees in the real space is reproduced on the virtual space as human figures that mirror the positions of evacuees; the positions of the subjects are acquired by sensors. The system commander assigns evacuation destinations and evacuation directions through the control interface shown in Fig. 2. The commander issues high level instructions to the guiding agents using a map.

The guiding agents that assigned to evacuees on a one-to-one basis provide individual navigation maps via GPS-capable cellular phones. An agent is instructed on a direction of evacuation by the control center. The agent retrieves shelters around the user, and selects a destination according to the ordered direction and distance between the user and each shelter. The agent also obtains the surrounding environmental data from a database. Then, the agent sends their users personalized navigation map showing a destination, the direction, impassible point, the current location and the movement history as indicated on Fig. 3.

3   Experiment of Pedestrian Navigation

3.1   Overveiw of Experiment

We conducted two navigation experiments in which pedestrians were guided by distant navigators using the large-scale evacuation navigation system. These experiments have two purposes. One is to investigate the information required by pedestrians, and the other is to analyze communication between the pedestrian and the navigator. May et al. already examined information requirements in an experiment of navigation based on turn-by-turn strategy [6]. However the human subjects did not take along a map showing the current location in the research.

We analyzed the information requirements with *think aloud method* [7] which was to observe what human subjects behave and think. The method has actually been applied to experiments in navigation systems. In the method, an experimenter instructs human subjects to think aloud while performing tasks. The experimenter observes the human subjects' behavior and thinking at the same

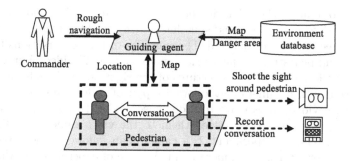

Fig. 4. Experiment 1: observation of conversation between pedestrians

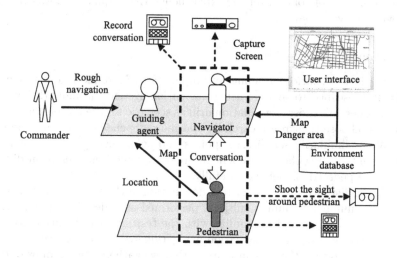

Fig. 5. Experiment 2: observation of conversation between pedestrian and navigator

time. The experimenter can combine human subjects' behavior with their feelings about the system which they have in mind. In these navigation experiments, we observed two kinds of conversations.

Observation of conversation between pedestrians. The pedestrians used navigation system which provided a map as Fig. 3. In the first experiment, we let human subjects to use system in pairs and instructed them to talk to each other (Fig. 4). We refer to this experiment as *experiment 1*.

Observation of conversation between pedestrian and navigator. In the second experiment, pedestrians used the navigation system and consulted with distant navigators via voice conversations (Fig. 5). We instructed pedestrians to talk to navigators anytime they have a question. We call this experiment as *experiment 2*.

In order to analyze the relativity between the conversation and the behavior, we needed to gather actions, speeches and eye sights of human subjects. Following three data were collected; 1) recordings of the conversations between pedestrians and pedestrian or pedestrian and navigator, 2) video pictures of the behavior of pedestrians, 3) video pictures of the sight pedestrians have seen.

In experiment 1, a cameraman followed a pair of pedestrians and shot their behaviors with video camera. We recorded speeches of the pedestrians with attached microphones and transmitted them to the video camera by Bluetooth audio transmitters. In experiment 2, a cameraman followed a pedestrian and shot his behavior with video camera as in the case of experiment 1. Maps provided to pedestrians and navigation screens were recorded by DV video recorder. Conversations between the pedestrian and the navigator were also recorded with call-recording microphone. After the experiments, the graphic data was synchronized with the voice data.

3.2   Scenario of Experiment

We assumed the scenario that a huge earthquake struck around Kyoto University and dwellers escaped to shelters using navigation system through GPS-capable cellular phones. We chose a evacuation drill as scenario for the reason that pedestrians must choose their route carefully and more depended on the system than usual. We preliminarily set disaster points and subsequently added secondary disaster points during the experiment in order to make route selection difficult and to make pedestrians behave carefully.

The direct distance from a start to a destination in the experiment was about 1.5 km. The number of human subjects performed as pedestrians was four. All of them were students and unfamiliar with the testing area. Additionally, they had no experience using the evacuation navigation system. In experiment 1, the pedestrians performed the task in pairs so that we gathered two groups of data. In experiment 2, the pedestrians performed the task alone so that we gathered four groups of data.

3.3   Task and Instruction

In experiment 1, pairs of pedestrians left start points and headed for destination points. They consulted a map showing the current location on a cellular phone and talked to each other on their travel. In experiment 2, pedestrians had two cellular phones so that they could consult with a distant navigator in parallel with reading a map. When they have any questions or any troubles, they could consult the navigator to resolve it.

In experiment 2, the task of a navigator was to answer questions from a pedestrian. The navigator was expected to make the maximum efforts to answer any questions from a pedestrian. The navigator should use information on the navigation system sufficiently. An information screen for a navigator is shown in Fig. 2. A navigator could view environmental information about a local area, the current locations of pedestrians and a map provided to a pedestrian. Considering

Table 1. Conversation about current location

> A: ((The corner to turn is)) here? What do you think about that?
> B: Further, isn't it further? Because it is still
> A: What? But it ((= map)) has not reloaded yet.
> B: I see.

those information, the navigator guided the pedestrian via voice conversation. The navigator answered the questions consulting a screen of navigation system. Experimenters who were familiar with the experimental area acted as navigators. Additionally they had practiced guiding pedestrians beforehand. They guided pedestrians one-on-one in the experiment. The purpose of the experiment is to analyze what kind of information pedestrians required. Therefore a navigator must not speak to a pedestrian voluntarily.

Pedestrians ware expected to be aware of the necessity to select routes carefully and to be encouraged to voice what they are thinking in these experiments. To ensure it, we gave the instructions below to the human subjects in the experiments; "This is an evacuation drill. Pedestrians are expected to act carefully and to commit themselves to reach shelters in safety", "Disaster points are impassable so that pedestrians must avoid them".

4   Result and Analysis

4.1   Information Required by Pedestrians

Conversations about questions, confirmations and trouble were extracted from pedestrians' speeches and transcribed. These transcripts were categorized according to pedestrian's intentions or pedestrian's demands. The result shows that the pedestrians required information about the current location, the current direction and a proper route to a destination. The information was used to confirm and trust a route as well as decide it. The information required by pedestrians are categorized into the following three types.

Current location. In Table 1 case, pedestrians could not have the confidence in correspondence between a map and the real world. Such cases were frequently observed when pedestrians could not recognize the corner that they had decided to turn as reading a map in advance.

Current direction. In Table 2 case, pedestrians could not understand a map properly because of losing sense of direction. Sense of direction was important for understanding maps.

Proper route toward destination. In Table 3 case, pedestrians were not only aware of the current location and the current direction but also read the map properly. However they had no concrete idea which route is optimal.

We describe the details about the three kinds of information with the transcripts that actually observed in the experiment. In the following transcripts, 'P:'

Table 2. Conversation about current direction

A: So, ((should we read the map)) in this direction? ((should we go)) in this way?
B: This way.
A: Is this OK?
B: eh?
A: ((We should read this map)) in this direction, don't you? Yes, yes, because we are walking this way now.
B: This way, this way, it's bad to read the map as it is.
A: Yes, it is.

Table 3. Conversation about route selection

A: Which route? This one?
B: How about downside? ((See the road heading southward)) this way?
A: I agree. Because the danger zone exists over there, this way is better

means an utterance of a pedestrian and 'N:' means an utterance of a navigator. Number in parentheses indicates elapsed time in silence by tenth of seconds and a dot in parentheses indicates a tiny gap within or between utterances. A phrase bracketed by '()' means unclear speech. A phrase bracketed by '(())' means a supplement by us. The plural sentences started with '[' means that they are started at the same time. ':' shows sounds are stretched or drawn out (number of : indicates the length of stretching). ',' means continuing intonation. '?' means rising intonation and '.' means closing or stopping intonation.

4.2   The Failed Case of Verbal Navigation

Questions about route selection were most frequently observed in experiment 2. A navigator tried to guide a pedestrian, but the navigator sometimes could not guide him to a proper route. Hereinafter, we discuss failure cases of verbal navigation and analyze why they failed communications.

Table 4 shows an example of failed navigation caused by a navigator that could not recognize a situation of a pedestrian. In Table 4, the pedestrian asked the navigator about route selection (see line 2). In the case, the navigator could not understand the pedestrian's situation and failed to navigate the pedestrian (line 4-11). The navigator ended the conversation with an instruction to check the current direction using the movement history. The map on a cellular phone showed an instruction to go southward but the pedestrian lost sense of direction and wrongly started going eastward as saying "I start walking randomly" (line 13). The conversation was started with the request for route guidance but the navigator could not meet the pedestrian's demand. The navigation failed due to the difficulty for the navigator to check the pedestrian's situation in the case.

Table 4. Failure case of navigation caused by obscurity of pedestrian's situation

```
 1  ((Pedestrian stops just after departure and ask the route to navigator))
 2  P: Now, which direction ((to go))? (0.5) Should I turn at first, leaving the park?
 3     (1.6)
 4  N: Well:, Can you see a road (.) heading southward straight?
 5  P: ((starts walking))Southward,((look around))((turn back))
 6  P: Well, maybe.
 7     (0.6)
 8  N: Well, hard to fi:nd?
 9  P: Yes. I can't grasp the direction.
10     (0.4)
11  N: Well.
12     (0.9)
13  P: Oh, now (.) I start walking randomly.
```

A map on a cellular phone was reloaded every one minute. Location measurement and a server access took about 15 seconds on the navigation system. Consequently, the map was updated every 75 seconds. Additionally, location measurement via GPS sometimes has a gap between the current location shown on the map and the current location in the real world. Resolving the gap, the navigator was required to ask some questions to the pedestrian about the pedestrian's situation at first. However, when the pedestrian was lost and asked the navigator for guidance, it was difficult for the navigator to get actual information from the pedestrian. The failure cases are considered to be caused by the lack of common basis between the pedestrian and the navigator.

4.3   The Successful Case of Verbal Navigation

Table 5 shows a transcript of information sharing based on a navigation map. First, the pedestrian asked the question "Does this bold black line mean this big street?" (see line 1). This question implied that the pedestrian believed to read the same map as the navigators. The navigator said "Go slightly leftward" (line 14) for guiding the pedestrian. The word "leftward" did not indicate "left side of the body (=eastward)" but "left side of the map (=westward)" in this conversation. In a word, he meant that the pedestrian had to go westward in the instruction. The pedestrian properly interpreted this confusing instruction and started heading westward without hesitation. It appears that they used the map as basis. Such a instruction was typical case when a pedestrian used maps and voice conversations.

Navigations based on a movement history also occurred several times in experiment 2. As described in section 4.2, a navigation based on a movement history sometimes failed due to the difficulty of understanding the pedestrian's situation. On the other hand, a navigation based on a navigation map often succeeded

Table 5. Navigation based on navigation maps

```
 1  P: Does this bold black line mean this big (.) street?
 2  N: Yes.
 3     (3.3)
 4  P: ((turn right)) We:[ll,
 5  N:               [If you go straight,
 6     (0.4)
 7  P: Yes.
 8  N: Well, fire [disaster, you will face the fire disaster,
 9  P:            [Do you mean fire disaster?
10  P: I see.
11  N:  Go, (.) slightly leftward.
12  P: OK.
```

because they can use the map as concrete common basis. Misconceptions were not likely to occur as long as a pedestrian can read maps properly.

4.4   Design Implication of Guiding Agent

We demonstrated that the kinds of information required by pedestrian were the current location, the current direction and a proper route toward a destination. Pedestrians wanted information related to the current situation but it is difficult to understand it by communication with a distant navigator. Therefore the navigation system is required to enable to check conditions of a pedestrian. Pedestrians who truly need the verbal navigation are ones who are bad at reading maps. We can support the map recognitions of such pedestrians who have a high tendency to get lost. With proper map recognition, the pedestrians can receive smooth verbal navigation from a navigator.

Pedestrians could not be convinced their location even if they could get their current location via GPS. Because GPS system had little measurement error and navigation system delayed of about 75 seconds for updating a navigation map. We can improve latter point to enable mobile phone to cache the static data and to receive only dynamically changing data.

Pedestrians also could not be convinced their current direction. Guiding agents calculate their current direction based on the movement histories. However, when a they just leaving a start or turning a corner, it is difficult for a guiding agent to calculate the current direction from the movement history. These days, cellular phones with electronic compasses are spreading. The system can capture precise direction of a pedestrian easily with them.

In addition, pedestrians wondered which route they should select. Because there ware plural courses that can arrive at a destination. For supporting route selection, guiding agents should be equipped a function to show a route which is suited to user preferences (e.g. movement distance or a number of turns).

5 Conclusion

Our approach to provide personal navigation is to build a multi-agent system that assigns one guiding agent to each human. This research attempts to demonstrate a design implication of the guiding agent. In the navigation experiments in which a pedestrian using a map on a GPS-capable cellular phone was guided by a distant navigator, we investigated the communication between them by conversation analysis method. The problems we tackled in this work are as follows.

Analysis of information required by pedestrian. We examined the information required by pedestrians using the navigation system. The result indicated that pedestrians required information about the current location, the current direction and a proper route to a destination.

Analysis of communication between pedestrian and navigator. Navigation maps and movement histories were used as communication basis in successful cases. When a pedestrian did not understand a map adequately, navigation sometimes failed due to lack of communication basis.

In this research, we analyzed the information required by pedestrians and the limitation of remote navigation using maps and voice conversations. Future works include determining how to reflect the result of this experiment to the guiding agents and how to support people who are not good at reading maps.

Acknowledgment

This work was supported by a JSPS Grant-in-Aid for Scientific Research (A) (18200009), a Grant-in-Aid for JSPS Fellows and Strategic Information and Communications R&D Promotion Programme.

References

1. Koyanagi, T., Kobayashi, Y., Miyagi, S., Yamamoto, G.: Agent server for a location-aware personalized notification service. In: Ishida, T., Gasser, L., Nakashima, H. (eds.) MMAS 2005. LNCS, vol. 3446, pp. 224–238. Springer, Heidelberg (2005)
2. Ishida, T., Nakajima, Y., Murakami, Y., Nakanishi, H.: Augmented experiment: Participatory design with multiagent simulation. In: IJCAI, pp. 1341–1346 (2007)
3. Nakajima, Y., Shiina, H., Yamane, S., Ishida, T., Yamaki, H.: Disaster evacuation guide: Using a massively multiagent server and GPS mobile phones. In: SAINT 2007, p. 2 (2007)
4. Sacks, H., Schegloff, E., Jefferson, G.: A Simplest Systematics for the Organization of Turn-Taking for Conversation. Language 50(4), 696–735 (1974)
5. Nakanishi, H., Koizumi, S., Ishida, T., Ito, H.: Transcendent communication: location-based guidance for large-scale public spaces. In: CHI 2004, pp. 655–662. ACM Press, New York (2004)
6. May, A.J., Ross, T., Bayer, S.H., Tarkiainen, M.J.: Pedestrian navigation aids: information requirements and design implications. In: PersonalUbiquitousComputer 2003, London, UK, vol. 7, pp. 331–338. Springer, Heidelberg (2003)
7. Ericsson, K.A., Simon, H.A.: Verbal reports as data. Psychological Review 87, 215–251 (1980)

Identifying Structural Changes in Networks Generated from Agent-Based Social Simulation Models

Shah Jamal Alam, Bruce Edmonds, and Ruth Meyer

Centre for Policy Modelling,
Manchester Metropolitan University Business School
Manchester M1 3GH, United Kingdom
{shah,bruce,ruth}@cfpm.org

Abstract. Finding suitable analysis techniques for networks generated from social processes is a difficult task when the population changes over time. Traditional social network analysis measures may not work in such circumstances. It is argued that agent-based social networks should not be constrained by *a priori* assumptions about the evolved network and/or the analysis techniques. In most agent-based social simulation models, the number of agents remains fixed throughout the simulation; this paper considers the case when this does not hold. Thus the aim of this paper is to demonstrate how the network signatures change when the agents' population depends upon endogenous social processes. We argue for a much wider attention from the social simulation community in addressing this open research problem.

Keywords: agent-based simulation, network analysis, Kolmogorov-Smirnov statistic.

1 Introduction

Many social simulation models assume a fixed number of agents, usually for simplicity's sake. As a result, only the degree distribution of the resulting social networks evolves over time, while the size of the network remains unchanged. Many agent-based social simulation (ABSS) models have shown that agents' local interactions can lead to structures such as *scale-free* and *small-world* networks, where the network stabilizes after a sufficient number of simulation runs (e.g. [6, 12]). However, it is usually an explicit algorithm and the network size that influences the simulation outcomes. Analyzing the networks where the size and structure of the agent population depends upon emergent social processes remains a largely open question for the social simulation community.

There are a variety of metrics measuring global properties of networks coming from two research communities. The 'complex network' community focuses mainly on size, density, maximum degree, average path length, connectivity, and degree distribution (e.g. fat-tailed) [10]. The 'social network analysis' (SNA) community have their own measures such as centrality, closeness, proximity, clustering, homophily, and community structure [13]. However, it has been shown that networks sharing similar global properties can have significantly varying local structures [5].

A. Ghose, G. Governatori, and R. Sadananda (Eds.): PRIMA 2007, LNAI 5044, pp. 298–307, 2009.

ABSS modellers face an even bigger challenge: characterizing the co-evolution of a dynamic network as the simulation proceeds. If agents are heterogeneous and able to join or leave the modelled system during the simulation run, the network characteristics may change completely over the course of a simulation run. Typically, snapshots of the simulated network are taken at regular time intervals. Such snapshots of the network can then be compared based on the SNA measures and other complex network characteristics. Performing a cross-sectional analysis of the network at the end of the simulation is inadequate to capture the underlying social process then. As Edmonds and Chattoe [4] have argued, in many cases an agent's behaviour cannot just be reduced to the notion of a mere node.

In the subsequent sections, we define the problem followed by a discussion on two agent-based models. We demonstrate how the use of some *a priori* assumptions can affect the evolved network's structure. In the end, we suggest a potential way in uncovering the effect of dynamic population on the generated social networks.

2 Networks from Embedded Social Processes

Consider a simulated network S (N, E) at the start of a simulation run, i.e. at time $t=0$. N is the set of nodes and E is the set of edges through which the nodes of the graph are connected. The agents are represented as nodes while the ties between them form the edges in the network. The network could be of any structure, e.g. unconnected $(E = \{\Phi\})$, a small-world network [14], or a scale-free network [3]. At every time step, $t: t \in (0,\infty]$ new agents become a member of N, while n already present agents leave: $n \in (0, |N|]$.

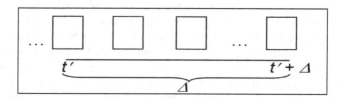

Fig. 1. A simulation run over time, where Δ is the lag size

With each time step, the network is likely to change. Changes may happen to the size of the agent population (number of nodes in the network) and also to the formation and breaking of ties among the agents (number and position of edges). The degree distribution of the network alters depending upon the type of relations that the edges represent.

In models where the joining and leaving of agents is driven by socioeconomic conditions, agents' decision choices are constrained. The resulting network structures in such case are hard to predict in advance. The shape and size of the network at a certain time t' could be radically different at a later time $t'+\Delta$ (where Δ is the possible time-lag of size ranging from *1, 2 ...* onwards; see figure 1). It is even possible that the network dissolves after some time and recovers later on.

Unlike physical systems, social processes tend to be modelled descriptively and validated qualitatively [8]. The evidence is often gathered through fieldwork. An individual's relations and actions are driven by their position in society and other factors affecting the system. Social systems do not remain in a stable state and are dynamic in nature. Events changing the structure of the network may occur any time during the simulation which might be missed when using global measures.

Keeping the number of nodes fixed could possibly increase the risk of type-II error or a 'false-positive' effect. For instance, it is possible that a network's convergence to a certain topology may be rigidly determined by the mechanism through which the agents interact. Ideally, one would apply a scheme that helps in understanding the interplay of the processes and remains robust to the changing network up to certain degree. Of course, in case the network degenerates, any such scheme is likely to fail.

3   Examples from Two Agent-Based Social Simulation Models

Two different agent-based models are presented to support our proposition. The first is a model developed by Jin et al. [6] about friendship networks generated from three simple rules. The second is being developed by us based on evidence from a real case study. The two models are different with respect to their purpose and complexity and are certainly not compared in this paper. Our purpose is to highlight the likely effect of a fixed agent population and *a priori* assumptions about the agents' interaction that may bias an evolved network structure.

3.1   A Model for Growing Social Network

An example of simple rules resulting in the emergence of highly-clustered network structures is explained in Jin et al. [6]. The model is based on three rules: "(1) meetings take place between pairs of individuals at a rate which is high if a pair has one or more mutual friends and low otherwise; (2) acquaintances between pairs of individuals who rarely meet decay over time; (3) there is an upper limit on the number of friendships an individual can maintain." Since the number of agents, i.e. nodes in the network remain fixed at all time, the building and breaking up of ties are solely dependent upon the algorithm used in the model.

Simulating this model with 250 agents and a friendship upper limit set to 5 resulted in a quick emergence of a 'small-world' like structure. Once converged to a certain value, the clustering coefficient varies [13] within a small range (figure 2). We have used the implementation of the simplified model included in the Repast [11] demonstrations package.

Next, we compared network snapshots $P= \{P_0, P_{0+\Delta}, P_{0+2\Delta}...\}$ where each element P_i represents a distinct population of agents at a particular time in the run, P_0 being the population at $t=0$. We performed the Kolmogorov-Smirnov (K-S) test [9] for each consecutive pair $(P_i, P_{i+\Delta})$ [1]. The K-S test belongs to the family of nonparametric statistics and is 'distribution-free'. Unlike classical statistical techniques such as e.g. the *t-test*, there is no prior assumption about the distribution of the population from which the data is sampled. A two-population K-S-test indicates the likelihood that two datasets come from the same distribution. A comparison of the nodes degree distribution based on the

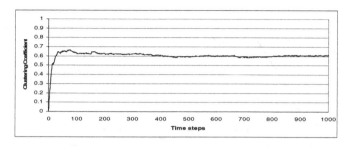

Fig. 2. Clustering coefficient of the friendship network [6] over a simulation run

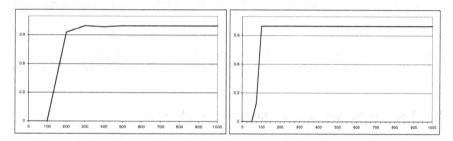

Fig. 3. Y-axis: P-score of the K-S test for the degree distribution of the friendship network compared for consecutive snapshots taken at every (left) 100th tick and (right) 25th time step

K-S statistic in figure 3 shows the network stabilizing after some time. The p-score (Y-axis) that can be calculated from the KS-test can be roughly interpreted as the probability that the two data sets have the same distribution. In our context, a value 1.0 (maximum) implies that there is no change in the degree distribution of the two consecutive snapshots of the agents' network. On the other hand, a low p-score is an indication that the network structure has changed from the previous snapshot even though, for example, the clustering coefficient remains the same. Figure 3 (left) illustrates the case when the snapshots were taken at every 100th time step. The network composition does change initially, but around the 500th time step, the degree distribution of the network stabilizes and there is no difference. Figure 3 (right) shows the comparison of networks snapshots taken at every 25th time step. As can be seen, the network starts to take shape increasingly and finally stabilizes in the distribution.

Choice of a lag does influence the outcome of the statistic when comparing consecutive snapshots of the degree distribution. With a smaller lag size in figure 3 (right), one may conclude that the network's composition stabilizes around the around 100th time step. Figure 4 shows the p-score for the K-S test statistic where we compared consecutive snapshots at the smallest possible lag size, i.e. every 5 time steps. This is due to the reason that the three basic actions 'random meeting', 'neighbour meeting' and 'random removal' occur at every 5th step in this model. The agents' network grew in the initial steps and the similarity in the network configuration continued to increase thereon. In all three different granularity cases (figures 3 and 4),

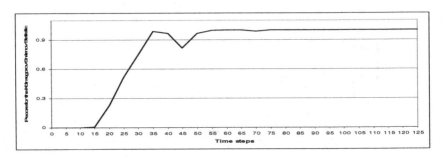

Fig. 4. P-score of the K-S test for the degree distribution of the friendship network compared for consecutive snapshots taken at every 5th time step for the first 125 time steps of the simulation

it is clear that once the network stabilizes, its structure remains the same. One may conclude this to be a consequence of a fixed population size, where only the ties are changed.

3.2 A Model of Socioeconomic Impact of HIV/AIDS

The second model is being developed based on a case study in the CAVES project[1]. It investigates the impact of HIV/AIDS on households and the overall community structure. The case study area is located in the Limpopo region in South Africa and is one of the most vulnerable areas lacking water, food security, jobs and other social infrastructure. Many households have female heads because the men are often living away from the house as migrant workers. State grants are the primary source of income of which a high percentage is spent on food, health and funeral costs. People try to cope with stressors via mutual help amongst neighbours, friends and extended family. A major concern is the number of orphans in the community that has increased mostly due to HIV/AIDS related adult deaths. The extended family by and large accommodates orphans of a dissolved household [15].

The model focuses on the behaviour of individual agents as well as that of households and thus attempts to take into account both the individual interactions and the decisions taken at the household level. We have adopted a multi-layer network approach to model the social networks. Individuals are represented as agents with a network of friends. Each individual is member of a household, with one of the household members acting as the household head. Households have a network of social neighbours with whom they interact. In addition, agents may join different groups like funeral clubs or savings clubs.

Agents and households are created based on the available demographic data. Both endogenous and exogenous factors influence the dynamics of agent interactions. As a result, the size of the generated networks changes over time. At creation agents are assigned some random friends. With the agents joining the clubs, the size of the friendship network remains dynamic. A high prevalence of HIV/AIDS affects the health of those who get infected resulting in a high increase death. Each individual

---

[1] CAVES (Complexity, Agents, Volatility, Evidence, Scale): http://www.cfpm.org/caves

agent is a member of a household. Households in turn form clusters which represent the extended family. This comes into play when a household dissolves when the parents have died; an accommodating household is looked for. This search uses the family hierarchy to determine the nearest living relative who is able to accommodate the surviving dependants [2].

The simulation runs evaluated in this paper were initialized with 30 households and about 150 adult and senior agents. These numbers were chosen because the online tool used in calculating the Kolmogorov-Smirnov p-score allowed only a limited data set size [7]. For future work, we will apply standard statistical software for a larger number of agents.

In this setup, only the friendship network of adult and senior agents has been considered. We added the three rules for growing the friendship network from the model by Jin et al. [6]. In contrast to the latter model, the size of the population is not fixed – agents die and are born over the course of the simulation. Agents' expected life was sampled from a normal distribution with a mean of 75 years and standard deviation 10 years. However, the actual lifespan of an agent may be shorter due to declining health. This is influenced both by the socioeconomic status of a household, which affects the food intake of its members, and the prevalence of HIV/AIDS. The birth rate was set to 15 children per 1000 individuals of a population. The size and the network composition resulting from this model cannot be assumed in advance.

To investigate the impact of HIV/AIDS, or in other words the impact of a rapidly decreasing agent population on the evolution of the friendship network we performed two batches of simulation runs, one without prevalence of HIV/AIDS and one with a prevalence of 14%. Agents were randomly assigned 1 to 5 friends thus using the maximum limit as in the model described in the previous section.

The first batch comprised of three simulation runs with slightly different settings regarding the rules governing the formation and breaking of friendship links. Figure 5 (left) shows the clustering coefficient of the agents' friendship network for the three different cases.

In the first case (Case-I), friendships are formed by two of the three rules from the Jin et al. model [6], the neighbour meeting and the random meeting rule. Agents also make friends when they join the same club. Friendship ties only break when agents die. Case-II incorporated the random removal rule in addition, whereas for Case-III, only the three rules from [6] were used and the same club membership was ignored

In all the three cases, the network remained sparse with a small clustering coefficient. Adding the random removal rule did influence the abundance of links initially, but was not significant in the long run. The relative changes in the friendship network's degree distribution were more evident when the Kolmogorov-Smirnov test was applied to all the three cases, as in the previous model. While a global property of a network, here the clustering coefficient, showed a similar pattern, networks actually changed in different ways for each case as shown in figure 5 (right).

In the next step, the simulation as in Case-III was run, but this time with an HIV/AIDS prevalence of 14%. The rapidly declining agent population causes the clustering coefficient (in figure 7; left) to decline much faster as compared to the three previous cases in figure 5. Most agents die around the 600th time step.

The p-score of the K-S statistic drops between time periods 350-450 indicating significant change occurring in the network. This happens due to increasing deaths in the system, which affects the degree distribution of the agents' friendship network. As the network becomes sparse after the 500th step, the corresponding p-value shows no change at all, followed by a sharp decline when the entire community structure collapses.

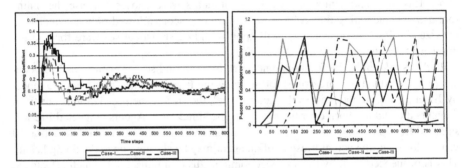

Fig. 5. (left) Clustering coefficient of the agents' friendship network; (right) P-score of the K-S test for the degree distribution taken at every 50th time step for the three different simulation settings

To further investigate whether the changes in the number of agents does really make an impact on the network signatures, we ran simulations for three additional cases without prevalence of HIV/AIDS. In Case-I, no birth of an agent was possible, so the agent population slowly declined Case-II used the opposite scenario with only births but no deaths happening during the simulation run. For Case-III we kept the initial population of agents constant throughout the run.

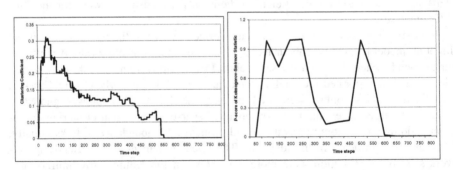

Fig. 6. (left) Clustering coefficient of the agents' friendship network; (right) P-score of the K-S test for the degree distribution taken consecutively at every 50th time step, with HIV/AIDS prevalence

Figure 7 (left) shows the clustering coefficients for these three cases. For the first case we get a similar pattern as in figure 6 (left). Whereas in Case-I no birth was allowed, in the latter case agents' fertility had declined due to the HIV/AIDS prevalence, thus equally constraining births. Case-II follows a similar pattern as the simulations displayed in figure 5, where the population is equally growing due to the high birth rate. Case-III however, shows a high clustering coefficient, well-above 0.5 after some initial steps. This is very similar to the clustering coefficient obtained for the Jin et al. model in figure 2. The reason for achieving a so-called 'small-world' effect is that the agent population remained the same in this case.

The p-score for the Kolmogorov-Smirnov (K-S) statistic for the respective three cases is shown in figure 8 (right). Similar network configurations may be observed for Case-I and the HIV/AIDS prevalence scenario shown in figure 7 (right). The K-S statistic for Case-II keeps changing over time which is due to the birth of agents during the simulation. For Case-III, the signature is again almost identical to the Jin et al. model run as shown in figure 3. Once the agents' friendship network stabilizes it remains the same for the rest of the simulation run.

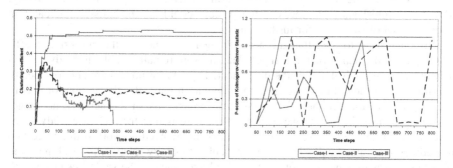

Fig. 7. (left) Clustering coefficient of the agents' friendship network; (right) P-score of the K-S test for the degree distribution taken consecutively at every 50th time step for the three different simulation settings

4   Discussion and Outlook

A very few papers about social network models assume that the number of agents will change over time. Models of network evolution, e.g. the Barabasi-Albert model of preferential attachments provide the mechanism whereby the number of agents monotonically increases (but does not decrease). Even so, such network evolution is deterministic and can be predicted in advance. On the other hand, agent-based models where an agent's membership in the network is constrained by its local interaction processes, the population size cannot be guessed for larger time lags in advance.

In this paper, we have discussed the issue of changes in the network structural signatures in case of a dynamical population. We have examined the stability of network measures on two different agent-based simulation models where networks evolve over time. The network measures, i.e. the degree distribution and the clustering coefficient are the most prevalent measures in the network analysis and we have applied them to the simulated networks as demonstration. It is shown that even the robust measures behave differently under varying population during the simulation despite similar generative mechanisms. Nevertheless, the instability of networks measures can be generalized to more advanced network measures that are used in analyzing the simulated networks.

The Kolmogorov-Smirnov (K-S) test is used to test if there is a difference in the distribution of two populations. The K-S test provides a means to look into the stability of measures on pure statistical basis and thus can be applied to any agent-based simulation case study. Previously, Kossinets and Watts [16] have used the K-S statistic for a longitudinal empirical friendship network of e-mail logs for fixed sized time windows. We have, in this paper, considered different network snapshots of the same simulation run as separate populations and compared the measures them using the K-S test. Our main motivation has been to look for techniques that can help keeping track of the network structure over the course of a simulation run. Observing the p-score for consecutive snapshots can indicate whether the network structure has changed or not. A high p-score is an indicator that there is no evidence from the distributions that the network has changed – a difference is possible but this is unlikely. Moreover, significant differences in the p-score could be one possible indicator in selecting a set of snapshots for further analysis.

It is interesting to note that the network measures such as the clustering coefficients vary as the denominator changes. The measure remains stable in the dynamical networks, when the isolated or the unconnected agents (or nodes) are not considered. The removal (or death) of an agent in the population may alter the number of unconnected nodes in the network. As a result, the transitivity in the network no longer remains the same. The point we want to make here is that for real case study problems, it might be a good idea to check whether the evolved network is due to certain procedures that specifically lead to a particular topology. Networks resulting from social processes may or may not produce topologies such as the *scale-free* or a *small-world* topology. We are working towards further results to support that this point holds for all the agent-based simulations in general and can therefore call for much wider attention of the MAS community.

Acknowledgments. Thanks to our colleagues at the Centre for Policy Modelling for their useful comments. This work is supported under the EU FP6 Project CAVES.

References

1. Alam, S.J., Meyer, R., Norling, E.: Agent-based Model of Impact of Socioeconomic Stressors: A Dynamic Network Perspective. In: Sixth Intl. Joint Conf. on Autonomous Agents and Multiagent Systems, Hawaii, USA, pp. 1079–1081 (2007)
2. Alam, S.J., Meyer, R., Norling, E.: Using Agent-Based Modeling to Understand the Impact of HIV/AIDS in the Context of Socio-Economic Stressors. CPM-06-167 (2006), http://cfpm.org/cpmrep167.html
3. Albert, R., Barabasi, A.: Statistical Mechanics of Complex Networks. Rev. Mod. Phys. 74 (2002)
4. Edmonds, B., Chattoe, E.: When Simple Measures Fail: Characterising Social Networks Using Simulation. Social Network Analysis: Advances and Empirical Applications Forum. Oxford, UK (2005), http://cfpm.org/cpmrep158.html
5. Faust, K.: Comparing Social Networks: Size, Density, and Local Structure. Metodološki zveski 3(2), 185–216 (2006)

6. Jin, E.M., Girvan, M., Newman, M.E.J.: Structure of growing social networks. Phys. Rev. E 64, 4 (2001)
7. Kirkman, T.W.: Statistics to Use (1998),
    http://www.physics.csbsju.edu/stats/
8. Moss, S., Edmonds, B.: Sociology and Simulation: Statistical and Qualitative Cross-Validation. AJS 110(4), 1095–1131 (2005)
9. Neave, H., McConwa, K.: Distribution free methods. OUP (1987)
10. Newman, M.E.J.: The structure and function of complex networks. SIAM Review 45, 167–256 (2004)
11. North, M.J., Collier, N.T., Vos, J.R.: Experiences Creating Three Implementations of the Repast Agent Modeling Toolkit. ACM Trans. on Modeling and Computer Simulations 16(1), 1–25 (2006)
12. Pujol, J.M., et al.: How Can Social Networks Ever Become Complex? Modelling the Emergence of Complex Networks from Local Social Exchanges. JASSS 8(4), 12 (2005),
    http://jasss.soc.surrey.ac.uk/8/4/12.html
13. Wasserman, S., Faust, K.: Social Network Analysis: Methods and Applications. Cambridge University Press, Cambridge (1994)
14. Watts, D.J., Strogatz, S.: Collective Dynamics of 'small world' networks. Nature 393, 440–442 (1998)
15. Ziervogel, G., et al.: Adapting to climate, water and health stresses: insights from Sekhukhune, South Africa. Stokholm Environment Institute (Oxford) (2006)
16. Kossinets, G., Watts, D.J.: Empirical analysis of an evolving social network. Science 311, 88–90 (2006)

Appendix: A Scheme for Comparing Changes in the Network Structure During a Simulation Run

I.   Choose a lag of size Δ for the comparison of network snapshots at different time steps.
II. For all time lags t_i ($i \leftarrow 0, \Delta, 2\Delta, \ldots$), obtain a corresponding series of the node degrees, P_i. (We call this the profile)
III. For all consecutive pairs (P_i, $P_{i+\Delta}$) ($i \leftarrow 0, \Delta, 2\Delta, \ldots$), compute the p-score for the Kolmogorov-Smirnov (K-S) test for 2-populations.

The K-S test gives an indication of the likelihood that the two series are from the distribution. A low p-score indicates that it is unlikely that the two series are from the same distribution, and hence that the degree distributions and hence the network type differs in some respect. A high p-score would mean that there is no evidence that the distributions are different and hence is a fairly tough test of network similarity. However it is still possible that the networks do differ, albeit in subtle ways. The webpage used for this test is: http://www.physics.csbsju.edu/stats/

Multi-agent Simulation of Linguistic Processes:
A NEPs Perspective

Gemma Bel-Enguix and M. Dolores Jiménez-López

Research Group on Mathematical Linguistics
Rovira i Virgili University
Pl. Imperial Tarraco, 1, 43005 Tarragona, Spain
{gemma.bel,mariadolores.jimenez}@urv.cat

Abstract. Networks of Evolutionary Processors (NEPs) –introduced in Castellanos et al. (2001)– are a new computing mechanism directly inspired in the behaviour of cell populations. NEPs, as well as generating devices, can be considered as bio-inspired context-sensitive multi-agent systems. This paper analyzes the agential features of NEPs and their special responses to the environment, which make this system specially suitable for description of Natural Language.

1 Introduction

In the last decades, biology has become a rich source of models for other sciences. The knowledge of the behaviour of nature has influenced a number of areas such as artificial intelligence, mathematics or theoretical computer science, giving rise to new perspectives in research, like *natural computing*. Neural networks [17], genetic algorithms [29], ants' theory [11] and L systems [27] are just some examples of this eclosion of new bio-inspired computational paradigms.

One of the most developed lines of research in natural computing is the named *molecular computing*, a model based on molecular biology, which arose mainly after Adleman's work [1]. An active area in molecular computing is *DNA computing* [26], inspired in the way DNA performs operations to generate, replicate or change the configuration of the strings.

Furthermore, during the last years, systems biology and cellular biology have achieved an important development. These advances have provided new models for computer science. One of them is *cellular computing*, that emphasizes the concept of microbiological populations as well as the equilibrium of the devices and the relationships between the elements. *P systems* [25] can be considered an example of this emerging paradigm.

On the other hand, natural computing has evolved from the first numeric models –like neural networks– to symbolic models –like cellular computing– which are closer to multi-agent systems.

Networks of Evolutionary Processors (NEPs) [3] are inspired in both, in bio cellular models and in basic structures for parallel and distributed symbolic processing.

A. Ghose, G. Governatori, and R. Sadananda (Eds.): PRIMA 2007, LNAI 5044, pp. 308–318, 2009.

The cellular basis of NEPs relate them with P systems, especially with *Tissue P systems* [24], a theory in the area of membrane computing whose biological referent is the structure and behaviour of multicellular organisms. In tissue P systems, cells form a multitude of different associations performing various functions.

From the computational point of view, NEPs are related to the Connection Machine [18] and the Logic Flow paradigm [12]. Another important theoretical relationship of NEPs is the theory of Grammar and Eco-grammar Systems [7], which provide a syntactical framework for communities of evolving agents and their interrelated environment.

With all this background and theoretical connections, it is easy to understand how NEPs can be described as *bio-inspired context-sensitive multi-agent systems.* Many disciplines are needed of these types of models that are able to support a biological framework in a collaborative environment. The conjunction of these features allows applying the system to a number of areas, beyond generation and recognition in formal language theory. Linguistics is one of the fields with a lack of biological models and with a clear suitability for agential approaches.

We introduce in this paper a method that aims not only to be implemented, but also to be able to generate a computational simulation of a number of language processes. Therefore, what we are not suggesting a new multi-agent theory that can help in the resolution of several open questions in linguistics, but a new method of linguistic research and simulation, which is based in a bio-cellular model with multi-agent capabilities. The introduction of such model can help to change the perspective of theoretical linguistics, causing that implementation could become a new central tool for the development of linguistic formal theories.

In the sequel, we introduce the computational definition of NEPs (Section 2), highlighting some of the most important features of this type of multi-agent systems (Section 3). After explaining what is the signification of such traits for linguistics (Section 4), we show a simple example of an implementation of the morphological component of language (Section 5).

2   NEPs: Definition

As it has been already pointed out, Networks of Evolutionary Processors are a new computing mechanism directly inspired in the behaviour of cell populations. NEPs can be defined as systems consisting of several devices whose communication is regulated by an underlying graph. Such devices, which are an abstract formalization of cells, are described by a set of words (DNA) evolving by mutations, according to some predefined rules. Their outcome travels to the other nodes if they accept it after passing a filtering process. At the end of the process, only the cells with correct strings will survive. This mechanism allows the specialization of each processor.

First precedents of NEPs as generating devices can be found in [10] and [9]. The topic was introduced in [3] and [22], and further developed in [2], [4], [8], and [23]. A new approach to networks of evolutionary processors as accepting devices has started in [20]. A scheme of the basic architecture of NEPs is shown in Figure 1.

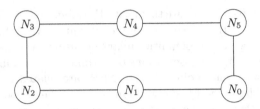

Fig. 1. Graph Structure

Following the basic definition of NEPs, a Network of Evolutionary Processors of size n is a construct:

$$\Gamma = (V, N_1, N_2, ..., N_n, G),$$

where:

- V is an alphabet and for each $1 \leq i \leq n$,
- $N_i = (M_i, A_i, PI_i, PO_i)$ is the i-th evolutionary node processor of the network. The parameters of every processor are:
  - M_i is a finite set of evolution rules of one of the following forms only
    - i. $a \rightarrow b, a, b \in V$ (substitution rules),
    - ii. $a \rightarrow e, a \in V$ (deletion rules),
    - iii. $e \rightarrow a, a \in V$ (insertion rules).
  - A_i is a finite set of strings over V. The set A_i is the set of initial strings in the i-th node.
  - PI_i and PO_i are subsets of V^* representing the input and the output filter, respectively. These filters are defined by the membership condition, namely a string $w \in V^*$ can pass the input filter (the output filter) if $w \in PI_i(w \in PO_i)$.
- $G = (\{N_1, N_2, ..., N_n\}, E)$ is an undirected graph called the underlying graph of the network. The edges of G, that is the elements of E, are given in the form of sets of two nodes. The complete graph with n vertices is denoted by K_n.

Configuration of a NEP is an n-tuple $C = (L_1, L_2, ..., L_n)$, with $L_i \subseteq V^*$ for all $1 \leq i \leq n$. It represents the sets of strings which are present in any node at a given moment.

A given configuration of a NEP can change either by an evolutionary step or by a communicating step. When changing by an evolutionary step, each component L_i of the configuration is changed in accordance with the evolutionary rules associated with the node i. The change in the configuration by an evolutionary step is written as $C_1 \Rightarrow C_2$.

When changing by a communication step, each node processor N_i sends all copies of the strings it has which are able to pass its output filter to all the node processors connected to N_i and receives all copies of the strings sent by any node processor connected with N_i, if they can pass its input filter. The change in the configuration by a communication step is written as $C_1 \vdash C_2$.

This formal definition of NEP, which has been developed in the last years by theoretical computer science, can provide a good framework for attempting a new description and formalization of linguistics. In the sequel, we discuss several features of NEPs, explaining why they are suitable for linguistics.

3 NEPs: Features

From the definition above, and taking into account their intrinsic characteristics, NEPs can be defined as *modular evolutionary environmental multi-agent systems*. They take the multiagent and modular features from classical theoretical computer science, while the environmental and evolutionary characteristics are typical of bio-inspired models. We describe the chief traits of such multi-agent systems as follows:

- *Modular*: NEPs are distributed systems of contributing nodes, each one of them carrying out just one type of operation. Every node should be defined depending on the specific domain we aim to tackle.
- *Multi-level modularity*: Every specialized processor can be modular as well. This architecture is quite suitable for linguistics, a science whose units in every level are obtained by gathering smaller segments up to reach, in the highest one, the most complex constructs. Such path, in linguistics, is reversible. In the present paper, we show an example of the morphological module understanding its internal structure as another NEP.
- *Evolutionary*: agents/nodes can change their definition during the computation. Such modifications can be caused by the context, by the elements inside or by the learning of the modules.
- *Environmental*: By this feature we explain that NEPs are systems-in-context. Context has an important influence in the behaviour of nodes/agents. By context of one node we understand: a) the other processors in the same system, and b) the environment in which the system is placed. Both elements are crucial for describing the state of an element in a given moment and its evolution in a time sequence.

Inside of the construct, every agent is *autonomous, specialized, context-interactive* and *learning-capable*. These features can be described as follows:

- *Autonomous*: Autonomy and specialization are strongly related in NEPs. Even if every agent depends on the other to accomplish the final objective, in order to improve the final result they can change the strategy and the own sub-goals.
- *Specialized*: Every processor is designed for a specific task, in a way that the final success of the system depends on the correct working of every one of the agents.
- *Context-Interactive*: There is a constant *contextualization* and *redefinition* of agent capabilities during the computation. In our model, we postulate that language and context modify each other, in a way that utterances imply an

action that modifies the ecosystem and has a global incidence. This is the way how NEPs can model evolution in both, the agents and the environment. The interaction with context implies three different abilities of agents. They are:

- *Context-sensitive*: Having a broad knowledge of the configuration of the environment and the other agents of the system
- *Context-reactive*: Changing their goal and behaviour depending on the configuration of the environment.
- *Context-modifier*: The productions and behaviour of a given cell are able to modify the general context.
- *Learning-Capable*: Evolution in nodes can be caused by learning. Unsuccessful computations can change the configuration or the interaction between processors.

Between the processors, there are social competences, specified by a Graph-Supported structure and Filtering-Regulated Communication and Coordination.

- *Communication*. Agents can interact in the consecution of the same goal, work for their own interests or even isolate.
- *Coordination*. It is necessary to define protocols for synchronizing the communication.

The two mechanisms that regulate the interaction in the multi-agent system –the graph structure and the filters– have an important role in both the specialization of the processors and the correct functioning of the device. These features are explained as follows:

- *Filter-regulated*: By means of input and output filters.
  - The objective of the *input filter* is to control the information or structures entering the node. This helps to the specialization, by the selection of the strings/structures the node can process, and protects the module from possible harmful items.
  - By the *output filter* the node selects the information it wants to share and also when it wants to share it.
- *Graph-supported*: The edges of the graph govern the communication. Non connected graphs do not communicate. This mechanism decreases the complexity of the working of the whole system and allows interaction between processors.

However, communication between nodes and the environment is not graph-supported. We establish that the agents know, in every moment, what is the configuration of the general cytosolic area where the system is placed.

Finally, in what refers to the functioning of the NEPs, two main features deserve to be highlighted.

- *Emergence*: The behaviour of the nodes is not necessarily pre-established. It depends on both, the evolution of the system and the conditions of the environment.

– *Parallelism*: Different tasks can be performed at the same time by different processors. Some of linguistic processes, as well as language generation in general are considered to be parallel. For apparently sequential interactions (i.e. dialogue) parallelism allows working with multi-modal exchanges.

4   NEPs for Modelling Linguistics

Because of the main features we have mentioned above, NEPs seems to be a quite suitable model for tackling linguistics. Human language is traditionally a difficult entity to deal with, to approach by formal methods, and to describe. One of the main problems of verbal language is that it is generated in the brain, and there is an important lack of knowledge of the mental processes the mind undergoes to, finally, bring about a sentence.

While expecting new and important advances in neuro-science and neuro-language, we are forced to use the models that seem to fit better to language generation and recognition. Such models are usually related to cognitive theories, that have also inspired different perspectives in computer science.

Up to now, one of the hypotheses that have produced the best approximations to natural language processing, as well as most of cognitive processes, is *modularity*. Even though the idea of modularity has been implicit in cognitive science for a long time, it is with the publication of *The Modularity of Mind* (Fodor, [15]) when those implicit ideas that had been current over the previous two decades crystallized into a single recognizable hypothesis.

In general, modular theories in cognitive science propose a number of independent but interacting cognitive 'modules' that are responsible for each cognitive domain. Specific arrangement of those modules usually varies in each theory, but generally each mental module encapsulates a definable higher mental function.

Fodor's theory is not by far the only one about modularity of mind. In fact, in the 1980s there started a new trend represented by authors such as Chomsky [6] and Jackendoff [19]. The theory of modularity is also present in linguistic approaches. In fact, the idea of having a system made up of several independent components (syntax, semantics, phonology, morphology, etc.) has been often assumed in linguistics. We may cite several modular approaches in Linguistics, from Chomsky's Generative Grammar [5] and Halle's Morphology [16] to Autolexical Syntax [28] or Jackendoff's view of the Architecture of Language Faculty [19] just to name a few. One of the main advantages of modular grammar is that they can reduce delays imposed by monolithic or non-modular grammars. This reduction of delays is due to the fact that, in modular grammars, subsystems of grammatical principles can be applied independently of each other and, sometimes, in a parallel fashion.

Therefore, taking the four main modules usually considered in linguistics – syntax, semantics, phonology, morphology– and considering the edges of the underlying graph as way for communicating or not communicating, a simple scheme of a "language generation NEP" can be drawn where N_0 stands for phonetics, N_1 represents morphology, N_2 is syntax and N_3 refers to semantics.

The semantic node is only communicated to the phonological and the syntactic ones because it seems there is not interaction between semantics and phonetics.

Modularity appears in linguistics together with a multi-level specialized structure. This implies that each one of the main modules could have also a modular structure [30,13,14]. A good example of that is the Chomsky's theory of Government and Binding [5], where several components can be found in syntax: government theory module, binding theory module, bounding theory, move-alpha, etc. In the same theory, there are several syntactic levels (D-structure, S-structure, and LF). Eventhough the first formalization of NEPs did not expect those type of constructions, there is no theoretical reason that prevents them. Multi-level modular NEPs could be designed in order to simulate the whole process of sentence generation, for example.

If NEPs are modular multi-agent systems, they have to communicate in order to exchange results. If we defend a specialized approach, we have to establish ways of interaction between the nodes of the computing device. Since the underlying graph of the systems is not necessarily complete, communication between two nodes can be regulated by the existence –or not– of an edge that unites them. Several protocols of creation or deletion of nodes have to be formalized as well, in order to increase the capacity of evolution and adaptation of the network.

Another chief problem for the formalization of human verbal language is its changing nature. Not only words change through the time. Also rules, meaning and even phonemes –the first components of language– can take different shapes during the process of computation. Formal models based only in mathematical (an extremely stable) language present a lack of flexibility to describe natural language. Biological models seem to be better to this task, since biological entities share with languages the concept of "evolution" as one of the main features of the system. A number of authors (McMahon [21] have adopted – or adapted – biological evolution itself in order to construct an evolutionary theory of language change. From this perspective, NEPs offer enough flexibility to model any change at any moment in any part of the system. Besides, as a bio-inspired method of computation, they have the capability of simulating natural evolution in a highly pertinent and specialized way.

However, many unexpected changes or strange uses of rules in language, are not caused by evolution, but by social constraints: historical context, interaction with other users, secret goals of the speakers... These features can be modelled by what we call *context-interactivity*. It is in this aspect where the classical theory of formal languages has achieved the worst results for dealing with natural language. Some linguistic disciplines, as pragmatics or semantics, are context-driven areas, where the same utterance has different meanings in different contexts. To model such variation, a system with a good definition of environment is needed. NEPs, which are based in colonies of cell populations that behave according to the configuration of the environment, seem to be able to offer some kind of solution to approach formal semantics and formal pragmatics from a natural computing perspective.

Moreover, linguistics has always been studied from a linear and sequential point of view. Indeed, the sound is produced in a sequential way, but many studies could suggest that the production could not be sequential. This is, for example, what the Chomsky's idea of rewriting seems to suggest. Furthermore, some linguistic theories, like autolexical syntax (Sadock, [28]), are defined by their authors as parallel, indicating that "natural-language expressions are organized along a number of simultaneous informational dimensions".

Finally, the multimodal approach to communication, where not just production, but also gestures, vision and supra-segmental features of sounds have to be tackled, refers to a parallel way of processing. NEPs allow to work in the same goal, but in different tasks, to each one of the modules. The autonomy of every processor and the possible miscoordination between them can also give account of several problems of speech.

5 An Example: Halle's Lexicalist Hypothesis

We have shown how the features that have been highlighted in the design of NEPs are also conditions that should provide a robust framework for linguistics. Many linguistic theories are based in these principles and, therefore, should be able of being formalized under these parameters.

So, to illustrate our proposal, we introduce an example of application of NEPs to language processing in a modular multi-level way. To do so, we take a classical and very fruitful proposal of Morris Halle about morphology. Halle [16] postulated the lexicalist theory for word formation. A rough explanation of the theory could say that words are obtained combining morphemes by means of word formation rules (WFR). But not every word generated by this method is good. There are actual words (un-happy-ness), potential words (un-dog-ly) and gaps (un-good-ly). To distinguish between them, it is necessary an output filter for these productions. But once filtered, these words could have to be modified by syntactic or phonetic rules (un-happi-ness). At the end of the process, we expect to get only the correct words of the language.

Keeping in mind these elements, we can define a second level modular system for Halle's lexicalist hypothesis as follows:

$$\Gamma = (V, N_1, N_2, N_3, G, E),$$

where:

- V is the set of morphemes of the language.
- $N_1 = (\text{WFR}, \emptyset, V^*, W \in V^*)$.
- $N_2 = (\text{SR}, \emptyset, W, Ws \in V^* \cup Wp \in V^*)$.
- $N_3 = (\text{PR}, \emptyset, Ws \in V^*, Wp \in V^*)$.
- $G = (V, E)$ is the underlying graph, being:
  - $V = \{N_1, N_2, N_3\}$.
  - $E = \{N_1 N_2, N_2 N_3, N_3 N_1\}$.
- $E \subset V$ is a set of morphemes over V.

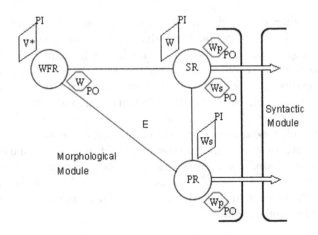

Fig. 2. Modular Architecture: Halle's Morphological Module

This formalization has added something to the basic computational definition of NEP, the environment (E), in order to increase the power of the context.

In our description WFR stands for Word Formation Rules, SR for Syntactic Rules and PR for Phonetic Rules. It is clear that the first node will compose words, but not all of them can be considered words of the language. A first filtering (W) does not allow 'potential words' and 'gaps' to leave the processor N_1. Some of the strings that are able to pass the filter will need a new processing in the syntactic module N_2 and others even a third processing in the phonetic module.

The configuration of the context establishes a set of morphemes that will be the initial input of the system.

Every node in the system is, by definition, an initial node. The input (morphemes) is taken from the environment, and every processor could do that. However, in this NEP, only the filter of N_1 allows the morphemes to enter the processor. Both, N_2 and N_3 are final nodes, and their productions, if correct, can leave the morphologic module and go directly to the syntactic module.

Halle's Hypothesis has been discussed and improved during thirty years, but it is a very good example of modularity, interaction between modules, and filtering. The NEP's design is shown in Figure 2. The example is simple, but it can illustrate the process and suggest more complex architectures for the future.

6   Final Remarks

The paper presents a quite new bio-inspired multi-agent method of computation, NEPs. After explaining some of the main features of the system, we remark its suitability for tackling several fields of linguistics that have been difficult to formalize.

The idea of a multi-agent modular approach to syntax has several exponents in the last years. But it is quite unusual to aim a formal and modular approach to semantics and pragmatics. We think NEPs provide the theoretical background to do that.

The coincidences between several structures of language and biology allow us to take advantage of the bio-inspired models formalized by theoretical computer science. Moreover, the multi-agent capabilities of these models make them a suitable tool for simulating the processes of generation and recognition in natural language.

From a theoretical point of view, maybe NEPs cannot be used to explain how language is generated (this is part of neurology and biology), but they can help to implement and simulate such processes. The results achieved can be a way to falsate, test and debug the formal weakness of current hypothesis as well as provide feed-back to suggest new lines of research.

So, the paper has two main interests: the first one involves language and computability; the second one is related to language and biology. First, the theory we present can show several methods for artificial intelligence to achieve an implementable formalization of natural language, capturing several aspects (i.e. context, evolution, meaning, etc.) that traditionally have been hard to manage for natural language processing. On the other hand, it can be a way to improve, by means of simulation of mental processes, the research on how language is generated and recognized.

The main idea for the future is to start an implementation of NEPs, in order to prove that the computational simulation of language by this mechanism is possible. For our purposes, we suggest to perform the following improvements in the basic design of linguistic NEPs: a) to strengthen the role of environment in the system; b) to take advantage of the idea of modularity, which is related to the architecture of NEPs and to symbolic conceptions of cognitive processes; c) to develop communication protocols using the underlying graph.

References

1. Adleman, L.M.: Molecular Computation of Solutions to Combinatorial problems. Science 226, 1021–1024 (1994)
2. Castellanos, J., Martín-Vide, C., Mitrana, V., Sempere, J.M.: Solving NP-complet Problems with Networks of Evolutionary Processors. In: Mira, J., Prieto, A.G. (eds.) IWANN 2001. LNCS, vol. 2084, pp. 621–628. Springer, Heidelberg (2001)
3. Castellanos, J., Martín-Vide, C., Mitrana, V., Sempere, J.M.: Networks of Evolutionary Processors. Acta Informatica 39, 517–529 (2003)
4. Castellanos, J., Leupold, P., Mitrana, V.: On the Size Complexity of Hybrid Networks of Evolutionary Processors. Theoretical Computer Science 330(2), 205–220 (2005)
5. Chomsky, N.: Lectures on Government and Binding. The Pisa Lectures. Foris Publications, Dordrech (1981)
6. Chomsky, N.: Modular Approaches to the Study of Mind. San Diego State University Press (1984)
7. Csuhaj-Varjú, E., Dassow, J., Kelemen, J., Păun, G.: Grammar Systems. Gordon and Breach, London (1993)
8. Csuhaj-Varjú, E., Martín-Vide, C., Mitrana, V.: Hybrid Networks of Evolutionary Processors are Computationally Complete. Acta Informatica 41/4, 257–272 (2005)

9. Csuhaj-Varjú, E., Mitrana, V.: Evolutionary Systems: A Language Generating Device Inspired by Evolving Communities of Cells. Acta Informatica 36, 913–926 (2000)
10. Csuhaj-Varjú, E., Salomaa, A.: Networks of Parallel Language Processors. In: Păun, G., Salomaa, A. (eds.) New Trends in Formal Languages. LNCS, vol. 1218, pp. 299–318. Springer, Heidelberg (1997)
11. Dorigo, M., Stützle, T.: Ant Colony Optimization. MIT Press, Cambridge (2004)
12. Errico, L., Jesshope, C.: Towards a New Architecture for Symbolic Processing. In: Plander, I. (ed.) Artificial Intelligence and Information-Control Systems of Robots 1994, pp. 31–40. World Sci. Publ., Singapore (1994)
13. Everaert, M., Evers, A., Hybreqts, R., Trommelent, M. (eds.): Morphology and Modularity. In: Honour of Henk Schultink, Publications in Language Sciences 29, Foris (1988)
14. Farmer, A.K.: Modularity in Syntax: A Study of Japanese and English. MIT Press, Cambridge (1984)
15. Fodor, J.: The Modularity of Mind. MIT Press, Cambridge (1983)
16. Halle, M.: Prolegomena to a Theory of Word Formation. Linguistic Inquiry 4, 3–16 (1973)
17. Haykin, S.: Neural Networks: A Comprehensive Foundation. Prentice Hall, Englewood Cliffs (1999)
18. Hillis, W.D.: The Connection Machine. MIT Press, Cambridge (1985)
19. Jackendoff, R.: The Architecture of Language Faculty. MIT Press, Cambridge (1997)
20. Margenstern, M., Mitrana, V., Pérez-Jiménez, M.: Accepting Hybrid Networks of Evolutionary Processors. In: Ferreti, C., Mauri, G., Zandron, C. (eds.) DNA 10. Preliminary Proceedings, Milan, University of Milano-Biccoca, pp. 107–117 (2004)
21. McMahon, A.: Understanding Language Change. Cambridge University Press, Cambridge (1994)
22. Martín-Vide, C., Mitrana, V., Pérez-Jiménez, M., Sancho-Caparrini, F.: Hybrid Networks of Evolutionary Processors. In: Cantú-Paz, E., et al. (eds.) GECCO 2003. LNCS, vol. 2723, pp. 401–412. Springer, Heidelberg (2003)
23. Martín-Vide, C., Mitrana, V.: Networks of Evolutionary Processors: Results and Perspectives. In: Molecular Computational Models: Unconventional Approaches. Idea Group Publishing, Hershey (2004)
24. Martín-Vide, C., Pazos, J., Păun, G., Rodríguez-Patón, A.: A new class of symbolic abstract neural nets: Tissue P systems. In: H. Ibarra, O., Zhang, L. (eds.) COCOON 2002. LNCS, vol. 2387, pp. 290–299. Springer, Heidelberg (2002)
25. Păun, G.: Computing with Membranes. Journal of Computer and System Sciences 61, 108–143 (2000)
26. Păun, G., Rozenberg, G., Salomaa, A.: DNA Computing. New Computing Paradigms. Springer, Berlin (1998)
27. Rozenberg, G., Salomaa, A.: The mathematical theory of L Systems. Academic Press, New York (1980)
28. Sadock, J.M.: Autolexical Syntax. A Theory of Parallel Grammatical Representations. University of Chicago Press (1991)
29. Schmitt, L.: Theory of Genetic Algorithms. Theoretical Computer Science 259, 1–61 (2001)
30. Weinberg, A.: Modularity in the Syntactic Parser. In: Garfield, J.L. (ed.) Modularity in Knowledge Representation and Natural-Language Understanding, pp. 259–276. MIT Press, Cambridge (1987)

A 3D Conversational Agent for Presenting Digital Information for Deaf People

Da Phuc Phan, Thi Nhat Thanh Nguyen, and The Duy Bui

College of Technology
Vietnam National University, Hanoi
duybt@vnu.edu.vn

Abstract. Sign languages appear to be the major communication tool for the deaf community. As a minor community, Vietnamese deaf people often have to rely on a small numbers of interpreters who are hearing people knowing sign language in order to communicate with hearing people. It would be very beneficial for deaf as well as hearing people to develop an automated translation system between spoken/written languages and sign language. In this paper, we present our attempt to graphically decompose the gestures in Vietnamese Sign Language so that they can be easily synthesized in a 3D conversational agent. In order to describe the signs in Vietnamese Sign Language, we proposed an animation-level markup language. Based on this, we presented our 3D conversational agent for presenting multi-modal information for deaf people. The 3D agent can assist deaf people easier and in a more natural way.

Keywords: Sign Language Synthesis, Human Computer Interaction, 3D Conversational Agents.

1 Introduction

Sign languages have the similar communication capacities to those of spoken languages. They appear to be the major communication tool for the deaf community [6,9]. Sign languages include finger spelling and gesture. In finger spelling, finger postures and motions are used to express letters. Through a letter sequence, a sign word is spelled. On the other hand, gestures and motions are used to express a word, or even a phrase. Each gesture is described by hand shape, location, movement, orientation, number of hands. Sign language has its own grammar based on spatial, physiological and temporal dimensions. For example, not only strongly recognized gestures, but also pronouns and index references, appeal to mechanisms involving the signers space. Beside finger spelling and gesture, other movements of the body, including mouth patterns, head and shoulder movements and facial expression are used in sign languages to express speaker's thoughts. These movements both play paralinguistic (kinetic stress, face expression) and grammatical roles (marking syntactic clauses).

In Vietnam, there are about 5.3 million disabled people, a large part of that are deaf people. As a minor community, deaf people often experience great difficulties

A. Ghose, G. Governatori, and R. Sadananda (Eds.): PRIMA 2007, LNAI 5044, pp. 319–328, 2009.

in communicating with hearing people. They have to rely on a small number of interpreters who are hearing people knowing sign language. As the society is paying more and more attention to deaf people in recent years, efforts have been made to produce tools that allow them to communicate easier with hearing people. Fortunately, recent advanced research in linguistics, machine learning and computer graphics have offered different models for automated translation between spoken/written languages and sign language. It would be very beneficial for deaf as well as hearing people to develop such a translation system.

As is the case in spoken language, Vietnamese Sign Language differs from one region to another. As in the past, gestures and signs of the deaf in Vietnam have developed the best in such places as Hanoi, Haiphong, Hochiminh City,... These gestures and signs are often natural, spontaneous or imported from over-seas and have not been systematized yet. In order to help the deaf have the opportunity to select the signs they wish to learn, a project has been deployed by University of Pedagogy, Ho Chi Minh City to develope a "Vietnamese Sign Language Dictionary For People With Hearing Impairment" [12], in which the signs of three aforementioned cities and the Common Signs have been recorded. The dictionary comprises popular notion in topics related to daily life to help the hearing and deaf people communicate and study more effectively.

In Vietnamese Sign Language, however, there have not been either any serious attempt of decoding of the language structure or synthesizing the language for automated translation. In this paper, we attempt to graphically decompose the gestures in Vietnamese Sign Language so that they can be easily synthesized in a 3D avatar. We propose an animation-level markup language to describe the signs in Vietnamese Sign Language. Based on this, we propose a method of presenting multi-modal information for deaf people with the use of a 3D conver-sational agent. The 3D agent is built based on Java3D, VRML (Virtual Reality Modeling Language) and H-anim, an abstract representation for modeling three dimensional human figures.

The rest of the paper is organized as follows. Section 2 summarizes some back-ground concepts on Sign Language and notations to represent Sign Language. We then review some related work in Section 3. In Section 4, we present our markup language for representing Vietnamese Sign Language. Section 5 shows how we present information for deaf people in a 3D agent.

2   Background

Following Stokoes footsteps [10], linguists have proved that sign languages, like oral ones, were articulated into phonemic and morphemic levels. At phonemic level, the basic movements - phonemes, which are formerly called cheremes, are functionally equivalent to the phonemes of spoken languages. It has been recognized that for phonemes in sign languages, the mental abstractions involved are essentially the same as in oral languages. Phonemes in a sign language are usually comprised of: hand shape, location, movement, and palm orientation. An individual hand shape means nothing out of context. It is only when we combine that hand shape with movement and a certain location that we able to determine its meaning. At morphemic level, a morpheme is the smallest linguistic unit that has semantic meaning. Similar to spoken language, morphemes are composed of phonemes.

Sign languages are often represented in some visual forms for the purpose of communication and education. There are three popular ways to represent sign languages, which are Stokoe Notation [10], Sutton SignWriting [2], and HamNoSys [8]. The Stokoe notation [10] for American Sign Language was created earliest for a sign language and is mostly restricted to linguists and academics. It it is arranged linearly on the page and uses elements of the Latin alphabet and is phonemic. This system only uses a reduced set of symbols to match the needs of American Sign Language. For example, only a single symbol is used for circling movement, regardless of whether the plane of the movement is horizontal or vertical because the other parameter of the motion is determined by American Sign Language phonotactics and need not be indicated in a phonemic system. Sutton SignWriting [2], created by Valerie Sutton in 1974, represent the gesture and movements of signed languages by visual symbols. It is based on a notation system for dance movements representation - Sutton DanceWriting. As a "movement-writing-alphabet", SignWriting can be used to describe any signed language in the world. The Hamburg Sign Language Notation System, HamNoSys [8], was created in 1989 by a group of deaf and hearing people. Unlike SignWriting, HamNoSys was developed for study and research purpose. HamNoSys breaks each sign down into about 200 characters in some components such as hand position, hand orientation, hand shape, motion, etc. All of signs are figure shape so it is easy to read by human.

3   Related Work

There have been a number of attempts in synthesizing sign languages. In Sign-Anim project (also known as Simon-the-Signer) [5,7,13], a signing avatar system based on motion capture is used. Each sign is represented by a data file recording motion parameters for the body, arms, hands, and so on. The corresponding sequence of such motion data files can be used to animate the 3D humanoid. In this way, accurate motions can be created. However, the major drawback of motion capture is that we have to record the large number of signs for a complete lexicon. To overcome the drawback of motion capture, some projects synthesize deaf signing animation from a high-level description of signs in terms of the HamNoSys transcription system [8]. This approach use the HamNoSys notation for transcribing signing gestures. This notation system breaks each sign down into components such as hand position, hand orientation, hand shape, motion, etc. Using HamNoSys notation can improve the disadvantage of motion capture. However, this notation is designed to be read by humans rather than computers. Therefore it is quite difficult to implement. Adding a new sign into this notation is also not easy. An example of this approach is the ViSiCAST project [1]. In this project, an XML-compatible notation, ViSiCAST-GML, is developed based on

HamNoSys [8] in order to produce adaptable communication tools allowing sign language communication where only speech and text are available. In Thetos project [11], input data in form of a text file in Polish is linguistically analyzed to produce the output in form of an animated sequence. All the existing work for sign language synthesizing, however, did not concentrate on creating an easy method for mapping sign language to animation sequence.

4   Animation Markup Language for Vietnamese Sign Language

Vietnamese Sign Language is based on the well-established American Sign Language. Thus, there are about more than 600 concepts in Vietnamese Sign Language, which can be decomposed into morphemes and phonemes [4]. For other concepts, it is possible to implement finger spelling of Vietnamese words similar to the American Sign Language system. Figure 1 shows the alphabet table of Vietnamese Sign Language.

Each sign/morpheme in Vietnamese Sign Language maybe a static shape or a dynamic gesture. A gesture starts with a static shape followed by a hand movement. In general, a sign /morpheme can be articulated into phonemes, which are: hand shape, palm orientation, hand position and hand movement.

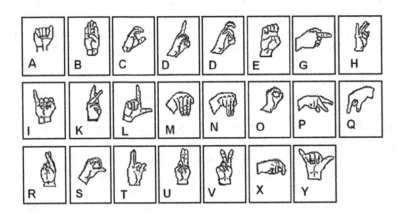

Fig. 1. The alphabet table of Vietnamese Sign Language

4.1   Hand Shape

There are many different types of hand shape in Vietnamese Sign Language. Some typical hand shapes are: hold shape, large open shape, small open shape, C shape (hand like C character), finger point shape and hook shape. Visibly, the hand shapes can be distinguished by the level of bending of each finger and the distance between fingers. We propose 5 levels of bending, ranging from very small to very big. These 5 levels are enough to describe signs in Vietnamese. The distance between each finger is small or big. The hand shape can also be used to describe postures in finger spelling. Here are how we describe a hand shape in XML:

```
<hand_shape>
    <thumb> very small/ small/ medium/ big/ very big </thumb>
    <index> very small/ small/ medium/ big/ very big </index>
    <middle> very small/ small/ medium/ big/ very big </middle>
    <ring> very small/ small/ medium/ big/ very big </ring>
    <pinky> very small/ small/ medium/ big/ very big </pinky>
    <distance> small/big </distance>
</hand_shape>
```

where <thumb>, <index>, <middle>, <ring>, <pinky> are the level of bending of thumb, index finger, middle finger, ring finger and pinky respectively; <distance> represents the distance between fingers.

4.2 Palm Orientation

The palm can be in some main orientations: inside, outside, up, down, left and right. Here are how we describe palm orientation in XML:

```
<palm_orientation>
    <X>0/-1/1</X>
    <Y>0/-1/1</Y>
    <Z>0/-1/1</Z>
</palm_orientation>
```

where the palm orientation is determined by three X, Y, Z values, with 0 meaning orientation independent, 1 meaning inside (for Z)/up (for Y)/left (for X), and -1 meaning outside (for Z)/down (for Y)/right (for X).

4.3 Hand Position

In Vietnamese Sign Language, the hand can be set into many position to represent different meanings. For example, pointing index finger to the nose describes the concept "smell". The position of the hand can be determined with regard to: head, left side of the head (l_head), right side of the head (r_head), chest, left side of the chest (l_chest), right side of the chest (r_chest), waist, eye, nose and mouth. Moreover, the dependency between two hands, e.g. left hand above right hand, is also a part of hand position. Here are how we describe hand position in XML:

```
<hand_position>
    <type> dependence/independence </type>
    <depend_post> up/down/equal </depend_post>
    <post>head/l_head/r_head/chest/l_chest/r_chest/waist/nose/eye/mouth </post>
</hand_position>
```

where <type> indicates the dependency between two hands; <depend_post> indicates the type of dependency between two hands; and <post> indicates the position of the hand with regard to the body.

4.4 Movement

Movements in sign language can be divided into 2 different categories: finger movement and hand movement.

Finger movement can be of several form: wave form, the thumb and index finger touch together, and so on. Finger movement can also be repeated several times. Here are how we describe finger movement in XML:

```
<finger_move>
    <type>wave/thumb_index/thumb_pinky/open/close/shake </type>
    <time> 1/2/3/4/5 </time>
</finger_move>
```

where <type> contains the form of finger movement, which can be wave, thumb_index (the thumb and index finger touch each other and move in reverse directions), thumb_pinky (the thumb in turn touches from index finger tip to pinky tip, and move in reverse directions), open (hand in closed position, then opening fingers out), close and shake; <time> contains the number the finger movement is repeated.

Hand movement is more complicated than finger movement. A hand movement can be described by trajectory (line, circle), direction (clockwise, anticlockwise), distance (short, medium, long) and number of movements. Here are how we describe hand movement in XML:

```
<hand_move>
    <type>line/circle/sin </type>
    <distance>short/medium/long</distance>
    <direction>
        <axis>X/Y/Z</axis>
        <dir>1/-1</dir>
    </direction>
    <time> 1/2/3/4/5 </time>
</hand_move>
```

where <type> indicates the trajectory of the movement, the value of which can be line, circle or sin; <distance> indicates the distance of the movement, the value of which can be short, medium or long; <direction> indicates the direction of the movement, which can be broken into two small parts: axis of the movement and orientation of the movement; and <time> indicates how many times the movement is repeated.

5   Synthesis of Vietnamese Sign Language on a 3D Conversational Agent

Based on the proposed animation markup language for the Vietnamese Sign Language, we propose a method of presenting multi-modal information for deaf people with the use of a 3D conversational agent. The information is now presented to deaf people in a 3D agent in several modals: text, sign language synthesis, lip movement and facial expressions. The 3D agent is built based on Java3D, VRML (Virtual Reality Modeling Language) and H-anim. The 3D model of the agent include a head and a body.

Table 1. H-anim joints that we use in our 3D agent for synthesizing Vietnamese Sign Language

Shoulder_XZ_Right	Shoulder_XZ_Left
Shoulder_Y_Right	Shoulder_Y_Left
Elbow_XZ_Right	Elbow_XZ_Left
Elbow_Y_Right	Elbow_Y_Left
Wrist_Right	Wrist_Left
ThumbJoint_1_Right	ThumbJoint_1_Left
ThumbJoint_2_Right	ThumbJoint_2_Left
IndexJoint_1_Right	IndexJoint_1_Left
IndexJoint_2_Right	IndexJoint_2_Left
IndexJoint_3_Right	IndexJoint_3_Left
MiddleJoint_1_Right	MiddleJoint_1_Left
MiddleJoint_2_Right	MiddleJoint_2_Left
MiddleJoint_3_Right	MiddleJoint_3_Left
RingJoint_1_Right	RingJoint_1_Left
RingJoint_2_Right	RingJoint_2_Left
RingJoint_3_Right	RingJoint_3_Left
PinkyJoint_1_Right	PinkyJoint_1_Left
PinkyJoint_2_Right	PinkyJoint_2_Left
PinkyJoint_3_Right	PinkyJoint_3_Left

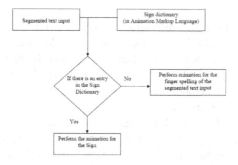

Fig. 2. Synthesis of Vietnamese Sign Language on a 3D conversational agent

The facial expression is produced with the muscle model proposed by Bui [3]. The animation of the body is performed with H-anim. Based on body segments and joints, H-anim supports a set of specifications for creating human animation in the virtual world. Human body is a composition of a number of segments (such as forearm, hand, and foot) connected by joints (such as elbow, wrist and ankle). As mentioned in the standard description, the main purpose of the H-anim is to create a humanoid with compatibility, flexibility and simplicity. In this framework, a human body is defined as a hierarchy of segments and articulated at joints; relative dimensions are proposed by the standard, but are not enforced,

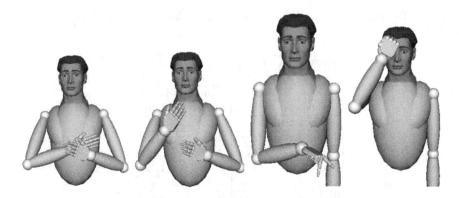

Fig. 3. The 3D agent signs the sentence "I go to school in the morning" in Vietnamese Sign Language

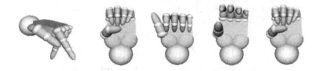

Fig. 4. The 3D agent spells the word "PEACE" in Sign Language

permitting the definition and animation of cartoon like characters. Humanoid in H-anim standard maybe have different levels of skeleton articulation (Levels of Articulation). Another feature of H-anim standard is that we can access the points on the human body via their names and actual locations in the skeleton definition. Table 1 shows the names of the joints that we use in our 3D agent to synthesize Vietnamese Sign Language.

The process of synthesizing Vietnamese Sign Language is described in Figure 2. The input of the process is the segmented text which is the result of some linguistic analysis module. The segmented text is then checked whether it exists in the sign dictionary. If so, the corresponded xml sequence for the sign is used to produce the animation on the 3D agent. Figure 3 shows how our 3D agent signs the sentence "I go to school in the morning" in Vietnamese Sign Language.

If the segmented text does not exists in the sign dictionary, the text will be broken up into characters, which are shown by the 3D agent in the finger spelling way. Figure 4 shows how our 3D agent spells the word "PEACE" in Sign Language.

Facial expressions can be shown in the head of the 3D agent (see Figure 5). However, we have not developed a mechanism to markup the synchronization between facial expressions and body gestures yet.

Fig. 5. Facial expressions can be shown in the head of our 3D agent

6   Conclusion

In this paper, we presented our attempt to graphically decompose the gestures in Vietnamese Sign Language so that they can be easily synthesized in a 3D avatar. In order to describe the signs in Vietnamese Sign Language, we proposed an animation-level markup language. Based on this, we presented our 3D conversational agent for presenting multi-modal information for deaf people. The 3D agent can assist deaf people easier and in a more natural way. In the future, we will extend our markup language in order to specify the synchronization between the facial expressions and body gestures. We also want to integrate other modules into the system such as voice recognition in order to create a fully functional application.

Acknowledgement

This work is financially supported by the Grant of Fundamental Research Funds No. 204006, entitled "Modern Methods for Building Intelligent Systems".

References

1. Bangham, J.A., Cox, S.J., Elliott, R., Glauert, J.R.W., Marshall, I., Rankov, S., Wells, M.: Virtual signing: Capture, animation, storage and transmission - an overview of the visicast project. In: IEE Seminar on Speech and language processing for disabled and elderly people (2000)
2. Bonow Boeira, V., Volz de Oliveira, L.R., Souza Madeira, D., da Rocha Costa, A.C.: Using signwriting as a phonetic notation system. In: Braffort, A., et al. (eds.) Atelier traitement automatique des langues des signes: TALS 2005 (2005)
3. Bui, T.D.: Emotion and Facial Expressions in Creating Embodied Agents. PhD thesis, University of Twente, The Netherlands (2004)
4. Inclusive Education For Hearing Impaired Children in VietNam. Signs of the Deaf in VietNam (1997)
5. Marshall, I., Pezeshkpour, F., Bangham, J.A., Wells, M., Hughes, R.: On the real time elision of text. In: RIFRA 1998 - Proc. Int. Workshop on Extraction, Filtering and Automatic Summarization (1998)
6. Neidle, C., Kegl, J., MacLaughlin, D., Bahan, B., Lee, R.G.: The syntax of American Sign Language: functional categories and hierarchical structure. MIT Press, Cambridge (2000)
7. Pezeshkpour, F., Marshall, I., Elliott, R., Bangham, J.A.: Development of a legible deaf-signing virtual human. In: Proc. IEEE Conf. Multi-Media (1999)

8. Prillwitz, S., Leven, R., Zienert, H., Hanke, T., Henning, J., et al.: Hamburg notation system for sign languages - an introductory guide. In: International Studies on Sign Language and the Communication of the Deaf, vol. 5 (1989)
9. Sacks, O.: Seeing Voices – A Journey into the World of the Deaf. The University of California Press (1989)
10. Stokoe, W., Kuschel, R.: For Sign Language Research. Linstock Press (1978)
11. Thetos: Text into sign language automatic translator for polish, http://sun.iinf.polsl.gliwice.pl/sign/
12. http://vsdic.net/english/default.asp
13. Wells, M., Pezeshkpour, F., Marshall, I., Tutt, M., Bangham, J.A.: Simon: an innovative approach to signing on television. In: Proc. Int. Broadcasting Convention (1999)

Multiagent-Based Defensive Strategy System for Military Simulation

Seheon Song[1], Seokcheol Shin[2], and Minkoo Kim[1]

[1] Graduate School of Information and Communication, Ajou University
Suwon, Gyeonggi, Korea
{lego,minkoo}@ajou.ac.kr
[2] Agency for Defense Development
Seoul, Korea
scshin@add.re.kr

Abstract. In ubiquitous computing, it needs to manage dynamic and various information from various sources and aware the situation. In the same way, it needs same capabilities including detecting and analyzing data from various sources, and recommending behaviors to a commander in a national defense domain. In this paper, we describe the adaptation of an open-source multi-agent architecture for a military defensive strategy system for battle simulation. We define the challenging problem of military defense. We take a community computing concept to adapt to handle dynamic environment, and the Cougaar framework to build our system which supports distributed multi-agent system.

1 Introduction

Since Mark Weise said, current computing paradigm becomes increasingly changed to ubiquitous computing. This change implies that applications and services must be aware and adapt to highly dynamic environments. In the same way, it is required to have capabilities including detecting and analyzing data from various sources, and recommending behaviors to military officers in military domain. And it needs to have scalability and survivability for the aware system. Context awareness is core concept in the vision of ubiquitous computing where networks of small computing devices are dispersed in the physical environment, operating autonomously and independently of centralized control. The fundamental objective of context awareness is to provide services not only to people at any time/where but specifically to communicate the right thing at the right time in the right way. In a context aware framework, devices and programs are no longer passive entities waiting for instructions or commands; instead it is as if they are alive and capable of intelligent behavior. The goal of context aware framework is to achieve this kind of autonomous behavior in software using context information.

In this dynamic environment, predictable or unpredictable ubiquitous services are dynamically requested. In PICO project, community computing was introduced as a framework for cooperation among agents in a ubiquitous environment. And other approach tries to define formal model for community computing. Community computing is a paradigm to solve complex and dynamic problems using cooperation with smart objects in ubiquitous computing environments. We adapt to this concept to

A. Ghose, G. Governatori, and R. Sadananda (Eds.): PRIMA 2007, LNAI 5044, pp. 329–338, 2009.

support context aware framework for dynamic environment. The Cougaar framework supports highly scalable, distributed systems, and is easy to deploy and configure systems, also can integrate with other technologies, and is proven survivability. It has tunable survivability including dynamic role assignment enables virtual organization of tasking, unconstrained, dynamic peer-to-peer functionally oriented groupings, survivability roles complement domain processing roles.

Our approach provides supports for most of the tasks involved in dealing with context – acquiring context from military units. We are developing such an intelligent information system using community computing and Cougaar framework. Our domain scenario is a battlefield composed of military units.

The rest of this paper is organized as follows. Section 2 discusses on related work. Section 3 describes our domain scenario. We present our implementation in section 4. Finally, we conclude in Section 5.

2 Related Works

2.1 Community Computing

The pervasive information community organization (PICO) is a middleware framework that enhances existing Internet-based services. PICO's objective is to meet the demands of time-critical applications in areas such as telemedicine, the military, and crisis management that demand automated, continual, unobtrusive services and proactive real time collaborations among devices and software agents in dynamic, heterogeneous environments. PICO creates mission-oriented dynamic computing communities that perform tasks for users and devices [2]. Another approach tries to redefine the concept of community computing as a new paradigm in which ubiquitous services are provided through cooperation among existing smart objects, and develop well-defined abstraction model for intuitive design of a community computing system [3].

In case of the military area, it seems to be dynamic information, and distributed devices including a variety of sensor and military units, therefore this model is enough to cover the dynamic situation in this area.

2.2 Cougaar: A Distributed Agent Infrastructure

Cougaar is a Java-based infrastructure designed to support large distributed multi-agent systems (DMAS). The architecture is the result of over seven years of DARPA-sponsored work exploring scalability and robustness in distributed-agent systems. Although the DARPA effort has focused on work in the domain of military logistics, the architecture is general and has been applied to domains ranging from project planning to sensor data fusion.

Cougaar could support highly scalable, distributed systems, and modular, parallel software development. It is easy to deploy and configure systems using this framework. And it can integrate with other technologies, and it is proven survivability.

The open source Cougaar agent framework [5] provides a hierarchy of modeling entities that can be used to effectively represent the hierarchy of business process elements in the military logistics domain. These three infrastructure entities are the

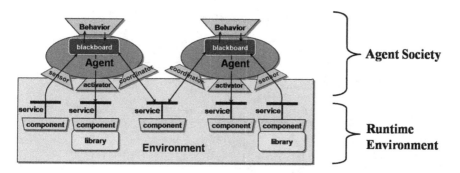

Fig. 1. Cougaar High-level Architecture

plug-in (at the lowest level), the agent (containing multiple plug-ins), and the community (containing multiple agents).

Individual agents are typically used to model individual organizational entities or functional entities. Cougaar agents are able to communicate directly with other Cougaar agents over point-to-point links established using agent-unique identifiers. The actual inter-agent communication mechanism is transparent to the agent and can include: in-memory dispatch, RMI over a network, or even SMTP over intermittent communications [6]. Agents contain assets, which can be either physical or conceptual entities managed by a particular agent. Common uses for assets within Cougaar when modeling military organizations are to represent other organizations relevant to the agent/organization, and the vehicles owned by that organization (which may in fact be represented as vehicle agents; see below).

An agent contains an arbitrary number of plug-ins, each of which implements a self-contained part of the application business logic. Unlike the peer-to-peer communications of agents, plug-ins communicate with other plug-ins (within the same agent) using a publish/subscribe mechanism on an agent-local blackboard. Because of this, the application developer must ensure that there are one or more subscribers for anything published to the blackboard.

At the top-level, a community is a collection of agents whose membership is based on a shared task or on a domain partition. Depending on the application domain, communities can be a useful abstraction, allowing the developer to treat a collection of agents as a single entity. Finally, the entire universe of plug-ins, agents, and communities in a given Cougaar-based application is called a society.

Comparing Java Agent Development Framework (JADE) and Cougaar, JADE is best suited to developers of relatively simple agent applications and developers that require FIPA compliance [8]. Cougaar is best suited to developers that want to customize the agent framework's core services or create complex, large-scale, robust or highly secure agent-based applications.

3 Domain Scenario

For the system simulation, we make a battlefield scenario. Fig 2 shows a hierarchy of military units, which have command center, division, scouter, infantry, tank, and

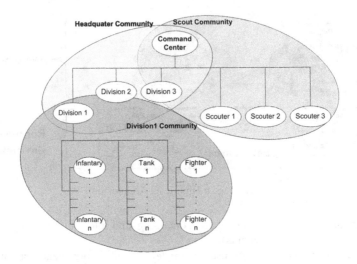

Fig. 2. Hierarchy of Military Units

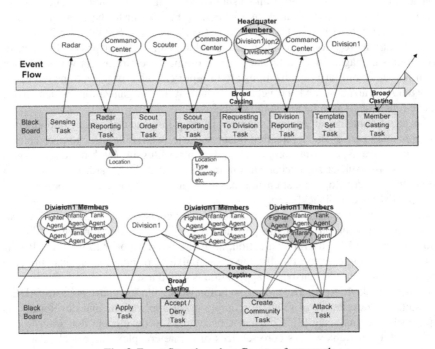

Fig. 3. Event flows based on Couggar framework

fighter. They could be reorganized into community by their own roles. In this scenario, Radar detects unidentified objects in the boundary of the country. Then, radar informs that information to the command center. The command center orders a scouter to collect information about unidentified objects. The scouter reconnoitered detailed information about unidentified objects. From collecting information, the command center decides that objects are enemy. They need to choose military units for efficiently exterminating the enemy. Using military organization template, they collect enable military units. After making an attack community, all members in the community get an attack order and fight.

Fig3 shows event flows in Cougaar framework followed by previous scenario. All of members are agents. They share their information including tasks through blackboard. All of message including information and order between agents are handled by task.

4   System Design and Implementations

Following our scenario, we define several kinds of agents such as radar, command center, scouter, 3 divisions, 5 infantries, 5 tanks, and 5 fighters. Based on cougar framework, each agent has several plug-ins like this:

Table 1. Plug-ins by Agent Type

Agents Type	Plug-ins	Plug-in Description
Radar	InformInvasionPI	Inform enemy invasion to command center
Command Center	RequestScoutePI	Collect information about invasion area through radar
	MakeForcePI	Command force attack
	SelectDivisionPI	Select suitable division and give force template to the division
	RequestDivisionInfoPI	Request division agent for division information
Scouter	ScouteEnemyPI	Scout enemy information in detail
	ReportDetailEnemyInfoPI	Transmit information to command center
Divisions	ReportDivisionInfoPI	Reply to requests from command center agent
	RequestForcePowerInfoPI	Request for force power like infantry, tank, and fighter
	CastAttackForcePI	Recruit military units for organizing force template
	CreateTeamCommunityPI	Create team community
	OrderAttackCommandPI	Order attack command to created team community
Infantries,	ApplyCastPI	Publish one's participation yes or no, and one's class
Tanks	ReceiveAttackOrderPI	Receive a attack order
	InviteTeamCommunityPI	Create team in dynamic
	AttackEnemyPI	Attack enemy though task attack enemy

Using this plug-ins, we make this system by four phases in our scenario.

Phase 1: Inform a enemy invasion using radar

Radar agent detects enemy's invasion, and first detecting information (distance, power). *InforInvasionPI* create *EnemyInfo* class which has variables of distance, power and enemy group list. It also assigns values of distance and power variables. Then, it transmits *EnemyInfo* to *CommandCenter* agent. *CommandCenter* agent receives enemy information and order a scouter agent to scouting mission.

ResponseInvasionPI receives *EnemyInfo* from radar agent. It transmits *EnemyInfo* to scouter agent. Scouter agent scouts specific information and report this information to command center agent. *ScouteEnemyPI* refines *EnemyInfo* through assigning values of the rest variables using scouting report. *ReportDetailEnemyInfoPI* transmit refined *EnemyInfo* to CommandCenter agent. Fig4 shows phase1 process in our system. In this situation, a goal which is exterminating enemy is created. As follows previous community computing research, it is a particular condition that a community should satisfy. In short, it is the objective of a community [3].

Phase 2: Select a division

Command center agent requests and reports each division's information about their military power. *SelectDivisionPI* broadcasts DivisionInfo relay to each Division Agent using *AttributeBasedAddress.getAttributeBasedAddress* method. DivisionInfo class has properties which are message sender info, division power and location. *SelectDivisionPI* chooses best suitable division considering power and location information of DivisionInfo object, then it transmit military template to the chosen division agent for member casting.

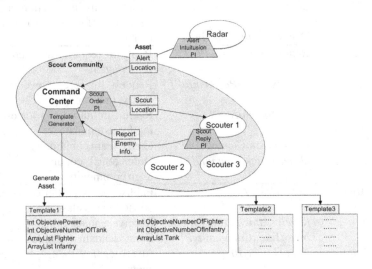

Fig. 4. Phase1 Process

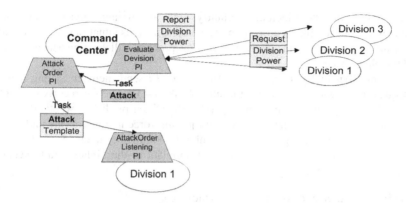

Fig. 5. Phase2 process

Division power is composed of force power information and location information. Then he selects appropriate division through evaluating this information and orders the chosen division to attack the enemy. *ReportDivisionInfoPI* replies to CommandCenter agent for an information which has the sum of member agent's power and division location. *RequestForcePowerInfoPI* gets powerInfo of member agent of each division when CommunityPlugin cannot get power information of each member agent.

Phase 3: Member Casting using member templates

After receiving attack order from command center, the chosen division agent starts to organize military force community. This process is composed of announcement and collecting/selection using member template. Member template has several kinds of

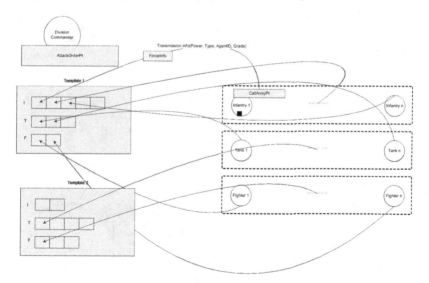

Fig. 6. Phase3 process

slots for unit or members including infantry, tank, and fighter. Division commander predefines various templates correspond to possible various situations. Adequate units are permitted to join the member, and casting process will be finished after being filled template space.

Assuming division2 is chosen, *CastAttackForcePI* send member casting message to adequate force agents including Infantry, Tank and Force. If it receives accepting message from force agents though *ApplyCastPI*, which publishes whether it accept casting or not, then it fills the template with joining force member to the end. During this work, it chooses the highest grade member to community manager. At the end, it transmits the list of member agents for the template to the highest grade agent for creating an attack community.

Phase 4: Create dynamic community & achieve goal

As follows previous community computing research [3], a goal dynamically arise, a community is dynamically generated to achieve the goal. Then the community is disorganized when the goal is attained. In this research, they assume that community templates and the structure of each community are predefined. When recruiting finishes, division commander agent finds the highest class unit, and appoints the highest unit as a forces manager. Division commander creates a community using community information. Forces manager is correspond to a community. It invites members in this division to collect community members, that is, forces manager sends 'community-join' task to each members. Each of members joins the community dynamically using Cougaar community service. After inviting and joining process, an 'attack-community' community is accomplished.

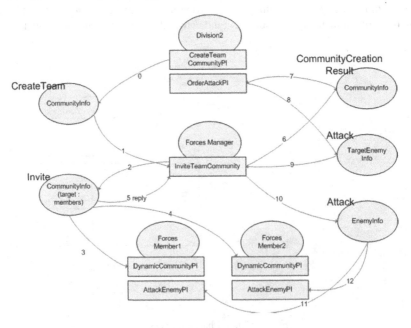

Fig. 7. Community Creation Process

CreateTeamCommunityPI receives *CreateTeamCommunity task* from *CastingPI*. *CreateTeamCommunityPI* orders casting members to create a community. *CreateTeamCommunityPI* transmits *CreateTeamCommunity* task to the highest grade agent. If an agent has this plugin, it becomes a force manager which requests inviting members of member list in *CreateTeamCommunity* task. If *CreateTeamCommunityPI* receives community creation message from *InviteTeamCommunityPI*, it transmits *OrderAttackCommand* task to *OrderAttackCommandPI*. *OrderAttackCommandPI* transmit *AttackEnemy* task to *InviteTeamCommunity*. *InviteTeamCommunityPI* dynamically creates a *TeamCommunity*. The other members dynamically join the community when they receive *Invite* task from *ForcesManager.InviteTeamCommunityPI*. Then it returns a result of creating community. *AttackEnemyPI* receives *AttackEnemy* task from *Division2.OrderAttackCommandPI*, it broadcast this information to members. *DynamicCommunityPI* receives *Invite* task from *ForcesManager.InviteTeamCommunityPI*, it makes member to join community. Using our simulation, fighter1 is chosen for forces manger, and community composed of fighter1, infantry2, tank1, and infantry3. Then Forces Manager (fighter1) orders to begin attack. When all of the community members received the attack order, they start to attack and report the result. In case of achieving goal like mission complete, community is destroyed. This is a cycle of attack community in a successful situation.

5 Conclusion

In this paper we have developed multiagent-based defensive strategy system. This is achieved using Cougaar framework in which provides an infrastructure designed to support large distributed multi-agent systems, and also it is convenient to realize community computing concept to our system. Comparing with Jade, Cougaar framework is more suitable to develop complex, large-scale, and highly secure agent-based applications. That's why we choose this framework for a military domain in spite of its complexity.

Our preliminary experiment has provided how the information system for military domain scenario operates on Cougaar framework in detail. But there are some limitations of number of agents, scenario complexity and scale, knowledge processing method, and validation for this system. For further studies we should adapt to current community computing concept and define context model using formal method like ontology and use knowledge process methods such as rule and ontology reasoning. It will guarantee a reasonable decision and context aware process.

Acknowledgement. This research was supported by Defense Acquisition Program Administration and Agency for Defense Development under the contract.

References

1. Weiser, M.: Some Computer Science Issues in Ubiquitous Computing. Commun. ACM 36(7), 75–84 (1993)
2. Kumar, M., Shirazi, B., Das, S.K., Singhal, M., Sung, B., Levine, D.: Pervasive Information Communities Organization PICO: A Middleware Framework for Pervasive Computing. In: IEEE Pervasive Computing, pp. 72–79 (July-September 2003)

3. Youna, J., Jungtae, L., Minkoo, K.: Multi-agent based community computing system development with the model driven architecture. In: AAMAS 2006, pp. 1329–1331 (2006)
4. Cougaar Open Source Web Site, http://www.cougaar.org/
5. BBN Technologies: Cougaar : A Scalable, Distributed Multi-Agent Architecture. In: IEEE SMC 2004 (2004)
6. Daniel, C., Anthony, R., Jeffrey, B.: A Cougaar-Based Logistics Modeling Tool for Highly Adaptable Military Organizations. In: AAMAS 2004 (2004)
7. Matthias, B., Schahram, D.: A Survey on Context-aware systems. International Journal of Ad Hoc and Ubiquitous Computing (2004)
8. Jade Agent Development Framework, http://jade.tilab.com/

Achieving DRBAC Authorization in Multi-trust Domains with MAS Architecture and PMI

Somchart Fugkeaw[1], Piyawit Manpanpanich[1], and Sekpon Juntapremjitt[2]

[1] Thai Digital ID Co.,Ltd., Bangkok, 10500, Thailand
{Somchart,Piyawit}@thaidigitalid.com
[2] Whitehat Certified Co.,Ltd., Bangkok, 10310, Thailand
Sekpon@whitehatpro.com

Abstract. This paper presents the approach of the distributed RBAC (DRBAC) access control of the multi-application delegated to the multi-user and multi-relying party federations. In our approach, DRBAC utilizes Public Key Infrastructure (PKI) and Privilege Management Infrastructure (PMI) to serve the authentication and authorization. We propose the dynamic mapping scheme based on the Attribute Certification model in handling user identification, role assignment, and privilege delegation. To encourage distributedness, better scalability and performance, as well as ease of management and extension, Multi-Agent Systems concept is applied for the automation of the authentication, authorization and accountability functionalities. For the trust management of multiple PKI domains, we employ the Certificate Trust Lists (CTLs) model to make the different PKI domains can interoperate effectively. Finally, our ongoing implementation is demonstrated to prove our proposed model.

Keywords: Distributed Role Based Access Control, Authentication, Public Key Infrastructure, Privilege Management Infrastructure, Multi-Agent Systems.

1 Introduction

1.1 Overview

Role Based Access Control (RBAC) is recognized as an effective access control management for a large number of users because it allocates permissions to roles rather than individuals, and there are typically far fewer roles than users [7]. The central notion is that permissions are associated with roles, and users are assigned to appropriate roles. In [9], the Distributed RBAC (DRBAC) is defined as a set of distributed roles which is employed and shared by both resource provider and resource subscriber. In general, distributed roles are determined by a resource provider and the subscribing organization will map its local roles to the distributed roles. Although RBAC itself is relatively well-studied and well-understood, the understanding of decentralized administration of RBAC is still at an early stage [11].

For the prominent example of works related to RBAC and X.509 certificate attribute have been discussed in [5, 7, 8, 9]. In [5], X.509 based identity/attribute certificates and use-condition certificates are used for the access control. In [7, 8, 9], the authors has implemented the PERMIS project that provides a policy driven role based

A. Ghose, G. Governatori, and R. Sadananda (Eds.): PRIMA 2007, LNAI 5044, pp. 339–348, 2009.
© Springer-Verlag Berlin Heidelberg 2009

access control system based on the X.509 Attribute Certificate. PERMIS applies the X.509 PMI to build an efficient role based trust management system and user role delegations. Those works inspire our research idea in applying the attribute certificate for authorization management. However, the integration function of authentication and authorization has not been provided. This brings up the idea of how we can achieve the SSO authentication and flexible authorization in the distributed system.

In [4], we proposed a model of attribute mapping between PKC, bridge AC and Role AC to support the authentication and authorization in the multi-user and multi-application environment. However, the model does not address the full deployment of RBAC in the distributed and multi-trust domains.

Recently, authors in security area have adopted MAS for the network security control, especially in the distributed computing systems. In [12], the authors proposed the design of flexible multi agent-based network security for authentication and authorization in mobile environments. The agent performs the contract-net protocol for communication process of dynamic authentication between network domains. So far, the DRBAC model supporting multi-SSO federations and multi-trust domains has not been addressed by any works.

1.2 Motivation and Contributions

The motivation of this research truly reflects the real need of today applications in distributed computing areas. We're motivated by the following questions:

1) How can we support the authentication and authorization in the distributed environment which has multiple applications, multiple users, and multiple administrative domains with least user impact? (For example, a user of Company A can use several allowed applications of Company B transparently with high trust in one sign-on.)

2) How to establish high trust among administrative domains (e.g. Companies) based on policy (not all is taken equal)?

3) How is the DRBAC handled and deployed to a number of users in a robust, flexible and efficient way?

4) How to make it as much distributed as possible to avoid single point of failure?

In this paper, we present the extended approach of the distributed RBAC access control of the multi-application delegated to the multi-user and multi-relying party federations. In our approach, DRBAC utilizes PKI to perform the authentication and authorization. X.509 certificate standard [6] is deployed by means of user certificate for the user identification and X.509 Privilege Management Infrastructure (PMI) is adopted for the authorization after the authentication is done. At a core, the multi agent system approach is applied for the automation of the authentication, authorization and accountability functionalities. In addition, our paper describes the full control and cross trustworthiness among different PKI domains. Finally, we introduce the technique of parallel agent processing to improve the system performance. As a consequence, this paper empowers the following contributions:

1) a high modularity and flexibility of the authentication and authorization model in the distributed system environment;

2) a scalable, decentralized trust management and access control in multiple SSO and PKI domains;
3) a development of a dynamic RBAC policy management tool.

2   A Framework of the Proposed Model

2.1   Overview of the Proposed Model

Figure 1 presents the conceptual view of our proposed model.

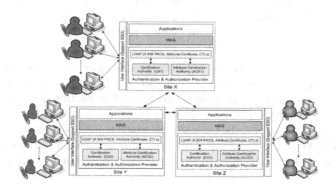

Fig. 1. A Framework of DRBAC based on MAS and X.509 PKI

The main components of each individual domain consist of three main parts:

1) **User Interface** is designed as an interface for the client who requests to use application(s) via the web pages. In our system, the clients need to authenticate themselves by using the certificate securely stored in a smart card or a token for two-factor authentication before accessing the application(s).

2) **Authentication and Authorization Provider** is a component that issues X.509 user certificates and attribute certificates [2]. These certificates are physically stored in the LDAP directory for further authentication and authorization. The management of privileges is done by the role assignment of PMI standard by means of the Attribute Certificate (AC) issued by the Attribute Certificate Authority (ACA). In our model, there are three certificate types as follows:

1. Public Key Certificate (PKC) or User Certificate is an X.509 certificate issued by the CA to identify the user of which the public key is bound to a particular Distinguished Name.
2. Role Attribute Certificate (Role AC) is an attribute certificate that holds user roles associated with applications.
3. Bridge Attribute Certificate (Bridge AC) is the other kind of Attribute Certificate designed to facilitate the mapping between the PKC and Role AC.

3) **Multi Agent System (MAS)** is the core platform that performs the authentication, authorization, and auditing function and closely works with the authentication and authorization provider module. Figure 2 shows the agent components constituting in MAS.

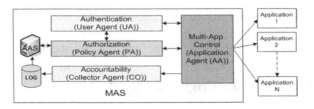

Fig. 2. MAS Component

The trust and security management of the MAS are also guaranteed by the PKI. At each MAS server of several organizations, the key pairs and certificates are installed to further use for securing and authenticating the communication process among agents. There are four types of agents:

- User Agent (UA) is responsible for authenticating user, validating client certificates, mapping user to role, verifying/authorizing client requests according to the user privilege profile obtained from the corresponding PA (through AA), and delegating corresponding application(s) to the client. Each UA will be dead after a complete logout, or after certain idle period, which is the SSO session timeout.
- Application Agent (AA) is mapped to a particular application and functions as the representative of an application in serving requests from UAs. Its job is to authorize requests according to the dynamic user privilege profile, schedule the sequence of clients connecting to applications, to support the multiple applications selection by clients, and to log on to the application on behalf of the client.
- Collector Agent (CO) interfaces with the log server. All local entities send activity logs to this agent for recording in the log server.
- Policy Agent (PA) figures out the effective privilege profile for the point of authorization (AA, UA). It combines the privilege profile obtained from Role AC, which is static, and Activity Analyzer Server (AAS), which is dynamic, to generate the effective privilege profile for a given user.

To enable activity-based policy enforcement, the following two servers are required:

- Activity Analyzer Server (AAS) performs two functions: analyzing logs and dynamically forming the dynamic privilege profile for a user based on his/her access request activities and the preventive authorization policy. For example, the preventive authorization policy could define that a user privileges will be degraded to 'guest' if it found that he/she requested for over-privileged accesses more than 10 times within 20 minutes. As the privilege profile is based on user activity, it is dynamic.
- Log server collects all activity logs from all entities through CO.

2.2 User Role Mapping

In [4], we defined the attribute mapping scheme between PKC, Bridge AC, and Role AC. The Bridge AC is used to map the user identification hold by the PKC to the privilege of the specific role retained in the Role AC. In the case that user role might be changed due to the role adjustment, addition or modification, it is simply done by the updating on Bridge AC and/or Role AC. Only affected Bridge AC or Role AC of the site that initiates the change the role will be updated locally. The attribute type and value can be updated all the time. PA will be responsible for the validation of privilege assignment engaging the Role AC. Figure 3 shows the example case of how multiple Bridge ACs are mapped to the Role ACs of the different organizations.

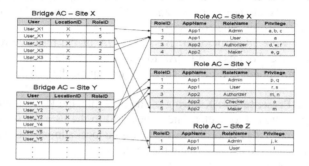

Fig. 3. Role Mapping between Bridge AC, and Role AC

2.3 Authentication and Authorization Process by MAS

Figure 4 illustrates relationships among MAS components for the authentication and authorization process.

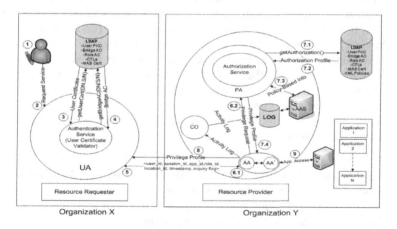

Fig. 4. A Model of X.509 Authentication, DRBAC Authorization, and Activity-based Policy

In the overall process, there are two major phases: Setup Phase and Runtime Phase. The steps are described as follow:

Setup Phase:

[Step1] Two-Factor Authentication: Client uses the smart card or Token in addition to the password to authenticate himself/herself via SSL to the Web Server. This step is normally supported by SSL technology.

[Step 2] MAS Construction: After the successful two-factor authentication, Web Server requests the MAS module to generate a UA. The UA is mapped to the client for managing all of its application requests. Logically, the MAS module, a trusted core component, will generate the UA whenever the client has successfully authenticated to the system. On this ground, this newly-created UA is automatically trusted.

[Step 3] Client Certificate Validation: The UA looks up the local LDAP, verifies the authenticity of the client certificate, and checks its validity against a pre-defined policy (e.g. CRL status, specific content rules).

[Step 4] User Role Identification: Basically, UA of the resource requester will lookup the Bridge AC from its own LDAP to find the user role. Then, the UA will get the role of the corresponding user and get ready to request the privilege from the resource provider.

[Step 5] User Presentation: Knowing of the user role, the UA can present the list of available applications (no matter where they are) to the user for selection of use. We assume this knowledge is locally available as the local administrator should know what his/her users need to use and where they are.

Runtime Phase:

[Step 6] Application Requesting and UA Message Verification: Once the UA recognizes an application access request (application and action) from the user, it will check if it knows about the privilege profile of the user role for the requested application.

If the UA has such knowledge, it will verify the request against the privilege profile and authorize or deny the request accordingly. To authorize the request, it will send the message with 'inquiry' flag unset to the appropriate AA. If the AA also agrees, to grant the request, this message will start the new session between the UA and the AA. If the UA has none of the user privilege profile (first request to the Resource Provider), it will proceed to send the message with 'inquiry' flag set (saying "I have no idea; please give me the privilege profile of the user for ALL applications at the Resource Provider site") to the appropriate AA. The AA will ask the local PA.

Thus the message that the UA sends to the AA serves for session initiation and privilege profile query at the same time.

The message includes <user_id, session_id, app_id, role_id, location_id, timestamp, inquiry flag> where

- *user_id* is the id of client or user asking for the request;
- *session_id* is the id of communication session of the request (this could be randomly generated at the beginning of the session);
- *app_id* is the id of Application which is requested by the user;
- *role_id* is the id of the role obtained from the Bridge AC;
- *location_id* is the 'from' id of the organization or the site of the relying party in the distributed systems;
- *timestamp* is the time that UA sends the request.
- *inquiry flag* indicates if the AA is to forward the privilege profile to the UA.

As we employ PKI as the tool enabling trust, when a UA message is sent out to an AA at another site, it must be signed by the local MAS. That is, MAS guarantees the UA message to the AA by signing it with its private key. The signed message is then encrypted with the AA's public key to ensure confidentiality. Thus, only legal AA can use its own private key to decrypt the message. Besides, trust between the CAs is ensured by CTLs stored in the local LDAP of all relying parties. All partner CAs are known and trusted for each other if they are registered in the CTLs.

[Step 7] Effective Role and Privilege Profile Formation: The local PA will look up for the associated Role AC of the Resource Provider where the application privileges of the given role are specified, and will consult the AAS for dynamic privilege profile of the role. Afterward it combines the two privilege profile to a single one (called the effective privilege profile) and sends back to the AA. If the AA checks the request against the effective privilege profile and found that it is allowed, it will start the new session with the UA. As the 'inquiry' flag is set, the AA will forward all of this to the UA, and keep only the part related to its responsible application locally. Owing to this, the UA will have the effective privilege profile of the role for all applications provided by the organization the AA resides in, while AA will have only the privilege profile of the user role for the corresponding application.

[Step 8] Application Delegation: To start a session, AA will accept the UA request by sending back the acknowledgement to the UA. AA will also send all activities of UA requests to CO for collecting in the log server.

[Step 9] Multi-Application Control: After the process in Step 8 is done, AA will then be responsible for controlling the use of multi-application requests by several users (UAs). It manages the application access queue and does the login task on behalf of the authorized users.

3   Implementation

3.1   Overview of the Implementation

The prototype has been developed as a system infrastructure to support the strong authentication, authorization, and accountability service for the multi-user and multi-application environment. Our current status of the implementation is to utilize the features of AmTRUE [4] in the distributed systems. The experiment was conducted to verify that our proposed DRBAC scheme can handle and delegate the roles of the number of users in a robust, flexible and efficient way. In the experiment, 50 clients of 3 organizations are assigned to register for the certificates and key pairs issued by their own CAs in order to use in the multiple SSO web-based applications autonomously. For the test, all relying parties need the core MAS module to install at their own site. MAS is developed by a Java-based API, so it can be connected into any applications that requires its secure functionality. Finally, we discuss the performance improvement method for the MAS communication process and show the simulation result.

3.2   Policy-Based and System Configuration Administration

To provide the effective way in configuring the role policy and MAS component, the MAS configuration interface is designed and developed. Figure 5 presents the DRBAC and MAS configuration screen.

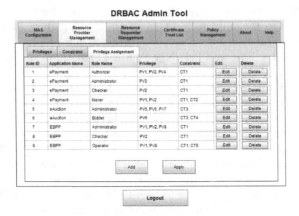

Fig. 5. DRBAC and MAS Configuration

From this screen, the system administrator can easily configure privileges and constraints of the Resource Provider. Also, the local role based policy and Bridge ACs are specified and maintained by this tool. This is necessary for scalability and role based control crossing independent security domains.

3.3   Performance Improvement by Multi-instance Processing

To deliver high performance, we introduce the multi-instance concept by having multiple AA's dedicated to an application. Each of them maintains its own queue. Initially an application will have only one "original" AA. When the queue length reaches a certain threshold, the AA will fork itself as a "replica" to accept future incoming requests, while the original still serves incoming requests if its queue has available room. Both the original AA and its replicas can do forking. To prevent wasting the resource, each AA replica instance has its own clock counting down and if the timeout is met, it will suicide. The clock will be reset for every request arrival to it. One may notice that the back-end application still processes in serial manner. This is left to the system administrator as it is trivial to establish server load balancing or clustering. Besides, as the serial processing still exists in Policy Agent (PA), PA is also multiplied, giving better performance.

In the simulation, we used the Java thread programming and applied multi-instance concept to AA (more than one AA dedicated to an application) and PA for performance improvement. Initially, multiple AA instances with 2 PA instances were deployed for the simulation. To start, we generate a number of requests and let them randomly to be sent to AA instances. The elapsed time from the start to successful connection of each request was captured. Then all times are averaged to produce the results as illustrated in Fig.6.

The graph confirms a good trend of processing time when we add more UA instances for 100, 500, and 1,000 requests. Thus, the finding reveals that the proposed performance improvement technique is sound and attractive in supporting a large

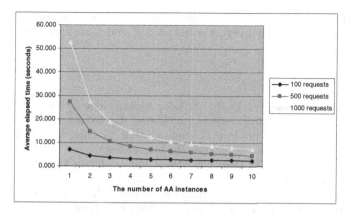

Fig. 6. Multiple Agent Instances Processing Time

number of requests with multiple instances. With cheaper hardware today, the agent-consumed resources are not that much, especially when compared to the number of requests and reduced processing time.

4 Conclusion and Future Work

We have proposed an architecture integrating PKI, PMI, and RBAC for the access control in dynamic distributed systems (multi-application and multi-user). MAS concept is applied for the automation of the authentication, authorization and accountability functionalities. In our model, the agent system is capable to work and adaptable well in the distributed environment by taking the following actions:

- Verifying trust among agents to ensure the authenticity and integrity of partners organizations;
- Monitoring the security sessions because the multiagents can more easily manage the detection and response to important time-critical information that could appear suddenly at any large number of users in the distributed systems;
- Renewing itself if any service disruption has occurred to support service continuity;
- Intervening any improper actions or illegal activities according to the activity-based policy enforcement.

For the trust management of multiple PKI domains, we employed the Certificate Trust Lists (CTLs) model to make the different PKI domains can interoperate effectively. In order to improve the performance, a multi-instance concept is employed to parallelize agents' activities. The simulation was conducted and confirmed a good performance in both speed and response time.

In summary, our proposed approach truly reflects the real need of the authentication and the authorization application in the dynamically distributed systems. For future works, we will focus on the full implementation of multiple system robustness and reliability. In terms of reliability, the system needs to be tested under a high number of clients and applications. We will test and evaluate the optimal threshold of the proper instances could be forked to the size of requests. The management of the complexity and heterogeneity of different access control models are also promising.

References

1. Lee, D.-G., Kang, S.-I., Seo, D.-H., Lee, I.-Y.: Authentication for single/Multi domain in ubiquitous computing using attribute certification. In: Gavrilova, M.L., Gervasi, O., Kumar, V., Tan, C.J.K., Taniar, D., Laganá, A., Mun, Y., Choo, H. (eds.) ICCSA 2006. LNCS, vol. 3983, pp. 326–335. Springer, Heidelberg (2006)
2. Farrell, S., Housley, R.: An Internet Attribute Certificate Profile for Authorization (April 2002), http://www.ietf.org/rfc/rfc3281.txt
3. Wang, X., Zhao, G., Zhang, X., Jin, B.: An Agent-Based Model For Web Services Transaction Processing. In: IEEE International Conference on e-Technology, e-Commerce, and e-Services (EEE 2005), pp. 186–189. IEEE Computer Society, China (2005)
4. Fugkeaw, S., Manpanpanich, P., Jantrapremjitt, S.: AmTRUE: Authentication Management and Trusted Role-based Authorization in Multi-Application and Multi-User Environment. In: IEEE International Conference on Emerging Security Information, Systems and Technologies (SECURWARE 2007). IEEE Computer Society, Spain (2007)
5. Thompson, W., Johnston, W., Mudumbai, S., Hoo, G., Jackson, K., Essiari, A.: Certificate-based access control for widely distributed resources. In: Proc. of the 8th USENIX Security Symposium, USA (1999)
6. ITU-T Rec. X.509, ISO/IEC 9594-8 The Directory: Authentication Framework (2000)
7. Chadwick, D.W., Otenko, A., Ball, E.: Role based access controls with X.509 attribute certificates. IEEE Internet Computing, 62–69 (2003)
8. Chadwick, D.W., Otenko, A.: The PERMIS X.509 Role Based Privilege Management Infrastructure. In: ACM Symposium On Access Control Models And Technologies (SACMAT 2002), pp. 135–140. ACM, USA (2002)
9. Zhou, W., Meinel, C.: Implement Role-Based Access Control With Attribute Certificates. In: International Conference on Advanced Communication Technology (ICACT 2004), Korea, pp. 536–541 (2004)
10. Freudenthal, E., Pesin, T., Port, L.: DRBAC: Distributed Role-based Access Control for Dynamic Coalition Environments. Technical Report TR2001-819, Department of Computer Science, New York University
11. Li, N., Mao, Z.: Administration in Role-Based Access Control. In: ACM Symposium on Information, Computer and Communications Security (ASIACCS 2007), pp. 127–138. ACM, Singapore (2007)
12. Santa, G.A., Higuera, D.: Mobile User Authentication Protocols. In: Proc. Of IASTED International Conference in Wireless and Optical Communication, Canada (2001)
13. Ma, M., Woodhead, S.: Constraint-enabled Distributed RBAC for Subscription-based Remote Network Services. In: IEEE International Conference on Computer and Information Technology (CIT 2006). IEEE Computer Society, USA (2006)

When and How to Smile: Emotional Expression for 3D Conversational Agents

Thi Duyen Ngo and The Duy Bui

College of Technology
Vietnam National University, Hanoi
{duyennt,duybt}@vnu.edu.vn

Abstract. Conversational agents have become more and more common in the multimedia worlds of films, educative applications, e - business, computer games. Many techniques have been developed to enable these agents to behave in a human-like manner. In order to do so, conversational agents are simulated with emotion and personality as well as communicative channels such as voice, head and eye movement, manipulator and facial expression. Up to now, creating facial expression from emotions has received much attention. However, most of the work concentrates on producing static facial expressions from emotions. In this paper, we propose a scheme for displaying continuous emotional states of a conversational agent on a 3D face. The main idea behind the scheme is that an emotional facial expression happens for a few seconds only when there is a significant change in the emotional states. This makes the emotional facial expressions of the conversational agents more realistic due to the fact that a facial expression only stay on the face for a few seconds.

Keywords: Human Computer Interaction, 3D Conversational Agents, Emotional Facial Expressions.

1 Introduction

Conversational agents become more and more common in multimedia world of films, educative applications, e - business, computer games and so on. The aim of these conversational agents is either to entertain or to interact with people. Many techniques have been developed to enable these agents to behave in a human-like manner. In order to do so, conversational agents are simulated with the same communicative channels as humans, such as voice, head and eyes movement, manipulator and facial expression [2,11,18,5]. Moreover, besides cognitive functions, they are also simulated with emotion and personality [7,13,28,31].

One particularity of humans is to have emotions, this makes people different from all other animals. Emotions have been studied for a long time and results show that they play an important role in human cognitive functions. Emotions are so powerful that they can affect creativity, evaluate judgement, rational decision making, communication, and other cognitive processes of people [15,14,9]. Picard has summarized this in her "Affective Computing" [25]. In fact, emotions

A. Ghose, G. Governatori, and R. Sadananda (Eds.): PRIMA 2007, LNAI 5044, pp. 349–358, 2009.

play an extremely important role during the communication between people. Everybody usually assesses each other emotional states, probably because of their good indication of how the person feels, what the person could do next, and how he is about to act. For this assessment, the human face is the most communicative part of the body for expressing emotions [12]. Recent findings show that facial movements play an important role in interpreting emotions. It is recognized that a link exists between facial activity and emotional states. This is asserted in Darwin's pioneer publication "The expression of the emotions in man and animals" [10]. It is undoubted that conversational agents need emotional states and a way to facially express emotions in a real way in order to improve their communication with humans. Therefore, the accurate selection as well as timing of facial expressions according to emotional sates would improve the realism of conversational agents.

Up to now, creating facial expression from emotions has been received much attention [24,17,29,6]. Most of the work concentrate on producing static facial expressions from emotions, e.g. [6]. For expressing continuous emotional states of an agent, not much attention has been paid besides [4]. In this work, Bui [4] brought out a scheme for generating facial expressions from continuous emotional states. In each small interval of time, emotional state is mapped directly to facial expressions which are then displayed on a 3D face. This one to one mapping, however, is not good in the case where there is a high activated state that lasts for a long time. In that situation, the a facial expression might stay on the face for quite a long time. This reduces remarkably the realism of conversational agents because according to psychological and biological research one emotional facial expression usually lasts for only three to four seconds [16].

In this paper, we propose a scheme for displaying continuous emotional states of a conversational agent on a 3D face. The main idea behind the scheme is that an emotional facial expression happens for a few seconds only when there is a significant change in the emotional states. More exactly, an emotional facial expression is activated when there is a significant increase in the intensities of emotions. For the rest of the time, the expressions in the face are kept at low level displaying moods rather than emotions even if the intensities of emotions are high. Our solution for creating real emotional facial expressions can eliminate the limitation of Bui's mechanism [4].

The rest of the paper is organized as follows. Section 2 presents a summary on related work. We then propose our model to convert continuous emotional states of an agent to facial expressions in Section 3. We then test our model in an emotional conversational agent and show result in Section 4.

2   Related Work

In the research field of conversational agents, creating and combining facial expressions have received quite a lot of attention. Many 3D models have been proposed to create realistic facial animation (see [23] for a summary). More and more attention has been paid to facial animation in synchronization with synthesized/natural speech and many talking faces have been developed [2,11,18]. Specifically, significant attention has been paid to visual speech [18,8]. For integrating all these facial movements, besides Bui's method [5], no appropriate methods have been proposed. Bui has developed a mechanism for combining facial movements on a 3D talking head. The system containing six channels is able to create realistic facial expressions and combine facial movements while taking into account the resolution of conflicting muscles/parameters temporally. Particularly, facial movements are broken up into "atomic" movements. Each atomic facial movement consists of three phases: onset, apex, and offset. Combination of movements is performed through two steps: combination of movements in one channel, and combination of movements in different channels. In one channel, the activity of each muscle involved the movements in that channel is modulated to create transition effects between movements. And then, in different channels, the conflicts between the parameters involved in different movements are resolved first. After that, the activities of parameters are combined by taking the maximum values.

One interesting research question which has also received attention is expressing emotions on faces of conversational agents. Until now, there are several proposed methods. These methods can be classified into two categories: static emotion representation methods and dynamic emotion representation methods. In the first category, static emotion representations, several researchers including Kurlander [20], Latta [21], Raouzaiou [27], Albrecht [1] used the emotional wheel described by Plutchik [26] to develop facial animation systems. This emotional wheel model enables researchers to create mechanisms to map emotional state to universally recognized facial expressions. However, this model is only static emotion representation. It does not provide any consistent mechanism for creating emotional facial expressions. So any facial expression can be displayed at any time, independently from the previous emotional facial expression. This is a considerable weakness. Another drawback of the static representation is that emotions vary relatively slowly, so a change of expression from an emotion (i.e. happiness) to the opposite emotion (i.e. anger) takes remarkable time, which is not very appropriate. The second method type, dynamic emotion representations, including the systems of Reilly [28], Velásquez [31], Kshirsagar and Magnenat-Thalmann [19], Paiva [22], Bui [6], and Tanguy [30], selects which emotional facial expressions should be displayed from emotions dynamically. Dynamic emotion representations keep track over time of changes in emotion intensities, represent emotional momentums, and therefore provide a consistent mechanism for creating emotional facial expressions and eliminate the limitation of static emotion representation methods. The system proposed by Kshirsagar and Magnenat-Thalmann [19] uses a Bayesian Belief Network representing emotional state to select the next facial expression that will be displayed on the face of a conversational agent. The advantage of this method is using previous states to select the next expression. However, the number of facial expression that can be displayed by the system is limited. The work described by Bui [6] uses two fuzzy rule - based systems to map an emotion state to facial expressions. There are six basic emotions used to generate an emotional facial expression, namely happiness, sadness, surprise, disgust, anger and fear. One interesting point of this method is using a fuzzy rule based system, which allows the system to incorporate qualitative descriptions such as "happiness is very high" with quantitative information such as emotion intensity or muscle contraction level. Based on Picard's description of emotion intensity and emotion filters [25], Tanguy [30] has developed a dynamic emotion representation. This model can represent any number of types of states, such as emotions, drivers, and so on.

It can be seen that dynamic emotion representation is better than static emotion representations. However, existing dynamic representation systems only deal with expressing emotions without real time conditions. In fact, human emotions are very complicated and we usually can not know in advance how one's emotion will occur. In case there is an emotion that lasts for a long time, mapping one to one from given emotions to facial expression will reduce the realism of conversational agents. In fact this is almost always true because emotions tend to decay slower than facial expressions do. Our solution in this paper will eliminate this limitation.

3   Proposed Model

In this section, we propose our model to convert continuous emotional states of an agent to facial expressions. Our model is based on the idea that an emotional facial expression happens for a few seconds only when there is a significant change in the emotional states, more exactly, a significant increase in the intensities of emotions. When there is not any significant change, the expressions in the face is kept at low level displaying moods rather than emotions even when the intensities of emotions are high. That means the emotional facial expressions appear only when there is a significant stimuli that changes the emotional states. The emotional expressions will not stay on the face for a long time while emotions decay slowly. However, the expressions of moods can last for much longer time on the face [16].

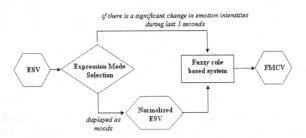

Fig. 1. Our model to convert continuous emotional states of an agent to facial expressions

Our model uses the system in [6] to convert a static emotional state to a facial expression. We also use the system in [5] to combine the emotional facial expressions with other movements of the face. The model, as shown in Figure 1, consists of four components:

1. The input is a series of Emotion State Vector (ESV) over time, resulting from an emotion component of a conversational agents such as [4]. Each ESV is a vector of intensity of the six emotions represented by real numbers at time t: $ESV^t = (e_1^t, e_2^t, \ldots, e_6^t)$ where $0 \le e_i^t \le 1$.
2. The output is a series of Facial Muscle Contraction Vector (FMCV) over time. Each FMCV at time t is described as: $FMCV^t = (m_1^t, m_2^t, \ldots, m_{19}^t)$ where $0 \le m_i^t \le 1$. This is a vector of contraction level of 19 muscles in the right side of the 3D face model in [3].
3. The Expression Mode Selection determines whether an emotional facial expression should be generated to express the current emotional state or the expressions in the 3D face kept at low level displaying moods rather than emotions. This component checks if there is a significant increase in the intensity of any emotion during last 3 seconds (the duration of an emotional expression), that is if $e_i^x - e_i^{x-1} > \theta$ where $t - 3 \le x \le t$, t is the current time, and θ is the threshold to activate emotional facial expressions. If there is a significant change, the ESV is converted directly to FMCV using the fuzzy rule based system proposed in [6]. If not, the ESV is normalized to lower intensity and then converted to FMCV using the same fuzzy rule based system. In this way, the emotions are displayed as moods, the low-intensity and long-lasting state of emotions.
4. The fuzzy rule based system to convert from emotions to facial muscle contraction levels, which is proposed in [6]. This system uses two collections of fuzzy if - then rules which are used to capture the relationship between the EVS and the FMVS. The Single Expression Mode FRBS maps a single emotion to its universally recognized facial muscle contraction levels, and the Blend Expression Mode FRBS maps the two emotions with higher intensities to a blend of their universally recognized facial muscle contraction levels.

4   Result

We use the emotional conversational agent presented in [4] to test our proposed model. The agent is situated in the domain of a football supporter. Football is an emotional game. There are many events in the the game that trigger emotions of not only players but also of coaches, supporters, etc. A last-minute goal triggers happiness or relief in some people whereas it triggers sadness, anger or disappointment in other people. Testing the football supporter's domain gives us the chance to test many emotions as well as the dynamics of emotions because the actions in a football match happen fast.

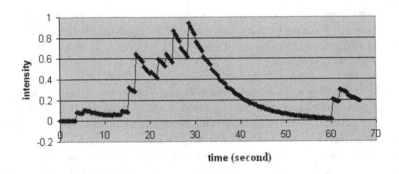

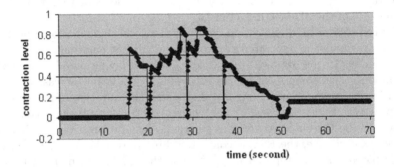

Fig. 2. The graph that shows the intensity of emotion Happiness of Obie during the football match (above) and the graph that shows the contraction level of Zymgomatic Major (below), the smiling muscle to express Happiness before applying our proposed model

The agent, named Obie, is a football (soccer) supporter agent. Obie is watching a football match in which a team, which he supports, is playing. Obie can experience different emotions by appraising events based on his goals, standards, and preferences. Obie can also show his emotions on a 3D talking head.

Before applying our model to convert continuous emotional states of an agent to facial expressions, Obie sometime displayed a visible facial expressions for a long time (such as happiness or sadness) as the emotions lasted for a long time. That gives the agent a mechanical look over time because a facial expressions just stays on a human face for a few seconds. This can be easily seen in the intensity graph of emotion Happiness and the contraction level graph of muscle Zymgomatic Major, the smiling muscle to express Happiness in Figure 2. From the graph, we can see that the contraction level of Zymgomatic Major stays high for a long period, from second 15 to second 45. That mean the 3D face "smiles" for about 30 seconds.

After applying our model, Obie now displays his emotions in his 3D face in a much reasonable way. Each emotional facial expressions just last for about 3 seconds. For the rest of the time, the 3D face display low level expressions as moods rather than emotions. This can be seen in the intensity graph of emotion Happiness and the contraction level graph of muscle Zymgomatic Major in Figure 3 and Figure 4. From the graph, we can see that, the 3D face only "smiles" twice, at second 15 and second 27, each time for about 3 seconds. The rest of the time, the face displays a happy mood when the intensity of emotion Happiness is high.

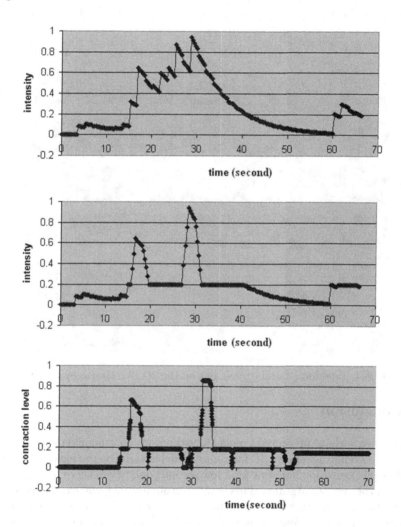

Fig. 3. The graph that shows the intensity of emotion Happiness of Obie during the football match (top), the graph that shows the normalized intensity of emotion Happniness by our model to display on 3D face (middle), and the graph that shows the contraction level of Zymgomatic Major (bottom) after applying our proposed model

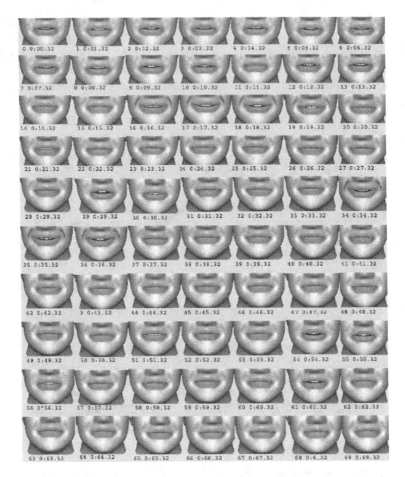

Fig. 4. Emotional facial expressions on the 3D face (frame by frame)

5   Conclusion

In this paper, we have presented a model for expressing continuous emotional states of a conversational agent on a 3D face. Our model is based on the idea that an emotional facial expression happens for a few seconds only when there is a significant change in the emotional states. This makes the emotional facial expressions of the conversational agents more realistic due to the fact that a facial expressions only stays on the face for a few seconds. We have tested our model on Bui's football (soccer) supporter agent [4] and produced more believable facial expressions.

Acknowledgement

This work is financially supported by the Grant of Fundamental Research Funds No. 204006, entitled "Modern Methods for Building Intelligent Systems".

References

1. Albrecht, I.: - Faces and Hands- Modeling and animating anatomical and photo-realistic models with regard to the communicative competence of virtual humans. PhD thesis, University at des Saarlandes (2005)
2. Albrecht, I., Haber, J., Kähler, K., Schröder, M., Seidel, H.P.: May i talk to you? facial animation from text. In: Proceedings Pacific Graphics 2002, pp. 77–86 (2002)
3. Bui, T.D., Heylen, D., Nijholt, A.: Improvements on a simple muscle-based 3d face for realistic facial expressions. In: 16th Int. Conf. on Computer Animation and Social Agents, pp. 33–40. IEEE Computer Society, Los Alamitos (2003)
4. Bui, T.D., Heylen, D., Nijholt, A.: Building embodied agents that experience and express emotions: A football supporter as an example. In: Proc. CASA 2004, Computer Graphics Society (2004)
5. Bui, T.D., Heylen, D., Nijholt, A.: Combination of facial movements on a 3d talking head. In: Proc. CGI 2004. IEEE Computer Society, Los Alamitos (2004)
6. Bui, T.D., Heylen, D., Poel, M., Nijholt, A.: Generation of facial expressions from emotion using a fuzzy rule based system. In: Australian Joint Conf. on Artificial Intelligence (AI 2001), Berlin. LNCS, pp. 83–95. Springer, Heidelberg (2001)
7. Bui, T.D., Heylen, D., Poel, M., Nijholt, A.: Parlee: An adaptive plan based event appraisal model of emotions. In: Jarke, M., Koehler, J., Lakemeyer, G. (eds.) KI 2002. LNCS, vol. 2479, pp. 129–143. Springer, Heidelberg (2002)
8. Cohen, M.M., Massaro, D.W.: Modeling coarticulation in synthetic visual speech. In: Magnenat Thalmann, N., Thalmann, D. (eds.) Models and Techniques in Computer Animation, pp. 139–156. Springer, Tokyo (1993)
9. Damasio, A.R.: Descartes error: Emotion, reason, and the human brain. G.P. Putnam, New York (1994)
10. Darwin, C.: The expression of the emotions in man and animals. Univerity of Chicago Press, Chicago (1872/1965)
11. DeCarlo, D.C., Revilla, M.S., Venditti, J.: Making discourse visible: Coding and animating conversational facial displays. In: Computer Animation 2002(2002)
12. Ekman, P., Friesen, W.V.: Unmasking the Face: A Guide To Recognizing Emotions From Facial Clues. Prentice-Hall, Englewood Cliffs (1975)
13. El-Nasr, M.S., Yen, J., Ioerger, T.R.: FLAME-fuzzy logic adaptive model of emotions. Autonomous Agents and Multi-Agent Systems 3(3), 219–257 (2000)
14. Forgas, J.P., Moylan, S.: After the movies: the effects of transient mood states on social judgments. Personality and Social Psychology Bulletin 13 (1987)
15. Galernter, D.H.: The muse in the machine. Free Press, New York (1994)
16. Hager, J.C., Ekman, P.: Essential behavioral science of the face and gesture that computer scientists need to know (1995),
http://face-and-emotion.com/dataface/misctext/iwafgr.html
17. Hayes-Roth, B., van Gent, R.: Story-making with improvisational puppets. In: Johnson, W.L., Hayes-Roth, B. (eds.) Proceedings of the 1st International Conference on Autonomous Agents, pp. 1–7. ACM Press, New York (1997)
18. King, S.A., Parent, R.E., Olsafsky, B.: An anatomically-based 3d parametric lip model to support facial animation and synchronized speech. In: Proceedings of Deform 2000, pp. 7–19 (2000)
19. Kshirsagar, S., Magnenat-Thalmann, N.: A multilayer personality model. In: Proceedings of 2nd International Symposium on Smart Graphics, pp. 107–115. ACM Press, New York (2002)

20. Kurlander, D., Skelly, T., Salesin, D.: Comic chat. In: SIGGRAPH 1996: Proceedings of the 23rd annual conference on Computer graphics and interactive techniques, pp. 225–236 (1996)
21. Latta, C., Alvarado, N., Adams, S.S., Burbeck, S.: An expressive system for animating characters or endowing robots with affective displays. In: Society for Artificial Intelligence and Social Behavior (AISB), 2002 Annual Conference, Symposium on Animating Expressive Characters for Social Interactions (2002)
22. Paiva, A., Dias, J., Sobral, D., Aylett, R., Sobreperez, P., Woods, S., Zoll, C., Hall, L.: Caring for agents and agents that care: Building empathic relations with synthetic agents. In: Proceedings of the Third International Joint Conference on Autonomous Agents and Multiagent Systems, pp. 194–201. IEEE Computer Society, Los Alamitos (1996)
23. Parke, F.I., Waters, K.: Computer Facial Animation. A K Peters (1996) ISBN 1-56881-014-8
24. Perlin, K., Goldberg, A.: Improv: A system for scripting interactive actors in virtual worlds. Computer Graphics 30(Annual Conference Series), 205–216 (1996)
25. Picard, R.: Affective Computing. MIT Press, Cambridge (1997)
26. Plutchik, R.: Emotions: A general psychoevolutionary theory. In: Scherer, K.R., Ekman, P. (eds.) Approaches to emotion. Lawrence Erlbaum, London (1984)
27. Raouzaiou, A., Karpouzis, K., Kollias, S.D.: Online gaming and emotion representation. In: García, N., Salgado, L., Martínez, J.M. (eds.) VLBV 2003. LNCS, vol. 2849, pp. 298–305. Springer, Heidelberg (2003)
28. Reilly, W.S.: Believable social and emotional agents. Technical Report Ph.D. Thesis. Technical Report CMU-CS-96-138, Carnegie Mellon University, Pittsburgh, PA, USA (1996)
29. Stern, A., Frank, A., Resner, B.: Virtual petz: A hybrid approach to creating autonomous, lifelike dogz and catz. In: Sycara, K.P., Wooldridge, M. (eds.) Proc. of Agents 1998, pp. 334–335. ACM Press, New York (1998)
30. EAR. Tanguy. Emotions: the Art of Communication Applied to Virtual Actors. PhD thesis, Universit of Bath (2006)
31. Velásquez, J.D.: Modeling emotions and other motivations in synthetic agents. In: Proc. (AAAI 1997/IAAI 1997), pp. 10–15. AAAI Press, Menlo Park (1997)

GAMA: An Environment for Implementing and Running Spatially Explicit Multi-agent Simulations

Edouard Amouroux[1,2], Thanh-Quang Chu[1,2], Alain Boucher[1], and Alexis Drogoul[1,2]

[1] AUF-IFI, MSI, ngo 42, Ta Quang Buu, Ha Noi, Viet Nam
[2] IRD, GEODES, 32 av. H. Varagnat, 93143 Bondy Cedex, France
edouard@amouroux.biz, ctquang@ifi.edu.vn, alain.boucher@auf.org,
drogoul@mac.com

Abstract. In this paper, we introduce the GAMA (Gis & Agent-based Modelling Architecture) simulation platform, which aims at providing field experts, modellers, and computer scientists with a complete modelling and simulation development environment for building spatially explicit multi-agent simulations.

The most important requirements of spatially explicit multi-agent simulations that our platform fulfils are: (1) the ability to transparently use complex Geographical Information System (GIS) data as an environment for the agents; (2) the ability to handle a vast number of (heterogeneous) agents (3); the ability to offer a platform for automated controlled experiments (by automatically varying parameters, recording statistics, etc.); (4) the possibility to let non-computer scientists design models and interact with the agents during simulations.

While still in its implementation phase, the platform is currently used for two main applications. One is about the modelling of the spread of avian influenza in a province of North Vietnam in collaboration with CIRAD (French Agricultural Research Centre working for International Development). Its goal is to simulate the poultry value chain of a whole province using geolocalised data, and to use this to optimise a monitoring network. A second application conducted with the Institute for Marine Geology and Geophysics (VAST, Hanoi) is about using an interactive simulation for supporting decision-making during urban post-disaster situations. This application relies on geolocalised data as well, and requires facilities of interaction between users and the simulation.

1 Introduction

The use of computer modelling and simulation for the study of complex natural or social phenomena has been gaining momentum since several years. This has been the case for traditional techniques, such as mathematical approaches based on system dynamics, but even more for the so-called Individual-Based Modelling (IBM) approaches. The first kind of models represents a system by a set of global aggregated variables, and its dynamics by equations or constraints that link these variables and express their evolution. They are interesting in that they can sometimes be solved analytically, but are very sensitive to local heterogeneities. On the contrary, IBM models are based on entities that represent individuals and their interactions in the system modelled. They can explicitly take the environment and the different actors of the system into account, with all their attributes and behaviours. They provide an interesting way for exploring, analysing and

A. Ghose, G. Governatori, and R. Sadananda (Eds.): PRIMA 2007, LNAI 5044, pp. 359–371, 2009.
© Springer-Verlag Berlin Heidelberg 2009

understanding situations of the emergence of global properties from the interaction of local components of the system. Finally, thanks to their fine-grained approach, these models enable the scientists to watch and follow various outputs (from global statistical results to detailed reviews of local behaviours) of the evolution from the system.

A subcategory of these IBM models concerns the ones based on "spatially explicit multi-agent systems (MAS)". Here the entities (or agents) are explicitly situated in a simulated environment, in which they can perceive the information available in their neighbourhood, act upon it, and interact locally with their neighbours. They are particularly well suited for fine-grained simulations based on realistic environments such as the ones represented in Geographical Information System (GIS). These simulations are becoming more and more popular nowadays, especially in the area of decision-support systems (DSS) for social, ecological, agricultural or biological concerns.

Unfortunately there are no real development environments available on the market for designing and implementing such simulations. Instead of focusing on high-level properties of the model, designers and modellers still have to deal with low-level constraints that are, moreover, remarkably similar from one project to another.

1.1 Requirements of a Modern Simulation Platform

A ready to use yet generic platform for the subgroup of situated agent-base model requires several issues to be addressed.

Environments. As we partly focused on the geographical data accessibility aspect, the platform has to support the main GIS file format. At the moment the most common GIS file format is that of the shape file, promoted by ArcGIS, but it is important to provide computation tools that can be adapted to handle other formats like OpenGIS.

Continuous environments like the one provided by the GIS are not the only kind of topological space in which simulated agents can behave. There are at least 2 others: discrete (i.e. grid) environments as well as network (i.e. social network) ones that are commonly used by modellers (see [1] for extended description of multi-agent's environments). A simulation platform must then provide sufficiently generic abstraction of the environment in order to allow modellers to manipulate them without hassle.

Agents. A modern tool should provide facilities to implement specific agent architecture but also the possibility to instantiate agents straight "out of the box" (like NetLogo) without much need for programming. The first point requires that abstractions like the decision mechanisms, the internal state, the relations with the outer world be clearly formalised, organised and reusable within the platform. They should be offered as a well documented meta-model and an easily extensible framework. The second point requires, at least, a specifically designed language to program agents without the complexity of a computer programming language. A graphical user interface could be added in order to ease further the modelling process. The definition of environment and of an agent architecture along with a simulation management defines a *meta-model* which is a very useful guideline for both developing a new specialisation (from a framework point of view) and for the modelling process (from a user point of view). We would now have a generic and useable platform but it still lacks ease of use for thematician. To address this specific issue, the platform should at least provide a simple way to instantiate simulations from a model. To do so a common yet efficient way is to develop an accessible modelling language that would be automatically instantiated as a simulation using already defined classes. These requirements have for main consequences that we should have a ready to be used platform, with the previously discussed features, and a framework organisation. This organisation will unbound the limits of the proposed platform when specific needs occur (depending on the modelled system, data availability, etc).

1.2 State of the Art

The multi-agent simulation platforms offer is huge but often those platform are quite specific in terms of application. However some platforms are mature enough but lack some important features while new platforms that are being developed to address some of these needs still lack maturity. In addition many multi-agent platforms, like Jade for instance, don't offer a good support of topological spaces or no environment at all and, consequently, have to be put aside.

Table 1. Agent-based simulation platforms review considering the previously defined requirements

	Swarm	NetLogo 3	Mason	RepastJ
GIS	Partial (uneasy)	Partial (raster)	No	Good (but only through Example)
Generic Environment	No	No	Yes	Yes
Generic Agent	No	No	Yes	Yes
Meta-model	Yes	Yes	No	No
Ease of use	No	Yes	No	No
Main strength	Swarm concept	Ease of use	Speed	Well developped libraries
Main weakness	Complexity	No complex model support	Complexity	Difficulty to use by modellers

Swarm [2] by its historical importance is the first to be reviewed (see [3] for extended review of several platforms). Indeed, there is two different implementations of this platform, the original one is developed in Objective-C and a new one in Java. They both lack real (easy / useable) GIS support. Although it provides a meta-model with the concept of Swarm, every agent of the simulation is both an agent and an environment for other agents, it is a very rigid and complex organisation. Finally it doesn't offer any easy way of modelling, especially for non computer scientists, they would have to learn a programming language. The second platform to review is Netlogo [4]. This is an educational platform and so it has ease of use in mind. Here there is no need to learn an obscure programming language, it offers a very easy and quick to learn language yet a quite powerful one. Although its potentiality is not as great as other platforms but it remains useable for many developments. The problem with Netlogo starts also with GIS support, only simple raster data can be used as an environment. The meta-model is also very simple consisting of only reactive agents, acting and interacting in a grid environment. The third one, MASON, has for main features its innovative design made for execution speed. The drawback of this is its complexity for programming a model, especially when using the scheduling mechanism. Another drawback is that it does not support yet GIS, although MASON is a recent platform.

Finally, RepastJ (version 3) is a bit older than MASON and so it already has much more developed features, especially a GIS support thanks to OpenMap. It still lacks ease of use but it has a well organised platform architecture and good documentation.

Considering all these advantages and defects we have chosen to base our development of an extensible yet generic platform on RepastJ having in mind the accessibility and re-usability of the developed platform.

2   GAMA's General Orgamisation

Our aim is to develop both a generic architecture for situated agent-based modelling and a ready to use platform. For this, we have the following strategy. Firstly, we chose to clearly separate the simulation process, managed in the *Simulation Kernel*, from the modelling process, managed in the *Meta-model*. Secondly, every first class entity (defined as "a program building block, an independent piece of software which [...] provides an abstraction or information hiding mechanism so that a module's implementation can be changed without requiring any change to other modules." in [2]) of the platform is thought to be re-definable resulting in the possibility to use GAMA as a framework and allowing developers to build their own simulation platform considering their specific needs.

2.1   Modelling Ontology

Our meta-model is thought as guidelines to build any kind of simulation from physical phenomena to social ones. Every model share a minimal set of concept, we generalised and organised them in a meta model (see Fig. 1). The two main concepts to consider are Agent and Environment at first.

In GAMA what we call *Agent* only takes care of holding the internal state of the modelled entity and a decision system. Consequently we will refer to common "Agent" sense in literature with "Entity". The decision system of an Entity can be of any kind, from cellular automata, rule-based system or complex cognitive system. To have an example of a possible decision system we will define the one used in conjunction with the GAma Modelling Language (GAML, cf section 3). The internal state is only a set of variables and is less likely to be redefined. To catch up the common agent paradigm we defined also two other concepts: the *Body* and the *Skill*. Entities are localised in an *Environment*, spatial or conceptual one. This localisation and actions within an Environment are done thanks to the *Body* class which acts as an interface between the Entities and the environment. The Body class offers the following localisation services:

– Communication and perception with the use of *Variables* (stigmergy) and signals
– Neighbourhood, which agents are around
– Movement possibilities

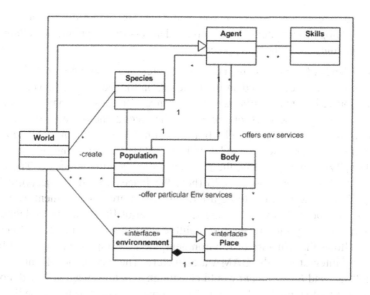

Fig. 1. Meta-model: a world managing agents and environments

Using the standardised basic low-level localisation services of any environment (that will be described below), the *Body* is generic to all environments defined in GAMA and is able to manage several environments at once. As an Entity can act on various environments at the same time, the *Body* will manage all the requests of the *Agent* and direct them to the relevant one. For example an ambulance can move in a city represented by a GIS while being localised in a communication network environment (each cell represents a rescue unit and is connected to the rescue units it can communicate with).

Skills are a set of possible actions for the Entity. These actions can be very different from interaction between Entities, action on the Environment or even with the GUI (e.g. reveal/hide the Entity). In GAMA, generic *Skills* have been already defined allowing common action for the Entity (for instance Carrying which allows the agent to carry other agents). Although new *Skills* would be needed to fulfil specific needs depending on the modelled system. More precisely *Skills* embed effective Java methods that will allow the Entity to do actions defined in the model and present what kind of variables are needed or optional for the Entity to fulfil those particular actions.

To allow Entities to perceive, act and interact they need a substrate to do so, that is where *Environment* come into the light. As defined in [5]: "An environment can either be represented as a single monolithic system, i.e. a centralized environment, or as a set of cells assembled in a network, i.e. a distributed environment". In GAMA every type of *Environments* are unified thanks to the generic network organisation consisting of an aggregation of *Places*. *Places* are where the Agents are effectively localised and where environmental data are stored. *Places*, in coordination with the *Environment*, also offer a minimum set of low level services to the Entity's *Body* as follow:

- Store and access (perception) environmental data (including stigmergic data)
- Space topology (movement constraints) and access to neighbourhood (*Places*)
- Which Entities are at the same place

There are 3 types of environment (network, discrete and continuous) to fulfil all the possible needs and we developed an implementation for each of these. The first one is a Network space, it connects *Places* without concern for any real physical space and is generally used to transcribe social relation. The second one is the Grid *Environment* consisting of regularly arranged cells. It allows simulation of the model when no real field data is needed or to test a model with forged data and has the benefit of being computationally efficient. Finally, the third one is the continuous space. The first implementation of this one relies on GIS (here the Places are GIS Objects), using the OpenMap library, and is ready to be used; which is a great requirement as we stated before. It is also possible to use the abstract concept of Environment to define a new implementation of any kind (even a monolithic one) of Environment. As long as the developer follows the structure of Environment, the new implementation will be fully and smoothly integrated in the GAMA architecture. These concepts of Entities (*Agent + Skills + Body*) and *Environment* would be enough to define an agent-based model but are not enough to do it efficiently. We added automatic mechanisms to ease the "model to simulation process". We did so with the three concepts as follows that will instantiate the Entities and then manage the evolution of the simulation. Generally Entities can be regrouped under a few different prototypes; we decided to formalise it and proposed an implementation of this mechanism (along the instantiation one). The *Species* is such a prototype it defines both the internal states and the behaviour. Though, the description of the behaviour depends on the decision system chosen in the *Agent*'s architecture. For example a generic vehicle in a simple model could be defined as an *Agent* with the following characteristics:

Internal state: fuel, speed, passenger capacity
Skills: move (on road), load and unload passengers
From this base we can build various models from traffic simulation with cars and trucks, to rescue situation with ambulance and military forces.

To instantiate or specialise this generic *Agent* we added the *Population* class. It is responsible for building a concrete *Agent* from the prototypical one (defined thanks to *Species*). It will specialise *Variables*, the behaviour (depending on the decision system) and sets the localisation. In the previous example, *the population would consist of 70% of ambulances (different types) and 30% military forces, localised uniformly on roads using GIS data, with fuel, capacity and speed distributed over field data.* It is possible to use mathematical functions to distribute parameters (random initial location) over a space. Finally, the *World* object is in charge of the instantiation of all objects (reading a parameter file) and their coherent interactions throughout the simulation. As the *World* is also an *Agent* it is possible to give it a behaviour. Actually its behaviour is to follow a predefined scenario (e.g. executes events) and to provide access to the current situation of the simulation to the GUI packages that enables the user to track the evolution of the system and eventually interact with it.

2.2   Simulation Kernel

The simulation kernel is in charge of the technical process to build a concrete simulation from a model. In fact, an agent-based model is a static object that describes a dynamic system. It consists of a description of *Environments*, Entities and their action on it and among them. Entities are all similar to the prototype defined in the model, to execute the simulation we need to create all the effective Entities with their specific variables values, localisation and behaviour as defined in the model. To do so, and to be able to monitor and control the run of the simulation, we developed a simulation kernel offering the full range of essential services.

The main class and the entry point of this kernel is the *Simulation* class (see Fig. 2). It is responsible for reading the parameter file (XML-based), instantiate all the needed objects and delegating the parsing of specific XML elements to the World object. The *Scheduler* is responsible for the correct execution of the simulation, it allows every *Agents* to execute their actions, manages coherently newly created Entities and disposable ones within the execution process. An Entity can be added to the simulation but usually has to fulfil conditions (e.g. not 2 entities at the same localisation) and can be discarded only when no other Entity is having an interaction within the first one. When all this technical work is done and the simulation is ready to start, the *Simulation GUI* comes onto the scene. Its responsibility is to allow users to monitor the evolution of the system. As various needs exist, depending on the purpose of the simulation, we had to allow monitoring from a single Entity (e.g. its internal state), using individual probes, to global (or group restricted) or statistical measures using graphs and statistical output (using the Colt library). It is also possible to track the spatial evolution of the system within the *Environment*, which a mathematical model cannot allow. For example, watch

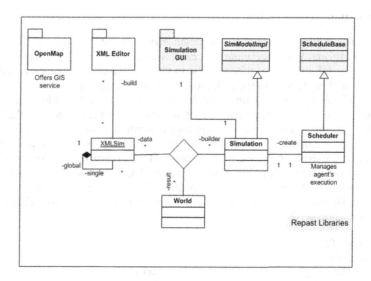

Fig. 2. Simulation kernel: providing services to execute a simulation

Entities' movements and track their trajectories over time. On top of visualisation we added the possibility to dynamically affect the simulation throw interaction mechanism. It is possible to check an Entity's internal state then change values and, more importantly, its behaviour. For example, in our rescue simulation, we will capture decision process throw interaction with the simulation. Decision makers will change Entity's behaviour on the fly to conform them to their own decisions. As you may have noticed along the description of these general mechanisms, the platform is generic for any situated IBM model. As long as developers follow the general guidelines of each modules, ascending and descending compatibility is guaranteed. In addition, if you need to model similar system with different data but same type of Entities (or even different Entities but with similar possibilities of action), only the configuration file has to be modified with the new parameters. For example if you have modelled the avian influenza propagation in a village of the North Vietnam, you can use the same model with field data from Thailand.

3   GAML: A Scripting Language for Developing Agents

GAML is a modelling language, inspired from the EMF (Etho Modelling Framework) language developed during the Manta project [6], based on XML formalism and is meant to define reactive agents. The idea behind it was to propose an easy to learn language, like the NetLogo one, but not a programming one. This langage is designed to be used with reactive agents, especially the architecture detailed in section 3.2. For instance, the *World*, which manage the simulation configuration as well as the scenario, is defined thanks to a light version of GAML.

3.1   Simulation Configuration

GAML defines a general formalism to parameterise all the first class entities of the meta-model (*Agents, Species, Population, Environments* and *World*). As *Agent, Species* and *Population* definitions are quite specific to the Agent architecture developed along GAML they will be defined in the following section. Consequently we will now focus on *World* and *Environment*. Defining an *Environment* is type dependent but is quite simple. In the case of a network *Environment*, we only define the topology of the *Places*. Concerning the grid *Environment*, the topology is implicit (4 or 8 neighbours) so only the dimensions and the metric (cell size) has to be defined. The GIS *Environment* is a bit more complex so we will look at an example. Here we just define a reference layer (as different layers are likely to cover different zones) plus drawing information and the 'type' argument defines which library (OpenMap here) to use to read the layers. We also define a simple grid with square cells to enable the use of localized data produce by Entities during the simulation.

```
<GIS type="OpenMap">
    <shapeLayers>
        <layer prettyName="road" isRef="true">
            <shapeFile value="data/gis/road.shp" />
            <lineColor value="#000000" />
            <fillColor value="000000" />
```

```
            </layer>
        </shapeLayers>
    </GIS>
    <GRID type="'square'" width="500" height="500">
    </GRID>
```

World which is the interface between the Simulation kernel and the Modelling ontology has also the responsibility to follow a predefined scenario and to track the evolution of the simulation. To do so the *World* is defined like an *Agent* to produce event in the simulation and to provide facilities to track any evolution of the simulation

```
    <event if="time = 10 hours * rnd">
        <do action="earthquake">
        <arg name="magnitude" value="rnd * 7"/>
        </do>
    </event>
```

As you can see in the example (an earthquake to happen randomly in the first 10 hours with random magnitude up to 7), an event is just a global action on the simulated system and as you will see in the next section it relies on the earthquake *Skill* (*World* specific ones) mechanism as *World* is a specific *Agent*.

3.2   GAML and Its Associated Agent Architecture

GAML is responsible for enabling the modeller to describe all the characteristics of the Entities. Concretely, GAML will offer a description formalism for the internal state of the Entity and for its behavior also based on the following decision system. The behavior of the Entity is split in 2 parts, *Reflexes* and *Tasks*. *Reflexes* are simple actions to be executed whenever a condition is fulfilled. Each Task implements a specific behavior, for instance looking for food, and consists of a sequence of actions and a motivation depending on internal state and perception of the Entity. At each timestep the Entity selects whether to continue the current *Task* or to start a new one depending of the motivations. The Actions are implemented (and described) in a *Skill* class which is referenced by the *Species*.

Species. As described in the meta-model the *Species* is the prototype of Entities and so this is where they will be defined in GAML. Here is an example from the AROUND project (cf. Applications section):

```
    <task name="driveVictim">
        <priority if="!self.empty" value="20" else="0"/>
            <duration max="2 hours" />
                <repeat action="goto">
                    <arg name="target" value="hospital" />
                    <arg name="speed" value="150 kmh" />
                </repeat>
                <do action="drop">
                </do>
    </task>
```

This Task makes the Entity (an ambulance for instance) go to a hospital then deliver its victim there at the condition the Entity carries a victim and no other Task is much motivated. The "goto" action is a repetitive one and will be executed as long as the entity has not reached the hospital (as defined in the "moveable" Skill class using the compulsory parameter "target"). The "do" is a non-repetitive action to "drop" (defined in the "carrying" *Skill*). As you can see this task will be executed if the Entity actually carries a victim. Another way to act for the Entity is reflexes. They are simple non repetitive action that are instantaneous action, an example could be:

```
<reflex if="context.fire">
    <do action="die" />
    </do>
</reflex>
```

Here if an ambulance is taken into in fire it will be destroyed. These examples show an Entity acting in its environment but interactions among Entities is addressed through communication (or with specific *Skills*) which is handled specifically as follows.

There are two main ways of communicating in our agent-based simulation platform, a basic message paradigm and the stigmergy. Here is an example for message:

```
<ask target="self.myHQ">
    <set var="rescuedVictims" value="self.myHQ.rescuedVictims + 1"/>
</ask>
```

Stigmergy relies on signals landed in the *Environment* which act as a shared medium and manages propagation of these signals. Like other environmental data those signals are used thanks to the Body.

Population. Here we defined the instantiation of Entities from the *Species*. We define groups of Entities sharing the same behaviour and localisation process, here is an example:

```
<group species="ambulance" size="10">
    <subgroup size ="5">
    <location ="hospital"/>
    <var name="fuel" init="100 * rnd"
    </subgroup>
</group>
```

Here we have a group of ambulances, starting in the hospital with a random quantity of fuel.

Though this modelling language is more accessible than a programming language, a graphical editor is currently under development to ease further the modelling process, especially for field specialists. This editor allows the "simulationist" to focus on modelling by managing low level coherency.

4   Applications

The development of GAMA has then been conducted in parallel with the implementation on the platform of four complex models with very different requirements, enabling us to make a clear distinction between generic structures and services and application-specific needs.

The first model concerns the simulation of the spread of avian influenza (AI) in North Vietnam [7]. It is built in collaboration with epidemiologists and veterinarians from the CIRAD. Mathematical models failed to represent the complexity of the real system and to predict correctly the spread of avian influenza. First, we are using IBM models and MAS based simulation platform so we can take into account the heterogeneity of agents (domestic and wild birds, humans and their different roles, etc). Second, the GIS-based Environment allows us to use geolocalised field data to take explicit account of the real environment. These two aspects are thought, by field specialist, to be the key factors in the spread of avian influenza. With this approach we will be able to propose an interactive tool (the simulation) to specialist to to develop further their insight of the dynamic of this system and to propose iteratively a more and more realistic model. Eventually when the model will be realistic enough for specialist, the simulation will be use as a "virtual laboratory" to test and optimise the deployment of a targeted monitoring network

The second model, part of a larger project called "AROUND" (Autonomous Robots for Observation of Urban Network after Disasters), concerns the simulation and optimization of urban disaster rescue operations. It is built in conjunction with geographers and rescue experts from the VAST (see for instance [8]), and specifically targets post-earthquakes situations in Hanoi city. As in RoboCup Rescue [9], realistic aspects of the disaster are taken into account: fire, housing and building damages, road disruptions, status of victims, localization of rescue centres, etc. The search and rescue operations are implemented through heterogeneous agents that represent firemen, ambulances, and policemen with realistic individual behaviours. The aim of the project is to learn the global strategy used by rescue experts in such situations in order to provide an efficient decision support system in case of real disasters. The learning process consists in letting the experts play with the simulation, alter the individual behaviours and decisions of the agents, and in inferring, by successive proposals, trials and validations, realistic decision rules. This application requires a high level of interactivity with users and the use of very precise field data.

The third model is about the simulation of daily household activities in order to test the effect of the introduction of in-house services and appliances. It is built in collaboration with ergonomists of EDF (Electricité de France), who provide real-life scenarios (translated from video shootings of French families). Each member of the household is represented by an agent, which can either play its behaviour as stated in the scenario or be controlled by an end-user and learn its behaviour by imitation. This participatory process (detailed in [10]) requires a high level of interactivity and a precise description of the environment surrounding the agents.

Finally, the fourth model is a reimplementation of the SAMBA model [11], originally implemented in the CORMAS environment [12]. SAMBA uses multi-agent modelling for testing hypotheses about agricultural dynamics and to better understand individual decision making and its consequences on agricultural dynamics and land use change in the Bac Kan province. The original SAMBA model was limited to the scale of a village; its reimplementation in GAMA aims at adopting a multi-scale approach by taking into account behaviours from other actors: local authorities, province authorities, inter-villages trade possibilities, changes of government policies, etc. The development of GAMA has then been conducted in parallel with the implementation on the platform of four complex models with very different requirements, enabling us to make a clear distinction between generic structures and services and application-specific needs.

5   Conclusion

The GAMA platform is still under development but already offers most of the requirements we described. GIS support is addressed thanks to the use of OpenMap while a generic environment support is developped as well as specific ones too. The agent architecture separating the internal state + decision system from the localisation one and from the action one represents a good guideline to implement a specific agent architecture while it is very generic. These 2 features result in a precise and generic meta-model.

From a more "end user" point of view, we added several facilities to use the platform for modelling and simulation with no programming need. GAML and the reactive agent architecture offers a ready to be use which is very accessible to non computer modellers with a minimum learning requirement. This architecture is not mandatory and the framework organisation allows re-using of previously defined model. Even simulation can be integrated without too much hassle in the framework.

The choice to base GAMA on open-source libraries like OpenMap and RePast allows us to benefit from their future enhancements while easily reusing and adapting most of the tools (visualization and manipulation tools, for instance) they already provide.

Finally Repast is going to evolve soon, we will have to review the new platform and decide whether to use it or not for GAMA. As we used Repast as a set of libraries, this would not be too complex.

Acknowledgements. We are very grateful to our partners, Stéphanie Desvaux (CIRAD – Hanoi), Nguyen Hong Phuong (VAST — Hanoi), Nicolas Sabouret (LIP6 — Paris, France), Yvon Haradji (EDF R&D — Clamart, France) and Jean-Christophe Castella (IRD – Montpellier, France) for their advices on the development of the platform. We would like also to thank François Sempé for his advices on this paper. This work is supported by a 3-years PhD grant from the IRD, an international volunteer grant from the French Ministry of Foreign Affairs, and a research grant from the ICT-Asia Programme.

References

1. Railsback, S.F., Lytinen, S.L., Jackson, S.K.: Agent-based Simulation Platforms: Review and Development Recommendations. SIMULATION 82(9), 609–623 (2006)
2. Weyns, D., Van Dyke Parunak, H., Michel, F., Holvoet, T., Ferber, J.: Environments for Multiagent Systems, State-of-the-Art and Research Challenges. LNAI, vol. 3477. Springer, Heidelberg (2005)
3. Minar, N., Burkhart, R., Langton, C., Askenazi, M.: The Swarm simulation system: A toolkit for building multi-agent simulations. Santa Fe Institute working paper (1996)
4. Tissue, S., Wilensky, U.: Netlogo: A Simple Environment for Modelling Complexity. In: International Conference on Complex Systems (2004)

5. Ferber, J.: Multi-Agent Systems, An Introduction to Distributed Artificial Intelligence. Addison-Wesley, Reading (1999)
6. Drogoul, A., Ferber, J.: Multi-Agent Simulation as a Tool for Modelling Societies: Application to Social Differentiation in Ant Colonies. In: Castelfranchi, C., Werner, E. (eds.) Artificial Social Systems, Berlin, vol. 830, pp. 3–23. Springer, Heidelberg (1994)
7. Desvaux, S., et al.: HPAI Surveillance Programme in Cambodia: Results and Perspectives. In: OIE/FAO international Conference on Avian Influenza. Developments in Biologicals, vol. 124, pp. 211–224 (2005)
8. Nguyen-Hung, P.: Decision support systems applied to earthquake and tsunami risk assessment and loss mitigation. Colloque international sur les Application de la télédétection, des SIG et des GPS pour la réduction des risques naturels et le développement durable (2006)
9. Kitano, H.: RoboCup Rescue: A Grand Challenge for Multi-Agent Systems. In: International Conference on Multi-Agent Systems, pp. 5–12 (2000)
10. Sempé, F., Nguyen-Duc, M., Boissau, S., Boucher, A., Drogoul, A.: An artificial maieutic approach for eliciting experts' knowledge in multi-agent simulations. In: Sichman, J.S., Antunes, L. (eds.) MABS 2005. LNCS, vol. 3891, pp. 75–87. Springer, Heidelberg (2006)
11. Castella, J.C., Boissau, S., Tran-Ngoc, T., Dang-Dinh, Q.: Agrarian transition and lowland-upland interactions in mountain areas in northern Vietnam: Application of a multi-agent simulation model. Agricultural Systems 86(3), 312–332 (1986)
12. Bousquet, F., Bakam, I., Proton, H., Le Page, C.: Cormas: common-pool resources and multi-agent Systems. In: Mira, J., Moonis, A., de Pobil, A.P. (eds.) IEA/AIE 1998. LNCS (LNAI), vol. 1416, pp. 826–837. Springer, Heidelberg (1998)

Multi-agent Based Incineration Process Control System with Qualitative Model

Hyeon-Kyeong Kim[1] and Seungdo Kim[2]

[1] Department of Information Science and Telecommunication, Hanshin University, Korea
hkim@hs.ac.kr
[2] Department of Environmental Science and Biotechnology, Hallym University, Korea
sdkim@hallym.ac.kr

Abstract. The expert knowledge about incineration process is often imprecise and of qualitative nature. In this paper, we present a framework for incineration process control based on qualitative incineration process model. Our framework is designed on the basis of multi-agent platform to apply to ubiquitous computing environment. Once end-user chooses a task, the framework is designed to provide remote context-aware services through cooperation between agents. The task is to correct undesired state of a chosen incineration plant, i.e., to change a physical parameter to some desired value. The framework finds appropriate services by analyzing causal relations between parameters. Since problem solving uses qualitative and common sense knowledge, interactions with users are natural and easily understandable. The framework has been implemented and test on several tasks.

Keywords: Qualitative Model, Ubiquitous Computing, Context-Aware Services, Physical System Analysis.

1 Introduction

Recently, computing-device-rich and communication-resource-rich environment has introduced a new computing paradigm called ubiquitous computing. The goal of ubiquitous computing is to provide seamless services to users by cooperation between various computing objects [1,2,3,4]. While a lot of work has focused on various aspects of ubiquitous computing, we are exploring the following three aspects among them in this paper: 1) natural interaction with users to enhance user participation in cooperation as active computing object 2) developing system in application domain that provides useful context-aware services 3) developing ubiquitous computing system based on multi-agent framework due to its communication ability with other agents and autonomous behaviors.

Qualitative models have been developed to formalize the intuitive and qualitative knowledge that people have about the physical world [5,6,7]. These models have provided computational models of human qualitative reasoning. This nature made qualitative models have played an important role in developing systems that require natural and easily understandable interactions with users. Besides natural interaction with users, qualitative models have been used in the areas where it is not easy to build

A. Ghose, G. Governatori, and R. Sadananda (Eds.): PRIMA 2007, LNAI 5044, pp. 372–379, 2009.

quantitative model due to lack of exact knowledge or data. The researches in qualitative models have focused on developing useful software systems, e.g., intelligent tutoring systems, engineering problem solving systems and robots. Especially engineering domain has been a major application field: diagnosis/troubleshooting, monitoring, design, and failure modes and effects analysis. Key ideas of qualitative models are to represent partial knowledge about domain and to solve given problems with the partial knowledge.

Lately, incineration has drawn attention because of its reduction efficiency of solid wastes and technical stability. A lot of incineration plants have been installed in Korea during the last two decades. However, incineration was blamed to generate air pollutants such as dioxins. Fig. 1 shows a simplified diagram for incineration process. Basically it consists of incinerator, 2nd incinerator and flue gas treatment train. Given solid waste and air, it finally produces gases through combustion and thermal destruction of incompletely combusted gas. Ideally if the working condition is controlled, this process should not produce air pollutants. But it is impossible in real world. What we can do is to control parameters of system to avoid undesired conditions as much as possible. While many efforts have been made to develop complete quantitative incineration process model, complicated thermodynamic nature of the process has made it difficult to build such a model. Although such a model has been developed, there are still difficulties to get complete and precise input data, i.e., complete data about solid waste supplied. In addition to this, it is not easy for non-expert to interpret numerical results.

In this paper, we present a framework for incineration process control based on qualitative incineration process model. Our system is designed with multi-agent platform to apply to ubiquitous computing environment. While our framework has some common ground with previous works in execution framework for ubiquitous computing and qualitative monitoring system, our framework is different with them: 1) Previous works in task execution framework in ubiquitous computing require developers to specify workflows for each task that achieve a certain goal. Workflow is composed of primitive activities that are also required to be predefined by developers. Each task should be carefully designed by developers. Our framework executes each task by searching causal relations between parameters. A task is mapped into to achieve a

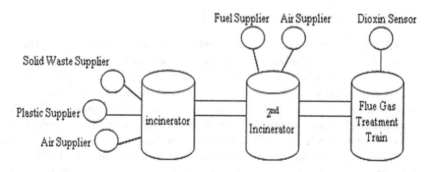

Fig. 1. Simplified Diagram for Incineration Process

change of a parameter and this is accomplished by tracing causal dependencies between parameters. Once qualitative model is built, causal dependencies for incineration process are automatically generated and any kind of dependencies can be traced to achieve a task. Unlike previous work that workflow and primitive tasks are predefined, our framework just traces causal dependencies of corresponding parameter of a task. 2) While qualitative approach to physical system has been actively applied to many domains, their applications for ubiquitous computing environment have been hardly tried. Our framework is designed to provide remote services through cooperation between agents on the basis of multi-agent platform.

The expert knowledge about incineration process is often imprecise and of qualitative nature. Our qualitative incineration process model captures the qualitative knowledge of the experts. Problem solving and services are based on qualitative and common sense knowledge. Our model is represented by causal relations between parameter and suggests solutions for a given situation with incomplete knowledge. In ubiquitous computing environment, each computing object plays an active role as an autonomous agent and communicates with others to collaborate and achieve a goal. People participate in the collaboration as an active computing object and sometimes as service receiver. It is important to have the interaction between man and machine that are adapted to user. We expect that reasoning based on qualitative models can help user to participate the collaboration in comfort.

2 Qualitative Model

Our system uses qualitative incineration process model that plays a key role to analyze the current state of an incineration reactor and to find proper services to fix the problem. Our qualitative model is built by using qualitative representation. One of the most successful approaches in qualitative representation is an approach based on qualitative process theory [6]. The basic idea of qualitative process theory is that all changes in world are caused by physical processes. Domain model consists of objects, relationships, and processes. Causal relations between parameters are captured by qualitative proportionalities and direct influences.

2.1 Qualitative Incineration Process Model

The incineration process system that our model is grounded on consists of the first and second incineration chamber, and flue gas treatment train. Our qualitative model captures complex interactions among thermodynamic processes: complete combustion, incomplete combustion, heat flow, gas flow, and thermal destruction of hydrocarbon gas [8]. Fig. 2 shows a part of causal dependencies generated from qualitative incineration model. + and − with arrow in the figure represent causal dependencies between parameters: while + describes positive influence, − describes negative influence. For instance, the figure shows incomplete combustion rate is positively influenced by proportion of plastic in solid waste. This implies that the incomplete combustion rate is increased as proportion of plastic in solid waste is increased.

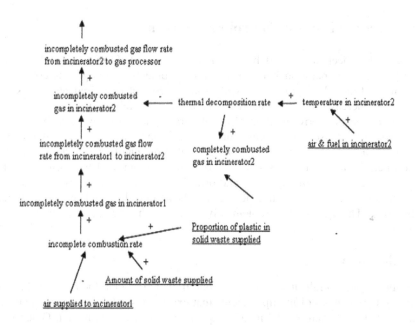

Fig. 2. A part of causal dependencies between parameter in incineration process

Decrease of the proportion results in decrease of the rate. Reverse relation is true for – dependency. For example, incomplete combustion rate is negatively influenced by air supplied. It implies that increase of amount of air supplied leads to decrease of the incomplete combustion rate and decrease of air leads to increase of the rate.

2.2 Planning with Qualitative Model

While human operators working at incineration plants do not have a complete and precise model for incineration process, they have abilities to handle many unusual and undesired conditions by using qualitative and incomplete knowledge. The qualitative incineration model captures the sort of knowledge that the operators have. Qualitative model can provide a useful ground for problem solving with partial knowledge.

Given a goal to achieve, causal dependencies are generated from qualitative incineration model. Then problem solver works backwards from the top-level goal to sub-goals by tracing qualitative influences through the causal dependencies. For example, as shown as Fig. 2 one way to decrease incompletely combusted gas in 2nd incinerator is to increase thermal decomposition rate. And the rate is increased by increasing temperature in the incinerator. And the temperature is increased by increasing air and fuel supplied to the incinerator. Then this task is achieved by primitive tasks to control air supplier device and fuel supplier device, respectively.

In Fig. 2, underlined parameters represent primitive tasks that are controlled by operating corresponding devices. Actions in our framework are primitive tasks performed by devices. To find tasks to achieve the top-level goal, reasoning agent regress back to the primitive tasks through causal model.

3 Incineration Process Control Framework

Our system has been developed based on multi-agent platform to provide remote services through cooperation between computing objects in ubiquitous computing environment. The tasks given to the system are to correct undesired physical situations such as increased dioxin generation. To correct an undesired physical situation means to change the corresponding physical parameter to a desired value. Given a task is chosen by a user, our system finds appropriate context-aware services for a given situation by tracing causal relations generated by qualitative model. Undesired situation i.e., values of a corresponding parameter is monitored by sensors and reported through agent communication platform. Execution of service is also done by sending messages to corresponding devices to take actions through agent communication platform. This qualitative problem solving approach gives users natural interaction with the system.

3.1 Architecture

Fig. 3 shows the overall architecture for our framework. Our Incineration Process Control system consists of multiple agents that execute tasks by cooperation between them. Qualitative domain model includes qualitative incineration model. Given task, reasoning agent finds solutions, i.e., proper services. Service consists of primitive tasks operated by devices such as "increase air supply by operating air supplier". Service also specifies its filtering conditions such as "dioxin amount is below threshold value". Filtering condition is monitored by related sensor. Incineration Process Control interacts with users to fetch a wanted task and resource choices for services. It

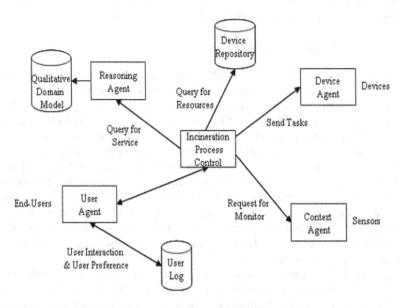

Fig. 3. Architecture of Incineration Process Control Framework

also provides feedback regarding the execution of the task. Device repository maintains a list of all entities such as incineration plants and their devices. Devices are the entities that can change the values of physical parameters such as air supplier and thermostat. The Incineration Process Control sends primitive tasks to device agent for relevant devices to perform operations as directed. Context agent is requested for monitoring filtering conditions by related sensor. We assume devices and sensors are connected to our framework.

3.2 Executing a Task

The system works as follows:

1. End users choose a task through user interface.
2. The system queries the reasoning agent for the service to execute chosen task. The task is mapped into a goal to change corresponding physical parameter. The reasoning agent figures out the necessary service by planning with causal dependencies generated from qualitative model. Solution consists of primitive tasks and their filtering condition with information about relevant devices and sensor.
3. User agent presents the end-users with possible values of related resources including plant name and devices. There are multiple numbers of plants, their devices. User chooses the plant, and devices among available devices.
4. The system requests context agent to monitor the filtering condition of the chosen plant. The context agent collects data from the sensor attached to the plant, detects the situation that service should happen and reports to the system.
5. Once filtering condition is detected, system requests to device agent for the corresponding device to perform primitive tasks as directed.
6. User agent provides feedback regarding the execution of the task.

3.3 Implementation

Our system has been implemented in Java. Qualitative incineration model and reasoning agent have been implemented by using Jess [9]. Jess is a rule engine for the Java platform. Agent communications has been implemented with JADE[10]. JADE is Java agent Development Framework that supports developing multi-agent system. User log and device repository have been built by using Access.

Our implementation has been tested on several tasks: Decrease Dioxin, Increase Complete Combustion, Decrease Incomplete Combustion, Increase Thermal Decomposition. Once qualitative model has been built, it is easy to add tasks since the same causal relations already generated are traced to change a corresponding parameter. Different tasks searches different parameters in the relations.

Fig. 4 show screenshot of user interface of user agent in the middle of the "Decrease Dioxin" task. This task is mapped into "decrease incompletely combusted gas in incinerator2". Reasoning agent find 4 available services: (DecreaseProportionOf-Plastic 3) (DecreaseSolidWaste 4) (IncreaseAir 2) (IncreaseFuel&Air 1). The numbers represent priorities of services. The system chooses the highest priority service, i.e., IncreaseFuel&Air. Once the service is chosen, reasoning agent returns: 1)

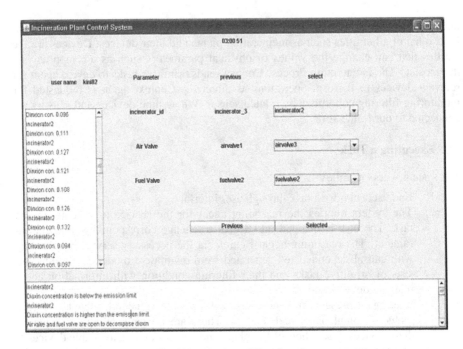

Fig. 4. Screenshot of User Interface

filtering condition and relevant sensor: the incompletely combusted gas in flue gas treatment train is greater than threshold 2) resources: plant name, air supplier and fuel suppler 3) action: increase air and fuel supply by control the valves. The plant name (incinerator_id in the figure), air supplier (Air Valve in the figure) and fuel supplier (Fuel Valve in the figure) need to be obtained in the service. The user's previous choices for this service are shown in the interface. For now user choose resources. We are planning an option for the system to choose automatically resources. The left window displays how dioxin level keeps changing by receiving the monitoring data from a sensor. Threshold value is assumes as 0.100. The window in the bottom displays explanation regarding the execution of the task.

4   Conclusion

In this paper, we propose an incineration process control system in ubiquitous computing environment. Our system is based on qualitative model and multi-agent platform. Unlike tradition approaches for physical system application, qualitative approach finds solutions by tracing causal relations between parameter. We believe the qualitative problem solving approach plays an important role for natural user interaction. Incineration process has a qualitative nature due to its complicated interactions of thermodynamic process and lack of complete input data. Multi-agent platform provides remote services in ubiquitous computing environment with communication abilities. Services require context-aware monitoring of a parameter by corresponding sensors through agent communications.

Our goal is to build a system to build an intelligent common sense reasoning system in ubiquitous computing environment that covers broad range of physical phenomena in various applications. We plan to keep expanding to achieve our goal.

Acknowledgments. This research is supported by ubiquitous Autonomic Computing and Network Project, the Ministry of Information and Communication (MIC) 21st Century Frontier R&D Program in Korea.

References

1. Garlan, D., Siewiorek, D., Smailagic, A., Steenkiste, P.: Project Aura: Toward Distractif-Free Pervasive Computing. IEEE Pervasive Computing, 22–31 (April-June 2002)
2. Roman, M., et al.: Gaia: A middleware Infrastructure to Enable Active Spaces. IEEE Pervasive Computing, 74–83 (October-December 2002)
3. Kumar, M., et al.: PICO: A middleware Framework for Pervasivc Computing 2(3), 72–79 (July-September 2003)
4. Ranganathan, A.: A Task Execution Framework for Autonomic Ubiquitous Computing. PhD thesis, University of Illinois, Urbana-Champaign, Urbana, Illinois (2005)
5. de Kleer, J., Brown, J.: A Qualitative Physics based on Confluences. Artificial intelligence 24, 7–83 (1984)
6. Forbus, K.: Qualitative Process Theory. Artificial Intelligence 51, 381–416 (1984)
7. Bobrow, D.: Qualitative Reasoning about Physical systems. The MIT Press, Cambridge (1985)
8. Kim, H., Kim, S., Kim, M.: Conceptual Modeling for Incineration Process. In: 4th International Conference on Cumbustion, incineration/Pyrolysis and Emission Control, pp. 117–120 (2006)
9. Jess, http://herzberg.ca.sandia.gov/jess/
10. JADE, Java Agent Development Framework, http://jade.tilab.com/

Engineering Adaptive Multi-Agent Systems with ODAM Methodology

Xinjun Mao[1], Jianming Zhao[2], and Ji Wang[1]

[1] Department of Computer Science, National Univ. of Defense Technology, Changsha, Hunan Province, P.R.China, 410073
mao.xinjun@gmail.com, jiwang@ios.ac.cn
[2] School of Computer Science, ZheJiang Normal Univ., Jinghua, Zhejiang, P.R.China, 410073
znuzjm@mail.zjnu.net.cn

Abstract. Agent orientation is believed as an appropriate and powerful paradigm to develop complex systems. In order to engineer complex self-adaptive multi-agent systems, we present dynamic binding mechanism and an agent-oriented methodology called ODAM that exploits the flexibility and high-level abstraction of agent orientation based on organization metaphors. The meta-model and modeling language of ODAM based on dynamic binding mechanism can effectively deal with the dynamic and self-adaptive aspects of MAS. Moreover, MDA approach and iteration development are integrated into ODAM to adapt to the variety of agent technologies and platforms, to deal with complexity of systems, and to simplify the development of MAS.

1 Introduction

Recently more and more software systems are with such complexity characteristics as situatedness, openness, autonomy, self-adaptation and self-organization [1][2]. Obviously, to develop such complex systems need novel and effective software engineering techniques [1][3]. Agent-oriented software engineering (AOSE) is considered to be an appropriate and powerful paradigm to develop such complex systems and in the past years many progresses have been made in this area. However, if we want the paradigm to be successfully applied in the development of complex systems, twofold should be considered when conducting researches on AOSE. Firstly, AOSE should borrow successful technologies and practices of software engineering so that it can integrate with main stream technologies, and benefit from good experiences and solutions of software engineering. Second, the potential and flexibility of agent orientation paradigm should be extensively exploited. Against the background, in this paper we present an agent-oriented methodology called ODAM to support the development of complex self-adaptive systems. The proposed methodology is based on organization metaphors and dynamic binding mechanism, and presents explicit models and notations to describe and analyze self-adaptation aspects of complex MAS.

A. Ghose, G. Governatori, and R. Sadananda (Eds.): PRIMA 2007, LNAI 5044, pp. 380–385, 2009.

2 Overview of ODAM Methodology

ODAM is an agent-oriented methodology that is based on organization abstractions and MDA. It contains three constituents as follows (see Fig.1).

(1) Agent-oriented modeling language
The modeling language is based on the meta-model of organization abstractions and dynamic binding mechanism. It provides multiple viewpoints and models to specify and analyze self-adaptive MAS in a comprehensive way.

(2) Agent-oriented software development process
The development process of ODAM covers requirement, analysis, architecture design, detail design phases. Each phase contains a number of development steps. Especially, ODAM distinguishes platform-independent models and platform-dependent models, and supports model transformation between different level models and iteration development.

(3) CASE Toolkits
The toolkits include a number of software tools to support the software development with ODAM methodology, such as virtual modeling tool, model consistency checking tool and model transformation tool.

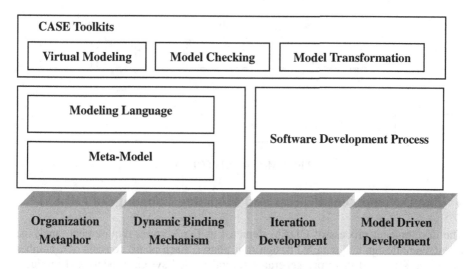

Fig. 1. The Framework of ODAM Methodology

3 Dynamic Binding Mechanism and Meta-model of ODAM

We present dynamic binding mechanism in order to interpret and analyze the dynamic and self-adaptive aspects of MAS. In complex MAS, agent can take actions to *join* a role or *quit* from a role, and consequently, it obtains or lose the structural and behavioral features defined by the role. When agent *joins* a role, we say that the role is to be bound to by the agent.

The status of roles that agent has bound to can be in active or inactive, and changed by taking actions *deactivate* or *activate*. Only when the role to be bound to is in active state, it can govern agent's behavior. For example, agent will take actions based on the behavior specification of the role, or own the resources specified in the role. Otherwise, when the role that agent binds to is in inactive state, it will not govern agent's behaviors. However agent still keeps the information of the role. Moreover, when the agent becomes actively binding to the role again by taking action *activate*, the information of role will be resumed to agent. Such scenario is different from one that agent quits a role. Fig.2 depicts the concept model of ODAM based on organization abstractions and dynamic binding mechanism.

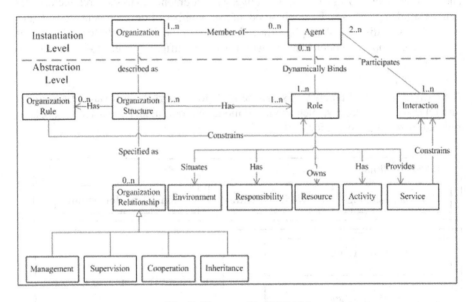

Fig. 2. Meta-model of ODAM

4   The Development Process and Modeling Language of ODAM

The development process of ODAM depicted as Fig.3 covers requirement, analysis, architecture design and detailed design four phases. Each phase consists of a number of related steps and therefore generates several related system models and products that can be specified by visual modeling language from multiple viewpoints and with graphic notations (see Fig.4). The whole development steps in requirement, analysis and architecture design phases can be iterated.

(1) **Requirement Phase**

The requirements of system to be developed should be identified and described by defining and analyzing organization scenarios of system. In ODAM, the system to be developed and its environment are taken as organizations. Organization scenario specifies the observable functions and behaviors of systems from the viewpoints of system environment.

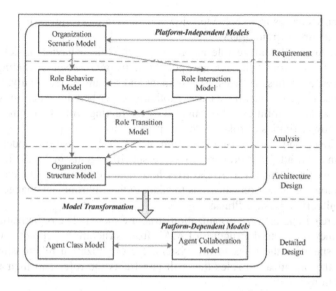

Fig. 3. The Development Process of ODAM Methodology

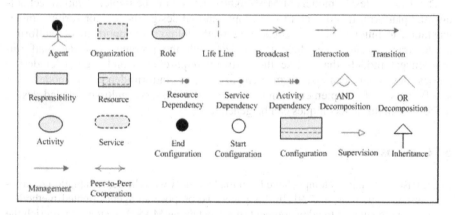

Fig. 4. Notations of Modeling Language

Step1. Define system's environment. The result of this step is a list of environment constituents.

Step2. Identify organization scenarios. The result of this step is a list of identified organization scenarios that define the high-level requirement from behavior viewpoint and in macro-level. Typically, organization scenario model describes the participated roles, pre-conditions, post-conditions, and event flows of organization scenario.

Step3. Describe organization scenarios. The result of this step is to get a number of organization scenario description tables.

(2) Analysis Phase

Step4. Create and analyze organization interaction model. Organization interaction model defines how agents in organization interact with each other to achieve organization scenarios from behavior viewpoint and in macro-level. It is the extension to the interaction diagram in UML.

Step5. Create and analyze role behavior model. Role behavior model defines the behaviors of role from behavior viewpoint and in micro-level, including role's responsibilities, activities, services, environment and resources. Especially, the relationships between these constituents are explicitly described in order to specify and analyze how responsibilities to be achieved by interacting with environment and using resources, how activities of roles to be encapsulated as services.

Step6. Create and analyze role transition model. Role transition model defines the dynamic and self-adaptive property of some specific agents in MAS from behavior viewpoint and in micro-level. It specifies how agent dynamically binds to different roles in various organization situations to adapt to the environment changes.

(3) Architecture Design Phase

Step7. Create and analyze organization structure model. The organization structure model defines the overall structure of MAS from structure viewpoint and in macro-level, and specifies the roles in the system, the organization relationships between them, and the organization rules that will constrains the roles and their relationship and interactions.

(4) Detailed Design Phase

The detailed design models of MAS tightly depend on the implementation technology and platform. It is difficult to develop a unified design models for various implementation techniques and comprehensive methodology to support all of platforms. Model transformation can help us to deal with the problem. For the platform-independent models that define the software requirements and high level design phases, developers can transform them to various platform-dependent models that satisfy the specific implementation techniques. If necessary, multiple detailed design models for multiple techniques can be generated.

5 Conclusion

In the past year, many attempts have been made to deal with the self-adaptation of complex systems, such as [4,6,8,9]. In this paper, we propose an agent-oriented methodology ODAM to support the development of self-adaptive MAS. We attempt to enrich the agent-oriented meta-model and modeling language to satisfy the development requirement for adaptive MAS, and integrate with successful software engineering technologies and practices such as MDA and iteration development. Comparison with existing agent-oriented methodologies [4,5,6,7,10], our proposed ODAM methodology has the following characteristics. (1) The environments of agents are explicitly modeled and investigated in role behavior model in order to investigate adaptive agents. (2) The dynamic binding mechanism is presented to interpret and analyze the adaptive behaviors of agents. The mechanism permits agent to change its roles in order to adapt to changes of situated environment and organization context. It also permits agent to change the status of roles that it has bound to. Such a mechanism can act as a basis of agent-oriented meta-model and modeling language for adaptive MAS. (3) The proposed meta-model of ODAM based on organization abstraction and dynamic binding mechanism are high-level and supports the natural modeling. Especially, we present role transition model to specify how agents evolve and adapt to changes in its lifecycle. (4) ODAM introduces MDA approach and iteration development. The models based on organization abstractions are taken as platform-independent models, and the detailed design models are taken as platform-independent models. The bridge between them is built by model transformation.

References

1. Zambonelli, F., Van Dyke Parunak, H.: Towards a paradigm change in computer science and software engineering: a synthesis. The Knowledge Engineering Review 18(4), 329–342 (2003)
2. Mao, X., Yu, E.: Organizational and social concepts in agent oriented software engineering. In: Odell, J.J., Giorgini, P., Müller, J.P. (eds.) AOSE 2004. LNCS, vol. 3382, pp. 1–15. Springer, Heidelberg (2005)
3. Luck, M., McBurney, P., Shehory, O., Willmott, S.: Agent Technology: Computing as Interaction (A Roadmap for Agent Based Computing), AgentLink (2005)
4. Cernuzzi, L., Zambonelli, F.: Dealing with adaptive multi-agent organizations in the gaia methodology. In: Müller, J.P., Zambonelli, F. (eds.) AOSE 2005. LNCS, vol. 3950, pp. 109–123. Springer, Heidelberg (2006)
5. Santos, D., Ribeiro, M.B., Bastos, R.M.: Developing a conference management system with the multi-agent systems unified process: A case study. In: Luck, M., Padgham, L. (eds.) Agent-Oriented Software Engineering VIII. LNCS, vol. 4951, pp. 212–224. Springer, Heidelberg (2008)
6. Ferber, J., Gutknecht, O.: A meta-model for the analysis and design of Organizations in MASs. In: Proc. Of ICMAS, pp. 128–135 (1998)
7. Zambonelli, F., Jennings, N.R., Wooldridge, M.: Developing Multiagent Systems: The Gaia Methodology. ACM Transactions on Software Engineering Methodology 12(3), 317–370 (2003)
8. Juan, T., Sterling, L.: A Meta-model for Intelligent Adaptive MASs in Open Environments. In: Proc. Of AAMAS, pp. 1024–1025 (2003)
9. Odell, J.J., Nodine, M., Levy, R.: A metamodel for agents, roles, and groups. In: Odell, J.J., Giorgini, P., Müller, J.P. (eds.) AOSE 2004. LNCS, vol. 3382, pp. 78–92. Springer, Heidelberg (2005)
10. Giunchiglia, F., Mylopoulos, J., Perini, A.: The Tropos Development Methodology: Processes, Models and Diagrams. In: Proc. Of AAMAS, pp. 35–36 (2002)

Integrating Agent Technology and SIP Technology to Develop Telecommunication Applications with JadexT

Xinjun Mao, Huocheng Wu, and Jie Li

Department of Computer Science, National University of Defense Technology, Changsha,
Hunan Province, P.R.China, 410073
mao.xinjun@gmail.com

Abstract. We present an approach by combining agent technology and SIP technology to develop complex telecommunication applications. Our approach is to encapsulate telecommunication applications as software agents, to create and control the communication sessions between agents based on SIP protocol, and to build a bridge between SIP technology and agent technology. We have developed an agent-oriented platform called JadexT by extending Jadex. An example is studied to illustrate our approach.

1 Introduction

With the evolution of telecommunication networks and demands of abstracting proprietary networks into converged next-generation service creation and delivery platform, it is necessary to develop platforms which enable vendors to interact and discover best solutions, and to share various resources and services to satisfy customer's requirements and lower the development cost. Against this background, SIP is proposed and plays an important role in telecommunication industry and has been chosen by the Third Generation Partnership (3GPP) as the call control mechanism for next-generation networks [1]. SIP is an application-layer control protocol and proposed as standard for initiating, modifying, and terminating interactive sessions with one or more participants. These sessions involve multimedia elements such as video, voice, instant messaging, online games, and virtual reality [6]. SIP works independently of underlying transport protocols and without dependency on the type of session that is being established.

It is still a challenge to design and implement next-generation telecommunication applications which exhibit new complexity features such as open, dynamic, autonomic, self-organized, self-adaptive. We believe that next-generation telecommunication applications not only need data-centric interaction (e.g., interchanging audio, image and video), but also need semantics-centric interaction (e.g., negotiation and cooperation between applications). To develop such applications requires effective approaches to ensure interoperability and resource sharing of applications, to control application complexity, as well as new tools and platforms to facilitate fast development and deployment of robust and extendable applications.

A. Ghose, G. Governatori, and R. Sadananda (Eds.): PRIMA 2007, LNAI 5044, pp. 386–391, 2009.
© Springer-Verlag Berlin Heidelberg 2009

In this paper, we present an approach by combining agent technology and SIP technology to develop complex telecommunication applications. We abstract and encapsulate telecommunication applications as autonomous agents which can interact with each other by both SIP protocol and ACL protocol. We have developed an agent-oriented platform called JadexT which provides SIP-based message transfer system, and combines BDI reasoning engine and SIP mechanism by extending Jadex to support the design and implementation of agent-based SIP User Agent (UA) when developing next-generation telecommunication applications.

2   JadexT: Integrating Jadex with SIP Technology

2.1   JadexT Architecture

Fig.1 depicts the framework of JadexT, which is compatible with FIPA Agent Management Model [5].

(1) Message Transport Layer
In such layer, JadexT provides SIP-based message transport system (MTS) and enables communications between software agents on different platforms and telecommunication networks.

(2) Rational Agent Layer
In such layer, JadexT provides rational capability of BDI reasoning and reactive reasoning. To support SIP-based interaction, JadexT supports the integration of SIP message transport system with Jadex reasoning engine.

(3) Platform Agent Layer
Such layer contains a number of software agents, including application agents and system agents. There are two specific system agents: Agent Management System (AMS) that manages the agents in JadexT platform and Directory Facilitator (DF) that provides yellow page services for other agents.

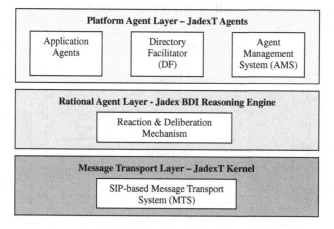

Fig. 1. Framework of JadexT

2.2 JadexT Message Transport System

The core technology that distinguishes JadexT from other agent platform (e.g., Jadex or Jade) is that JadexT implements a SIP-based message transport system which supports encapsulating native message to SIP message, sending it to receiver, and decoding the coming SIP message to native message and subsequently delivering it to receivers when a SIP message arrives. The architecture of the message transport system is event-driven and utilizes the Publisher/Subscriber event model (see Fig.2).

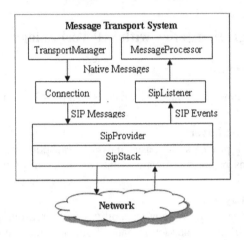

Fig. 2. Message Transport System Architecture

2.3 Integrating Jadex Reasoning Engine with JadexT Platform

JadexT supports the integration of rational agent reasoning layer and SIP-based message transform layer. Such integration consists mainly of three parts: (1) JadexT platform, (2) an Adapter Agent corresponding to JadexT platform, (3) the original Jadex Agent which encapsulates the BDI reasoning engine (see Fig. 3).

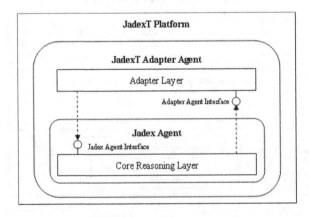

Fig. 3. Mechanism of Integrating Jadex Reasoning Engine with JadexT Platform

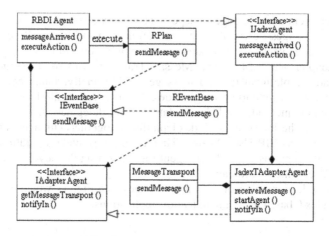

Fig. 4. Class Diagram of JadexT

In general, agent platform is the execution environment of agents, and only capable of executing certain type of agents (called Adapter Agents). Therefore, a Jadex agent has to be wrapped into a JadexT adapter agent before it could run on the JadexT platform. An Adapter Agent Interface and a Jadex Agent Interface are needed to provide useful services for Jadex agent as well as Adapter Agent. Generally, Jadex Agent Interface offers methods for performing reasoning, whereas Adapter Agent Interface provides notification and message sending facilities.

The class diagram of JadexT's core package in Fig.4 depicts how Jadex reasoning engine can be integrated with JadexT platform. The JadexT adapter agent uses the message transport system to provide message sending service for Jadex agents. It uses IJadexAgent interface to perform active and reasoning actions. In our approach, the Adapter Layer is not explicit defined as one class but implied in

Fig. 5. Software Development Packages of JadexT

JadexAdapterAgent and MessageTransport. The Jadex agent uses IEventBase interface to send messages during the plan execution, and the REventBase which is a concrete class of IEventBase delegates the sending action to the MessageTransport of JadexT adapter agent. Moreover, MessageTransport uses the message transport system of JadexT platform to send messages. Additionally, Jadex agent can also fulfill its notification function through JadexT adapter agent interface. After invoking "startAgent()" method, the JadexT adapter agent delegates all reactive and reasoning actions to the Jadex agent. JadexT platform, together with agents running on it, can be viewed as SIP User Agents. Therefore, we provide a solution to design and implement agent-based SIP User Agent for supporting the development of next-generation telecommunication applications.

JadexT provides a number of software packages (see Fig. 5), which can be reused to develop JadexT-based telecommunication applications.

3 Case Study

In order to testify the usefulness and effectiveness of JadexT platform, we have developed a personal assistant agent (called PAA) for end-users so that it can get useful information in the Internet, or to obtain telecommunication services from the world-wide, or to provide new telecommunication services that can be provided for end-users effectively even if they reside in multiple heterogeneous networks.

Let us consider the following scenario. An end-user wants to listen to a specified song, so the PAA will finds out the provider of song (called service provider agent, SPA) and get song by interacting with provider agent. After getting the song, PAA will play the song to the end-user. The cooperation between PAA and Provide agent is both a semantics-centric interaction process and a data-centric interaction process. The semantics-center interaction process can be explicitly specified by FIPA ACL and protocol that is inclined to express knowledge and semantic information (e.g., cooperation intention and content). However, it is difficult for FIPA ACL to express data-center information such as audio, video, image. The data-centric interaction process can be specified by SIP protocol. We have successfully developed a software prototype of the above case with JadexT.

4 Conclusion

In this paper, we make efforts to integrate agent technology and SIP technology together in order to present a solution to develop complex next-generation telecommunication applications. Such an attempt is under a project with Huawei Corporation that devotes to developing telecommunication devices and applications. The approach that we propose is to extend Jadex to develop agent-based telecommunication applications in SIP environment. We have developed an agent platform called JadexT which utilizes message transport mechanism based on SIP protocol and integrates with BDI reasoning engine, and therefore support software agents to interact with each other integrating data-centric and semantics-centric way. Our approach permits to integrate agent paradigm and SIP technology to create and delivery next-generation telecommunication applications across multiple heterogeneous networks in a cost-effective way. Based on JadexT, we have developed several applications of next-telecommunication services.

References

1. Third Generation Partnership Project, 3GPP Specifications,
   http://www.3gpp.org/specs/specs.htm
2. Gervais, M.P., Ruffel, N.: Design of telecommunication services based on software agent technology and formal method. In: Proceedings of the IEEE Globecom 1997, vol. 3, pp. 1724–1728 (1997)
3. Jennings, N.R.: An agent-based approach for building complex software systems. Communication of ACM 44(4), 35–41 (2001)
4. Telecom Italia, Jade - Java Agent DEvelopment Framework,
   http://jade.cselt.it/
5. Foundation for Intelligent Physical Agents, FIPA Agent Management Specification (2001/10/03), http://www.fipa.org/
6. IETF Network Working Group, RFC 3261 - SIP: Session Initiation Protocol (June 2002),
   http://www.ietf.org/rfc/rfc3261.txt
7. Pokahr, A., Braubach, L., Walczak, A.: Jadex User Guide (2006),
   http://vsis-www.informatik.uni-hamburg.de/projects/jadex/

A Generic Distributed Algorithm for Computing by Random Mobile Agents*

Shehla Abbas, Mohamed Mosbah, and Akka Zemmari

LaBRI, Université Bordeaux 1
351 cours de la liberation,
33405 Talence-France
{abbas,mosbah,zemmari}@labri.fr

Abstract. In this paper, we investigate the following problem: k mobile agents are placed in a network. The agents initially move in the network using random walks. They have unique identities and mark on the $\mathcal{WB}$ (memory location for nodes) on arriving at any node v. We give an algorithm for the agents to do random walk and mark nodes of the network. This has many applications such as constructing a spanning tree. The agents on entering a region of bigger identity agents transfer the knowledge and submit themselves to bigger identity agents hence reducing the number of agents in the network.

Keywords: Mobile Agents, Random Walks, Distributed Algorithms.

1 Introduction

Mobile agents are under consideration in many problems of research these days. We consider multiple mobile agents. The main advantage of using these agents is the ability to accomplish tasks which will be difficult and less effective in the presence of a single agent. These agents are not *heavy*; meaning they carry limited knowledge and computational abilities. However when they move in the network they make use of the resources of the nodes which provides the memory location and facilitates them to perform the tasks assigned to them. The agents get to know the existance of other agents upon meeting on any node as they have no other explicit means of communication.

Problem Definition. The problem we are presenting in this paper is of multiple mobile agents which are competitive having unique identities. These agents perform a Random Walk and move around in a network. Agents do the calculations on the basis of their identities. The bigger it is, the powerful it is. Hence when smaller identity agent enters on a node discovered by the bigger identity agent, they fight with each other making its place to stay in the network. The battle is won by the bigger identity agent. Therefore, an agent survives only till the time it does not enter a region of a bigger agent. They mark the edges through which

---

* This work has been supported by the french project "Agence Nationale de la Recherche ANR-06-SETI-015".

A. Ghose, G. Governatori, and R. Sadananda (Eds.): PRIMA 2007, LNAI 5044, pp. 392–397, 2009.

they come. The utility of this computation is to trace back to the root node from where they start their walks. They are compared on the basis of their identities and meet as an adversary to each other. Whichever wins makes its adversary as its slave. The algorithm continues till all the nodes of the network are being visited and there remains only one agent with biggest identity.

Related Works. The spanning tree problem has been studied extensively. Computing a spanning tree of a network is an important problem in distributed computing [6]. The spanning trees are also constructed using randomized techniques such as Random Walk [3,5]. Mobile agents being more efficient and not using much resources are also used for construction of spanning tree [1,4]. The complexity analysis has also been done by [2] in calculating the time for the mobile agents to meet and merge in the network, which will reduce the total number of agents from k to 1.

Contribution. Our contribution to this work is that we give an algorithm by random and memoryless mobile agents. After giving the generic algorithm we show in the following section how we can use the generic algorithm for the applications such as construction of a spanning tree using these random and memoryless mobile agents which mark on the $\mathcal{W}B$ of nodes.

Outline. This paper is organized as follows. In Section 2, we explain our model, giving details of assumptions and variables that will be used by our algorithm. In Section 3, we will be giving our main algorithm. After narrating the generic algorithm, we will be discussing an application which can be cater for using the generic algorithm. We will be concluding the paper in Section 4.

2   Model

We consider a *synchronous distributed* network of processors with an arbitrary topology. It is represented as a connected graph $G = (V, E)$ where V is the set of vertices representing processors, and E is the set of edges corresponding to communication links.

A *mobile agent* (MA) is an entity which moves in the graph. There are many models to study the movement of the agents depending on the parameters of interest and on the applications. In this paper, we consider the MAs with an identity whose storage memory can not deal with topological information of the network. This is useful for instance if the network is huge (e.g. Internet). We study in this work agents that do not store information about the visited vertices. One interesting model that we deal with is that of random walks. Hence, our MA moves randomly in the graph. The MA performs a *random walk*: when it is located in a vertex v, if $B(v, 1)$ denotes the ball of center v and radius 1, the MA chooses *uniformly at random* one of the vertices in $B(v, 1)$, if the chosen vertex is v, the MA does not move, else, it moves to the chosen vertex.

In our algorithm, the following assumptions are made:

- Each node v is equipped with a white-board $\mathcal{W}B(v)$ which is a memory location in a node and mobile agents can read and write the information from there, $WB(v)$ is a list (agent, parent, children) where the agent is the identity of the agent who has added any entry, parent denotes the channel that leads to the parent node and children denotes the set of channels that lead to children. These variables will be precised later.

- Agents have unique identities.
- An agent can move to any neighboring node that is the outdegree of the current node. It may also stay at the same vertex.
- Negligible time is considered in computation, i.e. agents can read and write in a WB in no time.
- $notVisited(a, v)$ is a local function to check if the WB is not already written by an agent a on the vertex v
- $visited(a, v)$ is a local function to check if the WB is already written by an agent a on the vertex v
- $locked$ is used as a mutual exclusion variable if any agent is writing on the WB.

3   Generic Algorithm

Each agent carries with itself few parameters such as its unique identity and the parent node from which it is coming. Initially the parent node will be null which makes it the root node, that is the node on which an agent is arbitrarily placed before the start of the alogrithm. An agent performs a Randow Walk. We consider a data structure white board $WB(v)$ for each node which is the memory location of the node on which the agent can write its identity, the parent node from where it is coming and the children nodes of that agent if there are any. An agent can come and write its entry on WB. However, if an agent a has already written on any vertex v then it does not write on that vertex again and this can be verified by the function $notVisited(a, v)$ described above.

Each MA a is either in a *master* or a *slave* state; the agents are considered in master state initially. The state of an agent defines its behaviour; for example, if an agent is in the master state, then it is free to move in the network by using random walk. It does not change its parent/root or identity. However, an agent changes to slave state when it enters into a node which has already been *visited* by an agent with bigger identity hence acting as a slave for that agent. It does not perform the random walk and its behaviour is changed as desired by the master agent.

The white board $WB(v)$ of nodes are empty initially indicating they are not yet written or visited by any agent, the parent and children fields are also empty. If the parent is ϕ (the empty set) for an agent a then this indicates that it is the root node of an agent a. The agents work in mutual exclusion, that is when an agent reaches any node, it locks itself before doing any calculations which is achieved by the variable $locked$.

Each master agent executes the generic Algorithm 1 till it changes its state to slave. The agents are placed on the network and from where an agent starts

Data: $state \in \{master, slave\}; init = master;$
a is initially at node $v_0, parent = \phi, children = \phi$;
$v.agent$ //agent on node v;
$v.parent$ //pointer towards the parent;
$v.children$ // pointer towards the set of children;
$masterchannel(w)$ //the channel for the master agent

```
1   WB(v₀) ← WB(v₀) ∪ (a, φ, φ);
2   locked = true;
3   repeat
4   │   choose a vertex v in B(u, 1);
5   │   if v ≠ u then
6   │   │   move to v;
7   │   │   if notVisited(a, v) or (visited(b, v) and (b < a)) then
8   │   │   │   v.agent ← a;
9   │   │   │   v.parent ← u;
10  │   │   │   v.children ← φ;
11  │   │   │   move to u;
12  │   │   │   u.children ← u.children ∪ {v};
13  │   │   │   move to v;
14  │   │   else
15  │   │   │   if visited(b, v) and (b > a) then
16  │   │   │   │   v.children ← v.children ∪ {a};
17  │   │   │   │   move to u;
18  │   │   │   │   masterchannel(w) ← v;
19  │   │   │   │   state(a) ← slave(b);
20  │   │   │   end
21  │   │   end
22  │   end
23  until state ≠ master ;
24  locked ← false;
```

Algorithm 1. Mobile Agent a (master) Algorithm at a vertex v

its random walk is the root node whose parent is empty. The agent can now move to a neighboring node or stay on the same vertex. If it chooses a vertex v which is not the same as on which it is present, then it moves to the vertex v. It checks in the $WB(v)$ if it is not already visited by same agent using the function $notVisited$ or visited by a smaller identity agent using the funtion $visited$. If this is the case then it adds its entry in the $WB(v)$ marking its identity and the parent node which is vertex u and children is empty. It moves back to its parent node to update the list of children of its parent node and return to vertex v. This way 1 round is used which consists of 3 units of time. This helps in removing the cycles and the edges are marked only once between nodes by one agent. If an agent decides to remain on the same vertex then it has to wait for 1 round (3 units) for next step of doing random walk. Else if it is visited by a bigger identity agent, then the state of smaller identity agent is changed to slave.

3.1 Applications

The algorithm described above can be used in various applications such as construction of a spanning tree, gathering and information collection. In the following section, we will illustrate our method by the computation of a spanning tree (Due to lack of space we do not give details of other applications). The functionality of slave agent will help in construction of a spanning tree.

When a smaller identity agent arrives at a node which is already written by a bigger identity agent then it changes its state to *slave*. The parent of the slave node will be changed from its own to the parent node of the *master* agent, the parent of the *slave* agent will be the children of the *master* agent, and the parent of the slave agent will be the new root node which will be considered empty.

Now the slave agent will move back to the parent node updating the list of parent and children pointing towards that of the master agent. The slave agent moves to the previous nodes updating each time the list of parent and children. This process will continue till it reaches the root node of the slave agent. After that it will move to the new root from where it changed its state. On returning to the new root, it will do the in-depth traversal of the sub-tree constructed by the slave agent using the function *traversal* which is a recursive function to change the orientation that is the list of parents and children of all the nodes which are part of the sub-tree constructed by the slave agent.

4 Conclusion

In this paper, we have discussed a generic algorithm for computing by random mobile agents which do not have memory. They are many in number and do the random walk. With multiple agents, our algorithm becomes more interesting and efficient. Our algorithm can be used in the applications such as construction of a spanning tree, the gathering problem and the information collection from the nodes of the network.

As a future work of this problem, we are studying the *broadcast* problem which can be done efficiently using these random mobile agents so that the information can be spread over the network.

References

1. Abbas, S., Mosbah, M., Zemmari, A.: Distributed computation of a spanning tree in a dynamic graph by mobile agents. In: Proceedings of IEEE 1st International Conference on Engineering of Intelligent Systems, pp. 425–430 (April 2006)
2. Abbas, S., Mosbah, M., Zemmari, A.: Collecte d'informations par des agents mobiles. In: Nouvelles Technolologies de la Repartition (NOTERE) (June 2007)
3. Aldous, D.J.: The random walk construction of uniform spanning trees and uniform labelled trees. SIAM Journal on Discrete Mathematics 3(4), 450–465 (1995)

4. Baala, H., Flauzac, O., Gaber, J., Bui, M., El-Ghawani, T.: A self stabilizing distributed algorithm for spanning tree constructionin wireless ad hoc networks. J. Parallel Distributed Computation 63, 97–104 (2003)
5. Broder, A.Z.: Generating random spanning trees. In: Proc. 30th Ann. IEEE Symp. on Foundations of Computer Science, pp. 442–453 (October 1989)
6. Gruner, S., Metivier, Y., Mosbah, M., Wacrenier, P.A.: Distributed algorithm for computing a spanning tree in anonymous t-prime graphs. Studia Informatica Univesalis 2, 141–158 (2002)

Coalition Structure Generation in Task-Based Settings Based on Cardinality Structure

She-Xiong Su[1], Shan-Li Hu[1,2], Sheng-Fu Zheng[1],
Chao-Feng Lin[1], and Xian-Wei Lai[1]

[1] Department of Computer Science and Technology, Fuzhou University,
Fuzhou 350002, China
[2] Key Laboratory for Computer Science, The Chinese Academy of Sciences,
Beijing, 100080, China
susx18@163.com, husl@fzu.edu.cn, sfz_roger@yahoo.com.cn,
lcf188@163.com, xianweilai@163.com

Abstract. Coalition formation is a key topic in multi-agent systems. To date, most work on this problem has concentrated on simple characteristic function games. However, this lacks the notion of tasks which makes it more difficult to apply it in many applications. Dang et showed that this problem was NP-hard and that the minimum number of coalition structures that need to be searched through in order to establish a solution within a bound from the optimal was $(2^{m+n-1}-1)$. Then Dang et presented an algorithm that takes a step further to search those task-based coalition structures whose biggest task-based coalition's cardinality is greater than or equal to $\lceil n(K-1)/(K+1) \rceil$ in order to attain the bound K, which is the best result known so far. Against this background, this paper reports on a novel anytime algorithm based on cardinality structure that only have to take a step further to search those task-based coalition structures whose cardinality structure is in the $CTCS(n, m, K^*)$. Finally via contrast experiment, the algorithm reported in this paper is obviously better than that of Dang et al. (up to 10^{19} times faster when $n=60, m=40, K=3$).

Keywords: Multiagent system, coalition structure, task, cardinality structure.

1 Introduction

Coalition formation has recently become an important topic in multi-agent systems. To date, most work on coalition structure generation has focused on simple characteristic function games (CFGs). In such settings, there is a value v(S) for each and every subset S of A, known as the value of coalition S, which is the utility that members of S can jointly attain:(1)optimal coalition structure generation[1][3]; (2) coalition structure generation with worst case guarantees[2]; (3) coalition structure generation with given required bound [4]. However, in many practical applications, it is often the case that a coalition is formed in order to perform some task from a pool of potential tasks that the agent system has to perform [5][6]. Recently, Dang et al. [5]presented an algorithm that searchs those task-based coalition structures whose biggest task-based

A. Ghose, G. Governatori, and R. Sadananda (Eds.): PRIMA 2007, LNAI 5044, pp. 398–403, 2009.

coalition's cardinality is greater than or equal to $\lceil n(K-1)/(K+1) \rceil$ in order to attain the bound K. Their algorithm is the best result known so far.

This paper is structured as follows. Section 2 introduces the task-based coalition structure and cardinality structure. Section 3 presents our algorithms. Section 4 evaluates the performance of our algorithm by comparing to that of Dang et al., and finally, section 5 concludes and presents future work.

2 Task-Based Coalition Structure and Cardinality Structure

We denote the set of all agents by $A = \{a_1, a_2, \cdots, a_n\}$, and $n=|A|$ is the number of agents. Let T be the set of tasks and m be the number of tasks: $T=\{t_1, t_2, ..., t_m\}$. For each subset $C \subseteq A$ and each set of tasks $V \subseteq T$ there is a task-based coalition(TC) value $v(C, V)$ for the task-based coalition (C, V).

Definition 1. A task-based coalition structure $TCS = \{(C_1, V_1), (C_2, V_2), ..., (C_k, V_k)\}$, $1 \leq k \leq n$, coalition C_i, $1 \leq i \leq k$, will do the set of tasks V_i such that the following conditions are satisfied:

- $C_i \subseteq A, C_i \neq \varnothing, \forall 1 \leq i \leq k$
- $C_i \cap C_j = \varnothing, \forall 1 \leq i, j \leq k, i \neq j$
- $\bigcup_{i=1}^{k} C_i = A$
- $V_i \subseteq T, \forall 1 \leq i \leq k$
- $V_i \cap V_j = \varnothing, \forall 1 \leq i, j \leq k, i \neq j$
- $V_i \neq \varnothing, \forall 1 \leq i \leq k-1$

The value of a task-based coalition structure is $V(TCS) = \sum_{i=1}^{k} v(C_i, V_i)$. Let TCS^* be the optimal task-based coalition structure and TCS_N^* be the partial optimal task-based coalition structure where N is the set of task-based coalition structure searched.

Assume $TCS = \{(C_1, V_1), (C_2, V_2), ..., (C_k, V_k)\}$, without loss of generality, if $V_k \neq \varnothing$ we can assume $|C_1| \geq |C_2| \geq \cdots \geq |C_k|$, if $V_k = \varnothing$ we can assume $|C_1| \geq |C_2| \geq \cdots \geq |C_{k-1}|$, of which $|C_i|$ is the number of agents in coalition C_i. Let $n_1=|C_1|$, $n_2=|C_2|$, ..., $n_k=|C_k|$, then TCS's cardinality structure $(CTCS)$ can be defined as $\{n_1, n_2, ..., n_k\}$. For example, in a multi-agent system composed of there agents $\{a_1, a_2, a_3\}$ and two tasks $\{t_1, t_2\}$, there exist three cardinality structures: $\{1,1,1\}$, $\{2,1\}$, $\{3\}$. And $\{3\}$ corresponds with $\{((\{a_1, a_2, a_3\}, \{t_1\}))\}$, $\{((\{a_1, a_2, a_3\}, \{t_2\}))\}$, $\{((\{a_1, a_2, a_3\}, \{t_1, t_2\}))\}$, $\{((\{a_1, a_2, a_3\}, \{\ \}))\}$.

Proposition 1. For each coalition structure $(C_1, C_2, ..., C_k)$ $(k \leq m+1)$, there are: $(k+1)^m - \binom{k}{2}(k-1)^m$ corresponding task-based coalition structures.

Theorem 1. The smallest number of task-based coalition structures that need to be searched in order to establish a bound from the optimal is $2^{m+n-1} - 1$. That is, search the following set of task-based coalition structures: $M=M_1 \cup M_2$ where M_1 is the set of task-based coalition structures$\{(A, V)\}$ in which V is a non-empty subset of T and M_2 is the set of task-based coalition structures$\{(C, V), (A \setminus C, T \setminus V)\}$ where C is a strict subset of A and V is a subset of T. And the bound is $\min(n, m)$[5].

3 The Algorithm

◆   Step 1. Search through the set M and those task-based coalition structures whose cardinality structure is$\{1,1,\ldots,1,n\text{-}\min(n\text{-}1,m)\}(M_{\min(n,m+1)})$.

◆   Step 2. Search those task-based coalition structures whose cardinality structure is in the $CTCS(n, m, K^*)$, with K^* running from $\min(n, m)\text{-}1$ down to 2 as long as there is time left, or until all task-based coalition structures(TCS) have been searched.

◆   Step 3. Return the task-based coalition structure that has the biggest value among those seen so far.

Definition 2. Let $h=\left\lfloor \dfrac{n}{K^*} \right\rfloor$, $d=n \bmod K^*$. Let $CTCS(n, m, K^*)$ be the set of cardinality structures, as follows:

(1) All cardinality structures who satisfy $n_1+ n_2 +\cdots+ n_i\geq h$ and $n_1+ n_2 +\cdots+ n_{i\text{-}1}<h$ ($n_i\geq 2$ and $n_{i+1}=1$), if $d=0$.

(2) All cardinality structures who satisfy $n_1+ n_2 +\cdots+ n_i\geq h$ and $n_1+ n_2 +\cdots+ n_{i\text{-}1}<h$ ($n_i\geq 2$ and $n_{i+1}=1$). Besides, $\{h, 1, \ldots, 1, n\text{-}\min(n\text{-}1,m)\}$ is also part of $CTCS(n, m, K^*)$, if $d=1$.

(3) All cardinality structures who satisfy $n_1+ n_2 +\cdots+ n_i\geq h+1$ and $n_1+ n_2 +\cdots+ n_{i\text{-}1}< h+1$ ($n_1<h$, $n_i\geq 2$ and $n_{i+1}=1$). Besides, $\{h, 2, 1, \ldots, 1, n\text{-}\min(n\text{-}1,m)\}, \ldots, \{h, d, 1, \ldots, 1, n\text{-}\min(n\text{-}1,m)\}$ are also parts of $CTCS(n, m, K^*)$, if $d\geq 2$.

For example:

$CTCS(13, 15, 3)=\{\{2,2,1,\ldots,1\}, \{3,2,1,\ldots,1\}, \{3,3,1,\ldots,1\}, \{4,1,\ldots,1\}\}$.
$CTCS(14, 12, 3)=\{\{2,2,1,\ldots,1\}, \{3,2,1,\ldots,1\}, \{3,3,1,\ldots,1\}, \{4,2,1,\ldots,1\}\}$.

The next step is to show that the solution generated by the algorithm is within a bound K^* from the optimal.

Assume TCS^* (the optimal task-based coalition structure) contains k task-based coalitions, and the cardinality structure of TCS^* is $\{n_1, n_2, \ldots, n_k\}$(If $V_k = \varnothing$, n_k will not participate in the following grouping). Now we can divide it into a groups according to the following rules: Firstly, let $\{n_i\}$ be a group for all n_i, if $n_i\geq h$. Secondly, let $\{n_{i+1}, \ldots, n_j\}$ be a group for all $n_{i+1}, \ldots, n_j$ if $n_{i+1} +\cdots+ n_j\geq h$ ($h+1$ if $d\geq 2$) and $n_{i+1} +\cdots+ n_{j\text{-}1}<h$ ($h+1$ if $d\geq 2$). Lastly, if $n_{p+1}, \ldots, n_k$ doesn't belong to any groups, let $\{n_{p+1}, \ldots, n_k\}$ be a group. Obviously, we have:

$$1\leq a\leq \left\lceil \frac{n}{h} \right\rceil, \text{ of which } \left\lceil \frac{n}{h} \right\rceil = K^* +1 (K^* \text{ if } d=0)$$

For example: $n=14$, $m=12,K^* =3$. If the cardinality structure of CS^* is $\{4,3,3,2,1,1\}$, it can be divided into $\{4\},\{3,3\},\{2,1,1\}$. If the cardinality structure of CS^* is $\{5,4,4\}$, it can be divided into $\{5\},\{4\},\{4\}$.

Lemma 1. Every group above has appeared in $CTCS(n, m, K^*)$ or in M, $M_{\min(n,m+1)}$.

Proof. If the group only has one member, for example, $\{n_i\}$, obviously it has appeared in $\{n_i , n-n_i\}(M_2)$. Otherwise there will be two or more members in the group, for example: $\{n_{i+1}, \ldots, n_j\}$. Now we can prove $\{n_{i+1}, \ldots, n_j\}$ has appeared as follows:

If $n_j \geq 2$, the group has appeared in $\{n_{i+1}, \ldots, n_j, 1, \ldots, 1, n-\min(n-1,m)\}$, according to definition 2, it has appeared in $CTCS(n, m, K^*)$.

If $n_{i+1}=1$, the group has appeared in $\{1,1,\ldots,1, n-\min(n-1,m)\}(M_{\min(n,m+1)})$.

If $n_q \geq 2$ and $n_{q+1}=1$ ($i+1 \leq q \leq j-1$), we can continue adding 2 to the group until $n_{i+1}+ \cdots +n_q+2+\cdots+2 \geq h$ ($h+1$ if $d \geq 2$). The group has appeared in cardinality structure $\{n_{i+1}, \ldots, n_q, 2, \ldots, 2, 1, \ldots, 1, n-\min(n-1,m)\}$ which is in $CTCS(n, m, K^*)$.

Lemma 2. If $d=1$, the new group by adding 1 to any group whose sum is h also has appeared in $CTCS(n, m, K^*)$ or in M, $M_{\min(n,m+1)}$.

Proof. As prove above.

Lemma 3. If TCS^* can be divided into a groups and these groups have appeared in $CTCS(n, m, K^*)$ or in M, $M_{\min(n,m+1)}$, then we have the bound $K \leq a$.

Proof. Assume the ith group is $\{n_p, \ldots, n_q\}$, we denote that:

$$V(g_i) = V(TC_p) + \cdots + V(TC_q), \ V(g) = \max\{V(g_i)\}(1 \leq i \leq a)$$

Because the ith group has appeared, $S_p, \ldots, S_q$ have ever appeared in the same task-based coalition structure. And these groups have appeared, so we have:

$$V(g) \leq V(TCS_N^*), \ V(TCS^*) = V(g_1) + \cdots + V(g_a) \leq aV(g)$$

$$\Rightarrow \frac{V(TCS^*)}{V(TCS_N^*)} \leq \frac{aV(g)}{V(g)} = a$$

That is, the bound $K \leq a$

Theorem 2. Immediately after searching through the set M, $M_{\min(n,m+1)}$ and those task-based coalition structures whose cardinality structure is in the $CTCS(n, m, K^*)$, the bound $K \leq K^*$ and it is tight.

Proof. According to the definition 2, we can analyze this theorem as follows:

(1) According to the definition ($d=0$), $a \leq \left\lceil \frac{n}{h} \right\rceil = K^*$, that is, TCS^* can be divided into K^* groups at most. From lemma 1 and lemma 3 we know that $K \leq K^*$. And there is a TCS' containing K^* coalitions whose cardinality structure is $\{h, h, \ldots, h\}$. Assign value 1 to each task-based coalition $TC \in TCS'$ and assign value 0 to all other task-based coalitions. According to the definition, no two of the task-based coalitions in TCS' have ever appeared in the same task-based coalition structure, $V(TCS_N^*) =1$. Therefore

$$\frac{V(TCS')}{V(TCS_N^*)} = \frac{K^*}{1} = K^*$$

and the bound is tight.

(2) According to the definition ($d=1$), If only there is a group whose sum isn't h, then TCS^* can be divided into K^* groups at most. From lemma 1 and lemma 3 we

know that $K \leq K^*$. Otherwise, the sum of every group except the last group is h, and the last group is $\{1\}$. We can merge the last two groups into a new group. According to lemma 2 we know that the new group also has appeared. From lemma 1 and lemma 3 we know that the bound is K^* and is tight.

(3) According to the definition ($d \geq 2$), if the group is not $\{h\}$, the sum of the group must be larger than or equal to $h+1$. Therefore, if there are not $\{h\}$ in all groups or there isn't the $(K^*+1)th$ group, there will be K^* groups at most. From lemma 1 and lemma 3 we know that $K \leq K^*$. Otherwise, without loss of generality, we can assume that the number of $\{h\}$ is p and the sum of the $(K^*+1)th$ group ($\{n_{i+1}, \ldots, n_k\}$) is q. From

$$p \cdot h + \left(K^* - p\right) \cdot \left(h+1\right) \leq n < K^* \cdot \left(h+1\right) \Rightarrow q < p$$

That is, the number of members in the $(K^*+1)th$ group is less than the number of $\{h\}$. For each member in the $(K^*+1)th$ group, we assign it to $\{h\}$. That is, $\{h, n_{i+1}\}$, ...,$\{h, n_k\}$. For each $\{h, n_j\}$ ($i+1 \leq j \leq k$), if $n_j = 1$, the group has appeared in $\{h, 2, 1, \ldots, 1, n\text{-min}(n\text{-}1,m)\}$ which is in $CTCS(n, m, K^*)$, if $2 \leq n_j \leq d$, the group has appeared in $\{h, n_j, 1, \ldots, 1, n\text{-min}(n\text{-}1,m)\}$ which is also in $CTCS(n, m, K^*)$. So we have the bound is K^* and is tight.

The bound decreases as K^* decreases, so that our algorithm is an anytime one.

4   Comparison of Algorithms Developed

We test the algorithm with the number of agents n=60, m=40. The result of test is presented in the following graph. As we can see from the graph, for large bounds, there is no significant difference among algorithms. However, for small bounds, our algorithm is obviously better than that of Dang et al.(up to 10^{19} times faster when K=3). In these cases, the number of task-based coalition structures that our algorithm has to search is much smaller because of the smaller granularity of searching.

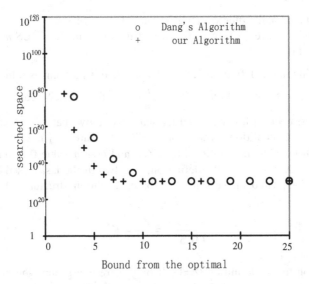

Fig. 1. The case n=60, m=40

5   Conclusions and Future Work

This paper analyzes the relations among task-based coalition structures in depth and presents the smaller granularity of searching ('cardinality structure' of task-based coalition structure). Then we presents an anytime algorithm based on cardinality structure that only have to take a step further to search those task-based coalition structures whose cardinality structure is in the $CTCS(n, m, K*)$ after searching the set M and $M_{min(n,m+1)}$. So that those coalition structures need to be searched are decreased greatly. Consequently, the algorithms reported in this paper are obviously better than that of Dang et al. Key properties are given and proved. Experimental results and analysis are given too.

As to future work, we intend to further reduce the complexity of the algorithm and we will try to present the optimal algorithm.

Acknowledgments. This paper is supported by the National Natural Science Foundation of China under Grant No. 60373079, No. 60573076; and by the Foundation of the Chinese academy of sciences under Grant No. SYSKF0505.

References

1. Rahwan, T., Ramchurn, S.D., Dang, V.D., Jennings, N.R.: Near-Optimal Anytime Coalition Structure Generation. In: 20th International Joint Conference on Artificial Intelligence, Hyderabad, India, pp. 2365–2371 (2007)
2. Su, S.-X., Hu, S.-L.: Coalition Structure Generation with Worst Case Guarantees based on Cardinality Structure. In: 6th International Joint Conference on Autonomous Agents and Multi-Agent Systems, Hawai'i, USA, pp. 1182–1184 (2007)
3. Su, S.-X., Hu, S.-L., Lin, C.-F., Zheng, S.-F.: A Coalition Generation Algorithm Based On Local Optimum. Chinese Journal of Computer Research & Development 44, 277–282 (2007)
4. Su, S.-X., Hu, S.-L., Zheng, S.-F., Lin, C.-F., Lai, X.-W.: Coalition Structure Generation With Given Required Bound Based on Cardinality Structure. In: 6th International Conference on Machine Learning and Cybernetics, Hong Kong, China, pp. 2505–2510 (2007)
5. Dang, V.D., Jennings, N.R.: Coalition structure generation in task-based settings. In: 17th European Conference on AI, Trento, Italy, pp. 210–214 (2006)
6. Li, C., Sycara, K.: A stable and efficient scheme for task allocation via agent coalition formation. Algorithms for Cooperative Systems. World Scientific, Singapore (2004)

A Specialised Architecture for Embedding Trust Evaluation Capabilities in Intelligent Mobile Agents

Justin R. Pike, Elizabeth M. Ehlers, and Ockmer L. Oosthuizen

University of Johannesburg, Academy for Information Technology, Auckland Park Kingsway
Campus. Kingsway, Auckland Park, Johannesburg, South Africa
{jrpike,emehlers,oloosthuizen}@uj.ac.za

Abstract. This paper proposes an approach to enhancing mobile agent protection. Mobile agents may come under threat from malicious hosts and unscrupulous agents. In an effort to reduce risk for mobile agents and improve the robustness of mobile agent systems - the proposed trust-based approach could be used to augment existing mechanisms aimed at mobile agent protection. The approach involves the development of a component that embeds an intelligent trust evaluation capability in a participating agent. This allows user agents to delegate the task of trust evaluation to specialised evaluator agents. These evaluator agents are a simple add-on to mobile agent systems - eliminating the need to redevelop mobile agent systems.

Keywords: Trust, Mobile Agents, Agent Architectures and Applications.

1 Introduction

This paper promotes the application of trust-related mechanisms as a 'soft' approach to augment existing approaches to mobile agent protection. Mobile agency has numerous benefits [1] unfortunately the applicability of mobile agent systems is (in some cases) inhibited due to the threats posed by malicious hosts and unscrupulous agents [2].

A potential solution is to endow agents with the capability to evaluate the trustworthiness of other agents and agent hosts. The capability will allow the agents to reach rational decisions relating to delegation and migration actions. It is expected that such a scheme will reduce the risks for the agent.

The suggested scheme is described in section 3. In particular, section 3.1 focuses on the addition of intelligent evaluator agent's to a generic mobile agent system. The evaluator agent is particularised in section 3.2. Section 3.3 elaborates on the embedded trust evaluation capability. Preliminary results and a conclusion follow in section 4. Firstly however, it is worthwhile to consider the state of the art from which some good ideas were gleaned.

2 State of the Art

This section classifies the literature into two topics: trust theoretic approaches and models (section 2.1); and mobile agent protection mechanisms (section 2.2).

A. Ghose, G. Governatori, and R. Sadananda (Eds.): PRIMA 2007, LNAI 5044, pp. 404–409, 2009.

2.1 Trust-Theoretic Approaches and Models

As far as trust-theoretic approaches are concerned, perhaps the most significant contribution is the cognitive trust theory proposed by Castelfranchi et al [3]. Most notably the work considers the beliefs of trust; the sources of trust; and the attribution of the success or failure of a delegated action/task/goal.

The above cited work also culminated in a Fuzzy Cognitive Map model [4, 5] for evaluating the trustworthiness of agents. Other trust and reputation models that are worthy of mention include TRAVOS [6] and FIRE [7].

More specialised contributions include an attempt at producing a shared semantics for communicating reputation information [8]. Another noteworthy contribution aims at using relationship analysis for the purposes of trust evaluation [9]. Another work suggests the use of broker agents in eliciting honest reputation reports from agents [10].

It would seem that despite these contributions – there are no trust models or systems that consolidate all (or even most) of these ideas. Furthermore, there is little or no evidence in the above cited literature that the mentioned mechanisms have been used to aid the protection of mobile agents from malicious hosts.

2.2 State of the Art in Mobile Agent Systems

Numerous mobile agent systems have been developed. An overview of some of these systems is provided by Karnik et al [11]. Agent protection support appears limited and is not augmented using trust-based measures in the systems considered. However, work aimed at overcoming these deficiencies has been carried out; Lin et al proposes a trust management architecture aimed at enhancing mobile agent protection [12]. Nonetheless, it would seem that few (if any) mobile agent systems offer comprehensive built-in support for the protection of mobile agents – particularly from malicious agent hosts. Nonetheless these systems are still of value. Therefore, instead of developing new mobile agent systems from scratch, a better solution is to develop generic add-ons to support mobile agent protection as described subsequently.

3 A Generic Mobile Agent System

3.1 System Architecture

The generic add-ons come in the form of service providing evaluator agents as depicted in figure 1 below. The service orientation of the proposed solution promotes autonomy (through a semantically enriched trust evaluation service). It also provides a high level abstraction that allows for improved handling of heterogeneity and thus takes a step towards handling the challenges of open environments.

Evaluator agents provide a trust evaluation service by evaluating the trustworthiness of other agents and agent hosts in the mobile agent system. Since the host controller agent (human or otherwise) controls the host, clearly the host is malicious if and only if the host controller agent is malicious. Therefore agent-oriented trust evaluation techniques can be applied.

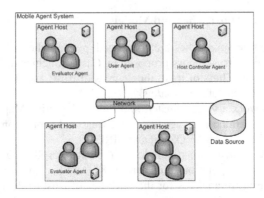

Fig. 1. A Generic Mobile Agent System

The evaluator agents, by providing a trust evaluation service, may act as brokers of reputation information (a similar scheme is proposed by Jurca et al [10]). The client user agent may ultimately decide to trust another agent or host partly on the basis of the provided reputation information. Thus, from the client user agent's perspective, the problem of evaluating trustworthiness of other agents and hosts has now shifted to the problem of deciding if the evaluator agent can be trusted.

One solution to the problem is to endow the user agent with intelligent trust evaluation capabilities – as provided by the component (section 3.3). This seemingly decentralised solution then brings into question the need for the evaluator agent. However, it should not be forgotten that the user agent's main purpose (its goals) do not relate to trust evaluation. The user agent can avoid the unnecessary burden on its resources by delegating the (typically secondary or supporting) trust evaluation goal.

The proposed evaluator agent model is discussed subsequently (section 3.2). A discussion of the design of a trust evaluation component follows in section 3.3.

3.2 Evaluator Agent Architectural Model

The evaluator agent mentioned previously exhibits a specialised BDI-theoretic architecture. The agent receives requests from user agents for trust evaluation services. The agent may also request reputation information from other trust evaluator agents deemed trustworthy (This can result in a so-called 'web of trust').

In order to service the trust evaluation requests (the agent's goal) the evaluator agent executes the appropriate plans. The evaluator agent's plan library contains procedural knowledge for evaluating the trustworthiness of other agents. For example one such plan allows the agent to categorise an agent on the basis of its relationships with other agents. This is achieved by categorising agents according to a domain ontology and then applying rules to the categorisation to infer relationships. It is also foreseeable that whenever the agent receives reports post the delegation of some action, task or goal, the agent will possibly need to execute a plan to attribute the success or failure to either environmental factors or agent internal factors. In fully observable environments, a rule-based approach for attribution may suffice. Alternatively, the use of a probabilistic approach (such as Bayesian network) is more

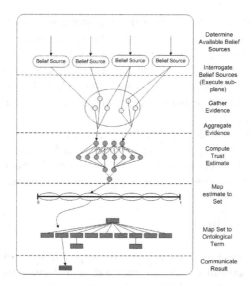

Fig. 2. Generic Plan for Trust Evaluation

suitable. The agent also has a generic plan for producing trust evaluation reports (trust evaluation). The generic plan (or meta-plan) is illustrated in figure 2 below.

The plan specifies the selection of sources of belief to base the evaluation upon. The sources of belief selected depend on the availability of those sources. For example the availability of reputation providers within the system constrains the use of reputation as a source of belief.

The agent then needs to interrogate the sources of belief in order to produce evidence. This may correspond to the agent requesting reputation information; retrieving knowledge of past direct experience from its knowledge base; and categorizing the agent according to its known relationships. All this so-called evidence can then be aggregated to form the strengths of beliefs. The beliefs correspond to the beliefs of trust as presented by Castelfranchi et al [2]. The aggregation of the evidence can be based on the perceived reliability of the evidence. The reliability estimates should decay over time, so that more recent evidence holds more weight.

Once the strengths (certainty) of the beliefs have been set, it is then possible to compute an estimate of trustworthiness. This can be achieved using the component discussed in the following section. Thereafter, a semantically enriched measure of trustworthiness is communicated to the client user agent.

3.3 Trust Evaluation Component

The evaluator agent ultimately needs to reason about the trustworthiness of other agents. This is achieved through some special purpose plans and the generic plan discussed above. The generic plan is supported by a trust evaluation component. The component provides an intelligent trust evaluation capability that, when embedded into an agent, allows the agent to rationally evaluate the trustworthiness of other agents.

The component provides an interface that requires certainty estimates for the beliefs of trust. At its simplest, the component includes a method for computing the estimate as the sum of a weighted product, based on the topology of a belief network. A more complex implementation of the component involves the use of a Bayesian network and an inference procedure such as the Monte Carlo Markov Chain (MCMC) algorithm for computing an estimate of the probability of betrayal (in its various forms) given the evidence.

The resulting estimate is then mapped to a set which corresponds to well defined semantics. Thus the client agents share a common understanding of the degree of trust, assuming they share the evaluator agent's ontology. If client agents implement their own ontology of trust then semantic mapping will be required.

4   Results and Conclusion

The above solution proposes a trust evaluation component that can be used to embed the trust evaluation capability into both user agents and evaluator agents. The user agents may use the capability in finding a trustworthy evaluator agent with specialised evaluation capabilities (more plans, and more advanced plans).

Since the component and the plans which it forms part of consolidate some proven ideas from the literature, promising results are expected. In particular, it is expected that the results by Falcone et al [5] will be readily transferable, due to the cognitive nature of the evaluator agent. Preliminary stages of prototype development show promising results with the evaluator agent outperforming a guessing evaluator agent in most instances.

This paper presents an approach aimed at reducing risk for mobile agents (and their owners), posed by malicious hosts and unscrupulous agents in mobile agent systems.

The proposed solution could be used to augment existing approaches to mobile agent protection, resulting in more robust mobile agent systems. Further benefits of this solution include the continued use of existing mobile agent systems (as opposed to reinventing the wheel). The reusability benefits of component-based architecture also apply.

References

1. Lange, D.B., Oshima, M.: Seven Good Reasons for Mobile Agents. Communications of the ACM, 88–89 (1999)
2. Bierman, E., Cloete, E.: Classification of Malicious Host Threats in Mobile Agent Computing. In: The 2002 Annual Research Conference of SAICSIT on Enablement through Technology, pp. 141–148. SAICSIT, South Africa (2002)
3. Castelfranchi, C., Falcone, R.: Social Trust: A Cognitive Approach. Trust and Deception in Virtual Societies, pp. 55–90. Kluwer Academic Publishers, Norwell (2000)
4. Castelfranchi, C., Falcone, R.: Trust in Information Sources as a Source for Trust: A Fuzzy Approach. In: 2nd International Joint Conference on Autonomous Agents and Multiagent Systems, pp. 89–96. ACM Press, New York (2003)

5. Falcone, R., Pezzulo, G., Castelfranchi, C., Calvi, G.: Why a Cognitive Trustier Performs Better: Simulating Trust-based Contract Nets. In: 3rd International Joint Conference on Autonomous Agents and Multiagent Systems, pp. 1394–1395. IEEE Computer Society, Los Alamitos (2004)
6. Teacy, W.T.L., Patel, J., Jennings, N.R., Luck, M.: TRAVOS: Trust and Reputation in the Context of Inaccurate Information Sources. In: Autonomous Agents and Multi-Agent Systems, pp. 183–198. Springer, Heidelberg (2006)
7. Huynh, D., Jennings, N.R., Shadbolt, N.R.: Developing an Integrated Trust and Reputation Model for Open Multi-Agent Systems. In: 7th International Workshop on Trust in Agent Societies, pp. 65–74 (2004)
8. Casare, S., Sichman, J.: Towards a Functional Ontology of Reputation. In: 4th International Joint Conference on Autonomous Agents and Multiagent Systems, pp. 505–511. ACM Press, New York (2005)
9. Ashri, R., Ramchurn, S.D., Sabater, J., Luck, M., Jennings, N.R.: Trust Evaluation Through Relationship Analysis. In: 4th International Joint Conference on Autonomous Agents and Multiagent Systems, pp. 1005–1011. ACM Press, New York (2005)
10. Jurca, R., Faltings, B.: An Incentive Compatible Reputation Mechanism. In: 2nd International Joint Conference on Autonomous Agents and Multiagent Systems, pp. 1026–1027. ACM Press, New York (2003)
11. Karnik, N.M., Tripathi, A.R.: Design Issues in Mobile Agent Programming Systems. In: IEEE Concurrency, pp. 52–61. IEEE Computer Society, Los Alamitos (1998)
12. Lin, C., Varadharajan, V., Wang, Y., Pruthi, V.: Trust Enhanced Security for Mobile Agents. In: 7th IEEE International Conference on E-Commerce Technology, pp. 231–238. IEEE, Los Alamitos (2005)

Reasoning with Levels of Modalities in BDI Logic

Jeff Blee, David Billington, and Abdul Sattar

Institute for Integrated and Intelligent Systems, Griffith University,
170 Kessels Road, Nathan, Queensland 4111, Australia
{J.Blee,D.Billington,A.Sattar}@griffith.edu.au

Abstract. Modelling real world problems using rational agents has been heavily investigated over the past two decades. BDI (Beliefs, Desires, and Intentions) Logic has been widely used to represent and reason about rational agency. However, in the real world, we often have to deal with different levels of confidence in the beliefs we hold, desires we have, and intentions that we commit to. This paper proposes the basis of a framework that extends BDI Logic to take into account qualitative levels of the mentalistic notions of beliefs, desires, and intentions. We also describe a set of axioms and properties of the extended logic.

Keywords: BDI Agents, Modal Logic, Nonmonotonic Logic, Belief Revision.

1 Introduction

Agent Technology is now well recognised, in the field of information and communication technologies, for modelling complex real world problems [6]. BDI Logic is one of the most widely studied formal languages that provides theoretical foundations for rational agents. This logic originated from the early work of Bratman [3], and was chiefly developed by Rao and Georgeff [10]. BDI Logic is used for several current agent languages and architectures, such as AgentSpeak [9], JASON [2], and JACK [4]. The main goal of agent frameworks is to model human-like reasoning by capturing the mentalistic notions of belief, desire, and intention. In the real world, these notions can not be simply evaluated in terms of true or false. We argue that, like humans, the agent must have an ability to reason with different levels of mentalistic notions. These levels of agents' attitudes reflect the degree of its confidence about its beliefs, desires, and intentions and thereby allow more versatility in modelling situations. As a simple example, let us introduce the personal assistant software of an academic (Helen). Part of the duties of this assistant software involves arranging Helen's academic schedule. The system receives email notifications of seminars, meetings, etc, and using its database of Helen's beliefs, desires, and intentions, it allocates a schedule for Helen. There may be several seminars, meetings, or combinations of these occurring at the same time that Helen desires to attend. Unfortunately, with standard BDI, the system is unable to decide which to schedule, at least not without a machine learning process to "teach" the system further differentiation. We propose a framework to integrate grading or levels of the BDI mentalistic notions and therefore give that differentiation and more versatility.

A. Ghose, G. Governatori, and R. Sadananda (Eds.): PRIMA 2007, LNAI 5044, pp. 410–415, 2009.

There have been many attempts to grade such mentalistic notions as belief, usually into different types of belief as in [14]. Some introduce actual levels of belief as in [13]. The most interesting work is that of Casali *et al* in [5] which extends the earlier work of Parsons & Giorgini [8]. Like the framework in this paper, Casali introduces levels in all the mentalistic notions of BDI, as well as, using numeric, possiblistic type functions in its semantics. However, the similarity ends there. Casali's framework uses multi-contexts with a different semantics for each of the mentalistic notions, though a common underlying multi-valued Lukasiewicz logic is used. This tends to make it overly complex, unwieldy and somewhat counter-intuitive. While there are nominally three modalities, they are more akin to possibility functions. Desires tend to be combined arbitrarily with no defined method for calculating the result.

The framework of our paper uses a common syntax and underlying logic for each of the mentalistic notions. The framework is extended loosely from the multi-modal BDI logic of [10] with each grading or level being a separate modality. It also introduces *doxastic ignorance*, an effective absence of real belief, and an example methodology defining dependencies of desires and their calculation. While the framework can have *n* levels of each of the mentalistic notions, we suggest five basic levels of each notion for ease of presentation and understanding, with two of the levels being able to be expanded into more levels if required. In section 2 we present the basic syntax of the framework, the modal levels and axioms and properties as they pertain to belief, and the framework extended to desires and intentions. The paper is concluded in section 3.

2 Basic Framework Syntax

The alphabet of this framework is the union of the following pairwise disjoint sets of symbols: a non-empty countable set $\mathcal{P}$ of atomic propositions; a non-empty countable set $\mathcal{A}$, of atomic actions; the set $\{\wedge, \vee, \rightarrow, \neg\}$ of connectives; the set of brackets $\{(, [,),]\}$; and a set of modalities $\{$BA, BU, BI, BW, BD, DA, DU, DI, DW, DD, IA, IU, II, IW, ID$\}$, described in Sections 2.1 and 2.2. The syntax of the language is as follows:

$$\varphi ::- \ p \mid (\neg\varphi) \mid (\varphi_1 \wedge \varphi_2) \mid (\varphi_1 \vee \varphi_2) \mid (\varphi_1 \rightarrow \varphi_2) \ ;$$

where $\varphi \in \mathcal{L}$ ($\mathcal{L}$ is the set of all formulae of the alphabet), and $p \in \mathcal{P}$.

2.1 Levels of Belief

As stated in the introduction, in realistic situations agents may have shades of belief. We note that in the nonmonotonic logic, Defeasible Logic [1, 7], situations may be believed to be *usually* true, (e.g. any random given bird is usually able to fly), or *usually not* true (weakly believed).

Definition 1: The five belief levels are defined as follows:

BAφ means that φ is Believed Absolutely and is the strongest level of belief (e.g. φ is "the sun will rise tomorrow").

BUφ means that φ is Believed Usually true (e.g. φ is "the bus will be on time") and this level can be divided (BU.$_8\varphi$ and BU.$_7\psi$ means φ is more strongly believed than ψ). For example, an agent's belief that a random bird can fly may be greater than the belief that the bus will be on time at the bus stop, but both beliefs are "usual" beliefs.

BIφ means that φ is not believed or disbelieved (e.g. φ is "the weather will be fine on Xmas day next year"). It is labelled as *Doxastic Ignorance* and is actually an absence of definite belief. *Doxastic Ignorance* is a term we introduce to denote something that is essentially neither believed, nor disbelieved and is similar to the logic presented in [12], but differs in that Doxastic Ignorance pertains to belief.

BWφ means that φ is usually not believed, only Believed Weakly, i.e. might be true (e.g. φ is "used car salesmen tell the truth"). This is the mirror opposite of BU and can similarly be divided into more levels if necessary.

BDφ means that φ is absolutely Disbelieved, i.e. believed false with the strongest level of belief, and is mirror of BA (e.g. φ is "a comet will hit my house tonight").

Doxastic possibility (P) is the $\Diamond$ (diamond) to belief's $\square$ (box) (P$\varphi \equiv \neg$B$\neg\varphi$).

There is a natural affinity between the BA level and the BD level (BA $\neg\varphi$ is the same as BD φ) as well as between BU and the BW. This suggests the ability to cut the five levels down to three basic levels. However, with three levels the direction of belief strength priority between levels could alter depending upon the inclusion of a negated formula. Therefore, five levels are retained here to simplify the reasoning.

Belief Axioms and Properties

In this section we present the major belief axioms, and properties that follow from those axioms. Axiom numbering is prefixed by the letter "A" and properties by the letter "P". Let φ and ψ be any formulae in $\mathcal{L}$.

$$\text{For each } \varphi \text{ in } \mathcal{L}, \ \text{BA}\varphi \lor \text{BU}\varphi \lor \text{BI}\varphi \lor \text{BW}\varphi \lor \text{BD}\varphi . \tag{A1}$$

$$\text{If } \Phi, \Psi \in \{A, U, I, W, D\} \text{ and } \Phi \neq \Psi, \text{ then } \text{B}\Phi\varphi \rightarrow \neg\text{B}\Psi\varphi . \tag{A2}$$

$$\text{If } \Phi \in \{A, U, I, W, D\} \text{ and } \varphi \equiv \psi, \text{ then } \text{B}\Phi\varphi \equiv \text{B}\Phi\psi . \tag{A3}$$

$$\text{BA}\varphi \equiv \text{BD}\neg\varphi . \tag{A4}$$

$$\text{BD}\varphi \equiv \text{BA}\neg\varphi . \tag{P1}$$

$$\text{BU}\varphi \equiv \text{BW}\neg\varphi . \tag{A5}$$

$$\text{BW}\varphi \equiv \text{BU}\neg\varphi . \tag{P2}$$

$$\text{BI}\varphi \equiv \text{BI}\neg\varphi . \tag{A6}$$

$$\text{B}\Phi\varphi \rightarrow \neg\text{BI}\varphi \land \neg\text{BI}\neg\varphi \ (\text{where } \Phi \in \{A, U, W, D\}) . \tag{P3}$$

$$\text{BI}\varphi \equiv \neg\text{BA}\varphi \land \neg\text{BA}\neg\varphi \land \neg\text{BU}\varphi \land \neg\text{BU}\neg\varphi . \tag{P4}$$

$$\text{BI}\varphi \equiv \neg\text{BA}\varphi \land \neg\text{BD}\varphi \land \neg\text{BU}\varphi \land \neg\text{BW}\varphi . \tag{P5}$$

Definition 2: P$\Phi\varphi \equiv \neg$B$\Phi\neg\varphi$ and so B$\Phi\varphi \equiv \neg$P$\Phi\neg\varphi$ [where $\Phi \in \{A, U, I, W, D\}$].

$$\text{BI}\varphi \equiv \neg\text{PI}\varphi . \tag{P6}$$

(P6) follows (A6) and $BI\neg\varphi \equiv \neg PI\neg\neg\varphi \equiv \neg PI\varphi$. Bearing in mind the relationship between the belief levels, let us look at the five doxastic possibility levels.

$$PA\varphi \equiv \neg BA\neg\varphi \equiv \neg BD\varphi \equiv (BA\varphi \vee BU\varphi \vee BI\varphi \vee BW\varphi) . \tag{P7}$$

$$PU\varphi \equiv \neg BU\neg\varphi \equiv \neg BW\varphi \equiv (BA\varphi \vee BU\varphi \vee BI\varphi \vee BD\varphi) . \tag{P8}$$

$$PI\varphi \equiv \neg BI\neg\varphi \equiv \neg BI\varphi \equiv (BA\varphi \vee BU\varphi \vee BW\varphi \vee BD\varphi) . \tag{P9}$$

$$PW\varphi \equiv \neg BW\neg\varphi \equiv \neg BU\varphi \equiv (BA\varphi \vee BI\varphi \vee BW\varphi \vee BD\varphi) . \tag{P10}$$

$$PD\varphi \equiv \neg BD\neg\varphi \equiv \neg BA\varphi \equiv (BU\varphi \vee BI\varphi \vee BW\varphi \vee BD\varphi) . \tag{P11}$$

KD45 Axioms

In multi-modal BDI logic, and doxastic logic, their axioms include the axiom system **KD45**. We now look at how closely **KD45** hold for our levels of belief.

It has been shown elsewhere, [11], that the strict **K** axiom does not hold over modality gradings. An example of the **K** axiom applied to the BD level of belief $(BD(\varphi\rightarrow\psi) \rightarrow (BD\varphi\rightarrow BD\psi))$ is that if we strongly disbelieve the rule *if the sun is shining then it is raining*, then it follows that if we disbelieve *the sun is shining*, this implies that we disbelieve that *it is raining*. This is plainly nonsense and the other levels (except for BA) have this problem to varying degrees. However, an altered **K** axiom of the form of (A7) makes much more sense.

$$B\Phi(\varphi \rightarrow\psi) \rightarrow (BA\varphi \rightarrow B\Phi\psi), \text{(where } \Phi \in \{A, U, I, W, D\}). \tag{A7}$$

By convention, (A7) can also be rewritten as $BA\varphi \wedge B\Phi(\varphi\rightarrow\psi) \rightarrow B\Phi\psi$. This is similar to Modus Ponens. So if we believe $\varphi\rightarrow\psi$ at the Φ level and we strongly believe φ, then (A7) allows us to derive ψ at the Φ level.

$$B\Phi \varphi \rightarrow P\Phi \varphi \quad \text{(where } \Phi \in \{A, U, W, D\}) . \tag{A8}$$

The axiom D (serial), can be applied to all levels except BI (A8). For example, using (P8), $BU\varphi \rightarrow PU\varphi$ is equivalent to $BU\varphi \rightarrow (BA\varphi \vee BU\varphi \vee BI\varphi \vee BD\varphi)$. $BU\varphi$ is included on both sides of the implication arrow and this is then a tautology. A problem with the BI level with D is that using (P9), $PI\varphi \equiv \neg BI\varphi$, so $BI\varphi \rightarrow PI\varphi$ is converted to $BI\varphi \rightarrow \neg BI\varphi$. This is obviously not what we want. However, it must be remembered that doxastic ignorance is not actual belief, but an effective absence of belief. Therefore D holds for all the levels of actual belief.

Normally, the axioms 4 (transitivity) and 5 (Euclidean) are used for introspection. To demonstrate the problem with transitivity for these belief levels, observe that $BD\varphi \rightarrow BD\ BD\varphi$ means if φ is disbelieved, then that disbelief is disbelieved. By converting through (P1), we get $BA\neg\varphi \rightarrow BA\ \neg BA\neg\varphi$, or, $BA\psi \rightarrow BA\ \neg BA\psi$. This is definitely not the axiom of transitivity, nor positive introspection. The Euclidean axiom 5 has similar problems. Using (P11), we can convert $PD\varphi \rightarrow BD\ PD\varphi$ to $(BU\varphi \vee BI\varphi \vee BW\varphi \vee BD\varphi) \rightarrow BD\ (BU\varphi \vee BI\varphi \vee BW\varphi \vee BD\varphi)$. So, if the disjunction of formulae on the left of the statement is true, then this implies that we disbelieve that same disjunction of formulae. This is not what we want and is not true negative introspection. However, we present altered versions of 4 (resp. 5) that allow introspection (similar to 'arbitary' introspection defined in [13]). By locking the first (resp. only) belief level on the right side of the axioms to absolute belief, we get true positive (resp. negative) introspection, which is what we are really seeking here.

$$B\Phi\varphi \to BA\ B\Phi\varphi \quad (\text{where } \Phi\in\{A,U,I,W,D\}) . \tag{A9}$$

$$P\Phi\varphi \to BA\ P\Phi\varphi \quad (\text{where } \Phi\in\{A,U,I,W,D\}) . \tag{A10}$$

2.2 Levels of Goals

Desires and Intentions can be described as weak goals and strong goals respectively (i.e. desire + commitment = intention) and an agent can conceivably have varying degrees of strength of these. The desire to live/survive is stronger that the desire to go to work, which in turn is stronger than the desire to be robbed. Having levels of desire gives an agent more versatility in representing a wider range of situations.

The framework of levels introduced for beliefs can be extended to desires and also intentions. Essentially, each goal level will have a similar meaning to similar levels of belief. While beliefs are usually held about current states in a world, goals are always held about future states. The difference between goal types is that a given desire, among several desires, becomes an intention if it is committed to by the agent. A rational agent may have conflicting desires, but not conflicting intentions.

Due to space limitations, we have omitted the definition of desire and intention levels, but they essentially mirror the levels presented for belief. Briefly, $DA\varphi$ denotes φ is absolutely desired, $DU\varphi$ means φ is desired, less than DA, $DI\varphi$ applies if neither φ nor $\neg\varphi$ is desired (*goal indifference*), $DW\varphi$ denotes φ is only weakly desired, and $DD\varphi$ means φ is *not* desired, or $DA\neg\varphi$. As with BU and BW, DU and DW may be subdivided if required.

So, after deliberation, an agent commits to a particular desire, thereby creating an intention of the same level as the relevant desire (e.g. $DU\varphi$ + *commitment* $\to IU\varphi$). The desire and intention axioms and properties are essentially the same as in belief. Naturally there are no goal equivalents to the introspection axioms (A9) and (A10).

3   Conclusion and Future Work

The framework undertaken in this paper provides a foundation for a layered BDI architecture. This essentially enables a rational agent to capture commonsense reasoning. We believe that representing and reasoning with levels of mentalistic attitudes significantly enhances an agent's ability to perform human-like practical reasoning in complex domains. The proposed framework has the prospect of being simpler and more intuitive than other BDI frameworks, including that of Casali. Intended future work includes extending the syntax to include plans, strictly defining a multi-modal BDI semantics partially based on [10], and introducing this basic framework into an existing BDI agent platform, most likely the AgentSpeak(L) platform, JASON. Naturally this will necessitate dropping any strictly modal aspects, but the logic, as stated, should be able to be easily adapted to JASON. We thank the Smart Internet Cooperative Research Centre (SITCRC) for their funding of this work.

References

1. Billington, D.: Defeasible Logic is Stable. Journal of Logic and Computation 3(4), 379–400 (1993)
2. Bordini, R.H., Hubner, J.F., Vieira, R.: Jason and the Golden Fleece of Agent-Oriented Programming. In: Bordini, R.H., Dastani, M., Dix, J., El Fallah Seghrouchni, A. (eds.) Multi-Agent Programming: Languages, Platforms and Applications, pp. 3–37. Springer, Heidelberg (2005)
3. Bratman, M.E.: Intention, Plans, and Practical Reason. Harvard University Press, Cambridge (1987)
4. Busetta, P., Ronnquist, R., Hodgson, A., Lucas, A.: JACK Intelligent Agents - Components for Intelligent Agents in Java. Agent Oriented Software Pty. Ltd., Melbourne (1998)
5. Casali, A., Godo, L., Sierra, C.: Graded BDI Models for Agent Architectures. In: Leite, J., Torroni, P. (eds.) CLIMA 2004. LNCS, vol. 3487, pp. 126–143. Springer, Heidelberg (2005)
6. Luck, M., McBurney, P., Shehory, O., Willmott, S.: Agent Technology Roadmap: A Roadmap for Agent Based Computing, AgentLink III (2005)
7. Nute, D.: Defeasible logic. In: Bartenstein, O., Geske, U., Hannebauer, M., Yoshie, O. (eds.) INAP 2001. LNCS, vol. 2543, pp. 151–169. Springer, Heidelberg (2003)
8. Parsons, S., Giorgini, P.: On using degrees of belief in BDI agents. In: Proceedings of International Conference on Information Processing and Management of Uncertainty in Knowledge-Based Systems (1998)
9. Rao, A.S.: AgentSpeak(L): BDI Agents speak out in a logical computable language. In: Perram, J., Van de Velde, W. (eds.) MAAMAW 1996. LNCS, vol. 1038, pp. 42–55. Springer, Heidelberg (1996)
10. Rao, A.S., Georgeff, M.P.: Decision Procedures for BDI Logics. Journal of Logic and Computation 8(3), 293–343 (1998)
11. van der Hoek, W.: On the Semantics of Graded Semantics. Journal of Applied Non-Classical Logics 2(1), 81–123 (1992)
12. van der Hoek, W., Lomuscio, A.: A Logic for Ignorance. Electronic Notes in Theoretical Computer Science. Elsevier, Amsterdam (2004)
13. van Ditmarsch, H.P.: Prolegomena to Dynamic Logic for Belief Revision. Synthese(Knowledge, Rationality & Action) 147, 229–275 (2005)
14. van Linder, B., van der Hoek, W., Meyer, J.-J.C.: Seeing is Believing, And so are Hearing and Jumping. In: Gori, M., Soda, G. (eds.) AI*IA 1995. LNCS, vol. 992, pp. 402–413. Springer, Heidelberg (1995)

A Distributed Computational Model for Mobile Agents

Med Amine Haddar[1,3], Ahmed Hadj Kacem[2], Yves Métivier[3],
Mohamed Mosbah[3], and Mohamed Jmaiel[1]

[1] ReDCAD Research Unit
École Nationale d'Ingénieurs de Sfax, Tunisie
[2] MIRACL Laboratory
Faculté des Sciences Economiques et de Gestion de Sfax, Tunisie
[3] LaBRI UMR 5800
ENSEIRB - Université Bordeaux 1 351 Cours de la Libération 33405 - Talence France
{haddar,mosbah}@labri.fr

Abstract. In this paper, a novel formalized mobile agent distributed computation model based on transition systems is presented. In our model, the mobile agent actions (e.g. computations, communication and migration) are described using transitions. Thus, a mobile agent algorithm is viewed as a transition system and the underlying distributed system is modeled by a connected graph. We exploit the high-level encoding of agent actions by transitions to prove the correctness of agent algorithms. We illustrate this approach with the distributed computation of a spanning tree.

Keywords: mobile agent, computations model, distributed algorithms, transition systems.

1 Introduction

1.1 Background

Nowadays, distributed systems are solicited in potential life services (such as banks, railway stations, airports, trade companies , etc). All of them need reliable applications to propose secure services to their clients. This aim can be realized by proposing powerful models which simplify the design and the proof of distributed algorithms. To formally describe distributed algorithms, several works have tried to propose a "standard" model for distributed systems. But, unlike sequential algorithms, there is not a "universal" model of computations for the distributed ones. Indeed, designing and proving distributed algorithms is still a hard task and they depend closely on the considered model. The mathematical *tool-box* provided by local computation model proposed an exciting proof approach for distributed algorithms [1]. Nevertheless, with the success of mobile agent based applications, regards are switched from classical systems (message passing, shared memory, remote procedure call, etc) towards this new paradigm.

A. Ghose, G. Governatori, and R. Sadananda (Eds.): PRIMA 2007, LNAI 5044, pp. 416–421, 2009.
© Springer-Verlag Berlin Heidelberg 2009

Among many others, the distributed computing community is presenting an increasing interest into mobile agents due to their considerable reduction of network load and their overcoming of the network latency. There are also new trends to use this technology in faulty distributed systems for which mobile agent gives a promoting solution for arising problems.

1.2   Related Works

Mobile agents technology, and in general agents, are not restricted to a specific domain. Rather, they are likely to play a key role in many aspects of programming and formal design. In the literature, mobile agents are mainly used in several areas. A first area focus on how to use mobile agents for improving computations power. By the wide requirements of the computational power and the programming benefits of mobile agent, many authors have motivated their works by the use of mobile agent to solve common problems [2]. In the distributed computing community, metrics are done to prove the positive impact in performances while using mobile agent for the computational and communication resources. These results have motivated researchers to perform computations by means of mobile agents [3]. An other important area of researches dealt with formal aspects in order to design mobile agent with a high level of abstraction [4]. A variety of models are proposed using various languages. The complexity to understand these models depends on the used languages. Indeed few tools are proposed to make automatic transition from formal model to implementation. To our knowledge, there are very few *computational models* which give a simple and easy way for designing mobile agents and provide a proof approach to verify mobile agent properties (e.g. correctness). In [5], the author proposes a computational model which simply emphasis the use of mobile agents for the stabilization of distributed systems. A mobile agent is formalized in an algorithmic fashion increasing the difficulty to proof mobile agent correctness and termination.

1.3   Motivations and Contributions

Our work is motivated by the increasing needs to develop distributed algorithms executed by mobile agents. Traditional distributed algorithms are based on the classical model of distributed systems, composed of permanently active processes communicating through established links. This model of distributed systems is no longer valid when dealing with mobile agents. Surprisingly, a recent result [6] proves the equivalence of computations between a mobile agent system and a message passing distributed system.

In this paper, we propose a *computational model* for describing, understanding and proving distributed algorithms for mobile agents. More precisely, using a high-level encoding of mobile agent distributed algorithms, by local rules, we show that we can benefit from mathematical properties of rewriting systems (or more generally *transition systems*) to obtain rigorous and formal proof of these algorithms. A mobile agent algorithm is formalized in our model by a transition system. We have proposed, to prove such a system, an approach based on *mathematical tool-box* provided by local computation theory.

Our model, in addition to benefits obviously inherited from the use of mobile agent paradigm, and unlike classical models based on message passing systems, does not require active processes in each host. The resources, on a given host, are solicited when a mobile agent arrives on it. To illustrate our model, we present in [7] a distributed algorithm to solve the spanning tree problem in an anonymous netwok. Such a problem is among the important problems in distributed computing. We present a description of the algorithm as a transition system. We simulated our solution in the VISIDIA platform [8].

This paper focuses on the proposed model. Due to lack of space, we give a general description of the model. Details of this model and examples can be found in [9]. The last section gives a conclusion and some prospects.

2   The Proposed Model

In order to formally describe a mobile agent algorithm, we define what we call a *Mobile Agent System*. We start this section by detailing this system entities. Then, we lay bare the definition of the mobile agent algorithm. Finally, we expose the graphic notation made to easily describe a mobile agent algorithm.

2.1   Mobile Agent System

A mobile agent system, as defined in [6], consists of:

- a collection $\mathbb{P}$ of places,
- a navigation subsystem $\mathbb{S}$,
- a collection $\mathbb{A}$ of mobile agents,
- an injection $\pi_0 : \mathbb{A} \longrightarrow \mathbb{P}$ describing the initial placement of mobile agents,
- an initial labeling λ of places and mobile agents.

The labeling λ of places and mobile agents can code anonymous places (all places have the same label), anonymous mobile agents (all mobile agents have the same label) or any initial knowledge of the mobile agent. As examples of initial knowledge, we can cite the number of places, the number of mobile agents, the diameter and the topology of the navigation subsystem, the placement topology of mobile agents and identities or partial identities of places or mobile agents.

The navigation subsystem is described by an undirect connected graph $G = (V, E)$, where the vertices V denote the places and the edges E denote the bidirectional channels operating between them. Each place u contains a set of ports. Every port represents an access point to a communicating channel. Let δ_u be a function of ports classification which assigns to each port representing a channel connecting u to a place v a unique integer $\delta_u(v)$ belonging to $[1, deg(u)]$. Each mobile agent which migrates from one place to another knows by which channel it leaves by choosing the adequate port number. Thus, the navigation subsystem is defined by $\mathbb{S} = (G, \delta)$.

Every place in the mobile agent system contains a *WhiteBoard* which is used to store the place state (label). It is accessible in a mutual exclusion way for reading and writing operations done by mobile agents. The *lock/unlock* operations are envisaged to manage the access to the *Whiteboard* and thus to prohibit the concurrent access (reading or/and writing) to the place state.

The mobile agent system is asynchronous: there is no access to global clock. The migration is asynchronous: a migrating mobile agent arrives on a place in a bounded but unknown time. A communicating channel is modeled by a FIFO (first in first out) queue: two mobile agents sent on the same channel must arrive in the same order in which they are sent. Every mobile agent arriving on a place waits its turn, in order to be executed, in the *Able-To-Run* FIFO queue. The computations done by a mobile agent in a place is an *atomic task*. This property is guaranteed by the *lock/unlock* operations systematically done by the mobile agent when it starts/stops running.

2.2   Mobile Agent Algorithm

Given a mobile agent system ($\mathcal{M}a\mathcal{S}$) according to the definition given in section 2.1, we propose a mobile agent algorithm which extends the one proposed in [6]. In $\mathcal{M}a\mathcal{S}$, a mobile agent performs several actions such as moving across a channel, waiting on a place, etc. These actions can be modeled in $\mathcal{M}a\mathcal{S}$ using transitions. Thus a mobile agent algorithm is described using a transition system. We associate to each mobile agent **a** a transition system $\mathbb{T}_a$.

The initial state of each mobile agent **a** is denoted by $\lambda(\mathbf{a})$ whereas the initial state of each execution place **p** is indicated by $\lambda(\mathbf{p})$. Let **a** be a mobile agent in the state s and let **p** be a place in the state q, an *elementary transition* associated to **a** transforms s into s' and q into q' indicates that:

– **a** is on **p** and it is still there.

$$(s,q) \quad \mathbf{a} \prod_{\mathbf{p}} \mathbf{a} \quad (s',q') \tag{1}$$

– **a** arrives on **p** through the port *in*.

$$(s,q,in) \quad \mathbf{a} \prod_{\mathbf{p}} \mathbf{a} \quad (s',q') \tag{2}$$

– **a** leaves **p** through the port *out*.

$$(s,q) \quad \mathbf{a} \prod_{\mathbf{p}} \mathbf{a} \quad (s',q',out) \tag{3}$$

– **a** is already on **p**, it creates a clone $\mathbf{a_c}$ in the state s_c.

$$(s,q) \quad \mathbf{a} \prod_{\mathbf{p}} \overset{\mathbf{a_c}}{\mathbf{a}} \quad (s',s_c,q') \tag{4}$$

— **a** is killed.

$$(s, q) \quad \mathbf{a} \prod_{\mathbf{p}} \quad (q') \tag{5}$$

In general, places do not have identities. However, to facilitate the presentation, a mobile agent **a** in transit is denoted by $(p, \mathbf{a}, p')$ where p is the starting place and p' is the destination place.

A configuration of a mobile agent system consists of the state of each place, the state of each mobile agent, a collection $\mathbb{A}$ of all mobile agents in the system, a collection $\mathbb{D}$ of mobile agents in transit (initially $\mathbb{D}$ is empty) and a projection π describing the placement of mobile agents which are not in a channel (several mobile agents can be on the same place).

An event in a mobile agent system is defined by an *elementary transition* **t** associated to a mobile agent **a** on a place **p**. The state of each mobile agent other than **a** is not affected, the state of each place other than **p** is not also concerned with such transition.

- If the *elementary transition* belongs to class (1) then π, $\mathbb{A}$ and $\mathbb{D}$ are not affected by the event.
- If the *elementary transition* belongs to class (2) then the set of mobile agents in transit after the event becomes $\mathbb{D} \setminus \{(\mathbf{p}', \mathbf{a}, \mathbf{p})\}$ (where $\mathbf{p}'$ is the adjacent place to **p** corresponding to the port *in*), $\pi(\mathbf{a}) = \mathbf{p}$ and π is not modified for other mobile agents. $\mathbb{A}$ is not affected by the event.
- If the *elementary transition* belongs to class (3) then the set of mobile agents in transit after the event becomes $\mathbb{D} \cup \{(\mathbf{p}, \mathbf{a}, \mathbf{p}')\}$ (where $\mathbf{p}'$ is the adjacent place to **p** corresponding to the port *out*), π is not defined for **a**, unchanged for other mobile agents. $\mathbb{A}$ is not affected by the event.
- If the *elementary transition* belongs to class (4) then π and $\mathbb{D}$ are not affected by the event and the set of all mobile agents becomes $\mathbb{A} \cup \{a_c\}$.
- If the *elementary transition* belongs to class (5), π and $\mathbb{D}$ are not affected by the event and the set of all mobile agents becomes $\mathbb{A} \setminus \{a\}$.

Remarks

- To resolve a large scale of problems where the coordination of mobile agents is needed, we are invited to control in runtime the mobile agents execution. To this aim, we design a set of *run-control-transitions* (see [9]). These transitions allow a mobile agent on a place to *wait* for an event (such as the change of local state) using the *standby/active* modes. *Run-control-transitions* allow also a mobile agent, on a given place, to notify the set of mobile agents standing by of occurred changes. The notification is done by means of *token*. A mobile agent, using the appropriate transition, *stands by* waiting for a *token* produced by another mobile agent. When it receives a token, it consumes it to reach the *active* mode. contor
- In order to simplify the description of mobile agent algorithms using transition systems, to follow the execution of these systems and to be able to check and to prove properties of elaborated algorithms we propose (see [9])

a graphical notation of the various classes of transitions. Indeed, we define what we call *composed transitions* and we give some examples of these transitions.

3 Conclusion

Attracted by the success of mobile agent paradigm in several domains, we proposed, in this paper, a *computational model* for describing, understanding and proving distributed algorithms for mobile agents. More precisely, by using a high-level encoding of mobile agents distributed algorithms, and by making use of transition systems, we showed that we can benefit from mathematical properties of local computations to obtain rigorous and formal proof of these algorithms. We looked in our model for the simplicity of formal notation. For this aim, we apply the notations of rewriting rules to describe the mobile agent actions. To illustrate our model, we present in [7] a solution to the problem of spanning tree in anonymous networks together with its correctness and termination proofs.

We plan, in the near future, to design and implement a framework which offers an easy-to-use graphical interface for programming and running mobile agents using the developed language.

References

1. Litovsky, I., Métivier, Y., Sopena, E.: Handbook of graph grammars and computing by graph transformation, vol. 3, pp. 1–56. World Scientific, Singapore (1999)
2. Abbas, S., Mosbah, M., Zemmari, A.: Distributed computation of a spanning tree in a dynamic graph by mobile agents. In: IEEE International Conference on Engineering of Intelligent Systems, pp. 425–430 (2006)
3. Pan, L., Bic, L., Dillencourt, M.B., Lai, M.K.: Mobile agents - the right vehicle for distributed sequential computing. In: Sahni, S.K., Prasanna, V.K., Shukla, U. (eds.) HiPC 2002. LNCS, vol. 2552, pp. 575–584. Springer, Heidelberg (2002)
4. Cardelli, L., Gordon, A.D.: Mobile ambients. Theor. Comput. Sci. 240(1), 177–213 (2000)
5. Ghosh, S.: Agents, distributed algorithms, and stabilization. In: Du, D.-Z., Eades, P., Sharma, A.K., Lin, X., Estivill-Castro, V. (eds.) COCOON 2000. LNCS, vol. 1858, pp. 242–251. Springer, Heidelberg (2000)
6. Chalopin, J., Godard, E., Métivier, Y., Ossamy, R.: Mobile agent algorithms versus message passing algorithms. In: Shvartsman, M.M.A.A. (ed.) OPODIS 2006. LNCS, vol. 4305, pp. 187–201. Springer, Heidelberg (2006)
7. Haddar, M.A., Kacem, A.H., Métivier, Y., Mosbah, M., Jmaiel, M.: Proving distributed algorithms for mobile agents: Examples of spanning tree computation in anonymous networks. In: Rao, S., Chatterjee, M., Jayanti, P., Murthy, C.S.R., Saha, S.K. (eds.) ICDCN 2008. LNCS, vol. 4904, pp. 286–291. Springer, Heidelberg (2008)
8. Bauderon, M., Gruner, S., Metivier, Y., Mosbah, M., Sellami, A.: Visualization of distributed algorithms based on graph relabelling systems. Electronic Notes in Theoretical Computer Science 50(3), 227–237 (2001)
9. Haddar, M.A., Kacem, A.H., Mosbah, M., Métivier, Y., Jmaiel, M.: Distributed algorithms for mobile agents. Technical report, Université Bordeaux1 (2007)

Belief-Based Stability in Non-transferable Utility Coalition Formation

Chi-Kong Chan and Ho-Fung Leung

The Chinese University of Hong Kong, Shatin, Hong Kong
{chanck,lhf}@cse.cuhk.edu.hk

Abstract. Coalition stability is an important concept in coalition formation. One common assumption in many stability criteria in non-transferable utility games is that the preference of each agent is publicly known so that a coalition is said to be stable if there is no objections by any sub-group of agents according to the publicly known preferences. However, in many applications including some software agent applications, this assumption is not true. Instead, agents are modeled as individuals with private belief and decisions are made according to those beliefs instead of common knowledge. Such belief based architectures have impacts on the coalition's stability which is not reflected in the current stability criteria. In this paper, we extend the classic stability concept of the core by proposing a new belief based stability criterion which we labeled the belief-based core.

Keywords: Coalition Formation, Stability, Non-transferable Utility Games.

1 Introduction

Intelligent agents often need to form coalitions in order to achieve tasks that cannot be done alone, or to maximize their own utility via mutually benefiting agreements. Various coalition stability solution concepts have been proposed in cooperative game theory [1][2]. So far, most of these stability concepts have a *common knowledge* assumption. However, this assumption is not realistic in some belief-based agents systems, where the agents' decisions are based on private beliefs instead of common knowledge.

In many applications, we are not able to assume such common knowledge preferences, and instead, agents often have to rely on their own internal belief during the coalition formation process. For instance, consider a typical propose-and-evaluate type mechanism (*e.g.*, [3][4]), where coalitions are formed in steps, and in each steps, agents are allowed to send proposals to others for forming new coalitions. Time constraints and other limitations (*e.g.*, problem size) often mean that, in practice, the agents can only make those proposals that have a reasonable chance of being accepted, according to the beliefs of the sending agent. Thus, during such a process, if a point is reached, such that each agent believes there is no better alternative solution than the current arrangement, for both himself and his partners, then the current solution should be regarded as stable, no matter whether those beliefs are true or not.

A. Ghose, G. Governatori, and R. Sadananda (Eds.): PRIMA 2007, LNAI 5044, pp. 422–427, 2009.

To model this situation, we are proposing a new stability criterion, the belief-based core that also takes into accounts the beliefs of the agents. We believe the proposed concepts can provide useful solution concepts for this emerging type of coalition games, which we call non-transferable utility games with private beliefs.

2 Motivating Examples

Example 1: *A belief-based dating game*

Consider an example dating game involving three agents, a, b, and c, who are considering to go to a movie. Their preferences are that each of them prefers to go in pairs (coalition of size 2) if possible. Failing that, their next choice is to go in a group of all three, and their last choice is to go alone. Furthermore, among the coalitions of size 2, agent a prefers to go with agent b, but agent b prefers to go with agent c, and finally, agent c prefers to go with agent a. In summary:

Agent a's preference: $(\{a,b\},\text{movie}) \succ_a (\{a,c\},\text{movie}) \succ_a (\{a,b,c\},\text{movie}) \succ_a (\{a\},\text{movie})$

Agent b's preference: $(\{b,c\},\text{movie}) \succ_b (\{a,b\},\text{movie}) \succ_b (\{a,b,c\},\text{movie}) \succ_b (\{b\},\text{movie})$

Agent c's preference: $(\{a,c\},\text{movie}) \succ_c (\{b,c\},\text{movie}) \succ_c (\{a,b,c\},\text{movie}) \succ_c (\{c\},\text{movie})$

Of course, such preferences are private information, not common knowledge. However, since the agents know each other and have interacted before, each of them also has a belief of the other two's preference:

Agent b's belief of a's preference: $(\{a,b,c\},\text{movie}) \succ_b^a (\{a,b\},\text{movie}) \succ_b^a (\{a,c\},\text{movie}) \succ_b^a (\{a\},\text{movie})$

Agent c's belief of a's preference: $(\{a,b,c\},\text{movie}) \succ_c^a (\{a,b\},\text{movie}) \succ_c^a (\{a,c\},\text{movie}) \succ_c^a (\{a\},\text{movie})$

Agent a's belief of b's preference: $(\{a,b,c\},\text{movie}) \succ_a^b (\{b,c\},\text{movie}) \succ_a^b (\{a,b\},\text{movie}) \succ_a^b (\{b\},\text{movie})$

Agent c's belief of b's preference: $(\{a,b,c\},\text{movie}) \succ_c^b (\{b,c\},\text{movie}) \succ_c^b (\{a,b\},\text{movie}) \succ_c^b (\{b\},\text{movie})$

Agent a's belief of c's preference: $(\{a,b,c\},\text{movie}) \succ_a^c (\{a,c\},\text{movie}) \succ_a^c (\{b,c\},\text{movie}) \succ_a^c (\{c\},\text{movie})$

Agent b's belief of c's preference: $(\{a,b,c\},\text{movie}) \succ_b^c (\{a,c\},\text{movie}) \succ_b^c (\{b,c\},\text{movie}) \succ_b^c (\{c\},\text{movie})$

In short, each of them wrongly believes that the others would prefer a coalition of size three to a coalition of size two. The game is denoted in Fig 1, where each node represents a possible coalition structure. For example, the top left node $\{(\{a\}, \text{movie}), (\{b\}, \text{movie}), (\{c\}, \text{movie})\}$ represents the outcome where each agent forms their own singleton coalition and go to the movie on his own, which is also the default outcome without any negotiation. Starting form the default outcome, the agents are allowed to make stepwise improvements by proposing alternative coalition structures. A proposal is considered successful if it is accepted by all the members of at least one coalition in the alternative outcome. In game theoretic terms, each successful proposal is called an *objection* to the original outcome. Objections are shown by both solid and dotted edges in Fig 1. The left most edge, for example, says that the outcome $\{(\{a\},\text{movie}), (\{b\},\text{movie}), (\{c\},\text{movie})\}$, is objected by the outcome $\{(\{a,b\},\text{movie}), (\{c\},\text{movie})\}$, which is because there exists a coalition $(\{a,b\}$ in this case) in the latter outcome such that each of its member prefers the latter to the former. As seen in Fig 1, each outcome is objected by at least one objection, so the core is empty in this case.

However, if the agents make the proposals according to their beliefs, that is, if each agent only proposes alternatives such that (i) he is better off in the alternative, and (ii) he thinks the proposal can be accepted by his new partners in the alternative outcome (perhaps in order to avoid the embarrassment of being rejected and to speed up the coalition formation process). Then there is actually a stable outcome for this game. Consider the dotted edge that leads from $\{(\{a, b, c\}, \text{movie})\}$ to $\{(\{a,b\},\text{movie}),(\{c\},\text{movie})\}$. This edge is no longer an objection in the belief-based game because each agent (wrongly) believes that the others would prefer a coalition of size 3 to a coalition of size 2. The same is true for the other two objections which are represented by dotted lines. So in this case, we can expect that the outcome $\{(\{a,\ b,\ c\},\text{movie})\}$, once reached, would in fact be stable.   ∎

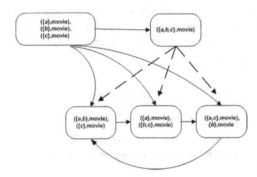

Fig. 1. A belief-based dating game

Example 2: *Randomized mechanisms*

In most distributed coalition formation mechanisms that employ propose-and-evaluate type protocols, one decision problem faced by the agents is what to propose to other agents. Naturally, one strategy for the agents is to only make proposals that are consistent with their belief regarding other agent's preferences.

Suppose that, in order to investigate the effect on stability caused by the above belief-based strategy, an analyst decides to implement and test the following two mechanisms as illustrated in Fig. 2. Both of them are randomized approaches for coalition formation games where the agents have difference preferences order regarding. the possible coalitional acts. The mechanisms, beginning with some initial coalitional action profile, are divided into rounds, and in each round, one of the agents is randomly selected. The randomly selected agent is then allowed make proposal for changes to the profile such that i) a new coalitional act is formed in the alternative profile, where the proposing agent is a member of the corresponding coalition ii) the proposing agent is better off in the new coalitional act than previously. If such an alternative is found, the agent then sends proposal messages to each member of the new coalition, and the new profile becomes effective if the proposal is accepted by each member of the new coalition. The recipient of such messages will then evaluate it, and accept it only if prefers the new coalitional act to the previous one that it was in. The mechanism terminates after a pre-defined number of rounds is reached (termination by time) or if no new proposals are accepted for a pre-defined consecutive number of rounds (termination by stagnant criterion). The different between the two mechanisms are that, in the first version (Random-N), the proposing agent makes proposal without considering his beliefs about the other member's preference (*i.e.,* he does not care whether his proposal is likely to be accepted or not, he just proposes it as long as he thinks it is beneficial to himself), while in the second version (Random-B), the agents carefully propose only the ones that are consistent with their beliefs (*i.e.*, each agent only proposes those proposals which he thinks will be accepted).

The analyst performs an experiment involving six agents. The agents' preferences regarding the candidate coalitional acts are randomly ordered. Each agent also has a belief of each other's preference, but subjected to a 25% error rate. The results are shown in figure 3 and 4. In Fig 3, we see the percentage of core-stable outcomes, out of 1000 repetition, achieved by both mechanisms after various numbers of rounds. The result seems to suggest that, according to the concept of the core, the belief-based version (Random-B) achieved larger number of stable results in the early rounds, but then loses out to the non-belief-based version (Random-N) in the long run. However, closer examination of the experiment data suggests that, in the long run, almost all games of Random-B terminates because no agent is able to make any more proposals. To see that, the analyst also measures the number of games that terminated by the stagnant criterion which is shown in Fig 4, which in fact suggests that the outcomes of Random-B should be at least as stable as Random-N in the long run, and outperforms it in the short run. Thus, this result is in contrast to the analysis as suggested by the core and we see that concepts like the core are insufficient in describing the stability of games such as this one.   ∎

What these two examples suggest is that the traditional stability criteria, which assume all preferences to be common knowledge, are inadequate in scenarios where private beliefs are important factors in determining the behavior of the agents. The reason is that we are facing a new type of games where the stability is based on private information instead of common knowledge. For these reasons, we are proposing a solution concept that is suitable for this new type of games.

3   Stability of NTU Games with Private Beliefs

The games depicted in examples 1 and 2 are examples of what we shall call non-transferable utility games with private beliefs (NTUPB games), which can be defined as follows. Again, let $N = \{1,...,n\}$ be a set of agents and let any subset $C \subseteq N$ be *called* a coalition. Each coalition is associated with a set of joint actions A_C. We define a *coalitional act* by a couple $x = (C,a)$, where $C \subseteq N$ *and* $a \in A_C$. The preference of each agent i is represented by a total ordered preference relation $\succ^i_i$ on the set of *coalitional act*, so that for any two coalitional acts $x_1 = (C_1,a_1)$ and $x_2 = (C_2,a_2)$, $i \in C_1 \cap C_2$, we have $x_1 \succ^i_i x_2$ if agent i prefers x_1 to x_2.

Unlike in traditional NTU games, however, the agents' preferences in NTUPB games are private information. So we also assume each agent i has a belief of other agent's preference relation $\succ^j_i$ for each agent $j \in N$, $j \neq i$. For instance, the notation $x_1 \succ^j_i x_2$ denotes "agent i believes that agent j prefers coalition act x_1 to x_2."

As before, we define the *coalitional action profile* (or *profile* for short) to be a profile S of coalition acts that corresponds to a coalition structure, *i.e.*, $S = \{(C_1,a_1), ... ,(C_k,a_k)\}$, and we use $C_i(S)$ to denote the coalition in S which the agent i is a member of, and $x(S)$ to denote its corresponding coalitional act.

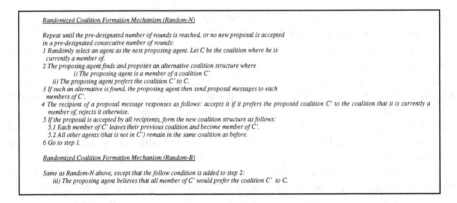

Randomized Coalition Formation Mechanism (Random-N)

Repeat until the pre-designated number of rounds is reached, or no new proposal is accepted in a pre-designated consecutive number of rounds:
1 Randomly select an agent as the next proposing agent. Let C be the coalition where he is currently a member of.
2 The proposing agent finds and proposes an alternative coalition structure where
  i) The proposing agent is a member of a coalition C'
  ii) The proposing agent prefers the coalition C' to C.
3 If such an alternative is found, the proposing agent then send proposal messages to each members of C'.
4 The recipient of a proposal message responses as follows: accepts it if it prefers the proposed coalition C' to the coalition that it is currently a member of, rejects it otherwise.
5 If the proposal is accepted by all recipients, form the new coalition structure as follows:
  5.1 Each member of C' leaves their previous coalition and become member of C'.
  5.2 All other agents (that is not in C') remain in the same coalition as before.
6 Go to step 1.

Randomized Coalition Formation Mechanism (Random-B)

Same as Random-N above, except that the follow condition is added to step 2:
  iii) The proposing agent believes that all member of C' would prefer the coalition C' to C.

Fig. 2. Two randomized coalition formation mechanism, one with belief consideration (Random-B), one without (Random-N)

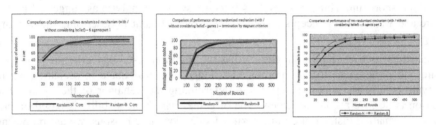

Fig. 3. (left). Comparison of Random-B and Random-N using stability concept of the core
Fig. 4. (middle). Comparison of Random-B and Random-N using the stagnant criterion
Fig. 5. (right). Comparison of Random-B and Random-N, according to the B-core

Before we define our main stability criterion, we first define two more concepts:

Definition 1 *(Domination Relation, dom)*. Given any two coalitional action profiles S_1 and S_2, we say S_1 is dominated by S_2 through a coalitional act $x = (C, a) \in S_2$, written $S_2 \operatorname{dom}_x S_1$, if , for each agent $i \in C$, we have $x \succ_i^i x_i(S_1)$.   ∎

Definition 2 *(Belief-based Domination Relation, B-dom)*. Given any two coalitional action profiles S_1 and S_2, we say S_1 is dominated by S_2 through a coalitional act $x = (C, a) \in S_2$ based on beliefs, written $S_2 \operatorname{B-dom}_x S_1$, if there exists an agent $j \in C$ such that, for each agent $k \in C, k \neq j$, we have $x \succ_j^k x_k(S_1)$ ∎

We are now ready to define our main stability concept:

Definition 3 *(B-core)*. A coalitional action profile $S = \{(C_1, a_1), \dots, (C_k, a_k)\}$ is in the B-core of an NTUPB game if there does not exist any alternative coalitional action profile S_2, so that we have both $S_2 \operatorname{dom}_x S$ and $S_2 \operatorname{B-dom}_x S$, for any $x \in S_2$.

Intuitively, we say a profile is in the B-core if there does not exist any alternative that satisfies the following two conditions: 1) every member of at least one coalition in the alternative prefers the alternative to the original profile and 2) at least one agent in that coalition correctly believes that point 1 is the case.

Example 3. Consider again the dating game example, the B-core consists of one coalitional action profiles, namely $\{(\{a, b, c\}, movie)\}$ ∎

Example 4. Consider again the two randomized mechanisms in example 2. This time, we measure the number of the percentage of stable outcomes according to the concept of B-core, out of 1000 repetitions, achieved after various numbers of rounds. The result, as shown in Fig. 5, suggests that belief-based version (Random-B) achieves larger number of stable results than the non-belief-based version (Random-N) throughout the execution of the mechanism, which is consistent with our previous observation in Fig 4. In fact, by comparing Fig 3 and Fig 5, we now know that Random-B tends to converge to a result in the B-core, whereas Random-N tends to converge to the traditional core. ∎

4 Conclusion

Most classical solution concepts in non-transferable utility coalitional game theory rely on a public information assumption. That is, they assume the agents' preferences to be publicly known. However this assumption is not practical in many software agent applications where intelligent agents have to rely on their private beliefs during decision making. In this paper, we propose a new type of game which we label non-transferable utility games with private belief, and provide a new concept for describing the stability of coalitions these games, namely, the B-core. By doing so, we are able to provide useful stability concepts for this new type of game which otherwise cannot be analyzed properly using the classic public information based approaches. We believe our model provide a useful tool in evaluating coalition formation algorithms for agent based cooperative games.

Reference

1. Gerber, A.: Coalition Formation in General NTU Games. Review of Economic Design 5, 149–175 (2000)
2. Vohra, R.: Incomplete information, Incentive Compatibility, and the Core. Journal of Economic Theory 86, 123–147 (1999)
3. Kraus, S., Shehory, O., Taase, G.: Coalition formation with uncertain heterogeneous information. In: Proceedings of the Third International Joint Conference on Autonomous Agents and Multiagent Systems, pp. 1–8 (2003)
4. Kraus, S., Shehory, O., Taase, G.: The advantages of compromising in coalition formation with incomplete information. In: Proceedings of the Third International Joint Conference on Autonomous Agents and Multiagent Systems, pp. 588–595 (2004)

Déjà Vu: Social Network Agents for Personal Impression Management

Chia-Chuan Hung, Yi-Ching Huang,
and Jane Yung-jen Hsu

Graduate Institute of Networking and Multimedia
Department of Computer Science and Information Engineering
National Taiwan University
r95944001@csie.ntu.edu.tw, r95045@csie.ntu.edu.tw,
yjhsu@csie.ntu.edu.tw

Abstract. As technology enabled new and faster modes of communication among people, it has become increasingly difficult to manage our social contacts effectively. Existing contact management tools lack the support for intelligent analysis of our social interactions. This paper introduces Déjà Vu, an intelligent system of social network agents for managing and analyzing personal social contacts over the web. Déjà Vu is designed to help users record and retrieve contact information by tagging via a simple user interface. In addition, it helps users acquire additional knowledge about their contacts through social computing and tagging analysis. Our preliminary study showed that tagging is a subjective behavior and the proposed social tagging mechanism can compensate for individual differences.

Keywords: multiagent, social network, social tagging.

1 Introduction

The Internet has transformed human communication. People nowadays communicate online with others through various ways, e.g. e-mail, instant message, or VoIP, etc. As a result, our social connections have become more complicated and difficult to manage. In daily life, our social interaction can be facilitated with knowledge about their names, interests, or topics in previous conversations. Given limited human memory, it can be difficult to recall a specific contact, especially when we are unfamiliar with him/her. A powerful contact management system may help record and retrieve contact information with ease.

Existing contact management tools often lack the support for analysis of social interactions. In this paper, we introduce *Déjà Vu*, an intelligent agent that analyzes a user's social contacts over the web.

Déjà Vu offers an intuitive user interface for recording personal impressions about our social contacts. According to Minsky's Society of Mind [1], people usually remember things or other people by associating meaningful words. Using Déjà Vu, a user can tag his/her friend with any description, and search for

A. Ghose, G. Governatori, and R. Sadananda (Eds.): PRIMA 2007, LNAI 5044, pp. 428–433, 2009.

specific contacts using descriptive words. For example, to remember the name of a person, where he/she comes from, what his/her interests are, and the recent topics of conversation, the user may tag "Janet" to be a "student" from "National Taiwan University", and Janet loves "sports", etc. During the next encounter, all relevant information about Janet may be retrieved from previous impressions.

Déjà Vu analyzes user-given tags and determines the relative importance using *social tagging analysis*. We apply semantic analysis to obtain the word meaning. Intuitively, a tag is relatively important for a particular person if he/she has been tagged with the same concept from most others. Similarly, a tag is important if relatively few contacts receive tags with the same concept.

The Déjà Vu agents are connected on a global social network. By exchanging tags annotated by users, agents can construct more objective impressions on a person. In addition, Déjà Vu recommends tags which are more frequently used by other users. We designed two experiments to verify that tagging is inherently subjective, and personal impressions can be improved by social tagging.

In this paper, we will start by briefly review some related work in next section. We present an overview of Déjà Vu multi-agent system in section 3. Next, section 4 describe social tagging more detail. In section 5, we verify the needs of social tagging in our experiments. Finally, we discuss some issues and make a conclusion in Section 6.

2   Related Work

There are many online websites that help people manage social contacts, such as MySpace[1] and Facebook[2]. They connect people together and exchange their experience by sharing profiles, photos, and etc. People can obtain their friends' information easily through these platforms.

On the other hand, constructing social networks automatically from various data is an important research topic. Several approaches have been proposed recently. For example, a social network can be extracted from mailing-list and web links [2]. A social network also can be mined from physical data, such as face-to-face social interactions [3].

In our approach, we use contact list to construct social network and apply tagging mechanism to manage social contacts. Users can describe a person as tags with any descriptive texts, which implies the impression on his contacts.

Ames and Naaman investigated the incentives for tagging [4]. They discover that personal and social purposes can emerge motivations for annotation. For personal purpose, we provide contact information management to help users recall memory of their friends. For social purpose, the common impression of people can be shared among the social network. Furthermore, we suggest people some recommended tags to reduce annotation loading. Users can select recommended tags by only one-click.

---

[1] http://www.myspace.com/
[2] http://www.facebook.com/

3   Social Network Agents

We utilize contact information to construct users' social network, and apply
social network analysis. A *social network* is an abstract representation of the
social relationships among individuals within a community. It is defined as a
directed graph where nodes are people and edges are relationships. Our system
Déjà Vu is designed as an intelligent system of social network agents. Each agent
represents a user and contains three modules: (1) contact management module;
(2) impression management module; (3) communication module. Each agent
collaborate with other agents and exchange information through communication
module. All agents could form a *global social network*. The following we describe
these modules respectively.

Contact Management Module. When a user adds contacts, contact management module would collect contact information and record the links between
user and his/her contacts. Communication module knows which person can be
accessed by these links. A directed contact link represents the familiarity from
user to a contact. The value of familiarity can be adjusted by user manually or
analyzed from email automatically. Frequent email communication indicates a
strong social relationship.

Impression Management Module. This module records tagging data in an
XML database. The tagging data includes all tags from user, self-description tags
from web mining, and common tags recommended from public. User given tags
would be analyzed and determined the tag weight by social tagging (in section 4).
Moreover, to reduce user's loading of tagging on a person, this module provides
recommended tags. They are obtained from: (1) contact's self-description on the
web. (2) common tags from social tagging.

Communication Module. Agents can share their tags and gather statistics
through communication module. Through query and response interaction, a
agent ask contacts' agents whether there exists a specific person on their personal
social network, and acquire common tags for this person.

4   Social Tagging

We apply tagging mechanism to manage contact information. People can describe their contacts as tags. These tags are attached to links between individuals on social network. Each individual has different opinions about a particular
person, thus we propose "*social tagging*" to integrate opinions in his/her social
circles. It collect and analyze tags from public to know the importance of each
tag to a specific person.

The main idea of social tagging is to calculate the rate of common tags on the
same contact, and also consider personal tagging frequency. We take the idea
of "*TFIDF*" (Term Frequency Inverse Document Frequency) [5] from document
analysis. As Figure 1 shows, suppose that user A tags his contact B with a tag
"x", we will check:

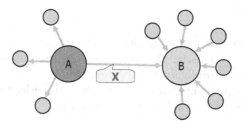

Fig. 1. Social tagging mechanism of Déjà Vu. Node A and B are two users in global social network, and user A has tagged a tag "x" on user B.

1. How many people have tagged B with "x"?
2. How many contacts have been tagged "x" by A?

The first measurement is similar to collaborative tagging, which is commonly used in social bookmarking tools, such as del.icio.us[3]. We calculate the tagging rate over all people's tagging data rather than an accumulative total. For everyone who knows B, it considers whether they have tags similar to "x" on B. If "x" has higher rate than a threshold, it will be added to the set of common tags of B. The second point is to measure the frequency that user A uses the tag "x". If A seldom uses "x" to tag on his/her social contacts, then we see the tag "x" has much importance when A tags this on B. According to these two measurements, we define tag importance as

$$w_{A \to B}(x) = \delta \times \frac{N_{tag\_B}}{N_{knows\_B}} + (1 - \delta) \times \frac{1}{N_{A\_tags}} \qquad (1)$$

where $w_{A \to B}(x)$ denote the importance of tag "x" which A tag B. N_{knows_B} is the total number of people who know B, and N_{tag_B} is the number of people who tag B with "x". N_{tag_B} means the frequency that A used tag "x". δ is an argument that can be adjusted. The value of $w_{A \to B}(x)$ becomes higher when B is tagged by many people with this tag, or very few contacts are tagged by A with this tag.

Semantic Analysis. Social tagging can be more efficiently and effectively with semantic analysis. We apply WordNet[6] and ConceptNet[7] to determine tag weights by concepts. WordNet is a lexical database which is based on the concept of synonym words. It is sufficiently structured and includes many lexical and semantic relation between words and *synsets*. ConceptNet is a freely available commonsense knowledge database. It provides a natural language processing toolkit which can support many practical textual-reasoning tasks. Given a particular word, ConceptNet returns a set of words with relevant concepts.

---

[3] http://del.icio.us/

5   Experiment

We design an experiment to justify the truth: tagging is a subjective activity. The experiment has two parts: One is to measure the differences between the common impression and individual perception, while we compare social tagging weight with people given importance; the other is to verify that differences not only exist on specific tag but generally on every tag.

Experiment Dataset.   Corresponding real world relationships, we construct a global social network consist of 19 people, then ask a group of 8 users to annotate (provide tags for) others. All these 8 users are on this social network, and they can choose some (at least 6) contacts to annotate. The average number of tags for each user to a contact is 7. Our social tagging mechanism automatically determines the tag weight for the user. The weight is assumed to be the tag importance of the user. Thus we want to know the distance between the user given importance and social tagging determined weight. According to his/her judgment, an experimenter gave a value (from 0.1 to 1.0) as importance for each tag. We apply our social tagging on each tag content, thus obtain tag weight for each tag.

Experiment Result.   After normalizing user grading preference, we average number of tag weight difference for each user, the result as Figure 2(a). It shows that it has a distance between user given importance (more subjective) and social tagging determined weight by common opinion (more objective). It is because experimenters may not familiar with or has incomplete knowledge about the tagging contact. Furthermore, for each tag, we calculate the average user difference as Figure 2(b) depict. It shows that common versus personal impression difference exists on every tag. Thus generally applying social tagging analysis on each tag is reasonable.

Tagging is a personal activity and it describe something or someone subjectively. Our social tagging mechanism can gather common impression to balance individual differences. Furthermore, it may help users know more about their contacts by recommending common tags.

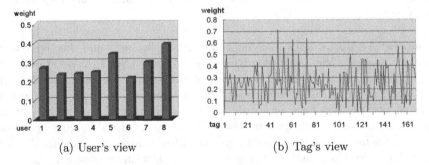

(a) User's view   (b) Tag's view

Fig. 2. These two images show the average tag weight difference between users given and social tagging calculated from user's view and tag's view respectively

6 Discussion and Conclusion

In our system, there are two issues that can be considered. First, we can include more factors, such as relation types (e.g. family, closed friends, business partners, etc.) and temporal change, to develop a more sophisticated function to upgrade performance and accuracy. Second, sharing all tags to everyone would face a privacy issues. One possible solution is to design two types of tag: public and private. An autonomic agent will determine tag type acording to some criteria, and then it only share users' public tags with anyone, preserving privacy.

Furthermore, FOAF[4] is a machine-readable ontology. It describes a person's profile and relations between him/her and other people. People only maintain their own foaf files. Based on foaf ontology, our designed agents could collect information to build social networks. Furthermore, people can share their comments or experience within social network. Applying social tagging computing on foaf ontology can help people know more about friends from others' viewpoints.

In this paper, we introduced our intelligent system Déjà Vu with multi-agents, which analyzes social contacts over the web, and provides a managing interface for users. It can help users retrieve contact information in an easy way. Furthermore, we apply social tagging and semantic analysis to analyze social connection and construct more complete contacts' information. Finally, we give an experiment to show that tagging is a subjective behavior and our proposed social tagging mechanism can compensate for individual difference.

References

1. Minsky, M.: Society of Mind. Simon and Schuster, New York (1986)
2. Culotta, A., Bekkerman, R., McCallum, A.: Extracting social networks and contact information from email and the web. In: Proceedings of the First Conference on Email and Anti-Spam (CEAS) (2004)
3. Gips, J., Pentland, A.: Mapping human networks. In: Proceedings of the IEEE International Conference on Pervasive Computing and Communications (2006)
4. Ames, M., Naaman, M.: Why we tag: Motivations for annotation in mobile and online media. In: Proceedings of the Computer/Human Interaction 2007 Conference (CHI 2007), San Jose, California, USA (2007)
5. Salton, G., Buckley, C.: Term weighting approaches in automatic text retrieval. Information Processing and Management 24(5), 513–523 (1988)
6. Miller, G.A., Beckwith, R., Fellbaum, C., Gross, D., Miller, K.J.: Introduction to wordnet: An on-line lexical database. International Journal of Lexicography 3(4), 235–244 (1990)
7. Liu, H., Singh, P.: Conceptnet: A practical commonsense reasoning toolkit. BT Technology Journal (2004)

---

[4] http://www.foaf-project.org/

Agent Dialogue as Partial Argumentation and Its Fixpoint Semantics

(Extended Abstract)

Takayoshi Suzuki[1] and Hajime Sawamura[2]

[1] Graduate School of Science and Technology, Niigata University
8050, 2-cho, Ikarashi, Nishi-ku, Niigata, Japan
takayosi@cs.ie.niigata-u.ac.jp
[2] Institute of Natural Science and Technology, Academic Assembly,
Niigata University
8050, 2-cho, Ikarashi, Nishi-ku, Niigata, Japan
sawamura@ie.niigata-u.ac.jp

Keywords: Argumentation, dialogue, agreement, fixpoint semantics.

1 Introduction

Dialogue and argumentation are basic components of MAS [10], and many models for them have been studied so far (e. g., [3], [8] for argumentation, and [6], [9], [5], [2] for dialogue systems). Those two are closely related to each other [13], and apparently the latter seems to be a special case of the former or one aspect of dialogue. However, it is not so clear how they are related to each other or simply how dialogue is different from argumentation. In this paper, we will consider an intrinsic relationship between them from a formal perspective.

Many argumentation models for agent-oriented computing have been developed so far [3][8][10]. Wherein, each agent is required to put forward its locutions in such a perfect form of argument that holds a logical consequence relation between a claim and reasons. Then every part of the argument are exposed to opponents and challenged by their counter-arguments (if any). This, in a sense, represents the way of argumentation in idealized situations. In our daily dialogue or argumentation, however, it happens very often that claims alone are spoken and their reasons are omitted often or added later if required. This might be said to be a sort of lazy computation in the world of dialogue and argumentation.

In Section 2, we describe a primitive but natural inter-agent dialogue model in which locutions such as inquiry, explanation, rebut, undercut, etc. are exchanged with each other in an imperfect or partial manner, where the explanation, for example, might not have the full reasons for the question. Such a dialogue turns out to get a benefit that it allows us to avoid excessive or unnecessary conflicts, increasing chances of agreement, and hence yields productive and rich outcomes for agents concerned. We, therefore, call such a type of dialogue agreement-oriented dialogue.

In Section 3, we are concerned with the semantics for such a type of dialogue. We then adopt the method of the fixed point semantics initiated by Dung [4]

A. Ghose, G. Governatori, and R. Sadananda (Eds.): PRIMA 2007, LNAI 5044, pp. 434–439, 2009.
© Springer-Verlag Berlin Heidelberg 2009

for our dialogue system. Theoretically and practically as well, it is an interesting and significant question if dialogue systems can have a formal semantics such as the fixpoint one since it is the well-known and established one, and the most successful one for computing in general.

2   Agreement-Oriented Dialogue

In this paper, we consider a dialogue whose participants consist of two agents, *proposer* and *partner* with their own knowledge in Extended Logic Programming (ELP) and the common argumentation framework [7].

2.1   Utterances

The utterances exchanged in the agent dialogue of this paper are *assertion*, *question*, and *explanation* that can be most seen in our daily dialogue. We view these as most primitive from the computational point of view as well as from the linguistic or communicational point.

Definition 1 (Assertion). *Let KB be a knowledge base of an agent, and Arg an argument in KB. The strong literals belonging to the conclusion of an argument Arg are called assertions in KB. The set of all the assertions in KB is represented by $Asts(KB)$.*

Definition 2 (Explanation). *Let a rule $L_0 \Leftarrow L_1 \wedge ... \wedge L_n \wedge not\ L_{n+1} \wedge ... \wedge not\ L_m$ be in KB. It is called an explanation of L_0 in KB if the strong literals $L_1, ..., and\ L_n$ are in $Ast(KB)$, the assertions in KB. $L_1, ..., and\ L_n$ are also called the assertions in the explanation, and the weak literals $not\ L_{n+1}, ..., and$ $not L_m$ are also called the assumptions in the explanation.*

Definition 3 (Question). *When L is a strong literal, $? - L$ is a question which asks for the explanation about L.*

In addition to these basic utterances, we introduce another kind of utterances that are intended to defeat assertions, which are to be uttered with arguments hidden behind.

Definition 4 (Rebut). *Let L_1 and L_2 be strong literals. Then, if $L_1 = \neg L_2$, L_1 rebuts L_2.*

Definition 5 (Undercut). *Let L_1 be a strong literal and $not\ L_2$ be a weak literal. Then, if $L_1 = L_2$, L_1 undercuts $not\ L_2$.*

Definition 6 (Attack). *Let L_1 and L_2 be literals. If L_1 rebuts L_2 or L_1 undercuts L_2, L_1 attacks L_2.*

Example 1. *Let $exl_1 = b \Leftarrow \neg a$ and $exl_2 = c \Leftarrow not\ a$ be explanations, and $ast = a$ an assertion. Then, the assertion ast rebuts the assertion $\neg a$ of exl_1, and undercuts the assumption $not\ a$ of exl_2.*

2.2   Agreement-Oriented Dialogue and Agreement

We define an agreement-oriented dialogue or simply an A-O dialogue as interacting relations between utterances described so far.

Definition 7 (Agreement-oriented dialogue (A-O dialogue). *Let α be a
proposer agent, β be a partner agent, $player_i$ be α or β, $utterance_i$ be an
utterance, ast_i be an assertionCask$_i$ be a questionCand exl_i be an explanation. An agreement-oriented dialogue is a finite sequence of moves $move_i =
(player_i, utterance_i)$ $(1 \le i \le n)$ such that*

1. *$player_i = \alpha$ iff i is an odd number, and $player_i = \beta$ iff i is an even
   number,*
2. *if $player_i = player_j$ $(i \ne j)$, $utterance_i \ne utterance_j$,*
3. *if $move_i = (player_i, ast_i)$ and $ast_i \notin Ast(KB_{player_{i+1}})$, then $move_{i+1} =
   (player_{i+1}, ask_{i+1})$,*
4. *the dialogue starts with $move_1 = (\alpha, ast_1)$, and then $move_2 = (\beta, ast_2)$,
   where ast_2 rebuts ast_1, or $move_2 = (\beta, ask_2)$,*
5. *if $move_i = (player_i, ast_i)$, where ast_i rebuts a strong literal asserted beforeC-
   then $move_{i+1} = (player_{i+1}, ask_{i+1})$,*
6. *if $move_i = (player_i, ast_i)$, where ast_i undercuts a weak literalCthen either $move_{i+1} = (player_{i+1}, ast_{i+1})$, where ast_{i+1} rebuts ast_i or $move_{i+1} =
   (player_{i+1}, ask_{i+1})$,*
7. *if $move_i = (player_i, ask_i)$, then $move_{i+1} = (player_{i+1}, exl_{i+1})$, and*
8. *if $move_i = (player_i, exl_i)$, where exl_i is not a fact, then either $move_{i+1} =
   (player_{i+1}, ast_{i+1})$, where ast_{i+1} attacks the antecedent of exl_iCor $move_{i+1}
   = (player_{i+1}, ask_{i+1})$.*

The condition 3 of Definition 7 above means that if an assertion put forward
is not included in the assertions in the hearer's knowledge base, questions are
always uttered (such a curiosity may be a kind of agent attitude or personality).
It should be noted that no moves are possible if exl_i in the condition 8 is a fact.

In what follows, we introduce a new notion of agreement for our dialogue,
which reflects an idea that we can understand things for the first time when we
can construct arguments on them.

Definition 8 (Agreement). *In an A-O dialogue, $player_{i+1}$ agrees (or attains
consensus or understanding) on the assertion by $player_i$ or the assertions in the
explanation by $player_i$ if $player_{i+1}$ can construct arguments on those assertions
under the knowledge base of $player_{i+1}$.*

Definition 9 (Agreement-oriented dialogue tree). *An agreement-oriented
dialogue treeisimply an A-O dialogue tree.jis a tree of dialogue moves such that*

1. *$move_1$ is the root, and*
2. *the children of $move_i$ are all $move_{i+1}$s that satisfy Definition 7, where*
   - *a child of $move_i$ is $move_{i+1} = (player_{i+1}, agreement\ ast_i)$ if $player_{i+1}$
     has agreed on the assertion ast_i or assertions in the explanation ast_i by
     $player_i$.*

- *a child of $move_i$ is $move_{i+1} = (player_{i+1}, disagreement\ ast_i)$ if $move_i$ $= (player_i, exl_i)$, where $exl_i = ast_i \Leftarrow$, i. e., the explanation exl_i of $player_i$ is a fact.*

We need definitions to specify the outcomes of A-O dialogues based on the A-O dialogue tree. The following notion is a counterpart of the notion of *dialectical justification* of arguments [7].

Definition 10 (Dialogical agreement). *Let Ast be an assertion put forward by a proposer. Ast is dialogically agreed if there exits an A-O dialogue tree whose root is Ast and every leaf of the A-O dialogue tree is a partner's utterance of the form (player, agreement ast).*

3 Fixpoint Semantics for the Agreement-Oriented Dialogue

We will consider the so-called fixpoint semantics for the agreement-oriented dialogue since it is the well-established and the most successful semantics for argumentation frameworks. It originates from Dung's influential work [4], and further has been applied to modified or extended argumentation frameworks so far by many authors (e. g., [7], [1], [12]).

First and foremost, we introduce the notion of 'agreeable' that is a counterpart of 'acceptable' in argumentation frameworks [3][8], and plays an essential role even in the development of dialogue semantics in what follows.

Definition 11 (Agreeable). *Let KB be a knowledge base, $Asts(KB)$ be a set of the assertions in a knowledge base KB (simply written as Asts), $S \subseteq Asts$, and $Ast \in Asts$. Then, Ast is agreeable with respect to S if and only if*

1. *if an assertion $\neg Ast \in Asts$ which attacks Ast exists, then both of the following conditions hold,*
   (a) *the antecedent of the explanation of $\neg Ast$ is attacked by the assertions in S [case of explanation for question $?\text{-}\neg Ast$].*
   (b) *all the assertions in the explanation of Ast are in S [case of question $? - Ast$].*
2. *if an assertion $\neg Ast$ which attacks Ast does not exist, all the assertions in the explanation of Ast are in S [case of explanation for question $? - Ast$].*

Definition 12 (Characteristic function). *Let S be a subset of Asts. F is a characteristic function such that*

- $F_{Asts} : Pow(Asts) \rightarrow Pow(Asts)$
- $F_{Asts}(S) = \{Ast \in Asts \mid Ast$ is agreeable with respect to $S\}$.

Proposition 1. *F_{Asts} is monotonic with respect to set inclusion.*

Proof. See [11] for the proof.

Since F_{Asts} is monotonic, it has a least fixpoint $\text{lfp}(F_{Asts})$, and can be constructed by the iterative method below. The following is a counterpart of the notion of 'justified' in argumentation frameworks [7].

Definition 13 (Agreed). *Ast is agreed iff the assertion Ast is in the least fixed-point of F_{Asts} (from now on, it is represented as JustAsts.) .*

Definition 14 (Finitary [4]). *Asts is finitary iff each assertion in Asts is attacked by at most a finite number of assertions in Asts.*

With these preliminaries, we can state the following proposition for our A-O dialogue, which allows for calculating the fixpoint in the iterative method.

Proposition 2. *We define a sequence of sets of assertions as follows:*

- $F^0 = Ast(KB_\alpha) \cap Ast(KB_\beta)$
- $F^{i+1} = F_{Ast(KB_\alpha)}(F^i)$ *(for $i \geq 1$).*

Then, if Asts is finitary, $\cup_{i=0}^{\infty}(F^i) = JustAsts$.

Proof. See [11] for the proof.

F^0 in Proposition 2 is unique and idiosyncratic in A-O dialogues, compared with its counterpart in argumentation frameworks [4][7], where it starts with $F_0 = \emptyset$ since justified arguments should be accrued from self-helped arguments. Our definition is based on the fact that in an A-O dialogue, when an assertion is dialogically agreed, the A-O dialogue tree must end with agreements of the partner at all the leaves of it.

For the agreement-oriented dialogue, we have the desirable properties: soundness and completeness, as in standard argumentation frameworks [4][7].

Theorem 1 (Soundness). *If an assertion is dialogically agreed, then it is agreed. See [11] for the proof.*

Theorem 2 (Completeness). *If an assertion is agreed, then it is dialogically agreed. See [11] for the proof.*

4   Conclusion and Future Work

We have presented a new type of dialogue system called agreement-oriented dialogue and its fixpoint semantics as a computationally feasible formal semantics for dialogues.

The contributions of the paper are summarized as follows:

- We characterized dialogue as partial argumentation, which we think is a natural aspect of human dialogues. We revealed a difference between dialogue and argumentation by exemplifying that there is an issue which is not justified with argumentation only but agreed in the context of a dialogue.

- We showed that the agreement-oriented dialogue system could have the fixpoint semantics, similarly to those for argumentation frameworks. This suggests a possibility of formal or mathematical semantics even for natural dialogues or conversations, together with the soundness and completeness theorems.

We will further develop the motto 'Dialogue as partial argumentation' to dialogues on uncertain issues under uncertain knowledge, using EALP (Extended Annotated Logic Programming) as a knowledge representation language and LMA (Logic of Multiple-Valued Argumentation) [12] as an argumentation framework for such an argument-based uncertain dialogue.

References

1. Amgoud, L., Cayrol, C.: A reasoning model based on the production of acceptable arguments. Annals of Mathematics and Artificial Intelligence 34, 197–215 (2002)
2. Amgoud, L., Maudet, N., Parsons, S.: Modeling dialogues using argumentation. In: ICMAS, pp. 31–38 (2000)
3. Chesñevar, C.I., Maguitman, G., Loui, R.P.: Logical models of argument. ACM Computing Surveys 32, 337–383 (2000)
4. Dung, P.M.: On the acceptability of arguments and its fundamental role in non-monotonic reasoning, logic programming and n-person games. Artificial Intelligence 77, 321–358 (1995)
5. McBurney, P., Parsons, S.: Risk agoras: Dialectical argumentation for scientific reasoning. In: Proceedings of the 16th Conference on Uncertainty in Artificial Intelligence (UAI 2000), pp. 371–379 (2000)
6. Parsons, S., Wooldridge, M., Amgoud, L.: Properties and complexity of some formal inter-agent dialogues. J. Logic Computat 13(3) (2003)
7. Prakken, H., Sartor, G.: Argument-based extended logic programming with defeasible priorities. J. of Applied Non-Classical Logics 7, 25–75 (1997)
8. Prakken, H., Vreeswijk, G.: Logical systems for defeasible argumentation. In: Gabbay, D., Guenther, F. (eds.) Handbook of Philosophical Logic, pp. 219–318. Kluwer, Dordrecht (2002)
9. Reed, C.: Dialogue frames in agent communication. In: Proceedings of the 3rd International Conference on Multi Agent Systems (ICMAS 1998), pp. 246–253 (1998)
10. Reed, C., Norman, T.J. (eds.): Argumentation Machines. Kluwer Academic Publishers, Dordrecht (2004)
11. Suzuki, T.: Agent dialogue as partial argumentation and its fixpoint semantics. Master Thesis, Niigata University (2007) (in Japanese)
12. Takahashi, T., Sawamura, H.: A logic of multiple-valued argumentation. In: Proceedings of the Third International Joint Conference on Autono mous Agents and Multi Agent Systems (AAMAS 2004), pp. 800–807. ACM, New York (2005)
13. Walton, D.: The New Dialectic: Conversational Contexts of Argument. Univ. of Toronto Press (1998)

Developing Knowledge Models for Multi-agent Mediator Systems

Cheah Wai Shiang and Leon Sterling

Department of Computer Science and Software Engineering
The Univeristy of Melbourne, 111 Barry Street, Carlton, Victoria 3053, Australia
{w.cheah@pgrad,leonss@}unimelb.edu.au

Abstract. Developing knowledge models for multi agent system is currently ad-hoc. Neither guidelines nor mechanisms nor techniques exist for developing the agent knowledge. This paper presents a conceptual architecture and implementation for a knowledge model for a class of multi-agent mediator systems. They arise from the prototyping of a multi agent system finding an adviser for an international student at an Australian University. The knowledge model development process is based on the quality criteria for knowledge based system of applicability and maintainability, as well as issues required by agents in dealing with knowledge. The process components are described and form the requirements for an agent developer in dealing with the development of agent knowledge from scratch.

Keywords: knowledge model, mediator, architecture.

1 Introduction and Motivation

Multi-agent systems constitute an important and growing current technology. While experience in developing multi-agent systems has grown, we are still a long way from having a well-defined methodology for developing them [1]. One of the least understood aspects of developing multi-agent systems is building the knowledge. Multi-agent systems need knowledge to work effectively. Over the past few years it has been realized that it is very difficult to get a single agreed ontology. Research has been devoted to mapping between existing ontologies. Ontology mapping is also very difficult. It is unclear how to divide effort between mapping ontologies and building from scratch. The research described in this paper arose from considering the task of building a multi-agent system for choosing an appropriate adviser for a graduate student. There is a need for a substantial amount of knowledge, including research areas, admission processes, and professional activities, usually described differently at different institutions. None of the existing ontology-related tools met our needs to build the knowledge for the multi-agent graduate adviser finder based on our early discussion. Neither methodology nor mechanism nor techniques existed for developing knowledge for agent system [7]. As a result, the contribution of this paper is to investigate requirements needed to develop agent knowledge models through prototyping. This paper describes the development process that has emerged from our prototyping

A. Ghose, G. Governatori, and R. Sadananda (Eds.): PRIMA 2007, LNAI 5044, pp. 440–445, 2009.
© Springer-Verlag Berlin Heidelberg 2009

of a graduate student adviser multi-agent system. A key issue is reconciling different descriptions of academics and their interests and activities at a range of universities. The process components have been described and will form a requirement to agent developers in dealing with development of agent knowledge from scratch. We believe that what we have learned will be applicable to similar systems where mediation is needed to match people such as an adviser to a student.

We observe from the literature that agent knowledge can be derived from multiple sources and multiple parties[8]; agent knowledge is user centric[5]; agent knowledge is diverse[9]; agent knowledge consists of two forms (e.g. what the agent understands and what the agent knows)[11] and agent knowledge must be accessible[10]. In this research, we model the knowledge development process explicitly based on these features. Additionally the knowledge model development process is based on quality criteria for knowledge based system (e.g. applicability and maintainability [12]). We believe that knowledge models need to be treated according to the software engineering paradigm. The knowledge model can be applied and behaves as expected and any changes and updates of the knowledge model can be easily traced.

Our research builds on lightweight methods for developing agent knowledge models (e.g. from EXPLODE [3]); having tabular l storage in managing the conceptualization of domain knowledge from EXPLODE (e.g. feature from Methontology); application centric in which the knowledge model will be based on the users' criteria [6]; having reconciliation consideration in knowledge model development and deployment by taking the benefit of distributed knowledge sources [8] and diversity management and finally considering the deployment issues of knowledge model to agent system [13]. This paper is organized as follows: Section 2 briefly describes our proposed knowledge model conceptual architecture. Section 3 discusses the knowledge components in detail, while Section 4 describes the practical aspects of the knowledge model. Section 5 concludes the paper.

2   A Knowledge Model Process Conceptual Architecture

2.1   Overview of Knowledge Model Development Life Cycle

Figure 1 shows our conceptual architecture for the knowledge model. The knowledge model development process comprises five sections. They are knowledge consensus within knowledge engineering; knowledge model control; knowledge model repository; knowledge model structure; and utilization of agent knowledge model within agent operation. The core of the development process is constructing a well-formed software-based agent knowledge model. The agent knowledge model is constructed through cyclic process, from a simple knowledge structure to a complete knowledge model representation of concepts, sub-concepts, attributes and relationship between a class and each of the individuals that comprise it. This operation involves iterative process from individual knowledge repository, knowledge consensus and agent knowledge repository in conceptualization of agent knowledge model, formation of agent knowledge model and elaboration of the agent knowledge model. The agent knowledge model is software-based in which the knowledge model can use, reuse,

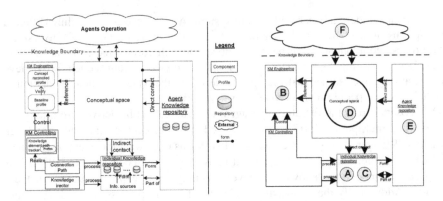

Fig. 1. Knowledge model process conceptual architecture

construct, re-construct, integrate, maintain and plug into multi-agent software application. The development process of knowledge model is labeled accordingly (e.g. A-F) as shown in Figure 1 right. In stage A, the process involves individual explicit knowledge interpretation and conversion. Stage B involves consensus logging and baseline hosting. The activities required in consensus logging are pattern extraction, establish reconciled concept, add reconciled concept as instance, verification and refinement. Stage C involves individual knowledge refinement based on the outcome from Stage B. It involves the process to embed a common element into the individual knowledge repository. Stage D is the agent knowledge model structure or conceptual space and it defines "what an agent can understand". Stage E is a process to form "what an agent knows" through knowledge model instantiation. The process involves forming the instances for each of the concepts within the knowledge model through connection path. Finally, stage F indicates how the knowledge model is used by an agent during the operation. Middleware is proposed for knowledge model utilization.

3   Knowledge Component Features

The KM controlling section is a core execution component during the development of the agent knowledge model. It consists of three sub-components. They are the knowledge director, knowledge path tracker and connection path. *Knowledge director* is designed based on the analysis results from knowledge sources through the user model, and the contextual knowledge derived from the task at hand. The input to the knowledge director is the explicit knowledge (e.g. information on web) and the output is an individual knowledge repository represented in XML. To form an individual knowledge repository, several activities are required by the knowledge director. These are preprocessing, concept extraction, concept instantiation and global integration. The preprocessing is a process that deals with conversion of individual explicit knowledge. Concept extraction is a preliminary stage to form an individual knowledge repository after preprocessing. The concept instantiation component is looking for instances that fall outside the concepts. The global integration is to position the concepts within a standard ontology. *Knowledge path tracker* serves as a connection point between KM engineering and knowledge repository sections. It reacts based on two profiles, a K-distribution profile and a C-profile. The C-profile or contributor profile records individuals that contribute towards a particular concept within a particular community. Meanwhile, the K-distribution profile or knowledge distribution profile indicates a community that contribute towards a particular concept or knowledge point that can be looked at before further processing. *Connection path* (CP) is a component that will coordinate concepts in the reconciled profile, baseline profile and individual knowledge repository. The CP component will realize the tracker component to process individual knowledge repository in order to form agent knowledge repository. Since the agent knowledge repository captures what others people know to enrich its knowledge model, the aim of the CP component is exploring knowledge items that exist among the individual knowledge repositories.

KM engineering will handle the diversity among the concepts and instances derived from the knowledge director. It consists of two profiles. The *concepts reconciled profile* enables an agent to know what other people said for a particular concept through collection of reconciliation list. Pattern matching has been used to reconcile the diverse concepts and instances in individual knowledge repositories. The *baseline profile* indicates general concepts that must exist within an individual knowledge repository and also influence the refinement of knowledge model. The baseline profile is derived from motivation analysis. It provides a platform to position the concepts that need to be taken into account but with no explicit indication among individuals. At the end of process execution, the elements within the baseline profile will be integrated into individual knowledge repository, agent knowledge model and agent knowledge repository.

Knowledge model repository section provides storage at the knowledge level. There are individual knowledge repositories, agent knowledge repository and agent knowledge model structure or conceptual space. The *individual knowledge repository* consists of knowledge for a particular individual. In this project, we have embedded the knowledge among the different individual into dedicated XML files. Since the individual is located within a community, the group of individuals that have the same location will form a larger repository, folder. The *agent knowledge model structure* consists of concept template for agents. The *agent knowledge repository* is the outcome from the instantiation of KM structure.

Two scenarios are described to simulate the utilization of knowledge model within multi agent system, multi agent interaction and human agent interaction. In multi agent interaction, a personal information agent (PIA) has been dedicated to perform the task of finding a potential advisor. The PIA uses motivation knowledge derived through motivation analysis. Once activated, by default the PIA would have complete knowledge for performing the task required when it entered a working environment. Logically, the PIA will inherit the knowledge model in a particular working environment. However, the knowledge it has is just a knowledge shell without knowing instances. The inheritance mode depends on what role an agent plays in the environment. From client and service aspect, a client agent will inherit with KM without instance. Meanwhile, a service provider will inherit with complete KM and instances. The overall execution of the agents are traversing the agent knowledge model, obtaining annotation to dedicated agent knowledge repository, comparing the returned knowledge items, ranking it and presenting to user or providing response to PIA. In human-agent interaction, the operation is still the same but more dynamic and complex agent development (e.g. degree of autonomy) is introduced.

4 Experiment

To illustrate the feasibility of our approach, a preliminary case study to find a potential advisor through a multi-agent mediator system has been developed. A sample of 60 data sets within 6 Australia universities was used in our case study. The knowledge model development process works with the data set. The result indicates the information obtained through each search within a university community from the outcome of knowledge modeling. Several motivation scripts had been obtained and used to exercise the utilization of knowledge model in the multi-agent system based on the requirements when choosing a potential supervisor [4]. To get an overall recommendation, we used a heuristic approach in which the highest-ranked information is considered most significant. The overall execution of the agents are traversing the agent knowledge model based on the motivation element within the motivation script; checking the motivation element within the reconciliation list; obtaining annotation to dedicated agent knowledge repository, comparing the returned knowledge items, ranking it and presenting to user.

5 Conclusion

We have presented a new process for developing a knowledge model for multi-agent systems and treating the knowledge model as a software artifact within overall development. This process can become the requirement for agent developer in order to develop agent knowledge from scratch. The conceptual architecture has extracted features from ontology methodologies [5] in supporting knowledge engineering tasks and supporting the ontology system. Through this project, we realized that our proposed knowledge model conceptual architecture consists of similar components as indicated in [5], an ontology maintenance subsystem. From [6], we interpret that our proposed KM engineering is hosting the criteria and issues editor in forming and refining agent knowledge structure; KM controlling is like a search engine to extract the most important concepts based on a given set of criteria; individual and agent knowledge repository is hosting the selected concepts and the agent knowledge model is a platform or acts as ontology editor enabling knowledge construction and refinement. The knowledge development process proceeds in a "spiral" way or cyclic process [2, 3].

The agent understand the concepts involved through traversing the agent knowledge structure. the meaning of the concept can be realized through its constituent instance. The agent knowledge model is software-based so that it can be used, reused, constructed, re-constructed, integrated, maintained and plugged into multi-agent systems. Finally, we have explicitly modeled the agent knowledge and provided a platform to manage it. We have achieved the applicability and maintainability of agent knowledge model. The knowledge model is flexible to use by agents without modifying the underlying multi agent system operation. Indirectly, it will reduce the development time and costs. In future, we will work toward proposing software methodology for the agent knowledge model.

Acknowledgements. This research has been supported by Australian Research Council Linkage grant LP0454027 and a Malaysian government scholarship to the first author.

References

1. Luck, M., McBurney, P., Shehory, O., Willmott, S.: Agent Techonology: Computing as Interaction: A Roadmap for Agent-Based Computing, Agentlink (2005)
2. Schreiber, G., Akkermans, H., Anjewierden, A., Hoog, R., Shadbolt, N., Velde, W., Wielinga, B.: Knowledge engineering and management,The CommonKADS methodology. MIT Press, Cambridge (2000)
3. Hristozova, M., Sterling, L.: An eXtreme method for developing lightweight ontologies. In: Workshop on Ontologies in Agent Systems, 1st International Joint Conference on Autonomous Agents and Multi-Agent System (2002)
4. Indgreen, A., Palmer, R., Vanhamme, J., Beverland, M.: Finding and choosing a supervisor. Journal of Marketing Review (2002)
5. Konstantinos Kotis, G.A.: Human-centered ontology engineering: The HCOME. International Journal of Knowledge and information system (KAIS), 109–131 (2006)
6. Chiu, D.K.W., Poon, J.K.M., Lam, W.C.: How ontologies can help in an e-marketplace. In: 13th European Conference on Information systems (2005)
7. Pinto, H.S., Martins, J.P.: Ontologies: How can they be built? Journal of Knoweldge and information system (2004)
8. Liu, D.R., Wu, I.C., Yang, K.S.: Task-based K-support system: disseminating and sharing task-relevant knowledge. Journal of expert systems with applications (2005)
9. Lister, K., Sterling, L., Taveter, K.: Reconciling Ontological Differences by Assistant Agents. In: Proceedings of the Fifth International Joint Conference on Autonomous Agents and Multiagent Systems, Future University, Hakodate, Japan (2006)
10. Preist, C.: Agent mediated electronic commerce research at Hewlett Packard Labs. Journal of SIGecom Exchange, 18–28 (2001)
11. Annamalai, M., Sterling, L.: Guidelines for constructing reusable domain ontologies. In: AAMAS 2003 Workshop on Ontologies in Agent Systems, Melbourne, Australia (2003)
12. Benjamins, R., Fensel, D., Pierret-Golbreich, C., Motta, E., Studer, R., Wielinga, B., Rousset, M.C.: Making knowledge engineering technology work. In: Proc. 9th Int. Conf. on Software Engineering and Knowledge Engineering (SEKE), Madrid, Spain (1997)
13. Corcho, O., Fernandez-Lopez, M., Gomez-Perez, A.: Methodologies, tools and languages for building ontologies. Where is the meeting point? Journal of Data and Knowledge Engineering 46(1), 41–64 (2003)

A Game Theoretic Approach for Deploying Intrusion Detection Agent

Yi-Ming Chen[1], Dachrahn Wu[2], and Cheng-Kuang Wu[1]

[1] Department of Information Management, National Central University
[2] Department of Economics, National Central University, Chung-Li 320, Taiwan
{cym,drwu}@mgt.ncu.edu.tw, 93443002@cc.ncu.edu.tw

Abstract. The proposed framework applies two game theoretic models for economic deployment of intrusion detection system (IDS). The first scheme models and analyzes the interaction behaviors of between an attacker and intrusion detection agent within a non-cooperative game, and then the security risk value is derived from the mixed strategy Nash equilibrium. The second scheme uses the security risk value to compute the Shapley value of intrusion detection agent under the various threat levels. Therefore, the fair agent allocation creates a minimum set of IDS deployment costs. Numerical examples show that the network administrator can quantitatively evaluate the security risk of each intrusion detection agent and easily select the most effective IDS agent deployment to meet the various threat levels.

Keywords: Agent deployment, Nash equilibrium, Shapley value, threat levels.

1 Introduction

To meet the threat of network attacks, enterprise network have built the security operation center of IDS to control and analyze intrusion events. For example, the Symantec threat advisory system provides recommended protective measures, according to the threat level, that aids the system administrator to prevent, prepare for, mitigate, and respond to network attacks. However, this system lacks specific measures for rational decision-making, and do not apply mathematical model to capture the interaction between attacker and defender.

Game theoretic tools provide analytical techniques of use in many areas of research where multi-agents compete and interact with each other in a system [2]. In most multi-agent interaction, the overall outcomes all depend on the choices made by all self-interested agents and make the choice that optimizes its outcome [7]. Therefore, we present the game theoretic framework for deploying alarm multi-agent using game theory (DAMAG), which analyze the detected threats and integrate with the existing IDS.

Our study is more closely related to the model proposed by Alpcan et al [1]. The proposed framework consists of two game theoretic models. The first scheme models the interaction process between the network attacker and the IDS agent as a

A. Ghose, G. Governatori, and R. Sadananda (Eds.): PRIMA 2007, LNAI 5044, pp. 446–451, 2009.

two-person strategy, that is a non-cooperative finite game. The proposed payoff functions utilize the security risk measures for two players. After this, the mixed strategy Nash equilibrium (NE) derived from these functions and assigned as a unique security risk value (SRV) for the agent. Then with the second scheme a cooperative IDS agent game is constructed and the powerful index the Shapley value [5] applied to calculate the marginal contribution between agent and mutually agreeable division of cost for IDS deployment. IDS agents are grouped into coalition groups by the various threat levels so as to provide fair and optimal IDS deployment. Numerical examples of the proposed framework compute the agents' SRV and verify that the computation of Shapley value does indeed obtain the quantitative value for decision and analysis of the IDS.

2 DAMAG Framework

2.1 The Security Risk Game

The security risk is measured by the expected cost of pay, or utilities from the security events multiple security event rates [8]. We define the security risk of IDS agent is its expected payoff which is measured from the rate of security events (i.e, attacker's breaches and agent's moves) multiple the cost per events. The following paragraphs discuss two players of this game.

Attacker. The user may become an attacker because of curiosity, to achieve self-respect or peer approval, etc. The attacker pays the cost, $-b_2$, which mean he gains a profit if intrusion is undetected. We define scattered attacks as penetration past the IDS agent; they can propagate malicious codes rapidly and widely. In contrast, the pure attack is a single event, which do not propagate viruses or malicious codes. When the attacker starts the propagation attack on the ith agent, its propagation rate is l_i. Moreover, the ease of user access to the network is related to network attacks. The f_i denotes the network bandwidth of usage rate for the ith agent residing at the network host (to demonstrate the influence between attacker and agent). We assume that when f_i increases, the probability of attack increases. On the other hand, f_i decreases, the probability of attack decreases. The propagation attack presents ëf$_i$ is multiple of pure attack f_i.

IDS agent. The set of IDS agents is denoted as $I = \{1,\ldots, i\}$. The parameter i refers to an agent residing at the IDS agent host I. The goal of the IDS agent, after investigation of the user's transaction, is to classify the user as a normal user or an attacker. Keromytis [3] proposed using an SOS architecture that requires the agent to frequently reconfigure the secure overlay network in order to prevent the attack. Thus m_i denotes the migration rate (mobility) of agent n_i at the host where the IDS agent moves to another host. The agent detection scheme commonly shows two types of errors: the classification of an attacker as a normal user (false negative or missing attack) and the classification of a normal user as an attacker (false positive or false alarm). For each agent's n_i security measures parameters there is an intrusion detection rate p_d, false negative rate $(1-p_d)$ and false alarm rate p_f. The cost value $-c_1$ is the gain of the IDS agent for the detecting of an attack while c_2 and c_3 are the costs paid by the IDS agent for false alarms and false negative.

The u_1 denotes the strategy of pure attack by the attacker with a probability of r_1, the u_2 denotes the strategy of propagation attack with a probability of r_2, and the u_3 denotes that the attacker does nothing and the probability is $1-r_1-r_2$. The d_1 denotes the strategy of the IDS agent which consists of detecting the attack and the alarm response. The d_2 denotes the strategy of the IDS agent, to do nothing following the attack. In addition, let q and $1-q$ be the probability of detection d_1 and no detection d_2, by the agent, respectively. Therefore, the normal form of the two player matrix game is shown in Table 1. The payoff matrix is expanded by adding a low and a column that represents a mixed strategy. The mixed strategy of the agent is called q-mix and that of the attacker is called r-mix [2].

Table 1. A payoff matrix for security game

Attack	IDS Agent		
	d_1	d_2	q-mix
u_1	$b_1 f_i, -c_1(1+p_d+m_i)$	$-b_2 f_i, c_3(1+(1-p_d))$	$b_1 f_i q - b_2 f_i (1-q)$
u_2	$b_1(1+\lambda f_i+l_i),$ $-c_1(1+p_d+l_i+m_i)$	$-b_2(1+\lambda f_i+l_i),$ $c_3(1+l_i+(1-p_d))$	$b_1(1+\lambda f_i+l_i)q$ $-b_2(1+\lambda f_i+l_i)(1-q)$
u_3	$0, c_2(1+p_f+m_i)$	$0, 0$	0
r-mix	$-c_1(1+p_d+m_i)r_1$ $-c_1(1+p_d+l_i+m_i)r_2$ $+c_2(1+p_f+m_i)(1-r_1-r_2)$	$c_3(1+(1-p_d))r_1$ $+c_3(1+l_i+(1-p_d))r_2$	

We assume the security risk game has no pure strategy equilibrium, so the analysis is extended by considering mixed strategies with the player probability distribution in the space of their pure strategies. The strategy pair (r^*, q^*) is said to constitute a noncooperative mixed NE solution to the matrix game. According to 3×2 matrix payoff functions described, the payoff for the each mixed strategy equal to each other. The mixed NE expressions can be written as:

$$b_1 f_i q - b_2 f_i(1-q) = b_1(1+\lambda f_i+l_i)q + b_2(1+\lambda f_i+l_i)(1-q) = 0, -c_1(1+p_d+m_i)r_1 - c_1(1+p_d+l_i+m_i)r_2 + c_2(1+p_f+m_i)(1-r_1-r_2) = c_3(1+(1-p_d))r_1 + c_3(1+l_i+(1-p_d))r_2. \tag{1}$$

where $0 \leq r_1, r_2, q \leq 1$. The equation (1) sovle the mixed strategy Nash equilibrium pair (r^*, q^*) which is the optimal attacking and detection. The prevent-exploitation method [2] finds r^* and q^* from these strategies' intersections.

We assume the game only exist a mixed NE pair (r^*, q^*) which is an optimal strategy. The mixed NE of the probability vector $r^*_i = \{r^*(u_1), r^*(u_2), r^*(u_3)\}$ with actions $\{u_1, u_2, u_3\}$ of the attacker and the vector $q^* = \{q^*(d_1), q^*(d_2)\}$ with actions $\{d_1, d_2\}$ of the IDS agent. Let v_i be the ith agent's SRV, which considers detection and attack probabilities. It is given by Equation (2).

$$v_i = \frac{r^*_i(u_1) + r^*_i(u_2)}{r^*_i(u_3)} + \frac{q^*_i(d_1)}{q^*_i(d_2)} \quad i \in N \tag{2}$$

2.2 The Deployment Game

In this section, we liken the interaction of IDS agent to the playing of a cooperative game in the IDS overlay network. A fair and efficient method is needed for deciding the number of and prioritizing the agents to be deployed for detection. The Shapley value is a powerful index for cost allocation [5]. The cooperative game provides a suitable model for the design and analysis of detection agent deployment, and it is shown that the famous Shapley value rule satisfies many nice fairness properties [9].

We define $y: V \rightarrow R^{+}$ as a one-to-one function by assigning a positive real number to each element of v and $y(0) = 0$, $V = \{v_1, v_2,...,v_j\}$, $j\in n$.. The security of IDS deployment is based on the concept of the threat level, h. The security threat levels, $H =\{h_1,..., h_H\}$, where $0< k_1 <k_2 < ... < k_H$ is the corresponding threshold values. In Equation (3), given the agent's output vector v, the security level, L, of the IDS is equal to h_j, if the sum of the SRVs of the agents is greater than or equal to k_j:

$$L = \begin{cases} h_1 & \text{if } \sum_{i=1}^{N} y(v_i) \geq k_1 \\ h_j & \text{if } \sum_{i=1}^{N} y(v_i) \geq k_j \\ h_{j+1} & \text{if } \sum_{i=1}^{N} y(v_i) \geq k_{j+1} \\ h_H & \text{if } \sum_{i=1}^{N} y(v_i) \geq k_H \end{cases}$$

(3)

where $k_j=2k_1, k_{j+1}=3k_1,..., k_H=Hk_1$ and $k_1 = \left(\dfrac{v_{Max} - v_{Mini}}{H+1} \right).$ (4)

The agents can be grouped into different security levels according to the average value of the interval k_1 of the threshold. It is divided by $H+1$ security threat levels from maximum SRV v_{Max} to minimum v_{Mini}.

The SRV of the agent can be modeled as an N-person game with $X = \{1, 2,..., N\}$, which includes the set of players (i.e., agent) and each subset $V \subset N$, and where $v_j \neq 0$ $\forall_j \in V$ is called a coalition [2], [6]. The coalition of X agent groups in the kth threshold of the threat level, and each subset of X (coalition), represent the observed threat pattern for different threat levels H. The aggregate value of the coalition is defined as the sum of the SRVs of the agent, $y(C) = \sum_{i \in C} y(v_i)$, and is called a coalition function. The different priorities for agent deployment are derived from the various thresholds. According to intrusion threat for each IDS host with respect to others and the effect of the threshold values on various threat levels, Shapley value represents the relative importance of each agent. Let $y(C) = \sum_{i \in C} y(v_i)$, $v_i \in V$, $C \subset X$ be the value of the coalition C with cardinality c. The Shapley value of the ith element of the agent vector is defined by

$$S(i) := \sum_{\substack{C \subset X \\ i \in C}} \frac{(c-1)!(n-c)!}{n!} [y(C) - y(C - \{i\})].$$

(5)

$$\Rightarrow S(i) := \sum_{C' \subset X} \frac{(c-1)!(n-c)!}{n!}. \tag{6}$$

Equation (5) can be simplified to Equation (6) because the term $y(C)\text{-}y(C\text{-}\{i\})$ will always have a value of 0 or 1, taking the value 1 whenever C' is a winning coalition but not $C\text{-}\{i\}$ [6]. Hence, Shapley value $S(i)$ where C' denotes the winning coalitions with $\sum_{i\in C'} y(v_i) \geq k_j$. The Shapley value of the ith agent output indicates the relative SRV for the various thresholds (i.e, threat levels) so as to provide a computation for choosing a reasonable agent for IDS deployment.

3   Numerical Examples

Twenty hypothetical numbers of parameters is given to model the matrix, and randomly generate simulation sets of security measures for agents and attackers. Then, we apply the GAMBIT [4] and Equation (2) to calculate twenty agent's SRVs from the numerical examples and create one Nash equilibrium by logit tracing in extensive game. Second, the SRV of each IDS agent is utilized for computing each agent's Shapley value. In this paper, four threat levels are designed for the distributed IDS (i.e., green, yellow, orange and red). We adopt the Matlab to find the Shapley value of agents for the four threat levels. Then simulations create four agent deployment sets for a secure IDS network.

Figure 1(a) shows the sequence of twenty agent SRV vector outputs, $V = [v_{20}, v_{19}, v_{10}, v_9, v_{18}, v_7, v_8, v_{16}, v_{15}, v_6, v_5, v_4, v_{14}, v_3, v_2, v_{12}, v_{17}, v_1, v_{11}, v_{13}] = [0.252, 0.38, 0.96, 1.009, 1.093, 1.264, 1.283, 1.461, 1.497, 1.589, 1.685, 2.11, 2.538, 2.925, 4.66, 5.799, 10.675, 10.913, 20.367, 50.638]$. According to the SRV vector output, we use Equation (4) to obtain four thresholds $k_{green} = 10.08$, $k_{yellow} = 20.15$, $k_{orange} = 30.23$, $k_{red} = 40.31$. Using these threshold values we apply Equation (6) to calculate the exact Shapley value of IDS detection agents as shown in Figure 1(b). It is interesting to note that the Shapley value of IDS agents with a low SRV is smaller for the red and orange threat level than the ones for the yellow and green threat level. This indicates that agents with low SRVs play a less significant role than others for switching to the red threat advisory.

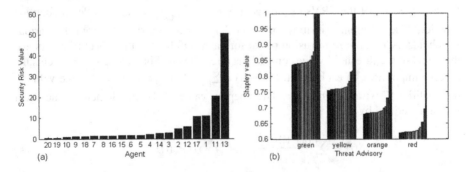

(a)   Agent

(b)   Threat Advisory

Fig. 1. Security value risk of the 20 IDS agents (a) and considering the four levels (b)

The threat levels are indicated from a comparison of Figure 1(a) with Figure 1(b) to be more objective and efficient deployment than pure SRV. The high SRV agents play a more significant role than do the lower ones in dangerous situations (e.g., red level). On the other hand, in gentle dangerous situations (e.g., green level) there is no particular difference between high and low SRV agents. Moreover, the proposed framework can also provide more quantitative values for various situations than in human decision-making, as is illustrated from a comparison of Figure 1(a) with Figure 1(b).

4 Conclusions

The proposed framework applies game theoretic models to solve IDS agent deployment problems. The experiments actually identify and provide encouragement for the use of the framework to connect the Nash equilibrium and Shapley value concepts, enabling the IDS to prioritize deployment for four threat levels. We present the static and complete information of security game. Future work will propose a Bayesian game which fall under the gambit of non-cooperative game with incomplete information, and present a simulation from an organization's security operational center.

References

1. Alpcan, T., Basar, T.: A Game Theoretic Approach to Decision and Analysis in Network Intrusion Detection. In: IEEE Conference on Decision and Control, pp. 2595–2600 (2003)
2. Dixit, A., Skeath, S.: Games of Strategy. W. W. Norton & Company (2001)
3. Keromytis, A.D., Vishal, M., Rubenstein, D.: SOS: An Architecture for Mitigating DDoS Attacks. IEEE Communications 22, 176–188 (2004)
4. McKelvey, R.D., McLennan, A.M., Turocy, T.L.: Gambit: Software Tools for Game Theory (2007), http://econweb.tamu.edu/gambit
5. Mishra, D., Rangarajan, B.: Cost Sharing in a Job Scheduling Problem Using the Shapley Value. In: Proceedings of the 6th ACM conference on Electronic commerce, pp. 232–239 (2005)
6. Owen, G.: Game Theory, 3rd edn. Academic Press, New York (2001)
7. Parsons, S., Wooldridge, M.: Game Theory and Decision Theory in Multi-Agent Systems. Autonomous Agents and Multi-Agent Systems 5, 243–254 (2002)
8. Schechter, S.E.: Computer Security Strength and Risk: a Quantitative Approach. PhD Thesis, Harvard Univ. (2004)
9. Zolezzi, J.M., Rudnick, H.: Transmission Cost Allocation by Cooperative Games and Coalition Formation. IEEE Transactions on power systems 41, 1008–1015 (2002)

Double Token-Ring and Region-Tree Based Group Communication Mechanism for Mobile Agent

Zehua Zhang and Xuejie Zhang

School of Information Science and Engineering, Yunnan University, Kunming, 650091,
P.R. China
{zehuazh,xjzhang}@ynu.edu.cn

Abstract. Many multi-agent applications based on mobile agents require message passing among group of agents. Although much work have been done on
the issue of reliable point to point communication for mobile agent, but how to
implement a group communication system for mobile agents still remains an
open issue. We propose a novel mobile agent group communication mechanism
DTRTGCM in this paper, by use double toke-ring and the dynamic commission
of the nearby communication support point RS and CC, the communication efficiency is considerably enhanced, messages can be multicasted more quickly
and the register cost of mobile agent is greatly decreased, DTRTGCM also supports the atomic and totally ordered message delivery.

1 Introduction

Communication is an essential ability for mobile agent; a reliable and efficient communication mechanism plays a very important role in the realization of mobile agent
system. A specific kind of communication, which is used in many multi mobile agent
systems (such as auction and information retrieval, etc.), is group communication, it
can also be used for implementing mobile agent fault tolerance. In group communication, a message is delivered to all the members of a group. In a mobile agent group,
mobility of the group members introduces new challenges for message dissemination.
Although group communications have been well studied for stationary process groups
systems [1,2], and much work have been done on the issue of reliable point to point
communication for mobile agent, but there were just a few works about the issue of
group communication for mobile agents, such as [3,4,5,6].

Existing group communication mechanisms suffer from low efficiency for large
group members in a large scale network, assumptions like specific services such as IP
Multicast, or don't support atomic and totally ordered message delivery (Atomicity
guarantees that any multicast message is eventually delivered to all mobile agents in
the group, total ordering ensures that all the multicast messages are delivered in the
same order to all the group members).

In this paper, we present a novel group communication mechanism Double Token-
Ring and Region-Tree Based Group Communication Mechanism for Mobile Agent
(abbreviated as DTRTGCM). It is more efficient, supports the atomic and totally

A. Ghose, G. Governatori, and R. Sadananda (Eds.): PRIMA 2007, LNAI 5044, pp. 452–457, 2009.

ordered message delivery, and has some merits which meet many requirements of group communication for mobile agent well.

The rest of this paper is organized as follows: Section 2 presents new Group Communication Mechanism DTRTGCM for Mobile Agent. Section 3 give the performance analysis and experiment results of DTRTGCM. Finally, the conclusions of or research are stated in section 4.

2 The DTRTGCM Group Communication Mechanism

2.1 Structure of DTRTGCM and Related Data Structure

As depicted in Fig. 1, a mobile agent computing network consists of many mobile agents and MAPs. A MAP is a mobile agent platform running on nodes in the network; it supports the execution, mobility, communication, and security of mobile agents, etc. In DTRTGCM, each region has a region server (abbreviated as RS) which maintains the addresses of the mobile agents (abbreviated as MAs) which immigrate in this region and the addresses of MAs which birth in this region, the RS also responsible for the delivery or buffering of the messages for the MAs who reside in this region, and sends out messages for them. One MA belongs to one RS at any time.

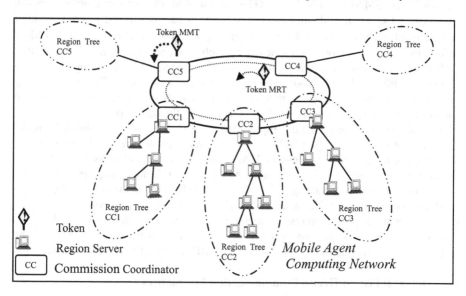

Fig. 1. The structure of DTRTGCM group communication mechanism

When a group is needed to be constructed over a large scale network (such as Internet), all MA's group communication request is send to their RSs(selected by the mobile agent, mobile agent's RS can be dynamically changed), and one or many RSs select a RS in the network as their Commission Coordinator (abbreviated as CC) according to efficiency, cost and security, etc. thus form a Region-Tree which use CC as its root. By negotiation among CCs, and use two token among the CCs, one for multicast messages and another one for the release of the received messages in the buffer, all CCs form a Double Token-ring overlay network

Let G = {A1, A2, ..., An}be a group of n mobile agents; let L be the locations of the MAPs, L = {L_1, L_2, ..., L_k}; and C={CC_1, CC_2, ..., CC_R} is the Commission Co-ordinators of the group. A group can be built temporarily by negotiation or by appointed beforehand, and its owner may not be informed about this even.

Each RS maintains a Region Server view RV for the MAs register to it, it is a tuple: RV = (GID, RMAlist, RSMB, RRMB, CCID), GID is the ID of the group; RMAlist = {(A_i, L_i) $\mid$ $A_i \in G$ and A_i register to this RV, L_i is the location of A_i} is the list of mobile agents who are members of this group and registers to this RS currently; RSMB buffers messages that have been sent out by mobile agents who register in this RS; RRMB buffers multicast messages which have been received from the RS's CC; CCID is this RS's Commission Coordinator's ID

Each CC maintains a coordinator view CV for MAs register to it, which is a tuple: CV = (GID, CMAlist, GMAlist, CClist, CSMB, CRMB, $Seq_{MaxReceived}$), GID is the ID of the group; CMAlist = {(A_i, L_i) $\mid$ $A_i \in G$ and A_i' s RS register to this CC, L_i is the location of the A_i's RS } is the list of all the group mobile agents whose RS commission this CC as their Commission Coordinator (i.e. the list of mobile agent who distributing in different regions in this Region-Tree, and this CC is the root of the Region-Tree); GMAlist = {A_i $\mid$ $A_i \in G$}is the list of all the member mobile agents in the group, a CC use it to distinguish if a message is sent out by the group's member mobile agent; CClist = {(C_i, L_i) $\mid$ $C_i \in C$ and L_i is the location of C_i }; CSMB buffers messages that have been sent out by mobile agents register in this CC's RSs; CRMB buffers received multicast messages which is sent to this group; In all the sequence numbers of the acknowledgement messages from this CC's RSs, $Seq_{MaxReceived}$ is the maximum sequence number which that the messages whose sequence number below or equal to it have all been received by the receivers.

A multicast message (MM) is a tuple: MM = (GID, Seq, Sender, Info), GID is the ID of the multicast group; Seq is the sequence number of message MM; Sender is the ID of the agent who send out message MM; Info is the content of message MM.

The message multicast token is a tuple: MMT = (GID, Seq_{Max}), Seqmax is the maximum sequence number of messages that have been multicasted in the group GID.

The message release token is a tuple: MRT = (GID, Seq_{MaxPR}, Seq_{MinCR}), Seq_{MaxPR} is the maximum sequence number of messages that have been delivered to all mobile agents in the previous rotation of token MRT; Seq_{MinCR} is minimum number of the $Seq_{MaxReceived}$ (defined in the CV) numbers that MRT ever met in current rotation

2.2 The DTRTGCM Group Communication Mechanism

A message multicast token MMT and a message release token MRT is initialized in a Commission Coordinator CC_o, then MMT begin to rotate in the CCs in C. a CC_0 is selected beforehand or is a negotiation result among the CCs.

Message Delivery algorithm:
(1) When a message is send out by a MA from a MAP on a node (it can also be the messages send out by a static agent or other entities), it is firstly delivered to the MA's RS, and the RS send this message to its CC's CSMB.

(2) A CC can multicast message only when it get the message multicast token MMT, once a CC get the MMT from other CC, it multicasts all the messages in its CSMB buffer to all the CCs in its CClist. Before the multicast of a message MM, set $MM.Seq = MMT.Seq_{Max}+1$, after sent out the message, set $MMT.Seq_{Max} = MMT.Seq_{Max}+1$.

(3) If the CC's CRMB isn't empty, every CC multicast messages in CRMB to all the RSs in its CMAlist

(4) If the RS's RRMB isn't empty, every RS multicast messages in RRMB to all the mobile agents in its RMAlist.

(5) Once a mobile agent get a message MM_i, an acknowledgement message AK_i for MM_i is sent to the RS, when a RS get all the acknowledgement message for MM_i from the mobile agents in its RMAlist, it send AK_i for MM_i to its CC. each CC set its $CV. Seq_{MaxReceived}$ as the maximum sequence number which that the messages whose sequence number below or equal to it have all been received by the receivers.

Buffer message release algorithm:

(1) In the first rotation of the message release token MRT, set $MRT. Seq_{MaxPR} = 0$, $MRT.Seq_{MinCR}= 0$, when the MRT back to CC_o, the second rotation begin.

(2) Every time MRT back to CC_o, set $MRT.Seq_{MinCR} = CC_o.CV.Seq_{MaxReceived}$, once MRT arrives at a new CC, compare $MRT.Seq_{MinCR}$ with this CC's $CV.Seq_{MaxReceived}$, if $CV.Seq_{MaxReceived} < MRT.Seq_{MinCR}$, set $MRT.Seq_{MinCR} = CV.Seq_{MaxReceived}$.

(3) When MRT arrives at each CC, release the messages in the CV.CRMB if their sequence number Seq is less than or equal to $MRT.Seq_{MaxPR}$.

(4) When MRT back to CC_o, set $MRT.Seq_{MaxPR} = MRT. Seq_{MinCR}$, then, MRT begin a new rotation, go (2).

MA's move mechanism:

The move of mobile agent is classified into three kinds: intra-RS, intra-CC and inter-CC, according to mobile agent's move scope.

If a mobile agent A_i performs an intra-RS move from MAP i to MAP j(move scope is in the same region), A_i send a message to its RS to inform its new location, RS modifies the corresponding record in its RMAlist from (A_i, L_i) to (A_i, L_j). No more work is needed to do in the system, and the mobile agent's move has no effect its CC and other CCs.

In intra-CC move, mobile agent A_i's move scope exceeds one region but still in the same CC, when A_i has finished its register to a new region RS k, RS k send a message, to its CC to inform the arrival of A_i, CC add a new record (A_i, L_k) in its CV.CMAlist, L_k is the Location of RS k. This kind of move has no effect on other CCs.

When A_i performs an intra-RS move from one CC u to another CC v, A_i sends a move request message to its RS, let the time T_d be the time that when RS receive the move request message, T_d is used is the dividing point, A_i must receive all messages in the buffer RRMB which have been received before T_d, then, A_i move to a new region RS' in CC v, after A_i has finished its register on RS' and RS' inform CC v about this A_i's immigration(get $CC_v.CV.Seq_{MaxReceived}$ at the same time), A_i sends an ACK knowledge to its former RS, suppose RS_{max} (RS'_{max}) is the maximum Seq of messages in the RS.RRMB(RS'.RRMB), A_{max} is the maximum Seq of messages which A_i has received. Now the situations and corresponding actions are shown in Table 1.

Table 1. Actions corresponding to different situations for intra-RS move

Situations		Actions
no message in RS.RRMB	$A_{max} >= RS'_{max}$	Do nothing and finish the move
	$A_{max} < RS'_{max}$	Keep receiving messages from RS until get the message with Seq = RS'_{max} -1
Have messages in RS.RRMB	$RS_{max} >= RS'_{max}$	Do nothing finish the move
	$RS_{max} < RS'_{max}$	Receives the cached messages in the former RS's RRMB(which is received after T_d), and keep receiving messages from RS until get the message with Seq = RS'_{max} -1

3 Performance Analysis and Experiment Result of DTRTGCM

DTRTGCM is more efficient. Firstly, compare with the mechanism GCS-MA [6], the message multicast process and message release process are detached, both two processes become more efficient. Secondly, a mobile agent can react quickly with the changes in its circumstance, since it can decide by itself to register to a RS and Commission any RS in a region-tree as its CC. Finally, when a mobile agent moves in a RS or CC, the cost for the mobile agent's register is restricted to the least degree.

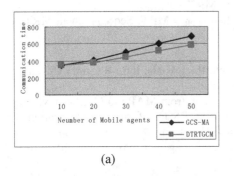
(a)

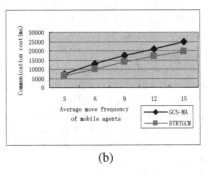
(b)

Fig. 2. The communication time and communication cost of GCS-MA and DTRTGCM

DTRTGCM supports the atomic and totally ordered message delivery, and each mobile agent can quickly know which messages have been received by other agents by consult the Commission Coordinator's CV.CRMB, this is very import merit in some applications such as E-business and auction; When a mobile agent is also a member of another group G_s which is resides in a LAN, the RS established formerly in this LAN can be utilized in G_s as the coordinator; moreover, most of the message cache operation is happed in the RS, this is more distributed and more conform to the design principles of distributed computing systems.

Another advantage of DTRTGCM is it combines group communication well with point to point communication for mobile agents, it coexisting well with the point to point mobile agent communication mechanism MRTBDCHP in our before work [7].

We have done the simulative experiment in our campus LAN by use IBM Aglets 2.0.2 and JDK 1.3.1. Compare with the mechanism GCS-MA [6], experiment result manifested that with the increase of the number of mobile agents, the increase of the average communication time of DTRTGCM is more slow, as shown in Fig. 2(a). When the number of mobile agents is fixed, with the increase of the average move frequency of mobile agents, the increase of DTRTGCM's communication cost is more slow contrast with GCS-MA, as shown in Fig. 2(b).

4 Conclusion and Future Work

We propose a novel mobile agent group communication mechanism DTRTGCM in this paper, by use double toke-ring and the dynamic commission RS and CC as the nearby communication support point, the communication efficiency is considerably enhanced, messages can be multicasted more quickly and the register cost of mobile agent is greatly decreased. DTRTGCM supports the atomic and totally ordered message delivery and coexisting well with the point to point mobile agent communication, it also has some merit which meets many requirements of group communication for mobile agent well. In our future work, we'll focus on the problem of the application of group communication and point to point communication for mobile agent in the agent organizations.

Acknowledgement

This work is supported by the National Natural Science Foundation of China (NSFC) (No.60573104).

References

[1] Moser, L.E., Melliar-Smith, P.M., Agarwal, D.A., Budhia, R.K.: Lingley-Papadopoulos CA, Totem: a fault-tolerant multicast group communication system. Commun. ACM 39(4), 54–63 (1996)

[2] Chockler, G.V., Huleihel, N., Dolev, D.: An adaptive total ordered multicast protocol that tolerates partitions. In: PODC 1998, Puerto Vallarta, Mexico, June 28–July 2, pp. 237–246. ACM, New York (1998)

[3] The mobile groups approach for the coordination of mobile agents. Journal of Parallel and Distributed Computing 65, 275–288 (2005)

[4] Jafarpour, H., Yazdani, N., Bazzaz-zadeh, N.: A scalable group communication mechanism for mobile agents. Journal of Network and Computer Applications 30, 186–208 (2007)

[5] Murphy, A.L., Picco, G.P.: Reliable communication for highly mobile agents. Autonom Agents Multi-Agent Systems, 81–100 (2002)

[6] Xu, W., Cao, J., Jin, B., Li, J., Zhang, L.: GCS-MA: A group communication system for mobile agents. Journal of Network and Computer Applications 30, 1153–1172 (2007)

[7] Zhang, Z., Zhang, X.: Multi region-tree based dynamic commission home proxy communication mechanism for mobile agent. In: Shi, Z.-Z., Sadananda, R. (eds.) PRIMA 2006. LNCS, vol. 4088, pp. 540–545. Springer, Heidelberg (2006)

Towards Culturally-Situated Agent
Which Can Detect Cultural Differences

Heeryon Cho[1], Naomi Yamashita[2], and Toru Ishida[1]

[1] Department of Social Informatics, Kyoto University, Kyoto 606-8501, Japan
cho@ai.soc.i.kyoto-u.ac.jp, ishida@i.kyoto-u.ac.jp
[2] Media Interaction Principle Open Laboratory,
NTT Communication Science Laboratories, Kyoto 619-0237, Japan
naomi@cslab.kecl.ntt.co.jp

Abstract. A method to calculate the semantic dissimilarity in two countries' pictogram interpretations is proposed. Two countries' pictogram interpretation words are mapped to SUMO classes via WordNet2SUMO. Appropriate concept weights are assigned to SUMO classes using the interpretation ratios. The edges between the two SUMO classes are counted to obtain the path length of the two classes. Three bipartite graphs are generated using the classes and edges to calculate the between-country vs. within-country dissimilarity in pictogram interpretations. Preliminary result showed that human assessment of interpretation dissimilarity does not always correspond to concept-level dissimilarity in the ontology.

Keywords: interpretation, cultural difference, detection, ontology.

1 Introduction

Our goal is to build an agent which can automatically detect cultural differences. Existing literatures on culturally-situated agents have tackled the problem of cooperation between agents with different cultural backgrounds[1] or the problem of bridging humans with different cultural backgrounds[2]. The former focuses on conflict resolution while the latter focuses on mediation. In this paper, we tackle the problem of automatically detecting cultural differences based on human-provided interpretations. We use pictogram as a symbolic medium to collect human interpretations from two different cultures.

Pictograms have clear pictorial similarities with some object[3], and one who can recognize the object depicted in the pictogram can interpret the meaning associated with the object. Pictorial symbols, however, are not universally interpretable. For example, the cow is a source of nourishment to westerners who drink milk and eat its meat, but it is an object of veneration to many people in India. Hence, a picture of a cow could be interpreted quite differently by Protestants and Hindus[4]. We conducted a human cultural assessment experiment using U.S.–Japan pictogram interpretations as stimulus. Experimental findings revealed that human subjects looked at similarities and differences in two countries' interpretations when assessing cultural differences. Based on this finding,

A. Ghose, G. Governatori, and R. Sadananda (Eds.): PRIMA 2007, LNAI 5044, pp. 458–463, 2009.

Table 1. A pictogram with U.S.–Japan interpretation words, SUMO classes, and ratios

U.S.				JAPAN		
WORD	SUMO CLASS	RATIO		WORD	SUMO CLASS	RATIO
talking	Speaking+	0.30		*speak*	Speaking+, SoundAttribute+	0.34
pray	Praying=	0.30		*announcement*	Stating+	0.25
thinking	Reasoning=	0.23		*thank you*	Thanking+	0.22
speaking	Disseminating+	0.17		*soliloquy*	Text+	0.19

we formulate a simple assumption that interpretation differences can be detected if semantic differences can be detected. To this end, as a first step, we propose a method to calculate overall semantic dissimilarity of pictogram interpretation using ontology.

2   Measuring Semantic Dissimilarity Using Ontology

The idea is to compare dissimilarity of pictogram interpretations on the semantic level by mapping interpretation words to an ontology. In this paper, we use WordNet2SUMO[5] to map pictogram interpretation words to SUMO[6].

2.1   Mapping Words to SUMO and Calculating Concept Weights

We assume that a pictogram has a list of interpretation words and corresponding ratios of each country (Table 1). Searching through the WordNet2SUMO using each interpretation word as input will return relevant SUMO classes, instances, properties and so forth, but here we will only use the SUMO class and instance mappings. Table 1 shows related SUMO classes for the U.S.–Japan pictogram interpretation words. The "+ (plus)" suffix in the SUMO classname denotes that given interpretation word is subsumed by that concept. The "= (equal)" suffix denotes that given word is equal to the SUMO class or instance. We calculate the *Concept Weight* or *CW* of each SUMO class related to each word by taking into account the ratio of the interpretation word. The concept weight *CW* of a given SUMO class can be calculated as follows:

$$CW(class, country) = \sum_{\forall word, word \in C(class)} \frac{Ratio(word, country)}{NumOfRelatedClass(word)} \quad (1)$$

For example, the concept weight of Speaking and SoundAttribute class assigned to Japan's interpretation word *speak* in Table 1 can be calculated as:

$CW(Speaking, Japan) = 0.34/2 = 0.17$
$CW(SoundAttribute, Japan) = 0.34/2 = 0.17$

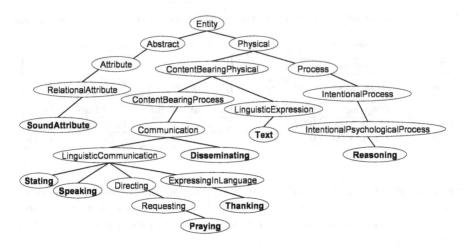

Fig. 1. Partial SUMO ontology containing SUMO classes given in Table 1

The result of the concept weight calculation will generate a list of SUMO classes with appropriate weights reflecting the conceptual interpretation of a given country. Once the list of SUMO classes with associated concept weights is obtained, we use the partial SUMO ontology containing the SUMO classes to leverage the graph structure of the ontology (Fig. 1). We count the number of edges between two SUMO classes to obtain the path length of the class pairs.

For instance, `Speaking` and `Stating` class in Fig. 1 has a path length of "2". Using the SUMO class and path length information, we generate a bipartite graph with left and right vertices representing each country's SUMO classes. Figure 2 shows three bipartite graphs, US–US, US–Japan, and Japan–Japan, generated using SUMO classes in Table 1. The vertices are connected completely in an *N-to-N* fashion, and each edge connecting the two vertices is assigned a path length of the two SUMO classes. Note that an edge connecting the same two classes is always assigned a path length of "0 (zero)" (e.g. `Stating` and `Stating` in Fig. 2 upper right is assigned "0").

2.2 Calculating Semantic Dissimilarity for Detection

The overall semantic dissimilarity in the two countries' SUMO classes is calculated by multiplying the concept weights of the two countries' SUMO classes and the associated path length, and adding up all possible SUMO class pair values.

Let $G(V, E)$ be a bipartite graph containing weighted SUMO class vertices $V = (V_1, V_2)$ where V_1 and V_2 denote $Country_1$ and $Country_2$ respectively and path length-assigned edges E. Using the concept weight equation CW in (1), the two countries' *Semantic Dissimilarity* or *SD* is calculated as:

$$SD(G) = \sum_{\forall v_i, v_i \in V_1} \sum_{\forall v_j, v_j \in V_2} CW(v_i) \times PathLength(v_i, v_j) \times CW(v_j) \quad (2)$$

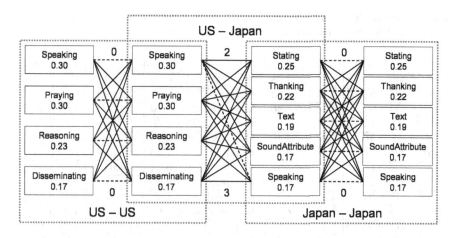

Fig. 2. Three bipartite graphs (US–US, US–Japan, Japan–Japan) with weight-assigned SUMO class vertices and path length-assigned edges (refer to Table 1 and Fig. 1)

The bipartite graph represents two countries' pictogram interpretations in terms of SUMO classes. Using the equation (2), we calculate the semantic dissimilarity values of the three bipartite graphs, namely, $Country_1 - Country_1$, $Country_1 - Country_2$, and $Country_2 - Country_2$. In the case of Fig. 2, the semantic dissimilarity values for US–US, US–Japan, and Japan–Japan are calculated as 4.92, 5.92, and 5.03 respectively. Note that multiplication between the same two classes will always return zero since the path length is zero. Hence, all class pairs connected with dashed lines in Fig. 2 will be zero.

Once the semantic dissimilarity values of the three bipartite graphs are obtained, we compare the *between-country* value with two *within-country* values. We assume that if the *between-country* semantic dissimilarity value is greater than the two *within-country* semantic dissimilarity values, then cultural difference exist in two countries' pictogram interpretations. This is based on the intuition that culturally-different pictograms will contain more varied *between-country* concepts than *within-country* concepts; that is, interpretations will center on similar concepts within the same country, but once the scope is enlarged to cover interpretations of the two countries, the concepts will become more varied for pictograms having cultural difference. In the case of Fig. 2, since the *between-country* value (US–Japan: 5.92) is greater than the two *within-country* values (US–US: 4.92, Japan–Japan: 5.03), "cultural difference exists" is returned.

2.3   Preliminary Result

We applied our method to thirty U.S.–Japan pictograms having human cultural difference assessment result. Table 2 shows the pictogram number (P#), human cultural difference assessment averages (AVG), three semantic dissimilarity values (US–US, US–JP, JP–JP), and hit or miss results of the proposed

Table 2. Human judgment averages (AVG), three interpretation dissimilarity values, and proposed method's performance of hits (H), misses (M), and false positives (FP)

P#	AVG	US–US		US–JP		JP–JP	H/M
P21	7.00	7.30	<	8.07	>	7.08	H
P1	6.83	5.31	<	7.73	>	5.63	H
P12	6.33	4.22	<	5.14	<	5.46	M
P2	6.17	5.83	<	9.30	>	5.35	H
P28	6.17	5.70	<	7.25	>	7.10	H
P11	6.00	5.77	<	7.33	<	7.54	M
P14	6.00	5.66	>	5.61	>	5.12	M
P13	5.83	5.16	>	4.55	>	2.99	M
P15	5.67	2.91	<	4.39	<	5.76	M
P10	5.50	5.63	<	5.88	<	5.94	M
P16	5.17	8.93	>	8.18	>	6.25	M
P30	5.00	5.64	>	5.21	>	4.43	M
P8	4.67	7.50	<	8.66	>	8.58	M
P9	4.67	6.96	<	8.60	>	8.20	M
P22	4.67	6.81	<	7.06	>	5.76	M
P23	4.50	6.75	<	8.43	>	8.24	M
P7	4.17	5.77	<	7.99	<	9.01	H
P3	4.00	7.90	>	7.58	>	6.47	H
P4	4.00	7.60	>	7.26	>	6.77	H
P5	4.00	6.55	>	6.10	>	5.42	H
P18	3.83	7.55	>	6.53	>	1.54	H
P17	3.67	3.24	<	5.02	<	5.80	H
P20	3.67	4.33	<	7.47	>	6.20	FP
P6	3.50	7.49	>	6.51	>	5.37	H
P19	3.50	7.65	>	6.82	>	4.90	H
P27	3.50	5.79	<	6.72	>	6.20	FP
P29	3.33	6.07	<	6.28	>	3.98	FP
P25	3.17	7.30	<	7.63	>	7.26	FP
P26	2.83	6.83	<	6.86	>	5.90	FP
P24	2.33	8.13	>	8.03	>	4.87	H

method when compared to the human assessment (H/M). Pictograms with averages (AVG) greater than or equal to 5 are judged by humans to have some kind of cultural difference. Initial findings of the result is discussed next.

3 Discussions

Existing researches propose node-based and edge-based approaches to measure concept (dis)similarity within a taxonomy[7] or a concept net[8] respectively, and we extend these approaches to group-level semantic dissimilarity measurement. Since our approach postulates a correspondence between human perception of pictogram interpretation and SUMO classes, we analyzed the missed cases for reasons for failure. One reason for failure is that in some cases, humans may perceive clear difference in interpretations, but ontology may not reflect this difference; that is, even if difference between two SUMO classes is small, interpretation difference perceived by humans may not be small. For example, Table 2 P13 (AVG: 5.83) is judged by humans to have cultural difference since a major U.S. interpretation word, *happy*, which captures emotional state, is clearly perceived as different when compared to major Japanese interpretation words, *pretty* and *cute*, which captures outward appearance. However, when the three words *happy*, *pretty*, and *cute* are mapped to SUMO, all are mapped to `SubjectiveAssessmentAttribute` class rendering the difference indistinguishable. So, for these kinds of pictogram interpretations, our method is not effective.

Another reason for failure is that for some interpretations having largely different SUMO classes, humans may not perceive such differences. For example, the top ranking US.–Japan interpretation word for Table 2 P29 is *carnival* and *amusement park* respectively, but humans see little cultural difference in the two. This is because association is used when humans compare these two words. However, at the SUMO-level, *carnival* and *amusement park* are mapped to `RecreationOrExercise` and `Corporation` class respectively which are very different classes; association is not incorporated in the ontology.

4   Conclusions

We proposed a way to calculate semantic dissimilarity in two countries' interpretations by mapping interpretation words to SUMO classes via WordNet2SUMO. Appropriate weights were assigned to mapped SUMO classes by distributing interpretation ratios. The edges between the two SUMO classes were counted to obtain path length of the two classes. The concept weight and path length information were used to calculate the semantic dissimilarity of the two countries' pictogram interpretations. Our approach is ontology-dependent and for those pictograms with interpretation differences indistinguishable at the ontology level, cultural difference detection is difficult; one reason is due to disagreement between human perception and ontology. Future work will focus on implementing an agent which can automatically detect cultural differences in interpretations.

Acknowledgements. We give thanks to Yumiko Mori and Toshiyuki Takasaki at NPO Pangaea, Tomoko Koda at Osaka Institute of Technology, Rieko Inaba at NICT Language Grid Project, and Satoshi Oyama at Kyoto University for discussions on the initial research result. *All pictograms presented in this paper are copyrighted material, and their rights are reserved to NPO Pangaea.*

References

1. Chaudron, L., Erceau, J., Tessier, C.: Cultural differences? An opportunity for a mutual knowledge enhancement. In: PRICAI 1998 Workshop on Issues in cross-cultural communication: Toward culturally situated agents (1998)
2. Ishida, T.: Communicating culture. IEEE Intelligent Systems, Special Issue on the Future of AI 21(3), 62–63 (2006)
3. Marcus, A.: Icons, symbols, and signs: Visible languages to facilitate communication. Interactions 10(3), 37–43 (2003)
4. Kolers, P.A.: Some formal characteristics of pictograms. American Scientist 57, 348–363 (1969)
5. Niles, I., Pease, A.: Linking lexicons and ontologies: Mapping WordNet to the Suggested Upper Merged Ontology. In: IKE 2003 Proc. of the Int'l. Conf. on Information and Knowledge Engineering (2003)
6. Niles, I., Pease, A.: Towards a standard upper ontology. In: FOIS 2001 Proc. 2nd Int'l. Conf. on Formal Ontology in Information Systems (2001)
7. Resnik, P.: Using information content to evaluate semantic similarity in a taxonomy. In: IJCAI 1995 Proc. of the Int'l. Joint Conf. on AI, pp. 448–453 (1995)
8. Rada, R., Mili, H., Bicknell, E., Blettner, M.: Development and application of a metric on semantic nets. IEEE Transaction on Systems, Man, and Cybernetics 19(1), 17–30 (1989)

Ontology-Based Emotion System
for Digital Environment

WooYeon Hwang and Jung-Jin Yang

School of Computer Science and Information Engineering
The Catholic University of Korea
43-1 Yeokgok 2-dong, Wonmi-gu, Bucheon, Gyeonggi-do, Republic of Korea
Tel.: +82-2-2164-4678
{hwangwooyeon,jungjin}@catholic.ac.kr

Abstract. Internet development has changed the whole aspect of our lives and it is not too much to say that we are currently living in a cyber community represented by Internet. In this kind of environment, interactions with the others and various services are established and a character in the cyber community substitutes a person. In expressing oneself with defined personality, emotion plays an essential role. Nowadays, avatar and emoticons function as primary sources for expressing feelings but more mutual level of expressing interactive emotions among cyber subjects are not examined in depth. This paper proposes emotional system which actualizes more detailed schemes to express emotions based on both psychological theory of emotion and ontological representation of their relationship. The system is constructed to express individual's emotion by realizing contextual information and applying OCC Model. It is expected to express oneself precisely, exploit a market for characters and enable human services.

Keywords: Emotion System, Ontology, Inference Engine, OCC model.

1 Introduction

Nowadays cyber community, which includes online games, movies, and animations, is becoming a place of social interaction that makes possible self-expression and formation of human relationship. A good example of a cyber community is a role playing game in which characters that represent real human beings and game characters that are created artificially combine and interact to form a relationship. The endeavors to approach the consumers using characters is continuously working not only in computer games but in the fields that provide more practical service through order systems and reservation systems. In situations like these, a system that has the ability to read emotional state and express it is being required. Further, in a ubiquitous era, emotional element itself will be an important criterion of service. This paper concretizes the theories presented in the previous research, 'Ontology-based Emotion Engine for Digital Character' [1], and deals with the possibility of using emotion system by creating real simulators. In this paper we examine emotion model and ontology-based representation that is essential for emotion system including the ontology

A. Ghose, G. Governatori, and R. Sadananda (Eds.): PRIMA 2007, LNAI 5044, pp. 464–472, 2009.

repository technology to save the ontology. Further, we introduce the architecture of emotion engine along with preliminary result of the simulator.

2 Emotion Model

In an emotional situation a model for interpreting outer event and deciding how it will affect current emotional state is required. As a matter of fact, there are many models for emotion and among those, we determined emotion using Ortony, Colins, Clore (OCC)Model[2] and Emotion Mixture Model. These emotion models satisfy emotion category defined in facial animation standard [3].

3 OCC Model

Instead of trying to list all emotions created by human, the OCC Model categorizes emotions that are produced and caused by similar reasons and defines them as Emotion Types. The OCC Model has advantages of saving space for storing emotion form resulting from emotion types and determining emotion in a short period of time because the criterion for emotion is relatively simple.

3.1 Elements of Emotion Evaluation

The OCC Model categorizes the factors that evaluate emotion as Event, Object, and Agent.

Event: The actions that are related to the purpose of agent
Object: The Individuals that exist with the same level of qualification
Agent: The Subject of the actual emotion, its emotion type is based on event and object

3.2 Process of Emotion Evaluation

The process used in the OCC Model is composed of Classification, Quantification, Interaction, Mapping, and Expression.

Classification: The character determines which emotional category is affected by event, action, and object.
Quantification: Determines the degree of intensity of effects on emotional categories.
Interaction: Forms Emotional Value of current event, action, and object in classification and quantification. The emotional value has effects on the character's emotional categories.
Mapping: Defines 22 emotional categories of OCC model. These require at least one different matching emotional expression.
Expression: Emotional State can be seen in a facial expression and may affect the condition of the character.

4 Mixed Emotion Model

Composition of primary emotional state	Words for mixed emotions
Pleasure + accommodation	Love, friendship
Fear + surprise	Alarm, dread
Sadness + dislike	Blame
Dislike+ anger	Disdain, hatred
Pleasure +fear	Guilt
Anger + pleasure	Pride
Fear + dislike	Shame
Anticipation + fear	Anxiety, prudence

In Plutchik's work [4], emotional word list, as shown in the table left, is presented to the evaluators and made them pick two or three components of each of the eight primary emotional states.

Another method of mixture of emotion is using emotion circle. Words that show emotion are categorized in a circle by Whissel[5].

5 Ontology

In W3C, XML is recommended as a prototype for describing Meta-data. XML is defined as a structure that can be recognized by a device. It can describe sentence structures, by using Cardinality Restriction, and along with XML Schema, it can give an account of meta-data vocabulary in the form of Element and Attribute. RDF[7] declares material and immaterial sources as triple, based on a subject, a predicate, and an object.

RDF Schema is used as Meta-data in order to define light-weighed ontology, which denotes terminology and concepts of roles. In applied hierarchy, each concept specifies declared ontology, and the class itself is guaranteed with meaningful mutual operations. OWL[7] is ontological language recommended by W3C and it can be used as structural data for logical expression and rational system by proposing Description Logic.

Since the handling memory of stationary model taken by ontology is inappropriate to accept broadly designed knowledge, the use of ontology repositories is required and inference engine is used for consistency checking of logically expressed knowledge and deducing knowledge. In order to satisfy functional demands and capacious demands of ontology repositories, the work emphasizing Abox reasoning like Minerva [8] was researched.

In this emotion engine, OWL is used to describe information on emotions. The Minerva system is utilized for ontology repository purpose.

6 Expression of Emotional Knowledge System by Using OWL

In emotion engine, sharing and reuse of knowledge are allowed. We designed ontology, based on components of each module, and used Protégé 3.1[9] to check validity of knowledge models and to facilitate expansion of knowledge by logic-based deduction.

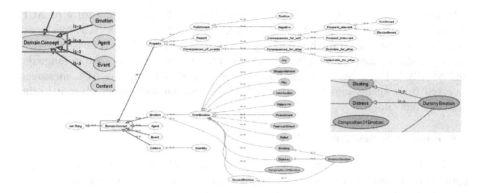

Fig. 1. Emotion and Emotional Decision Ontology

As shown in Figure 1, primary emotions, secondary emotion, and contents about criterion of judging emotions are created. The main functions of ontology designed by using Protégé 3.1[9] are shown below.

- Ontologicalization of emotional contents
- Framing rules for logical and rational ways of deducing emotions
- Guaranteeing semantic interoperability between applications
- Reusing of designed ontology

7 Application of Ontology Repository and Inference Engine

Emotion models designed in ontological forms are stored in ontology repository through provided API. To expand logical design knowledge and to check consistency, deduction through inference engine can be performed at the points of time for loading of ontology, correction and meaningful inquiry. It uses a policy that exchanges saving space and deduction time by achieving deduction. IBM DB2 is used for DBMS, which is for saving ontology. In order to store design knowledge expressed into relational database, DB Schema and loading module provided by ontology repository are used.

7.1 Ontology Loading Process

OWL files are converted to the form of relational data base (RDB) and are stored. Reasoner, provided by Minerva, is activated and then Abox deduction and Tbox deduction are performed. They are converted to RDB form and saved in DB.

7.2 Process of Inquiring and Answering to Ontology Repository

Each character that is the subject of emotions can be treated as agents. Various ways in approaching ontology repository are required to decide emotions of characters.

Each agent sends out queries to access ontology repository of which ontology is saved and the result of inquiry received is transferred to ontology repository and it is delivered back to the agent that sent out the query in the first place. Ontology Agent performs these processes.

Ontology Agent receives inquiring requests from each agent in the form of ACL messages that is used as prototype of FIPA-Compliant Agent. With ACL messages, usage of communication methods among common agents by agents is possible. ACL messages should have parser which is responsible for conversion of inquiry language and SPARQL[10] is used for handling the queries. Parser converts ACL messages received from agents into the form of SPARQL and ontology agent saves it in the ontology repository.

7.3 Emotion System Architecture

As shown in Figure 2, Emotion system architecture can be divided into four different parts. It is composed of context module, recognizing context, context analysis module, which decides emotions by analyzing context, Character Emotion that is responsible for mixing emotions and deciding final emotion, and emotion repository, which contains emotion model, the criterion of judging emotions.

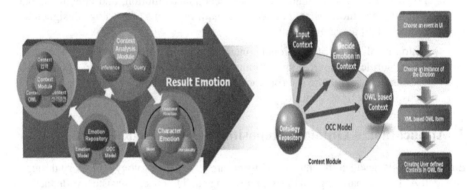

Fig. 2. Architecture for Emotion System   **Fig. 3.** Context Module

◆ **Context Module:** Context module defines characteristics of incoming circumstantial information. Each character recognizes situation that one is in and produces a certain type of emotion based on their recognition. Context collection agent recognizing peripheral context and delivering information about the circumstances to context module is, therefore, required. Context collection agent decides the kinds of object that is interacting with the character and effects to the character. These influential factors include conversations in the form of texts, actions and reactions of the character, and information about environment of which the character is placed in. The gathered information is sent to context model through ACL messages. ACL messages include XML documents about circumstantial information. Before revealing assembled circumstantial information as emotion, characters decide what kind of personalities they would be given and characteristics about the circumstances are determined by having instances of evaluation elements within emotion repository. The context character decided at this point is not the finalized form of character but it acts as the base of final emotion. In context module, event-related matters are either chosen or created and the character of the event is defined as previously mentioned.

◆ **Context analysis module:** Context analysis module asks SPARQL queries developed from context to ontology repository to discover size and kinds of emotion in the context. In the process of question transfer, detailed information is obtained through a deducing apparatus.

◆ **Character emotion module:** Character emotion module is a part deciding peculiarity of the character, saving the condition of emotion, composing emotion with base on the pre-saved emotion, and producing a new emotion. Character emotion module is divided into personality module and mood module. Figure 4 shows character emotion module.

Personality module uses EFA space[11] to indicate peculiar characteristics of each individual and it saves three different kinds of information, extroversion, fear, and aggression, to constitute spacer.

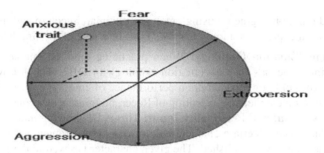

Fig. 4. EFA Spacer

In Figure 4, for instance, an anxious character is deduced with 30 extroversion, 70 fear, and –10 aggression. With this EFA space, actual emotion value that would be applied is decided. An anxious person has elevated level of uneasiness and fear and much lower level of emotions according to happiness and self-confidence than that value given in the original context module. Even in the same situation, emotional expressions might vary. The ratio of EFA spacer decides the character and the size shows the character's power of expression. Even the level of timidity differs from person to person. Figure 5 shows different ways of expressing emotion in the same circumstances. This depends on personalities.

In mood module, historical events affected the character are saved and administer condition of mood that the character is having. Mood saved in mood module is a assembly of primary emotions. In order to change mood, the only thing that has to be done is to change primary emotion that wanted to be changed. When module notifies the condition of mood, it mixes two different primary emotions that have the largest numerical values among the mood values. Mix of emotions can be obtained by calculating emotional degrees in emotion circle created by Whissel. For example, Angry is 212° and disappointment is 136.7°. The average value of these two is 174.35° and the emotion circle tells that this is indignant. This kind of relationship between the primary emotion and secondary emotion is saved in emotion ontology and emotion types are determined be asking questions.

First Emotion	Angle	First Emotion	Angle	Second Emotion	Angle
Angry	212	Disappointment	136.7	Indignant	174.35
Joy	323.4	Remorse	123.3	Mostile	223.35
Disappointment	136.7	Satisfaction	326.7	Aggressive	231.7
Resentment	176.7	Satisfaction	326.7	Wondering	251.7

Fig. 5. Secondary Emotion

7.4 Emotion System Simulator

We designed emotion engine by using emotion system architecture and made a simulator for emotion expression. Figure 6 shows User Interface of the simulator.

◆ **Loading Emotion Ontology:** When practicing emotion engine for the first time, one has to load emotion ontology in DB2. The following screen shows ontology loaded upon performance of emotion engine, the action of emotion engine, and execution of Racer, an inference engine.

◆ **Context Input and Personality Input:** This is UI showing input of context. In this process, certain characteristic of context is granted and a definite circumstance is established. The given character is saved in the form of OWL document. It is a part deciding personality of a character. Inputting values for extroversion, fear, and aggression, which are required for determining EFA space, continuance value that maintains the personality, and personality expression index value showing the degree of expression is achieved at this point.

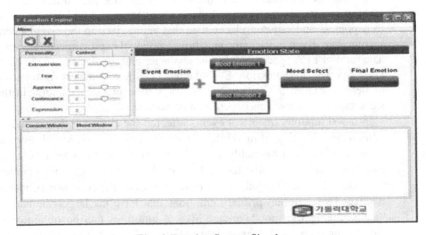

Fig. 6. Emotion System Simulator

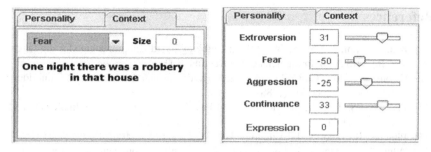

Fig. 7. Context Input and Personality Input

◆ **Deducing Emotion:** After context information is entered, with personality as a criterion, the quantity of emotion changes, affects mood of the character, and then develops a mixed emotion with the mood that the character is having currently. A most appropriate emotion can be deduced along with context recognized as represented in Figure 3.

◆ **Expressing Emotions:** The final emotion delivered as XML form is applied to the character through expression engine. Below shows an emotion has been applied to the actual character.

8 Result

This research proposes ontology-based emotion engine as a scheme to judge emotion of digital characters. We mentioned about a general concept of ontology and established techniques and tools for embodiment. We succeeded in expressing contents of emotion engine by ontology and deducing rules for inference and system architecture that are based on logical description. We also actualized architecture-based emotion engine and designed simulations for the emotion circumstances in this paper. It is shifted from existing digital characters with blank expression and passive characteristics to more active characters. These characters are to be applied in various types of services including games and movies.

More emotion models that could be added and methods to link emotion models organically should be considered in further studies. A better way of expressing emotions of human beings with detailed partition of personalities of character should be taken into account as well.

Acknowledgments

This research is supported by the ubiquitous Autonomic Computing and Network Project, the Ministry of Information and Communication (MIC) 21st Century Frontier R&D Program in Korea.

References

[1] Kim, J., Choi, J., Cho, S., Yang, J.-J.: Ontology-based emotion engine for digital characters. In: KIIS 2006 Spring Science Convention (2006)
[2] Ortony, A., Clore, G., Collins, A.: The Cognitive Structure of Emotions. Cambridge University Press, Cambridge (1988)
[3] Pandzic, I.S., Forchheimer, R.: MPEG-4 Facial Animation: standard, Implement and Applications (2002)
[4] Plutchik, R.: Emotional Psychology, HakJi Corporation (2004)
[5] Whissel, C.: Mate selection in popular women's fiction. Human Nature 7, 427–447 (1996)
[6] W3C RDF Primer W3C Recommendation (February 2004),
    http://www.w3.org/TR/2004/REC-rdfprimer-20040210
[7] W3C OWL Web Ontology Language Overview W3C Recommendation (February 2004),
    http://www.w3.org/TR/2004/RECowlfeatures-20040210
[8] IBM Integrated Ontology Development Toolkit (March 2006),
    http://www.alphaworks.ibm.com/tech/semanticstk
[9] Protégé 3.1, http://protégé.standford.edu
[10] W3C SPARQL Query Language for RDF (February 20, 2005),
    http://www.w3.org/TR/rdf-sparqlquery
[11] Wilson, I.: The Artificial Emotion Engine: Driving Emotional Behavior. AAAI, Menlo Park (2000)

An Agent Approach for Distributed Job-Shop Scheduling

Claudio Cubillos, Leonardo Espinoza, and Nibaldo Rodríguez

Pontificia Universidad Católica de Valparaíso, Escuela de Ingeniería Informática,
Av. Brasil 2241, Valparaíso, Chile
{claudio.cubillos, nibaldo.rodriguez}@ucv.cl,
leo_espinoz@yahoo.es

Abstract. The present work details the experience on designing a multiagent system devoted to a dynamic Job Shop setting using the PASSI methodology. The agent system is in charge of the planning and scheduling of jobs and their operations on a set of available machines, while considering the materials assigned to each operation. Dynamicity concerns job orders scheduling on-the-fly and the re-schedule caused by changes to the original plan due to clients, machines and material stocks. The system has been modeled with the PASSI Toolkit (PTK) and implemented over the Jade agent platform.

1 Introduction

The agent paradigm has leveraged as an important modeling abstraction, in areas such as web and grid services, peer to peer and ambient intelligence architectures just to mention some cases. To get more mature and widespread, the use of agent-oriented software engineering (AOSE) methodologies and tools are a key factor of success.

Hence, the present work describes the design of a multiagent system using a particular AOSE methodology called PASSI [2]. The chosen domain corresponds to the job-shop scheduling problem under a dynamic scenario in which job requests coming from clients must be processed on-the-fly and where re-schedule can occur due to changes in the environment (e.g. materials stock-out), problems with the service (e.g. machine delays or break down) or client eventualities (e.g. due-date change, job cancellation).

2 The Dynamic Work-Shop Problem

The traditional Job-Shop Scheduling Problem (JSSP), can be described by a set of n jobs $\{J_j\}_{1 \leq j \leq n}$ which is to be processed on a set of m machines $\{M_r\}_{1 \leq r \leq m}$. Each job has a technological sequence of machines to be processed. The processing of job J_j on machine M_r is called the operation O_{jr}. Operation O_{jr} requires the exclusive use of M_r for an uninterrupted duration p_{jr}, its deterministic processing time, and each operation O_{jr} has pre-assigned materials $\{W_i\}_{1 \leq i \leq k}$. In addition, each job has a due-date $\{D_j\}_{1 \leq j \leq n}$. A schedule is a set of completion times for each operation $\{c_{jr}\}_{1 \leq j \leq n; 1 \leq r \leq m}$ that satisfies those constraints. The considered JSSP involves the scheduling of n jobs J on the m

A. Ghose, G. Governatori, and R. Sadananda (Eds.): PRIMA 2007, LNAI 5044, pp. 473–478, 2009.
© Springer-Verlag Berlin Heidelberg 2009

machines M and consuming k materials W while minimizing the total tardiness regarding the due-dates.

On the other hand, the dynamic variant of the problem adds the fact that the jobs to be processed are not known in advance and that they must be scheduled as soon as they arrive. In addition, environmental changes can cause some events to happen, such as a machine delay or breakdown, a client canceling/modifying a job order, among others. Therefore, the objective is to obtain a schedule that also minimizes the number of non-placed jobs. It is one of the most hard NP-complete combinatorial optimization problems.

3 The Agent Architecture

The multiagent job-shop scheduling system has been developed using PASSI, a step-by-step methodology for designing and developing multi-agent societies (please refer to [2] for more details) and stands over the Jade Agent Platform [1]. In the following subsections, the agent architecture is described in terms of the PASSI methodology phases. In order to provide the reader with an appropriate level of detail in the design while considering space restrictions, only the most relevant diagrams will be presented focusing in the System Requirements for JSSP and the Agent Society architecture models.

3.1 Agent Identification (A.Id.)

At the present step the use cases capturing the system requirements are grouped together to conform an agent. The diagram in Figure 1 shows the identified use cases for this job-shop system and the leveraged agents.

Firstly, the Client agent is a GUI agent in charge of the communication between an actual client and the rest of the system, providing the possibility of generating a job order, and to communicate inbound/outbound eventualities regarding such order due to changes in the environment (e.g. order modification/cancellation from client, order delay/reject from the system).

Order agents are devoted to the job order management, its breakdown into operations, the request to Stock agents of the necessary materials for each operation execution, and the request to Machine agents for the scheduling of each operation. For the interaction with the Stock agents the FIPA Query Interaction Protocol [4] standard is used. In the latter case, the FIPA Request Interaction Protocol is used [3].

Machine agents encapsulate each real machine, being primarily in charge of its schedule management. This involves processing requests coming from Order agents and performing the scheduling process.

Additionally, it also manages eventualities that can cause schedule changes due to the machine itself (e.g. delay or breakdown), due to material supply problems (e.g. delay on delivery), or even due to client changes (e.g. order cancellation or modification). For all the above, an optimization heuristic presented by Yoo et al. [5] and inspired in simulated annealing was used.

Finally, Stock agents main goal are to maintain adequate levels of materials by generating supply orders (to the Stock Administrator), and to provide the necessary materials for the execution of each operation.

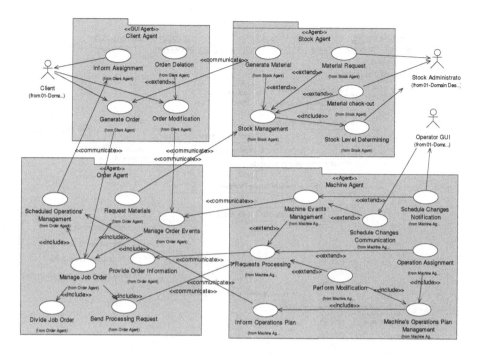

Fig. 1. Agent Identification Diagram for the Job-shop scheduling system

3.2 Roles Identification (R.Id.)

Roles Identification consists in exploring all the possible paths of the preceding Agents' Identification Diagram in Figure 1. In fact, each "<<communicate>>" relationship among two agents can be in one or more scenarios showing interacting agents working together to achieve certain desired system behavior.

The Figure 2 shows the scenario in which the Client actor requests the system to process its job. Each object in the diagram is described following the *<role>:<agent>* convention.

This scenario involves all actors and agents in the system. It starts with the Client requesting its order processing through the GUI (Client agent), the interface generates a *JobOrder* with all the details and forwards the request to the manager role of the Order agent. This agent breaks down the job obtaining an *Operation List* containing the sequence of required operations and related materials. The manager role queries the Stock agents for the availability of the materials needed for each *Operation*. On its turn, the Stock agent checks the *Stock Level* of each item in the operation's *Material List* and reserves the required amount.

With the materials availability confirmation the Order agent starts sequentially requesting Machine agents to schedule its operations. The scheduler role of the Machine calls the optimization heuristic to search for feasible alternatives selecting the best one according to the active *UtilityFunction*.

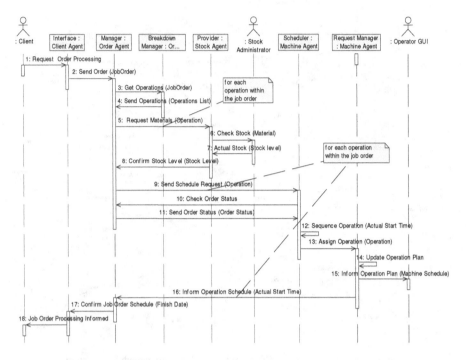

Fig. 2. Roles Identification Diagram for the "Client Requests Job Processing" scenario

Once found, the operation is programmed into the actual *MachineSchedule*, then the new operation schedule is informed to the operator (through the Operator GUI actor) and the corresponding Order agent is informed about the scheduled operation indicating its *Actual Start Time*.

Finally, once all operations were successfully scheduled, the Order agent informs the Client about the *FinishDate* for the entire job.

3.3 Ontology Description (O.D.)

In this step the agent society is described from an ontological perspective, providing them with a common knowledge of the job shop domain, and thus, enabling communication among involved actors and agents.

The following Figure 3 shows a portion of the Domain Ontology Description regarding the concepts, while leaving away the actions and predicates for space reasons. In the upper part of the diagram we can identify the *Event* concept hierarchy providing all the concepts needed to express any eventuality due to Machine or Client changes. On the center are depicted the Machine and Client concepts. Both have a *Utility Function* consisting in a set of *Utility Properties*. Each one contains a *Property* plus its weight in the utility function (e.g. Tardiness:3.4, Non-PlacedJobs:5).

JobOrders are decomposed into *Operations*, each of which has a *MaterialList* that needs to be available upon start. Each *Material* type is managed by a *Stock* that

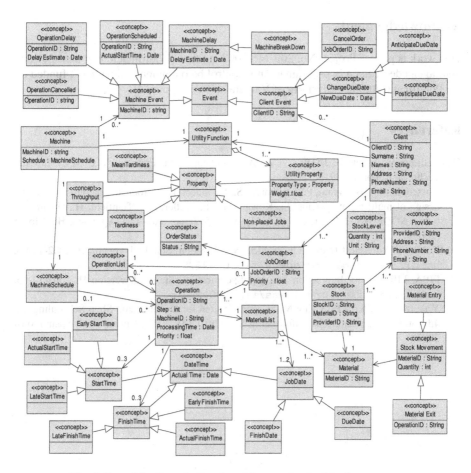

Fig. 3. Part of the Domain Ontology Diagram for the Job-shop system

monitors its *StockLevel* and generates *Stock Movements* for handling the *Material Entry* into the stock from suppliers and the *Material Exit* from the stock to supply the operations' processing.

Finally, the *Operation* has also associated a set of *Start Times* and *Finish Times* useful for its schedule minimizing the violation of the *Due Date* imposed for the entire Job.

4   Conclusions

An agent-based software architecture for dynamic job shop scheduling was described. It provides a transparent and flexible way to make interoperate clients, machine operators and stock administrators into a single architecture.

The specification of a domain ontology allows a clear understanding of the knowledge model that agents must "understand" in order to communicate within the agent society. In this way, the system openness is encouraged.

Acknowledgement

This work is part of Project No. 209.746/2007 entitled "Coordinación en una sociedad multiagentededicada a la programación y control bajo ambiente dinámico", funded by the Pontifical Catholic University of Valparaíso (www.pucv.cl).

References

[1] Bellifemine, F., et al.: JADE - A FIPA Compliant Agent Framework. C SELT Internal Technical Report (1999)
[2] Cossentino, M., Burrafato, P., Lombardo, S., Sabatucci, L.: Introducing pattern reuse in the design of multi-agent systems. In: Kowalczyk, R., Müller, J.P., Tianfield, H., Unland, R. (eds.) NODe-WS 2002. LNCS (LNAI), vol. 2592, pp. 107–120. Springer, Heidelberg (2003)
[3] FIPA. FIPA Request Interaction Protocol Specification, Standard, version H, 2002-12-06, http://www.fipa.org/specs/fipa00026/
[4] FIPA. FIPA Query Interaction Protocol Specification, Standard, version H, 2002-12-06, http://www.fipa.org/specs/fipa00027/
[5] Yoo, M.J., Müller, J.P.: Using Multi-agent System for Dynamic Job Shop Scheduling. In: 4th Int. Conf. on Enterprise Information System (ICEIS 2002), Ciudad Real, Spain (April 2002)

Author Index